HISTORY OF BIBLICAL INTERPRETATION

VOLUME 4: FROM THE ENLIGHTENMENT
TO THE TWENTIETH CENTURY

Society of Biblical Literature

Resources for Biblical Study

Susan Ackerman, Old Testament/Hebrew Bible Editor
Tom Thatcher, New Testament Editor

Number 63

History of Biblical Interpretation
Volume 4: From the Enlightenment to the Twentieth Century

HISTORY OF BIBLICAL INTERPRETATION

VOLUME 4: FROM THE ENLIGHTENMENT TO THE TWENTIETH CENTURY

By

Henning Graf Reventlow

Translated by

Leo G. Perdue

Society of Biblical Literature
Atlanta

HISTORY OF BIBLICAL INTERPRETATION
VOLUME 2: FROM THE ENLIGHTENMENT TO THE TWENTIETH CENTURY

Original title: *Epochen der Bibelauslegung Band IV: Von der Aufklärung bis zum 20. Jahrhundert*, by Henning Graf Reventlow, copyright © Verlag C.H. Beck oHG, Munich 2001. English translation produced under license from the publisher.

Library of Congress Cataloging-in-Publication Data

Reventlow, Henning, Graf.
  [Epochen der Bibelauslegung. English]
  History of biblical interpretation / by Henning Graf Reventlow
     p. cm. — (Society of Biblical Literature resources for biblical study ; no. 50, 61–63)
  Includes bibliographical references and indexes.
  ISBN-13: 978-1-58983-202-2 (paper binding, vol. 1 : alk. paper) — ISBN 978-1-58983-455-2 (paper binding, vol. 2 : alk. paper) — ISBN 978-1-58983-459-0 (paper binding, vol. 3 : alk. paper) — ISBN 978-1-58983-460-6 (paper binding, vol. 4 : alk. paper)
  1. Bible—Criticism, interpretation, etc.—History. I. Title.
BS500.R4813 2009
220.609—dc22
                                                  2009045014

18 17 16 15 14 13 12 11 10   5 4 3 2 1
Printed on acid-free, recycled paper conforming to ANSI/NISO Z39.48-1992 (R1997) and ISO 9706:1994 standards for paper permanence.

CONTENTS

Abbreviations

Primary Sources

Ant.	Josephus, *Antiquitates Judaicae* (*Jewish Antiquities*)
AW	Ferdinand Christian Baur, *Ausgewählte Werke in Einzelausgaben*. Edited by Klaus Scholder. 5 vols. Stuttgart-Bad Cannstatt: Frommann, 1963–1985.
Canon	Johann Salomo Semler, *Abhandlung von freier Untersuchung des Canon*. Edited by Heinz Scheible. Gütersloh: Mohn, 1967. [Orig. 4 vols., 1771–1775]
Commentary	Heinrich Eberhard Gottlob Paulus, *Philologisch-kritischer und historischer Commentar über die drei ersten Evangelien*. 3 vols. Lübeck: Bohn, 1800–1802.
Essay	John Locke, *An Essay concerning Human Understanding*. Edited by Peter H. Nidditch. Oxford: Clarendon, 1975.
GV	Rudolf Bultmann, *Glauben und Verstehen: Gesammelte Aufsätze*. 4 vols. Tübingen: Mohr Siebeck, 1933–1965.
Hdb	Heinrich Eberhard Gottlob Paulus, *Exegetisches Handbuch über die drei ersten Evangelien*. 3 vols. Heidelberg: Winter, 1830–1833. *Handbuch über die drei ersten Evangelien: Wohlfeile Ausgabe* [*WA*]. 3 vols. Heidelberg: Winter, 1842.
KD	Karl Barth, *Die kirchliche Dogmatik*. 5 vols. in 14. Zollikon: Verlag der Evangelischen Buchhandlung, 1932–1970.
SW	Johann Gottfried Herder, *Sämtliche Werke*. Edited by Bernhard Suphan et al. 33 vols. Berlin: Weidmann, 1877–1913. Repr., Hildesheim: Olms, 1967–1968.
Treatise	John Locke, *Two Tracts on Government*. Edited by Peter Laslett. Cambridge: Cambridge University Press, 1967.
WA	See *Hdb* above.

Secondary Sources

AR	*Archiv für Religionswissenschaft*
ATA	Alttestamentliche Abhandlungen
BBKL	*Biographisch-Bibliographisches Kirchenlexikon.* Edited by Friedrich Wilhelm Bautz. Hamm, Westfalia: Bautz, 1970–.
BevT	Beiträge zur evangelischen Theologie
BHTh	Beiträge zur historischen Theologie
BZAW	Beihefte zur Zeitschrift für die alttestamentliche Wissenschaft
EHS	Europäische Hochschulschriften
EvT	*Evangelische Theologie*
FRLANT	Forschungen zur Religion und Literatur des Alten und Neuen Testaments
FSThR	Forschungen zur systematischen Theologie und Religionsphilosophie
HCNT	Hand-Commentar zum Neuen Testament
HKAT	Handkommentar zum Alten Testament
HNT	Handbuch zum Neuen Testament
JSOTSup	Journal for the Study of the Old Testament Supplement Series
KEK	Kritsch-exegetischer Kommentar uber das Neue Testament
KHC	Kurzer Hand-commentar zum Alten Testament
MThSt	Marburger theologische Studien
NovTSup	Supplements to Novum Testamentum
OTE	*Old Testament Essays*
SBLMS	Society of Biblical Literature Monograph series
SHCT	Studies in the History of Christian Thought
SNTSMS	Society for New Testament Studies Monograph Series
SThGG	Studien zur Theologie und Geistesgeschichte des Neunzehnten Jahrhunderts
StPB	Studia post-biblica
ThB	Theologische Bücherei
ThSt	Theologische Studien
ThZ	*Theologische Zeitschrift*
UTB	Uni-Taschenbücher
VTSup	Supplements to Vetus Testamentum
ZThK	*Zeitschrift für Theologie und Kirche*

INTRODUCTION

The depiction of the epochs of biblical interpretation concludes with this fourth volume. The principles of this volume are unchanged from the preceding installments. As in them, my intention here has been to trace in the life's work of selected theologians and laity their developing understanding of the Bible in the context of the particular periods in which they lived. The combination of the biography and work of an author indicates a connection between the author's circumstances of life, the intellectual and cultural background of the author, and the view of the Bible prevailing at the time.

As with previous volumes, one could object this time that certain significant theologians and biblical interpreters have been passed over, but this criticism would miss the express purpose of the presentation. It is not only for reasons of limited space that the history of interpretation has to be set forth by presenting selected authors who are in a certain way representative. There are, for example, Old Testament scholars more significant than Ernst Wilhelm Hengstenberg, some even theologically close to him, for example, Franz Delitzsch. Yet it was Hengstenberg in particular who represented most clearly a direction that is usually neglected in the history of interpretation.

This volume covers authors from the different countries of Western Europe in terms of their significance for the development of biblical understanding. If, from chapter 5 on, attention concentrates on the development in Germany, this corresponds to the leading role that German theology and exegesis played from the end of the eighteenth century to the middle of the twentieth century. It was only after the Second World War that Anglo-Saxon research entered the conversation in a more important way. The same holds for Roman Catholic exegesis, which, apart from some outsiders like Richard Simon, was long hemmed in by dogmatic restrictions. Therefore, only a few Catholic biblical interpreters are mentioned.

Within the time frame delineated for this volume, the work reaches its conclusion with the two significant theologians and biblical interpreters Karl Barth and Rudolf Bultmann. Most of the generation of interpreters following them are still among the contemporaries of the present writer. A greater interval of time seems necessary to evaluate them adequately.

Once again, the bibliographical references for the individual sections are intended to document citations and offer suggestions for further work. The secondary literature for many authors is vast and is frequently compiled in special bibliographies or bibliographical periodicals. This presentation is often based on a selection of this literature far more extensive than could be listed in these references.

Upon the work's conclusion, thanks go to the Deutsche Forschungsgemeinschaft for supporting its continuation for two years and the Fritz Thyssen-Stiftung for supporting its completion. Thanks are due also to the publishing house C. H. Beck, which made possible its printing, and to the editors who watched over it attentively throughout its development. Its completion would not have been possible without the help of the assistants to the professorial chair and the project as well as the ever-courteous support of the staff of the library of the University of Bochum, and especially for the extensive interlibrary loan service that was necessary. Sincere thanks are extended to them as well.

1

Lutheran Hermeneutics in Germany

1.1. The Reformation's Understanding of the Bible Methodologically Established: Matthias Flacius Illyricus

Matthias Flacius Illyricus was born in 1520, the son of a landowner of Croatian descent in the city of Albona (today Labin) in a region of the Istrian peninsula belonging at the time to the Republic of Venice. His mother came from the patrician Venetian family Luciani. Following the humanistic custom of the time, he latinized his personal name and homeland and called himself Matthias Flacius Illyricus Albonensis. His father died early on, and his maternal uncle provided for his basic education and had a significant influence on him personally as well. As a humanistic reformer, this uncle, the Minorite (Franciscan) provincial Bildus Lupetinus, kept his ear open to the Reformation. He was later imprisoned for decades and finally executed. Instead of granting Flacius's wish to enter the cloister, he directed his nephew's attention to Luther and in this way pointed him toward his later path in life. After attending school in San Marco in Venice and concluding his studies with the famous humanist Giovanni Baptista Egnatius (Cipelli), Flacius, following the advice of his uncle and his teacher, went to Augsburg in 1539 and from there to Basel. In Basel he matriculated at the university. Simon Grynaeus (1493–1541), the successor to Erasmus as professor of Greek, and later New Testament, also a famous philologist, accepted him fondly. Johannes Oporinus (1507–1586), humanist and printer, became his friend and publisher. In 1540, Flacius moved to Tübingen and then to Wittenberg in 1541. After his foundational study of the three biblical languages and the acquisition of a sufficient ability to write German, he received the Magister (master) degree in 1543. A personal meeting with Luther, who impressed upon him the existential significance of justification, finally pulled him out of the religious self-doubts that had afflicted him since Basel. He developed a close friendship with Melanchthon. In 1543, he was sent as a messenger of the Smalcaldic League to the Doge at Venice, where he met once again with his imprisoned uncle. In 1544, he became professor of Hebrew. He lectured on the Old Testament, but also on the Pauline letters and on the writings of Aristotle. In 1545, he married a pastor's daughter in a ceremony attended personally by Luther. During these years he also wrote a study on the concept of faith (*De vocabulo fidei* [1549; expanded in 1555]), which was the first sign of his philological and theological interest and his proficiency in Reformation theology.

The death of Luther in 1546 marked for Protestantism the beginning of a turn for the worse. Emperor Charles V (ruled 1519–1556), perceiving a political constellation of advantage to him after the deaths of his chief rivals, Francis I of France and Henry VIII of England, believed he could restore religious unity in Germany, if necessary by force. In a confidential arrangement with Pope Paul III (1534–1549), who had opened the Council of Trent, he made preparations for war against the Protestant princes and cities joined together in the Smalcaldic League. The outcome of the Smalcaldic War (1546–1547)—the defeat of the Protestants at Mühlberg—affected Wittenberg also. Duke Moritz of Saxony (1521–1553) had fought on the side of the emperor and was rewarded with parts of the Ernestine region and the electorship. Wittenberg too thereby fell to him. When the university closed during the war in 1546, Flacius fled the city with the other professors and proceeded to Braunschweig. He returned to Wittenberg when the university reopened in 1548. At that time he began his battle against the "Augsburg Interim."

Since doing away with the Reformation by force no longer appeared possible, Emperor Charles V relied on the Council of Trent in order to achieve his desired reunification of the two confessions. A "provisional" regulation for confessional relationships in Germany, the "Augsburg Interim" that Charles V brought before the Diet of Augsburg (1547–1548), contained the attempt to establish theologically a mediating doctrine of justification (faith and love act together in justification) and, in ecclesiology, the ratification of the Catholic order. Notwithstanding the original intention of introducing reforms into Catholic regions as well, the regulation became legally binding only in the Protestant territories and cities. Though Protestantism was suppressed in many places during the temporary dominance of the emperor, it was interpreted in Electoral Saxony in terms of the so-called Leipzig Interim. In keeping with the elector's promise to the classes (i.e., gentility, citizens, and farmers who had certain rights for partaking in the government of the country) to respect the

Protestant faith, nothing changed with respect to questions of doctrine. It was nonetheless conceded, on the basis of an advisory of Melanchthon and most of the Wittenberg theologians, that rites that did not contravene evangelical faith (*adiaphora,* or "indifferent things," such as confirmation and final unction, prayer at Mass, priestly vestments, fasts, and hours of prayer) could be retained.

Flacius vehemently opposed these regulations. He sought in vain to persuade his Wittenberg colleagues to repudiate the *adiaphora* provision completely. When the Leipzig Interim had passed, he fought on by means of a (pseudonymous) printed polemic (1549), the republication of Luther's letters to the theologians at the Augsburg Imperial Diet of 1530 (with attacks on Melanchthon in the foreword), as well as personal protests. At last, before the Interim was introduced, he resigned his professorship in Wittenberg and went to the city of Magdeburg with its famous publishers. There resistance to the Interim was carried on under the leadership of theologians such as Nikolaus von Amsdorff (1483–1566) and Nikolaus Gallus (1516–1570)—the later so-called Gnesio-Lutherans ("authentic" Lutherans). Flacius lived there until 1557, earned a living as a book seller, and together with like-minded associates fought above all for the freedom of the church from the power of the state. He also contended with Georg Major (1502–1552) of Wittenberg and (despite the offer of a position by Duke Albrecht of Prussia) with Andreas Osiander (1496–1552) of Königsberg. These conflicts always had to do in one way or another with the doctrine of justification, and especially the relationship between justification and good works. On this issue, Flacius and the Gnesio-Lutherans averred "by grace alone."

Despite the tone of the polemics of the time, which often spilled over into personal smear tactics, Flacius and his fellow combatants cannot be denied credit for having saved the Lutheran subject matter, which otherwise would have passed away in the compromises that Philipp Melanchthon and his followers (the "Phillippists") were ready to make with the politicians. Against the mystical spiritualism of Caspar Schwenckfeld (see *History,* vol. 3), Flacius stressed the necessity of Holy Scripture and the publicly proclaimed Word of God for the faith ("Von der Heiligen Schrift und ihrer Wirkung" [1539] and additional tracts; see Keller, 25–92).

In the meantime, the entire political situation changed. First of all, Moritz of Saxony had changed sides and driven Charles V as far back as Innsbruck. The subsequent development led to the Augsburg Religious Peace (1555) and the emperor's abdication (1557). He resigned over the failure of his efforts to reunify the German church. Protestantism in Germany was secure for decades thereafter, the Interim obsolete. Flacius was largely responsible for the fact that it was no longer effectual, though he did not receive the credit.

In 1557, he was called to Jena as professor of New Testament at the university newly founded by the Ernestine Duke Johann Friedrich II (1554–1595), called "the middle," because he ruled between the two dukes who bore the same name. This ruler at first followed the Gnesio-Lutheran line; strict Lutheranism became the territorial church's confession in the so-called Book of Confutation. During his time in Jena, Flacius contributed considerably to a general church history divided into the centuries and prepared by different colleagues called the "Magdeburg Centuries" (some thirteen volumes appeared from 1559 to 1574, published by Operin in Basel). In this work church history was always to be measured against the norm of Scripture (see *History*, vol. 1). In Weimar in 1560, he disputed with the Philippist Victorinus Strigel (1524–1569) on original sin. According to Strigel, original sin was an *accidens* (an inessential element) in humanity, while Flacius stressed that it belongs to the nature (*substance*) of fallen humanity who live in the "Kingdom of the Devil."

A crisis came when, in the course of the development toward a territorial church, the ruler introduced a consistorial constitution for the control of the church by the state (by means of pre-censorship, church discipline, and jurisdiction over doctrinal disputes). Flacius and the Gnesio-Lutherans, however, emphasized the freedom of the spiritual office for pastoral church discipline. The conflict led to the dismissal of Flacius and several colleagues in December 1561. From then on he was a restless refugee.

He found refuge first in Regensburg, where at the time Gallus was the superintendent. There, among other things, he worked on the "Key to Holy Scripture" (*Clavis Scripturae sacrae*), which appeared in 1567. His attempt to found an evangelical university in Regensburg (and a daughter university in Klagenfurt) failed. For political reasons the senate of the city enjoined him from activity in church politics and also from publishing anything in Regensburg. This notwithstanding, the combative Lutheran published a profusion of theological polemics elsewhere, against the Reformed doctrine of the Eucharist, the Heidelberg Catechism, and the Council of Trent, among other things. His first wife died in 1564 at the birth of their twelfth child; he remarried soon afterwards. Half of the children died young—a fate common at the time—or were sick. His own health, too, was likewise affected. The hatred of the Saxon elector August (ruled 1553–1586) pursued him, because of advisors who persuaded August that Flacius especially was to blame for the disunity among Protestants. In 1566 at the Imperial Diet, when Flacius handed Emperor Maximilian II (reigned 1564–1576) his work "Concerning the Transference of the Roman Empire to the Germans (*De translatione imperii Romani ad Germanos*) and asked for the convocation of a Protestant Council, he was almost imprisoned immediately at the instigation of the elector. Finally, the intimidated council of Regensburg would no longer offer him any protection there.

At just the right time, in the autumn of 1566, a call reached Flacius to come to Antwerp to serve as pastor of the Lutheran church, where among other things he wrote a confession and liturgy for the church. Yet the advance of the troops of the Duke of Alba forced the Protestant preachers to leave the city at the beginning of 1567. After stopovers in Frankfurt am Main and other places, he set out in autumn for Strassburg. While Flacius was in Antwerp and Frankfurt he had published the two volumes of his *Clavis* (published by Oporinus in Basel). He found safety in Strassburg for several years. Yet in time his obstinacy and the enmity of elector August caught up with him even there. In a tractate on original sin, which Flacius published as an appendix to his *Clavis*, he once again spoke of original sin (with Aristotelian concepts) as the "substance" of fallen humanity. This provoked the Gnesio-Lutherans too against him. "Did then God's creation," the complaint ran, "fall in a Manichean way into a Kingdom of Good and a Kingdom of Evil?" The strict Lutheran theologian Tilemann Heshusius (1527–1588) vainly sought in 1568 to dissuade him from using this terminology. Among the writings Flacius produced in Strassburg, one should mention especially the *Glossa* to the New Testament, which appeared in 1570. Finally, the constant pressure of the elector August on the council led Strassburg to expel him in 1573, along with his sick wife and his children. He found his last refuge in Frankfurt am Main, where Catharine of Meerfeld, the courageous prioress of the Cloister of the Weissen Frauen (which had become Protestant), accepted him along with his family. Not even her action could prevent his expulsion in the end. Though he had been severely ill since the autumn of 1574, the deadline for expulsion was set at 1 May 1575. He died before that, in March 1575.

Of his numerous writings, his major work on hermeneutics, the *Clavis*, has been best remembered. Although there are all sorts of later writings about the book and numerous new editions of the work appeared until the beginning of the eighteenth century, there is no modern critical edition. A partial reprint with a German parallel text (Geldsetzer) appeared in 1968, followed in 1993 in Flacius's native land by a reprint of the Latin text with a Croatian translation in memory of this famous son of the Croatian people.

The motto in volume 1 already indicates the point of departure: according to Mark 4:10–13, expanded in Luke 24:45, Jesus discloses the meaning of the parables to his disciples. Flacius (together with Luther) understands the Scriptures christologically. The preamble, which dedicates the book to Duke Christoph of Württemberg, explains how Flacius interprets the Scriptures. In spite of the natural knowledge of God that is open to all (Ps 94:8–9; Isa 40; Rom 1:20; Acts 14:16–17; 17:26–27), God has also spoken to humanity publicly and altogether humanly: through patriarchs, prophets, his own son, and the apostles. God also had this revelation set down in writing. Scripture is inspired, because the Holy Spirit has spoken it through the mouths of human instruments and written it down by their hand. Cited as scriptural proofs from the Old Testament are Jer 36:5; Deut 17:18; 27:26; 31:12; and Josh 1:7. With regard to the indissolvable unity of both Testaments, he also refers to New Testament texts: Luke 16:29; 2 Pet 1:19; 2 Tim 3:16–17; Matt 5:18; Luke 16:17; and 24:44. In opposition to the decision of the Tridentine Council stating that tradition is necessary for understanding Scripture, Flacius explains that Scripture is understandable in and of itself, if one compares its passages with each other. The answers drawn from the Bible that Jesus gives to the devil in Matt 4 or to the Sadducees in Matt 22, as well as John 5:39 ("you search in the Scripture…") are proof of this. Flacius also objects to the imposition of Aristotelian concepts on the Scripture, as among the Scholastics. Thus, Luther was the first to rediscover that the expression "righteousness of God" (*iustitia Dei*) means the righteousness given by God to humans and not that God himself is righteous. A glance at the history of theology teaches that the Bible was often forgotten and had to be rediscovered again. Flacius named his work, as he remarks, *Clavis,* that is, the "key," to Scripture, because only the Lamb of God could open the closed book (cf. Rev 5:1–14); he hoped, nevertheless, that his book might help in opening it.

Volume 1 contains a biblical dictionary in the biblical-theological sense of the term. It is biblical-theological and not purely philological in that it explains the individual biblical concepts (in alphabetical order) first in the literal sense and then in their pictorial-figurative meaning within the framework of the Bible as a whole. The point of departure for biblical interpretation from individual concepts follows a methodological procedure that derives from Aristotle: the synthesis. This method shows how time-bound it is in that it applies to the biblical text the principle that the meaning of the whole can be to some extent assembled from the individual building stones, that is, the meaning of the particular concepts. Comparisons of innerbiblical parallel occurrences are continually referred to as the way to clarify difficulties of interpretation. In the case of concepts that played a special role in dogmatic controversy, for example, covenant, law, and testament, Flacius offers more lengthy short treatises. In addition, purely dogmatic, technical concepts such as *adiaphoron* (see above) are taken up (1:22–23) and explained biblically. The article *analogia fide* ("analogy of faith," 1:36) is important for hermeneutics. Its starting point is Rom 12:6, a formulation already traditional that was now (mis) understood dogmatically by Flacius in the sense of "agreement with the confession of faith." Flacius here emphasizes, in agreement with Luther's teaching, the doctrine of justification by faith as the decisive standard for the interpretation of Scripture.

Volume 2 of *Clavis* then offers a series of treatises about the interpretation of Scripture. In the foreword directed to the landgraves of Hesse, Wilhelm (ruled 1567–1592) and Ludwig (1567–1604), Flacius speaks of the Holy Spirit as the true interpreter of Scripture whom one must implore in prayer for grace. He rebukes Catholic theologians for deviating from Christ as the sole *scopus* ("goal") of Scripture. He called on the landgraves to convene a synod so that the purity of doctrine and faith could be maintained in their lands and contested questions could be decided. He again stresses that Scripture is to be interpreted from itself alone, because only the Holy Spirit can interpret it, and Jesus Christ is the center of Scripture.

The first tractate of this volume takes up the topic "Concerning the Epistemological Foundation of Holy Scripture" (*De ratione cognoscendi sacras literas*; the edition and translation of the first four sections are by Geldsetzer). It gathers together some major problems of biblical interpretation and gives methodological rules to solve them. Hence, this tractate particularly has often been considered a fitting introduction to Flacian hermeneutics.

In focusing on the difficulties in understanding the Bible as his starting point, Flacius is led by a pedagogical concern: "On the contrary (I say this) in order to arouse the reader all the more to diligence and by attending to the difficulties [the reader] may therefore learn all the more exactly the aids that I will present. With diligence and prayer one can discover in them the most certain truth about all things necessary" (Geldsetzer, 5). The fact that the language and meaning of Scripture are not immediately evident is due to "our guilt." A remedy is possible, however. Flacius seeks the clarification here in deliberate opposition to the Catholic polemical theologians who recommend popes and councils as the most reliable interpreters, since the meaning of Scripture is obscure. Flacius explicitly reproaches the Jesuits of Cologne (unknown to us), because out of "ignorance and wickedness" they would have so distorted the Scriptures by the imposition on them of philosophical-Aristotelian meanings or subject matter that they now seem "to give prominence and glory to Moses and the good works and merits of humans" (Geldsetzer, 7).

As one sees, all the technical-methodological instructions that Flacius thereafter proposes stand, from the outset, under a theological banner. In hermeneutics particularly, the concern of the Reformation is put to its decisive test by the man from Illyria: "Scripture alone" represents the foundation of the evangelical confession.

In subsequent sections, Flacius lists an entire series of reasons for the difficulties that impede access to understanding the Bible. Among them is, first of all, the linguistic form of the Bible: its antiquity in respect to the changing meaning of the words, the varying style, the linguistic diversity of the individual writers and especially the Old and New Testaments, and their figurativeness. This humanist, schooled in ancient rhetoric, also mentions the different tropes and metaphors, the partially incomplete or abbreviated sentences, and so forth. "It is however puzzling to us why God has transmitted the Scripture virtually sentence for sentence and so tightly compacted in fixed sections, just like imperial law is written" (Geldsetzer, 17). Leaps in train of thought, as well as things, places, and customs that are unknown to the reader, add to the difficulties.

For the Lutheran Flacius, all the linguistic problems eventually culminate in the theological contradiction that, for the ill-informed, exists between law and gospel. "Their unity and their difference is the most certain key for the entire Scripture" (Geldsetzer, 21). The thesis is Lutheran when he argues that the law, in lieu of its life-giving function, which was forfeited as a result of the fall, performs only one additional function: humans are led by the law's revelation of their sins and of the wrath of God to the "doctor" Christ (*paedagogus ad Christum* [Geldsetzer, 20; cf. Gal 3:24]). But what is decisive is "that the gospel is superior to the law and gives the life that the law only promises" (Geldsetzer, 21). Flacius extols the fact that God desired to transmit his secrets (*mysteria*) to us in such a way that we should expect them "only out of his gracious hand." In addition: "Much is concealed even from the pious so that they will search the Scriptures all the more zealously" (Geldsetzer, 23).

This leads to the section in which Flacius identifies the means of salvation. The first of these is Father, Son, and Holy Spirit. Additional means of salvation are based on this trinitarian foundation: instruction imparted by officeholders (i.e., experienced servants of Christ) about the things that are dealt with in Scripture, knowledge of the biblical languages, meditation over Scripture, prayer, and experience. Comparisons of passages and good translations are added as methodological aids for investigating unclear statements (see above). Flacius must of course grant the pope's followers that these means are not suitable for the uneducated. But at this point he refers to Luther's translation, which has already explained many things, and to the true officeholders (*ministri*) and doctors of the church who explain the difficult passages of Scripture.

Flacius then sets forth the rules for the knowledge of Scripture drawn from the Scripture itself. The professor speaks openly: the rules for the study of Holy Scripture are fixed (Geldsetzer, 44–45; this has to do with "teaching and learning"). Flacius again begins with the trinitarian foundation and the notion that all wisdom is based in Christ. Also belonging here is God's covenant with humanity. Furthermore, the sum of Scripture is to be ascertained. For this, Flacius makes use of the logical three steps of the *syllogismus* customary in Scholasticism. The first major premise reads: "What God says is true" (Geldsetzer, 35). It "requires no proof," for it is the foundation of all theology. The minor premise affirms: "our words (say Moses and the prophets) are the words of God." The conclusion is, "Therefore our words and writings are … all true" (Geldsetzer, 37). The second syllogism (which is demonstrated by the miracles in the history of Old Testament Israel) reads: "everything the Old Testament or the prophets have spoken about the Messiah … is completely true" (major premise). Our Jesus, however, is certainly a person such as the prophets have depicted as the Messiah. Thus, the subordinate premise is that this has been fulfilled. Conclusion: "Therefore this man Jesus himself is the true Messiah" (Geldsetzer, 37). For Flacius, these two syllogisms were closely connected, with the second reinforcing the first. "God, however, confirmed the public speech of Jesus by his own testimony, by calling down three times from heaven (Matt 3:17; 7:15; John 12:28) and in addition by so many and so great wonders" (Geldsetzer, 39). Doubt whether these miracles had actually happened was still unknown in the sixteenth century. As the concluding proposition of the two syllogisms together, which Flacius called "the sum of the entire Old and New Testament," he remarked: "Therefore, what Jesus and his apostles said and taught is completely true" (Geldsetzer, 39). The christocentric starting point (altogether in harmony with Luther) leads thus to a totally biblical theology. In what follows, Flacius goes into the relationship of law and gospel in still more detail in order to round out the Reformation doctrine

Flacius emphasizes later on that every interpretation of Scripture has to be made in accord with the "analogy of faith." Corresponding to the explanation of this concept in volume 1, he means a dogmatic foundation. Flacius recommends this foundation to students of theology as the point of departure for their exegesis of Scripture. Flacius thinks concretely of Genesis 1–3, where he finds a foundational confessional statement "of the one God, creation, the fall and salvation by means of the blessed seed (Gen 3:15, traditionally interpreted christologically, as the so-called Protoevangelium)." He then points to the Decalogue, the Lord's Prayer, and finally the Words of Institution (Geldsetzer, 46; [the parallel translation is misleading here]). He takes Paul (1 Tim 1:7) and Cicero together as witnesses (Geldsetzer, 49–51) that we must know exactly whereof we speak when we consider all of the Scriptures or only sections of them (contemporary hermeneutics would say that we have a pre-understanding). In this connection, Flacius refers once again to Christ as the true source of all doctrines in biblical theology. "We received from heaven a doctrine that was already composed and contained in a book" (Geldsetzer, 55). Philological and theological points of view are closely combined. So, when drawing a conclusion from 2 Tim 2:15, one derives not only a "solid knowledge of words and meanings, clauses and sentences, and the overall disposition of each Scripture," but also "a precise differentiation of the subject matter and objects that are contained in the Holy Scripture" (Geldsetzer, 51). Here once again this means the distinction between law (promise) and gospel (Geldsetzer, 53). In this connection, Flacius emphatically admonishes that doctrines are to be sought from Scripture and not from tradition (i.e., the fathers). Christ and the apostles did not wish to cite any fathers (Geldsetzer, 57). In comparison with Aristotle and philosophers, who require capable and insightful listeners, Flacius stresses that the biblical message seeks simple listeners whom God then makes capable of understanding. Yet here too learning is necessary, its goal being the knowledge of God, justification of sinners, and glorification of God.

In the case of knowledge of the Scriptures, a distinction is to be made between what God says clearly and unambiguously and what we derive from God's statements. Flacius repudiates the third type of theology, namely, drawing conclusions out of philosophy.

To be sure, he also objects to the "fanatics" (Geldsetzer, 79) who consider the human sciences useless or even harmful for knowledge of Holy Scripture. Above all, knowledge of language is important, but so are dialectic and rhetoric; and now even philosophy is designated as useful, although, like Hagar in the house of Sarah, it is the handmaiden of theology. In this connection, Flacius also requires instruction and examinations, and he names in particular a "content examination" (Geldsetzer, 83). Here he means an examination in which the pupils must show that they themselves can apply what they have learned instructively.

The next section, too, which contains "Instructions" for correct readings of Scripture (see Geldsetzer, 88ff.), is directed to students of theology. Here reference is made first of all to the high value of the subject, the Bible as the Scripture of the living God himself. Therefore, one must ask for God's help in order to understand the Bible. But then altogether concrete statements follow. It is important that Flacius designates the literal meaning as the "simple and precise meaning of Holy Scripture" (Geldsetzer, 89) and warns against allegories. After he speaks briefly about techniques of memorization, he recommends that in dealing with any book (*alicuius libri*) and not only the Bible, one should commit first the intention and then the main argument of the entire book to memory, and subsequently one should put its outline and finally the whole into a table. A further step consists in ascertaining the form (*genus*) of the text: "whether it has to do with narrative or history, an instruction or some doctrine, a writing of comfort or threat, the description of some subject matter, a speech or something similar" (Geldsetzer, 97). It is remarkable to observe that form criticism is not a modern discovery but is already found here, at least as a postulate. Additional steps of investigation are directed to questions of dialectic: logical forms of the text, definitions, and syllogisms. Readers should commit all these to memory and reflect on them. To the concise, "anatomical" (Geldsetzer, 101) record, a more detailed one can then be added. By means of these considerations, which are then illustrated in a few textual examples, Flacius desires to provide his students with some practical aids for carrying on their biblical studies fruitfully. Reflected here also are some of the instructional practices of the time.

1.2. Defending the Bible as the Word of God: Johann Gerhard

Johann Gerhard was born on 17 October 1582, the son of a patriarchal family of Quedlinburg. His father, Bartholomew, was the council treasurer of the city and the bursar of the prince-mother superior of Quedlinburg.

His mother was the daughter of the mayor of Halberstadt. At the time when the Thirty Years' War broke out, prosperity was increasing in the empire, and Quedlinburg was a wealthy city. There the young Johann attended a gymnasium until 1598. A severe illness in his fifteenth year brought about an inward change. Johann Arndt (1555–1621), at the time a pastor in Quedlinburg, visited the youth, who was undergoing this difficult internal trial. The young man believed that he was experiencing the illness as God's punishment for his sins. Arndt bound his sermons into the *Four Books of True Christianity* (1605) along with a Lutheran confession that broadly reverberated with a warm, mystically impressed practice of faith. (Approximately fifty editions of this work were published). When Gerhard regained his health after a year and understood this as salvation given through grace, Arndt obviously influenced him to dedicate his life according to the "holy doctrine." In 1598, the plague broke out in Quedlinburg. Though Gerhard became ill once more, he was able to recover. His mother sent him to Halberstadt for the remainder of his time in school. In 1599, Gerhard began the usual basic university studies in Wittenberg. Instead of continuing with theology, however, he changed to medicine in 1601, owing to the counsel of an influential relative. When this relative died in 1602 and Gerhard reflected on the vow he had made to Johann Arndt (who had moved in 1599 to Braunschweig), he took up theological study in Jena in the following year. In June 1603, he received the promotion to a master of philosophy, and he began to lecture on metaphysics. The rediscovery of the metaphysics of Aristotle was very much the fashion of the period. It supplied for Lutheran theology some fundamental presuppositions that Gerhard also appropriated, such as the teaching of material reality in the categories of the motives of deeds (*causa efficiens*), the giving of form (*forma*—an inner power), the setting forth of purpose (*causa finalis*), and the knowing of truth from which theological truth may not be separated. In the same year, Gerhard became severely ill once again and believed he was near death, a fact indicated by a testament handed down from this period. When he became well once again, he moved to Marburg, which at the time was a Lutheran university (later it became Calvinist; see below) to pursue further study. It was here that Balthasar Mentzer (1565–1627) became his teacher. Gerhard accompanied him to other Lutheran centers at Stuttgart, Tübingen, and Strasburg. Soon after his return, an uproar broke out in Marburg on account of the Calvinism that Count Moritz (reigned 1592–1627), who had converted to the Reformed tradition, forced on the city. This uproar was forcibly crushed. The Lutheran professors were expelled, and they founded a new academy in Giessen. Gerhard returned to Jena, following the wishes of his mother. After a brief time as a *Dozent*, in 1606 he accepted a call from Johann Casimir, duke of Saxony-Coburg, to be the superintendent of Heldburg. The faculty of Jena bestowed upon him an honorary doctorate of theology. In addition to his usual official duties in Coburg, once a month he held theological disputations, during which he treated all standard *loci* in four years.

In the years 1602–1610, he produced fifty-one Meditations (*Meditationes sacrae*), which were translated numerous times. This was an extensive construction of mystical contemplation. Subsequently, Gerhard was unable to accept a variety of calls to positions in the church and the university in other places, because his duke would not allow him to go. Instead, the duke required Gerhard to undertake the post of general superintendent in Coburg (1615). Between 1613 and 1615, he visited all of the churches of the duchy. The result was an ecclesiastical order designed by him to address the flagrant, deplorable state of affairs in the clergy and the community (1615). Finally, Casimir agreed to allow Gerhard to accept the position of professor on the faculty of Jena. In the years following Heldburg, Gerhard worked on his major theological work, the *Loci theologici*, which appeared in nine volumes from 1610 to 1622. Already in the spring of 1610, Gerhard had brought out a special tractate, "Concerning the Legitimate Explanation of Holy Scripture." His major work of theological polemic, in which he defended Lutheran teaching against the criticism raised by the Catholic theologians (short title: *Confessio catholica*), appeared in four parts from 1633 to 1637. He also completed the Lutheran harmony of the Gospels begun by Martin Chemnitz (1522–1586). This harmonization was to demonstrate the error-free nature of the Gospels. In addition, during the last years of his life, he supervised the redaction of the so-called Weimar Bible, a work that was initiated by Duke Ernst the Pious of Saxony-Gotha (1601–1675, duke since 1640). This Bible was expressly written for non-theologians. In addition to these undertakings, a series of notes and commentaries on biblical books were published posthumously.

Throughout his life, Gerhard experienced many difficulties both individually and in his family. Gifts from his landlords, recommendations, and so on brought him considerable wealth; however, the restless times also occasioned economical losses. His first wife, who was fourteen years old when they were married (1608), died in 1611, soon after the death of their firstborn child. His second wife was seventeen years old when they were married in 1614. Of the six surviving children, a son also became a professor of theology in Jena. In the period after the conclusion of the *Loci* in 1622, which he celebrated with a gala for the senate of the university, Gerhard did not lack for work. In his home, he continued to house numerous students as renters or boarders. He contributed to a better financial position of the university by visiting the courts of princes who were in the vicinity. He turned down numerous calls to other schools, including some that were outside of Germany. During the turmoil of the Thirty Years' War, he repeatedly adopted a position advocating peace. In 1636, the Swedes, wishing to capture him because of his interventions, sent Swedish soldiers to plunder and torch his manor, Rosslau. In addition, in the spring of 1637, imperial troops stole many of his expensive gifts of honor (golden and silver cups) and even took his household goods. Toward the end of his life, he no longer harbored any illusions about the possibility of controlling the human propensity for violence. This tended to contradict his Lutheran view of human nature.

Johann Gerhard died on 17 August 1637, after a brief, feverish illness, surrounded by his family, servants, and both of his theological faculty colleagues, Johann Major and Johann Himmel.

When he entitled his main theological work *Loci theologici*, Gerhard followed, as we already noted (see *History*, vol. 3), an old rhetorical model that had reached with Melanchthon a specifically biblical-theological high point. Gerhard's *Loci* differ from Melanchthon's *Loci*, which he follows in what had become the traditional arrangement of systematic themes. Gerhard's work, however, is distinguished from Melanchthon's in that he places in his *Loci*, as the first locus, his own comprehensive section dealing with Holy Scripture (*De Scriptura Sacra*). This initial principle is clear in Gerhard's first sentence in Locus 1 (Cotta 1.1; cf. Preuss 1:13): "We rightly begin with Holy Scripture, which we recognize as the only principle of theology, … since it is upon this acknowledgment that all else is dependent." The placement of this principle at the beginning rests upon the new foundation of Aristotelian logic as a theoretical method by the philosopher Giacomo Zabarella (1533–1589), who was professor of logic in Padua since 1564. According to his theory, which reaches back to Aristotle, one must proceed from the first principles to the later principles and the conclusions that are developed. Zabarella deals here with the contemplative disciplines that have to do either with things that are eternal or are not dependent on the human will. Familiar with Aristotelian thought, Gerhard openly adopted Zabarella's methodology, which conformed to his Lutheran understanding of the significance of Holy Scripture as the only basis of faith (*sola scriptura*). The renaissance of Aristotelian thought offered for him, then, the appropriate methodology. Additionally, in the period of the Counter-Reformation and the great war of faith, the defense of this principle of Scripture against the Catholic position played an important role. This emerges more clearly in the previously disseminated "Tract Concerning the Explanation of Holy Scripture" (literally reproduced in the edition of Cotta 1.42–49, as Locus 2), which was shaped as a debate of the author with polemical theologians like Bellarmine (see *History*, vol. 3) and Thomas Stapleton (1535–1598). The *Loci* also consider both the Socinians and the Reformed Church. In following the rhetorical scheme of objection and answer, he enters into the objections raised against the Lutheran position that the Scripture interprets itself. Without an authoritative interpretation, so Catholic theologians asserted, the Bible would become a "dead letter" and frequently unclear. Additionally, Scripture may not be sufficient in and of itself to judge all questions of faith and ethics. Therefore, the authority of the church and of the papal teaching office are necessary for its understanding. The thesis of the "clarity" (*perspicuitas*) of Scripture (Preuss 1.20) plays in this regard an important role: the Scripture is itself clear when it says that the corporal spirit is so corrupted by sin that we are unable to recognize the divine mysteries. This means that we are led to the recognition, as Gerhard himself says concerning the conclusion in Luther's *De servo arbitrio* ("Concerning the Lack of Free Will"), that the enlightenment of the Holy Spirit is necessary (Tract [= Cotta, Locus 2] §§48–51)

In comparison with the older *descriptions* such as those of Johann Wigand's (1523–1587) and Matthew Judex's (1528–1564) *Syntagma* (1568), it is striking that Gerhard does not distinguish any longer between the Word of God and the Holy Scripture (Preuss 1.1.7). In the period of orthodoxy, Scripture is the Word of God (cf. Preuss 1.27.539). Catholic theology widely distinguishes between the two. Important also is the formal separation between the external form of Scripture (the "sign") and its content (the "signification"; Preuss 1.1.7). For Gerhard, Holy Scripture means theologically only the content by which it comes to him, although he has a great deal to say about the external form (as, for example, the Hebrew and Greek texts of the two Testaments [Preuss, 1.12–16]). Scripture is the Word of God, "which in the past was proclaimed orally by the prophets and the apostles" (Preuss 1.6). The written form has the same authority. Formulated in Aristotelian terminology, this is connected with the idea that God is the "primal cause" (*causa efficiens*) of Scripture in the sense of the "first cause" (*causa principalis*). Scripture is only an instrument (*causa instrumentalis*; Preuss 1.2.12). As an instrument, nevertheless, it is credited as the means by which the Spirit effectuates its power of activity (Preuss 1.2.456). The ideas of *forma* and *materia* can be applied, notwithstanding, to Scripture. As the internal form (*forma interna*), the Holy Spirit is the formative power of Scripture. The languages are the external form in which the Scripture is contained and its style (Preuss 1.12.305–9), while the material consists of "the sacred things that are written down according to God's will" (Preuss 1.4.52). The contents of Holy Scripture, therefore, are defined essentially through its theological statements. In this regard, Gerhard names two possibilities of organization: (1) the one according to history (*historiae*) and doctrine (*dogmata*), and the other (2) according to law and gospel (ibid.).

Against the Catholics, and in particular the spiritualists, Gerhard stresses that the Spirit and the Scripture closely belong together. Nothing from the outside is to be applied to it (Tractatus [= Cotta, Locus 2], §21). This is connected to Gerhard's view of the inerrancy of Scripture, although this idea is limited fundamentally to include only the necessary truths of salvation and does not pertain to the matters of chronology and physical (natural scientific) data in the Bible. In the later polemic of the Enlightenment against orthodoxy, this usually was overlooked. Certainly, there were additional problems, for example, how far the authority of Scripture should be extended. The Catholic polemical theology brought attention to obvious errors: for example, Matt 27:9 attributes a passage from Zechariah (11:13) to Jeremiah. In the harmony of the Gospels edited by Gerhard, he rejects the possibility that there could exist an error here. Much more, the evangelists knowingly exchanged the names in order to draw attention to the fact that one and the same Spirit is the actual author of all prophetic words. This explanation contained a real weakness that would later lead either to the stinging criticism of the Enlightenment or to an anachronistic fundamentalism that viewed the Bible in all of its historical and natural scientific statements to be unlimited in its veracity.

The thesis of the inerrancy of Scripture necessarily led Gerhard to deal with the state of the Hebrew and Greek texts (Preuss 1.14). Against the objections brought forward by the Catholic polemical theologians that the Hebrew text is corrupt in numerous places, Gerhard appeals to Origen and primarily points back to his assertion that the Old Testament text may have been distorted by the wickedness of the Jews. He is prepared to admit, however, that individual mistakes in the text likely are due to the carelessness of copyists. It is decisive, however, that "mistakes like these are not particularly significant … for they do not relate to matters of faith and ethics that would place in question the integrity of Holy Scripture" (Preuss 1.14.333). The affirmation that the pointing of the Hebrew text may be as old as the consonantal text originates from the same motivation and provides certainty for the clarity and perfection of Scripture. In addition to this, Christ's statement in Matt 5:18 plays a role: neither a jot nor a tittle will pass away until the end of the world (Preuss 1.15.336). In response to the objections of Bellarmine, Gerhard expresses his view more briefly about the integrity of the Greek text of the New Testament (Preuss 1.16). In regard to the Greek text, Gerhard in essence remarks that one could not exclude from corruption individual manuscripts of the New Testament, since better preserved ones may be used to make improvements (Preuss 1.16.356). He especially concerns himself with the sinful woman in John 8, which is absent from many manuscripts, and with the concluding formula of the Lord's Prayer in Matt 6, which, according to Bellarmine, has been added. Gerhard considers it to be original, since it exists in trustworthy manuscripts (Preuss 1.16.361).

Ultimately one expects the Aristotelian method to inquire about the purpose (*finis*) of Scripture. In respect to God, its purpose is both "the recognition that he brings about salvation, and his glorification." While in respect to humanity, its final objective, which is reached through the "means" of teaching, discovery of guilt, improvement, and education (according to 2 Tim 3:16), consists of faith, love, and hope (Preuss 1.17.362–63). Gerhard's hermeneutics, contained in the "Tract" of 1610, are of special interest. It is important that he, in reference to Luther's *De servo arbitrio* ("Concerning the Lack of Free Will"; §§48–54), views prayer and enlightenment by the Holy Spirit as necessary preparation for the interpretation of the Bible. These things are necessary, because the divine secrets contained in Scripture are concealed by the fact that human nature is corrupted by sin. The Holy Spirit is necessary above all for the recognition of the secrets of faith. Even so, the enlightened are still not able by this means to understand fully the doctrines of Scripture and to have a "historical faith through the external employment of the Word" (§54). This is a far cry, however, from concluding that this attributes obscurity to the divine Scriptures. They have much more power to enlighten our understanding, since the Spirit accomplishes this through Holy Writ (§56). Gerhard stresses that the Spirit wishes to enable us to arrive at this enlightenment by means of our "treatment of the Word." This is something one achieves through reading, meditation, and examination of Scripture (§57). It is important that everything is spoken in clear and understandable words according to their lexical meanings, which do not stand in need of any farfetched explanation (§58).

From these clear, fundamental statements, the rule of faith (*regula fidei*) yields a "summation of the heavenly teaching delivered from the clearest statements of Scripture" (§61). Therefore, one must be on guard against the interpretation of unclear places that allows something to emerge that disputes this rule. Since Scripture is given by the divine Spirit, it may contain nothing that is contradictory (§63). For the explanation of these obscure places, Gerhard provides a series of technical instructions: thus, there may be places where statements of faith are formulated and expressed in clauses. These may be taken as useful axioms for understanding (§66). They may be considered a correlation of beliefs and not simply as providing the meaning of a word. For this, Gerhard provides in §70 additional rules. Important is the distinction drawn between concrete and figurative words. For those that are concrete in meaning, the grammatical signification and the consideration of the emphasis are important. Thus, one is to examine where the same word occurs in other places, and whether with the same or different meaning (§68). Where Scripture speaks metaphorically or in parables, knowledge of natural things is of utmost importance (§69). Gerhard speaks in another place even more expressly over the different meaning of Scripture, which he primarily divides traditionally, in accordance with Bellarmine, into literal, spiritual, allegorical, typological (moral), and analogical (to refer to eternal life) understandings (§131). Gerhard agrees with Bellarmine and Jerome that fixed and certain arguments may be obtained from the meaning of a word (§136). Therefore, one must begin with the lexical meaning that may be obtained from the words and their context, coupled with the meaning provided by the Holy Spirit. "The different teachings, admonitions, rites, and refutations of opponents may be obtained from this lexical meaning" (§139). If the Holy Spirit itself explains something to be typological or allegorical, then we may certainly follow the path of allegory" (ibid.). However, one may never consider ethical commands, promises, threats, and dogmatic expositions to be allegory. By contrast, ceremonial instructions of the Old Testament may be explained allegorically, "for they are shadows and types of future things." Narratives may be understood in the same way: David's victory over Goliath signifies that Christ is victorious over the devil or the pious over fleshly desires. On the whole, the use of allegory may be more appropriate for proclamation than for opposition against opponents. An allegorical interpretation is necessary, in the following circumstances:

1. when Scripture has stated something somewhat incorrectly (e.g., Ps 91:13 indicates that Christ has tread on snakes and adders, something he had never done),

2. when the lexical meaning expresses something absurd: thus, when human passions like wrath, rage, or disgust are attributed to the immutable God. Here, Gerhard is bound to the philosophical (metaphysical) conception of God! On the other hand, he differentiates between them, when he later reflects on the relationship between philosophy (still meaning at that time a common designation for all theoretical and practical sciences) and theology (§§165–78). Philosophy examines things that are accessible to human reason, while theology is occupied with the revelation that is set down in Scripture and the divine secrets that are present in it. Scripture requires enlightenment through the Holy Spirit. Subsequently, Gerhard began the process of interpretation always with prayer (see above)! For this reason, the sphere in which reason is valid is limited.

3. when the lexical meaning stands in opposition to the rule of faith. The meaning of the *regula fidei* for Gerhard's understanding of Scripture once more appears here. Gerhard also holds that the use of allegorical meaning is possible when the lexical meaning appears not to offer any useful teaching. However, the allegorical interpretation brings forth a richer understanding. Thus, in the narrative concerning Laban, when he substitutes Leah for Rachel and gives her to Jacob (Gen 29:23–25), Gerhard suggests that this story could mean that God in a similar way disappoints many people. Rachel stands for lasting things that God appears to allow people to have, but then, when they awaken from their sleep, they recognize that it was Leah (something without value) (§144). One sees in this example that Gerhard's precritical exegesis, although it adheres fundamentally to Luther's emphasis on the lexical meaning, is still oriented primarily to dogmatics. In the case of a passage that produces a valuable teaching with the help of an allegorical interpretation, allegory is also permitted.

All of this is shown in connection with the rule of faith, which is stressed as the most important principle (which, as we saw, is taken as far as it is concerned from Scripture). Gerhard is convinced that, if Scripture also uses in some places in the articles of faith an improper (perhaps an allegorical) formulation, then this is expressed in other places in clear language (§§148, 149). The rule of faith is, however, to be accepted in its entirety, not simply in various parts, for it is clear that the Holy Spirit is not able to contradict itself (§150). In addition, no meaning may originate from obscure passages that contradict the analogy of faith. We encountered this idea already in Flacius (stemming from Rom 12:6, however, reshaped here to receive a more technical meaning).

It also is important to observe that, in following what Gerhard considers to be one of the most important methods for comprehending the meaning of unclear statements of Scripture, he time and again recommends comparison with other passages of Scripture. Since Scripture is a unity and therefore is not able to contain actual contradictions, unclear passages may be explained from their respective parallel statements. In answer to the objection of Thomas Stapleton that this may be an uncertain method, Gerhard responds that this comparison must be without prejudice or any preconceived meanings and must be related to the circumstances of the respective passages. Aside from this, the method may be combined with other methods but must be controlled in any case by the rule of faith (§§117–19). Incidentally, this provides parallels not only in respect to the words, but also in regard to the facts (§120).

All in all, the teaching of Johann Gerhard is a self-contained, impressive system based on Scripture. By means of revitalized Scholasticism, this system seeks to integrate the fundamental statements of the Lutheran Reformation and to oppose the contrary understandings of the Counter-Reformation as well as the Reformed Church and the spiritualists. He has to a great extent largely succeeded in this effort. If one reads Gerhard's edifying writings, one will not be able to reproach him for being remote from reality or articulating an abstract dogmatic paradigm. He was also engaged in a lively church that was living by means of the spirit of Scripture. For us as readers who are living long after his death, the decisive weakness of the system to be sure immediately comes into view: the idea of the historicity of the faith and the church is still strange to Lutheran orthodoxy in its understanding of the Bible. This was its Achilles heel, which has become apparent to later readers. The worldview of the Enlightenment, with its understanding of history, had not yet appeared. This weakness finally broke down the entire system, although much of the knowledge produced would have merited preservation.

2

The Bible in England from the Sixteenth to the Eighteenth Centuries

2.1. Ordering the Church according to a Biblical Pattern: Thomas Cartwright

In the summer of 1572, a sensational, anonymous, subversive writing of a group of Puritans appeared: an "Admonition to Parliament" to fundamentally reform the church. Queen Elizabeth I (reigned 1558–1603), however, already had intervened in Parliament, denying it any right to deal with religious matters. This demand was nothing new. Ever since the English church's separation from Rome beginning with Henry VIII (reigned 1509–1547), which was initially based purely on dynastic reasons, there were reforming impulses, at first Lutheran and then later Zwinglian and Calvinistic. These impulses started in the universities and were especially noticeable in Cambridge, strengthened by the emergence of strongly anticlerical feelings in the cities, especially in London. The pre-Reformation Lollards had sustained their position in the underground in some of the rural areas. Aside from abolishing the cloisters in 1536, the structure of the church of the Middle Ages was largely untouched, particularly in regard to the external forms of worship, the sacraments, and the hierarchical leadership under the archbishops of Canterbury and York, together with their bishops. The two brief periods of rule of the adolescent ruler King Edward VI (reigned 1547–1553) and "bloody" Queen Mary (reigned 1553–1558) were characterized by enormously contrasting religious fluctuations in the monarchy. Edward was open to the Reformation, while Mary was a Roman Catholic. Her execution of Protestants led to her notoriety, captured in the descriptive adjective "bloody." Consequently, Elizabeth I, during her lengthy reign, created the basic framework for the new structure of the church, which she did not allow to undergo any noticeable alteration. This new order was approved by Parliament. In essence, this structure was related to the efforts at reform during the reign of Edward VI. To this structure belonged the renewed supremacy of the crown over the church and the requirement that the clergy had to conform to the liturgical order of the church regulated by the "Book of Common Prayer."

The Elizabethan church, which presented itself at least outwardly as a unity, comprised rather early these two contrasting tendencies. What united them was the emphasis on reform that had been operative as early as the sixteenth century. One of these two tendencies was known by what originally was a term of reproach: "Puritans." To term their opponents "Anglicans" would be anachronistic. In modern times, one certainly uses the terms "conformists" and "nonconformists," that is, those who, on one side, defer to the rules of the state church, and those who, on the other side, seek rigorous reform.

One of the first expressions of the Puritan attitude occurred in response to the affair set in motion by John Hooper (1495–1555), when the Diocese of Gloucester was offered him. Hooper declined for some length of time to wear the prescribed liturgical vestments, because they were not scripturally based, until he finally yielded to the pressure, conceding that this matter was not decisive for issues of faith (*adiaphora*). This controversy calls attention to two key issues that pertain to the Puritans and their enemies. The fight over whether established liturgical forms required scriptural authority had started already during the reign of Queen Mary, when English Protestants had begun to flee to Frankfurt am Main. This issue sprang to life once again during the 1570s and came to involve an especially important figure, Thomas Cartwright.

Cartwright likely was born in Royston, near Cambridge, to a well-to-do farming family in the year 1535. He matriculated in Clare Hall College, Cambridge, in 1547. In 1550, he transferred to St. John's College, which, at the time, was under the direction of a radical Protestant, Thomas Lever (or Leaver, 1521–1577). In 1554 he graduated with a bachelor of arts (liberal arts) degree. In 1556 (during the reign of Queen Mary), he left the college and studied law with a lawyer. He returned to the college in 1559–1560, became a fellow there, and soon received his master's degree. In 1562, he then transferred to Trinity College.

Already by this time, the queen had required of Archbishop Matthew Parker and the bishops measures to enforce conformity in the churchly rites and ceremonies. The official issuing of such articles, which one sought under pressure to enforce, called forth the resistance of a party that soon came to be known as the Puritans. The opposition was especially articulated in the universities. Theologians from the Continent, for example, Theodor Beza (1519–1605), Heinrich Bullinger (1504–1575), and his later successor, Rudolf Gualther (1519–1586), were asked to support their colleagues by correspondence.

In 1565, Cartwright became for two years the house chaplain of the archbishop of Armagh in Ireland, Adam Loftus (ca. 1533–1605). When Loftus moved to Dublin, Cartwright returned to Cambridge. There he was chosen to be the university preacher for 1567–1568. Not least because of the substantial impression he made as a preacher, he became Lady Margaret Professor of Divinity. This chair, endowed by the mother of Henry VII, is held in high esteem even today.

In his first series of lectures in 1570, which dealt with Acts 1–2, Cartwright aroused controversy with his thesis that the order of the ancient church described there should be the model binding on the church of every period of time, and therefore also must be introduced into the English church. Thus, congregations are to have a say in the choice of their pastor, who must be competent to preach (something that was not always the case at that time). The congregations were to be led by elders (presbyters). Bishops should possess only spiritual functions, and the offices of the archbishop and the archdeacon (since they are not mentioned in Scripture) are to be abolished. All ecclesiastics should have equal rights. Additional criticism was directed against obvious abuses in the church, including the possession of several ecclesiastical benefices ("pluralism") or the continuing absence of the holders of a possession from their parishes ("absentism"). Cartwright was a capable speaker, and students streamed to his classes. The university became divided over his theses. The leadership of the opposition party fell to John Whitgift (ca. 1530–1604), the director of Trinity College and, since 1570, the vice chancellor of the university. Cartwright was finally dismissed from his university post. He went to Geneva, where he was warmly received by Beza. He gave lectures in the academy located there and became intimately familiar with the Presbyterian model of the church in practice.

When Cartwright returned to Cambridge a year later, Whitgift initiated against a suit him under the pretext that he had not been ordained to the priesthood in the space of time prescribed by his oath. Whitgift led the judicial proceeding against him that would withdraw his fellowship and therefore his livelihood. Cartwright then lived with several of his prosperous followers, sustaining himself in part by becoming the teacher of their children. In the following period, there was an exchange of pamphlets with Whitgift (see below). At the same time, the beginning of the official persecution of the Puritans also affected Cartwright. In order to escape the threat of incarceration, he fled in late 1573 to Germany and enrolled in the University of Heidelberg, which, at the time, was under the protectorate of the prince elector, Friedrich III of Kurpfalz (ruled 1559–1576). Heidelberg was the citadel of Reformed theology. In 1563, the Heidelberg Catechism had appeared in the frame of a new church order. When a Lutheran prince elector (Ludwig VI, 1576–1583) followed, the Calvinists, among whom Cartwright had taken refuge, had to leave Heidelberg. He enrolled in Basel. His next position was in Middelburgh in Holland. Initially he was the chief sales officer for the English merchants who resided there. In 1580, beginning as proxy, he became the pastor of the English community first in Antwerp and then from 1582 in Middelburgh. He declined calls to be a professor, first at Leiden and later at St. Andrews. As a result of the urging of his friends, he returned to England in 1585, in spite of poor health. Arriving there he was immediately taken prisoner. While in prison, he was, nonetheless, visited by masses of people who wished to greet him. On account of this popularity, the queen obtained his release. Being a wise politician, she reached the conclusion that treating him well would make him less dangerous.

When Whitgift became archbishop of Canterbury in 1583, he immediately introduced sanctions against the Puritans. To this end, he published three articles to which every priest in all of his archdioceses was to subscribe by oath. This meant that the priest had to accept the Book of Common Prayer in its totality and could not use any other form of worship. A refusal meant the threat of dismissal, which happened to about three to four hundred clergymen. A storm of protest, which reached as high as the royal counsel of the government, forced Whitgift to withdraw his sanctions in part. In spite of persecution, the Puritan activities continued, especially in the regular, local meetings of pastors, the so-called *classes*, an early form of Presbyteries. Influential patrons held their protective hand over the Puritans. Still, their efforts to achieve in Parliament a Presbyterian system continued to be fruitless, largely owing to the position of the queen and the parliamentary majority.

In the year 1586, the Earl of Leicester, who was the leading Puritan at court, named Cartwright the principal of the military hospital in Warwick, which was endowed by the earl himself. Cartwright preached in a nearby church every Sunday and was now recognized as the uncontested leader of the Presbyterians. Numerous queries reached him on a regular basis, through which he was requested to offer his insight on the numerous problems of the Christian order of life.

At the same time, various events had weakened the Puritan cause. The Earl of Leicester died in 1588, as did his brother, the Earl of Warwick in 1589 (or 1590). John Field, one of the important spokespersons of the Puritans, likewise died shortly before, in 1588. Using the pseudonym Martin Marprelate, Job Throckmorton, who was probably a member of the Puritan laity, wrote satirical attacks against the conformist priests at the time the Puritan cause was strengthening. The excess of these attacks alienated conventional believers more than strengthening the Puritan position. The state church authorities used the situation to strike a decisive blow. Leading Puritans, among them Cartwright, were hunted down, arrested, and indicted. In October of 1590, Cartwright was imprisoned. Various charges were brought against him in the High Commission, which he was required to refute. Among them was the charge that he had refused the loyalty oath, to which he largely refused to give an answer. He comported himself in a similar fashion when he was interrogated by the highest court, the Star Chamber. Although he was never found guilty, he remained in prison with other Puritans until 1592, when he presumably returned to Warwick. He received a chaplain's post with the chief magistrate of the Island of Guernsey in 1595, a position that he held until 1601. He spent the last years of his life, prior to his death in December 1603, back in Warwick. He had survived into the beginning of the reign of James I (1603–1625) and even received an invitation to speak at the conference of Hampton Court that was held in 1604, when the hope was that a new regulation of churchly measures would be approved. He died before this conference was held, and the reform did not materialize. During the 1590s, the Puritan activity had shifted from a churchly, political polemic to the moral theology set forth by William Perkins (1558–1602), which emphasized the majesty of God in opposition to fallen humanity and accentuated the double predestination of salvation and damnation, rebirth, the conscience, and the covenant as the obligatory basis of action. These were typically Calvinistic theological doctrines (originating with Zwingli, Bullinger, and Calvin and continuing with Beza).

The "Admonition to the Parliament," which, as we have already noted, appeared in the summer of 1572, is still attributed by some scholars to Cartwright. However, most have concluded that its authors were John Field and Thomas Wilcox (ca. 1549–1608). Presumably Cartwright was the author of a second "Admonition," which appeared in October of 1572, along with the publication of the written disputations he had with Whitgift (which he published in his *Works*). The authorities attempted to associate all three (Field, Wilcox, and Cartwright) with operating an illegal printing shop, but these efforts were in vain. A widespread group of followers consisting of Puritan laity and pastors arranged for the distribution of these writings.

Even if the "Admonition" did not likely originate personally with Cartwright, it is still the most clearly articulated witness of the Puritan-Presbyterian position. In the "Admonition," the authors primarily stress that "nothyng in this mortal life is more diligently to be sought for, and carefully looked unto than the restoration of true religion and the reformation of Gods Church." The gathered Parliament should be responsible for this. This reformation, to which the Parliament must concentrate all of its efforts, is to seek "not only in abandoning al popish remnants in ceremonies and regiment, but also in bringing and placing in Gods church those things only, which the Lord himself in his word commandeth" ("Admonition," Frere and Douglas, 8). For we in England are so far from having a church rightly reformed on the basis of God words "that we are not [the second edition inserts 'scarce' for 'not'] yet come to the outward face of the same." Three things are to be considered the characteristics of the church. The two fundamental characteristics both wings of the classical Reformation churches emphasize: the unadulterated preaching of the word and the correct administration of the sacraments. Church discipline is added, "which consisteth in admonition and correction of faults severelie" (9). For the service of the word it is to be conceded "that the substance of doctrine by many delivered is sound and good, yet here in it faileth, that neither the ministers thereof are according to Gods word proved, elected, called, or ordayned: nor the function in such sorte so narrowly looked into, as of right it ought, and is of necessitie required."

Subsequently, the practice of the early church is contrasted to the present situation in the Church of England. During the early period, a rigorous selection of servants of the Word for teaching and conduct was undertaken, and no one would be admitted who had offered sacrifices to idols or had functioned as a pagan priest. Now priests who were active during the reigns of Henry VIII, Edward VI, Mary, and Elizabeth were in office, chosen on the basis of private recommendation. These included all sorts of persons who were incapable of giving instruction and were even in need of teaching themselves. In contrasting the ancient church with its present form, the pamphlet reads:

> Then, the community had authority to call ministers: instead thereof now, they run, they ride, and by unlawful suit and purchase of position, they also prevent other suitors. In the time of the ancient church, no

pastor could be placed in any community without the agreement of its members. Now total power resides within the hand of the Bishop, who by his authority imposes people upon them, whom they legitimately reject as pastor on the basis either of a dishonorable life or the lack of a proper education.... In the ancient Church, after just trial and vocation ... [ministers] were admitted to their function, by laying on of the hands of the company of the eldership onely: now ther is ... required an albe, a suprplesse, a vestiment, a pastoral staffe, beside that ridiculus, and ... blasphemous saying, receave the holy gost.... Then every pastor had his flocke, and every flocke his shepheard, or ells shepheards: Now they doe not only run fyskying from place to place (a miserable disorder in Gods church) but covetously joine living to living, making shipwrakce of their owne consciences, and being but one shepherd ... have many flockes. Then the ministers were preachers; now bare readers.... In those dayes knowne by voice, learning and doctrine: now they must be discerned from other by popish and Antichristin apparel, as cap, gowne, tippet, etc.... At that time the office was painful, but now it is gainful (word-play). At that time it was a service of poverty and shame, but now it is one of wealth and fame. Therefore, they are assigned titles, properties, and offices, which are devised by the Antichrist. These include metro-politan bishop, archbishop, gracious lord, lord bishop, suffragan bishop, dean, archdeacon..., etc. All of these, which are foreign to the Church of Christ, are expressly forbidden in God's Word, and must be promptly and completely removed.... (10–11)

In addition, it is necessary to abolish a number of things from the pre-scribed order of worship and set of requirements found in the Book of Common Prayer, for they stand in "contradiction to God's Word. These include baptism performed by women, private communion, Jewish rites of purification, observance of feast days, and so forth" (11–12).

All of these statements are rhetorically and skillfully crafted and effec-tively argued by setting forth the contrast between the "then" and "now," something that calls forth an impressive form of propaganda. It is no wonder that this pamphlet was propagated so quickly, and the church's establishment sought to suppress the writing's circulation by every avail-able means.

Among the presuppositions of the argumentation, many motifs attract attention that derived from Christian humanism. To these belonged pri-marily the comparison with an ideal period of the early church to which people are called to return immediately. The present situation of the church is experienced as the period of dissipation, characterized by every kind of abuse, and these abuses are required to be totally set aside. Anticlericalism is the motif that stands out most in this text. This motif found fertile ground in the hierarchical structure of the church. Reform, not reformation, is the actual purpose of the humanistic criticism of the church (see *History*, vol. 3). Furthermore, it is characteristic, as already noted with regard to Bishop Hooper, that the criticism is directed toward liturgical vestments. The Puritans reject them as "papist." Actually they were preserved in the Church of England from the time prior to the period of the Reformation. The still fresh memory of the Catholic threat posed by Mary made this criticism a popular argument. Even so, behind this critique lay a fundamental anti-ceremonialism. For the Conformists (similarly true of Luther), liturgical forms and vestments were not believed to be relevant (*adiaphora*). This is also a central point made by Whitgift for rejecting the Puritan's demands, and such an argument, deriving from humanistic ideas, had played a role earlier in Melanchthon's disputation with the Gnesio-Lutherans (see *History*, vol. 3).

In addition to the humanistic presuppositions, biblical ones are also to be considered. For the Puritans, the Bible, in particular the New Testament, was literally authoritative in the entirety of its wording. Today one would call this attitude fundamentalism; however, in that period it is simply precritical. Although observations made possible by historical-critical methodology—differentiations, awareness of the contradictions in Scripture, historical nuances, and, related to these, different valuations of the text—resided outside the horizons of the biblical scholarship of the time, perceptive observations were often made. But for all that, the Puritans' view of Scripture was in no way impartial. Decisive was the view that Scripture is completely identical to the Word of God. As such, all of its various parts are equally authoritative. Therefore, Scripture was interpreted literally and construed as expressing a complete harmony. A presupposition was that, in terms of its content, the Bible was considered to be a book of law to instruct its readers in their obligations to God. Corresponding to this, the concept of covenant was interpreted in the sense of a contract, the requirements of which were imposed upon the Christians. Similar ideas are found already in Calvin (see *History*, vol. 3). For the Puritans, however, these obligations carried considerably greater weight. This orientation to deeds was left untouched by the Reformation's doctrines of justification and grace when considering the laws of the Old Testament. This allowed a mixture of a Calvinistic theological foundation with the humanistic tradition continuing since Erasmus in the English population. This is clear when the moral law of the Old Testament, in particular the Decalogue, is seen to be identical with the natural law. In addition, Cartwright and Perkins also regarded the Jewish civil law as binding not only in ancient Israel but also in their own day. Moreover, it goes without saying that the entire Scripture was interpreted christologically.

The "Admonition" further criticizes the practice of the Eucharist in the church. In this case, too, the demand for celebrating the Lord's Supper according to that practiced in the Bible stood at the center of contention. Issues included the use of bread instead of the host, the receiving of the elements while sitting instead of kneeling, the forbidding of private communion, the use of the exact words of Christ in the language of institution, and the removal of sins (13–14).

A third point in the "Admonition," which was the most important, was the order of the church (15–19). In this matter, the Presbyterian model was defended as the only one that was scriptural. The order, which Calvin had introduced in Geneva, was to be in force also in the Church of England. According to the Bible, there are only three offices— preachers (pastors), elders, and deacons—and these are to return to their biblical functions. Thus, pastors are to proclaim the Word; elders are to lead the community; and deacons are to attend to the care of the poor. The collectors of the offering are to assume only this role; they are not to usurp the office of the deacon. Hierarchy was rejected; the "equality of the servants" (16) was the primary requirement. In addition, a strong churchly discipline was demanded. Excommunication (exclusion from the Eucharist) was rigorously enforced against all sinners, and this was handled impartially.

In the concluding literary feud between Cartwright and Whitgift, the latter foreswore the possibility of finding a thoroughgoing New Testament justification. His central point reads: "I find in the Scriptures not *one* certain and ideal form of leadership that is proscribed or commanded to Christ's Church, which must be seen as unquestionable or as a necessity for the salvation of the Church" (*Works* 1:184). The view of Cartwright is diametrically opposed to this position. He emphasizes that "matters of ceremonies, order, discipline and (church) government belong to … matters of faith and salvation." If the position introduced by Whitgift were allowed to become pervasive in the Church of England, the consequence would be that the church would lack any biblically based order. Instead, this order would be shaped according to tradition and practice. In his theology, Whitgift was no less a Calvinist than his opponent. Other theological considerations would be established in the next century that would allow the unity of the church finally to be maintained, and the Puritans around Perkins would draw back into the sphere of personal piety. Cartwright likewise was energetically opposed to a separation from the official church, which was the aim of the radical Congregationalists and especially the followers of Thomas Brown (ca. 1550–1633), that is, the so-called Brownists. The day of the Puritans as a political power dawned with the English Revolution around 1640, yet their misuse of power led finally to their failure in 1660.

2.2. Instituting the "Mortal God" as the Lord of Refuge: Thomas Hobbes

Thomas Hobbes was born in Westport, a suburb of Malmsbury in the county of Wilshire, near Bristol. He was the second son of the curate of the local parish. As he wrote in his autobiography, composed in Latin, he came too early into the world on 5 April 1588, for his mother had given birth to "twins," "himself and apprehension" (*Opera latina* 1:lxxxvi). Hobbes brings (chronologically imprecise) his birth into direct correspondence with the setting sail of the Spanish Armada against England (May 1588). Thus, according to his own awareness, his birth was connected with an important moment in world history. His father, a theologically uneducated clergyman who scarcely knew how to do anything more than to follow the prescribed liturgy (something not unusual for that period), died early, and the gifted youth received the patronage of a well-to-do uncle who provided him with the means for his education. Early on he mastered Latin and Greek in the primary schools and, following additional private tutoring, was accepted into Oxford University after he was presented with a "school certificate" by his teacher for his Latin translation of the play *Medea*, by Euripides. In Oxford he studied in Magdalene Hall and received the bachelor of arts degree in 1608, following his basic studies. The troublesome conflicts between the Puritans and the followers of the state church at the beginning of the reign of James I flowed into the University of Oxford. The Military Petition, which was signed by eight hundred Puritan clergy and presented to the new king, led to the defeat of the Puritans at the conclusion of the Hampton Court Conference. The king empowered the system of the see of bishops with his famous declaration: "No bishop, no king." In Oxford the ideology of the state church was enforced through corresponding measures of censure and discipline. Still, Hobbes should have been able to detect in Magdalene Hall the Puritan spirit, which was dominant there. But we hear almost nothing about those years.

Hobbes's life took a decisive turn when he was employed by William Cavendish (Baron of Hardwick), the head of one of the most wealthy and influential families in the country, as tutor of his young son, who was only two years his junior. Hardwick became the Earl of Devonshire in 1618. Hobbes's appointment was due to the recommendation he received from the leader of the Hall. Hobbes thereafter spent a great part of his life in the two country estates of the family, Chatsworth and, above all, Hardwick Hall (the main estate) in Derbyshire. He continued to serve three successive generations of the Cavendish family. After two years of residency in Hardwick, he set out with his ward on an educational excursion, which was obligatory for young nobles, traveling to Germany, France, and Italy. This trip lasted from three to five years. Back at home in Hardwick and during an even longer residence with his lord in London where he was the accompanying steward, he had a great deal of time for his own activity that included reading in the well stocked library of the manor. Here he was especially occupied with reading the Greek and Roman classics. One fruit of his labors was his translation of the history of the Peloponnesian war written by Thucydides (ca. 460–403 B.C.E.), published in 1629. For a while, he served as the secretary of Francis Bacon (1561–1626), who had been dismissed as lord chancellor in 1621. Hobbes translated for him some essays written in Latin. He also represented his lord in the management of the Virginia Company, which invested in the newly established colonies in Virginia and Bermuda. In 1626, the first earl died, and Hobbes's student succeeded him as the head of the family. But he soon died in 1628. Hobbes thus dedicated his translation of Thucydides to the second earl's eleven year old son and successor.

The second earl had left behind considerable debts. Facing financial difficulties, his widow at once reduced the number of employees, including the post held by Hobbes. Subsequently, he assumed new duties as the tutor of the seventeen-year-old son of Sir Gervase in Nottinghamshire, whom he accompanied for a year and a half on a grand tour to France and then to Geneva. It was during this trip, likely in Geneva, that he accidentally came across an opened volume of the "Elements" of Euclid in the library of a host. From this reading, he came to be impressed by the geometric method of proving mathematical theorems by the use of reason. Euclid taught how to dismantle complex theorems into their most simple, basic elements, and then, starting from the fundamental one, to construct a new synthesis. This awakened in Hobbes an interest in geometry (mathematics) and especially the natural sciences, which he was able to develop through exchanges with other intellectuals during his later stays in Welbeck and Paris. He sought, then, to translate Euclid's method into a political philosophy and to establish it on a more geometrical (i.e., mathematical) basis.

Not long after his return in 1631, so it seems, he was recalled to Hardwick by Lady Devonshire, the widow of the deceased earl, and he soon became the tutor of her son, the thirteen-year-old third earl. While there, he also met relatives of the family, including William, Earl (later Duke) of Newcastle (1593–1676), whom he visited rather frequently at his country estate in Welweck, and his younger brother, Sir Charles Cavendish. A circle of intellectuals came to Welweck, among whom were the poet Ben Johnson (1573–1637), Sir William Davenant (1606–1668), and the optician Walter Warner (ca. 1570–1643). Interested in the natural sciences, among other things, Hobbes studied, for example, the works of Galileo Gallilei (1564–1642), who is important above all as the founder of the mathematical-natural, scientific method. Hobbes presumably also visited the country estate of Lucius Cary (Lord Falkland [1610–1643]), the lord of the manor of Great Tew in Oxford, a meeting place of liberal followers of the state church and the monarchy. In 1634, Hobbes embarked with his young lord on an impressive tour to the Continent that lasted for two years. In Paris he met the Franciscan Martin Mersenne (1588–1648), who was occupied especially with mathematical-natural scientific studies, and his circle of scholars, among whom was Pierre Gassendi (1592–1655). Philosophically these thinkers were in many cases skeptics who raised doubts about the prescribed ontic and moral truths fostered by Aristotle, and at the same time sought a new basis for knowledge in reason. On his way to Venice, Hobbes also visited Galileo at his country villa in Florence. On the return trip, Hobbes and his charge took up residence yet again in Paris for eight months by renewing the contacts, including Mersenne and his circle. He added to this a personal, Europe-wide exchange of letters with foreign scholars. After his return (1636–1637), Hobbes played with the idea of ending his service to the Devonshires. He moved to Welwick, where he stayed for a lengthy period; however, he continued to live in Chatsworth. The third earl asked him to assist him in the expansion of his library holdings.

Hobbes was already busy in preparing his philosophical life's work in the form of a trilogy, which would bear the name *Elementa philosophiae*. He was unable to publish the first two major sections, *Concerning Matter* (*De corpore*) and *About Man* (*De homine*), before 1655 (the first) and 1658 (the second). For an anticipated volume on political philosophy, he had completed in May 1640 a preliminary study (*Elements of Law, Natural and*

Political). Aristocratic friends pressured him to disseminate it in a hand-written form.

This transpired during an explosive political time. King Charles I (reigned 1625–1649), who ruled with absolute political control, had by that time fallen into increasing difficulties. Many members of Parliament inclined to Puritan thinking, being scandalized by the Archbishop of Canterbury, William Laud (1573–1645), who was a supporter of the tradi-tional Church of England's views of liturgy. In order to carry out his wars against the Scots and the Dutch, Charles I required the financial support from Parliament. The "Long Parliament" (1640–1648) exacted from the king severe concessions: the removal, imprisonment, and finally execu-tion of Laud and the king's chief political advisor, the Earl of Strafford (condemned and executed in 1641). Since Hobbes's suggested resolution in his political writing amounted to giving total authority to the ruler who was in office, he felt himself severely threatened by the Parliament and thus fled to Paris. He lived there for the next ten years. The royal succes-sor, the later Charles II, also was sheltered in Paris by his tutors, for he was still young. Hobbes was called temporarily to the exiled court in Saint Germain to instruct the young man in mathematics.

During this time, civil war broke out in England in 1642. When Oliver Cromwell (1599–1658) led the victorious army of the Parliament against those loyal to the monarchy, Charles I fled to Scotland, whose leaders pro-ceeded to deliver him back to England. His execution resulted in the final victory of Parliament in 1649. The abolishment of the system of bishops sealed at the same time the provisional victory of the Puritans, although the Independents led by Cromwell, not the Presbyterians, comprised the major force of his army.

In Paris, Hobbes again met together with his old discussion part-ners, including Mersenne and Gassendi (since 1645 a professor in Paris). He published in Amsterdam as a private printing the social, theoretical portion of his life's work under the title *De cive*. This new edition was disseminated in a limited circulation only under his initials. Later there were additional printings (1647) produced in Amsterdam. Hobbes suf-fered from a severe illness for several months in 1647, which brought him close to death. Thereafter he was afflicted with gradually increasing trem-ors of the hands that continued for the remainder of his life. In his last years, he could write only with the help of secretaries. When Mersenne died in 1648, Hobbes became increasingly lonely. In the spring of 1651, there appeared in London an authorized English translation of *De cive* (*Philosophical Rudiments concerning Government and Society*). During the same year, Hobbes also composed a new volume, which the same house published under the title, *Leviathan; or, The Matter, Forme and Power of a Commonwealth Ecclesiastical and Civil*. A splendid copy of this work was presented to the pretender to the throne (the later Charles II) at the court of Saint Germain, but Hobbes was no longer received there after October. *Leviathan* had triggered vehement accusations against Hobbes as a professed atheist. The high Anglican clergy especially resented his presence at court, since he wished to place in question the subjection of the church under the direct lordship of the sovereign. This corresponded to the system of *independence* introduced by Cromwell: the freedom of the congregations under only a very loose political oversight. Hobbes wanted not only to renounce external church oversight but also to deny the sovereign the authority to make decisions about Christian dogma. Furthermore, he set forth a natural religion that barely referred to a personal God, thus strengthening the accusation of atheism. A ruler scarcely could associate any longer with such a person.

After a declaration of loyalty to the Republic (Commonwealth) under Cromwell's rule, Hobbes believed he could live again in England without risk. He returned there in the winter of 1652 and was soon received again by the Earl of Devonshire on his manors and lived there and sometimes in London until his death. Meanwhile, Cromwell had erected his sole rule as "Lord Protector" in 1653, which endured until his death in 1658 but collapsed soon thereafter.

In 1660, Charles II was called back to the throne by the people and the army and moved into London. Hobbes presented himself on the roadside to the king, and when Charles II passed by in a coach he greeted Hobbes graciously. The king granted Hobbes free access to the court and offered him a yearly pension, although it frequently was not paid. Hobbes's enemies, however, had defamed him as both a nonbeliever and a father of immorality such that it became fashionable among the wanton courtiers to call themselves "Hobbists" in order to provoke the clergy. The clergy, on the other side, blamed the conflagration of London in the year 1666 on the licentious deeds occasioned by Hobbes's influence and called this fire a punishment of heaven. Although legal proceedings that had been initiated against Hobbes for the illegal distribution of printed material (especially the *Leviathan*) were quashed through the influence of powerful friends, the king forbade him to publish additional compositions.

Hobbes's later years were made miserable by the constant fear of persecution. Uncommon for that time, he reached an advanced age and lived longer than most of his adversaries. In 1675–1676, at the age of eighty-seven or eighty-eight, he even translated the entire work of Homer into Latin. He also composed a text entitled *Behemoth* (in spite of the fact that the king previously had denied him permission to write an official publication) in the year of his death. This book dealt with the dissolving of any kind of political order during the period of the civil war of 1640–1660, especially during the time of the "Long Parliament." On 4 December 1679, he died following a stroke.

Especially illuminating for the role of the Bible in Hobbes's thought is *Leviathan*, which points to the mature, final stage of the edifice of his philosophy, the structure of which was already begun in *De cive*. Since his opponents had already defamed him as an atheist, *Leviathan* suffered a great deal of injury at the hands of its contemporary interpreters. Even so, an entire school wished to enlist Hobbes in a positive manner as a thinker removed from theology and as the originator of a modern, secular conception of the state. New editions and translations of *Leviathan* continued to appear for many years, although only the first two major sections were transmitted. The remainder of the book (two additional main sections that constitute more than half of the complete volume!) was judged to be of little interest for the modern reader and thus was omitted. In the meantime, it seems to have become widely recognized that the sources were clearly falsified by this position. Hobbes himself several times rejected the charge that he was an atheist. Philosophical historians accustomed to reasoning on a secular level considered the argument in the first half of *Leviathan* to be most important, and they believed that they could ascertain his positions by "intrinsic" arguments.

At the same time, it is clearly mistaken to identify in Hobbes's philosophy a single strand of thought that provides a consistent perspective for his social, theoretical system. For all of his originality, he was a Christian thinker of the seventeenth century, dependent on the cosmological presuppositions and different traditions of his age. The seventeenth century primarily expressed its thoughts theologically, and these theological influences are clearly evident in Hobbes's work. Thus, he was under the impress of Calvinism (Hobbes belonged to the Calvinistic High Church) as well as humanism, which was especially vital in England during this period. Influential humanists included John Colet (see *History*, vol. 3), Erasmus (see *History*, vol. 3), and Thomas More (1478–1535). In addition, although newly founded in England, a monarchy ruling both state and church was not an innovative concept. Hobbes was not the first to emphasize the imposition of a monarchy that ruled both state and church as the only possible result. This view resulted in part from

Hobbes's experience of the break-up of any kind of political order during the period of the Long Parliament (cf. *Leviathan*). Thomas Erastus (ca. 1523–1583), one of the Heidelberg reformers, had already developed the theory of the right of the ruling sovereign over the church (called Erastianism), a view that found wide distribution in England and Scotland.

New, however, is Hobbes's rational procedure of argumentation, which he used in developing his theses. This approach was based on the method taken from the natural, scientific, and mathematical discourse. This mode of discourse was the object of his occasional expression that the subject of philosophy "excludes theology" (*English Works* 1:10), which was frequently taken as evidence of a rejection of any kind of theology. Although Hobbes is original and subsequently consistent in the use of philosophy in an entirely new field, he still places alongside it many traditional, theological ways of argumentation. His practice is in no way a purely opportunistic, external alignment of the two fields, nor is it a concession to human irrationality, as has been recently argued.

The structure of *Leviathan* is instructive. in the opening segment ("Of Man") of part 1, "Commonwealth," Hobbes develops initially the anthropological process of argumentation. At the same time, the third major section, "Of a Christian Commonwealth," sets forth in parallel fashion the concept that both state and church stand under a ruler, a reality that depicts the unity of the state church in England. The fourth major section reinforces the third, when Hobbes describes the "Kingdome of Darknesse." Here we recognize a polemical description of the negative counterpoint to the ideal Christian commonwealth set forth by the Roman Catholic Church. Hobbes's theory about the origin of the state in *De cive* and in *Leviathan* is well known. According to the *natural human condition* (certainly not a historically conceived, primeval state, but rather a theoretical model), a war of everyone against everyone prevails (part 1, ch. 13). The freedom to seek out self-preservation is a natural right, and therefore opposing enemies of this right is a prerogative of and appropriate for every individual. However, there is no security that prevails in this situation (1.14). Obviously shaped by Calvinism, this thoroughly pessimistic assessment of human nature is striking. Hobbes mentions three major motifs of human actions: "First, competition; secondly diffidence; thirdly, glory" (*Leviathan, English Works* 3:112). To desire to be like God is hubris, according to the Bible's understanding of the classical sin of humanity. From the seeking of self-preservation, there follows the fundamental law of nature "that every man, ought to endeavour peace, as far as he has hope of obtaining it" (117). From this first law of nature, there follows a second. Each person should speak out in the interest of peace his renouncement of reciprocity in claiming his right of everything in order to enable the other to practice his own natural right. This is the rationale for the so-called social contract. It is to be noted that Hobbes soon moves from the idea of "contract" to that of "covenant," thus providing a theologically constituted expression. The difference, according to Hobbes, is that there is a chronological aspect bound up with a covenant: "The matter, or subject of a covenant, is always something that falleth under deliberation; for to covenant, is an act of the will; that is to say, an act, and the last act of deliberation; and is therefore always understood to be something to come; and which is judged possible for him that covenanteth, to perform" (126). The further consequence (2.17) is the transfer of total power to a sovereign (a man [cf. the parallel expression] or a group of men; the absolute monarchy is therefore not theoretically the only conceivable form of the state), which henceforth the subjects must obey, at least if the commandments of God are not violated. Here (158) we find the famous definition of Leviathan as the "*mortal God*," "to which we owe under the *immortal God*, our peace and defense." The choice of the name Leviathan, who is the monster of the sea in the book of Job (with the motto from Job 41:24 on the book's artificially styled title page), is not accidental: God encounters Job with the sheer demonstration of power, which is sufficient for his submission. Hobbes consciously reaches back to biblical mythology in order to designate his teaching concerning earthly and heavenly power.

At the end of the major section, we find the chapter (2.31) entitled "Of the Kingdom of God by Nature" (343–58). It is characteristic for Hobbes that he here defines the natural relationship to God through the connection between power and obedience. Earlier (*Elements of Law*, ch. 18; *De cive*, ch. 4) Hobbes had identified the natural law directly and conclusively as the divine law. Here, however, he places the corresponding chapter at the conclusion of the main section. In doing so, civil law is included within its own sphere. With this Hobbes already appeals to the commandments of God in Scripture in the *Elements of Law*. While this appears to modern readers to be alien and extraneous to the modern legal system, it was consistent for Hobbes. Because humans either wanted or did not want to be subjected to the power of God, they must know as citizens of the state what God's commandments are, and they must neither "by too much civil obedience offend the Divine Majesty" nor "act contrary to God out of fear," thus fearing God to transgress "the commandments of the commonwealth" (*Leviathan*, 343) For the passage, Hobbes cites statements out of the royal psalms (Pss 97:1; 99:1)! The concept of "kingdom" for the power of God over the entire creation certainly must be only metaphorical: "For he only is properly said to reign, that governs his subjects by his word, and by promise of rewards to those that obey it, and by threatening them with punishments that obey it not." Irrational creatures, but also "atheists or those that do not believe that God has any care of the actions of mankind" (343), are therefore not subjects in the kingdom of God (344).

Hobbes again makes a connection with the Protestant tradition when he emphasizes the Word of God. He understands the term, however, in a broad sense. He speaks of a threefold Word of God, which comes through three sources: through natural reason (the rational), through revelation (inspiration through the senses), and through a human voice (the prophetic). The second possibility (through inspiration and supernatural experience) is actually eliminated, since God speaks in this way only to an individual person. Therefore, there remain two kinds of Word of God, which correspond to "a twofold kingdom, *natural* and *prophetic*: natural, wherein he governeth as many of mankind as acknowledge his providence, by the natural dictates of right reason; and prophetic, wherein having chosen out one peculiar nation, the Jews, for his subjects, he governed them, and none but them, not only by natural reason, but by positive laws, which he gave them by the mouths of his holy prophets" (345). Later (*Leviathan* 3.36; 407ff.) he adds, as a precise philologist, that the concept "Word of God" may have a double meaning in the Bible, thus following the sense of the Greek *logos theou*: "The words spoken by God, and concerning God, both are called God's word in Scripture" (*Marginalie*, 407). One could speak of the entire Bible as the Word of God only in the second sense.

In a characteristic manner, Hobbes stresses that the natural law, on the basis of which God reigns over humanity, and the obedience that is due him cannot derive from thankfulness for his blessings, but rather from his omnipotence, which allows him "the right of afflicting men at his pleasure" (346). Thus, Hobbes refers to a guiltless Job whom God nevertheless punished! The God of Job was at the same time a main witness to divine incomprehensibility (383): "We understand nothing of what he is, but only that He is"). Since everything spoken about God is only the transmission of human characteristics, one reaches the logical conclusion that one comes to understand God only through the negation of what is human (thus, one has the transient and the eternal, and the mortal and the immortal, that is, a so-called negative theology). "And therefore, the name of God is used, not to make us conceive him, for he is incomprehensible;

and his greatness, and power are unconceivable; but that we may honour him" (17). To the laws of nature or the commandments of natural reason, which have been given to humans without an additional Word of God, belong also the honor owed to God (again a central Calvinistic concept) and its different symbols.

But Hobbes was familiar not only with "the God of the philosophers," who evades every understanding, but also with the God who revealed himself in history. Therefore, Hobbes comes to speak about the Bible in the third main part, which leads to the concluding chapter (2.31). He does not attempt to connect both concepts about God.

He takes up the theme of this section in the first chapter (3.32). In the initial marginal comment (359), Hobbes summarized his theme: "The word of God delivered by prophets is the main principle of Christian politics." This was the reason why Hobbes occupied himself expressly with establishing his teaching about the state by connecting it with the Bible (for many modern interpreters this is incomprehensible or objectionable). In a second marginal remark, he adds: "Yet, is not natural reason to be renounced?" If something beyond reason is found in the Word of God, this means only that Scripture contains something that is neither demonstrated rationally nor refuted by natural reason. Even so, there is nothing in the Bible that runs contrary to reason (360). Thus, in the concluding observation (712), Hobbes contends: "all truth of doctrine dependeth either upon *reason* or upon the *Scriptures*." In making this argument, Hobbes moves along two planes. On the one hand, the newly revealed method of natural reason ought to prove in the sphere of the Christian theory of state that which the Word of God contains and the manner by which it may be transmitted authoritatively. On the other hand, Scripture thoroughly confirms what has been demonstrated in the preceding, main sections through the arguments of reason. Already in the previous main sections, including section 2 (which is the one most frequently read), the rational arguments concerning the state were treated, although the Scripture was frequently cited. For example, after the rational reasons were given for the distinction developed between the fatherly and despotic types of rule, one reads: "Let us now consider what the Scripture teacheth in the same point" (2.20, 191), and the argumentation has the identical result to what is taught by the process of human thought (i.e., the absolute power of the sovereign). Thus, "it appeareth plainly, ... both from reason, and Scripture" (194). It is striking that Hobbes takes his arguments from Old Testament passages and not from Rom 13. Perhaps his opponents had used Rom 13 too much in making their arguments in order to stress the divine, sacred worth of the king. Hobbes seeks to limit this affirmation by arguing that the king was chosen by his subjects according to the natural state of affairs. Even the "natural laws" are grounded in two ways. On the one side, they are the concluding results of reason and therefore should have been rather called "theorems," while, on the other side, they can be called "laws," "if we consider the same theorem, as delivered in the word of God, that by right commandeth all things" (1.15, 147).

In 3.32, Hobbes takes up once again ideas that he had expressed in the preceding chapter: God is able either to speak directly to a human being or indirectly through a person to whom he had previously spoken. The first alternative does not help, if one cannot convince others that God had addressed him. Moreover, the Scripture expressly warns about false prophets who only pretended that God had spoken to them (Deut 13:1–5). A miracle in and of itself cannot prove anything, since the Egyptian magicians also could perform wonders. Jesus likewise (according to Matt 24:24) warned about miracles. Since one may not always be able to wait for the fulfillment of a particular prophecy (Deut 18:21–22), Scripture indicates that the existence of a true prophet, that is, one who received a direct revelation, can be presupposed only when "the teaching of the religion which God hath established, and the showing of a present miracle" coincide (365).

Miracles now have ceased for a lengthy period of time. This means that "miracles cease, prophets cease, and the Scripture supplies their place" (marginal note, ibid.). Therefore, we lack the signs that enable us to recognize revealed speech of any private person. Since Jesus Christ, Scripture has taken the place of direct revelation, "from which by wise and learned interpretation and careful human reasoning we easily may derive all necessary rules and precepts that allow us to recognize our obligation toward God and people" (ibid.).

Here, as a result of the humanistic tradition, the Bible is understood as a book of law in which the obligations toward God and humans are mentioned in the same breath. The moral teaching given this way supplements the one provided by natural laws. Correspondingly, Hobbes writes over a later section (ch. 42; in the context of the question concerning the power of the church) with a note on the margin: "Of the power to make Scripture, law" (marginal note, 512). This concerns the Decalogue, the first tablet of which was a special law for the people of God who were obliged to be obedient to Moses (Exod 20:19), since they were placed under his power. The same is true for the law of the judges and priests, as well as the "Second Law" (Deuteronomy). The Old Testament as a whole was regarded as the law of the Jews since Ezra (the one who was given the power to serve in the role of high priest by the sovereign of that day). The New Testament became at first obligatory as law, when sovereigns were installed who were authorized to proclaim it as such. Since the apostles did not possess this mandate, during their time it held only the rank of good advice (441 = 519).

Hobbes clearly indicates why he draws on the Bible for this political philosophy: "And this Scripture is it, out of which I am to take the principles of my discourse, concerning the rights of those that are the supreme governors on earth of Christian commonwealths; and of the duty of Christian subjects towards their sovereigns" (365). Even if his remaining principles might not be reasonable, they are principles of Holy Scripture, as he would demonstrate, when he would come to speak about the kingdom of God among the Jews (2.30, 325). Hobbes desires to establish his absolutism also biblically, because the state was secular and Christian at the same time. At the end of chapter 43 he emphasizes once again that he only wanted "to show what are the consequences that seem to me deducible from the principles of Christian politics, (which are the holy Scriptures) in confirmation of the power of civil sovereigns, and the duty of their subjects" (602). For Hobbes, the Bible was, as it was for the Puritans, an unconditional authority. He does not attribute to the Bible the previously mentioned skepticism toward dubious receivers of revelation. He operates with the general principle that faith depends on a person's authority and our ability to trust that person, when arguments not based on reason are made (56). He emphasizes as early as in the first part (1.7, 55: "And, consequently, when we believe that the Scriptures are the word of God, having no immediate revelation from God himself, our belief, faith, and trust is in the church; whose word we take, and acquiesce therein").

Hobbes mentions expressly the entire horizon of the viewpoint from which he approaches the Bible. The accusation that he has knowingly concealed central statements of the Old and New Testaments, for example, in offering an extremely selective portrait of Moses who was not discussed as a leader of the exodus from Egypt (cf., however, 484) or as a sufferer who was similar to the suffering Jesus, fails to consider his clearly articulated purposes. He follows much more a typology of kingship that was widespread during his time, which he thought the Old Testament patriarchs, Moses, and the "good" kings of Judah exemplified. He regards them as patterns of the English rulers. He also seeks out passages from the New Testament that portray Jesus as the king of the end-time (e.g.,

Luke 1:32–33; the inscription on the cross; Rev 17:7 [3.35, 401–2]). In the modern view, this emphasis signifies naturally a very one-sided preconception. It should not to be forgotten, however, that there are also in our time rather one-sided, ideologically shaped approaches. That the Old Testament rendered the model according to which the New Testament was also assessed was nothing new, but rather corresponded to the Reformed tradition in place since Calvin.

While Hobbes places the general derivation of the commonwealth along with the commands of the sovereign and the obedience of subjects into the social contract, he establishes the foundation of the *Christian* community on the authority of the Bible. The commonwealth and the church are thereby connected. Hobbes makes the biblical canon dependent on the authority of the commonwealth to which he had before assigned the sphere of earthly rule. He explains that as a subject of the commonwealth, "I can acknowledge no other books of the Old Testament to be Holy Scripture, but those which have been commanded to be acknowledged for such, by the authority of the Church of England" (3.33, 366–67). It should be noted that here he was speaking of the state church as a whole and not of the sovereign as a person. His conclusion, which initially appears to be almost arbitrary, loses thereby much of its sharpness. Earlier (*De cive* 17.28; *Opera latina* 2:413) Hobbes had still expressly said that in regard to the secrets of faith the one who wields the power in the state has the obligation to allow the clergy who are properly ordained to explain the Holy Scriptures. Whether he had altered fundamentally his earlier attitude is a question that remains unanswered. In addition, Hobbes stresses that the Old Testament books named by Jerome, in contrast to Josephus, were identical to those translated in the Septuagint. However, he notes that there is no canonical problem when it comes to the New Testament.

In his further statements, Hobbes expands his expressed concerns beyond what was customary for him. Now he shows interest in historical questions. We confronted this in similar fashion in the writings of Hugo Grotius, who lived at approximately the same time (see *History*, vol. 3). The humanists had limited themselves to matters of text criticism. In a further development of 3.33 (368–74), Hobbes scrutinizes the time period and authority especially of the Old Testament books and, among other things, comes to the conclusion that the Books of Moses could not have been written by him: first, because Gen 12:6 indicates that "the Canaanites dwelt at that time in the land," a comment that presupposes that at the time of the narrator they no longer dwelled there; second, because in Num 21:14 another, older, book, called the "Book of the Wars of the Lord," is mentioned. Yet what is to be attributed to Moses is the main part of the law in Deut 11–27 (cf. Deut 31:9, 26). Corresponding to this is the fact that the book of Joshua is written after him, while the books of Judges and Ruth belong to a period after the exile (especially on the basis of Judg 18:30). Somewhat similar are the books of Samuel. These elements mean that the title of a book should not be considered to indicate the author of a biblical book, but rather points to the main person who is active in the text. Among other things, Hobbes associated with the books of Kings and Chronicles the fundamental conviction that specified that facts are always older than the things that are narrated in texts. And these are always older than the books in which they exist. In addition, there is a list of older books, for example, the books of the Annals of the Kings of Israel and Judah, which are mentioned in later biblical books. Interesting is Hobbes's assessment of the form of the book of Job. Although Job may not have been a fictitious person (see Ezek 14:14 and Jas 5:11), the book is not a history. The story derived from a much-discussed question in ancient times: why the godless often have had success in this world, while good persons frequently have been distressed (372). Further, the actual discussion of the issue may be contained in the verses outside the Prologue and the Epilogue. These verses do not address the problem of suffering per se, but rather are in the typical form of moral philosophy that was used in antiquity.

In the New Testament (374–75), Hobbes is faced with fewer difficulties: each of the authors had either seen Jesus himself or had been one of his disciples (save for Paul and Luke). Therefore, what they have written is as old as the apostles. The acceptance of these writings certainly occurred later. Their final confirmation as canon followed perhaps at the earliest in the Synod of Laodicea in the year 364. Hobbes did not consider them to be forgeries.

It is striking that Hobbes does not make explicit use of the dark passages of Scripture. He acknowledges their presence, but they do not further interest him. He pursues a specific purpose: to ensure the absolute authority of the sovereign over the state and church through biblical passages.

In spite of his criticism of a fundamentalist view of the Bible, which, for example, regarded Moses as the author of the Pentateuch and considered the entire text to be authentic, he did not question its authority. The books may be Holy Scripture, even though they were written by different authors. They still were all written by *one* Spirit. Hobbes does not wish to cite indiscriminately this or that passage. Rather he chooses to follow the meaning, "which is entirely clear and conforms with the harmony and the purpose of the entire Bible" (602). The biblical books describe a condensed history and have "one and the same purpose, i.e. to turn humans to obedience to God: first, by Moses and the priests; second, by the human Christ; and third, by the apostles and successors of the apostolic authority" (377). In his view of a history running through both Testaments, Hobbes strongly resembled Calvin. Hobbes also understood, as did Calvin, the content of the Testaments as law (cf. *History* 3:120–23). This confirms once more that there appear in Hobbes both Calvinistic and humanistic influences.

A remarkable distinction between Hobbes and Calvin was associated with Hobbes's specific intention. He turns now to the question: "by what authority are they [the Scriptures] made law?" (378). He answers that insofar as they conform to the laws of nature they were without doubt the law of God and were understandable by humans who were given the gift of reason. However, if God himself has produced the Scriptures and yet has not revealed them by supernatural means, then they are not binding, especially if the Christian community united in their ruler or the church did not recognize them as authoritative.

Here emerges the struggle between the Church of England (and other communities), which the English sovereign, according to Hobbes, rightfully rules with absolute authority, and the Roman claim to be the universal Church. The latter would then also have the mandate to decide about the authority of the Bible.

Hobbes deals with this problem in 3.35 (396–406). Accordingly, the concept of the Kingdom of God is to be understood in its actual sense. God had his own concrete, earthly kingdom—namely, Israel—which he established by means of the covenant with Abraham (Gen 17:7–8) and renewed with Moses at Sinai (Exod 19:5). Through Israel, God had chosen his king. Until the time of the New Testament, this sense of the kingdom proved to be correct. According to Hobbes, this ended, however, with the selection of Saul as King (1 Sam 12:2). The renewal of the kingship is announced to come not before the end-time. From the Lord's Prayer, "thy kingdom come," Hobbes concludes that it no longer exists in the intervening time. In the intervening period, that is, in history, earthly kings are set up in order to administer lordship over the church in their particular sphere of rule. Therefore, Hobbes later (ch. 39) defines the church as "a company of men professing Christian religion, united in the person of one sovereign, at whose command they ought to assemble, and without whose authority they ought not to assemble" (459–60). Free churches are thereby illegal; however, at the same time no single, universal church exists, since there is no power on earth to which all kingdoms are subject. With this, the front line against Rome is clearly drawn as well as against the Presbyterians.

In prophecy (3.36) Hobbes distinguishes between extraordinary or sovereign prophets, to whom God spoke through dreams or vision, and prophets with a continuing, however inferior, calling. To the sovereign prophets belonged Moses, the high priests, the pious kings, and finally Jesus Christ. How God spoke to Moses on Sinai and the high priests on the throne of grace cannot at all be determined. An example of inferior prophets are the seventy elders, upon whom the spirit of Moses was placed (Num 11:25). According to Hobbes, "spirit" can mean nothing other than being obedient to the divine purpose, which in this case indicates that the elders are witnesses for the sovereign role of Moses. In the New Testament, God spoke to Mary, Joseph, Paul, and Peter through visions. On account of the rare occurrence of authentic visions, except for those of the sovereign prophets and the Lord, each one should be examined carefully by means of the application of reason to determine its authenticity. Since prophecy, originally limited to Israel, had ceased to occur in the Jewish religion, this examination proved to have negative results. Every vision concerning Christ was referred back to the Old Testament. Hobbes was familiar with the prophets who appeared in the period of the monarchy; however, he kept quiet about the fact that they delivered messages of judgment to rulers. So the ideal depiction of was not destroyed.

A miracle (3.37) according to Hobbes is "a work of God..., done, for the making manifest to his elect, the mission of an extraordinary minister for their salvation" (432). Hobbes advises that care should be taken when dealing with many, but suspicious, miracles.

Hobbes locates the future and eternal life, corresponding to the Old Testament statements, on earth (3.38). The eternal life lost by Adam already was itself an earthly paradise. In his typical fashion, Hobbes argues that an ascension of humans to heaven "can hardly be drawn from any text, which I am able to discover" (341). Even as the place of eternal punishment, "hell" will be present on the earth, so then the future kingdom of God will take place in an earthly Jerusalem when Christ returns to reign there. From here, salvation will go forth to the heathen nations. All of these assertions are substantiated by corresponding scriptural passages.

The rulers in the kingdom of God (3.40) comprise the following series: Abraham, Moses (to whom special significance is attributed), the high priests, and the kings of Judah. Abraham, along with his successors, was required to follow the divine commandments because God concluded a covenant with him. These commandments included not only the moral laws of nature but also the commandments revealed to Abraham by God through visions and dreams. The notion of covenant, which comes from the Old Testament, contradicts logically the thesis of Hobbes that divine sovereignty proceeds from God's absolute power. The most important renewal of this covenant by God occurs with Moses. God's "lieutenant was Moses, for his own time: and the succession to that office was settled upon Aaron, and his heirs after him" (463). Moses was the (representative) sovereign also in regard to questions of religion. "For Moses only spake with God, and therefore only could tell the people what it was that God required at their hands" (466). High priests and later judges followed in the role of the representative of God. With Saul's kingdom, this period came to an end. The subsequent kings were intermediary rulers whose commandments were to be obeyed. After this period of monarchic rule, there followed a time (after the exile) in which the Jews did not have a fixed community. Then came Christ (3.41), who had the threefold office of the Messiah (475): savior, shepherd or teacher, and, finally, the future, eternal king ruling under his Father. Hobbes points expressly to the fact that Christ had done nothing to diminish the laws of the Jews and the Caesar. His kingdom would begin only after the resurrection of the dead. His power is not of this world. In challenging (Robert) Bellarmine (1542–1621), the "champion of the Papacy against all other Christian princes and states" (584), Hobbes determines that the power of the church consists only in teaching (baptizing and only through penance [!] forgiving sins), while Christ had consigned political power to the princes. Power is not bequeathed to those in the church who preach. Nor can churches excommunicate one another.

In the concluding chapter of the third major section (3.43), Hobbes discusses the things that may be necessary for salvation. These include faith in Christ and obedience to the commandments. Human rulers cannot identify and determine interior faith (according to 3.40, 462). Rather, this faith is dependent on the will and power of God, even if instruction by others supervenes (312, 589–90). It is different when it comes to obedience. Since we are all sinners, "there is required at our hands now, not only *obedience* for the rest of our time, but also a *remission of sins* for the time past" (585). The difference with Luther is remarkable. Obviously, for Hobbes one does not have reckon on new sins after forgiveness occurs. Obedience is now possible without any problems. To this corresponds also Hobbes's characteristic evaluation of the sacrifice of Christ. Hobbes explains that God has resolved that Christ's sacrifice occurred "for the reduction of his elect to their former covenanted obedience" (480). Here one also finds Hobbes's typical statement that thereby God accepts the desired responsibility for the deed (586). Likewise, already the typical, rational, "Anglican" theologian William Chillingworth (1602–1644) stresses for the first time in 1537 in a published work, *The Religion of Protestants a Safe Way to Salvation*, that God makes accommodation for weak mortals and does not demand from them anything more than what they are in a position to perform. As it already was touched upon with Chillingworth, Hobbes also limits the fundamental Christian articles necessary for salvation to the confession "that Jesus is the Christ." He discovers this already in the First Epistle of John (1 John 4:2–3; cf. 5:1 [386, 425–26, 507]). But in the light of other statements, this is hardly convincing. Beyond this, Hobbes also concludes that the description of the life of Christ in the Gospels and the apostles' preaching of the kingdom of God were intended to justify this confession (590–94), and here are accrued a series of individual passages. Closely associated with this, Hobbes also sets forth reasons why this confession was sufficient for salvation. The common tendency corresponds to the position that was practiced by the church and state, shaped by theologians of a liberal vintage. John Locke also would later explain that this confession if necessary was effectual for salvation.

In the fourth major section of *Leviathan*, Hobbes launches a polemic against the Roman Church. In contrast to the typically sweeping comparison of the pope with the Antichrist, Hobbes takes another direction. Atheists constitute the most deleterious part of the "kingdom of darkness." However, this enemy has penetrated into the church. The "spiritual darkness" was especially caused by appropriating Hellenistic philosophy. Among the works of this "spiritual darkness," the most severe are a lack of knowledge and the false interpretation of Scripture. Chapter 44, the first in this section, bears the superscription: "Of Spiritual Darkness, from Misinterpretation of Scripture." The most significant misuse of Scripture for Hobbes consists in the postulation that "the Kingdom of God ... is the present Church" (605). Because the kingdom was constructed by Moses for the Jews, it was, as was previously mentioned, brought to its end with the choice of Saul. It will be rebuilt not earlier than the end-time. Therefore, the pope's claim to be the ruler and the Roman misdeeds in the church, especially those having to do with ceremonies, sacraments, and so forth, are illegal. The same is the case with teachings that are weakly grounded in Scripture, including those having to do with purgatory, exorcism, and prayer to saints. In this summary, Hobbes expresses also his theory of death and resurrection. He denies the (Greek) concept of the eternal life of the "soul" by explaining: "The *soul* in Scripture, signifieth always, either the life, or the living creature; and the body and soul jointly, the *body alive*" (615). In 3.38 and again in 4.44, Hobbes develops his concept of "mortality." This is the teaching that at death the entire person dies, while in the resurrection one awakens as a complete human being with body and soul. This led to Hobbes's being accused of atheism by his contemporaries, since he pointed to passages such as Qoh 3:19: "That which befalleth the sons of men, befalleth beasts … as the one dieth, so doth the other" (622–23). He certainly came to this position as a consequence of his view that Scripture exists on a single plane. Thus, he cannot regard Qoheleth's position as exceptional. Because of his materialist philosophy, in his comments about demons and spirits in 4.45, he cannot accept the notion of the existence of bodiless spirits. Rather, these expressions must be reinterpreted according to corresponding New Testament passages. Thus, Matt 4:1-11 indicates that Jesus was led by the spirit into the wilderness. This reference was to the devil, who then led Jesus to the pinnacle of the temple. According to Hobbes, the Matthean passage could not mean that Jesus was demon-possessed, but only that he on his own accord had decided to go out into the wilderness where he finally received a vision (641–42). With this interpretation, he anticipated the manner of arguing assumed by the later rationalists.

The disputation with Catholicism, which in England amounted to preaching to the choir, was pursued by Hobbes totally on the basis of Scripture. He opposed the grasping of lordship in the church by its own clergy: "For it is not the Roman clergy only, that pretends the kingdom of God to be of this world, and thereby to have a power therein, distinct from that of the civil state" (700). He names expressly the Presbyterians as representative of the view that the kingdom of Christ already has come on the earth (690).

Hobbes argues on the whole on two planes. On one plane, he seeks to establish his theory of the state with rational argumentation ("according to a geometrical manner"), and on the other plane he depends on the Scriptures. These two planes of argumentation he does not consider to be contradictory, for reason and Scripture could never stand in opposition to each other. Above all, he draws on the Old Testament. Its "earth-bound" background especially conformed to his materialistic philosophy, while the (at least at first glance) "spiritualistic" characteristics of the New Testament he regarded as suspect. Thus, the kingdom of Leviathan has two sides: the worldly and the spiritual. That the king (i.e., the sovereign) was through personal union the ruler over both corresponds to the actual situation. In addition, the people of the state and the people of the church were identical, according to this theory. Even the great revolutionary chaos in England could not dissuade Hobbes from holding to these fundamental views.

2.3. CREATING ETHICAL COMMANDMENTS FROM THE NEW TESTAMENT: JOHN LOCKE

John Locke was born August 28, 1632, as the son of a country squire who bore the same name. The elder Locke was a justice of the peace and a small landowner in Wrington in Somersetshire (not far from Brighton). The younger Locke was baptized by the Puritan Dr. Crook. The family moved to Belluton, where Locke spent his childhood. During the civil war, his father served in 1642–43 as an officer in a cavalry regiment of the army of the Parliament. This regiment was commanded by an influential Somerset nobleman, Alexander Popham, who created for the younger Locke a stipend to attend the Westminster School in London, at that time a first-class school for the elite. The best students were even offered the opportunity to add Hebrew and Arabic to their studies. At the end of his studies, Locke was able to deliver an address in Hebrew. On the basis of the relationship of his school with Christ Church, at that time the most significant Oxford college, led by John Owen (1616–1683), a follower of Cromwell and an advocate of tolerance, he was able to receive in 1652 a stipend, a so-called King's Scholarship, extended in 1666 to a lifetime award. He began the usual basic curriculum with a heavy emphasis on Scholastic philosophy as well as an investigation of natural scientific and especially medical instruction. In the notebooks from his semesters of advanced study are found numerous extracts taken from medical books of instruction. After 1660, he became familiar with the new mechanical philosophy, which was represented by, among other scholars, the Oxford "virtuoso" (a pious, natural scientist) Robert Boyle (1627–1691). Having befriended Locke, Boyle continued this relationship until his death. Locke occasionally weighed the possibility of becoming a medical doctor; however, he never entered this career. He succeeded in obtaining his bachelor's degree in 1656, followed by a master's degree in 1658. He never strove to receive ordination as a clergyman, which presumably his father hoped he would obtain. Small academic offices followed: in 1661–1662, he was a reader of Greek, of rhetoric in 1663, and a censor for moral philosophy in 1664. He was also a tutor, beginning in 1661. In addition to these positions, in 1661 he inherited houses and estates from his father, with whom he had a deep relationship. Thus, he always had a moderate, additional, private income.

During this time, he was not untouched by political circumstances. After the death of Cromwell and the resulting disturbances, which directly affected Oxford, he welcomed the return of Charles II to the throne in 1660. In the same year, he took a stand on the relationship between state and church. He spoke (like Hobbes) of this in his *Two Tracts on Government*, which gave the state the right to determine external matters in worship (*adiaphora*). An additional manuscript, composed in Latin, from the year 1661 bore the superscription, "An infallible interpreter of Scripture not necessary," and was directed against the claim of Rome to papal infallibility. A more traditional discussion of questions of natural law (1663–1664) appeared under the title *Essays on the Law of Nature*. According to this work, reason is able to recognize that there is a God who has given us rules for our attitudes, which are subject to rational examination. He spurned therewith the Platonic-Stoic concept of "inborn ideas" (*ideae innatae*), in which it is alleged that humans are already imbued with fundamental, moral ideas.

In August 1665, Locke accompanied as a secretary an English diplomatic legation to Cleves, which was ruled by the great prince elector Friedrich Wilhelm von Brandenburg (ruled 1640–1688). In the Brandenburg-Prussian districts ruled by this prince elector, Locke came to know the common life of the Lutheran and Reformed confessions. He chose, however, not to continue in diplomatic service but rather returned to Oxford. While there, in 1666 he came to know the politician Lord Anthony Ashley Cooper (1621–1693; after 1672 Earl of Shaftesbury). The latter was at that time chancellor of the treasury and pursued private financial dealings in the American colonies. Locke and he became friends, and Locke was invited as Ashley's doctor (and secretary) to come to his house in London. There he read a great deal of medical and natural scientific literature and met the famous doctor Thomas Sydenham (1624–1689), whom he accompanied on visits to sick patients. In 1668, Locke advised his employer, who had an abscess of the liver, to undergo a surgery that Locke himself took part in supervising. The surgery was successful, and Ashley regarded him as the saver of his life. It is likely that Locke took part in Ashley's Green Ribbon Club, the early cell of what later became the Whig Party. This was the beginning of Locke's later activity as a Whig politician. In addition, he experimented in Ashley's chemical laboratory located in his house and was even elected to the Royal Society, in which the modern natural scientists were members. Furthermore, he undertook once again in 1667 the theme of "tolerance," this time in the sense of Ashley's liberal position in the *Essay concerning Toleration*, in which he recommended forbearance of groups insofar as they did not disturb the public peace. Atheists and Catholics, because they are intolerant themselves, are certainly to be excluded from forbearance. After 1671, he was interested also in the problem of epistemology and produced for a later composition on this topic, *Essay concerning Human Understanding*, several incomplete drafts (draft A, B, C). Since 1672, Locke had completed a great deal of administrative work for his employer, the Earl of Shaftesbury (1672–1673) and now, lord chancellor. Thereafter Locke was, until 1674, secretary and bursar of the Council for Commerce and Plantations. This established the basis for a published treatise on finance in 1693. He also invested in the commerce occurring with the Bahamas.

On account of his asthma, Locke undertook a trip to France at the end of 1675 and traveled through Paris to Montpellier, a center of medical science, where he remained until 1677. Except for trips into the province, he remained in Paris until 1679. While abroad, everywhere he came to know other scholars, and he occupied his thinking with philosophical questions. Working with the followers of Descartes and Gassendi, he examined primarily the problem of epistemology.

When Locke returned to England, he was met with a political crisis. The difficulty developed from the fact that King Charles II had no legitimate son. His brother, Jacob, who was a Roman Catholic, stood first in the line of succession to the throne. The rumor that there was a Catholic conspiracy led to significant disturbance. In 1673, the first Earl of Shaftesbury was discharged and imprisoned in the tower. After his release, he served again as chairman of the crown council and introduced a bill to the House of Commons, demanding that Jacob be removed from the succession. Charles II, however, blocked this bill each time it was introduced, keeping it from being passed. The more radical Whigs, under the leadership of the Earl of Shaftesbury, then hatched a plot to revolt against the king. In connection with these confrontations, Locke published *Two Treatises of Government*. The first Earl of Shaftesbury, facing the threat of a charge of high treason in 1682, fled to Holland, where he died in 1683. After the revelation of the murder plots of other radicals in 1683, a swell of imprisonments began that led Locke also to flee to Holland.

In Holland, Locke traveled to Amsterdam by way of Rotterdam. His contacts in Holland were with other English exiles seeking to avoid the English monarchy. At the end of 1684, he was denied his status as a member of the Oxford student association. During the spring of the following year, when his name appeared on a list of exiles who were to be arrested when they returned to England, he went underground and remained in hiding in different locales until May 1685. During this period, his *Essay* was completely finished (1685), although it was not published until 1689. Locke had already sent copies of the finished sections to England. He also came to know Philipp van Limborch (1633–1712), who was a professor in the Remonstrant Seminary. He represented a theology in the spirit of Erasmus and distinguished between necessary and unnecessary dogmas. He thought that the doctrine of the Trinity, the two natures of Christ, and the (Calvinistic) teaching of predestination were not necessary for salvation. While in Amsterdam, Locke wrote and published in addition an anonymous *Epistola de tolerantia*, which soon appeared in English translation (1689). Two further "Epistles" followed in 1692 as an answer to the attacks of the Oxford theologian Jonas Proast. In 1687, Locke resided once again in Rotterdam and stayed with the wealthy Quaker Benjamin Furly (1636–1714), whose extensive library was available to him.

The successful Glorious Revolution, occasioned by the victorious campaign led by William III (ruled 1689–1702) made it possible for Locke to return to England in 1689. Although he turned down the offer to become an ambassador, he nevertheless, exerted political influence. He first lived in London. Earlier, after 1682, he had had a continuing friendship with Damaris Cudworth (1658–1708), the daughter of Ralph Cudworth (1617–1688), a Cambridge philosopher who was an expert on Plato. As a result of this relationship, Locke received a pension and a friendly welcome from Damaris and her husband, Sir Francis Masham, to reside at their country estate of Oates in Essex. For a time, he resided also in London, since he belonged to the royal Board of Trade, beginning in 1696. This board gave its attention to the economic situation in England and trade relationships with the Colonies, Scotland, and Ireland.

By the 1690s Locke had become a famous author. Among his friends was Archbishop John Tillotson (1630–1694), who shared with Locke a latitudinarian (liberal) theology. In order to understand Locke's religions attitude, one must consider the proximity of his view to that which dominated the English church and expressed the theological inclination of the Whig political views. Through his theological inclination, Locke became involved in conflicts.

After his various writings concerning toleration, he still found it necessary to engage in efforts opposing polemics directed against him. In 1695, he again published an anonymous piece, *The Reasonableness of Christianity*. This occasioned considerable criticism in several writings produced by the Calvinist John Edwards (1637–1716). Edwards upbraided Locke for his denegation of the ideas of the firstborn and the Trinity as well as for his taking up Hobbes's teaching of limiting faith to an article of confession (see above). Locke answered in *Two Vindications* (1695–1696). He fought also with Edward Stillingfleet (1635–1699 [he finally became bishop of Worcester]), who compared Locke's expressions in his *Essay* with John Toland and maintained that he was a Unitarian who denied the reality of the Trinity.

After his resignation from the Commission on Trade (1700), Locke moved back to Oates, where he mostly remained. His health seriously declined, and when King William III in the especially frigid winter of 1697–98 bade him come to Kensington, presumably to offer him a diplomatic post, Locke had to turn down the offer. Still, he received many prominent visitors in Oates. After a lingering illness, he died at Oates on 28 October 1704.

For a long period of time, Locke has shared the same consideration given to Hobbes in the fields of philosophical history and political science. The important role that theological considerations, and above all the Bible, played in his thinking has often been misjudged by secular-minded scholars who have been blind, at times deliberately it seems, to the importance of these influences. It is rare that the lengthy biblical exegetical expressions present in many of his works have evoked any real interest. It is remarkable that many scholars have dwelled exclusively on Locke's contributions to epistemological theory, political science, and the theory of property. Recently, however, one can detect a change: it is more and more clear that Locke, while not a theologian by profession, possessed a significant theological education and was intimately familiar with the Bible.

The important of this quality was apparent already in the *Two Tracts on Government*, which engaged the crisis involving the succession to the throne. Locke became involved in a dispute with the theses of Sir Robert Filmer (1588–1653). This gained new intensity when Filmer's son posthumously published his father's work *Patriarca; or, The Natural Power of Kings* in 1680, to support the succession of the future James II. Filmer, who had fought on the side of the king during the civil war, had defended the divine right of kings to possess absolute dominion by referring to the status of Adam, the first man. All political power accordingly was conferred by God on fatherly dominion, which the first man exerted over his wife, his children, and his servants. Adam was the first patriarch and king. This authority was conferred upon his successors in the human race. This power was inherited by the sons of Noah, the Old Testament kings, and later the kings of all lands. Also in cases where this authority had resulted from usurpation of the throne or when a ruler's origins were not known, one must proceed with the view that this occurred according to the will of God and that such rulers were to be treated as legitimate rulers. The right of ostensibly free individuals to elect their own ruler was therefore excluded.

Locke could rebut this very influential thesis in political discussions only on the basis of the reasons stipulated in the Old Testament. The marks of a typological royal ideology did not appear to Locke's contemporaries to be as absurd as they do to us today. He devoted to this topic the first comprehensive treatment. It was relatively simple to rebuff Filmer's argument that royal dominion may be continually inherited by the progeny of Adam in a largely single line of succession. Since Adam was the father of all humanity, all humans are the legitimate heirs of his dominion: "In plain English, everyone can possess it, for there is no living person who does not possess the right to belong to the line and offspring of Adam" (*Treatise* 1.11.111, Laslett 240). This statement is especially important, for it sets forth the biblical basis for the political theory that Locke, as the father of liberalism, found to be valid: since all successors of Adam are the same and have equal rights, this is equally foundational in their claim to participate in political power. Subsequently, as Locke convincingly demonstrated, Filmer's thesis of an unbroken line of succession from Adam to the present monarchs could not be demonstrated. Above all, moving from the idea of the right of assets to the right of rule requires a logical leap. Locke especially points (*Treatise* 1.11.159–69) to the thesis of Filmer that God in the establishment of the Israelite monarchy recovered the previously interrupted succession (*Patriarcha*, 9). Locke noted that Filmer's position indicated that the English ruler was linked to the Old Testament kings as a typological prototype. Locke was obliged to examine also Filmer's interpretation of the texts in the primeval history. For example, in opposing Filmer, Locke argued concerning Gen 1:28, "This lordship over all of the world, which Adam possessed through means of creation, refers not only to Adam, but also to all human beings. This is clearly demonstrated by the wording of the verse, which has the plural" (*Treatise* 1.4.29, 179). Similarly Locke argued that Gen 9:1–3, the blessing of Noah, included also his sons. Filmer had explained this in the sense of the "subjection or blessing in the line of succession" ("Observations concerning the Origin of Government" [1652], Sommerville, 184–234, esp. 217). However, Locke pointed out here that the reading once more assumed the form of the plural (*Treatise* 1.4.32, 181). "This means nothing other than the fact that humans, i.e. the entirety of the human race, as the most important inhabitants of the earth, are made in the image of God and receive sovereignty over the other creatures" (*Treatise* 1.4.40, 186–87). Genesis 3:16 does not establish the lordship of Adam over Eve (i.e., women), as Filmer had maintained (*The Anarchy of a Limited or Mixed Monarchy* [1648], ed. Sommerville, 131–71, esp. 138, 145), but rather relates only to the natural dependence of a wife on her husband. If the two queens, Mary and Elisabeth, had married subjects, they still would not have had their political sovereignty affected. Furthermore, one must give attention to the situation of the biblical statement: if it had indicated that Eve was affected by being driven out of paradise, at the same time it is obvious that Adam scarcely could expect to be granted any privileged position! (*Treatise* 1.5.44–49, 189–94). Most important is the frequently stated basis of Locke's interpretation: the meaning of words. When God speaks to humans, he uses the same rules of speech as humans do in talking with each other (*Treatise* 1.5.46, 191). The actual standard for the interpretation of the meaning of words is reason, in conformity with Scripture ("Scripture or Reason," *Treatise* 1.1.4, 161; "Reason and Revelation," *Treatise* 1.6.60, 202), which makes accessible their import. These rules serve here to reject the biblical foundations of Filmer's argumentation. Locke could then develop, in the second treatise (which he had presumably composed already at an earlier time), his own teaching about society. His fundamental views of the natural freedom and equality of all humans, who possessed the same political and economic rights, originally rested not on a biblical foundation but rather on modern theories of natural rights.

Locke did not, however, engage in biblical arguments only on the basis of Filmer's positions. It was only after the release from private possession of Locke's voluminous handwritten manuscript that everything was available for review. Now one could know considerably more about Lock's great interest in the Bible and how intensively he occupied himself with its study for many years. In his diaries were found numerous references to biblical commentaries and other theological writings. In addition, he possessed a Bible and two New Testaments with inserted pages, in which he, even as one would do in a notebook, wrote down references to theological literature as well as his own remarks about the respective biblical passages. With these, a little-known side of Locke's thinking has now been revealed. This interest in biblical interpretation and theology had considerable influence as well on his philosophical views.

The role of the Bible grew more prominent for Locke during the course of his life, especially in the area of ethics. In the earlier *Essays on the Law of Nature* (composed in Latin during the years 1661–1664), he proceeded from the traditional interpretation that the law of nature, which was obligatory for all humans, could serve as the basis of an ethical system. He was especially occupied with its perceptibility. The essays dealing with this provide different answers. In Essay 7, the traditional teaching of the law of nature is represented: the law of nature is valid for all human beings; since harmony exists between this law and the rational nature of humans, it can also be recognized by reason (*Essays*, ed. von Leyden, 198). Locke further asks in Essay 2 how the law of nature could then be recognized. The path to this passes through discursive reason, which continues from the known to the unknown. More expressly disclosed in Essay 4 was Locke's elimination of inborn ideas and tradition. Thus, reason alone (or the "light of Nature") provided the ability to recognize that the coordinated, well-ordered movement of creation could point to an originator of the marvelous construction of the world. From the recognition that there must be a God, the view follows that this one must be a wise creator, who has given to humans in the law of nature a guide to their acts that correspond to his will. Throughout, Locke made ethics dependent on the will of God (what corresponds to the voluntarism of nominalism), and thereby rejected the thesis that human standards rested on the corresponding judgment of human beings as to what is good. This made once more acute, then, the question of revelation, which Locke, however, deferred to a future discussion. Later he busied himself repeatedly with the question of the deducible character of morality, whereby he especially pursued a double path in the *Essay concerning Human Understanding*. To begin with, there was a simpler plane; that is, humans themselves compiled moral ideas. The combination of and reflection on more simple characteristics of things mediated through the senses offer through the intellect a "mixed means" to which belong especially the designs for human behavior. They also depicted for Locke the abstract concept of a demonstrable morality (*Essay concerning Human Understanding* 2.22). Since such possibilities of combination remained in the sphere of the abstract, they could not advance to an associated law of nature, for "that which is an obligation cannot be understood without a law, nor may a law become known or assumed without a lawgiver, or without reward and punishment" (*Essay* 1.3.12, Nidditch 74). For the time being, however, Locke could still offer the following definition: "the law which God has set forth for the actions of humans is announced to them either through the light of nature (reason) or the voice of revelation" (*Essay* 2.28.8, 352). Since the idea of God, as was true of all other ideas, was not inborn, there was no direct way to the law of nature. Thus, Locke became increasingly doubtful as to whether it was deducible at all. The possible answer is "that God has provided a rule by which humans should regulate themselves. No one is as animal-like to deny" he possesses this. Humans may have the kindness, the wisdom, and the power to do so, but this is only a mere assertion." These views in general were already found in his *Essay* concerning the limits of human knowledge and the extent of what is unknown (*Essay* 4.3.22–23). In 4.16 Locke examined the degrees of knowledge and the acceptance of witnesses from the past. Since it was unquestionably true that witnesses are found in tradition, they still were distant from the original truth and deserved less acceptance.

> There is still a category of statements which demand the highest degree of our acceptance. These belong to a pure witness and do not depend on whether or not the proposed matter conforms with usual experience and the typical course of things. The basis for determining this is that the witness stems from someone, who is not deceptive and cannot be deceived, and that is God himself. (*Essay* 4.16.24, 667)

This witness is called "revelation," while our acceptance of it is "faith." This offers "certainty without doubt." However, whatever would fall outside the structure of conceivable experience would simply be incapable of being understood, and whatever would oppose simple, intuitive knowledge, could not be recognized as true (*Essay* 4.18.3–5). Therefore, the critical standard is valued:

> Whatever God has revealed is certainly true; no doubt can be raised against it. This is the actual subject of faith. However, whether it is a divine revelation or not reason must determine, for it can neither allow the understanding to cast aside something that is more appreciably evident in favor of accepting something that is less evident, nor can it allow the adoption of something that is in opposition to knowledge and certainty. (*Essay* 4.18.10, 695)

The method of the Enlightenment's biblical criticism was defined in this way. Locke once commented to Stillingfleet that he was certain that all in the Bible is true, and he complied with the view that the Scriptures have an inspired author. Locke remarks: "I still use the same manner of explaining the meaning of this book that I use for any other thing" (*Second Reply, Works* 4:341). Certainly there also is a sphere for which we have no natural conception. Thus, revelation must inform us, for instance, about the fallen angels (cf. Isa 14:12ff.; Rev 12:9) and the resurrection of the dead. They belong to the specific area of faith (*Essay* 4.18.7; 4.17.23). In the fourth edition there is an addition to 4.19, in which Locke turned his attention to the spiritualists who traced their knowledge to an "inner light." Locke referred to *two* entities that were able to create certitude when it comes to revelation: "Where reason or Scripture is clear for some kind of comprehension or action, we can accept this as coming from divine authority" (*Essay* 4.19.16, 706). We are able to see here that Locke at this stage (the addition was made in 1695) had removed himself from his earlier, purely rational standpoint.

In the same year, he wrote his work the *Reasonableness of Christianity* (the edition is *Works*, vol. 7). He opens his foreword with the remark that, since he was disappointed with most theological systems he had encountered, he had turned himself to his "sole reading of the Scriptures" (*Reasonableness*, 3). Similar expressions are found in earlier letters. This brings to mind the Protestant affirmation of "Scripture alone" in contrast to the Roman Catholic position that tradition provides the standard for the interpretation of Scripture. To be without presuppositions admittedly is an illusion, as one may see from the examination of any writing. But Locke himself was not aware of this.

As long as Locke's notebooks with their remarks on certain biblical texts were not available for study, one could have been surprised at how impressive the biblical knowledge is that is displayed in this writing, the subject of which, as noted in the conclusion, was justification (*Works* 7:158). As he himself noted in the preface of "A Second Vindication of the Reasonableness of Christianity" (*Works* 7:186–87), the work was occasioned by the controversy between dissenters concerning justification. They were a group about whom he had heard incidentally. In this lengthy controversy, which reached its high point in 1694–1695 with a flood of pamphlets, the issue had to do with the opposition between the strict Calvinists (mostly Congregationalists and Baptists), who opposed any combining of justification with works (Antinomians), and the moderate Presbyterians, who included confession and sanctification in the faith that brought about justification. On this matter, Locke sought to gain a discerning clarity. "The Scripture was direct and plain that it was faith justified. The next question then was, What faith was it that justified? What was it that, if a man believed, it should be imputed to him for righteousness? To find out this, I thought the right way was to search the Scriptures; and thereupon betook myself seriously to the reading of the New Testament." Beyond this, as may be seen from a letter to van Limborch (*Correspondence*, de Beer 5:1901), Locke wished to write a complete description of the Christian faith. Thus, Locke wrote for his own knowledge his work in the calm of the estate at Oates. He proceeded from the fall of Adam and the consequences this had for humanity (*Works* 7:4ff.). His readings of the narrative in Gen 2–3, in association with Rom 5:12 and 1 Cor 15:22, led to the result that humanity, after the banishment of Adam from access to the tree of life, had inherited mortality. However, humanity did not inherit the guilt of Adam's sin. Mortality is not a punishment, but rather was imparted to humanity by the omnipotent God, because he already had presented them with finite life. Each person was punished for his own guilt (Rom 2:6; 2 Cor 5:10; etc.). This argumentation is similar to that which is encountered in the teachings of the Socinians, whom Locke had reproached. Christ redeemed humans from the fate of death through the resurrection (1 Cor 15:21–22). This held true for the righteous (Rom 4:4, Rev 22:14; etc.), since sinners (Jas 1:15; Rom 6:23; etc.) were excluded from paradise. However (according to Rom 3:20–23; Gal 3:21–22), all humans have sinned against the law of works. God's purity was required to remove it. Locke could speak throughout of a "corrupted state of human depravity" (*Works* 7:140). Subsequently, no one could have succeeded in gaining eternal life, if God had not given the "law of faith" (Rom 3:27). Its rules are the same as those in the "law of works," for the moral (not the ceremonial or political) law is still valid. "But, by the law of faith, faith is allowed to supply the defect of full obedience" (*Works* 7:14). This faith was faith in Jesus, and that meant Jesus as the Messiah. This finally led Locke to undertake a detailed journey through the Gospels, resulting in his narrating what might be called a "Life of Jesus," which showed Jesus to be the Messiah. This is what the apostles had preached about him.

In a second line of argumentation (*Works* 7:103ff.), Locke explains that, in addition to faith in Jesus as the Messiah, confession is also constitutive for the covenant of grace. He writes, "These two, faith and repentance, i.e. believing Jesus to be the Messiah and a good life, are the indispensable conditions of the new covenant, to be performed by all those who would obtain eternal life" (*Works* 7:105). "For if they believed [Jesus] to be the Messiah, their King, but would not obey his laws ... they were but the greatest of rebels" (*Works* 7:111). "The duties of that law ... are of eternal obligation; nor can it be taken away or dispensed with, without changing the nature of things, overturning the measures of right and wrong, and thereby introducing and authorizing irregularity, confusion, and disorder in the world" (*Works* 7:112). In his second text of defense, Locke remarked that he may have found in the Gospels an answer to the problem of justification, which he discovered led to "the redemption" in attitude and teachings. This is "the necessity that such a law-giver should be sent from God for the reforming of the morality of the world" (*Works* 7:187). "Such a law of morality Jesus Christ hath given us in the New Testament.... We have from him a full and sufficient rule for our direction, and conformable to that of reason" (*Works* 7:143). "And then there needs no more, but to read the inspired books, to be instructed: all the duties of morality lie there clear, and plain, and easy to be understood" (*Works* 7:147). Anything like this did not exist before; the explanations of the heathen philosophers lead only "into a wild wood of uncertainty" (*Works* 7:147), The term "simple" is used time and again by Locke. The Gospels transmit the only admissible teaching of morality, which, as Locke repeatedly explains, can be understood by the simplest, uneducated people: "day-labourers and tradesmen, the spinsters and dairy-maids" (*Works* 7:146). By designating the morality taught by Jesus "suited to vulgar capacities" (*Works* 7:157), Locke presumably alludes to Erasmus (see *History* 3:56). This was obviously an element of the humanist tradition. Locke appears even to include himself, when he remarks that gifted humans are provided with leisure for learning and logic" (ibid.). They are finally not able to derive the binding elements of morality from the law of nature. Locke rejects a request to write a book with the remark: "But the Gospel contains so perfect a body of ethics, that reason may be excused from that enquiry, since she may find man's duty clearer and easier in revelation than in herself" (*Correspondence* 5:593–96, esp. 595). It is doctrinally sufficient for simple people to believe in Jesus as the Messiah and to recognize him as their king. A thoroughgoing eudaemonistic feature in Locke's deliberations is found also in the view that one may gain eternal life only by means of this obedience. All in all, Locke's position regarding justification was similar to that of the moderate Presbyterians and the Latitudinarians of the state church in England and the Arminians (Remonstrants) whom he had come to know in Holland. He is in no way original in this line of argument.

Locke was still precritical in his biblical views, different from those of his student Toland (see below), when he mentioned in *Reasonableness* that miracles attested to the sending of Jesus: "The evidence of our Saviour's mission from heaven is so great, in the multitude of miracles he did before all sorts of people, that what he delivered cannot but be received as the oracles of God, and unquestionable verity" (*Works* 7:135).

Toward the end of his life, Locke occupied himself with a thorough study of the letters of Paul. In *Reasonableness*, he had still designated them as occasional writings that were suitable for the audience composed of those who already were Christians (*Works* 7:151–52). He had then, however, felt compelled to examine more closely the teachings of the Pauline corpus, since his critics used them against him. Locke made notes in his paraphrases and remarks concerning Galatians, 1 and 2 Corinthians, Romans, and Ephesians (all of which he understood to be genuine letters of Paul). These notes appeared shortly after Locke had died. In a detailed foreword, he explains the purpose and methods of his interpretation. Letters are difficult to understand. Among other things, many of the circumstances of their origins and details, of which their original recipients were aware, are not known by the letters' modern readers. A historical report of the letters' background, as in Acts, is lacking. The style of Paul and the necessary understanding of many of his ideas render it difficult to grasp his views. Nevertheless, it was Locke's intention to come to an understanding of Paul. The motif from the foreword of *Reasonableness* recurs in a modified form. One must read the corpus as a whole time and again in order to determine the purpose and goal of each of his writings (*Paraphrase*, Wainwright 110). A single reading is not sufficient. It is clear from this approach that Locke presupposed that Paul was a consistent thinker. The attentive reader will determine "how the dispersed portions of his discourse come together in a meaning that is coherent and conforms wells to his entire thought, making his writings a consistent unit" (*Paraphrase*, 104). Not so novel were Locke's efforts to ascertain the situation in which the five letters were written, especially determining who the opponents of Paul were. Other interpreters had already been occupied with this prior to Locke. Locke was of the opinion that the opponents may have been Judaizing Christians.

Of course, throughout his explanations Locke most certainly used previously written commentaries, as the catalogue of his library and the remarks in his Bibles and New Testament notebook demonstrate. The customary form of paraphrasing allowed him to make clear in the text the process of argumentation present in the letters as he understood it and, where there appeared to be gaps, to produce the coherence for which he strove. The structure of the Locke's sections usually follows the same pattern: after a short listing of the contents comes an English translation of the text accompanied by a paraphrase supplemented by his notations. At the beginning of each letter, there is a short synopsis of the circumstances leading to its composition and its purpose. Locke could express his theological understandings in the freely composed paraphrases (for some passages he keeps his views close to those in the original text) and in his remarks. Locke considered to be true (probably in a historical sense) all that the Bible transmits as true. He makes only one exception to this view (although he states this indirectly). In the Pauline epistles, he notes that Paul erred in expecting an imminent return of Christ (remarks on 1 Cor 1:7; etc.). At the beginning of each letter (except Ephesians), Locke placed the datum "the year of our Lord." Thus, for example, "the year of our Lord, 57, the year of Nero, 3." Accordingly, he introduces these letters as all coming from the same year, and the place of the sending is given as Gaul and Rome. On the one hand, a historical interest is clear from these remarks. On the other hand, Locke, who had so strongly underlined the role of reason in his *Essay*, now exposes clearly the supremacy of revelation. The expressions of Paul in 1 Cor 2:1–5 and 2:6–16 offer Locke the occasion to stress "that the knowledge of the Gospel is not sufficient for our natural abilities, even though they are enhanced by science and philosophy, but rather we are entirely dependent on revelation (*Paraphrase*, "Contents," 1 Cor 2:6–16; 172–73). Concerning the "wisdom for those who are perfected," about which Paul spoke in 1 Cor 2:6, Locke remarked in his notation: one may be perfected "when he is so convinced of the divine nature and origin of the Christian religion that he sees and recognizes that it all is the pristine revelation of God" (173). Here Locke spoke of his own changed conviction with which he placed himself especially in opposition to the deists (cf. below). Reason was certainly not devalued by stressing the insight of Paul's ways of thinking.

In his perceptions of sins, redemption, and the path to salvation, Locke in his paraphrases deviated from the Calvinistic view. While he did not deny that all humans are sinners (cf. his remarks concerning Rom 6:8; 533), he rejected the view that their sinfulness was inherited from Adam. They have only inherited his mortality (Rom 5:12–19, "Contents," 522–23; paraphrase of 5:12, 523). In addition, the view that Christ was punished for the guilt of humanity was rejected by Locke. He paraphrased Rom 8:3 to read instead: "This means (God sent) his Son into the world in his own body, in which the flesh never gained the upper hand

and thereby would generate evil, but rather for the purpose that by means of his example of a fleshly body, which could rule perfectly over sins, we should ourselves conform to the moral righteousness of the law" (552). In one annotation, Locke remarked concerning this: "To *fulfill* signifies here not a completely precise obedience, but rather means that such an irreproachable life through serious strivings for righteousness displays what it meant for believing subjects of Christ to be free from the dominion of sin." Locke could combine his own efforts with a doctrine of the justification by faith: "Jews and pagans are to be saved when they believe in Jesus Christ and strive seriously for justification, although they shall not obtain this salvation, until faith as justification is reckoned to them" (annotation to Rom 2:26; 502). Locke does not take over the statement "faith alone." The study of the Pauline letters had not resulted in his becoming a theologian following the views of Paul. He ultimately remained in the humanistic tradition.

2.4. Discovering Only What Is Reasonable in the Bible: John Toland

John Locke had some adherents, whom by the end of his life he would have liked to disavow, because they used his principles to reach particular conclusions that he himself was not prepared to draw. Among these belonged John Toland. Toland was a man of wide interests, and his early work, in which he was engaged with the study of the Bible, depicts only a part of his rich, literary creations. His book *Christianity Not Mysterious* is the clearest example of the interest of a so-called freethinker or deist in understanding the Bible. It is not easy to characterize this early expression of the Enlightenment that developed especially in England. Exponents of this line of thought as a rule understood themselves as Christians, although they turned against the hierarchically structured church, the representatives of which they suspected of "priestcraft." The well-known accusations directed against the Roman Catholic Church they now turned against the Church of England. The inheritance from the Puritans in this respect is unmistakable. In addition, the ethical orientation appealing to natural religion was not peculiar to the deists. We encountered this already in Locke. New is the increased role of reason, which appears clearly in Toland.

John Toland presumably was born on 30 November 1670, on the peninsula of Inishowen in Ireland. He always veiled his origins. According to one polemical rumor, he was the illegitimate son of a priest. Raised initially as a Roman Catholic, he transferred his allegiance at an early age to Protestantism. He found a patron who financed his education at a school in nearby Redcastle and then his pastoral studies at Glasgow College (the early unit of the later university) in 1687 or 1688. Then, beginning with the fall of 1689, his patron paid for his studies at the University of Edinburgh. In 1690, after the usual study in the liberal arts, he received a master's degree. Supposedly, he may have joined there the Rosicrucian order, although proof of this is lacking. Following the conclusion of his studies, he made his way to London, where he found an entrée to well-to-do Presbyterian residents and became the tutor in the house of a rich widow. An influential Presbyterian clergyman endowed him with a stipend for pursuing studies at the Universities of Leiden and Utrecht in Holland (beginning in the fall 1692). There he came to know Jean le Clerc (1657–1736) and Philipp van Limborch. In addition, he studied with the famous church and biblical historian Friedrich Spanheim the Younger (1632–1701). In Rotterdam he became acquainted with Benjamin Furly. When Toland returned to England in the summer of 1693, he visited, among others, John Locke, to whom he presented a letter of recommendation from Furly and a book of van Limborch's.

In England, Toland had no inclination to assume a pastor's office. Instead, he resided first in London and then later in Oxford, earning a living from literary orders of different patrons. In coffeehouses and pubs, he caused quite a sensation by expressing radical political views and uttering criticism of the state church. In the autumn of 1692, he returned to London, where he sought the companionship of confidants of Locke, including Anthony Ashley Cooper, who later became the third Earl of Shaftesbury (1671–1713). He likely also made contact with Locke himself, although the latter denied later having established a close friendship. His republican leanings (which were clearly evident in the publication of the works of the Republican James Harrington [1700]), led to his meeting with people of the same opinion in the Greek coffeehouse in London. The rumor circulated that he belonged also to the Calves' Head Club, which celebrated annually in the Black Boy tavern the execution of Charles I (1649).

As a result of his initial work, *Christianity Not Mysterious*, which appeared anonymously in 1695 and was soon followed by a second edition under his own name, Toland fell into disrepute. When he made his way to Ireland in 1697, possibly with a secret political commission that may have involved espionage, he was officially pursued there. The Irish House of Commons condemned his book as heretical, ordered it to be publicly burned by the executioner, and sought to arrest the author. Toland hurriedly fled back to England. When he put out a *Life of Milton*, in which he expressly said that not all of the writings written under the name of Christ or of the apostles may be authentic, he was heavily criticized and fled again, this time to Holland. Le Clerc, van Limborch, and Locke now distanced themselves from him. Only Shaftesbury was willing to continue to have contact with him, but this was done in secret. In the year 1700, the Lower House of Convocation (the synod of the clergy) of the Church of England condemned his work *Christianity Not Mysterious*. Even so, the more liberally situated bishops in the Upper House abstained from any persecution of Toland. For Toland, therefore, there was hope, in spite of his persecution: the influential Tory politician Robert Harley (later the Earl of Oxford [1661–1724]), had recognized his talents and often used him for political missions (presumably involving espionage) in spite of his liberal and republican inclinations. Thus, Toland, because he had defended in his *Anglia libera* (The Free England) the Protestant succession of the Welf dynasty in Hanover, was commissioned to be a member of the delegation sent to Hanover. This delegation presented the document of succession to the electress princess, who, at that time, was Sophie (1630–1714). However, when Queen Anna (ruled 1702–1714) ascended the throne in England, Toland fell into disfavor once again, because he had, only a short time before, pleaded for the succession of the House of Hanover. He traveled once again to Germany, this time privately. He initially came to Hanover, where he engaged in discussions with the philosopher G. W. Leibniz (1646–1716) over problems of metaphysics (thereafter followed a lengthy correspondence). Finally he came to Berlin, because the daughter of the princess electress, Queen Sophie Charlotte of Prussia (1668–1705), wife of Friedrich I, was interested in philosophy. His correspondence with her was published under the title *Letters to Serena* in 1704. Because of his uncontrolled behavior and incautious political pronouncements, however, he soon had to return home once again.

During numerous journeys to foreign courts by order of Harley (secretary of state, beginning in 1704), Toland frequented many foreign courts, including Vienna where he met with the free-spirited circle around Prince Eugen of Savoyen (1663–1736), the victor against the Turks in Belgrade. Documents preserved in Vienna continue to speak of this encounter. Toland's hope for a government post, following the victory of the Tories in 1710, which brought Harley into office as prime minister, was met, however, with disappointment. His situation became completely hopeless when, in 1714, George I from the House of Hanover followed

Queen Anne to the throne, leading to the beginning of a lengthy period of Whig dominance. On account of his activity on behalf of Harley, Toland fell under the suspicions of the Whigs. In addition to this, he was regarded as an incorrigible freethinker. During the last years of his life, he sought tirelessly to keep his head above water as a writer who delved into politics, including those of the church, and theology. His most famous work during this period was *Pantheisticon*, which appeared under a pseudonym in 1720. In this writing, he described the teaching and ritual of a pantheistic association, of which he evidently was a member. The apparently irreconcilable opposition between the pantheistic theory emerging in several other works and the work *Christianity Not Mysterious* (along with other later writings), which had an undeniable Christian foundation, cannot be solved simply by accepting the notion of an inner development. Rather, this points to a separation between religious and philosophical thinking.

In his last years, Toland increasingly suffered from illness and debts, which accrued as a result of one unfortunate speculation in stocks. He died in March 1722.

Toland's book *Christianity Not Mysterious* is in a special way representative of the deist view of the Bible. Toland obviously proceeds from Locke's theory of epistemology in his *Essay* and applies it to the New Testament (the Gospel).

In the preface (iii–xxx), Toland explains his intention when expressing a judgment about the Bible: one need accept only what is evident to one's own God-given reason. The Bible is darkened by Scholastic disputations and metaphysical speculations. In this utterance Toland's humanistic orientation becomes transparent. In contrast to these two things, the articles of Jesus and the apostles can be apprehended rationally, since they are simple and understandable. Toland argues that, on the basis of the divine nature of the New Testament, the alleged secrets of the Gospel may be explained, while he contends that the Bible sets forth the truth of the divine revelation. These arguments offered a defense against the atheists and the enemies of revealed religion. There is no reason to doubt the apologetic goal of Toland in this writing. The accusation raised by his opponents that he is an atheist cannot be justified by reference to his very first publication.

Toland at first defines "reason" entirely in the sense of John Locke (§1, 7–22). Perception consists of observing the conformity or nonconformity between ideas. These are noticed either intuitively, thus immediately, or transmitted through cognition based on the senses. The primary ones (as, for example, the recognition that two plus two are four) are unmistakable contrasted with the ones transmitted by the senses. Information results from experience or authority, whereby divine authority unfailingly contrasts with that of humans, for God, unlike humans, cannot lie (here Toland cites Num 23:19; cf. 33).

In the second section of his volume (§2, 23–66), Toland undertakes to demonstrate that nothing in the teachings of the Gospel stands in opposition to reason; that is, nothing conflicts with our clear, understandable ideas and general concepts. Only by conformity with our reason are we capable of determining the divine nature of the Scriptures, not because the authority of the church has determined it to be so.

> But if we believe the *Scripture* to be Divine, not upon its own bare Assertion, but from a real Testimony consisting of the Evidence of things contain'd therein; from undoubted Effects, and not from Words and Letters; what is this but to prove it by *Reason*? It has in itself, I grant, the brightest Characters of *Divinity*: But 'tis *Reason* finds them out, examines them, and by its Principles approves and pronounces them sufficient.

Playing a role here is the principle that the sense of the words in the biblical text "must be always worthy of their author." This would not be the case, if statements must be accepted literally (and not figuratively), as, for example, the notion "that God is subject to passions, is the Author of sin, that *Christ* is a Rock, was actually guilty of and defil'd with our Transgressions, that we are Worms or Sheep and no Men" (32–34). God, it is true, is omnipotent, but omnipotence cannot contain in itself that which is contradictory. "To say, for example, that a thing is extended and not extended, is round and square at once, is to say nothing; for these Idea's destroy one another, and cannot subsist together in the same Subject" (39).

The significance of the Scriptures resides above all in the fact that they transmits additional information, which reason in and of itself cannot obtain. Thus, only God as the creator can provide information about creation, as well as the last judgment and other important truths (40-41; Toland cites 1 Cor 2:11). If, however, something was revealed, it must be both possible and knowable. Thus, it must stand the test of rational examination. Toland seeks to demonstrate this from Scripture itself, as, for example, the commandment to stone false prophets (Deut 13:1–3) and the statement in Deut 18:21–22 that the truth of a prophecy is demonstrated by its prediction coming to pass (43). Toland recognizes also the miracles of Jesus as demonstrating the divine character of his teaching

(46ff.). There was still no critical questioning of miracles as was done in the later Enlightenment. In regard to the whole of his argument, there was a fundamental methodological principle: the interpretation of Scripture follows the same rules of interpretation that apply to all other books (49).

However, from where do such affirmations come? As a deist, Toland places the blame on the priests. Actually, he has in mind the clergy of the Church of England, but it was advisable for a theologian of the seventeenth century to avoid mentioning them in any discussion of a pagan priesthood. One encountered them in the ancient mysteries and recognized the intended secrecy in which they were involved. The "cunning *Priests*, who knew how to turn every thing to their own Advantage" (70), divulged nothing of the obligations experienced by the initiates. The attentive reader heard throughout Toland's book that the English theologians led their sheep astray by maintaining that they were imparting a mystery not subject to criticism. The ones in view were perfectly aware that they were meant. It requires no explanation that what Toland asserted led to the outrage against him. According to Toland, those he blamed treated as a "mystery" a matter that was "a thing intelligible of it self, but so vail'd by others, that it could not be known without special Revelation" (72). This was true also of the New Testament, which has nothing that could not be understood: it was said to require revelation, but once revealed it is no longer a mystery.

Toland rejects the objection that something could still be regarded as a mystery, because we could not know all of the characteristics of a matter, let alone its nature. He continues, arguing that we know only what is necessary for us. Toland then expresses his own view of understanding Christian teaching: (1) "That no Christian Doctrine ... can be reputed a mystery, because we have not an adequate or compleat Idea of whatever belongs to it"; and (2) "what is revealed in Religion ... must and may be as easily comprehended, and found as consistent with our common Notions, as what we know of Wood or Stone, of Air, of Water, or the like" (80). Toland once again turns in a more detailed manner to the topic that we (according to Locke, to whom he makes reference as an "excellent modern Philosopher" [83]) do not know anything of the essence of things. Therefore nothing can be called a mystery, because we do not know its actual essence (89). Concealed from the earlier people of God under the Mosaic order are finally things that have been imparted in parables. They were, however, also "not in and of themselves incapable of being understood, but rather were *mysterious* only for those to whom they were not enfolded" (108).

After answering additional objections, Toland comes to his final conclusion: "Now since by Revelation Men are not endu'd with any new Faculties, it follows that God should lose his end in speaking to them, if what he said did not agree with their common Notions" (133). In the same place, Toland defines faith as consisting of two parts, knowledge and affirmation. Without the evidence of the first, faith will not be possible. In order to dispense with the objection that Abraham believed blindly when he stood ready to sacrifice his son (Gen 22), Toland falls back on Heb 11:17–19: Abraham may have been capable of doing this, because he considered that God was able to awaken him from the dead (136–38). Faith in the New Testament also was "a most firm Persuasion built upon substantial Reasons" (138). Self-contradiction and "mystery" are basically one and the same (140). Why, then, is revelation needed at all? There are facts that cannot be known without revelation; however what is known must stand the test of reason. If it is objected that reason is more important than revelation, that would mean also that Greek grammar is more important than the New Testament, for Greek is the precondition of being able to understand this text. "We make use of Grammar in order to understand the Language and of Reason in order to grasp the sense of that book" (146). Besides, reason came from God as a light for everyone who comes into the world. The allusion here to John 1:9 is unmistakable!

Miracles do have their place in Toland's approach. In his view, they can in no way be contrary to reason. A miraculous action must therefore be "something that in itself is intelligible and possible; tho the manner of doing it being extraordinary" (150). If someone is able to walk through flames unharmed, it is both possible and a miracle when he is protected by supernatural powers. In contrast to this, if Christ were born without the opening of his mother's womb, being contrary to nature, this would consequently be impossible.

In addition to reason, it is the area of ethics that characterizes Toland as an Enlightenment theologian. For him, morality is incorporated in the teaching of Jesus: "He fully and clearly preach'd the purest Morals, he taught that reasonable Worship [alluding to Rom 12:1, a favorite text of Enlightenment theologians] ... So having strip'd the Truth of all those external Types and Ceremonies which made it difficult before, he rendered it easy and obvious to the meanest Capacities" (158).

While Toland still did not yet practice historical criticism, he did prepare the way for the early beginnings of the application of characteristics of Enlightenment thought and standards for making judgments about the

Bible. To these belong the concentration on the New Testament and the understanding of Jesus according to the paradigm of a moral teacher.

The connection of the deists with the Puritans on the one side and the Latitudinarians on the other is unmistakable. Finally, this approach proceeded from the humanists. The deists have only formulated it more consistently and radically. If they understood faith primarily in the sense of morality, they felt they were in accord with their environment. Since the anticultic and anticlerical feeling was expressed more clearly and was directed against the clergy of their own church, conflict between the two was unavoidable. At the same time, they felt that they were unquestionably Christians, thus distinguishing themselves from the more radical Enlightenment in France.

3

THE BATTLE FOR THE TEXT OF THE BIBLE

3.1. ARGUING ABOUT VOWEL SIGNS AND ACCENTS: ELIAS LEVITA, LOUIS CAPPEL, AND THE BUXTORFS

The struggle over the dating of the vowel signs and accents in the Hebrew Bible began with the work of the Jewish philologist and humanist Elias Levita (1469–1549), who published, in addition to Hebrew and Aramaic grammars and lexicons, a study of the Masorah (the rabbinic commentary to the Bible), entitled *Masora ha-Masoret* (Commentary of the Commentary) in 1538. In this latter book, he contended that the origination of vowel signs and accents was not established in their final form by Ezra and the men of the "Great Synagogue" (to whom also the final establishment of the canon customarily had been attributed), but rather by rabbinic commentators (the Masoretes) in the city of Tiberias, perhaps in the fifth century C.E. Elias believed in the human origin of the Bible and knew of no theological reasons residing behind the development of the text. His works were known also by Christian Hebraists, including Sebastian Münster (1489–1552) and Paul Fagius (1504–1559), who published the most important bilingual editions (Hebrew and Latin). The interpretation of Elias was used also by scholars such as J. J. Scaliger (1540–1609) and Jan van Drusius (1550–1616), who likewise did not give any attention to dogmatic concerns. The debate over the significance of the vowel signs first developed in the orthodox period as a background for the dogma of inspiration, for the interpretation of the text often depended on knowing the proper vowels of the Old Testament text. Thus, strong advocates of the divine gift of the Scriptures viewed inspiration as questionable if the vowel signs were added only later. It is understandable that this was taken up in Roman Catholic theological disputation with the Protestant emphasis on *sola scriptura* (Scripture alone), inasmuch as the later adding of the vowel signs would devalue the church's central teaching concerning authority. If the vowel signs were later, then this would make untenable the contention that the Bible is the only basis of faith.

The best-known defender of the orthodox position was Johannes Buxtorf (1564–1629). Born in Kamen (Westphalia) as the son of a preacher, Buxtorf came to the University of Basel after studying at Herborn. In 1590 he graduated with a master of arts degree. Thereafter, he became professor of Hebrew at Basel and remained there until his death from the plague. He composed workbooks for biblical and postbiblical Hebrew, biblical and talmudic Aramaic, and Syriac. During his time, he was the leading Christian authority on rabbinic literature. He increased his familiarity with these languages by his direct association with Jews, and he carried on an extensive correspondence with Jewish and Christian scholars. He advocated his position for the great age of the masoretic pointing in his work *Tiberias* (1620; new ed., 1665). At this time Elias Levita was the only prominent opponent of his position. Buxtorf, however, lamented in his foreword that many Christian theologians and philologists had accepted his opponent's biases. His main defense was that there is the possibility that the meanings of many passages may have been altered arbitrarily. Thus a particular reading would be uncertain should the vocalization be regarded to be so late.

Buxtorf thought he could demonstrate his position with strong scholarly arguments (instead of polemicizing) by focusing on the history of the Hebrew text. "I shall demonstrate with copious examples from the Talmud that the great part of the Masorah had come into existence prior to the Jewish Talmud." The Masoretes, having at hand vowels and accents that existed prior to their work, added their notes containing their judgments, thus demonstrating that they could not have been altered. The vowel and accent system originated with Ezra and the men of the "Great Synagogue." Buxtorf was aware of the fact there were two major schools of Masoretes, Ben Asher and Ben Naphtali, one existing in Israel (Tiberias) and the other in Babylon, but he contended that both had come into existence long after the discovery of the vowel and accent signs.

Following these affirmations, Buxtorf displayed his rich knowledge about the Masoretes, their schools, and their works. He determined that the pointing of the vowels is inconsistent (47–60). The same is true of *dagesh* and *mappiq* (60–65) as well as the accents. Earlier rabbis would speak against the judgment made by Elias that nothing in the Talmud addresses vowel points and accents (70–71). There is evidence that for arguing that "the men of the Great Synagogue" under Ezra must have been the devisers or tradents of punctuation, whereas the decision whether this was still older must remain open. For the canonical authority of the Scriptures, this does seem to have been a matter of consideration for Buxtorf.

Louis Cappel (Cappellus) was the next to take up the issue. The Latin title of his work was *Arcanum punctationis revelatum* (The Mystery of Punctuation Revealed). Louis Cappel was born in 1585, probably in the vicinity of Sedan in France, to a family of Protestant jurists. His parents fled from France when they came under persecution for their confession. After the early death of his father (1586), his mother returned to France and placed the younger children under the care of a Catholic tutor. The older brother, James, had remained in Sedan, where he became a minister and then, in 1599, a professor. He sent for Louis to come to Sedan for studies at the academy that was located there at the time. After the conclusion of his studies in Sedan (1607–8), Louis initially became the housemaster of the grown children of the Duke of Bouillon. In 1610, Cappel started the usual study journey for three years, spending two years in Oxford and one year in Leiden. In 1613, the congregation of Bordeaux provided him with the opportunity to study at the academy in Saumur, the leading educational institution of the Protestant church in France during the seventeenth century. This academy became well known and sometimes was feared because of its liberal spirit. There Cappel was professor for Hebrew until his death in 1658, and he held the additional academic post of professor of theology from 1626 to 1657. For a brief time he served as the pastor of Saumur.

The *Arcanum* appeared as an anonymous book in 1624. When he wrote this text, Cappel had been convinced for some time that the vowel signs and accents in the Hebrew biblical text were relatively late. Before the publication of his book, he sent the completed manuscript to Buxtorf to review, who after considerable procrastination returned it with a negative evaluation. He alluded to the fact that such a pronouncement would lead to dangerous consequences. In spite of this, the well known Orientalist Thomas Erpenius (1584–1624) published it with his own foreword in addition to the anonymous one written by Cappel. In it Erpenius explained, as had already Cappel in his own foreword, among other things, that in spite of expected disagreement, one may not keep silent about the truth.

The evidence is presented in a historical and rational manner. In the initial main and thematic chapter, Cappel contends that the data from the Jewish grammarians (Ibn Ezra, Kimchi, and Judah Levita), the unpointed Torah scrolls of Jews, the kabbalistic and talmudic writings, and the ancient Hebrew signs found in the Samaritan texts, taken together, demonstrate the lateness of the pointing system. The first exemplar of the Samaritan Pentateuch arrived in Paris in 1623, where Jean Morin (see below) published it and thereby made it accessible to western critics. Thus, this was a new argument, about which Buxtorf in 1620 could not yet have known. What Cappel regarded as a powerful historical factor was the recognition that these writings were not familiar with any pointed biblical text. The second section set forth a rejection of the arguments of his opponents.

Cappel seeks in the beginning of this section (1–5) to dispel the orthodox scruples that led to the arguments of Elias Levita, who, in arguing against an origin of the pointing system in 500 C.E., did so because this late date could militate against the authority of the Bible. That this is not the case is a position supported by Luther and a succession of Protestant Hebraists, including K. Pellikan (1478–1556), S. Münster, P. Fagius, and others, as well as Catholics such as Reuchlin (see *History*, vol. 3). To these can be added the Jewish witnesses. Elias had enlisted Ibn Ezra as a witness and turned to Kimchi for an interpretation of the Jewish opinion that Ezra reconstituted the readings of the text that had been forgotten in the exile, but this knowledge then would have been transmitted orally until the Masoretes of Tiberius developed a system of vowels and accents.

In the addendum Erpenius published once again an address already given by Cappel in 1612. He argued at that time that the customary Christian practice of pronouncing the divine name as *Jehovah* was not accurate. Rather, *Adonai* had been read. In fact, as one knows today, this was the reading suggested by the Masoretes.

After the death of Buxtorf, his son (1599–1664), who bore the same name, succeeded to his position. Not until 1648 did the latter Buxtorf take up once again the disputation and wrote *Tractatus de punctorum vocalium et accentuum in libris Veteris Testamenti hebraicis, origine, antiquitate et authoritate...* (Tractate on the Origin, Age, and Authority of the Vowel Points and Accents in the Books of the Old Testament). The arguments were approximately the same as those made by his father.

Later Cappel composed a comprehensive work on Old Testament textual criticism, the *Critica sacra* (Sacred Criticism). The manuscript, which was finished by 1634, was not published until 1650 in Paris with Catholic support on account of the objections of Protestant orthodox theologians. Cappel explained the textual variants in the Hebrew Text, in the readings of the Hebrew text and the Old Testament citations in the New Testament, and in the Hebrew and Greek Old Testament by recourse to the traditioning process. Some errors developed in the process of copying manuscripts.

Nevertheless, the authority of the Bible was not diminished. Many of his contemporaries, however, were not able to come to such an unshackled judgment.

Jean Morin (1591–1659), the Oratorian who had converted from Protestantism, sought above all in his work *Exercitationes biblicae de Hebraei Graecique textus sinceritate* (Biblical Exercises concerning the Originality of the Hebrew and Greek Text [1633]) to show that the Hebrew biblical text was distorted because of many errors introduced by copyists and the vowel system. Instead of the Hebrew text, Morin argued for the superiority and inspiration of the Septuagint (from which the Vulgate originates). In the course of the Counter-Reformation in France, Catholic theologians sought to demonstrate that the idea that the Bible alone is the foundation for faith is not sufficient owing to the erroneous character of the text. Rather, the authority of the teaching of the church must come into play. Therefore it proved easy to take up the observations of the Protestant Cappel and to repeat many of his arguments, as Morin had done. This approach would be fundamentally altered in the nineteenth and early twentieth centuries.

3.2. Recovering the Text of the New Testament: John Mill, Johann Albrecht Bengel, Jakob Wettstein

The text of the New Testament represented a more difficult challenge. The recovery of the New Testament text in its original form, in so far as possible, was complicated by the large number of copies of existing manuscripts produced in the monasteries. In the west, the first printing of the Bible was the Vulgate at a time when this text stood at the forefront of interest owing to its use in church. Lorenzo Valla and initially Erasmus had wished to use only the Greek text in their revision (see *History*, vol. 3). Accordingly, for his edition of the New Testament, Erasmus hastily compared the Greek manuscripts available to him at the time and noted their differences, although these were produced in the twelfth and thirteenth centuries and were of poor quality.

The better composed version of the *Biblia polyglotta complutensia* (see *History*, vol. 3), on account of its delayed appearance and smaller circulation, was unable to gain acceptance as long as the Basel printing inundated the market. Thus, the text of Erasmus became widely known as the valid one (Textus Receptus, "the received text"). Later, even Brian Walton (ca. 1600–1661), composer of the famous *Polyglot Bible* (six volumes, 1654–1657), which had up to nine different languages for the entire

Bible, retained the Textus Receptus in the critical apparatus for the New Testament, although he increased the number of variants. Under these circumstances the need for an edition of the Greek New Testament became increasingly recognized in the seventeenth century. At this time the most important initiatives were carried out in England. When he was bishop of Oxford, John Fell (1625–1686), dean of Christ Church College in England since 1660 and vice chancellor of the university since 1666, entrusted John Mill with the production of a critical edition of the text of the New Testament. He could have selected no better person.

John Mill was probably born in 1645 as the son of simple parents; he came to Queen's College in Oxford when he was sixteen years old as the holder of a stipend. Afterwards he moved up in rank to fellow. After he had distinguished himself as tutor, Latinist, and academic disputant, he was ordained and then served as a chaplain to several lords and finally to King Charles II and his two successors. In 1681, he was promoted to doctor of divinity. In 1685, following the early death of his wife, he became principal of St. Edmund Hall, a student residence, and continued in this office until his death in 1707. All in all he lived the quiet existence of an Oxford scholar who, in addition to his administrative activity, had ample opportunity to spend a good deal of time in study. Mill devoted it entirely to his edition of the New Testament.

The text of the edition that was finished shortly before Mill's death offers the Textus Receptus with a few small changes. The text-critical footnotes on which Mill had worked for thirty years, however, contain the variants of a large number of new manuscripts that Mill had compiled and compared. The creation of the text and the apparatus dragged on for decades. French and English editions of R. Simon's *Histoire critique du texte du Nouveau Testament* were published in 1689 (see below). Mill used the work (presumably the English translation) immediately and was greatly impressed with it. It is difficult to say whether Mill or Simon should be given priority, since they made some of the same observations on the New Testament text. The monumental character of Mill's work is shown by the 168 two-column pages of introduction ("Prolegomena"), which Mill wrote last. First (part 1) he describes the emergence of the canon, including the noncanonical and apocryphal writings, in each case together with their historical setting, and mentions the reasons why a book was considered to be inspired. Part 2 contains a complete history of the text until Valla. Next he describes the printed editions since the *Complutensia*, including the edited versions and manuscripts, and then the edited manuscripts, editions, versions, and citations from the church fathers that were treated in his own edition. All of this contains a considerable amount of information. In addition, he develops the principle that the more difficult reading is to be preferred when a choice must be made between two different readings. Admittedly, Mill did not read any Oriental languages, except for a little Hebrew, and therefore he was dependent on the Latin translations of the corresponding versions. In spite of this deficiency, his significance as a pathfinder for New Testament textual criticism is not to be undervalued.

The project announced by the famous philologist of ancient texts Richard Bentley (1662–1742), which would have also presented a revised edition, was never realized. Even so, he deserves our eternal gratitude for his work on the textual criticism of the New Testament. The library of Trinity College in Cambridge, which was under his control due to his role as the college's master, housed one of the oldest and best biblical manuscripts, Codex Alexandrinus. A fire broke out one night, and he was observed wearing his nightgown and carrying out of the burning building the four heavy volumes of this priceless text.

The textual critical edition of the Greek New Testament (1734) by Johann Albrecht Bengel (1687–1752), the well-known Schwabish pietist, brought together for the first time an arrangement of the different groups of manuscripts in "nations": an Asian (Byzantine) and an African (Alexandrian) group. Later this division into textual "families" brought about the creation of a more refined order of manuscripts, which even today is recognized as a valid, differentiated classification. In its significance, Bengel's edition was exceeded only by the edition of Johann Jakob Wettstein.

Johann Jakob Wettstein was born in 1693, the son of a pastor in Basel and the scion of a learned, well-known family who had lived there for a long period. Already at the age of thirteen (1706) he began his foundational studies at Basel University. Beginning in 1709, he also studied theology (including Aramaic, Syriac, and Talmud). His uncle, Johann Wettstein, librarian in Basel, permitted him to compare the New Testament manuscripts that were collected there. From this research grew his dissertation, *De variis Novi Testamenti lectionibus* (Concerning the Different Readings of the New Testament), on the basis of which he was promoted to doctor of philosophy in 1713, which marked the completion of his studies. He defended the thesis: "The integrity of the Scriptures does not waver due to the variety of textual readings." This occasioned for him, however, severe difficulties with the orthodox clergy in Basel who defended the literal inspiration of the words of the text. In the years 1714 and 1715, he undertook a student journey to Zurich, Bern, Geneva, and then Lyon, Paris, Leiden, London, Cambridge, and Oxford, everywhere collating and copying New Testament manuscripts. He also designed the system, which continues to be used today, in which the manuscripts written in capital letters (uncials) were noted with Latin alphabetic signs, while minuscules were designated with Arabic numbers. From 1715 to 1717, he was an army chaplain in a Swiss regiment in service in the Netherlands. Beginning in 1717, he was a curate in Basel, where in 1720 he succeeded to the office of pastor and was connected to the University of Basel as a *Dozent* (private lecturer) for philosophy (including physics, astronomy, cosmogony, and dogmatics). A legal proceeding before the church council of the city of Basel, where he was attacked for his alleged interpretations of the Trinity and Christology, ended with his dismissal from his office as pastor in 1730. Immediately after the end of this process, he moved to Amsterdam, where the printed records of the proceeding were forwarded to him. He circulated them among the Remonstrant brotherhood. In 1731, after he had explained his conformity with Remonstrant toleration and especially the teaching of van Limborch, the general assembly of this church nominated him to be the successor to the ailing emeritus Jean le Clerc, the lector of Latin, Greek, Hebrew, and church history. However, the more orthodox city council required him to clear up the charges against him that had been raised in Basel. He succeeded in doing this in 1731 with a "Declaration," in which he distanced himself from, among other things, Socinianism (see below). In 1733, Wettstein finally moved to Amsterdam in order to succeed to his office, in spite of far-ranging quarrels, but he apparently did not receive the title Professor until 1737. In spite of some later applications to chairs that became vacant in Basel, he continued in his professorship in Amsterdam until his death in 1754. During his lifetime, he had become personally acquainted with many foreign scholars and had engaged in an expansive scholarly correspondence.

The result of the work of Wettstein on the text of the New Testament over several decades is available in a two-volume edition of the *Novum Testamentum Graecum* (1751–1752). For that period of time, it represented formidable progress and received international acclaim. Wettstein was inducted into membership in both the Royal Prussian Academy of Scholars in Berlin in 1752 and a year later into the Royal Society in London. In a section of the addendum, "Concerning the Interpretation of the New Testament" (2:874–89), Wettstein mentioned once again the most important rules of interpretation. He repeats in particular the following: "As we read, however, with the same eyes the holy books, the decrees of the princes, and all old and new books, so must the same rules of explanation [of the New Testament writings] be applied, which we use for their understanding" (875). Thus, there is required a neutral, common, and secular hermeneutic for interpreting all texts. Another modern rule was anticipated when Wettstein argued that the meanings of words and sentences are not understood according to the etymologies of words and their derivative sequence, but rather from their use and examples first by the same author, then by other biblical writings, and then by the Septuagint and other contemporary writings. Consequently, he stressed the important role of context. Wettstein, however, did not place the main emphasis on hermeneutics, choosing instead to focus on the corresponding literature.

Nor had Wettstein been so bold as to attempt to revise the actual text in his edition. Instead, he printed in the main section the Textus Receptus in the version that appeared in Amsterdam in 1624, by the publishing house of Elzevier. Between the text and the critical apparatus placed under it, he mentions here and there a reading that he held to be original. Even that was viewed as risky in his day, because of the orthodox clergy who regarded the biblical text as the literal inspired word given by God. Many of the text-critical details of Wettstein were surpassed in due time by the availability of better manuscripts or were reworked over a lengthy period of time in well-established handbooks. Still today the original "Wettstein" is valuable (republished in 1962!), which, in a second apparatus below the text, brings together numerous data from the works of Greek and Latin authors, Jewish-Hellenistic writings, rabbinic literature, and the church fathers. These data are offered from Wettstein's unparalleled erudition. Above all, religio-historical, comparative criticism can profit from these parallels. Many efforts undertaken to adapt these citations to the modern critical editions of the text, thus to produce a "new Wettstein," have failed either because of the constraints of the time needed to carry out this project or because of the premature death of the responsible editors.

4

France and the Netherlands in the Seventeenth and Eighteenth Centuries

4.1. Applying Historical-Philological Criticism to the Bible: Richard Simon

Richard Simon was born on 13 May 1638, in Brittany, in the harbor port of Dieppe, the son of a simple craftsman (his father probably was either a smith or a tailor). There he attended the community school and served as an acolyte in Catholic worship. The gifted youth attracted the attention of his parish minister, the Oratorian Adrien Fournier, who sought to influence the boy to seek the priesthood, especially of the Oratorian order. Moreover, the call of the church was the only way for a penniless young student to finance an education. Thanks to the recommendation of Fournier, Simon entered the college of this order in Dieppe, where he spent the first year of his philosophical studies. Besides the obligatory Latin, he continued with Greek. His philological and historical leanings were already apparent. He spent his second year of study (1657–1658) in the Jesuit College in Rouen. Their practical directed behavior, which stressed moral action, he found to be more to his liking than the mystically shaped clergy of the Oratorians. In the fall of 1658 he returned to the Oratorians and entered their new house in Paris as a novice. While there he decided not to complete his novitiate and, by 1659 was again in Dieppe. He found for himself a new patron, the well-to-do abbot Hayazinth de la Roque. The abbot offered to finance a course of study in Paris, and Simon continued his studies there during the years 1659–1662. Besides the usual Scholastic course of studies, in which Thomas Aquinas stood at the center, Simon occupied himself with church history, biblical studies, Hebrew, and Syriac. In 1662, Simon again took up a novitiate among the Oratorians, and once again he experienced several difficulties—above all, the instruction to read during the trial year exclusively literature of meditation. Finally, he was allowed to read the Bible in its original languages, the writings of the church fathers, and commentaries. He received honorific tasks in the order: he was *Dozent* (private lecturer) for philosophy in the college in July (1663–1664 and again in 1668–1671) and had to produce a catalogue in the library of the main building of the order in Paris consisting of a collection of Oriental manuscripts from Constantinople (1664–1666 and again 1668–1671). These tasks still allowed him time for his own work in the libraries of Paris, especially the royal one, which today are the National Library. After his ordination as a priest in 1669–1670, he experienced several quiet years during which he could carry out his main work, the *Histoire critique du Vieux Testament* (Historical Criticism of the Old Testament). In 1670, he became acquainted with the Jewish scholar Jona Salvador, with whom he would read passages from the Talmud every week. From him Simon learned a great deal about Judaism. For the Jews in Metz, who were embroiled in a legal process, he wrote an essay of defense.

This period ended with a scandal. During the early part of the year 1678, the authorization of the censor of the theological faculty and the superiors of the order had arrived for Simon's work that was in press for the production of thirteen hundred copies—the title page and the dedication excepted. Simon had hoped to gain the approval of the dedication to King Louis XIV, when the monarch returned to France from Flanders. In the meantime, a copy of the table of contents, which had been distributed for purposes of advertisement, came to the court and fell into the hands of the influential Jacques-Bénigne Bossuet (1627–1704; later bishop of Meaux), who considered himself to be the defender of the faith. A glance at the superscription of the fifth chapter of volume 1 was enough for Bossuet to order work's impoundment and official vitiation: "Moses cannot be the author of all that exists in the books attributed to him." He ordered the confiscation and official destruction of nearly the whole edition. One of the few copies that were saved formed the basis for the second printed edition, which was published in Rotterdam in 1685. Following its publication, Simon fell into controversy with orthodox Reformed theologians, including Ezechiel Spanheim (1629–1710) and le Clerc. Le Clerc wrote an anonymous work, *Sentimens de quelques théologiens de Hollande...* (Opinions of Some Theologians from Holland regarding the Historical Criticism of the Old Testament), which assumed the form of imaginary speeches that were placed in the genre of disputations.

The official condemnation led to the immediate expulsion of Simon from the order. He then took on a small pastoral appointment in Normandy (Bolleville), but soon gave it up and returned to Dieppe in 1682.

While there he continued to say Mass and understood himself to be a true Catholic. He hoped to return to the order or to be reconciled with Bossuet, but these desires were not fulfilled. In this period Simon composed his writings about the New Testament and, in addition, engaged in polemics against different authors. In 1694, he suffered a difficult blow: a great many of his possessions, among them books and manuscripts, were destroyed in the bombardment of Dieppe by the British and Dutch flotilla. Simon composed, among other things, a French translation of the New Testament, which he published in the independent principality of Dombe, thus free from French censorship. He failed in his attempt to have it also officially accepted in France.

According to a note of his biographer, Simon, following a severe case of anxiety about his possible persecution, rolled several barrels filled with paper over the city wall and burned them in an open field. He remained personally unharmed. The barrels held, among other things, the manuscript of a translation of the Pentateuch, which was to be part of a planned translation of the entire Old Testament. Simon died on 12 April 1712, shortly after making a will, leaving to the cathedral church of Rouen his valuable library, including manuscripts. Unfortunately, most of this was lost during the French revolution.

For a long time, Simon was a little-known figure. He was given significant attention only following World War II, especially by French Catholic scholars. This led to the reprinting of some of his major writings, and Simon then became regarded as the father of French biblical scholarship. This is understandable when one recalls that in Catholic, absolutist France during the seventeenth century an independent biblical critic was subjected to great difficulties. Further, his *Histoire critique du Vieux Testament* was the first example of something like an introductory handbook. This form came into prominence around a century later. The term "criticism" was immediately misunderstood by the orthodox opponents. Ezechiel Spanheim (see above) read into the term the view that Simon's work transmitted a harmful disparagement of the biblical authors themselves and thereby sought "to destroy every certainty and evidence of the Holy Scriptures" ("Lettre à un ami" [Letter to a Friend], published in Simon, *Histoire critique du Vieux Testament*, 568). After some positive words concerning this view, Simon gave a comprehensive description of the problems associated with the Old Testament, "which would be useful for the public" (*Histoire critique du Vieux Testament*, 2).

According to the state of biblical study at the time, it was little wonder that the entire first book was dedicated to textual criticism. Still, it proceeded time and again in a decisive way to set forth the debate between the Buxtorfs (father and son) and the French challengers Cappel and Morin (see ch. 3 above) concerning the degree of inspiration of the vowel points of the Hebrew text. Over against Morin's thesis that the Hebrew text was so completely corrupted that only the Septuagint (as the foundation of the Vulgate, which was the standard text in the Catholic Church) had maintained the original text, Simon emphasized the view that neither the presently existing Hebrew text nor the Greek version (perhaps the Vatican's Septuagint manuscript) conformed with the original version, but rather both had experienced numerous alterations. In his foreword (folio 3c), he stressed that this awareness destroyed the entire principle of the view of Scripture by both Protestants and Socinians. From the present exemplars of the Bible, it is clear that the contention that the Scriptures alone are "clearly the only sufficient basis for the truth of faith" cannot be maintained. This was not simply an effort to defend the Catholic view, although he believed throughout that he did support Catholicism with his views. At the same time, however, he depended especially on Jewish and rabbinic witnesses to demonstrate the view that numerous alterations had entered into the Old Testament. But there were no known falsifications or evidence of significant changes in meaning. The authority of the Bible was not destroyed, for "it is necessary that these additions and changes had the same authority as the remainder of the Scriptures." Otherwise, one would be forced to say that not everything in the Bible had the same divine and canonical status (foreword, folio 2a). Today, when the differences between "authentic" and "secondary" materials have begun to lose their theological significance, this statement appears to be very modern. On the whole, Simon represented a moderate position. At the beginning of the third book, he gives comprehensive details for the treatment of text-critical problems. It is important that one proceed from the Masoretic Text, which he considered to be the most trustworthy in spite of the many errors found in it (335), and for its improvement one could still refer to the remaining versions. One should indicate the different readings "in accordance with the rules of criticism, which one is accustomed to use in other books" (354). Philology is a science that, free of preconceptions, serves as a credible instrument that offers one the ability to produce a trustworthy text of the Bible.

Simon's theory of the origin of the Pentateuch especially received attention. He tries to solve the problem in part by noting there are many particular examples in the Pentateuch of materials that could not come from Moses (as, for example, the account of his death in Deut 34; and places where Moses is mentioned in the third person). Still, he held to the traditional attribution of Mosaic authorship by offering an original suggestion: there are "public scribes" (he also calls them "prophets," since they were also inspired) who had "the freedom to make collections of older documents. These were maintained in the state archives, and gave them a new form. They added or omitted materials depending on their appropriateness" (foreword, folio 1b; cf. 1.1, 3–4). The present form of the Pentateuch (and the remaining books of the Old Testament) is a result of their work. Among the materials edited by them, above all Genesis, there are texts primarily original to Moses, while others, for example, the history of creation, contain still older traditions. Repetitions within the Books of Moses may have been generated through parallel editing of the same kind of acts. There was not in this writing any division into sources in the manner of the nineteenth century, although this work was certainly a predecessor to that development. It has been noted that Simon, to a certain degree, may have effectively displaced the principle of tradition in the Catholic Church (Scripture and tradition of the church, according to the Council of Trent, are parallel sources of faith) with the principle of the Bible alone, thereby recommending the tradition of Scripture based on its sources and chronology.

In his efforts to deal with the problems of the form of the text in which the biblical writings exist—that is, in manuscripts and translations—Simon was the paradigm of a humanistic philologist. For example, the question about the authors of the biblical writings fits this approach, and Simon extended his view to the New Testament. While the subject of criticism in the Old Testament is presented in three sections of one volume, New Testament criticism is produced in several volumes. Thus, there appeared in Rotterdam in succession the following books concerning the New Testament: the *Histoire critique du texte du Nouveau Testaments* (Historical Criticism of the New Testament [1689]) and the *Histoire critique des versions du Nouveau Testaments* (Historical Criticism of the Translations of the New Testament [1690]). Finally, Simon brought out a history of the interpretation of the New Testament, the *Histoire critique de principaux commentateurs du Nouveau Testament* (Historical Criticism of the Principal Commentators of the New Testament [1693]).

It is revealing to see that Simon in his volume on the historical criticism of the New Testament (*Histoire critique du texte du Nouveau Testaments*) undertakes initially a delimitation of the canon. Only on this basis is an inner criticism of the canon possible. The Gospels are, as Simon correctly recognized, the writing down of apostolic preaching

(1). The heretics have sought vainly to put in their place some apocryphal texts. The Gospel of Matthew was written originally in Aramaic, as Simon saw things, and was in the possession of Nazarenes who were the first Christians from Jerusalem (ch. 5, 33–38). If the Greek version is only a translation, it achieves apostolic authority through its lengthy use in the church. Matthew is the oldest Gospel, a long-held interpretation. Mark offered, according to the tradition of the ancient church, the contents of the message of Peter, although it was a Gospel originally written in Greek. It is not an abbreviated version of the Gospel of Matthew (chs. 10–11). Simon recognized also the problem of the ending of Mark (Mark 16:9–20), which, according to Jerome, did not appear in the oldest manuscripts. If it was added later, Simon thinks that one need not doubt the authenticity of this section, "for it was just as old as the Gospel of Saint Mark" (84). Here he demonstrates a conservative attitude in spite of his literary-critical method. The Gospel of John is the most recent Gospel. Agreeing with Jerome, Simon held that it was written in Ephesus. Simon also notes here that some heretics rejected this Gospel. He determines (99–100) that the section about the "sinful woman" in John 7:53–8:11 was not part of the older manuscripts of the Gospel, according to Jerome, other church fathers, and Maldonatus (*History*, vol. 3). With Maldonatus he stresses, however, that this in no way affects the authority of the canon in its present expanse, established by the Council of Trent (100).

As for the origins of the Letter to the Hebrews (ch. 16), Simon follows the view of Origen that the author was a disciple of the apostle Paul. He astutely remarks that "the entire difficulty is reduced to knowing whether the church, in which the writings of the Old and New Testament were used, has explained at the same time that they originated from the authors whose name they bore" (129). Here in fact the distinction between faith in the canon and fundamentalism is defined.

According to present understanding, one is astonished that Simon experienced the degree of persecution that he did. In truth, he knew very well how to separate critical observations from faith in the biblical canon. Corresponding to his own claim, he had remained a thoroughly loyal Catholic.

Simon's history of interpretation of the New Testament provides evidence of his astonishingly precise knowledge of patristic literature and the more recent interpreters of his own time. Whoever seeks to obtain a first look at the older history of New Testament exegesis and to become familiar with the many interpreters who today are forgotten only has to take up this handbook. It shows once more the great erudition of these exegetes, who were wrongfully persecuted.

4.2. DISTINGUISHING REASON FROM REVELATION: BARUCH DE SPINOZA

The life of the famous philosopher Spinoza initially moved in rather restful circumstances until a great disruption occurred. The son of Michael de Spinoza, a merchant, and his second wife, Hanna Deborah, Baruch (Spanish Bento, Latin Benedictus) was born in Amsterdam (in the Jewish section of Vlooienburg) on 24 November 1632, according to existing reports. He came from a Marianist family, that is, Portuguese Jews who were forced to undergo superficial conversion to Christianity as a result of the Inquisition, but who secretly continued to belong to Judaism. After the family emigrated to a relatively tolerant Holland, it joined the Jewish community in Amsterdam. The internal situation of this community was complicated: after a lengthy period of underground life, the majority of its members hardly knew anything of Jewish teachings and practices. Only a few, aside from the leading rabbis, could even read Hebrew. The young Baruch attended the elementary school of the community ('ēṣ ḥayyîm, "tree of Life"). He soon achieved a distinguished reputation owing to his brilliant intelligence and ambition for learning: in seven years of school he learned to read and write Hebrew, afterwards to read and translate the Bible (Pentateuch and Prophets) into Spanish (the language of the educated members of the community), and even to translate a little from the Talmud. Even the Kabbalah (Jewish mysticism) became familiar to him. Moreover, he appeared to have become familiar already with the commentaries of Maimonides (Rabbi Moses ben Maimon [Ramban]) and Ibn Ezra (see *History*, vol. 2). He did not begin training to become a rabbi, but rather left the school presumably around 1648. His mother died when he was six years old, and his father later remarried. In addition to the Jewish school, he pursued learning in a Latin private school. Following the death of his half brother Isaac in 1649, Baruch had to work in the commercial business of tropical fruits with his father. After his father's early death (1654), Spinoza continued in the business together with his younger brother, who was still a minor. Debts that he had inherited came due in 1656, and he could survive financially only by being legally acquitted from the inheritance of his father. A judicial remission allowed the conferment of the business to a guardian.

In the meantime, Spinoza internally had dissociated himself from the Jewish tradition. Nothing is known about the developments leading to this, since he himself never mentioned anything about it. It is clear that the head of the Jewish community became increasingly disturbed over this progression. Spinoza was finally excommunicated (1656). Since the decree speaks only in general terms about the reasons for this condemnation and mentions no concrete teaching of Spinoza, we know nothing about what the specific reasons were. Spinoza's defense, composed in Spanish, may have contained the particulars, but unfortunately it was lost.

Spinoza now learned the craft of grinding optical lenses and lived by selling optical implements such as microscopes and telescopes, which were highly valued by well-known doctors and astronomers. In 1671, Leibniz consulted him in a letter about optical questions (Letter 45). He lived some years in Amsterdam, before pressure from the rabbis on the city leaders forced him to relocate to Rijnsburg near Leiden. He Latinized his forename to Benedictus. The record of his correspondence indicates that he kept company with members of the Christian free churches such as the Mennonites and the Quakers. While it is not expressly stated, he may also have participated in meetings (*collegia*) with religious freethinkers. There are several questions that continue to be debated: Had he already done this before he was excommunicated? And, during which period in his life did he become familiar with natural science and the philosophy of Descartes? His friends and correspondents included the Cartesian doctor Lodewijk Meyer (1629–1681), who composed the book *Philosophia Sanctae Scripturae Interpres* (Philosophy as an Interpreter of Holy Scripture [1666]) and Heinrich Oldenburg of Bremen (ca. 1615–1677), who, along with J. Wilkins, served as secretary of the British Royal Society. Oldenburg visited Spinoza when he was residing in Rijnsburg, which is where, beginning in 1601, Spinoza wrote the first part of his major work *Ethics*. In 1663, he resettled in Voorburg, near The Hague. Here Jan de Witt, the Council Pensionary of the Dutch Republic, visited him following the death of William II, Prince of Orange (1650). De Witt was also the political leader of the land as the representative of the well-to-do citizenry, the Regents Party, and the one who guaranteed freedom of religion, while the nobles, the reformed clergy, and the more simple people were the supporters of the House of Orange. De Witt is supposed to have provided Spinoza with an allowance of two hundred guilders. Shortly thereafter, in 1663, Spinoza published the only work that appeared in his lifetime and bore his own name, *Renati Descartes principiorum philosophiae more geometrico demonstrata* (Descartes' Principles of Philosophy Demonstrated in a Geometrical Way). The rest of Spinoza's life was modest and uneventful. He often spent the day working in his room, where he even had his meals brought. After June 1665, he interrupted his work on his *Ethics* in order to write the *Tractatus Theo-logico-Politicus* (A Theological-Political Tractate). In 1670, it was published anonymously, using a faked publisher's name: "Apud Hericum Künrath," and a false place of publication ("Hamburgi"). Actually it appeared with Jan Rieuwertsz in Amsterdam. When Spinoza heard that a Dutch transla-tion was in preparation, he sought in vain to prohibit its publication, since he feared the work would be completely prohibited to be read. His caution was well advised. Soon the volume received severe criticism from theolo-gians, and requests were made to the synods that it be banned. Although in the beginning, the defense of the work by Jan de Witt and other influential friends of Spinoza prevented its impounding, in 1674 an order came from the court to forbid its use. Still, the publisher published additional editions, partially in England; thus, its distribution could not be stopped.

During the same year (1670), Spinoza moved for the last time. He took up residence in The Hague, where he continued to live until his death in 1677. A series of events that occurred during this period are known. In 1672, after the seizing of power by William III of Orange, who became the "governor" of the state, Jan de Witt was murdered along with his brother Cornelius by a mob on an open street. It is said that Spinoza, being deeply affected by this event, intended to go into the streets with a placard, for he wished to brand the doers of this deed as the "Last of the Barbarians." His landlord, however, hindered this effort by locking the door of the house. A year later, Spinoza returned from an unsuccessful attempt to visit the Prince of Condé, the commander of the French troops in occupied Utre-cht. The prince had demanded to see him, but he was met at the door by a crowd of people who suspected that he was a spy. He was, nevertheless, successful in convincing them to break up and leave.

When Spinoza was offered a professorial chair of philosophy at the University of Heidelberg in 1673, he turned it down (Letter 48) for the reason "that it has never been my desire to teach publicly." In addition, he was uncertain how much freedom would be guaranteed him to engage in philosophy without being disturbed because of his well-known religious position. This proved to be a wise decision on Spinoza's part, for as soon as the following year, the troops of Louis XIV attacked the palatinate, and Heidelberg University was closed.

In 1675, Spinoza moved to Amsterdam in order to look for a publica-tion of his *Ethica, ordine geometrico demonstrata* (Ethics, Demonstrated in Geometrical Order). Nevertheless, since the controversy still continued to disseminate a rumor that "I have sought to demonstrate in a book in press that there was no God" (Letter 68, to Heinrich Oldenburg), he refrained from the project. The work was first published posthumously. In the last decade of his life, Spinoza began to write a "Political Tractate" (*Tractatus politicus*), although he did not finish it. In the autumn of 1676 he received a personal visit from Leibniz. He died unexpectedly, following a year-long bout with tuberculosis, on 26 February 1677.

Spinoza belongs to those authors whose intentions were seriously misunderstood by his contemporaries and by many others until the recent past. In the latest period of critical scholarship, however, there are different approaches that are considerably more suitable. Spinoza betrayed his intentions by writing them down in a letter to Oldenburg (Letter 30). According to this, he was mostly moved by

> 1. the presuppositions of theologians, since I know that these presuppositions keep most people from turning their spirit to philosophy…;
> 2. the view, which people have of me, that I unceasingly am held to be guilty of atheism; I feel compelled to reject this view where ever possible;
> 3. the freedom to engage in philosophy and to say what one thinks; to defend this freedom, since it is suppressed in every possible way by the exaggerated sense of self-importance and impertinence of the preachers.

The "Theological-Political Tractate," in which Spinoza described his view of the Bible, cannot be understood without referring first to the philosophy developed in his *Ethics*. When he interrupted the work on *Ethics* in order to write his "Theological-Political Tractate," there was a pressing necessity behind this decision: the attitude of biblical revelation in the eyes of his contemporaries required a "thinker." Apart from this, there was also the publicity surrounding his excommunication from the Jewish community. Consequently, the view that he was an atheist was widespread. In spite of his outspoken views expressed in the letter to Oldenburg and the "Theological-Political Tractate," he was not successful in dispelling this stubborn judgment. As the strong outcry against his views demonstrates, the contrary was the case. Even in recent times a view that above all goes back to Leo Strauss sees in the "Tractate" an extroverted writing, behind the wording of which Spinoza hides his genuine, basically secular position. This view is occasioned by the work's apparent contradiction to the philosophy developed in his *Ethics*.

As the title of the work shows (*Ethica, ordine geometrico demonstrata*), Spinoza wished to develop his philosophy in a geometrical, mathematical way similar to Hobbes's approach *more geometrico* ("in the geometrical manner"). This meant in practice proceeding in a deductive manner: from an initially developed definition axioms and propositions unfolded from which further results are obtained and so on. Yet, in addition, ancient presuppositions play a role: the initial postulate is presupposed, because all humans possess common presumptions (*notiones communes*), a thesis that originated with Aristotle. Spinoza begins, following several explanations of ideas, with a definition of God. Behind this lay the conception of God that stems from the pre-Socratic Parmenides (ca. 540–460 B.C.E.) and is found in the classical understanding of ontological metaphysics. According to this understanding, there is one, eternal being. This was transmitted in the Christian Middle Ages and developed by Jewish exegetes and the philosopher Maimonides, with the assistance of Aristotelian categories. Spinoza appropriated these: "By God I understand the eternal being" (*ens absolute infinitum* [1.1.6]). This becomes even clearer subsequently: "this means the substance, which consists of eternal attributes." Hence all additional conclusions ensue as a result from this. However, Spinoza draws from this proposition the most extreme consequences. To this belongs theorem 8: "Every substance is necessarily eternal"; theorem 14: Apart from God there is no additional substance that exists and can be grasped"; and from this is the directly deducible theorem 15: "All is in God and nothing can be or be grasped without God." This last sentence, which reflects a mystical conclusion, Spinoza develops from his own conception of substance. He has often been understood to be a pantheist, although doubts have been raised about this recently. An expression of Spinoza found in a letter to Oldenburg (Letter 73) speaks clearly against this earlier view: "Although there are people who have the opinion, derived from the 'Theological-Political Tractate,' that God and nature are one and the same, they are entirely wrong." "I regard God as the internal and not the external cause of all things." It is worthy of note that Spinoza refers this theorem to (the Lukan) Paul ("In him we live, move, and are," Acts 17:28), in addition to the ancient philosophers and the correctly understood Hebrew tradition. In spite of the mystical formulation, the opposition between God and nature is not moved aside; and yet the moment of the timelessness of God conditions his omnipresence and his comprehensive activity. For Spinoza, a radical separation of God from the world was not possible. Spinoza has pressed a commonly accepted ontology to its logical conclusion; he has not said anything that was fundamentally new. He explains what he thinks in the note (*scholium*) given to the twenty-ninth theorem in part 1 of his *Ethics* by means of the distinction between a "creating nature" (*natura naturans*) and a "created nature" (*natura naturata*) or through the distinction between the eternal nature of God and his *modi*, that is, the things "which are in God and without which God still cannot be grasped" (*Ethics*, Blumenstock 132, Latin 133).

The purpose of the freedom to engage in philosophy, already combined in the subtitle of the "Theological-Political Tractate" with the peace of the state and with piety, arrives at its conclusion in the last section of the book. Through the corresponding chapters (16–20), the Tractate does become a political writing concerning the state, but in the first instance it is a disquisition of revelation. The two themes are brought into association. It should come as no surprise that the same combination can be found in both Hobbes and Locke. Further, legal questions of the state in the seventeenth century were not settled without recourse to the widely recognized authority of the Bible. That Spinoza expressly enters into this position is not merely to be seen as an external concession to his readers to address the openness of his views or to provide the authorities responsible for censorship with the opportunity for evaluation: he himself did not wish to abandon his views, but rather he sought to bring them into conformity with his philosophical approach.

Already in the preamble, in which Spinoza offers to the "philosophical readers" the opportunity to assess his views (*Tractatus*, Gawlick and Niewöhner 22/23 [Latin/German]), his methodology of proceeding, informed by the Enlightenment, becomes evident. He begins with "superstition" (*superstitio*), to which all humans are subjected because of fear (for example, Alexander the Great, who consulted an oracle at a critical juncture). In order to guard against this fear, one has outfitted religion with cult and customs, which should induce humans to demonstrate reverence toward it. Since "we" (i.e., Spinoza and his readers) live in a free state (Holland), he wishes to show that the freedom to judge "not only may be considered to be harmless for piety and peace in the state," but also can even be abolished at the same time only along with peace in the state and piety itself (10/11). For this purpose it had been necessary first to point out the main prejudices (*praejudicia*) concerning religion—here is the second principle shaped by the Enlightenment! The causes of these prejudices he found especially in the imperiousness of the clergy of all religions, who confirmed the biases of many by stressing the "secrets" (*mysteria*) of Scripture and condemning the natural light of reason. The result of his examination of Scripture therefore led to the conclusion "that the authority of the prophets is of significance only for questions of moral conduct and true virtues." This opened the way for him to discover the recognition that "in that which the Scripture expressly teaches nothing that would fail to agree with reason or that contradicts it" (16/17) can be found. Much here evokes the first publication of the young Toland, which appeared only a short time later (see above).

Also in the "Theological-Political Tractate," Spinoza builds on the foundations laid down in his *Ethics*. This becomes clear as early as the beginning of the actual text, which Spinoza opens with two chapters about prophecy. Already the initial definition incorporates Spinoza's philosophical approach: "prophecy" is, as the beginning sentence of the Tractate formulates, only a word for revelation: "Prophecy or revelation is the certain knowledge revealed by God to humans that makes known a sure knowledge of a particular matter" (ch. 1, 30/31). The prophet is defined in Exod 7: 1, where Aaron is introduced as the prophet of Moses, that is, as a "translator" (ibid.). Spinoza concludes his definition of prophecy with the statement "that one is able to call natural knowledge prophecy. For what we recognize through the natural light depends only on the knowledge of God and his eternal decree" (30/31–32/33). The "natural light," or reason, holds the position of primacy and is comparable to biblical prophecy, "for all which we clearly and lucidly recognize is provided by the idea of God ... and nature, which are one to us. This knowledge is certainly not expressed with words, but rather in a much more perfect way that completely harmonizes with the nature of spirit" (34/35). Nevertheless, biblical prophecy also brings to us, in spite of the imperfection of transmission, a certain knowledge. Prophecy is required only for those who are not capable of acquiring philosophical insight: "A prophet ... is the one who interprets what God has revealed to those who do not have a certain knowledge of what God has revealed and therefore are able only to accept it through faith" (30/31). The consequence is that one is unable to determine qualified differences between natural and prophetic knowledge:

> With respect to certainty..., which is intrinsic to natural knowledge and the source (namely God) from which it originates, it is in no way inferior to prophetic knowledge, even if someone would like to conceive that it is or should wish to dream that it is, thinking that the prophets possessed a human body, but no human spirit, and their experiences had been of an entirely different kind than our own. (32/33)

A difference from natural knowledge one can see only in the fact that "it [prophetic knowledge] extends beyond the limits of natural knowledge and that the laws of human nature, considered in themselves, cannot be its origin" (ibid.). In addition, the motto of the work, taken from 1 John

4:13, "Therefore we know that we continue in God and he in us, for he has given to us from his spirit," betrays Spinoza's essentially spiritual approach to knowledge. The same is clear in the sentence at the beginning of chapter 12: "the eternal word, the eternal covenant of God, and true religion … are inscribed in the human spirit by God himself" (392/393). In both of these affirmations, the superiority of the natural over revealed knowledge and the emphasis on the humanity of the recipients of revelation, Spinoza dared to take a revolutionary step. In orthodoxy, as represented in Holland by the Reformed theologians, one looked for the content of revelation only in Holy Scripture, for Scripture was the book that contained this revelation. In addition to this, orthodoxy had strictly separated natural from supernatural knowledge, even if it did not factor out the role of reason from biblical exegesis. Spinoza had even desacralized the Bible itself, in that he made its holiness depend entirely on its use: Scripture is "holy and its speeches are divine only so long as they have directed humans to the worship of God" (398/399). It is not a priori. "Therefore the divine character of Scripture must be based only on the fact that it teaches true virtue" (234/235). The storm of protest that was raised against Spinoza after the appearance of the book and when the name of its author became known was understandable from the side of theologians. On the other side, Spinoza still grants to the Bible an exceedingly high position: he stresses "that I value very highly the Holy Scripture or revelation with regard to its usefulness and necessity." "For, since we are unable to grasp through means of natural light that simple obedience is the way to blessedness, it is only revelation which teaches that this happens by the grace of God which human reason cannot understand. This results in the fact that Scripture grants a very great consolation to mortals" (ch. 15, conclusion, 464/465).

The concept of "prophecy" was, however, more broadly conceived than is typical for current biblical scholarship: placed under this category are not only Noah, Abraham, Moses, and Aaron, but also Hagar, Gideon, and King Solomon, all known to be rather different among recipients of revelation. Spinoza stresses that "prophecy did possess, not a more spiritual character, but rather a more vital power of perception" (65/66). The prophets received revelation only through the power of imagination (*imaginatio*), and not from the principles and ideas upon which is built entirely our natural understanding" (60/61–62/63). What was revealed to them came through words and visions (*figurae*; 36/37). Revelation conformed to their temperament and the capacity of their imagination: "If the prophet received a revelation in a sanguine disposition, there were revealed victory, peace, and what moves humans to joy…; if the prophet, by contrast, bore a tragic disposition, then there were revealed to him war, the punishment of judgment, and all kinds of damnation" (70/71). Correspondingly valid for visions was the observation that "if the prophet was a farmer there were shown to him oxen, cows, etc.; if a soldier, then the leader of the army and the Lord of Hosts; and finally if a courtier then a royal throne and similar things" (72/73). Moreover, the contents of Scripture, on the whole, conformed to the apprehension and the meanings of the nation (444/445). In the same way, Christ conformed in his pronouncements to the manner of thinking of his hearers. Thus, one may not conclude on the basis of Matt 12:26 that he believed in a kingdom of demons, or from Matt 18:10 in an angel (96/97). Spinoza places great weight on the fact that the prophets (recipients of revelation) in no way had possessed a comprehensive knowledge. Thus, Joshua could not know the true cause of what appeared to him to be the standing still of the sun (Josh 10:13). Noah was of the opinion that the entirety of humanity was destroyed, because he held that the world outside of Palestine was uninhabited, etc. The thought that God himself had conformed to the apprehension of the recipient of revelation is certainly nothing new. We saw this notion already in Irenaeus (see *History,* vol. 1). However, in Spinoza this thought is certainly altered. It provides the proof that biblical revelation uncovers no supernatural truths. This revelation can contain nothing that moves beyond the human capacity to know, although this varies for different individuals. This resides also in the purpose of God:

> that the prophets were not required to know anything about things that are mere speculation…, and actually did not know anything.… There is no idea therefore that one may see among them knowledge of natural and spiritual things. I conclude, therefore, that we are obliged to believe the prophets only in regard to that which constitutes the purpose and the kernel of revelation; in regard to all other matters we are free to believe what each one prefers. (94/95)

Thereby an important purpose was achieved: the worldview that presupposed that the Bible, the church, and believing humans were authoritative and binding in their requirements, both before and after, was forfeited. Since this worldview was explained as bound to the past, it no longer stood in the way of modern, natural scientific bodies of knowledge.

As regards the content of revelation, the prophets had nothing more to offer than moral certainty. They could obtain this, because their intention was directed only to the accomplishment of what was good. Spinoza stresses that the true prophets served as the instruments of divine grace, while false prophets were those who were the executors of God's wrath (68/69). The purpose of their message is observable in their moral conduct. In this respect the *imaginatio* is in no way devalued! Spinoza explains expressly that he is not interested in the form of the prophetic experience of revelation: "By the way, we need not know in the main the cause of prophetic knowledge because ... I shall merely investigate the documents of Scripture and draw from them my conclusions in the same way I do in regard to the data of nature. I do not care about the origin of these documents" (60/61).

A special place is granted only to Christ, "to whom has been revealed directly the plan of the salvation of God apart from words and visions. God has provided revelation through the spirit of Christ to the apostles even as occurred to Moses through the voice from the wind. Therefore, the voice of Christ can be called the voice of God, which Moses also heard" (44/45; cf. also 148/149: Christ the "mouth of God"). Christ is not dependent on the imagination as were the prophets; much more he had "grasped things truly and adequately" (148/149). He is therefore the ideal philosopher! He appears as the true teacher, who certainly accommodated himself to his audience, as, for example, he sometimes taught the law. He was sent "not only for the instruction of the Jews, but also for all humanity" (ibid.). His message was, in the main, moral instruction (384/385). As regards the doctrine of the incarnation, however, Spinoza did not believe it, and he explained Christ's resurrection in allegorical fashion (as a "second resurrection = the spiritual love of God; see Letter 75, to Oldenburg). As a result, Spinoza also stripped away Christ's role as savior. In the specific place that Spinoza assigned to Christ, Spinoza revealed his own fundamental view: although keeping his official distance from the church, he was a Christian humanist. Contrary to different-sounding affirmations, one can thoroughly accept the argument that here he expresses his actual meaning.

Later, in chapter 3, Spinoza gives an account of his views concerning Israel's election. He contends that Israel was called to be only a political kingdom, which was to enjoy corporeal amenities, and not for matters that bore on virtue and understanding. Thus, these specific qualities would not have made Israel exceptional among other nations.

In chapter 4 ("Concerning Divine Laws"), Spinoza distinguishes between human and divine law. "Under the category of human law, I understand the way of living, which serves only the securing of life and the state. Under divine law, however, there is the aim only for the highest good, namely true knowledge and the love of God" (136/137). The divine law is nothing other than the order of nature, from which the equation of Spinoza's philosophy arose. He had disclosed his definition of God in his *Ethics* (see above). Human law served only to support the earthly existence of human beings within the context of state and society (cf. ch. 3). For their obedience to this law, the patriarchs were promised security and well-being in life. Further, the Jews, because they lived in a special kingdom, maintained particular laws, which served the internal and external support of the state. Viewed historically, as Spinoza expressed later in chapter 16, the law of the Hebrews given by Moses as the intercessor to God was a completed social contract, which depicted the fundamental features of their special type of state. According to the preamble, "the laws, which God revealed to Moses, were nothing different ... than the sole order of justice of the Hebrew kingdom" (16/17). After its end, this order lost its validity. For the divine law, by contrast, Spinoza (without having mentioned its provenance) contended that the classical teaching of Greek philosophy was valid, according to which the intellectual recognition, in this sense the love of God, was the highest blessedness, which was the foremost purpose of human action. As such, this blessedness was true for all humans. The law is then only an aid for all those not able to achieve such a purely intellectual knowledge of God as eternal truth. Therefore, the love of God must be experienced as a commandment. Spinoza subsequently recommended following the natural light and the natural divine law by reference to biblical passages, from which he drew, in particular Pauline passages such as Rom 9:18 ("Paul therefore teaches exactly what I maintain" [124/125]) and above all Solomon in Proverbs. In certain sections, the Bible became the principal witness of reason. One who followed the natural law through means of natural light did not require revelation. Here, rationalism and spiritualism (cf. Sebastian Franck, *History*, vol. 3) were extremely close. In fact Spinoza described this form of knowledge in *Ethics* as intuitive (book 2.2, *scholium*, Blumenstock 226/227). Even so, there arose here a contradiction that Spinoza could not resolve: if natural law is identical to the omnipotence of God and if, therefore, all occurrences, including human actions, are predetermined, then what of human freedom, a characteristic that Spinoza considered to be very important?

Spinoza's interpretation of ceremonies (ch. 5) was typically humanistic and echoed the Puritan view (see above). Their occurrence in the Old Testament was merely related to the corporeal well-being of the Hebrews and the temporal welfare of the state. They did not belong to divine law.

Following the destruction of their state, the Hebrews (Jews) were no long required to observe the ceremonies (166/167). It was only consistent (if also rather bold) for Spinoza to classify under ceremonies the Christian sacraments (baptism and the Eucharist), for they do not "contribute to blessedness or hold within themselves any kind of holiness (176/177). As a divine command, they possess only a pedagogical purpose. In addition, the biblical stories (*historiae*) that the Bible reports are for the apprehension of common people (*vulgus*) and serve the purpose of narratives of example in which it is shown that there is a God who has created everything and cares for humanity: "it is understood that people are to live piously and righteously, while God afflicts the others with many punishments" (180/181). Faith in these stories, however, does not belong to the divine law, nor does it lead to blessing.

Spinoza's position on miracles (ch. 6) is what one would expect, given what has already been said. The description of certain events as miracles (as, for example, the sun standing still in Josh 10) is either expressed in poetic language or to be explained from the erroneous views and assumptions of the witnesses of the events at the time. It is fundamentally true "that all actual events, which Scripture reports, actually occur of necessity according to the laws of nature" (214/215). Therefore supernatural events cannot be. Spinoza notes expressly that he has followed a method different from that used in the assessment of prophecy: "I have maintained nothing as regards prophecy, which I could not have concluded from the fundamentals revealed in Holy Scripture. Here, by contrast, I have derived what is essential simply out of the principles, which are known to us through natural light" (222/223). At the beginning of this chapter, he repeats once more his philosophical definition of God, according to which God follows all laws of nature out of the necessity of his existence and the perfection of his nature (192/193). Of course, he maintains that biblical texts have defended his interpretation: above all, statements from Qoheleth (1:10–12; 3:11, 14; also Ps 148:6; Jer 31: 35–36) were mentioned (222/225). Therefore, miracles were excluded. The theme of miracle was touched on incidentally also in his exchange of letters (Letters 51–56) with Hugo Boxel. His correspondence with this high ranking politician, who was the secretary of the city of Gorkum, involved Gorkum's beliefs about ghosts. Spinoza strictly rejected this belief.

But what is the core of revelation? Spinoza handles this for the first time in chapter 13. Before taking this on, however, he composes a detailed middle section in which he enters into biblical, exegetical questions. Although the content of most of these chapters has been taken into consideration in the history of interpretation, Spinoza's position in these chapters is the least original. Furthermore, it has often been noted that his composition at this juncture possesses only a loose association with the other parts of the strikingly uneven tractate. Most of the judgments concerning religion and revelation have already been explained when he turns to the individual questions of exegesis.

Chapter 7, with its fundamental methodological points of view on biblical exegesis, precedes this section. The fundamental issue stands at the beginning: Spinoza determined "that the method of the explanation of Scripture does not differ in any way from the methods of the explanation of nature" (230/231). The term "history" can be used both for the critical examination of nature and for the exegesis of the Bible. Primarily, it is important to work out "a true history of Scripture in order to derive from this the certain dates and principles to acquire correctly the meaning of the authors of the Scriptures" (230–33). This was here formulated in a clear fashion for the first time, although it had already been observed by Grotius (see *History*, vol. 3), Hobbes (see above), and even the Jewish exegetes of the Middle Ages, to whom Spinoza harked back. To be sure, the modern concept of "history" did not reside at the basis of this view. Lacking, above all, was the idea of development, which would appear only in the eighteenth century. The meaning of the term "history," for Spinoza, corresponded to the fundamental basis of the Greek *historein*, the critical examination of facts. For him there was a close analogy between the sphere of nature and the past events as facts to be transmitted. More precisely, history has to do with obtaining the true definition of the phenomena that were common in nature. By analogy, this was true also for the criticism of Scripture. Important, in addition, was the distinction between "meaning" and "truth": "for we are concerned merely for the meaning of the speech, but not about its truth" (236/237). By "meaning" is understood solely the statements set down by the authors in the texts, originally having nothing to do with the speech (*oratio*) and its significance, while the (absolute) truth alone is to be transmitted through philosophical speculation (see under the rules of interpretation in ch. 7, 233/235–236/237). Therefore, one may not question the Bible in regard to truth. Meaning depends on the authors. This concentration on the authors of the biblical writings, as we have already seen, was found not only in Spinoza but also often in later biblical interpretation. It became a strong component of Idealism and Romanticism in the nineteenth century, although it has given way in the more recent period to other considerations.

In his disputations with contemporary theologians, in Holland especially the Reformed orthodox theologians, whose critical discord he addressed in the beginning of the chapter, Spinoza formulated the demand "that one should ascribe nothing as being taught in Scripture, which cannot be produced with full clarity from its history" (234/235). The analogy between the criticism of the "history of nature" and the history of Scripture is important, a point with which one must begin, in order to transmit "what is received as the most common, basic, foundation of the entire Scripture … and ultimately what in it is determined to be eternal and thus the highest salvific teaching for all mortal people (240/241). The contents that remain are not only made relative by this, but also lose their normative significance. Spinoza formulates additional rules for carrying out this view:

1. One must enter into the languages in which the biblical books are written, meaning then that the history of the Hebrew language is required, since, according to Spinoza, the New Testament books have characteristics of the Hebrew language. In the modern period, this thesis has been confirmed by the development of the so-called Koine Greek, the language in the New Testament that is partly influenced by Hebrew and Aramaic features. In the following context, Spinoza then returns to the difficulties that originated from an incomplete knowledge of Old Hebrew (250/251ff.), which did not allow a complete history of this language to be composed. He also raises the point (against the orthodox faith in the divine character of the Masoretic pointing; see above) of the later origin of this form of the language and therefore its lack of trustworthiness (254/255).

2. The statements (*sententiae*) of each book must be arranged in orderly fashion according to the main points of view in order to detect the sense of the more obfuscate passages of the particular usage of speech. Interpretation through the comparison of biblical statements is an ancient rabbinic method. With the emphasis on the particular usage of speech, Spinoza turns against the theses of his friend Lodewijk Meyer, who wanted to elevate reason as the standard for the transmission of the meaning of every biblical statement.

3. Spinoza requires a history of Scripture in the sense that first one handles "the life, customs, and interests of the writer of each book, who he was, what was the occasion from which he spoke, when he lived, for whom he wrote, and finally in which language he composed." In addition, Spinoza requires a history of the canon: "the occurrence of every single book, namely, how it was first obtained and into whose hands it had come. Further, it is necessary to determine how many readers of it there

were, who made the decision that it be taken into the canon, and finally, in which way all of the books, which we today call holy, have been incorporated into a whole" (238/239).

At the conclusion of this chapter, Spinoza defends against the traditionalists, who maintained that they possessed a sure and certain knowledge of the meaning of Scripture through means of tradition. It is striking that Spinoza speaks so often of the "Pharisees," obviously a code word for his earlier Jewish co-religionists. When he polemicizes against the affirmation that they possess an unassailable tradition for the interpretation of Scripture and against the corresponding claim of papal inerrancy in securing the true understanding of the Bible (246/247), he also has the Protestants tacitly in view, although it would have been inappropriate to make this known. It is both obvious and painful for contemporary Jewish interpreters that he distanced himself and his origins from rabbinic Judaism.

In spite of this comprehensive program, in the wider course of the chapter Spinoza is skeptical about whether it would be possible for this approach to be realized. Besides the difficulties of the Hebrew and the many ambiguities of its expressions, he mentions the obscure content of numerous biblical books and the fact that many New Testament writings (e.g., Matthew and Hebrews) exist only in translation. Yet he also holds that the obscurities of many fields are secondary to the fact that "we can achieve certainty in acquiring the meaning of Scripture in relationship to matters, which are necessary to lead to salvation and blessedness" (262/263). The key expressions, "ethical texts," "piety," and "rest for the soul," signify what Spinoza thinks about these passages.

In the subsequent passages (266/267–272/273), he engages in a dispute with Maimonides, who had maintained that each passage of Scripture allowed different sorts of meanings, and if they did not conform to reason, they must be explained allegorically. Maimonides facilitated allegorical interpretation at a time when Jewish scholars continued to discover standard Aristotelian-Averroistic philosophy in Scripture. In contrast to this, Spinoza sets forth his thesis that the meaning of Scripture results from itself and can be determined from the context. This view calls to mind less the Reformation's thesis that Scripture interprets itself (scriptura sui ipsius interpres) than the ancient exegetical practice existing in Judaism: harmony proceeded from the entirety of scriptural statements (see History, vol. 1). In chapter 15, Spinoza argued against Jehuda Alfachar, the medieval Jewish theologian who maintained that only those scriptural passages may be metaphorically interpreted that are themselves contradicted by clear statements in the Bible. This would mean favoring reason in interpreting the Bible!

Concerning the prehistory of the criticism of Mosaic authorship of the Pentateuch, Spinoza collects in chapters 8 and 9 everything that had been expressed concerning this idea that was accessible to him. He clearly refers to Ibn Ezra's objections against the Mosaic authorship of the Torah and adds his own observations, for example, the judgment that " the author of these books" speaks about Moses in the third person and testifies to many things about him (286/287). Locations are mentioned with their much later names, for example, the city of Dan in Gen 14:14 (cf. Judg 18:29). More recent sections of history appear, for example, in Gen 36:31, where the kings of Edom are enumerated prior to the conquest of this country by David. Books that were not identical with those of the Pentateuch were ascribed to Moses as the author, for example, the "Book of the Law of God" (Deut 31:9). The role that Spinoza allocates to Ezra is interesting. From the observation that the biblical books of history form a connection coursing through reconstituted transitions, and the recognition that a type of legal core seems to appear in Deuteronomy, he concludes that Ezra wrote down the different sections that had been handed down to him for the purpose of explaining that the tragic fortune of Israel in history was a result of their disregard of the law (301/302). Differing from R. Simon, Spinoza knows of no intermediate instances between Moses and Ezra. Deuteronomy may have been the book of the Torah that Ezra recited according to Neh 8 (302/303). In chapter 10 the investigation is expanded to the prophetic books and Chronicles–Nehemiah. At the end, Spinoza appropriates the thesis first stated by the apocryphal book of 4 Ezra that it was Ezra who had completed the Old Testament canon in its final expression through the recovery of lost books. Admittedly, Spinoza did not provide evidence for this.

The fact that biblical interpretation involves only meaning and not truth allowed Spinoza to deal with the contradictions within Scripture, and he takes this topic up in chapter 9. Here Spinoza demonstrates that the materials not only in the Pentateuch but also in the historical books had been brought together from different origins. An example is the transition from the book of Joshua, where, at the conclusion, the death of Joshua is mentioned (24:29–30), to the book of Judges, where (in 2:6–9) this is reported once again. The same thing occurs in the different narratives in 1 Samuel, which contain two different reports concerning the appearance of David in the court of Saul (1 Sam 17:18ff. and 1 Sam 16; 316–31, 318/319). In the following, Spinoza deals with the well-known question of biblical chronologies and their contradictions, which at the time was fiercely debated by many scholars. The starting point (see Josephus, *Ant.* 8.3.1 §§61–62) was the contradiction in the dating of Solomon's building of the temple in 1 Kgs 6:1 some 480 years after the exodus of Israel out of Egypt and the much greater number of years mentioned in other books. In the New Testament, it was, for example, the discovery that the four Gospels only partially conform to each other. "Who shall believe, however, that God wanted to have narrated the history of Christ four times and desired four humans to impart it in writing?" His point concerning the origin by human hands is decisive: "Each of them [the evangelists] has preached his Gospel in a different place, and each has written it down exactly as he preached it" (406/407). Even so, one does not have to know all of this. With respect to the orthodox teaching of the literal reading (verbal inspiration), all of these questions lose their significance, if only the recognition of different human authors is reflected. The orthodox position therefore can make no obligatory claim. Rather, the point of it all is whether the Bible opens a way to blessedness.

After the preceding critical observations, the conclusion comes rather unexpectedly: the Bible should be understood by reference to the meaning intended by its authors. By this, Spinoza means that, as for the divine law, it comes to us unaltered. Its basic statement is "that there is one God who cares for all things, that He is almighty, and that it goes well with the pious who follow well His counsel, while it goes badly with the godless" (408/409). His continuing statement, "and that our salvation depends only upon his grace [*a sola ejus gratia!*]" cannot weaken this view. Already earlier, he had expressed that there is *one* sphere in which total certainty may be possible: "that we are able easily to infer the sense of Scripture in relation to the moral teaching issued from its history and are in a position to derive the Bible's true meaning" (262/263). This was expressed with the most simple, commonly understood words. Even so, Spinoza did not mention the biblical statements concerning creation. They would have contradicted his concept of the eternity of nature.

According to Spinoza, the aim of speculative philosophy was to acquire the state of blessedness. The common people (*vulgus*), however, who are not capable of speculative achievements, cannot be required to attain a rational knowledge of God (422/423). Nevertheless, Spinoza thought that they were capable of moral behavior. This is expressed in chapters 13 and 14, where he argues in a purely rhetorical manner: "Who could not see that the two Testaments are nothing else than a teaching of obedience? … No one possibly could deny this" (428/429). The acceptance of the Bible as a book of moral instruction also does not stand in opposition to reason: "Therefore, we can accept this foundation of all theology and Scripture by means of rational judgment, even if this foundation may not be mathematically proven. It would be sheer folly not to recognize something as true, which has been affirmed through the witness of many prophets, which brings great solace to those strong in the spirit, and which is useful to the state" (460/461). For Spinoza, it is obvious that revelation taught that faith in God, worship, and obedience are one and the same. Obedience was known by means of the natural, divine law grasped by reason, was produced by the knowledge of unalterable rules of nature, was the reaction to the disclosure of the will of God known only through revelation, and led to love (490/491 n. 34). Corresponding to this, Spinoza defines faith: "Faith means nothing other than to think that of God, by the ignorance of which the obedience toward God is abolished, and what is necessarily given with this obedience" (430/431). It is valid, therefore, to say that "faith of itself does not produce blessing, but rather is only the means to obedience" (432/433). This is precisely the opposite of the outlook of the Reformers. To support his position Spinoza appeals to Jas 2:17 and 1 John 4:7–8; 2:3–4. In terms of content, the commandment to love the neighbor is "the only norm of the whole common faith" (430/431). For Spinoza, the meaning of the whole Scripture leads to one thing: "There is a highest being who values justice and love and whom all have to obey, so that it goes well with them, and whom they must worship through the practice of justice and the love of neighbor" (436/437; cf. 408/409). This statement, which was yet to be developed into seven points of a fundamental confession, reminds one of the deist Herbert von Cherbury (1583–1648), who also appropriated elements of Stoic philosophy. Spinoza also integrates the message of the apostles as well as that of Christ himself in this view. Chapter 11 explains that the apostles were mainly teachers and not prophets. The content of their message was only in their oral sermons, where they confirmed it by signs, received through revelation. "However, what they taught (in their letters) simply and without confirming signs, they have said or written on the basis of their (natural) knowledge" (382/383). In his preamble Spinoza criticizes the teaching of the (Reformed) theologians, who argued that human reason was corrupted and was not in a position to lead to salvation (382/383). Spinoza explains that he had found nothing expressly taught in Scripture "that was not in agreement with or that contradicted reason" (16/17). This was connected to the statement "that the subject of revealed knowledge builds only upon obedience" (18/19). Here he was suddenly no longer engaged in criticism!

By assigning the teaching of morality to the Bible, he pursues at the same time the aim of a strict separation of philosophy and revelation. That was in his own words the "main purpose of the entire work" (428/429). Already in the preamble, he states "that Scripture leaves reason completely unaffected and has nothing in common with philosophy, for Scripture and philosophy are fully different in regard to both their fundamentals and means" (18/19). Thus, the superscription of chapter 15 reads: "It is shown that theology does not serve reason and reason does not serve theology" (444/445). In different places (389–91, 598/599), it becomes clear that, for Spinoza, "superstition" was identical to the mixing of religion and philosophical speculation. Correspondingly, he defines the idea of "theology" in the following way: "I understand here under theology more precisely revelation in so far as it points to the final purpose, as already said, that Scripture has in mind (namely the form and manner of obedience)" (454/455). Nevertheless, Spinoza also builds a bridge: he stresses that the prophets (the recipients of revelation) "did not teach any morality, which did not fully conform to reason" (460/461; as well as the continuation of the above citation, 456/457). The teaching of the apostles "can be accepted by everyone who is guided by the natural light" (384/385). This also means that the moral teaching of the New Testament (of Christ and the apostles) has a universal character, while, by contrast, the law in the Old Testament was connected to Israel. In this place he still implements his main view "that theology has granted to everyone the freedom to philosophize" (466/467). This is possible only if every rivalry between theology and philosophy has been excluded. By contrast, it is wrong to maintain, even as the charge continues to be made, that Spinoza has secularized the Bible completely. This was not the objective of humanists. Like Erasmus, Spinoza was, in his own way, a pious man! Whoever does not allow for this seriously misunderstands his intentions.

The concluding section of the work is of interest to us for its entirely different relation to the Bible. This comes to expression above all in chapters 17 and 18. In the background stands a rather ancient approach to the Bible, which emerged for the first time with Eusebius of Caesarea (ca. 264–340): the typology of a state. This had to do with the exemplary character of the Old Testament orders for the present political order. Customarily, the view of rule found in contemporary monarchies (see Eusebius's view of Emperor Constantine) was compared with that of Old Testament kingship, particularly idealized in kings like David. In the Reformed Church of the Netherlands, a different model was frequently followed: there, Christ stood in the central position as the son of David; his lordship as king placed him in the succession of the Hebrew monarchy. From this understanding also was derived the divine right of earthly rulers, such as those of the House of Orange over the Netherlands. It was almost essential for Spinoza, when he opposed this, to develop his own opinion concerning this relationship of contemporary and Old Testament monarchies. As an adherent of the Regent Party, he saw the republican order as the ideal that reached back to the early time of Israel and now served as exemplary for the present period. Decisive for him was the fact that in this theocracy (in which God was the only king), a balanced distribution of power reigned. After the exodus from Egypt, the Hebrews were not bound together in any kind of constitutional law and shifted again into a, so to say, natural position, being free to set forth a preference for the type of rulership they preferred. On the basis of the counsel of Moses, they assigned lordship to God and not humans. Therefore, civil justice and religion were one and the same in their state. In reality "the Hebrews had initially reserved for themselves the right of government without limitation" (512/513). However, since they were excessively afraid of God's voice, Moses was named to be the only one who made requests of God, the only interpreter of the divine laws, and the only judge. He was, so to say, the representative of the most exalted majesty (God). Accordingly, Moses had possessed near-monarchic power, but he did not name a successor who would have the same degree of power. Joshua was his successor, but only as the commander of the army during the period of the conquest. However, Eleazar, the successor of Aaron, had been given the place to serve as Joshua's priest. Now only the priests were the interpreters of the law of God. In addition, the priest alone was the one who could transmit divine answers, when he was questioned. Thus, there already was a division of power: "For the right to interpret the law and to impart the answers of God resided in one, while the right and the power to lead the government according to the interpreted laws and the transmitted answers in the other" (516/517). Later (what is meant is the period of the judges) there was not at one time a supreme commander over all, but rather only individual leaders of tribes. Spinoza envisioned expressly, then, the advantage of this state in which all were of equal standing and were guided by the same love of the homeland (which was at the same time piety, since theocracy reigned). The army was formed from citizens (thus they were those who must have wished more for peace than war), and all citizens owned similar possessions, which, if taken, were to be returned during the year of Jubilee. They all belonged to the same circle of obedience, which governed their lives. Subsequently, Spinoza names the causes that led to the downfall of this form of the state. One important reason was the privileged status of the Levites, under whom not a few "pseudo-theologians" (*theologastri*) must have existed (ibid.), and in addition who without engaging in any of their own work must have been supported by others. This developed into a continuing dissatisfaction on behalf of the people. It became easy for one to recognize in them the contemporary clerics! In any case, Scripture gave witness to the continuing uproar of the people, who finally voiced their desire to choose an earthly king (see 1 Sam 8). This led to the failure of the theocracy.

In the following chapter (18), Spinoza came directly to the judgment that "an imitation of the same is neither possible nor advisable" (555/556). A biblical reason for this is that (according to 2 Cor 3:3) the covenant with God no longer can be written with ink and on stone tablets. In addition, such a political order was suitable only for a secluded land and not for the Netherlands, which was open to the world. Spinoza wished, however, still to draw some lessons from the history of the people of Israel, which the present country of the Netherlands may use. Above all was the lesson that it was disastrous to elect a king if a land has never had one before. So long as Israel had no king, Spinoza argued, Israel enjoyed a lengthy period of peace. War began only with the kings. It was also calamitous for the late period, when the priests had the capacity to take for themselves political power, for then came the sects and continuing religious dissension. In addition, "[h]eretics and the godless were first encountered among the High Priests of the Hebrews, who had acquired by crooked means the high priestly office" (274/275). For the downfall of the priests in the late period, Spinoza refers to the prophet Malachi (2:1–9; 558/559). The states of Holland have never had kings; therefore, they should not install a monarchy. Conversely (see the execution of Charles I in England and its consequences), it would also be disastrous to get rid of a king, if one possesses one, even if he were a tyrant. The conclusions from his criticism of priestly rule Spinoza leaves to his readers—they will perceive the actual references! On the whole, it ensued "that each state must continue by necessity its own form of government and that it is impossible to change it without the danger of a complete collapse" (570/571). The early period of Christianity is further evidence against a monarchy: "The Christian religion was not taught initially by kings, but rather by private individuals, who preached against the will of those who had the power of government. The Gospel was preached for a long time in private churches" (592–95).

In conclusion, it must be noted that Spinoza, like Hobbes, targeted another form of government, democracy, for the rule of *jus circa sacra* (the right for the rule to determine external forms of the exercise of religion) in chapter 19, while the "inner worship" and mainly piety remained a matter of private conscience. Since the external forms of religious practice exist legitimately only in the sphere of ethical activity, the absurd conclusion could be maintained "that justice and love could maintain their legal power only through the authorization of the government" (574/575). Applicable here is the reason for the existence of the state: "If that is so, then the well-being of the people must be the highest law.... Since now it is incumbent only upon the highest power to determine in which way the individual may practice piety toward his neighbor, this determines the way one should be obedient to God" (582/583). Thus, a special kingdom of God on earth is thereby excluded (574/575).

If one places Spinoza in his time, much of what appears to be unusual for the period is lost. Instead, the influences on his thought emerge much more clearly. One is not to ignore the fact that he worked in Holland, where the inheritance of Erasmus was strong both before and after him. This is evident even when he believed he was entirely able to have examined the Bible "with an impartial and free spirit" and to have taken what he "with full clearness could draw from it" (preamble, 16/17). Only that to which he failed to give consideration demonstrated his one-sidedness.

Confessionally, he was a maverick. He did not belong to rabbinic Judaism, which made him an outcast, nor could he feel at home in orthodox Reformed Christianity. He did not continue with binding relationships to free church circles like the Quakers and Kollegiants. In spite of this, Spinoza was not an atheist, as his opponents maintained. His image of God, however, continued to be a divided one: he could not reconcile the metaphysical God of the classical tradition and the biblical God who required moral obedience through the prophets, Christ, and the apostles. Thus, he raised the separation between philosophy and theology to a premise.

4.3. Defending Christian Truth with Biblical Prophecy: Pierre-Daniel Huet (Huetius)

Pierre-Daniel Huet was born on 8 February 1630, the son of a wealthy, patrician family in Caën (Normandy). At the age of three, he lost his elderly father, who had long ago been converted from Calvinism to Catholicism. His father was an advisor to the king and an administrator of the community of St. John's in Caën, where Huet was baptized. When Huet was six years old, his mother died. The care of him and his three sisters was undertaken by his uncle, a professor of astronomy, and, after his death, by his aunt. At the age of eight years, Huet was admitted to the Jesuit college, where he made quick progress, studying under outstanding teachers. He learned Latin and Greek in addition to the normal course of studies and passed through the curriculum with exceptional performance. In the study of philosophy (the standard for the Jesuits was still Aristotle), for which he obtained his degree, he developed a strong interest in geometry, which had become an important philosophical model at the time. The strict method for this type of mathematics appeared to him to be the pattern also for philosophy, which, according to the example of Plato, operated mostly in the form of dialogues. In addition to (Ptolemaic) astronomy, theoretical mathematics was also taught. This intelligent schoolboy ambitiously assimilated the entirety of an exceedingly conservative range of courses. The program of a public defense in 1646 by the scarcely sixteen-year-old graduate, who responded to questions in the areas of mathematics, astronomy, and philosophy, is still preserved. After the conclusion of his education, he began a course of study in both civil and canon law at the University of Caën, which was enhanced through many and various types of private lectures. Descartes' *Principia philosophiae* (1644) shaped him into a Cartesian at the age of eighteen. He devoured the work of the Reformed pastor and scholar Samuel Bochart (1599–1667), who taught in Caën and whose work appeared in 1646: *Phaleg et Canaan seu Geographia sacra* (Geography of the Holy Land). Bochart taught the youth Hebrew, while the Jesuit Parvilliers instructed him in Syriac and Arabic. He became accomplished in Greek by means of lectures on Homer and listened to the teachings of the geographer Antoine Halley. These studies reflected the academic pursuits of the perfect humanist. A friendship with Bochart developed, who marveled at his young protégé's intellectual abilities. Sacred geography offered stimulating problems: Where was the location of the earthly paradise? Where may one find Mount Ararat on which Noah's boat came to rest? Reports coming from travelers to the Orient were popular and increased the knowledge of this subject.

In 1650, when he had come of age, the young Huet undertook several journeys to Paris and acquired for himself a comprehensive library from his own resources. In Paris he came into contact with numerous famous personalities of the capital city by association with the "Academy" (a type of intellectual club) of the brothers Du Puy, royal bibliographers.

Huet was invited by Bochart in 1652 to accompany him on a trip to Sweden to visit Queen Christine (1620–1689) who ruled from 1644 to 1654. He describes this journey in his memoirs. He traveled from place to place, met scholars and paid his respects to princes, visited libraries, and made copies of the manuscripts housed there, including those by two *erudits* (scholars) of the late Renaissance, one famous and the other younger but already known. Huet was received in a friendly manner and could carry on conversations about scholarly questions with the queen, who was a lover of the sciences, in French, Latin, Greek, and Hebrew. On the return journey, he stopped in Amsterdam, where he visited, among others, the famous rabbi, Manasseh ben Israel. This encounter with a "Jew who was an astute and sensitive man" (*Demonstratio*, 2) became, as Huet would report later, an impetus for his investigations of the Bible, which he developed many years thereafter in the *Demonstratio evangelica*.

In December 1652, following his return, Huet was soon accepted into the newly founded Academy, in which the intellectual elite of the city of Caën, both scholars and artists, met weekly in the hotel Grand-Cheval. A well-to-do young gentleman without occupation and who enjoyed a great deal of leisure, Huet composed poetry after the example of the pastoral idylls of Theocritus (ca. 300 B.C.E.). His Latin *Carmina* (Songs), first published in 1664, went through several editions. While suffering from an eye problem, Huet wrote a Latin poem, *Epiphora*, about the possibilities of treatment by reaching back to the ancient recommendations of Hippocrates and Galen. As a typical humanist, he lived with his thoughts roaming about in antiquity. In addition, he was interested in astronomy and geometry, about which he corresponded with specialists. During frequent excursions to Paris he was introduced to the literary salons of noblewomen, such as Mademoiselle Madeleine de Scudery and Countess de La Fayette. He dedicated amorous verses to the Marquise de Montespan, the longtime mistress of Louis XIV. He chatted and wrote "Portraits," literary descriptions of the personalities whom he met. There exists a "Portrait" from the pen of "Madame de Caën," the abbess of the city's cloister of women; another is by "Princess Marie-Eléonore de Rohan" about Huet, and another composed by Huet in return about her. On the basis of his experiences with the text of Origen, Huet wrote a treatise *De interpretatione* (1661) about the art of translation. He is critical of a far too free rendition of the texts that were used, especially the Bible. From his encounter with the literary dames and gentlemen of society, Huet produced the work that gained for him significant notoriety in the history of literary scholarship, which continues to this day. This is his unique history of the novel, *Lettre-traité sur l'origine des romans* (Treatment of the Origins of the Novels), which appeared in 1670. In 1662, he founded in Caën his own *Academie de Physique* in which physics, mathematics, and other sciences such as biology and astronomy were to be discussed and practiced. After his departure to the French court in 1670, this academy quickly ceased to exist owing to weak leadership.

To this point, Huet had not yet obtained a job. After his father had converted from the Reformed confession to Catholicism, Huet always considered himself a true Catholic. His earlier inclination to assume a churchly office had not been realized, although he had received the tonsure as a first step through the efforts of the archbishop of Rouen. For a long period of time, Huet was positioned for a possible career as a jurist. He had turned down the offer to serve as advisor in the parliament of Rouen, because his occupation as a literary specialist stood in the way. His life took a turn in 1670 when he was named an assistant instructor of the dauphin (Crown Prince Louis [1663–1711]), who was at the time seven years old. This led to his becoming famous for the publication of a collection of classic texts that had been cleansed of scandalous passages: *ad usum delphini,* "for the use of the dauphin." This activity as assistant tutor ended when the crown prince married in 1680. In 1674, Huet was accepted into the Academie Française. As its senior president in 1720, when he was ninety, he greeted Czar Peter the Great during the latter's visit to Paris. Previously, in 1671, Huet had received his minor orders for the priesthood, and some years later was ordained a priest. For the reward of his activity at court, he received a benefice in 1678 that had recently become open in the Abby of Aulnay-sur-Odon, where he stayed in the summer. At the end of his occupation as an assistant tutor in 1680, he moved there. In 1685, the king recommended him to become the new bishop of Soissons. After a lengthy period of exchanges because of the long-enduring conflict between Louis XIV and the curia, in 1692 Huet took instead the Diocese of Avranches (after the resolution of the dispute). He performed his administrative duties throughout this time with zeal, as can be seen from the many synodal statutes that emerged, and he sought to reconstitute the discipline that had become lax in his diocese. He gave up his office in 1699 for reasons of health, but more probably because the life of the scholar appealed to him more. For his provisions, he was entrusted with the Abby of Fontenay, near Caën, and then in addition with the one at Aulnay. In the year 1701, he moved to join the Jesuits in Paris and lived with them some twenty years, finally becoming deaf and blind. After relocating to Paris, he wrote his comprehensive memoirs in Latin (*Commentarius de rebus ad eum pertinentibus* [1718]). He died, having almost reached the age of ninety-one, on 26 January 1721, in Paris. His last work, the *Huetiana,* a collection of fragmentary pieces, he handed over to his friend the abbot d'Olivet for publication. This work appeared in 1722.

Huet was one of the last true Renaissance scholars. He was comparable in knowledge and intelligence to Leibniz. However, while the latter was considered to be one of the most significant philosophers of his period, Huet was generally regarded as a second-order philosopher. At any rate, he always participated in writing many works that partook in philosophical discussion. In this regard, he entered into a disputation with the philosophy of René Descartes (1596–1650) and the formulation of his own philosophical approach. This he brought before the public in the *Censura philosophiae Cartesianae* (1689). Among others, Huet opposed Descartes' teaching of "inborn ideas." "It is wrong to argue that something exists in the understanding that was not perceived by empirical means" (*Falsum est, esse aliquid in intellectu, quod non fuerit in senso* [90]). Huet was an empiricist, admittedly only in a certain sense, for in his disputation with Descartes there was already apparent the "skepticism" that was rather widespread in France in the late Renaissance. This came to light especially in his writing *Traité de la faiblesse de l'espirit humain* (Tractate over the Weakness of Human Understanding), written in 1693 and published posthumously in 1723. For Christians, even as for Renaissance philosophers, skepticism certainly could not lead to the negation of all knowledge. To be sure, Huet, while granting the weakness of human reason, still contends that it allows us to rest assured that the impressions, which external objects dwell in us as ideas, for the most part transmit an appropriate picture of the world around us. At the same time, they freely make room for faith, which entirely transmits certainty (*Traité* 1.1.7, 16–21; cf. 3.7, 235–40).

This is a purely philosophical investigation, unlike the *Demonstratio evangelica* (1679), Huet's most important apologetic work. He composed the *Demonstratio* at the end of his time as the assistant tutor to the grown dauphin and dedicated it to him. In this comprehensive and at the same time multilayered writing, the elegance of the language reflects the comprehensive education of its author. The book presents the Bible as the actual subject. Moving out from this, Huet seeks to demonstrate the truth of Christianity. As he briefly explains in the preamble, it is his purpose to produce the ancient Christian arguments from the fulfillment of Old Testament prophecies in Jesus as the Messiah, which were viewed by many as refuted. "The truth of the Christian religion can be shown by way of demonstration, which is not less certain than any geometric argument" (*Demonstratio*, 3, marginal note).

It is all the more astonishing that Huet precedes his investigation by introducing the deductive method of geometry with a number of definitions, postulates, and axioms. Behind this construction is concealed Aristotelian thought. This shows that Huet still came out of Scholasticism. Such definitions are:

> 1. An authentic book is that which is written by the author, and it is said that he has composed it; 2. It is a book that is written in the contemporary period and the events described in it mainly occur at that time; 3. A history [*historia*] is the narration of things which have occurred at the time the book is written; 4. A prophecy is a narrative of future things, which have not yet occurred at the time they are proclaimed; 5. The true religion is that in which only true things are recommended to believe; 6. The Messiah is the God-Man, sent by God for the salvation of humans, and predicted by the prophets in the Old Testament; and 7. The Christian religion is the one, which determines that Jesus of Nazareth is the Messiah, and maintains as true what is written about him in the sacred books, both the Old Testament and the New. (6–8)

With this, the most important features of the program of Huet have been stated. The first five definitions one could designate as methodological principles, and the last two as the summary of the main contents. This is, as Huet also stresses, nothing new, but takes up once again what is known about the Christian faith. The fundamental principles are noteworthy. Huet's lack of philosophical acuity behind these formulations has been mentioned. More precisely, they should be regarded as a sign of his traditionalism. Obviously he believed in the dependability of the historical facts that are reported in the witnesses of Scripture, if these facts originated with identifiable composers (Definition 1) and the reported events are approximately contemporaneous (Definition 2). Huet had already remarked previously (4) that we are also to hold things to be true that we know only from hearsay, for example, that Constantinople is the capital city of Turkey and Augustus was Caesar in Rome. This knowledge is equivalent to the knowledge that derives from experience. Definition 3 is obviously to be seen in association with Definition 4: since a history over the period of its composition reports things that have already occurred, they rest therefore on historical facts. Prophecy alone was a description of the form of future things. That they nevertheless continued not as fiction but rather could be true, if what is predicted comes to pass, is a view that Huet gleaned only from the Bible. Historical narrative and prophecy transmit historical truth. They are distinguished for this reason from pure fiction, for example, that which is stated in novels. Striking is the mixture of rationalism and faith. Faith is, according to Huet, possible only if the historical truth of what was reported beforehand and what had been predicted (prophecy) had been demonstrated. This was an attitude that is found in particular among present fundamentalists.

While the postulates demand that readers approach the reading with authentic zeal and take the things that are demonstrated there to be true in the same manner as the things determined on the basis of reason, the axioms repeat, for the most part, only what was said in different words in the definitions. Only the sentence that states "all prophetic ability stems from God" (Axiom 4 [12]) is new. Evidently he felt that he was obliged to comply with what the structure required, thus leading to this division between definitions and axioms.

The actual content follows in the main section (17ff.). Here Huet formulates the entire ten propositions, which are expounded more precisely in what follows. The first proposition reads: "The books of the New Testament are authentic." It repeats what was said in Definition 1: They are therefore authentic, because "the subsequent period believed that they were written by the authors who are said to have composed them and conform to the time in which they were to have been written" (17). This is underlined by the evidence of the church fathers. Further evidence is related to the extent of the canon. The fact that the apocryphal Gospels and other noncanonical writings were rightly excluded from the canon can be demonstrated by the judgments of the following periods. Textual differences in the New Testament manuscripts, even when they affect the Gospels, are not significant for the central statements of faith. Finally, the agreement of the New Testament citations in the church fathers confirms the canon's integrity. Proposition 2: That the books of the New Testament are contemporary, follows from their authenticity. Proposition 3: "The narratives written in the New Testament are true" (23). This results from the conformity of the New Testament to its witnesses. Among other questions, Huet discusses whether the darkness of the sun and the quaking of the earth, which are to have happened according to Matt 27:45, 51–54 at the time of the death of Jesus, may be identical to the things mentioned by Phlegon, the ancient writer, and he points back to the divergent dating of Johannes Kepler and Gerhard Vossius. The complete discussion of this problem (25–37) shows a clash of conservative thought with modern astronomy. If all of this is true, Jesus must have been a divine man. "In addition to that, he confessed himself explicitly as the Messiah. Therefore, he was the Messiah" (37).

Then follows the demonstration of Proposition 4. "The books of the Old Testament are authentic. They are namely written by the composers who were said to have written them and approximately at the times in which they were to have been written" (38). Here are found above all two arguments: (1) All books that were contained in Ezra's canon were older than he; and (2) all books that are contained in the Septuagint are older than the time of Jesus Christ. In addition Huet considers the superscriptions of all books to be authentic. He concludes that inner-biblical witnesses demonstrate the authenticity of the Books of Moses. In regard to the question whether the entire Pentateuch or only Deuteronomy was found in the temple during the time of King Josiah by the priest Hilkiah (2 Kgs 22:8), Huet places himself on the side of Josephus, who assumed that it was the entire Pentateuch. Huet thus opposes Athanasius and Chrysostom, along with more recent scholars. One of the reasons is that the entire law was placed in the ark of the covenant (see Exod 25:16; Num 10:6). Huet names expressly the Jewish exegetes Abrabanel and Gerson as witnesses to this interpretation. On the other side, the Commentary of the Talmud *Debarim rabbah*, Maimonides, and Ephanias say that only the stone tablets were preserved in the ark, in contrast to the entire Torah. Huet then follows this with a statement about the authenticity of the Books of Moses (42–45). This, he says, is demonstrated by a witness of authorities, consisting of an almost endless chain of names. They begin with Sanchuniathon (second millennium B.C.E.), Homer, Hesiod, and the Samaritan Pentateuch, continue through the philosophers Thales (sixth century B.C.E.), Solon, Pythagoras, Plato, and Aristotle, and end with the translators Aquila, Theodotion, and Symmachus. In chapter 3, Huet, influenced by Vossius and Bochart, presents the view that he did not develop but that he made especially famous: "almost the entire theology of the heathen originated from their imitations of Moses, Mosaic deeds, and Mosaic writings" (56). Heathen deities such as Tammuz and Adonis may actually be the same as Moses, deified heroes who were also lawgivers, as was the Hebrew leader. Phoenicians and Canaanites must have taken notice of Moses, as did the Egyptians during the residence of the Israelites in Egypt. The Persians brought the Mosaic knowledge to India and the Greeks to Rome. The heathen fables appropriated this knowledge. According to chapter 4 (60ff.), Moses was accepted by the Egyptians as one of the gods. "Thoth ... is the same as Moses.... Osiris is the same as Moses" (60). Chapter 5 (72ff.) indicates that "Old Persian religion flowed from the Books of Moses.... Zoroaster is the same as Moses" (72–73). These theses are demonstrated with many learned citations, from which similarities between the fortunes of both emanate, for example, the parallels between their laws (76).

Chapter 6 shows in a similar way how the most ancient Indian religion emerged from the Mosaic religion. Chapter 7 indicates in corresponding ways the same for western peoples: Thracians, Germans, Gauls, Britains, Spaniards, and even Americans. For example, the Mexican god Teutl reflects the Egyptian deity Thoth (83). The barbarity of the Mexican religion (including human sacrifices) may have been appropriated from the Phoenicians, who had traveled there. The prescriptions of purity in many parts of South America (the menstruation of women, touching the dead) stem from the law of Moses. Chapter 8 suggests that even the Greeks have transmitted in their fables Mosaic instructions. Cadmos (legendary founder of Thebes), a contemporary of Moses, expelled by Joshua and the Phoenicians, cultivated the barbaric Greeks. Various Greek gods and goddesses (Apollo, Pan, even Priapus) emulated Moses and his wife Zipporah. Chapter 9 argues that the same thing occurred in terms of Rome and its gods. "Also in the Penates and Lares Moses is hidden" (108). By way of summary, one can say that Moses was disguised in all (discovered) gods, while Zipporah was behind all goddesses, since these women were wives of gods (118).

In retrospect, these chapters may be viewed to be somewhat like the design of a comparative history of religion. Admittedly it operated on the basic presupposition that all nonbiblical deities were fictitious (or divinized heroes). Another presupposition is that Moses and the religion of Israel historically antedate all heathen religions and therefore become their pattern. Both of these affirmations are dogmatic allegations, and in this respect the entire premise is precritical. Nevertheless, Huet was convinced he was right. Already in 1670–1671 the chronology was turned upside down by the Englishmen John Spencer (*Dissertatio de Urim et Thummim* [Cambridge, 1670]) and John Marsham (*Canon chronicus aegyptiacus, hebraicus, graecus* [London, 1671]). According to them, Moses borrowed his cultic law, which he transmitted, from the Egyptians. By contrast, in 1709 Jacobus Fayus defended Huet's chronology against Toland. Another aspect is Huet's enormous knowledge of classical tradition, which lies behind this description. Huet was a humanist in a comprehensive sense, a universal scholar in the old style. Leibniz had admired this about him in a letter that he, having perused the *Demonstratio*, had written to Huet (Letter 203).

Chapter 11 (124–25) points out that "many laws, rites, and stories of the various nations originated from the Books of Moses" (124). Huet names especially Greeks, Athenians, and Romans. The question of how the sacred books of an insular people like the Jews could be employed by the nations (ch. 12) is answered by reference to the exile by the Assyrians, Egyptians, Chaldeans, and so forth. The Phoenicians had disseminated the Books of Moses throughout all the world. Chapter 13 (134ff.) contains thorough discussions of the Hebrew language. Was it spoken by all people prior to the Babylonian confusion of tongues (Gen 11)? This assumption Huet repudiates with comprehensive arguments. A widespread interpretation was that Hebrew was as old as the world, was already spoken by Adam, was transmitted to Abraham through Shem and Eber's family, and eventually made its way to the Israelites. As for the so-called Hebrew alphabet, Huet knew that it would be better to name it Chaldean, which at the time of Ezra was taken over from Babylon (thus Origen, Jerome, and "the clever group among the rabbis"). The old Hebrew alphabet was Samaritan, which was generally widespread before the exile. In making this point, Huet was especially well instructed! He wishes, however, to present his own opinion: the Hebrew language is Canaanite, one of those that resulted from the Babylonian confusion of tongues. Abraham, whose mother tongue was Chaldean, learned the language of Canaan when he migrated there.

In chapter 14, Huet turns to oppose the arguments against the authenticity of the Books of Moses. His main opponent was Spinoza (*Tractatus theologico-politicus*), whom he did not name. In addition, he also considered Ibn Ezra, de la Peyrère (also anonymous), and Hobbes. There follows a detailed discussion of the passages already mentioned, which, according to Spinoza, spoke against the Mosaic authorship of the Books of Moses. Huet deals with all of these. He agrees that there are some anachronistic passages that are later explanations, probably made by Ezra. Similarly, the report of Moses' death would have derived from Joshua. However, he often regards Moses as possessing the gift of prophecy (as in Exod 16:35–36), a view that supported his presumption of Mosaic authorship. Finally, if in a few small details a textual corruption might have occurred, these do not affect in any way passages that are related to teachings of faith. In individual details, Huet is rather broad-minded. He does not see any of these problematic cases as endangering the authenticity of the Books of Moses.

In connection with the Books of Moses, he investigates the remaining books (in the breadth of the Vulgate canon) and confirms the authenticity of all of them. This section concludes with a look at the Hebrew canon, which was put together by Ezra (4 Ezra 14, among others) and may have been approved by the "Great Synagogue" (Gemara, Tractate Megillah).

In what follows, Huet turns to his main objective: prophecy. The authenticity of the prophetic books he had already demonstrated. Proposition 6: "Many prophecies of the Old Testament are true ones," is confirmed by fulfilled prophecies. Examples are Gen 9:24ff.; Lev 26:33, 44; and others. The main point Huet reaches, however, is Proposition 7: "There are many prophecies about the Messiah in the Old Testament." The demonstration of this point begins with this sentence: "The Old Testament is the design [forma] and the preparation [apparatus] of the New Testament" (271). There follows the consideration that there were two kinds of predictions, those given with signs and those with words. The New Testament statements in Rom 16:25–26; 1 Cor 2:7; and 1 Pet 1:20 are important, for they speak of an eternal predetermination of Christ. The passages that relate definitely to the Messiah, although lacking chronological denotation, are Gen 49:10; Dan 9:25; Zech 11:12–13; 9:9; and Pss 68 (69):22 and 22:18–19. Ancient church theologians such as Augustine, Eusebius, Lactantius, and Irenaeus assert that faith begins with the prophecies concerning Christ. The Jews, who expected a different Messiah, deny that these prophecies refer to Jesus. Whoever believes in Christ and yet denies that Jesus was predicted by the prophets, as did Theodore of Mopsuestia (see *History*, vol. 2), is a "disreputable heretic" (277). Subsequently, Huet undertakes a journey through the entire Old Testament during which he treats all the passages that were understood to be messianic prophecies, beginning with Gen 3:15. This section reaches as far as Proposition 8: "The Messiah is the one to whom all the prophecies of the Old Testament conform" (328). Proposition 9 follows in the steps of this one: "Jesus of Nazareth is the Messiah" (330). To demonstrate this point, Huet seeks to undertake a more precise comparison of Old Testament prophecies with what was reported in the New Testament, according to the motto of Augustine: "The Old Testament is the concealment of the New, and the New Testament is the revelation of the Old." Proceeding from additional remarks, Huet desired to consider not only words but also signs that the types have included (for typology, see *History*, vol. 1).

The following part is the result of a rather extraordinarily indefatigable effort. Through almost three hundred pages (330–619) in 169 chapters, Huet displays parallels in a broad sense between the Old Testament and the New. These are arranged across from each other in left- and righthand columns. For example, the passages of the genealogy of Jesus in Matt 1 and Luke 3 refer back to Abraham, Isaac, and Jacob (Gen 22:13). Chapters 1–3 mention the corresponding Old Testament passages on the left and the passages from Matt 1 and Luke 3 on the right (330–31). Chapter 170 contains the types beginning with Adam and followed by Abel, Noah, Melchizedek, Isaac, the ram sacrificed by Abraham (Gen 22:13), Joseph, the paschal lamb, and so forth. In connection with the discussion of Deut 18:15, which Huet interprets as Moses' prediction of Jesus (625), he also addresses the basis for the selection of the title of his book: Eusebius demonstrated in a carefully made comparison (*Demonstratio evangelica*) that Peter and Stephen had confirmed the proof of this prophecy (Acts 3:22; 7:37). "I wish to follow the most significant traces of this investigation." In this place, it became clear that the most important purpose of Huet was not to discover something that was new but rather to rediscover the old. He was a conservative thinker in a twofold sense: he was a humanist and a churchly traditionalist who sought to preserve both the truths of antiquity and the ancient church.

In chapter 171 (630ff.), in which Huet collects the essential marks of a prophet, it is important for him to affirm that the prophecies had offered not only a shadow (adumbration) of the future Messiah but also an exact description:

> a sprout of primal origin, the time of his birth, homeland, names, customs, values, studies, activities, deeds, the general results of life, death, even the form of his death, burial, what follows death, the miraculous return to life, and why Jesus took upon himself life and death. Finally, there are all the characteristics by which Jesus could be distinguished and understood as exceptional. (634)

This result comes when one classifies both prophecy and other types. There are prophecies that refer directly to Christ (e.g., Dan 9), while others have a twofold meaning: they possess both a literal sense and an allegorical meaning. The literal meaning can point in direction other than Christ, but the allegorical meaning can speak of him. An example is Ps 21 (22):19: the dividing of the clothes means literally Christ, but indirectly refers to David. By contrast, 2 Sam 7:12 contains a meaning that points directly to Solomon but also indirectly to Christ. In addition, Christ was prefigured by a type, as in the case of the rise of Solomon. These statements concerning Proposition 9 end with the conclusion that Jesus was in fact the Messiah. *Quod erat probandum* ("Something that was to be demonstrated!" [630]).

Huet finally comes to his main purpose, which is apologetics. Proposition 10 reads: "The Christian religion is true." The reason given the following:

> [W]e have defined the Christian religion as the one that has determined

... that Jesus of Nazareth is the Messiah, and what has always been written about him in the sacred books, whether the Old or the New Testament, holds true. Therefore the faith of the Christian religion alone is occupied with true matters.... Thus, it corresponds ... to our definition ... that the true religion is the one that suggests to believe only things that are true. From this is the result that the true religion is the Christian one. That was to be demonstrated."(640)

A final conclusion reads: "All religions, outside of Christianity, are false and godless" (ibid.).

If one considers the fact that this work was written a little later than Spinoza's *Tractate* in order to oppose it, one is astonished at the intellectual distance between the two. Spinoza, who is not free from a humanistic heritage, nevertheless has a distinctly different understanding from that of Huet. The difference, however, resides on different planes. Spinoza as a philosopher believes in the possibility of a rational knowledge of God and is distinct from Huet in pointing to the understanding that the Bible is a book of morality. Huet as a philosopher follows the ancient skepticism in his fundamental mistrust of rational knowledge. He understands the Bible precisely according to traditional church dogmatics, focusing on the teaching of Jesus as the Messiah. However, he uses the rational method of deduction from prescriptively formulated sentences (definitions), because they confirmed his view concerning the Bible. His view is that the Bible depicts the basis for a truth that was historically grounded. Moreover, if the Bible is understood as prophecy and the fulfillment of prophecy, it bears what may be demonstrated to be both a supernatural and a rational character. Like a typical Catholic theologian, Huet characterizes the way to proceed by referring back to primitive Christianity and the ancient church (where the church fathers also have a say in addition to the New Testament). Therefore, although both Spinoza and Huet are characteristic thinkers of the seventeenth century, of the two, Spinoza only seems to stand closer to us in the present.

Huet also has written a "Tractate on the Location of the Earthly Paradise" (*Traité de la situation du paradis terrestre* [1691]), demonstrating thereby that he was a type of Renaissance scholar with a biblical foundation. In this tractate he sought to bring the biblical narrative into conformity with geographical facts. He located paradise close to the confluence of the Euphrates and Tigris rivers. The work became very popular and underwent numerous editions.

5

The Bible in Pietism and the German Enlightenment

5.1. Bringing the Word of God More Amply among Us: Philipp Jakob Spener

Philipp Jakob Spener was born in 1635 in Rappoltsweiler in Alsace, the residence of the baronets of Rappoltstein. His father, Johann Philipp Spener, was councillor of the baronet of Rappoltstein, and his mother, Agatha Saltzmann, was the daughter of Johann Jakob Saltzmann, a councillor of Rappoltstein and reeve of Rappoltsweiler who later became the city syndic of Colmar. Thus, he came from a well-known patrician family in Strassburg with close relationships to the knightly family. Instructed by a private tutor, the young Philipp soon attracted attention because of his outstanding memory. While at the court of Rappoltstein, Spener was at the same time an orthodox Lutheran who possessed a Puritan piety. His piety was cultivated by Johann Arndt. In addition, Spener read two books of meditation from English authors in German translation that were widespread in Lutheranism: Lewis Bayly's (1565–1631) *Praxis pietatis* (The Practice of Piety), a pseudonymous work, *Güldenes Kleinod* (The Golden Jewel), and *A Book of Christian Exercise*, ascribed to G. Parson [1585], translated into German in 1612), which underwent several editions. This type of influence Spener experienced from his early youth. Also important for him was the example of the learned court preacher Joachim Stoll (1615–1678), especially his sermons. Through his private study, he deepened his knowledge of philosophy. By 1648, he had already matriculated in the University of Strassburg; however, he did not begin his course of study there until 1651. Strassburg was famous because of its (humanistic) scholarship in the discipline of history, but also because of the Lutheran theologian Johann Schmidt (1594–1678), who was also president of the church. Schmidt was an orthodox Lutheran and above all outstanding because of his piety, his activities on behalf of the Strassburg church, and his preaching. Also well known were Johann Conrad Dannhauer (1603–1666), who was Johann Gerhard's student, an orthodox Lutheran dogmatician and especially a polemicist, and Johann Georg Dorsche (1597–1659).

Spener remained in Strassburg until 1659. Already by 1653, he had received the master's degree in philosophy (with a dissertation on natural theology). After that he studied (especially German) history. From 1654 to 1656, he was the teacher (informant) of the Counts Palatine, Christian and Johann Carl bei Rhein. In this connection, he worked in the area of genealogy, at that time an important subject of the discipline of history and also gave lectures about this. Later, he added the study of heraldry. Even today he is regarded as one of the most important representatives of genealogy in the seventeenth century. In the field of theology, which he never pursued for a lengthy period, Johann Conrad Dannhauer was the most important of his teachers. Dannhauer's theology continued to be influential on Spener through the remainder of his lifetime, but Dannhauer did not share Spener's pre-pietistic inclinations. Spener learned biblical exegesis from Sebastian Schmidt (1617–1696), who frequently composed scriptural commentaries, which continued to appear in new editions. In contrast to the orthodox exegetical approach focusing on individual ideas and their dogmatic agreement (see Flacius above), Spener particularly pointed to the significance of the use of words in their present context in order to determine their meaning. In 1659, Spener concluded his course of study in Strassburg with a disputation. He moved to Basel in order to study rabbinic and talmudic literature with Johannes Buxtorf the Younger. In the ideal of a biblical theology purified from Scholasticism, which Buxtorf shared in the late phase of life, was what Spener would later represent. In addition, Spener also appropriated from Buxtorf both his perpetuation of the teaching of verbal inspiration and his rejection of the textual criticism of Cappel (see above).

Upon the conclusion of his studies in Basel, Spener undertook the usual educational journey. Although his destination was France, in particular Paris, he traveled only as far as Geneva. While there, he was influenced by the penitential sermons of Jean de Labadie (1610–1674) and learned more about him from one of his enthusiastic disciples, who provided Spener with French instruction. Labadie demanded in his sermons a reform of the church according to the pattern of the early community in Jerusalem, which was regarded as the ideal. Spener distanced himself from the later (1669) formation of a separatist community by Labadie and his followers in Holland, but wrote a volume entitled *La Pratique de l'oraison et meditation chrétienne* (The Christian Practice of Prayer and Meditation), which appeared in 1660. This work proved so captivating that it was published in a German translation. A difficult illness chained Spener to his bed for a period of three months so that he had to abandon his plan to take a trip to Paris. Even so, he met at Lyon with the Jesuit Claude-François Menestrier, an expert in heraldry, who advised him to introduce this profession to Germany. Afterwards Spener presented lectures in Strassburg. In the spring of 1662, Spener undertook a wider journey, this time primarily with the baronial brothers of Rappoltstein to the Württemberg Court in Stuttgart, where he met in particular with the learned Princess Antonia von Württemberg (1613–1679), who was interested in the Kabbalah. Spener himself, by contrast, was more reserved in his view of this Jewish mystical text. Finally, he spent several months in Tübingen, where he presumably read in the areas of heraldry and genealogy. He would have been offered a professorship in these fields by Duke Eberhard III, if he had not been called back to Strassburg, where he was offered after some uncertainty the position of a free preacher. In addition to occasional sermons in the minster and substitute sermons, he had a great deal of time to pursue his scholarly work. However, he did not abandon the work of the pastor. In 1664, he was promoted and married at the same time Susanne Ehrhardt, the daughter of a Strassburg patrician. She bore him eleven children, eight of whom survived. After his promotion, he also could offer lectures.

In 1666, Spener was surprised to receive a call to the position of senior pastor of the Frankfurt clergy. A lengthy, though futile, search by the Magistrate of the free imperial city for a foreign, promoted theologian had been conducted. Spener assumed this influential post in Frankfurt am Main at the age of thirty-one. He remained there until 1686, and these were his most productive years. Numerous letters and opinions from this period show Spener's widespread activity. In addition to these, he published many of his sermons. In connection with his plan, never fully realized, to write a work on Luther's biblical commentaries, he became thoroughly acquainted with the Reformer's thought and became an outstanding Luther expert. Still, he published none of his own writings. His church office, which consisted of serving as the chair of the ministerium of preachers, delivering regularly weekly sermons, providing spiritual guidance, and handling numerous administrative duties, required a great deal of time. He voluntarily preached rather frequently, even during the week.

Spener's activity of preaching led also to his criticism of the lectionary, which prescribed exclusively the ancient church pericopes from the Gospels for weekly Sunday worship. Spener discovered in the Gospel texts little encouragement for growth in piety. The Epistles, which appeared appropriate for such purposes, were never preached. Beginning in 1676, Spener addressed this issue by including in the introduction (*exordium*) of his sermons a progressive treatment of the Pauline letters so that he could read successively through the Letters of Romans and 1 and 2 Corinthians in one year. Here one is able to recognize an important shift from the orthodox practice.

A decisive stage for the origin of pietism is the establishment of the *Collegium pietatis* (perhaps "Meeting for the Advancement of Piety"). The impetus for this foundation came not from Spener but rather from the churchly community. A group of men who were dissatisfied with the trivial contents of daily conversations appeared before him in 1670 with the request to establish a communion that would be devoted to the cultivation of piety. Spener invited them into his parsonage and insisted that he would participate. They met twice a week. An initial prayer followed the reading of some pages from the book of meditation and a discussion. The purpose was to urge one another to practice piety, the love of God, and obedience to his commandments. The originally planned limitation to a circle of friends and those who were like-minded had soon to be abandoned. Everyone was allowed entrance in order to fend off the suspicion of an unlawful and secretive religious meeting that followed the image of Labadie.

At the end of the year 1674, the transition was made from books of meditation to readings of the Bible. From the discussion circle developed the "Bible hour." This practice, also performed by Labadie, appears to go back to the jurist Johann Jakob Schütz (1640–1690), who worked actively in the *Collegia pietatis*. It was probably Schütz who published anonymously in the same year a German translation of a piece of propaganda written by Labadie for such a gathering (*L'exercise prophétique* [The Prophetic Exercise]). Indirectly, therefore, the Reformed separatism of Labadie influenced the Bible movement of Lutheran pietism. In contrast to Schütz, who later founded his own separatist community, Spener thought of affiliating his assemblies with the official Lutheran Church. The simple people participated increasingly in these assemblies and soon replaced more and more theologians and the well educated. Correspondingly, the style became increasingly edifying.

Spener could not oppose the jurist Christian Fende and Eleonore von Merlau (1644–1724; in 1680 married to Johann Wilhelm Petersen

[1649–1727]) in their developing in the Hall Court, a separatist circle around Schütz. In this group, the teachings of a thousand-year reign of Christ (based on Rev 20:1–6), which was oppressed in Lutheranism, and of the restoration of all humanity were taught. In 1682, Spener and his *collegium* met in the Barefeeters Church. In this instance it was virtually only theology students who participated in the discussion. In Frankfurt following this separation, Spener had to confront considerable difficulties. His suggestions pertaining to reform, such as the introduction of confirmation, led to resistance from the city council. When the call came to Spener in 1686 from the Saxon elector George III (1647–1691) to become the high court preacher in Dresden, he was happy to accept it. Yet he never found the right access to the elector. The elector had, toward the end of the Dresden period, often complained that if he had to continue to see Spener and to listen to his preaching, he would have to move his residence to Torgau or Freiberg! However, Spener found an open ear with the noblewomen of the court.

Spender did not reestablish his *Collegia pietatis* in Dresden. Instead, he began to engage both adults and children in catechetical exercises according to Luther's Small Catechism, which soon attracted a great throng of people. As a result of the decision of the Diet in 1688, such exercises were introduced to all of Saxony. During Spener's residence in Dresden, the first debates between the Lutheran orthodoxy and the widely spreading pietistic movement took place in Leipzig with August Hermann Francke (see below). Spener often sought to persuade the elector to enlist associates who shared his pietistic thought to participate in these debates, but his efforts were in vain. In the ensuing expanding conflicts between orthodoxy and pietism in Lutheranism, the question of chiliasm was the main point of contention. Over against the crass chiliasm of Petersen, Spener represented a moderate teaching, which advocated "hope for a better time" (see his writing, "Maintaining Hope for a Better Time" [1692]). With this he clearly differentiated himself from orthodoxy, in which Luther's hope in the "happy last day of judgment" survived without the biblicists' acceptance of an intervening kingdom. In the background stood an image of humanity that was characteristically optimistic, for it at least held to be possible the common working together of human efforts for the "fruit of faith." Still, Spener considered himself to be a true Lutheran. Against a catalogue of the theological faculty in Wittenberg, which accused him of 284 errors, 263 of which were infringements against the Augsburg Confession, he defended himself with a "Sincere Conformity with the Augsburg Confession" (1695). On account of the situation in Dresden, Spener accepted the call of the Brandenburg elector, Friedrich III (who held this position from 1688 to 1713 and in 1701 became King Friedrich I of Prussia), to the position (less honored) of provost in the Nickolai Church in Berlin and counselor of the consistory. He arranged in the early years of the Reform University of Halle for the call of A. H. Francke, at first as a philologist, to the post of professor in 1691. Spener often supplied expelled pietistic preachers to numerous places. He then engaged in the publication of detailed letters and theological opinions. His last treatise was against the Socinians, who were expelled from Poland and denied the Trinity. He was able to complete it in spite of a long and finally deadly illness. He died in February 1705.

Spener's publisher, J. D. Zunner, planned a new edition of the popular tract of Johann Arndt in 1675 and invited Spener to write the preface. In this he succeeded in delivering a short, convincing description of his own reform program. Six months later, Spener added to the special edition (*Pia desideria*, ed. K. Aland) a dedication to his brothers in the office of the clergy. In making allusion to Eph 1:18ff. (2.8–14), he reflects on his hope in the divine call and the wealth of the divine inheritance, thus starting with a Lutheran approach. He indicates that faith is a work of God, from whom are received all the signs that follow. These are diligence and zeal, power and courage, blessing and the continuation of the Word of God, and complete satisfaction in the knowledge that the three first requests of the Lord's Prayer should be fulfilled. These are the consequences of this faith, which is a work of God (2.15–3.12). In the opening address (3.13ff.), there is by contrast a lament over the affliction of the body of Christ, the church. When illness occurs, it is the duty of all the clergy (who are presented in the image of doctors) to give consideration to medicine (3.23–4.2), thereby fulfilling their task in the shepherd's office to pasture the community (7.21–23). Both of these bind together the hope: "What is impossible for humans is possible for God!" (9.1ff.). And all that happens should be for the glory of God (4.36; 9.19; cf. 85.2). The following main section of the *Pia desideria* is divided into three subsections: the first is occupied with the description of the corrupt condition of the church. Pointing out the ideal condition of the ancient church (11.20–24), Spener indicates that the spiritual suffering of the present Evangelical Church (11.15–16) originated because of previous persecutions (referring especially to the Counter-Reformation and its consequences). These are now occurring more through internal shortcomings. In the worldly class (in Lutheran understanding Christian government; 14.10–15), Spener pillories the luxurious (salacious) court life, even more the neglect of the actual duties of the ruling class to care for the well-being of the clergy in favor of pure political convictions, or, by contrast, "Caesaropapism" (the assumption of purely spiritual responsibilities by the secular rulers).

Spener was even more extensively occupied with the corruption of the spiritual class (of the preachers; 15.20–28.3). According to him, the majority is in need of a living faith and is reproached for lacking a "deep inner godliness" (18.25), in addition to an excessive inclination to theological strife. The guilt Spener observes occurs in turning away from the study of the Bible to an addiction to disputation, whereby the "Scholastic theology, which Luther had driven out the front door, was allowed back in through the backdoor by others" (25.21–23). With this he seizes on the return to Aristotelianism in Lutheranism, as we already observed in Flacius and J. Gerhard. Instead of this, the "correct biblical theology should be brought back once again" (25.25–26.1), something that Spener detects especially in Luther (22.15–23.2). What is meant is a theology that is obtained directly from the Bible. For this theology, "the proper simplicity of Christ and his teaching" (27.2) should deliver the standard in contrast to Scholastic theology. For the term "biblical theology" in contrast to "Scholastic theology" Spener cites an expression of Jakob Weller (an orthodox Lutheran high court preacher in Dresden [1602–1664]) as evidence. It is therefore no pietistic new creation! All the same, there is clearly a distance from orthodoxy's use of the Bible. With respect to the third class (the ordinary citizen), Spener laments the common decay of moral behavior, especially drunkenness. Spener clearly underlines the Lutheran foundational statement of justification occurring only through faith without works (32.22ff.), as well as the effects of baptism and the Lord's Supper (33.1–20). However, he repudiates the widespread opinion that the mere participation in worship, confession, and the Lord's Supper is sufficient (35.1–11) when fruits do not consequently follow (35.9–10; cf. also 17.22; 61.14; 79.3, 37). Here Spener takes over the (originally) Reformed theology of covenant: from the side of God the covenant is a covenant of grace, but from the side of the Christians the covenant is a "covenant of faith and a good conscience" (35.23–24).

After this, Spener proves his hope for a future in a "better condition of the Church on earth" (43.31–32), including a return of all Israel (43.35–44.16), by reference to the witnesses of Scripture. In addition, he expresses the expectation of another collapse of Rome and notes the demand for Christian perfection underlined by citations of Paul (47.30–49.5), which are drawn from the ideal of the ancient church (49.6–52.13). Spener now comes to the third section, where he expresses the means by which an improvement of the condition of the church can be effected. Here only the preachers and the laity are addressed.

Decisive at this point is the first suggestion for improvement, which especially has made Spener the founder of pietism. It stands under the famous major premise (blocked out in the original) "that one therefore is intent on bringing the Word of God more richly to us" (53.31–32). Spener continues that the Word is the decisive means to ignite faith from the Gospel, although "the law, however, provides the rules that result in good works, and it is a very admirable impulse to pursue the same. The more richly the Word dwells amongst us the more we believe and the more fruits of faith we achieve" (53.36–54.1). However, good works belong necessarily to Lutheran theology. Their accentuation and the emphasis on "fruits" signify (prepared by reform Lutheranism) a recognizable shifting of weight over against Lutheran tradition.

The following suggestions as to how "to bring the Word more richly among us," Spener draws from his pastoral office. With this he concretizes the concept at the same time. He had nothing against Sunday sermons, although he did not find them satisfying. The community would come to know by means of the prescribed lectionary only a small part of Scripture, while the remainder they would never hear. Spener thinks that only through the epistolary texts does one discover the bases for sermons of meditation. Moreover, when one reads the Bible at home, it is "marvelous and commendable," although it is still not enough (54.23–25). Therefore, Spener recommends additional efforts for the church to undertake, besides simply the sermon, to introduce the people to the Bible. First of all, the father of the household should make the effort to read the Scriptures daily, especially the New Testament, or, if he cannot read, to allow it to be read to him. Second, the biblical books should be publicly read in succession with explanation (if need be by summaries), especially for the illiterate or for people who do not own a Bible. This should remind us that in the seventeenth century the printing of Bibles was still very expensive, and a Bible could not be the property of many people. For the first time, in pietism, the founding of the Bible Institutes made Bibles and parts of their text accessible for everybody. Third, Spener recommended (carefully done, because of the possible misuse threatened by spiritualists) assemblies of communities according to the pattern in 1 Cor 14 (see above). These should not occur without a preacher; however,

> where at certain times differing interpretations issue from the ministry [namely, orders where consisting of several ministers] or when

under the guidance of the preacher, several others from the community, whom God endowed with considerable knowledge or who are zealous to increase their understanding, come together to resolve to do what is taught in the Holy Scriptures. They are to read publicly from it and any passages of the same for the simple-minded, for any and all our edification is to be serviceable, and we are to converse as brothers. They are to state what they doubt and to require its illumination. Thus, those who come together with the preacher are to state their understanding, which they are able to bring. What each one brought forth may be examined according to the meaning of the Holy Spirit in the Scriptures. Others, especially the called teacher (preacher), examine what is offered and thereby the entire community is edified. (55.22–56.7)

As a typical pietistic keyword, "edification" is to be accentuated. While the concept refers in its New Testament usage to the constitution of the church and of the individual within it, it had already experienced in the pre-pietistic period an individualistic transformation in the sense of a psychological act. In pietism it became a prevalent catchword. The program of the pietistic Bible hour practiced in the conventicles (assemblies) was formulated with this understanding of edification. It is remarkable that Spener wished to place these gatherings under the collaboration and oversight of the clergy. In addition, he sought to hold these conversations in churchly settings and to restrict separatist leanings. Aside from this, he sought in a lengthy citation from Luther (57.9–32) to show that this reformer already had wished to have everyone intent on reading the Bible. This look backward not only served to deflect the suspicions of the orthodox Lutheran opponents of pietism, but also corresponded to Spener's fundamental conviction, which was continually emphasized. Characteristic for Lutheran pietism (in contradistinction to the Reformed Church) is also the point that the New Testament, in particular the New Testament Epistles, were to be stressed to the detriment of the Old Testament.

Spener's remaining suggestions for reform are bound closely with the first one. In the second suggestion, concerning the "spiritual priesthood" (58.13–60.29), which for Spener means the Lutheran priesthood of all believers, three times the charge "to study assiduously the Word of God" stands in the center (59.4–5, 24, 35–36). Love (third suggestion, 60.30–62.13) according to Rom 13:9 (61.18) is the content of all of the commandments. For religious conflicts (the fourth suggestion), where likewise loving action is advised (63.23), mere disputations are required instead (see above). Thereby, one does "the will of the Father" by fulfilling the commandments (Spener appeals to John 8:31–32 [66.17–23]), in order to convince the nonbelievers of the validity of the change in behavior brought about by believing in the Gospel. The section on the reform of theological studies (fifth suggestion, 67.17–23) contains, among other things, the encouragement to participate in Bible exercises, which a pious professor should conduct with his students (76.17–78.26). Spener especially recommends a cursory reading of the New Testament in order to determine what in it may be "serviceable for the edification" of the participants. Further, this should allow the reader to express his opinion concerning the meaning of individual verses. This simply transfers the practice of the Bible hour to the academic sphere. Finally, Spener's emphasis on the special preparation of students for their later assumption of the office of preacher (sixth suggestion, 78.27ff.) allows "the Word of the Lord simply but powerfully to be proclaimed" (79.18–19) and contrasts with the Baroque practice of the sermon, which especially accumulates in its introductory section (*Exordium*) all kinds of learned knowledge and demonstrates the rhetorical artistry of the preacher.

This is not possible, however, without an inner reform of the rank of the ministers. Spener undertakes the criticism of most ministers, who lack "the correct illumination, witness, and seal of the faith awakened by the divine word" (17.24–25). Nevertheless, they can learn the correct teaching "from Scripture; however, they can learn only its letters which come from human industry and not from the working of the Holy Spirit" (17.26–28). Thus, they are still distanced from the true faith. Spener strongly stresses the role of the Spirit for the understanding of Scripture and faith. This coheres also with his strong recommendation to read mystical literature, including the *Theologia Deutsch* and the writings of Johannes Tauler (ca. 1300–1361). Once again in this regard he appeals to Luther (74.9–75.20). He disregards the fact that Luther and the other Reformers had soon held their distance from mysticism. Spener offers a definition of Christianity that makes clear the association with Lutheranism as well as underscores the difference. "The whole of our Christianity consists in the inward or new humans, whose souls are faith and whose workings are the fruits of life" (79.35–37). In the following, Spener highlights the view that this inner human being becomes strengthened through the hearing of the word in the Holy Spirit and that "its witness must be demonstrated by the outer life" (80.20). Overall, especially in the "hope of better times," an optimistic image of humanity prevails, which is based admittedly on the biblical promises of God.

5.2. COMBINING PHILOLOGICAL-HISTORICAL AND CONSTRUCTIVE INTERPRETATION OF THE BIBLE: AUGUST HERMANN FRANCKE

August Hermann Francke was the offspring of a family of craftsmen in Lubeck. His grandfather, a master baker, had acquired financial means by his marriage to a rich woman, and he financed his son (the father of Francke) to study law. Francke's mother was the daughter of the city's syndic and later mayor, Gloxin. In the second generation, the parents therefore already belonged to the upscale citizenry. August Hermann was born in 1663. Already by 1666 his father was called to serve as counsel to the court of Duke Ernst the Pious, of Saxony-Gotha (reigned 1640–1675). The duke was a Lutheran prince known for his piety and zeal for reform. In his Thuringen duchy he successfully attended to the alleviation of the difficult economic consequences of the Thirty Years' War, in addition to dealing with forced schooling, church discipline, and other measures for secular and churchly education through liturgy, the printing of Bibles, and hymnals for the development of the church. The youthful Francke therefore was raised in a church-influenced milieu. For his later reforms, he has always referred to the example of the duke. After his father died in 1670 at the age of forty-five, his pious sister Anna, who was five years older than he, became his example. When he was older, she gave him Arndt's *Wahres Christentum* (True Christianity) and Puritan literature of edification. He experienced a first conversion. He was instructed by private tutors until he moved to the Gotha gymnasium. After two years, the gifted youth was ready to enter university. Since he had not yet reached the required age for attendance at the university and also lacked the financial means, he had to engage in private study while waiting for his opportunity. Francke later appraised his school period as a time of temptation. The enticement of reading ancient writers and the ambition to become a great scholar distracted him from pursuing pious goals in life. In 1679, he began his course of study at the nearby University of Erfurt, having received a stipend from his uncle, Dr. A. H. Gloxin, who administered the Schabbel Family foundation. This stipend imposed on him an attachment to the Lutheran Symbolic Books and an austere lifestyle. As usual, Francke began his studies with the faculty of arts. At the advice of his uncle, along with the fact that Erfurt offered him very little, he transferred to Kiel after one semester. Here he lived in the house of Christian Kortholt (1632–1694) and was supervised by him. Kortholt was a church historian and practical theologian who was influenced by Johann Arndt, a scholar bearing the impress of Lutheranism and a friend of Spener. Francke studied philosophy and history, learned English, but insufficient Hebrew, thus incurring the anger of his uncle. Although he participated in churchly life, he did not discover an existential faith. Because Dr. Gloxin was dissatisfied with the course of studies and the attitudes of his nephew, he withdrew Francke's stipend. Thereupon, Francke moved to Hamburg in order to study Hebrew with the Orientalist Esdras Edzard(us) (1629–1708), something he completed in two months. Edzard's method of reading texts that belonged together (first, Gen 1–4) convinced Francke so much that he would later appropriate it for the training of the students of theology in Halle. Owing to his lack of funds, Francke first was forced to return to his mother's house in Gotha to spend two years in private studies. During this time, he claims to have read through the Hebrew Bible six times. His interest in biblical philology had been awakened by Edzard. Still he could not take the step to find a vital faith.

In 1684, the opportunity presented itself for him to take up residence in Leipzig, financed by giving private lessons in Hebrew. Already in January 1685, he received the master's degree from the faculty of philosophy. According to the law of that time, he had the right to offer lectures, presenting besides Orientalist lectures also philosophical-exegetical ones on biblical texts. At the encouragement of Johann Benedict (II) Carpzov (1639–1699), who later became the bitter opponent of pietism, Francke founded the *Collegium Philobiblicum,* together with Paul Anton (1661–1730), later a colleague in Halle, and Hermann von der Hardt (1660–1746). The *Collegium* was an association of eight people who held master's degrees. They met once each week for scholarly exegesis of a chapter from the Old Testament and another from the New. This caused quite a stir; at Leipzig during that time debates concerned only dogmatic and controversy theology. The *Collegium,* however, was not different from other similarly organized groups of Leipzig graduates who held master's degrees. Spener had already once briefly visited it in order to provide the *Collegium* with a more strongly inspired character. When he came to Leipzig in 1687 and visited the *Collegium,* he repeated his admonition, which met with modest results. Nevertheless, this was the beginning of a theological course of study that was more strongly built on exegesis.

In the autumn of 1687, Francke's uncle, Gloxin, granted him for his accomplishments once again the Schabbel stipend—under the condition, however, that he further his education in biblical exegesis in Lüneburg with the superintendent, Caspar Hermann Sandhagen (1639–1697). In Lüneburg the decisive inner experience took place for his further career. Francke was required to preach a sermon on John 20:31: "These are written so that you may come to believe that Jesus is the Christ and that you will obtain life through faith in his name." With respect to this command, Francke recognized that neither the orthodox teaching nor the Bible (was it actually the Word of God and not the Quran or the Talmud?) still offered him a firm footing. However, even the existence of God was questionable for him. His own reputed faith appeared to him a delusion, his life a sin. Sinfulness he could not integrate as did Luther with faith. Only a conversion could help him. He reported that he was suddenly grasped by the certainty, which had been answered in prayer, that he could name God as his Father. His distress was turned into boundless exhilaration. From then on all uncertainty was gone. He wished henceforth especially to act to serve the neighbor, for scholarly fame meant nothing more to him.

In the spring of 1688, Francke had to leave Lüneberg, since Sandhagen had become the general superintendent in Schleswig-Holstein. In Hamburg, where he met several radical pietists, he wished to study the Bible without the scholarly apparatus, depending only upon the will of heaven. Against the protest of his uncle, he taught in the school of for poor children established by the head pastor Johann Winckler (1642–1705), a friend of Spener. Winckler's pedagogical ideas, so it seems, influenced Francke's later educational plans. A two-month visit in Dresden to Spener (January–February 1689) established a lifelong friendship between the two.

Having returned to Leipzig, Francke resumed his exegetical lectures in the philosophical faculty. The (Latin) interpretation of the New Testament letters now held practical consequences for him. Francke always followed his exegesis with instructions for piety. When Francke transferred his instruction to a baker's room, a German colloquium ensued and citizens of the city joined, among whom were craftsmen. His pietistic friends, who also had master's degrees, acted in similar fashion. When Johann Caspar Schade (1666–1698) transformed his college into an hour of awakening for hearers from all faculties, the number of participants became so large that the students founded small groups (conventicles) in which the biblical text was interpreted to relate it to their own lives. Since the lectures of the professors were unattended and the students shunned church attendance in favor of the conventicles, the resistance of the university and the clergy of the city was to be expected. This grew in intensity, since the students also engaged in pastoral care by visiting the sick. An investigation was undertaken by the theological faculty, but they could not demonstrate that any heresy had occurred. In terms of dogmatics, Francke and his friends remained Lutherans, and he probably would have remained unaffected had it not been for Christian Thomasius (1655–1728), a philosopher of the Enlightenment and and a lawyer. Thomasius was an adherent of natural law and made a report in the favor of Francke that contained excessive accusations against theologians. Francke also defended himself in an *Apologia* to the elector. From that time, Thomasius was forbidden to be active in offering lectures and left Leipzig. When Francke was in Lübeck in March 1690 on account of the death of his uncle, the same interdict (at the request of the theological faculty) reached him. Moreover, he was forbidden to organize conventicles. The Wittenberg theological faculty agreed with the judgment rendered by the theological faculty at Leipzig about the pietists. Thus occurred the break between pietism and Lutheran orthodoxy, even though Spener's suggestions for reform had largely been sympathetically received.

Francke's next station was Erfurt, where Joachim Justus Breithaupt (1658–1732), a follower of Spener, was senior pastor and professor. He provided Francke with a parishioner's position, but even here he soon made himself unpopular. He fell into disfavor with the pastors, because he invited, without consideration to congregational boundaries, children and adults to engage in catechetical exercises and to study in assemblies of edification (for whose participants he made available copies of the New Testament). He also was shunned at the university (where Erfurt pastors were allowed to hold lectures), since an enormous throng (including students from Jena and Leipzig) attended his presentations. The conflicts ended in September 1691 with his banishment, which had been requested by the city council through the prince, the Catholic archbishop and elector of Mainz.

Francke, at the invitation of Spener, who for a brief time had been in Berlin, visited him there. This introduced him to the minister president E. von Danckelmann, to the court counselor C. von Kraut, who was responsible for the development of the newly founded University of Halle, and to other influential personalities. Spener also managed to have Francke installed as a pastor in Glaucha, on the outskirts of Halle, and to serve as an unpaid professor of Greek and Oriental languages on the philosophical faculty. In the background operated the politics of Brandenburg-Prussia. Through the call of pietists to Halle in opposition to the orthodox Lutherans who were in control of the country estates and the surrounding universities, a tolerant climate should be created toward the Reformed court. Thus, already in 1691 Breithaupt was called to Halle to be the first professor of theology.

Following the initial controversies with the city's clergy, which had to be mediated by a commission appointed by the elector, Francke set to work to become primarily active in reforming his community, which was ruined by alcoholism. He also sought to implement Sunday sanctification, to increase church attendance, and to enforce with fines the practice of confession. He only had partial success. With the distribution of alms to poor children, which he combined with questions from the catechism, Francke detected an enormous lack of knowledge. His attempts to enable them to attend school by means of financial support failed. Thus, for example, when he purchased schoolbooks, which he made available to the children, they sold the books. Thereafter, in 1695 he founded first a boarding school for the poor (from which an orphanage developed) and employed needy students as teachers. Shortly thereafter he set up a public school and finally a boarding school for children of nobles, officers, and high officials (named in 1702 *Paedagogium Regium*). A sophisticated, rigorous, educational system with the (if not theoretically formulated) purpose of conversion and sanctification was established. With the endowments he erected an extensive building complex (recently restored). The whole operation, financed through gifts and personal income, grew into a large institutional operation, to which belonged a bookstore, a printing house, and an apothecary.

Most important for the expansion of the Bible into wide circles was the founding of the Bible Institute, in which Baron Carl Hildebrand von Canstein (1667–1719) was decisively involved, although the institute did not bear his name until 1775. Through the copious production of New Testaments and the entire Bible in the institute's own printing house and cheap prices, the pietistic goal was to place a Bible in every household.

In 1694, Francke was married to the orphan Anna Magdalena of Wurm, and in 1698 he became a professor of theology. He had to endure additional battles with the orthodox, which he could overcome only by means of the support of the state. On the other hand, Thomasius criticized sharply the rigorous educational and supervisory methods of Francke and his coworkers. The philosopher Christian Wolff (1679–1754), who represented an optimistic view of human nature, was expelled from Halle in November 1723 at the instigation of Francke and his pietistic colleague Joachim Lange (1670–1744; from 1709 professor at Halle). Francke's pietism had a broad influence that was not limited to Prussia and its army (through the pietistic chaplains from Halle) under Friedrich Wilhelm I (reigned 1713–40). It was widely dispersed in other European countries like Bohemia, Russia, and England.

After the conclusion of his strenuous prorectorate, Francke undertook in 1717–1718 a holiday journey that led him through middle and southern Germany. Everywhere he appeared, he preached, distributed tracts, and celebrated the apparent triumph of pietism. It became apparent that he could not impede the forward march of the Enlightenment, which Wolff's return to Halle announced, supported by Friedrich II as soon as he began his government. Francke did not live to see that. He died in 1727.

To the wide-reaching undertakings of Francke belonged also a reform of the study of theology, which he realized together with Breithaupt and the other professors at the University of Halle. Already in Leipzig he had implemented his idea, borrowed from Spener, that the study of theology must be fundamentally formulated around the Bible. Beyond that, the fact that he had occupied a professorship in philosophy in Halle for years, brought with it the obligation to present exegetical lectures. For Francke, exegetical lectures certainly could not be given without taking into consideration theological aspects. Of the three public lectures at the University at Halle, two were devoted to the Old Testament and the New Testament, and the third was "thetic," that is, on dogmatics. Francke placed more and more emphasis on the Old Testament. For capable students there were in addition opportunities for special studies, such as the Septuagint, the Apocrypha, the early church fathers, and Oriental texts. At the beginning of the course of study, everyone must study—if not completely master—Hebrew, along with the possibility of taking additional languages like Aramaic, Syriac, Arabic, and Persian. Cursory readings of the Bible in the original text should provide the basis for familiarity with the Bible throughout the entire course of study. This would be amplified by cursory lectures over the entire Old and New Testaments. In 1702, he founded a special institute, the *Collegium Orientale theologicum,* whose purpose was to deepen the study of the Holy Scriptures through the production of an edition of a new Hebrew text (appearing in 1720). This was to be supported by the greatest possible knowledge of many Oriental languages and the production of corresponding texts that served the same purpose. This should result not only in the increase in the fundamental, philological-historical knowledge of Scripture, but also in allowing students to "be able to understand and recognize in such a way Christ and the entire economy of salvation from the Scriptures of the apostles and prophets that through them a true basis of correct wisdom and divine learnedness is laid in their souls" (*Idea studiosi theologiae* [1712], according to Peschke, *Studien* 2:156 n. 14). In order to serve this objective, Francke presented an additional lecture (published later as tractates), possessing a special, paraenetic (ethical-admonishing) character, in which the students were given instruction about the formation of their studies and their conduct of life. This was scheduled so that it would not conflict with any other lecture. This allowed all students to participate.

Francke several times expressed his views concerning the fundamental principles for the interpretation of the Bible (hermeneutics). His first treatment of this topic was set forth in a lecture in 1693 that was published at once: *Manuductio ad lectionem Scripturae sacrae* (Assistance for the Reading of the Holy Scriptures). Francke did not produce a comprehensive hermeneutic but only a practical guide for students (Vorrede, 4–5*). Francke's understanding of the Bible (originating from spirituality; cf. Sebastian Franck, *History,* vol. 2) is fundamentally the distinction between the "frame" and the "kernel." The work on the frame is historical, grammatical, philological, and logical, while the study of the kernel is exegetical, dogmatic, elucidative, and practical (1–2).

The historical investigation transmits the *summa* (overall view) of Scripture, the difference between the Old and New Testaments, and the events reported in the Bible. In addition, it traces the basic concepts of individual books, the content of individual chapters, and the main passages of biblical statements of faith. A cursory reading, instruction, and reciprocal inspection by the students enable them to discover this overall view. The examination of manuscripts, additions, translations, text criticism, historical and ancillary disciplines of study, and natural science, which assist the determination of places, times, customs, and coins, are added to this approach. Even so Francke warns against an overestimation of historical exegesis and the acquisition of superfluous information, which contribute nothing to the actual reading of the Bible. The necessary grammatical knowledge one obtains best through the cursory reading of the New Testament in its original language, which requires the learning of its words. He brings attention to the numerous stylistic features of the New Testament and the impact of Hebrew (32–33), which one must know in order to understand the New Testament. Although these questions obviously interest him, he still issues a warning about them. These features may cause one to lose the joy of discovery in the study of the kernel by concentrating too much on the frame. This is especially true for the occupation with rabbinic literature, which is attractive to experts but of little use to others.

Analytic reading belongs to the preparatory phase of exegesis. It investigates the structure and inner connection of the biblical books as well as individual passages (48–49). They are analyzed differently according to the type of the writings (51ff.). In regard to the dogmatic writings of the New Testament (Francke thinks here of the Epistles), one must consider whether they treat respectively one theme (as, e.g., 1 Corinthians) or several. For a single theme one must work out its scope in Scripture. If several exist, one must clearly distinguish between them. In addition, one must treat the individual events of each of the historical books. This is the case also with the prophetic books. The Psalms must be individually examined. This type of analysis is true only for the frame and not for the kernel. Francke distinguishes between the purely grammatical "sense of the words" (*sensus litterae*) and the meaning of the word and the matter (*sensus litteralis*).

According to Francke, there exist both internal and external means of assistance for the investigation of the meaning of words (he follows the traditional distinctions). The internal means are the actual contents of the points of view that are derived from the text itself (since the Scripture is supposed to interpret itself [72–73]). These include things such as the scope, summary, and parallel passages. The analogy of faith assists further by its treatment of the knowledge that is necessary for eternal life. With the aid of the external means (the mentioning of places, customs, etc., in the Scripture), one can then proceed to the inspection of the order of things and circumstances. Proven rules of experienced exegetes can also be used that are especially helpful in interpreting books in which allegories, typologies, and parables occur (85–90).

Francke, in accord with the Lutheran tradition, stresses that each statement contains only *one* literal sense (68; cf. 71, 87). Added to this is his distinction between natural and reborn human beings. Those who are not reborn can participate in the discussion with the help of the hermeneutical means of the literal sense, but they cannot grasp spiritually the ways intended by the Holy Spirit. This is possible only through divine enlightenment (68–69). Since this is also accessible to every plain Christian, the simple reading of the Bible is necessary (71), since it involves the spiritual grasping of truth. Francke also has unequivocally warned against overestimating the value of scientific commentaries, since the external knowledge of interpretation of Scripture can stand in the way of edification and eternal salvation (91ff.).

Francke's dogmatic reading appears somewhat strange when compared with his manner of understanding the role of scriptural interpretation. Francke combines his special view with the practices of the orthodox operation of schools and the Lutheran tradition. The purpose is the recognition of the divine nature and will (99). For Francke, however, piety and a spiritual understanding are necessary to translate theological doctrines into practice. It is advisable to proceed from the dogmatic writings of the New Testament (see above). Methodologically this involves primarily the transmission of the major doctrine of a text and the combining of his special formulation of doctrines with it. The text contains both clearly expressed and concealed doctrines. The distinction between law and gospel is important (101ff.). As a result, Christ must emerge as the kernel of Scripture and the way to life, since otherwise every labor is in vain (104–5).

Following a dogmatic perusal, there is a particular type of interpretative reading of Scripture. This is the deduction of theoretical and practical correlations from what is previously known in order to serve a practical, religious edification. Already applied in orthodoxy, this method is at the same time complex and unclear. However, Francke pursues it with a great deal of joy (109–28). These readings lead to the final kind of reading, a practical one, which is the climax of the educational interpretation. Through this means the exegetical knowledge obtained is applied to the life of the interpreter, not discounting the emotion of the reader, which plays an important role (132ff.). Laity also who do not possess a knowledge of language are able to implement this understanding fully. This has to do with an action and not with a statement (139) and should extend to the whole of life. On the whole, biblical study for Francke is an organic development (142ff.). Its actual purpose is the promotion of God's honor through one's own and the neighbor's edification, which leads to eternal life.

In a section on the affects or emotions of the human soul (149–250), Francke emphasizes their significance for the interpretation of Scripture. Valid for the natural affects is that they are transacted directly through speech ("Out of the abundance of the heart the mouth speaks" [Matt 12:34]). Biblically based, a two-sided understanding of affects and word is valid: the affects of the biblical writers, whose underlying words, which are inspired by God, require us not to continue to remain in the frame but also push us forward to the kernel, which emerges in these affects (154). Against the objection that the author of these writings is, however, the Holy Spirit, Francke stresses that the biblical writers certainly did not simply write down everything that was dictated to them without feeling. Rather, their spirit and will have been moved by the Holy Spirit (159–60). In this regard, the traditional thought of the accommodation is helpful: the Holy Spirit had adapted itself to the temperament of the writers. Therefore, one must be occupied with their affections. Contrariwise, it is valid, then, for the interpreter to recognize that his emotions also are important for the understanding of the biblical writings. In addition, Francke distinguishes here between the one who is not reborn, who only approaches the Scripture with natural reason and cannot recognize the affects of the reborn (165–66), and the reborn, who alone advances to the meaning of Scripture. Thus, it is also the case here that affects and the Word belong closely together.

In the theory of the affects, Francke follows the spiritualizing tradition, which he develops even more widely in that he connects it with the understanding of the biblical words. While the early spiritualists placed Spirit and Word in opposition, Francke introduced the distinction between the external sense of the letter of the Word and the literal sense, that is, the material sense, and comes thus to an intrinsic combination of Lutheran and spiritual traditions.

In brief German tractates, Francke further developed individual aspects of his approach through the combination of exegesis as the ascertainment of the contents of Scripture and the subjective presuppositions of a fruitful interpretation by the reader's disproportionate *Manuductio*. The tractate "Simple Instruction on How One Should Read the Holy Scripture for One's True Edification" (1694; *Werke*, Peschke 216–20) stresses the distinction between a false purpose—that is, to read Scripture for a pastime, on account of the stories it contains, or to gain a reputation as a scholar— and a proper one, that is, to become a believing Christian. The reading of Scripture must begin with prayer, continue with meditation, and end with prayer. The cross and suffering, which God will impose on this type of pious reader, will teach one to understand Scripture correctly. In the "Introduction to the Reading of the Holy Scriptures, in Particular the New Testament (1694; *Werke*, 221–31 [excerpts]), he explains by contrast what the purpose of the entire Scriptures and the individual New Testament books may be. In his eyes, this is admittedly only a means of assistance derived from the "external scholarship" for the unlearned, teachers, and students in order to prepare them for the "simple" way of contact with the Bible, which can open up its "kernel" (preface; 221–23). The main purpose of all of Scripture (3) is "our blessedness," for it is the way to "faith in Jesus Christ" through expiation and good fruits. In both Testaments, this content consists of both law and gospel (4). From both of these, one primarily becomes familiar with the New Testament (6), because this "places most clearly before our eyes the recognition of Jesus Christ and the entire teaching of justice" (225). Then follow considerations about the purpose of the Evangelists (9) and the remaining biblical books. Further, the tractate "Christ, the Kernel of Holy Scripture" (222–48 [excerpts]), by which Francke obtains decisive, fundamental thoughts through a detailed exegesis of the Prologue of the Gospel of John (232, 243), underlines the distinction between theoretical knowledge about Christ and the true acquisition, which is achieved only through the Spirit—which in turn is obtained only through the way of prayer, suffering ("cross"), and introspection (243–48).

While Francke in his paraenetic lectures also continued later the work he had begun in Leipzig, that is, the interpretation of New Testament writings, evidently because the admonitions contained in them could be transferred almost directly to the present, he kept to the Old Testament in the pursuit of his scholarly interpretation. From the preserved accounts, we know the titles of his lectures, and some were published as records by students. He presented an introductory lecture on the Old Testament, as well as others on the Psalms and the prophets, additional interpretations of individual books, and once an overview of important theological sections of the Old Testament. Based on this activity with the Old Testament, he also produced a new hermeneutical approach, which was prepared in the years 1701–1707. In addition to the verbal meaning of Scripture (*sensus litteralis*), there is the deeper or mystical sense (*sensus mysticus*). With this idea, Francke adopted from the Middle Ages once again the three divisions of the planes of meaning, which Luther had dropped. This was almost inevitable from Francke's subjective approach to the understanding of Scripture.

He set forth a significantly altered approach in his new "Hermeneutical Lectures" (*Praelectiones hermeneuticae*) concerning the understanding of Scripture, presented initially in 1709 and then several additional times, before they were published in 1717. This approach contrasted with the earlier *Manuductio*. Admittedly, Francke limited himself here to the discussion of the interpretation devoted to the "kernel." Therefore, the distinction between the "frame" and the "kernel" is no longer decisive. Instead, Francke now handles the opposition between the "authentic" (*genuinus*) and the "false" sense of Scripture. The authentic sense is the one supplied and willed by the Holy Spirit; the false, which contradicts it, can be identified by Scripture (7). The "authentic" and the "false" senses can now be discovered on the plane of the verbal (grammatical; *sensus litterae*), by the literal and material meaning (*sensus litteralis*), and by the mystical or spiritual sense of Scripture (*sensus mysticus* or *spiritualis*). In addition, the readers are important: the reborn and those who are not reborn are to be distinguished (22–23). Only the reborn can know the spiritual sense. Those who are not reborn or the unconverted can grasp only an external meaning, like the Pharisees and scribes, who strove to obtain such an understanding. Students of theology should surely meditate on the three senses in their outer form, but the most important is the living knowledge of the truth (26–28). In addition, one must distinguish between the true and false scope (28–29). Francke points to numerous examples of how one is able to explore the three senses of Scripture with the question concerning the scope. Those who are not reborn also can do this, but only by penetrating a natural knowledge. The authentic, spiritual knowledge is possible only for the reborn, who are enlightened by the Holy Spirit. This truth is recognized at a distinctive level of understanding (57–60).

The context (what precedes and what follows) is important for the understanding of a biblical passage, as is demonstrated by numerous examples (61–94). The same is true for parallel passages (61–94). There are also lexical and factual parallels. Lexical parallels enlighten the literary sense (*sensus litterae*), while factual parallels illuminate the lexical and literal sense (*sensus litteralis*) and the mystical or spiritual sense. In the section concerning the analogy of faith (*analogia fidei* [166–92]), Francke rejects the characteristically orthodox Lutheran definition according to which the common meaning of Scripture conforms to Lutheran teaching (67). He claims, rather, that one is to evaluate it by reference to Scripture, because in the appeal to the commitment to the church is discovered only a subtle form of papism. Rather, the analogy of faith is the entire purpose of Scripture that is expressed in its symphonic harmony (174–75). If one strives for the order of salvation, one discovers it in accordance with the analogy of faith, because this is Scripture's aim (189).

On the whole, Francke was a transitional figure who brought together orthodox Lutheran, typically pietistic, and occasionally critical aspects to address the verbal sense of Scripture.

5.3. Battling against the "Bible Idol": Johann Christian Edelmann

Johann Christian Edelmann was born in 1698 in Weissenfels, a residence city on the Saale River. It was here that his father was a chamber musician in the court of Duke Johann Georg of Sachsen-Weissenfels. His mother was the daughter of a fodder marshal in the neighboring duchy of Sachsen-Zeitz. The duke and his half brother Christian were godfathers of those children who received their names. Later, two brothers and a sister (she died young) were born. In 1711, when Prince Christian, in spite of considerable debt, constructed a second residence in Sangerhausen, Edelmann's father, together with his family, followed the Prince there and became his court secretary. When Christian became duke himself in 1712 and returned to Weissenfels, the father left his family in Sangerhausen and accompanied his lord to his new residence. Since the father never received his salary from the duke, the financial position of the family was catastrophic. Edelmann's father eventually died in 1731, as a rental clerk in Eisenach. As a result of these circumstances, the young Edelmann spent his childhood in an oppressive state of poverty. In addition, his mother suffered for years from a severe case of tuberculosis. In spite of these adversities, Edelmann enjoyed the benefits of a good public education. He studied Latin and rhetoric, initially in Sangerhausen (1711–1715), then in Lauban, where he lived with his uncle, a pastor. His mother especially hoped he would study theology. Lutheran students, mainly coming from Silesian noble families, were sought out to receive an education in the Lauban Lyceum (Gymnasium). In 1717, owing to a conflict, Edelmann asked his father to remove him from Lauban, and he subsequently moved to Altenburg to attend its gymnasium (1717–1719). There, and then later in Weissenfels, he tutored the children of another uncle. In 1720 he began his theological studies in Jena (provided by an attestation of his poverty), which had the most popular theological faculty in Germany on account of the theological openness of the Lutheran Johann Franz Buddeus (1667–1729). His son-in-law, Johannn Georg Walch (1693–1775), a church historian, was one of its most famous professors. At the same time, Edelmann kept his head above water partly by activities as a house instructor; however, he studied sluggishly. After the death of his mother in1723, who had wished him to take up the life of a pastor, and after discouraging experiences in the pulpit, Edelmann abandoned his studies in 1724, being equipped only with a certificate as preacher. From 1725 to 1728, he was the private tutor of the (secretly) Lutheran Count Kornfeil in Würmbla (by St. Pölten in Lower Austria), where he enjoyed a great deal of freedom. Then he assumed a similar post with the pietistic Viennese merchant, Mühl. August Hermann Francke had gained a substantial number of followers among the Austrian Protestants and preachers in the Lutheran mission. Edelmann felt disgusted by the pietistic practices of prayer and the extreme confession of sins by his employers. After six months, he obtained the recommendation that allowed him to work in the service of the brother-in-law of Count Kornfeil, the Count of Auersperg in Purgstall. Here he worked as the house instructor under pleasant circumstances from 1728 to 1731. Still he hoped one day to be able to become a pastor. On account of a large surplus of theologians at the time, this proved to be very difficult for one who had not concluded his studies. In 1732, therefore, he became an instructor in a pastor's household in Bockendorf by Freiberg, Saxonia. A comprehensive reading of theological literature, however, caused him to develop deep-seated doubts as to whether he would ever be qualified for such a pastoral office. Of his readings, he was influenced most of all by Gottfried Arnold (1666–1714), who wrote *Unpartheyische* (= *überkonfesselle) Kirchen- und Ketzer- Historie* [Unbiased History of Churches and Sects], 1699–1700), a work of mystical spiritualism, in which Arnold flatly took the side of the oppressed heretics and sectarians. Edelmann himself came close in this phase to radical pietism or mystical spiritualism. He intensified his asceticism and his ethical rigor. This signified to him an experience of awakening. The Lutheran message of justification no longer offered him any consolation, since he understood it as a pretense for moral laxness. The existential problem of becoming a "true" Christian in his inward being concerned him, even when he had found a new employer. In 1732 he changed his employment to Count Callenberg in Dresden. While there he established an association with other spiritualists, especially the so-called *Engelsbrüder* (Brethren of the Angels) or Gichtelians, named after their founder, Johann Georg Gichtel (1638–1710). During his visit to Herrnhut in 1734, he abandoned his temporary plan to affiliate with the Brethren community of Count Zinzendorf (1700–1760). In 1735 he resigned from the employment of Count Callenberg and moved to the attic room in the house of the Gichtelien Grosskurth. He had already secretly composed the manuscript containing the first four sections of a work named *Unschuldige Wahrheiten* (Innocent Truths) and had anonymously sent it to press. Here is found (in the classical form of the dialogue, which was the mode of the period) the acceptance of Arnold's positions and the writings of the radical pietist Johann Konrad Dippel (1673–1743). These presented the usual spiritualistic criticism of the official church, which, according to the interpretation of Edelmann, had strayed into corruption, including their practices of infant baptism, the clerics, and the orthodox doctrines (like the dogma of justification), while the "enlightened" spiritualists (as Edelmann understood himself to be) are described as the true Christians and the "witnesses of the truth." That most of these statements were copied and not original to Edelmann did not play a role.

In the house of Grosskurth, Edelmann continued working on his manuscript of *Unschuldige Wahrheiten*, until he was sacked at the inducement of Grosskurth's wife. The first sections of the work were handed on to the radical pietistic book seller Andreas Gross in Frankfurt am Main, who published them in Büdingen (in the religiously liberal county of Isenburg-Büdingen) and exposed them at the Leipzig New Year's Mass in 1736. Gross asked for additional sections and invited him to work with the Berleburger Bible. Under the effort of Johann Heinrich Haug (1680–1753), this Bible work was a translation of the Bible following the Latin text, the translation of Luther, and the Zurich Bible. It was published between 1726 and 1742 in Berleburg and stood out for its adoption of a secret third meaning of Scripture (beside the verbal and the spiritual-moral ones) as well as for its polemic against the official church. The County of Sayn-Wittgenstein-Berleburg, during the rule of Count Casimir (1694–1741), was a free state for all religions and confessions, connected with a reduction in taxes. As in Isenburg-Büdigen (where the Berleburg Bible was printed), this was a way for poorer landlords to bring crafts and trades to their territory. Edelmann received for his collaboration a salary and moved to Berleburg in 1736. However, he did not maintain this connection very long. Coming into conflict with Haug and keeping his distance from the project of the translation of the Berleburg Bible, Edelmann by 1737 dissolved the association. The meeting with Johann Friedrich Rock (1678–1749), errant leader of the sect of the Inspired from the Wetterau, with which Edelmann associated for a time, ended in a confrontation. Edelmann's intellectualism separated him from the ecstatic mysticism of the Inspired. In his autobiography, he speaks of his deep crisis in the early part of 1739. What helped him to escape this predicament was the insight that the Logos in the Prologue of the Gospel of John may be identified with reason (as he later described at length in his work *Die Göttlichkeit der Vernunft* (The Divinity of Reason [1742]). He also experienced an external crisis. An acute lack of money forced him at the end of 1738 to hire on as an apprentice to a ribbon weaver. However, already by 1739 his works were so well known in radical pietistic circles that he was supported financially by numerous followers so that he could live as an unattached author. A rich merchant from Berlin, Pinell, especially supported him and asked him to travel to Berlin. Edelmann accepted his offer. In 1740, Pinell procured for him the posthumous works of Spinoza, which were difficult to acquire. After reading the *Tractatus theologico-politicus*, Edelmann began with the drafting of his own *Moses mit Aufgedeckten Angesichte* (Moses with Revealed Countenance), which led to the printing of the first three "countenances" in November 1740 and their distribution through middlemen in various cities. Shortly thereafter, on the basis of the prescriptions of the Imperial Police Order, legal proceedings were initiated against him with the Imperial Court Council on the charge of blasphemy, and the confiscation of his *Moses* throughout the empire was ordered. Following the limited distribution the work, Edelmann arranged to have it appear throughout the empire. Count Casimir, it is true, had some copies confiscated, but allowed the author to remain undisturbed. Edelmann in the meantime had become well-to-do through his book sales. He soon left Berleburg secretly, following the death of Count Casimir in 1741, because the count's successor wanted to tax him dearly. He traveled to the nearby County of Hachenberg, where he could live undisturbed. He moved to Neuwied from there in 1744, because the house in which he lived was sold. At this time, this was also a place of religious tolerance. However, Count J. Friedrich Alexander of Wied (1706–1791) could not resist the pressures of his consistory to require from Edelmann in 1745 an initially confidential confession of faith. Because inauthentic versions were circulated, he published it in a broader form in 1746 as *Abgenöthigtes Jedoch Andern nicht wieder aufgenöthigtes Glaubens-Bekenntnis* (A Confession of Faith That Is Wrung from Someone, However, Cannot Be Forced on Other People). In the following year, he decided to leave Neuwied and came in the autumn to Berlin after several trips. He dwelt with Penell in Cölln. The provost there, Johann Peter Süßmilch, (1707–1767) soon published a pamphlet opposing *Moses*. After further trips (for a while he lived in Altona) and the publication of additional writings, in 1749 Edelmann settled finally in Berlin. In the meantime a second legal proceeding, this time before the Imperial Chamber Court, was initiated against him, directed against his *Glaubens-Bekenntnis* (Confession of Faith). This procedure ended with a festive burning of his books in Frankfurt am Main in 1750 at the decision of the emperor's Book Commissariat. For permission to continue to reside in Berlin, he apparently was required not to publish anything more. Nevertheless, he continued to write surreptitiously at least until 1759. There were additional "appearances" of *Moses,* along with his own autobiography, which reached as far as the year 1744. In Berlin, well-to-do patrons supported him so that he had an adequate livelihood. He died in February 1767 due to apoplexy. His handwritten will was preserved in the possession of the librarian of the Hamburg academic gymnasium, Johann Christian Wolf (1690–1770), who later bequeathed it to the Hamburg State Library, where it survives still today, in spite of the ravages of the war.

The significance of Edelmann for biblical criticism in Germany, in contrast to that of the famous Hermann Samuel Reimarus (1694–1768), has not become well known until more recently. His works, including most of the manuscripts, are now accessible in a new printing. In contrast to Reimarus, who kept his *Apologie* hidden during his lifetime, Edelmann was more courageous in that what he wrote he published, at least during his younger years.

In our context, *Moses* and *Glaubens-Bekenntnis* are especially significant. Edelmann had begun to compose *Moses* in 1740 even before he came to know Spinoza's *Tractatus Theologico-Politicus*. Still, he strongly agreed with what the latter wrote and seldom disputed any of his ideas.

Following what at the time was the prevailing preference in composition, *Moses* is set forth in the form of a dialogue between "Light Loving" and "Blindly," whose names already suggest the direction in which he is proceeding. The illumined "Light Loving" tries hard, finally with success, to convince "Blindly," who was primarily faithful to the church and a student of the orthodox Lutheran pastor "Pitch-Dark," that the opinions of his teacher were irretrievably obsolete. The traditional anticlerical position, which we encountered already in the deists, is a thoroughgoing fundamental motif in the entire collection of Edelmann's works. The polemic, characteristic of deists as well as spiritualists, is uttered against the "ceremonies and the external, so-called worship features" (*Moses* 2:5). However, this is not central for Edelmann.

Edelmann attacks first the two main pillars of the orthodox view: the acceptance of verbal inspiration, which includes the entire biblical text, and, bound with it, the authorship of a historical Moses. The Lutheran equation of the authority of Holy Scripture with the Word of God is the underlying object of this attack. Edelmann is aware that he does not bring forward in any way new findings with his critical perspective. He can refer to "heretics" like Spinoza and recognized biblical scholars like Richard Simon, Campegius Vitringa (1659–1722), and C. M. Pfaff (1686–1760) (1:57–58). His argument, however, assumes a popular character. Against the orthodox point of view that the biblical text contains up to the present unaltered information, Edelmann cites the fortune of the tablets of the law (cf. Exod 31:18; 34:1): "when the great God treated the law that he himself had twice inscribed in a way that we in the present day have neither dust nor vestige of these, he certainly did not endearingly bypass human writings, whether they originated with Moses or someone else" (1:15). Against the orthodox's appeal to Matt 5:18, Edelmann refers to the loss of many legal and prophetic writings mentioned in the Old Testament (1:18–19). In his *Glaubens-Bekenntnis* (46), he points out that, according to the information of the best scholars, nothing more exists of the originals of the biblical books. It is no wonder, then, that the numerous interpretations and translations of the biblical text create a great deal of confusion among people. The fight over the correctness of the biblical text that occurs among Lutherans, Presbyterians, and Catholics only results in strife and conflict (*Moses* 1:80; 2:8), which appears ludicrous. To the demonstration that the Bible cannot be identical to the Word of God, Edelmann mentions his observations about the content. Among these belong the chronological contradictions, which he discovers in the books of Kings and Chronicles (*Moses* 2), as well as the atrocious ordinances of Moses that speak against the love commandment such as Deut 7:2 and Num 31:17, as when, following the victory over the Midianites, their women and children who previously had escaped are ordered to be killed (1:107). In his *Glaubens-Bekenntnis* (42), Edelmann says about the Bible: "I take it for a collection of ancient writings, whose originators have written according to the degree of their knowledge of God and divine matters, and for the most part have reported magnificent truths, for which I bear the greatest esteem. However, they have never had in mind … that they should force their insight forever upon posterity as an unerring standard and rule." Since the Bible in no way has been dictated by God, and yet "has been disastrously disguised and mutilated" (*Moses* 2:43), it thus is to be dismissed as the only standard of faith. "The idol of the Bible must fall, while humans should know the living God in a vital and convincing manner, and the true worship of God in spirit and truth should be established again in all the world" (2:45).

The second, often repeated theme echoes this first one: the service of the Bible is contrasted to the service of the living God. For this living God, Edelmann has continued to seek an apt expression. We do not go wrong, if we seek for this an inheritance from the spiritualists. Already with Sebastian Franck we discovered a similar contrast between the "letter" and the inner Word (see *History*, vol. 3). For Edelmann, the "living God" is a power that is active in us. However, the transition from spiritualism to the Enlightenment is demonstrated in the fact that, corresponding to the experience of his call, he could compare the "Word" from John 1 with reason and then could speak of the "divinity of reason." With this he then associates his thinking about the "truth," which he could find by all means in the Bible. "Light Loving" instructs "Blindly": "Therefore, it is entirely in vain…, if you want to conclude from the fact that I demonstrated to you that the Bible is not unharmed, if the truths contained in it were not supplied by God" (1:37). However, it is not only there, but also if one finds the same, for instance, in Ovid (ibid.). "For the truth is always from God, whether it is stated by Aesop or Paul, Christ or Confucius"

(1:51). Nor is the Qur'an excluded (1:99–100). On account of these statements, Edelmann has been called a protagonist of tolerance. "On account of the excellence identified in a matter, one should regard it as divine truth grounded in reason" (1:88–89). Therefore, Edelmann can demand that the Bible should not "be regarded differently than any other human book due to the likelihood of things recited, which have been examined in the light of reason (*Glaubens-Bekenntnis*, 69).

With Spinoza, Edelmann understands truth in ethical terms. In the second view of the understanding of God, this becomes clear in his discussion of the connection with the concept of conscience, to which Edelmann grants a central place in reference to the confessed atheist Matthias Knutzen (1646–?). Edelmann reproduces Knutzen's three tractates (a letter and two dialogues) verbatim. In contrast to Knutzen, who denied the existence of God and substituted for him a collective conscience, Edelmann states "that this is … the conscience or the enlightening reason of the living God" (2:65). However, a clear identification does not exist, as one is able to see in the thoughts developed by Edelmann in the third view of the definition of God. He comes close apparently to Spinoza's perspective (see above), when, on the one hand, he speaks of the "all accomplishing, all invigorating, and moving being" (2:161) and, on the other hand, emphasizes that while God is the "being and nature of all things," he must, however, in no way be the identified with creation itself" (2:161). Edelman apparently fluctuates between different influences, which he encounters, one after another, on his path of life: the personal God inherited from the Lutheran tradition and the "God in us" from spiritualism, which he identifies with reason. Both are mixed together with the Stoic-moral God, whose origin from classical antiquity Edelmann, as a theologian shaped by humanism, does not deny.

Edelmann confidently affirms in the introduction of his *Glaubens-Bekenntnis* that he would not withhold anything, even if this would result in his persecution (24). This was because, already in the preface, he gave free reign to his scolding of "clerics." Of particular interest is his portrait of Jesus. It is not surprising that Edelmann, given his presuppositions, cannot do anything with the atoning death of Christ for the sins of humanity. To those who were priests against their will, he wishes to give the opportunity to regain for themselves "the honorable title of an actual teacher of virtue." Additionally, he wants to make it comprehensible "that it is completely vain and useless babble, on one side … to admonish people to be virtuous, while on the other side to make them aware that they are corrupt to the core and incapable of any good thing" (13).

He finds it to be even more absurd, if people hear that their good creator "has given them a redeemer who must take upon himself their sins and bear their punishment. If that were true one would be a real fool, if he wished to trouble himself with virtue" (13–14). Therefore, this view is connected with his retaining nothing of the eternal damnation of sinners (83). Much more he plainly denies that there could be sinners: "God, as the completely perfect Good, could not possibly have made creatures who hate him or could revolt against him" (91). Proceeding from the presupposition that everyone at least grants that God is good, then one could not hate him.

> There is no person living on the earth who should be able to hate the good of one kind or another, which he actually experiences. Since he does not hate the good, it is therefore impossible that he should be able to transgress against it. If he is not able to transgress against it, then he is not able to sin against it. And if he cannot sin against it, then he has no need of propitiation. (91; cf. in addition under point 6)

After his disposing of the official Christology of the church, he formulates in twelve points his own confession of Christ: "[1.] I believe that he was a true man like we are and in all of his elements, nothing excepted, he had our nature and character" (93). In his comments that he added during the printing (94–101), he seeks to prove this by comparing the biblical narrative of the virgin birth of Jesus to similar stories from heathen sources (e.g., the birth of Romulus). This demonstrates that the Bible is not more creditable than other texts. For the view that Joseph was the true father of Jesus, he refers to the title of appropriate literature from England (which he knew from catalogues and newspapers) as well as to the lost sectarian literature of the early church, which is known through the apologetic refutation. The designation "Christ" = the "Anointed" [2.] indicates only that Jesus is a human being among those who are endowed by God with special gifts and virtues. The assumption that he may have been the Messiah is not believable and goes back to an "ancient Jewish sage" (120). [3.] "I believe that his disciples also in this proposition named him the Son of God. However, this means nothing more than the fact that they wished to give recognition to his excellence before other human brings" (123). This use of speech corresponds to a biblical custom to assign admirable features to the designation of "God." Because of many heathens joining Christianity, this term may have been misunderstood, because they customarily deified their heroes. There are once again numerous proof-texts in the following notes, and Edelmann comes again to speak of the virgin birth as an especially unbelievable basis for this appellation. The next principle [4.] is associated closely with the third: "When He names God his father, He has done so in no other understanding than we all have when we name God in the Lord's Prayer our Father. God has in actual understanding neither one son nor many" (136).

Then Edelmann comes to speak of the sending of Jesus. He recognizes "[5.] that the main intention of the Lord Jesus has been to unite in love again the human minds that were divided one against the other by the many kinds of misguided opinions about God, thus ending all religious squabbling. These should be abolished in order that humans may be united in love. This should also be taught by their clergy." In the notes we read the following as the basis: "For it is absolutely impossible that humans are able to bear a common love for one another, as long as they are taught by their priests that God hates and damns eternally all who do not profess their own particular understandings" (143). As a discouraging example from the Bible, in addition to the Protestant controversial literature, Ps 139:21–22 is mentioned. From this ensues [6.] the point that it cannot have been Jesus' purpose to found a new religion, but rather to show that the unchangeable God cannot possibly be offended. Therefore, he cannot in any way be angered over human sins, needing subsequently to be appeased (147). In the notations to this, Edelmann disputes not only original sin but also the punishment of hell and that Christ could have suffered for sins vicariously. Jesus earned therefore the titles of healer and savior, because he had abrogated sins by teaching that one cannot sin against God [7.]! This thought had been presented already around 1700 by Johann Konrad Dippel (1673–1734), the radical pietist who composed his writings under the pseudonym "Christianus Democritus." This could be demonstrated by the narrative of the woman taken in adultery in John 8! Edelmann was also aware of New Testament textual criticism: in alluding to Bengel's critical apparatus he noted that this pericope has been viewed as authentic according to the "recent clergy," while the "older clergy" had removed it as objectionable (165). The following proposition reads: "[8.] He must have been willing to suffer death for no other reason than because the priests at that time were afraid he may have turned aside the crowd and therefore would have diminished their revenues" (182). This demonstrates Edelmann's enmity toward the priests. He explains then that this concern at that time was unfounded, since Jesus directed the disciples to the priests (see Matt 8:4 par.), and they were commanded to contribute the gifts that were stipulated in the law, "which also I and all of his true disciples have done and will do" (183). Here Edelmann intimates that already only a few were allowed to open their eyes to the truth. As a rationalist he thought as an elitist!

The following two sentences (190) contain the clearest reference to the apostolic confession of faith: "[9.] That He not only was resurrected again in the spirit from the dead, among whom he lived at that time, after having shed his mortal flesh...." "[10.] That He returned in this spirit not only long ago, but returns also daily in many thousands of his witnesses in order to judge the living and the dead." Edelmann, the rationalist and spiritualist, cites 1 Pet 3:18 and argues against the resurrection of the flesh, since there are lacking reliable witnesses. He notes that in this passage, the statement is made that Christ has died according to the flesh but was resurrected according to the spirit. If the resurrection of Jesus according to the flesh is a central statement of faith, then why does Peter, reputed to be an eyewitness, say just the opposite! (191). Why had the resurrected Christ not showed himself to impartial observers? Why have the Romans reported nothing about the supposed, egregious event? The sentence "everything that has a beginning in nature must also find in time its end" has to be valid also for the flesh of Jesus; immortal flesh is unthinkable (201). Once more Edelmann knows of an entire series of parallels for the ascension from the history of religion. These include narratives concerning Zoroaster, Hercules, and Apollonius of Tyana, which are displayed as "fairy tales" (204). In addition, Edelmann can only ridicule the apostolic confession that Jesus is to sit at the right hand of God in order to represent us to him: "This would certainly be a thousand times more useful and necessary on the earth than in heaven..., if God had delivered to him the Kingdoms of the world." "Why does He call him to heaven?" (206). Why is the devil to reign a thousand years until Christ returns? It would be more real to expect this to occur on St. Never's Day (a German expression ridiculing imitation of Catholic saints' days).

Edelmann understands the day of judgment or the last judgment "to concern any person, since he arises from the amazing sleep of former errors in order to recognize God and himself and to begin a rational life" [11.] (121). He is also able to say "that God always allows humans to perform judgments against other humans on this very earth, under which we all presently dwell" (255). In the notes, Edelmann expressly grounds his view that as God is eternal so creation endures without beginning or end and thus is also eternal. Things are subjected to a continuous growth and decay (222ff.). God and His works are to be observed in nature (227). Edelmann requires of his readers, who are endowed with happiness from

God, to enjoy what presently exists and to reject superstition. As for this happiness, he believes "[12.] that it must begin in the present, only to continue after this life, and become ever more highly driven by the unending benevolence of God" (244–45). Further, he rejects the existence of the devil as a bogeyman (261ff.). Edelmann himself avows the religion of love, "which is as old as the world, and which our Jesus did not establish, but rather renewed" (317). The faith that one is obligated to love would be the greatest enemy of love (317ff.), for it has originated the greatest divisions.

5.4. Installing Rational Religion as Judge: Hermann Samuel Reimarus

Hermann Samuel Reimarus was born 22 December 1694 (according to the old Julian calendar), in Hamburg, the son of a teacher, Nicolaus Reimarus, who was employed in the Academic Gymnasium, the Johanneum. His mother, Johanna Wetken, came from an old Hamburg family. Educated first by his father, he attended the Johanneum in 1708 and then in 1710 the Academic Gymnasium, to prepare for the university. His most important teachers were the classical philosopher Johann Albert Fabricius (1668–1736) and the Hebraist Johann Christoph Wolf (1690–1770), who had edited a comprehensive collection of rabbinic literature (*Bibliotheca Hebraica*). Both were adherents of the so-called Physicotheology, which sought to discover God in nature. Among Reimarus's later Hamburg friends was the poet Barthold Hinrich Brockes (1680–1747), who was well known for his collection of poetry entitled *Irdisches Vergnügen in Gott* (Earthly Delight in God), which comprised nine volumes [1721–1748]). Beginning in 1714, he attended the University of Jena, where he studied the Bible in the original text. He listened to the lectures in systematic theology by Buddeus, who combined a Lutheran, orthodox, basic way of thinking with moral, rational, and historical concerns. Reimarus admittedly was more interested in philological and philosophical questions and gave up his theological studies while in Jena. Following this change in direction, he moved to Wittenberg in 1716, where he soon received his master's degree and turned to the study of philosophy. He presented his defense in this discipline on the subject "Machiavellismus vor Machiavell" (Machiavellianism before Machiavelli), which is now published in Schmidt-Biggemann, *Kleine gelehrte Schriften*, 69–130). In 1729, he became an adjunct advisor on the philosophy faculty. From 1720 to 1722, he undertook the customary study journey, which led him to Leiden, London, and Oxford. While in England he became familiar with the writings of the English deists, with whom he agreed later in many of his critical biblical arguments. After returning to Wittenberg, he assumed his activity as an adjunct and presented philosophical lectures and exercises. During this period, the strife between the pietistic theologians of Halle and the rational philosopher Christian Wolff (1679–1754) was moving ahead at full steam. In 1723, this conflict temporarily came to an end following the expulsion of Wolff from Prussia. Wolff's teaching that all may be proved by means of (mathematical) reason thoroughly occupied Reimarus's attention. In the same year, he became rector of the great city school located in Wismar; however, he rejected this school method in a writing that appeared in 1727, which is apparently lost. Later, he often explained that he wished to support instead perceptions that are comprehended on the "Bases of Sound Reason" ("in general experiences and known principles") (*Vornehmste Wahrheiten der natürlichen Religions* [Preferred Truths of Natural Religion], Gawlick, *Vorbericht*, 1:63). He did not become a consistent disciple of Wolff nor his student. In another respect, however, over the years he became more extreme than Wolff. Wolff had always given theology its own role in addition to that of philosophy. On the one hand, he explained that when God's Word exceeded reason then the Word provided a greater amount of knowledge. On the other hand, he also presented positive criteria by which a supernatural revelation must be judged: what contradicted reason or God's perfection or what required humans to engage in an action that spoke against the laws of nature cannot be a divine revelation. In the course of time, Reimarus secretly radicalized this position. For him, reason also served as the final arbiter for the criticism of the Bible. Wismar, who had moved to Sweden in 1648, had suffered a great deal during the northern war (1705–1721), including in the area of cultural standards. Reimarus was able successfully to raise the level of the city school. Among other things he expanded instruction in mathematics and science in the manner of Leibniz and Wolff and introduced the study of political science and history. In 1727, he was called to the post of professor of Oriental languages in the Academic Gymnasium in Hamburg, an office in which he served until the end of his life. He taught Hebrew philology and philosophy. In 1728, he married Johanna Friederike, the daughter of Johann Albert Fabricius. His only surviving son, Johann Albrecht Hinrich, was born in 1729 (died 1814). His only surviving daughter, Elise (1735–1805), became especially connected to Lessing.

Reimarus was a scholar of wide interests. The investigation *Allgemeine Betrachtungen über die Triebe der Thiere* (General Observations concerning the Instincts of Animals [1760–1762]) was regarded as a groundbreaking precursor of research in behavior, based on a physical-theological view of the world. *Vernunftlehre* (Theory of Reason [1756]) is, with its two fundamental rules of conformity and antithesis, a hand-book of logic. It originated from Reimarus's activity of teaching Latin. *Vindicatio dictorum Veteris Testamenti in Novo allegatorum* (The Defense of Old Testament Statements Cited in the New Testament [1731]) was a published lecture in which Reimarus still tried as an apologist to save the traditional christological, prophetic evidence from the Old Testament. This had been a prevailing position in Lutheranism since Flacius. Apparently Reimarus had not yet developed his own critical approach. A short time later, he devised the basis for his criticism. As the original plan of the *Apologie* shows (in the introduction by Alexander, 11–13), he had already planned in the 1730s as parts of his larger work the *Vernunftlehre* (Theory of Reason) and *Abhandlungen über die vornehmsten Wahrheiten der natürlichen Religion* (Essays concerning the Most Distinguished Truths of Natural Religion [1754]). While he concealed his volatile biblical criticism, the separate publication of these works was one of the maneuvers by which he kept from the public his true attitude. Thus, he gave the impression that he adhered to the broad opinion of orthodox theologians, in which natural religion is a kind of preamble (*preambula*) to Christian faith, based on the Bible and revelation. It became clear after his death, however, that he held the position that natural religion was all-sufficient. According to his definition (1.1, §69), natural religion is a living knowledge of God, which is acquired through reason. His interpretation that the world is a planned creation, recognizable from its order, offers the foundation of his thinking. In addition, Reimarus combines with this a human perspective, which sees happiness as the purpose of human life, and he supports his optimistic view of humanity on both faith in God's providence and the teaching of the immortality of the soul. The work is an example of the Enlightenment's teaching of religion. This indirectly explained biblical revelation as superfluous, an idea that was not shared by his contemporaries. Instead, Reimarus came to be regarded as a defender of the Christian faith against atheism. Actually he had prepared a frontal attack on the Bible as the source of revelation and thereby Christianity as religion of revelation. He continued to work secretly on the corrected manuscript of his *Apologie oder Schutzschrift für die vernünftigen Verehrer Gottes* (Apology or Writing of Defense for the Rational Worshipers of God), dealing with the source of revelation and the Christian religion of revelation until shortly before his death. His son handed over the final copy of this manuscript in 1814 to the Hamburg city library with a request of confidentiality. In 1972 it was completely printed.

After he had invited his closest friends to share a meal in February 1768, he explained to them that this was his final meal. Reimarus died peaceably on March 1 as a respected citizen and scholar. The scandal concerning him was not to break out until after his death.

When Lessing published a first imprint in 1774, it went virtually unnoticed, and neglected. In 1777, however, additional fragments of an allegedly unknown author, said to have been found in the Wolfenbüttel library (this text actually contained sections of an earlier version of the *Apologie*, which Lessing presumably had acquired from the family of Reimarus), an intense controversy broke out between Lessing and numerous opponents. These included, among others, the senior pastor of Hamburg, Johann Melchior Goeze (1717–1786), who was a defender of Lutheran orthodoxy. The publication was abruptly ended by the sovereign's prohibition (see below).

The existing version demonstrates Reimarus's criticism of the official theology and the entire Bible of the Old and New Testaments. However, the prepublication of his positive views of reason and natural religion tended to alleviate to some extent the disquiet tht the critical position had aroused. In Reimarus's Old Testament explanations, there is a thoroughgoing tendency to condemn morally the humans who appear in the Old Testament as witnesses of revelation. From Adam to the late kings and prophets, Reimarus sifts through the behavior of the biblical persons and demonstrates that all of these do not satisfy the moral demands that should characterize the divinely gifted bearers of revelation. His general judgment is scathing:

> There is certainly … no book, indeed no history of the world … in which the name of God is misused so frequently and shamefully, and in which all the persons who are identified as men of God and are determined with their conduct to love honor and virtue still create such terrible scandal, offence, and disgust. (*Apologie* 1:672)

This moral criticism of Old Testament persons, which is typical of the Enlightenment, is found also in the view of Pierre Bayle's (1647–1706) *Dictionnaire historique et critique* (1692–1695) about Abraham and David. The judgment is extended to the entire nation of Israel:

> However, I am upset sometimes at the unfathomable evil of the Israelite nation, which is constantly revolting against God in the wilderness and

later becomes addicted to idolatry. I find it difficult to make sense out
of the fact that a God has elected from among so many wise and docile
peoples a people to be his possession who are so obdurate in their dealings with him. (*Apologie,* "Vorbericht," 1:51)

The background is also the traditional anti-Semitism that Lessing had
first opposed. Reimarus also criticizes the ostensible miracles of the Old
Testament, which he either traces to natural processes or condemns as
deceitful reports. The best-known example is the narrative of the passage
through the Red Sea. In the fragment published by Lessing (*Werke,* Gopfert, 7:388–98, which Reimarus expanded in the final version and revised
in part: *Apologie* 1:299–326), Reimarus attests to the impossibility of this
narrative. This criticism begins with Exod 12:37, where six hundred thousand male participants (not taking into consideration both women and
children) are mentioned. Through statistical reckonings, Reimarus argues
that this number exceeded the time span that was available for the reputed
results to occur within this narrow expanse.

More important is the rejection of the New Testament explanation
of the Old Testament's messianic prophecies concerning Christ in which
orthodoxy offered one of its most important, apologetic arguments. Earlier, Anthony Collins (1676–1729) had indicated (*A Discourse on the
Grounds and Reasons of Christian Religion* [1724]) that these arguments
rest on an allegorical interpretation and thus one should return to a literal
understanding of the respective Old Testament passages. Perusing one
after another the series of Old Testament passages that are interpreted by
orthodoxy as referring to Christ, Reimarus agrees and says that he does
not discover one that refers to Jesus. For example, Isa 7:14 has in mind the
crown prince Hezekiah; the so-called *Protoevangelium* in Gen 3:15 could
only have been explained by blind-reasoned commentators as referring to
Christ; and the connection of Psalm 2 to Christ made in Acts 4:25ff. and
13:33 can be the result either of gross ignorance or an intentional misunderstanding of the Hebrew style (*Apologie* 1:721–55). In addition to the
points made by Collins, Reimarus also refers expressly to Grotius (see
History, vol. 3), who already had explained the historical sense of most
passages (*Apologie* 1:728). Even though these observations are found in a
polemical context, Reimarus still can be regarded as an important precursor of the historical criticism of the Old Testament.

This interlinking of observations concerning history and ideology
is true also of the section that Lessing published as the fourth fragment:
"The books of the Old Testament have not been written to reveal a reli-

gion" (*Werke* 7:398–426, revised by Reimarus, *Apologie* 1:769–819). The ideology is inserted in the assumption placed in the beginning of this section: "That the soul of a human being … is determined by nature to be a spirit immortal and imperishable and destined to a perpetual life by the creator following this temporality"(*Apologie* 1:769). Reimarus is even more precise in the previous version (Lessing, *Werke* 7:398):

> A supernatural, beatific religion must reside at the basis of all things and requires knowledge of the immortality of the soul, which receives either reward or punishment for one's behavior in a future eternal life. Further, this type of religion must involve the association of pious souls with God, which would lead to an increasingly greater glorification and blessedness."

This teaching of the immortality of the soul was of Platonic and Neoplatonic origin and was already widespread in the ancient church. It was a favorite teaching of the theology of the Enlightenment. Reimarus himself had offered a detailed treatment of this teaching in his work *Die vornehmsten Wahrheiten der natürlichen Religion* (The Most Important Truths of Natural Religion, X, Addendum, 2:691–766). Reimarus demonstrates by means of a correct historical argument that this teaching was alien to the Old Testament and concludes "that the books of the Old Testament do not contain divine revelation and that Moses and the prophets were not sent by God to reveal a beatific religion, because none of them considers the immortality of our souls and eternal life…. Rather many of these directly deny these affirmations" (*Apologie* 1:770–71). According to the fragment published by Lessing, Reimarus stresses that it can be only a "wicked and scurrilous religion, which can maintain scarcely more than the appearance of a religion (Lessing, *Werke* 7:399). How long such a condemnation endured may be seen in the fact that Emanuel Hirsch (*Das Alte Testament und die Predigt des Evangeliums* [1936; rev. ed. edited by Hans Martin Müller; Tübingen: Katzmann, 1986]) set this view forth as a main reason for the devaluation of the Old Testament.

More significant for the history of interpretation were Reimarus's statements concerning the New Testament. The section concerning the narrative of the resurrection of Jesus, published by Lessing in 1777 as the fifth fragment (*Werke* 7:426–57), was left out in 1778. However, in the final version it appears again in its original place (*Apologie* 2:179–271). It is important, not because Reimarus follows the older thesis (see Matt 28:13) of Thomas Woolston (*The Moderator between an Infidel and an*

Apostate... [1725; 3rd ed., 1729]) that the grave had been empty, because the disciples had stolen the corpse of Jesus (2:198–271). Rather, what is new is the method of argumentation against the resurrection of Jesus. This consists of the contradictions in the reports of the Gospels, which here for the first time are expressly mentioned. One has to consider that Johann Albrecht Bengel as late as 1736 published his *Richtige Harmonie der 4 Evangelien* (An Accurate Harmony of the Four Gospels), and this was certainly not the last of its kind!

The best-known and novel assertion, at least for Germany (at approximately the same time, Thomas Chubb had written a similar book, *The True Gospel of Jesus Christ* [1738], in which he asserted and similarly argued the same point), was the view that there is a difference between the purposes and words of Jesus himself (later one would say "the Jesus of history") and the theological conceptions of his disciples. With these views, Reimarus exerted a decisive influence on the life-of-Jesus research in the nineteenth century.

In respect to the teachings and views of Jesus, Reimarus's thought is divided already in the fragment edited by Lessing, *Vom Zwecke Jesu und seiner Jünger* (Concerning the Purpose of Jesus and His Disciples [1778]). Here, Jesus is the teacher of a true, "natural"—that is, moral—religion: "Thus, the intention of the preaching and teaching of Jesus is directed to an honest, active character, to a change of mind, to an unfeigned thought of the genuine love of God and of neighbor.... These are all moral instructions and obligations of life, which should improve humans inwardly and externally (*Werke* 7:501). Reimarus follows this interpretation, which was widespread since the birth of humanism. In another line of thinking, however, he attributes to Jesus the understanding that he regarded himself, in a worldly and political sense, as the Messiah who had been promised to the Jewish people. Jesus considered himself to be the king of the end-time who would deliver the Jews from the Roman yoke and who wished to establish his own lordship. In addition, the disciples imparted the hope in a worldly dominion in which they would obtain their own positions. It was only after the ignominious failure of the effort and the death of the master that they covered up in their reports the event and the true purposes of Jesus. This entirely different view of the person of Jesus is connected with the purpose of Reimarus to refute the official, spiritual interpretation of the messianic role of Jesus. Jesus may have been an extraordinary man and may have possessed the characteristics that one expected the Messiah to have, "however, at the same time, everything remains within the limitations of humanity" (Lessing, *Werke* 7:512).

Jesus did not in any way wish to found a new religion. Rather, as Reimarus proves above all with quotations from Matthew, Jesus was aware of his ancestral Jewish religion: "By the by he was born a Jew and wished to continue as one, for he came not to dispense with the Law, but rather to fulfill it (Lessing, *Werke* 7:502). In the final version of the *Apologie*, this argument is substantially extended. If earlier in the version of the fragment he had seen the teaching of Jesus summarized in the saying of Matt 1:14: "Repent, for the kingdom of heaven has drawn near," he now divides this verse by taking it to refer to two different addressees: "'Repent' addresses all humans and their common religion; 'the Kingdom of Heaven has drawn near' ... belongs to the positive religion of the Jews" (2:173). At the same time, Reimarus wishes to suggest by this argument that it is not forbidden for Jesus to observe Jewish ceremonies. They are partial, time related, and connected to a human form of religion. The *Apologie* presents a more negative portrait of the historical Jesus. He remains the teacher of an exemplary morality that, however, is still thoroughly compromised. This is due to the argument that the purpose of repentance was only a preparation for its main objective, that is, to present himself as an earthly pretender to the throne at the head of a revolution against the Romans and the Jewish Sanhedrin. He used, in addition, questionable means: first, he connected himself to the Old Testament passages traditionally explained as relating to the Messiah; and, second, he simulated miracles. It is also suspicious that he could not perform these miracles when he was confronted by someone's lack of faith, as, for example, that of his relatives or of the high council (*Apologie* 2:130–35). Thereby, "the great character suffers immensely, a limitation that would have been avoided, if one only had dealt with his work of conversion alone" (2:174). Further, Jesus pursued this objective by ambiguous means. This is noted, for example, when he induced John the Baptist, his cousin, to speak as if he did not know Jesus and was made aware of who he was only by means of the voice from heaven (see Mark 1:7, 11 par.). It is seen also when he exploited common superstitions in telling of alleged miracles or when he was banding together with the common people against the authorities. Reimarus concluded with this observation:

> that the high council had not been able to help from dealing with Jesus according to how he had acted. Thus, this one was not innocent, and had suffered on account of his own criminal actions.... It is to be lamented that the residual merits of Jesus concerning the active religion of humans had been stained and blackened through his intention to

become a Messiah of the Jews and through the suspicious and seditious measures due to it." (*Apologie* 2:176)

In the version of the fragments, this criticism is still completely missing. Because he could no longer view Jesus as exemplary on account of moral scruples, Reimarus obviously in the long run rejected Christianity lock, stock, and barrel. Since he retained the traditional, humanistic perception of Jesus as the teacher of an ideal morality, a conspicuously fractured image of Jesus is apparent in his writings.

Emphasizing the worldly character of the messianism of Jesus, Reimarus wanted to refute the teaching of Christ as the spiritual redeemer of humanity through two antitheses: worldly, not spiritual; particularly Jewish, not universal. In addition to this, Reimarus made use of a second line of argumentation: the distinction between the objective of Jesus and the objectives of his disciples. An entire chapter of the *Apologie* is devoted to the question of "whether Jesus, by means of his reformation of Jewish superstition, outside of reasonable religion, also had introduced supernatural mysteries" (2:39–72). The answer is that it is not heard in his original teaching. We should remind ourselves of Toland's work *Christianity Not Mysterious* (see above). For Reimarus, the parables of Jesus cannot be brought into play in order to oppose this, for in them Jesus spoke to the "common people," while he unveiled everything to his first disciples (2:45–46). In regard to the expression "supernatural mysteries," Reimarus understood in the first place the teaching of the Holy Spirit and of the Trinity (2:73–96). According to Old Testament linguistic use, the Spirit cannot be a person. The term has more to do with the ordinary and extraordinary gifts of God, something that is repeated in the New Testament. One may see the Trinity only in the baptismal formula at the end of the Gospel of Matthew (28:19). The ancient church had known only baptism in the name of Jesus (Acts 2:38; 22:16; *Apologie* 2:86–90). This trinitarian formula could only have been inserted into Matt 28 at a later time.

Everything in the New Testament that is specifically Christian goes beyond natural religion or contradicts it. Reimarus traces this Christian content back to the program of the apostles. The disciples had hoped, at least until the crucifixion, for nothing other than the earthly reign of the Jews under Jesus as the Messiah. When their hopes were disappointed as a result of his death, they fled and carved out a new plan: they made from the earthly Messiah a spiritual redeemer, who, according to the predictions of the prophets, must suffer for the sins of humanity, be resurrected, and then journey to heaven. From here he would return in power and majesty in a short time.

According to Reimarus, this entire system rests on the alleged facts of the resurrection. Since these facts were false and fictitiously invented by the disciples, "so is all of Christianity, which has been built on them from the ground floor up (i.e., what namely concerns the doctrines of faith). Thus its initial construction is demonstrated to be groundless" (*Apologie* 2:306). The view of the content of faith as facts and a coherent system in and of itself Reimarus shares with the orthodox apologists of Christianity. Since this understanding of faith is defended by the demonstration of facts, it can be dismantled by means of the refutation of established facts. As regards content, Reimarus ascribes everything to the teaching of the apostles, which speaks against what is considered to be normative, natural religion, and he therefore devalues it. For Reimarus, this oppositional teaching refers to what is the "purpose" (or "program") imposed by the apostles. This teaching is Jewish in its essential form: the proclamation of the spiritual redeemer who suffers for the sins of humanity, is resurrected, journeys to heaven, and comes back again from the clouds is tied up with Jewish views (the Pharisaic view of the resurrection of all humans from the dead at the end of time and the apocalyptic expectations of the return of the humble, suffering redeemer in majesty from the clouds).

In actuality, for Reimarus the contents of the faith are involved in his critical assessment. In his "preliminary report," which he only later placed at the head of the *Apologie*, he describes how he had come to doubt the systematic edifice of teaching rehearsed when he was a child. Besides, he observes that this program cannot be documented from the Bible and is actually incompatible with the thoughts about a most wise, extremely virtuous, and highest being who wishes to impart knowledge that brings about blessing (*Apologie* 1:47). Thus he could not accept particular doctrines such as the incomprehensible, certainly irrational teaching of the Trinity; or what speaks against the natural feeling of morality, for example, the God who punishes eternally or the doctrine of original sin (2.451–74); or what directly repudiates the Enlightenment's optimistic view of human nature. Reimarus came to these views during his decades of critical study of the Bible. It is also clear from his earlier manuscripts (*Kleine gelehrte Schriften* [Small Learned Writings]), which also are accessible in print, that texts like John 3:16 and 1 John 4:16 depict the starting point in his view of God: God is love, and, as a perfect being, he desires the eternal good fortune of his creatures (cf., *inter alia*, *Apologie* 2:415).

For individual observations, Reimarus often could refer to precursors. New was the radicalism with which he advanced the consequences of his criticism, extending to a complete rejection of the view that the revelation of Christian faith was based on the Bible. He certainly was not an atheist, but rather he believed in an all-wise, completely good God who reason may determine is present in creation and whom humans may serve properly only by means of moral acts. He could not make sense out of the depth of the biblical image of humanity. Therefore he could not understand the Lutheran doctrines of justification and reconciliation, which in his view the representatives of orthodoxy in Hamburg at that time presented in a rather distasteful manner.

Tensions in his thoughts are obvious. To be noted, however, are his important historical observations, including the continuing recognition of the distinction between the teaching of the earthly Jesus and the message of his disciples. In addition, he provided insights into the numerous contradictions in the Bible. To be sure, the literary problem of the origins of the Gospels and their mutual dependence was still unknown to him. Given his timeless, systematic thought, he could not understand the witness of a historical religion, which is what the Bible describes. His great editor, Lessing, had precisely and clearly known of this problem, but also could not discover a solution.

5.5. Supporting the Spirit against the Letter: Gotthold Ephraim Lessing

We already have become familiar with Lessing as the editor of the fragments of Reimarus. He was born in 1729, the son of a Lutheran pastor and a pastor's daughter in Dimenz (Upper Lusatia). Raised in a moderate form of Lutheranism, he attended a primary Latin school of his home city, where he already attracted attention on account of his outstanding gifts. By means of a stipend from the sovereign, the elector Friedrich August II of Saxony, he was able to attend the elite school of the state of Saxony from 1741 to 1746, the Prince's School St. Afra in Meissen. Afterwards, he completed his studies in Leipzig. Because his family had many children, he was able to go to Leipzig by means of a stipend from the city of Kamenz. Primarily owing to his father's wishes, he began with the study of theology. But he soon abandoned theology and considered other disciplines. He quickly made contacts with the theater. The charm of the stage of the famed "Neuberin" (Friederike Karoline Neuber [1697–1760]) attracted many students. Inspired by her performances, he came to develop a personal relationship with her. In 1748, she performed along with her ensemble the debut of his first comedy, *Der junge Gelehrte* (The Young Scholar). Later, Lessing began the study of medicine, but he did not finish this course. Then he was active as a journalist. When the theater of the Neuberin went bankrupt in the fall of 1748 and the actors left him as the guarantor for their debts, he was forced to flee via Wittenberg (where he briefly studied) to Berlin. There he made the risky choice to enter the life of a private journalist. In the *Berlinisch Privilegierten Zeitung* (Privileged Newspaper of Berlin; "Privileged" means that the newspaper received a special royal privilege to appear), he wrote under the rubric of "Scholarly Things," and then later in the *Vossischen Zeitung* he added "Das Neueste aus dem Reich des Witzes" (The Newest from the Realm of Wit). He was further occupied as a writer for the theater, and his critical reviews were feared. In addition, he cultivated social contacts, above all with other writers in the pubs located in the old city. A stopover in Wittenberg in the winter of 1751–1752 brought his studies to a conclusion, allowing him to earn a master's degree in liberal arts. After having returned to Berlin, Lessing resumed his activities as a journalist and writer. In 1752, he came to know Moses Mendelssohn (1729–1786), philosopher and pioneer of Jewish emancipation. This developed into a lifelong friendship. He also made friends with the Enlightenment book seller and writer Friedrich Nicolai (1733–1811). He joined with these two to edit "Briefe, die neueste Literatur betreffend" (Letters concerning the Newest Literature), beginning in 1759. This became the organ for his many-sided activities as a reviewer. The bourgeois tragedy *Miss Sara Sampson*, created during this period, was one of his best-known pieces for the stage.

A world trip with a wealthy man of Leipzig, Gottfried Winkler, was planned in 1756 to last for three years. However, this journey ended prematurely in the Hague owing to the outbreak of the Seven Years' War (1756–1763). Prussian troops had marched into Saxony. Lessing returned to Leipzig immediately with Winkler and remained there until 1758, when he returned to Berlin. In 1760, he received an offer from General von Tauentzien, governor of Silesia, in Breslau, to become his secretary. Lessing accepted this post and spent five years there, free of material needs. He worked privately on the play *Minna von Barnhelm*. However, he came down with a serious fever in the summer of 1764. In 1765, he returned to Berlin and had to struggle with financial concerns once again. To deal with his most pressing needs, he was finally forced to sell his library. *Minna von Barnhelm* was completed, and it debuted in 1767. In addition, he finished the writing *Laokoon*, which deals with the theory of art.

In 1767, Lessing accepted an invitation to come to Hamburg as a consultant for the newly founded *Deutsche Nationaltheater* (German National Theater). The most important production during this three-year residency was the *Hamburgische Dramaturgie* (Hamburg Dramaturgy), in which he critically reviewed the performances of this theater. In addition, he almost completed the tragedy *Emilia Galotti*. After a relatively short time, this theater also went bankrupt. The same thing happened to a press in which Lessing had invested the last of his funds. In this cosmopolitan city, he had come to know the Reimarus family and his future opponent, the senior pastor Goeze, and Eva König, whom Lessing later married. At that time she was the wife of a rich merchant, whose death soon left her a widow with four children.

Finally, in the year 1770, Lessing found a continuing position as a librarian in the famous Ducal Braunschweiger Library in Wolfenbüttel, which today still keeps alive his memory. Lessing's private home, to which he moved after some years, opposite the then-empty castle (the court had moved to Braunschweig years ago), commemorates his residence in the town. During his several years in Wolfenbüttel, his theological writings, a topic in which we are especially interested in our context, were composed. In the series *Zur Geschichte und Literatur: Aus den Schätzen der Herzoglichen Bibliothek zu Wolfenbüttel* (Concerning History and Literature. From the Treasures of the Ducal Library in Wolfenbüttel), having been freed from the limitations of censorship by his duke, he published a series of "rescues of texts," which included among others the preservation of the instruction of the Lord's Supper by Berengar of Tours (ca. 999–1088) as well as Leibniz's teaching concerning the punishments of hell. His activities were interrupted by a journey to Italy with Prince Maximilian of Braunschweig, during which he was received in Vienna by Empress Maria Theresia and Emperor Joseph II, and in Rome by Pope Pius VI. However, he was more interested in the libraries and scholars and brought back with him to Wolfenbüttel a valuable collection of Italian books.

By 1774, Lessing had begun to publish anonymously in his series the first fragments of Reimarus. Initially there was little public commotion over this. By the end of 1777, however, when Lessing had put out an additional four fragments, including in particular the provocative fifth one, which denied the resurrection of Jesus and represented the disciples as deceivers, the chief pastor in Hamburg, Johann Melchior Goeze, published his first article against Lessing and began to collect a number of these under the title, "Lessings Schwächen" (Lessing's Weaknesses). The storm broke with fierce vehemence, when in 1778 a special separate publication of the fragment *Vom Zwecke Jesu und seiner Jünger* (Concerning the Purpose of Jesus and His Disciples) was available for purchase. This fragment attacked the core affirmations of the New Testament (see above). The flames of the famous controversy concerning the fragments began to burn brightly. This happened directly after Lessing, who had married Eva König in 1776, experienced the greatest catastrophe of his life: the death of his newborn son during Christmas 1777, and the loss of his wife in the beginning of January 1778 as a consequence of the birth. In response to Goeze's criticism, Lessing answered in the form of a letter, "Anti-Goeze." This was followed in turn by the tractates *Parabel* and *Axiomata*. Important for Lessing's lay theological statements are the *Gegensätze des Herausgebers* (Oppositions of the Editor), which he published with the fragments of 1777. Already at that time he made it clear that he did not concur with the position of the "Unnamed." In addition to his opposition to Goeze, he contended also with Wolfenbüttel's superintendent, Heinrich Ress, who had published anonymously a polemical pamphlet against the fragment on the resurrection. Lessing replied with a "rejoinder" to this pamphlet and also wrote in opposition to Johann Daniel Schumann from Hanover the essay "Über den Beweis des Geistes und der Kraft" (Concerning the Evidence of the Spirit and Power).

In August of 1778, the controversy came to an abrupt halt, when the duke, through an order of the cabinet, forbade Lessing to write any further, uncensored publications in religious affairs either within or outside of the state. In addition, Lessing was required to deliver promptly the manuscript from which the fragments had come. Even so, Lessing's creativity was not stifled. He still completed his last drama, *Nathan der Weise* (Nathan the Wise), in which he developed the motif of the three rings from Giovanni Boccaccio's (1313–1375) *Decamerone* into a parable for religious tolerance. The popular interpretation of the drama as a plea for tolerance does not seem correct. In the context of Lessing's earlier utterances on the problem of truth, it rather appears as a witness of Lessing's resignation: if the truth remains lost forever, to keep peace between the adherers of different beliefs is the only solution that remains. This was a manner of thinking that originated with the Freemasons. In 1771, Lessing had become a Mason; however, he had soon distanced himself from the lodge on account of certain disagreements he had with their thinking. In 1780 the final version of *Die Erziehung des Menschengeschlechts* (The Education of Humankind) appeared. Lessing had already published the first fifty-three paragraphs in 1777 in his "Gegensätzen des Herausgebers" (Oppositions of the Editor, *Werke* 7:476–88). He referred to himself in the final publication of this work only as the editor, although his author-ship is almost certain as well. In the year 1780, Lessing's bodily strength noticeably decreased. Afflicted by various illnesses, he died on 15 February 1781.

For Lessing's theology and his final interpretation of the Bible, the writing *Die Erziehung des Menschengeschlechts* (The Education of Human-kind) is the classic document. The final version is divided into one hundred paragraphs and follows the form of a rationalistic, philosophi-cal treatment. In content, to be sure, it does not conform to this formal approach, but rather reflects, especially toward the end, many subjective thoughts and feelings of its author.

Already in the preface (*Erziehung*, Helbig, 9), Lessing uses a stylistic device by which he distances himself from the content. As the "editor," he contrasts himself to the author of the treatise, from whom he expects a hint concerning the historical significance of religions. From a lofty point (the "hill"), he wants to obtain an overview that reaches beyond the day. Certainly, we may not expect this to be a comprehensive treatment of the history of religion (one has wished on occasion to designate Lessing as the first historian of religion). In actuality, irrespective of a postulated polytheism of the primeval period, the essay concerns only the religions of Judaism and Christianity, which, in the structure of a religious-phil-osophical design, have been placed in a historical progression. This is compared with the history of humanity. The general theme is a theory of history: Lessing understands the history of humanity as consisting of stages of a process of education. He takes up a widespread understanding of the Enlightenment that can be found already in the writings of several church fathers up to Augustine and is evidenced in pietism (see *Univer-salverbesse rung* [Universal Improvement], by A. H. Francke). In §§1–3, Lessing reflects on the role of revelation in regard to this fundamental notion:

> What involves the education of individual humans is also a revelation for the entire human could not obtain from himself, but it provides that, which he could obtain from himself more swiftly and easily. In the same way also revelation provides nothing to humanity, which human reason, left to itself, would not have obtained, but it provided it earlier and con-tinues to provide the most important of those things.

One has frequently pointed to the difference from §77, where Lessing, in the form of a rhetorical statement, says about the Christian religion that it had been capable of coming "by all means to a closer and better idea of the divine nature, our nature, and our relationships to God than human reason can come." However this statement is to be understood within the frame of the dialogical form, which carries through the entire writing. Thus, Lessing engages in discourse at the same time with himself and with the reader. In §4 Lessing is clearly a man of the Enlightenment: the distinction between "accidental truths of history" and "necessary truths of reason" is also found in the well-known sentence in Über den Beweis des Geistes und der Kraft" (Concerning the Demonstration of the Spirit and the Power), which appeared in 1777: "Accidental truths of history can never demonstrate the necessary truths of reason" (Werke 8:12). Overall, the tractate Die Erziehung des Menschengeschlechts is not to be understood without looking at the other polemical writings in the period of the debate concerning the fragments. As a man of the Enlightenment, Lessing explains human history or the Jewish Christian history of religion as reflecting an increasing development in the knowledge obtained through reason. Islam and Asian religions are not to be found in this treatment, while the religions of other heathen peoples are placed on the periphery (§§20–21). To ask about the role of revelation in this development, Lessing found it necessary to accept the views of Reimarus, which he came to know in his publication of the Reimarus fragments. Using these, he consciously challenged the protest of Goeze and other critics. There are questions involved that bother him existentially. Thus, he stresses already in the Gegensätzen des Herausgebers (Oppositions of the Editor) that reason has its limits. For example, one may note his statement that "a *certain* apprehension of reason simply rests beneath the obedience of faith in the essential ideas of a revelation" (Werke 7:463; cf. 462). Revelation, as a means of education, becomes integrated into the process of the development of the stages of human reason.

The basic division of history into three periods provides the tractate with its essential structure. Lessing may have appropriated these from Joachim of Fiore (§§87–89, and later; see History, vol. 2). Following a polytheistic, primeval beginning, the three periods are (1) the period of the Israelite (Jewish) people (§§8–50), (2) the period of Christianity (§§51–75), and (3) the expected period of the "eternal gospel" (§86; according to Rev 14:6–7). The characterization of the Israelite people as "the most brutish and the wildest" (§8) and as "crude" (§§11, 16) is traditional. God worked as the educator of this coarse group of people, who "were still in their infancy" (§16). Here "education and revelation coincide" (§17). The law, which Moses gave to the people, served as the means of education.

Its observance or nonobservance was alone decisive for the nation's fortune (§17). "Thus, the people's point of view, as of yet, did not go beyond
this life, since they had no conception of a future life" (ibid.). The English
deists (especially Thomas Morgan, *The Moral Philosopher* [1738–1740])
had objected to the lack of the expectation of eternal life and to the sacred
character of the Old Testament. The English apologist William Warburton
(1698–1779), in his three-volume work *The Divine Legislation of Moses*
(1737–1741, reprinted 1978), had, in a paradoxical way, introduced the
same elements into the discussion as a positive evidence for the divine
nature of the Old Testament. Because, in his view, there was no knowledge
in the Old Testament concerning reward and punishment in the world
beyond, Israel had been able to survive only by means of divine providence. Without viewing the future in terms of reward and punishment,
an understanding that provides the normal condition necessary for the
maintenance of ethics, Israel could not have continued apart from providential guidance. While Lessing finds Warburton's arguments excessive
(§24), he agrees with him that the lack of this teaching's view of the future
attests to nothing negative concerning the sacred nature of the Old Testament (§22). His reasoning is that Moses was sent only to the Israelite
people *of that time* (§23) and wrote something comparable to an elementary book for children. Thus, he passed over elements of science and art
(§26), which were still not suitable for a particular age. It is for this reason
that the teaching of the future life could be lacking in the Old Testament.
However, the Old Testament should contain nothing that would have
delayed the people on their upward journey to obtain their proper goal.
"And what would have delayed it more than if this wondrous recompense
would have been promised in this life and by one who does not promise
anything that he does not fulfill?" (§27). Added to this is the consideration that the pious man who was fortunate and died in old age, tired of
life, would hardly long for another life. Even less would the evildoer, who
already cursed his present life because he felt the punishment (§30).

Lessing sees a new phase for the Israelites occurring "during the cap-
tivity under the wise Persian" (§35; Cyrus II [559–530 B.C.E.] is meant; cf.
§39). Whereas previously the people's ideas about Jehovah (Yahweh) were
restricted, because "he was more feared than loved" (§34), they now "began
to measure him against the conception of Being of all Beings, providing a
more proficient reason to recognize and worship him" (§35). "Revelation
had guided its reason, and now reason has enlightened revelation once
again" (§36). When they came to recognize "in Jehovah not simply the
greatest of all national gods, but rather God," whom they recovered once

more from their sacred writings" (§39), they returned as a purified people." One no longer was to think of idolatry and apostasy (§40). Because of their teaching of the immortality of the soul, the Jews came to be known among the Chaldeans (Neo-Babylonians), the Persians, and the Greek philosophical schools in Egypt. This faith in a universal God, however, could never find a firm footing in the entire nation, but rather was expressed only "in a certain sect" (presumably he means the Essenes) (§43). Lessing finds, then, all kinds of "preliminary practices, reflections, and hints" (§47) in the "elementary book," which possessed "every good attribute for a childish people" (§50). However, these were still reserved for "a certain age," that is, for a "childish people" (§51). "A better pedagogue must come and tear from the hands of the child the creative elementary book. Christ came" (§51). With his coming, the "elementary book," that is, the Old Testament, was no longer used.

For the "part of humanity whom God wished to engage in an educational plan" (§54), that is to say, "who needed and wanted nobler, worthier, reasons for moral actions, were motivated by more than temporal rewards and punishments" (§55). But then "Christ became the first *credible and practical* teacher of the immortality of the soul" (§58). Christ becomes believable through his miracles and his "resuscitation" (§59). Lessing characteristically allows the question to remain unanswered whether we can demonstrate this. "Everything then could have become important, which leads to the *acceptance* of his teaching. Now it is no longer so important to come to the acknowledgement of the truth of his teaching" (ibid.). As a *practical* teacher, Christ can be deemed to be effective, because he has taught that the immortality of the soul is to be assumed, not only as philosophical speculation but also by corresponding actions (§61). He was especially the first "to recommend an inner purity of the heart in the view of another life" (§61). The apostles have propagated this teaching and increased it with the addition of other doctrines. The New Testament writings, which have originated from them, have "delivered the second, improved elementary book for humanity" (§64), which "for seventeen hundred years has engaged human understanding more than all other books" (§65). The fact that so many nations have entered into disputation with this book has "led to the recognition that human understanding has been more assisted by this engagement than would be the case if each nation would have had especially for itself its own elementary book" (§66). And even in the present, it is still necessary. Lessing warns against impatience those who perhaps may already have advanced beyond the New Testament: "Take care, more capable individual, you who stamp excitedly and radiate enthusiasm when arriving at the last page of this elementary book; take care not to allow your weaker classmates to perceive what you sense or already are beginning to see" (§68). This statement obviously is not meant to be taken literally, that is, that a "more capable individual" reads the last page of the book of Revelation. Rather, the respective reader is eager to gain the knowledge that goes almost beyond the New Testament and therefore is like an impatient, waiting cart-horse, which burns with the desire finally to be able to move forth. To do so would be premature. In the paragraphs that follow, Lessing mentions examples of why it is still profitable in the present to be occupied with the New Testament. It is because it contains truths, "which we ... should as long gaze upon, until they learn to derive reason from their other perceived truths and then combines them" (§72). Such examples are the doctrines of the Trinity, original sin, and the atonement of the Son. Speculating over this matter, Lessing considers it legitimate, because "the development of revealed truths into the truths of reason is absolutely necessary, if humankind shall be helped by this" (§76). The relativism concerning history, which stands behind these convictions, is immediately discernible when Lessing next asks: "And why should we not consider the possibility that it could be through a religion about the historical truth (which is critical if one so desires) that humans are led, nonetheless, to convergent ideas about the divine nature and our nature which human reason would never have come to realize?" (§77; see above). Speculations of this kind are useful, because they exercise reason in dealing with spiritual matters, which reason needs "if it is to succeed in reaching its complete enlightenment and generate that kind of purity of heart which makes us able to love virtue for itself" (§80). The time of completion will come, expects Lessing, when man "will do the good, because it is the good, not because arbitrary rewards are offered" (§85). The proximity to Kant's ethics is clear here.

According to Lessing, this will be the time of the "eternal gospel," which, however, is not yet here. In this hope, the "enthusiasts of the thirteenth and fourteenth centuries," of which Lessing speaks in §87, erred; and yet, however, it is to be expected in a still unknown future. Lessing essentially agrees with their statement "that the new covenant must become *antiquated* as well, when it also has become old" (§88). The error of the enthusiasts (§90) consisted only in their proclaiming that the advent of this time has drawn near (§87). This was premature, because humans in that time were still without the necessary enlightenment (§89). Even now this will proceed very slowly and "imperceptibly" until this time will come. But then, even the second elementary book (i.e., the New Testament), shall be overtaken!

Finally Lessing draws the conclusion that actually the individual also must reproduce the entire process of this development. He argues that this may be possible only through repeated returns from the dead (§94), a much-considered thesis. This would make possible the securing of new understandings and abilities that one cannot reach in a *single* lifetime (§98). These are the thoughts that Lessing grasped at the end of his life. The premonition that he would not continue to live many more months had become a certainty for him. His bold hope allowed him a final perspective: "And what have I to miss? Is not the whole of eternity mine?" (§100).

With his recollection of the enthusiasts of the thirteenth and fourteenth centuries, especially Joachim von Fiore, Lessing provides us with an indication of his presuppositions. Fiore was a spiritualist, and Lessing becomes more and more like one in the later pages of his writings, which are also increasingly formulated in a manner more personal than one would expect. Like Fiore, he also expects a time, not too distant in the future, when not only the Old but also the New Testament would be superfluous. Already in the *Gegensätzen des Herausgebers* from 1777, he had expressed that Reimarus's attacks on the Bible could not irritate him, even if his criticisms are correct, for "the letter is not the Spirit; and the Bible is not the religion. Accordingly, objections against the letter and against the Bible are not objections against the Spirit and against the religion" (*Werke* 7:458). In this matter, he opposes primarily the orthodox, his critics on the right, who sought to maintain the authority of the Bible through clinging to the inspiration of the "letter." Additional arguments included, for example, the view that "religion precedes the Bible" (because the oral proclamation is prior to it), that it "obviously contains more than what belongs to religion," and that it is purely a hypothesis that the Bible must be infallible (ibid.). Nevertheless, these do not allow one to misjudge the kernel of his approach.

This is not the first time that rationalism and spiritualism have touched one another. On the one hand, Lessing formulates the view that "[r]eligion is not true, because the Evangelists and the apostles have taught it. Rather they have taught it, because it is true" (*Werke* 7:458; cf. also "Axiomata," *Werke* 8:148). On the other hand, he criticizes the rationalistic practice of preaching performed by his contemporaries. "The pulpits, instead of renouncing the entrapment of reason under guise of the obedience of faith, now resound with nothing but the inner ties between reason and faith." Thus, he advocates that reason very probably finds "things ... which exceed their perception.... For what is a revelation that does not reveal anything?" (*Werke* 7:461–62). He seeks to establish a middle path (7.461) between the "decrying of reason in the pulpits" (7:332) and its opposite. That he is willing to make room for even traditional dogmatic teachings such as the Trinity, original sin, and the atonement of the Son ("Erziehung," §§73–75) points to a Lutheran background from which he will not depart. This is further indicated by his plan to write a biography of Luther, which he never carried out. However, the Bible continues, including the New Testament, to be a historical witness, in the same way that all written traditions are able to be explained by reason of their "inner truth" ("Axiomata," X; *Werke* 8:149ff.).

Contemporary scholars noted mostly that Lessing provided for the first time a universal, historical design. The interpretation of nineteenth-century history took this up. However, his especially religious-philosophical theories receded from view. In the history of biblical interpretation, what has mainly been remembered about Lessing is that he regarded the Old Testament as an "elementary book" and therefore saw it as having become obsolete. He also regarded the New Testament as an "elementary book" that in time would be surpassed in an anticipated future, which continues to go forward.

5.6. Understanding the Biblical Writings from Their Period: Johann Salomo Semler

Johann Salomo Semler, born in 1725, was the son of a Lutheran pastor and a pastor's daughter. His birthplace was Saalfeld (Thüringen). During his school years in Saalfeld, at the time a small residential city of a duchy, pietism was gaining social influence, in part owing to the favor of the court. Compelled by his father's wish, the young Semler participated in the pietistic hours of edification. He found the piety that was practiced there to be hypocritical. While historical criticism and academic theology were repudiated by the pietists of Saalfeld, Semler, by contrast, found himself to be attracted to historical work. From 1743 to 1750, he studied in Halle, especially classical philology, history, logic, and mathematics, and, beginning in 1744, principally theology. Professor Sigmund Jacob Baumgarten (1706–1757), a famous scholar who possessed an orthodox outlook but also had historical interests, contributed to Semler's theological study. Baumgarten was indirectly a patron of the Enlightenment against his own intentions. By means of his *Nachrichten von einer hal-*

lischen Bibliothek (Reports from a Library in Halle), he informed experts in Germany, among other places, about deist works in England. Baumgarten became aware of the gifts of the young Semler, took him into his house, and entrusted the youth with many kinds of small, remunerated assignments to assist him. Among these were work on the *Nachrichten* and editorial work on a new edition of the Lutheran *Book of Concords* (1749; 2nd ed. 1761). This allowed Semler to provide his parents with a little financial assistance toward his education. In one work, he sought to demonstrate the originality of 1 John 5:7, a passage in which orthodoxy found evidence for the Trinity. This earned Semler a master's degree in 1750, thus concluding his studies. Up to this point he followed completely the orthodox views of his teacher, Baumgarten. Subsequent to the end of his studies, he accepted a position as editor for the *Coburger Staats und Gelehrtenzeitung* (Coburg State and Scholars Newspaper). By 1751, however, he was called to the post of professor of German legal history and Latin poetry at the University of Altdorf (near Nuremberg). His assignment as a historian pleased him very much, and his scrupulous devotion to his work at Altdorf led him to tarry in accepting the call to the theological faculty at Halle, which he had received in the spring of 1752. His ideas at the time were so provocative, and he was not yet to receive his doctor of theology degree from Altdorf until 1753. After he had been promoted, he finally accepted the call to Halle. While he kept his distance from his pietistic colleagues there, he remained in close contact with his teacher, Baumgarten. After Baumgarten's premature death, Semler published several of his works posthumously. Baumgarten has been labeled a transitional theologian who maintained his Lutheran-orthodox approach even though he tried to explain its positions with rational arguments. Nevertheless, Semler soon began to withdraw from his teacher's theological position.

Outwardly, Semler's life proceeded along rather peaceful paths. He held the chair in theology at Halle until the end of his life. A theological professor at that time had to cover a broad spectrum of areas in his teaching. Thus, Semler was expected to present lectures over hermeneutics and church history. In addition to the teaching of dogmatics, moral theology, apologetics, the interpretation of biblical books was to follow. Semler also authored numerous writings that contained readings not always simple to understand owing to the complexity of his style. His reputation at the university is demonstrated by the fact that he was the prorector during the years 1761–1762, 1770–1771, and 1789–1790. He was the representative of the king as the official rector, and this was the highest elected office of the university. He often was the dean of the faculty. He experienced an affront when, in spite of his opposition, along with that of the theological faculty, the minister Karl Abraham of Zedlitz (1731–1793), approved the appointment of the notoriously radical Enlightenment theologian, Karl Friedrich Bahrdt (1741–1792) as a private lecturer to the theological faculty. As a result, in 1779 Semler was removed as seminar director, a post he had held for many years. Because of this, he refused to accept the position of prorector in 1780. Still, he did not resign, and the vitality of his intellect did not decrease. He published many additional writings during the last decade of his life. His last work, *Letztes Glaubensbekenntnis* (The Final Confession of Faith), was published posthumously in 1792. Semler died after a brief illness on 14 March 1791.

One usually and correctly associates the significance of Semler for the history of biblical interpretation with his four-volume work *Abhandlung von freier Untersuchung des Canon* (Treatise on the Free Investigation of the Canon [1771–1775]). One can with certainty evaluate correctly Semler's intentions, if one correlates them with his theology as a whole. At first glance, many things appear to be contradictory. Some have even spoken of a break between the earlier and the later Semler. A closer inspection, however, indicates that he did not fundamentally alter his point of view. The different influences that acted upon him, one can easily perceive. It is hardly correct to call him a Lutheran, a point often made by later scholars. Formally he belonged to a Lutheran faculty, and in official declarations (as in the case of Bahrdt) these professors appealed customarily to the Augsburg Confession. And when the opportunity arose, Semler himself invoked a similar loyalty to Lutheran teaching and tradition. In reality, however, he viewed Lutheranism from a particular angle. For his personal view, he refers to Luther, for instance, in respect to pointing to his unencumbered judgment about some of the books of the Bible. Luther is decisively important for him insofar as he had overturned the authority of the church, which was based on the theology of the church fathers of the first five centuries and taught humans, with respect to the dogmatic contents of the Bible, "to follow alone their own unfettered conscience" (*Einleitung in die dogmatische Gottesgelehrsamkeit* [Introduction to Dogmatic Instruction], in Baumgarten, *Glaubenslehre* 2:143–44). Semler values similarly, among other things, the Augsburg Confession. He considers that this document presupposes only general rules of interpretation and is without "any dependence upon a learned or pious authority" (145). That he had a general rapport with Luther's key affirmation of the justification of the sinner through faith alone (see *History,* vol. 3) is doubtful,

even if he occasionally defends this teaching, for example, in his arguments against Emanuel Swedenborg (1688–1772; *Unterhaltungen mit
Herrn Lavater* [Conversations with Mr. Lavater, 1787], 7–8 263, 416–17,
426ff.). When he occasionally comes to speak at length about biblical
passages, for example, "Christ has died for our sins" (1 Cor 15:3) or "my
blood is poured out for forgiveness of sins" (Mark 14:24 par.), he strives
to move beyond the literal understanding held by others that he tolerates
for such passages. He explains them accordingly: "what is general in these
texts is the teaching of the previously unknown moral goodness and the
grace of God towards humans who wish to exchange their morally corrupt
condition with the free enjoyment of a moral order and the true worship
of God" (*Letztes Glaubensbekenntnis,* 167). It is also noteworthy that he
integrated the teaching of the atonement of Christ for sins (197) into the
public forms of the teaching of Protestantism. In his view, this teaching
of the atonement possesses value above all as a sign of difference from
Catholics and Socianians. In contrast to this, his high value placed on
Melanchthon and his students is striking: "Melanchthon's writings merit
the same kind of attention given to others" (in Baumgarten, *Glaubenslehre*
3:31). Judgments such as these can be multiplied easily from other writings of Semler. This is unusual for a time in which Melanchthon's standing
in both orthodoxy and pietism was not very high. However, Melanchthon
is the theologian who most closely related Lutheranism to humanism.
Semler was especially critical of Flacius (see above) and his disciples(see in
Baumgarten, *Glaubenslehre*, 3:43 and n. 20). Humanism as the ideal both
of education and of a strong moral character permeates his work. Admittedly, it has been noted that the term "moral" at this time was understood
more as a designation for the spiritual realm (in contrast to the physical
world). Semler often uses the term "spiritual" when speaking of the moral.
Subsequently, the improvement of humans in respect to ethical actions,
frequently found in Semler's utterances, is their actual "spiritual" goal. He
squares this with humanistic concerns. Finally, one should observe what
has been regarded frequently as a special doctrine of Semler: his distinction between a "private religion" and a "public" (or "church") religion.
Beginning in the 1770s there appears in Semler's writings (initially noted
in his *Letzte Glaubensbekenntnis*) the presupposition for his much-noted
position on the so-called Woellnersche Religionsedikt of 1788 (Woellner's
Religious Edict). In the edict, decreed by Friedrich Wilhelm II through his
minister, Johann Christoph of Woellner (1732–1800), reference is made
to church confessions and a peaceable association among the churches is
demanded. Polemics from the pulpit and the making of proselytes is for-

bidden. Surprising to many, Semler in his *Vertheidigung des Königl. Edikts vom 9te Jul. 1788* (Defense of the Royal Edict on the 9 July 1788) expressly consented to this edict. He could do that because he subjected the outward expression of religion completely to the view of the state. The state could not touch the private religion of the individual. This reminds one of the debate between Melanchthon and the so-called Gnesio-Lutherans under Flacius concerning the *adiaphora* (see *History*, vol. 3), in which his answer, influenced by humanism, was that many external rites in the church are inconsequential for the faith, for example, those that were central to the controversy between the Anglicans and the Puritans (see above, 24, 30, 52).

In Semler's *Letztes Glaubensbekenntnis*, which contains most of the discussion about this issue, Semler characterizes at the outset (1ff.) the two different forms of religion generally in a religio-historical fashion. These forms occur in all religions (Judaism, Islam, Brahmanism [Hinduism], and natural religion). While external religion is clearly defined on the basis of a particular, locally established, historical tradition of a faith community civically ordered and jointly shaped through public servants of a religion for a community's cultic rituals performed in worship, private religion is described as "inward," "moral," and "resting on continuing self-understanding and usage." (8). The latter, however, is never entirely specified. Apart from what is stressed about the individual distinctiveness of the forms (5, 65, 69–70, etc.), what is said about private religion becomes lodged in insinuations. It depends on ongoing, personal knowledge and its exercise (8). It is built on experience, namely, on a "freely invisible power of God, which we ourselves experience and which makes us blessed through Christ" (162).

However, individual religion also issues from "the new and personal certain recognition that God is the gracious, holy, and infinite God of all humans and looks only upon the doings of humans as far as they recognize the good" (73; cf. 102). This personal religion is "an individual, inner movement of one's understanding, judgment, and inclination toward God, Christ, and the Spirit of God" (76). With this Semler appears, on the one hand, to mean an ethically practiced Christianity in the sense of Erasmus (whose *Ratio* [see *History*, vol. 3] he published anew in 1777!). He names it on one occasion "practical religion" and points to the commandment to love God and to love the neighbor (134). The ideal would be when "all Christians exhibited their Christian worship of God by means of their ever more worthy moral behavior in fulfilling all ethical requirements" (109; cf. also the citation found in *Canon* 1.9). On the other hand, the remarks about the experience of God and the inworking of the Holy Spirit as characteristics of private religion signify the spiritual heritage that was continued through the pietism of Halle. In spite of his distancing himself from its excesses, Semler did not remain untouched by pietistic influences. As we saw, a strong individualism was a characteristic of spiritualism and pietism. To spiritualism also belonged the distinction between the Word of God and the Holy Spirit, even if Semler himself did not take this decisive step for understanding the purpose of Scripture. Together with his teacher, Baumgarten, Semler came to the distinction between the inspiration of Scripture and the direct, divine revelation (which at the same time was more narrow as well as broader than it was perceived in prescriptural forms; see Baumgarten, *Glaubenslehre* 3:32–35). This marked an important step away from the orthodox understanding of the Bible (on Johann Gerhard, see above, 13–22).

Finally, individual knowledge, which is frequently mentioned as the premise of accessing personal religion, is also the typical, key term of the Enlightenment. Semler understands this in terms of the different stages of personal, intellectual ability ("at least neither Christ nor an apostle has demanded that all Christians must have … the same degree of knowledge" [*Letztes Glaubensbekenntnis*, 171–72]). One who is deficient in it may nevertheless be content and still engage in the public practice of religion! Behind the separation between public and private religion is concealed the Enlightenment's thesis of priestly deception. The accusation, which on the surface is directed only at the Catholic clergy (pope, bishops, and monks), that the clergy have suppressed the freedom of Christians to favor their own claim to power in the church, veils imperfectly Semler's reservation about "popery" (112) or "clericalism" (156). On the other side, Semler still emphasizes expressly the necessity of "the public form of religion" as well as responsible, public religious servants (ibid.). However, "ceremonies" are external features and do not belong to the essence of religion. On the contrary: "These ceremonies attributed much more the propensity of behavior to the sensual desire among the Jews and the heathens, rather than to a moral sense that would have made it a personal obligation for all the participants in this public exercise of religion" (212). In other places (e.g., the preface to Baumgarten's *Geschichte der Religionspartheyen*, 12), Semler says even more clearly that this external form of religion may be grounded "in this incapacity and inactivity of the powers of the soul." Instead of these external rites, one "should have attempted, as far as possible, to induce humans to the exercise of their own powers of the soul." At the same time, he recognizes in this same connection that the introduction of ceremonies into ancient Christianity for people of that time may have been necessary, since these people were less disposed to an inner regard and practice of general truths" (5–6). In regard to the Catholics of the ancient church, Semler remarks that it is said they were "not half as able as Pelagius (whom Augustine opposed) to cultivate the inner Christian religion" (14).

Taken together, there was a rather colorful array of the different influences on Semler along with other theologians whom he met in 1770 in Magdeburg: August Friedrich Wilhelm Sack (1703–1786), Johann Joachim Spalding (1714–1804), and Johann Friedrich Wilhelm Jerusalem (1708–1789), all subsumed under the name of "neologs" ("teachers of new things"). Among the New Testament scholars of hermeneutics one may mention in addition Johann August Ernesti (1707–1781). These theologians cultivated a moderate form of Enlightenment understanding. As a moderate, Semler could still be understood for his separation between public and private religion. This allowed him tolerance toward the official church. Likewise, he circumscribed his thinking compared to that of the more radical deists ("naturalists"), as becomes clear especially in his engaging in the controversy concerning the fragments (see above; *Beantwortung der Fragmente eines Ungenannten*, [Response to the Fragments of an Unnamed Writer], 1779; 2nd ed., 1780). Here he rejects the thesis of the disciples' deception and defends the reality of the resurrection of Jesus.

From this background, one also is able to understand the intention of his major work concerning the Bible, the often inconsistent *Abhandlung von freier Untersuchung des Canon* (Treatise on the Free Investigation of the Canon [4 vols.]). The content of this work demonstrates that its biblical hermeneutic places its main emphasis on the Old Testament. Especially of interest is the first treatise in volume 1 (*Von freier Untersuchung des Canons* [On the Free Investigation of the Canon] 1:1–128), which provides the title for the entire work. After this there follow other, equally comprehensive materials. In the second volume, the first treatment, which responds to two reviews, continues to elaborate the history of the understanding of inspiration and canon (1–236). In what follows, Semler responds to additional reviews. The third volume is structured in a similar fashion, while the fourth contains exclusively his remarks directed to the work of the professor of theology at Greifswald, Johann Ernst Schubert (1717–1774), and his volume *Abhandlung von der heiligen Schrift und deren Kanon* (Treatise on the Holy Scripture and Its Canon [1774]). Semler once again defends his position. For Semler's interaction with the Bible, two fundamental presuppositions are important. One is his avoidance of the orthodox Protestant interpretation of inspiration, and the other is the understanding of the canon that accompanies it. For Semler this concrete perspective was initiated already in the edition of Baumgarten's *Glaubenlehre*. However, this subject still remained up in the air in the second half of the eighteenth century. The abstruse extremeness of the theory of verbal inspiration was refuted by the textual criticism of the two Buxtorfs. Considerably earlier, they had dealt it a deathblow. We already have come to know about its effects on the New Testament. German biblical scholarship, in comparison with that of Western Europe, had to be viewed at the time of Semler almost as a straggler. As Semler's "historical introduction" to Baumgarten's *Glaubenslehre* shows, he was a distinguished expert of the diverse, yet hardly monotonous Protestant orthodox theological literature. He already had access to comprehensive information on the entire breadth of the Christian and non-Christian religions and confessions in Baumgarten's lecture *Geschichte der Religionspartheyen*.

Orthodoxy understood the Bible as the means of salvation (*medium salutis*), word for word, without any differences. Semler could not agree with this position, since he had learned to think historically. Already as a student studying under Baumgarten, Semler had worked as one of the editors of the German edition of the *General World History*, and even after his teacher's death he continued with the further editing of this work between 1758 and 1766, publishing numerous preambles and notations. Nor could he see the Bible as a timeless and uniform book, but rather came to a differentiated position about the origins of the individual books. The problem of the historical development, in and of itself, did not concern him, but rather it was the question of an outspoken theological and at the same time enlightened pedagogy that led him to ask: What are the contents of the individual biblical writings, and how far can their reading edify spiritually the contemporary student of the Bible? This means: "help that such a selective reader … be led to perform all good works, in which virtues and merits become shrewdly and capably performed? What belongs to the final objective and consequences of the established and rational religions and still more the Christian?" (*Canon* 1:9/Scheible 18). This depends on the content of the biblical writings, which may be designated as the Word of God. This examination should be recommended, contended Semler, immediately at the beginning (4/14), to such Christians who "should actually desire to use their capacity for evaluation. They are able to make about one and the same object rather different observations and perceptions, which most other so-called Christians are not capable of doing." We have to do with a thoroughly elitist undertaking! If now the different groups of Jews within Palestine (Sadducees, Pharisees, and Samaritans) and outside of Palestine (Hellenistic Jews in Egypt and elsewhere) had a thoroughly different canon and still were considered Jews, it is not stipulated that after the decision of the Protestants (e.g., Lutherans) to appropriate the canon of the Palestinian Jews, because it contains exclusively divine books, that this dismisses the larger canons of the Roman, early occidental, and Greek churches. Therefore, the examination of whether this is the case should remain open, since the church fathers at that time leave the matter to every insightful reader. The examination should be directed to the already mentioned purpose of the readings of these Scriptures. Later, in the third volume of his investigation, Semler delivered a response to the reviews of the first volume (in the form of an extract from Jacob Basnage's [1653–1723] church history [*Histoire de l'Église depuis Jésus Christ jusque à present*, History of the Church since Jesus Christ until the Present, 2 vols., 1699]). This contains a lengthy description of the controversy in the early church concerning the development of the canon (*Canon* 3:1–189). By his use of the historical perspective, Semler brought an entirely new point of view to the previously purely dogmatic discussion. Admittedly, in the occidental church, there had been an agreement about the more extensive (as compared with the Palestine/Hebrew) canon that was based on the Latin translation of the Septuagint. In spite of this, "it is certain that the general concept of the steady uniformity and equivalence of the canon is without a basis in fact and does not reflect historical accuracy, when it is understood differently by the *public* community and the *public* practice of religion." Thus, individually thinking Christians may not always have bound themselves to public practice. Publicly this means that the clerics may use Scripture for public reading and instruction within the official ecclesiological structures. This means, however, that "the special investigation of these books for all reflective readers, as regards their private use, has remained free. It could not be cancelled by the canon that is introduced for *public* use" (1:19/24). Once again the distinction between public and private religion is helpful, for it creates free space for private people. Besides, Semler stresses that the result of historical investigation also is involved (1:17); the second edition (Scheible 23) adds to this: "in seriousness and without personal prejudice." "The personal Christian religion of each *Subjecti* (person)" is not bound to the canon (1:20/25).

For the acceptance and handling of the biblical statements by an individual, Semler reckons (1:5, 21–22/26–27) with a divine process of education for humanity. This occurs first for the Jews and then for the pagans, who (according to Paul in Rom 2:14) can succeed to eternal happiness apart from the Jewish Torah and the taking over of the entire Old Testament, because they already had used the gifts of natural truths with which God had provided them. However, when pagans were motivated by such "moral ideas and principles," that is, possessed "a moral improvement and active ability in a virtuous behavior," they did not need to use the Jewish canon in any way. Admittedly, they could rejoice in the principles and corresponding attitudes present in some persons appearing in various books of the Jews. "However the question is whether these pious and honest experts of the inner virtue must and should consider all of these books to be divine according to their content, which the Jews use to have" (1:23/27). It is important that here the *content* of these books is made into the critical standard, and the key word *virtue* points at the same time in the direction where it is thought to reside. For Semler, who always maintains a critical distance from Judaism, those books of the Old Testament are ruled out as divine, if one is unable to discover in them preeminently ethical statements. For this, he mentions repeatedly the books of Ruth, Esther, Ezra, Nehemiah, and the Chronicles (1:23/27; see above). The books of Ruth and Esther, in which unimportant, purely Israelite events are narrated, are examples of texts that are not able to contribute anything to the enhancement of *moral* knowledge and therefore are useless for non-Jews (1:8, 34–38/35–38). This is true also for all of the "narratives and descriptions of the history of the exodus from Egypt, the establishment of policy, and the entire state of the Israelites, including their wars with the contiguous peoples, the separation of the twelve tribes, the inner disruption of both kingdoms, the Babylonian imprisonment, and the rebuilding of the city of Jerusalem once again,… since these are and remain common human changes" (1:24/27). Thus, every feature of salvation is denied to the entire sphere of the events of history. It should be added that these are special processes of Jewish history, which are without relevance for those who belong to other nations. From this the question answers itself: "Therefore what is the valid conclusion? Is it because the Jews hold these books to be *divine and sacred writings*, that other peoples must regard their content as divine and much more worthy than the narratives of history and special events occurring among other peoples?" (1:24/28). The main objection is that in Jewish history we have to do with a *particular* history, which signifies nothing for humanity as a whole, for it contains no *general* truths. It is obvious that there exists also in the background of Semler's thought what was also the case with Spinoza's understanding: there is an observable opposition between general (both philosophical and ethical) truths and accidental truths of history. Lessing gave this principle its classical formulation. Semler mainly relates this insight to the history of Israel. However, that he holds this truth to be more fundamentally valid becomes apparent in that he also can name in the New Testament the Letter to Philemon as an example for a text that originated for a special situation and is irrelevant to the contemporary reader (1:25/28).

It is only the church, by means of a historical notation, that can testify for the prior *existence* and former acceptance of these biblical books by the larger part of Jews and Christians, and then place them in this or that time" (1:27/29). Further, only the church may presently fix a canon for the exercise of external religion. In addition, one may observe that historically a large number of canonical limits can be observed for the inner private religion that determines which biblical texts are considered divine according to the criterion of their content. This thus deals with "interior obligation" (1:30/32). However, the traditional criteria for inspiration used for establishing canonicity are not sufficient. These are "(1) a divine book must not contradict the natural, generally *moral*, or other types of knowledge; (2) it must contain more than the natural knowledge of God contains; and (3) it must have originated in a supernatural manner" (1:30–31/32). Decisive for Semler is the view that the perfect religion of Christians long ago must have surpassed the religion of the Jews and natural religion and therefore only truths that correspond to this perfect knowledge are fitting criteria. Subsequently, some writings in the canon are eliminated, for they do not contain "*moral*, noble concepts and principles for the improvement of all humans in every age" (1:34/35). In the background stands Semler's "idea of perfectibility." This means that humanity on the whole is found to be engaged in a continual process of improvement in an ever more perfect form of religion. Thus, Christianity represents a higher stage than Judaism and heathenism, and within Christianity its early stage (in contrast to the traditional theory of degeneracy found from Tertullian to Gottfried Arnold) appears in a still imperfect form.

Abraham serves as an example for Semler. Abraham is a person "of moral knowledge and practice" (1:38/38) who displays in his behavior "the depiction of the concept of the perfect creature" (ibid.; cf. also: in "accord with the idea of a *morally* perfect creature" [1:40/39]), who has achieved such perfection partially through "his own considerations of God and his perfection and purposes" (1:39/38), partially through other persons, and partially through dreams (Scheible 38). He could obtain thereby the certain conviction that God is the originator of these ideas. Revealing here is the mixture of traditional, dogmatic convictions with the philosophical thoughts of God as the perfect being. We encountered this already in Spinoza, who used this mixture as the starting point of his "ethics" (see above). The consideration by that time, also traditional, was that the transmission of the knowledge of moral perfection to other people could also be understood as the continuing Word of God. There exists no difference in quality between the oral instruction and its eventual recording in written form.

Connected with this is the development of the idea of adaptation. It only now becomes effective in the history of exegesis. Already Abraham, in his oral instruction followed by its being written down, has adapted himself to meet the circumstances of the present hearers (1:40/41). Accordingly, there may be in addition to the revealed, general truths, which are authoritative for the employment of all readers in every period of time and various regions those contained "in all writings of this so-called canon, such places and parts of the texts and their composition, which virtually pass away with this period" (1:42/40). To the latter belong especially the particular narratives of Moses and the other historical books concerning the history of Israel, in which all fortune and well-being are imparted only to the chosen people of God, while one hears nothing of the political and moral history of other nations. This corresponds to the "uncultivated form of thought" of many Jews (1:44/41). To be sure, the Jews, who then were living among other nations and assumed the "culture of understanding" (1:45/41), later sought to discover through allegory general truths even in the historical narratives. Semler willingly allows that the "undeniable principles of real spiritual perfection and improvement of humans" are "not seldom in these books" (in the Old Testament)" (1:46/42) and characteristically names books that do so: Psalms, Proverbs, Ecclesiastes, and Job. He says of these, "It is certain that they were unquestionably from God!" (1:46/42–43; see also 1:46, 60/42, 50, among others). Semler, among others, especially values Solomon's prayer of the dedication of the temple (1 Kgs 8:14–53) (1:60; cf. 3:563). However, that could certainly not be the case of all twenty-four books of the Old Testament canon. Semler then mentions an entire series of narratives that do not serve "*moral* improvement" (1:47/43), and therefore it is not necessary to have knowledge of them. He suggests, in reference to Jean Morin, that older educated Jews already had distinguished between things that were important only for a time and things that continued to be indispensable

(1:48–50/44–45). Conversely, Semler is convinced that "reasonable, honorable, virtuous *naturalists* among the heathen have received by all means their moral knowledge from God and could actually have learned from the writings of the Jews and Christians, without appropriating the particular parts (1:55–57/48–49). This culminates in the saying: "So *Pythagoras, Plato, Cicero*, etc. could have sung many songs in their hearts, if they had known them" (1:60/51).

Since Semler saw himself as a catechetical teacher incapable of using the entire Old Testament, he suggested that one should produce an outline for preaching and meditation at home: "in which the narratives and places are to be dismissed that are intended only for Jews and clearly bear the stamp of their time and location" (1:70/ 57; cf. 86/67). In the so-called Former Prophets (i.e., the historical books from Joshua through Kings), one discovers only the writing of the national history of Israel, which does not contain general truths. According to Semler, the basis for this was the writing of annals, which (as he means in allusion to Richard Simon's thesis of the "public recorders"; see above) were produced by prophets. Through their own teachings, the prophets had promoted a superior knowledge of God, for instance, through the knowledge that "*moral* circumcision, *spiritual* sacrifice, and honorable observance of obligations toward other people" may be a more preferable type of worship than Jewish sacrifice, circumcision, and ceremonies (1:80/63). This is true especially of the later, so-called writing prophets of whom one therefore could say: "the spirit of Christ was in the prophets" (ibid.). However, while the message of the prophets concerned mostly changing political circumstances, for example, the servitude of both kingdoms to foreign rule, the prophets also address the reconstruction of Jerusalem and the temple. The fanatical mass of the Jews always had hoped for a political liberator. This is true today, as many Christians, for instance in the Turkish war, hope for present fulfillments. However, the fulfillment of the prophetic writings and speeches at that time in the framework of "other events, *in entirely different lands*," is not at all thereby assumed. Now outside of Palestine, Christians who were formerly heathens become instructed by the teaching of Jesus. Activities of the Holy Spirit are now at work in all peoples, and therefore a precise knowledge of every book is not necessary. "It is an *historical* and superfluous knowledge for many people, which they do not need to add to their own experience and for the achievement of Christian perfection" (1:86/67).

Subsequently, Semler investigates the continuing history of the canon among the Jews and Christians, whereby he attributes to the assumption of divine inspiration of the Septuagint a fatal influence in appropriating the entire Old Testament in the church (17; 1:88ff./68ff.). The Jewish Christians already brought with them their canon (18). Jesus and the apostles therefore were engaged in discussions with Jews on the basis of this canon. Jesus disputed with the Sadducees' decision to limit their canon to the five Books of Moses. Paul cites the Apocrypha, including Enoch, as did 2 Peter and Jude, and others. These things are explained by the accommodation made to the respective addressees, but they say nothing about the divinity of the cited books. The Gnostics, by contrast, have thoroughly rejected the Old Testament books (19). To instruct common Christians and to convert the Jews, these goals required the perpetuation of these books. Clement of Alexandria and Origen, among others, have sought to provide for Christians a more significant meaning through the use of allegory. Semler argues that only the lower-level teachers (according to Paul the "fleshly Christians") have taught according to the verbal meaning, while the more noble ones (in Alexandria, Rome, and Antioch)—including incidentally many learned rabbis—have used allegorical interpretation to glean moral truths from the histories and prophecies (20). To use this approach, "the Jews actually do not have to thank their books…, but rather it comes from the sound, rational kinds of knowledge, which many rabbis have collected as academics" (1:109/81).

Correspondingly, this is true also for the New Testament: the oral teachings of Jesus and the apostles were adapted to their contemporary audiences. The Jews heard the narration primarily of the miracles of Jesus, which place him above Moses and all the prophets. This emphasis on speaking to the Jews originated in the "literary treatise" of Matthew, who wrote for the Jews in Arabia, while John presupposed readers, "who according to their circumstances … were already more familiar with meditation over truths" and therefore were taught more from the speeches and teachings of Jesus. Mark composed an abridgment of Matthew (as, among others, Jerome thought); Semler denies that he was an independent author. Fundamentally, Semler cannot accept the view that a comparison of the Gospels could be detrimental to any of them (1:114/84). For historical descriptions (as sitting at the customs control, casting a net, and crucifying someone), the Evangelists did not need divine inspiration, "but rather … for living knowledge and an accurate, straightforward state of mind" (1:115/84).

With respect to the inspiration of the New Testament, it is necessary to recognize that, even if with the writer's original composition had been articulated in words, "it now is past and inspiration no longer remains in the words which we presently read" (1:116/85). This results from the recognition that the present transcriptions often deviate from the original text, as the knowledge of textual criticism bears out. It may be mentioned here that in Semler's conclusion (24) he rejects the book of Revelation as Scripture.

In a concluding comparison of Semler with Spinoza, it is clear that they are not very distant from each other in spite of their different assessments of the Bible. Both share the philosophical conception of God as the perfect being as well as the general truths, which bear a moral character. However, while Spinoza develops his own philosophical system in his *Ethics,* he also understands the Bible (the Old Testament) as a book of moral instruction. Semler is interested only in moral truths, which he believes he can find in the Bible (above all the New Testament). Historical processes are devalued; as such they are considered to be secular and possess no religious significance. They carry weight certainly in providing background presuppositions for the oral proclamation of Jesus and the apostles and the origin of the biblical writings. The presentation of general truths is the only means to counteract both the historical relativizing of the Bible and the argument of the particularity, which to a great extent concerns the Old Testament. Outside of this, Semler is engaged in the religious education of the individual (in which the thought of perfectibility plays an important role). The difference between the private religion of the individual and public religion allows him a measure of freedom, which Spinoza, the excommunicated Jewish philosopher, did not possess. Officially, Semler could be understood as a true servant of the church (in spite of considerable hostility and suspicions from many sides), and he understood himself as such in rejecting extreme "naturalists" like Reimarus. Semler typically is considered to be the "father of historical criticism." This assessment, however, has to be given greater precision. It is correct that his great opponent was orthodoxy, whose idea of a pervasive inspiration of the entire Bible still exerted its influence into the eighteenth century. However, by prying open its uniform thinking in stressing the different historical presuppositions of oral proclamation and the written composition of individual biblical books, he created the final condition for a differentiated, historical assessment of the Bible. In fact, he composed in Latin a handbook of the New Testament (*Apparatus ad liberalem Novi Testamenti interpretationem* [Handbook of the Free Investigation of the New Testament], 1767) as well as the Old Testament (*Apparatus ad liberalem Veteris Testamenti interpretationem* [Handbook of the Free Investigation of the Old Testament], 1773), which possess the character of introductions to the respective Testaments. His own engagement lay, however, not in the sphere of history; historical events remained to him accidental and particular. For him what was important were the general, ethical truths around a corresponding piety of the individual and a continuing improvement of humanity. This thought of progress was quite modern in his time. By contrast, however, most of his interpretations are determined by the influences of the past.

5.7. Understanding the Bible as a Human Document: Johann Gottfried Herder

Johann Gottfried Herder was born on 25 August 1744, in Mohrungen (East Prussia), the son of an elementary teacher and sexton, Gottfried Herder, and his wife, Anna Elisabeth, the daughter of a shoemaker. Herder was the third of five children. The ownership of a small timbered house and of some farmland contributed to the modest livelihood of the family. The spiritual atmosphere at home was imbued with Lutheran pietism, especially that of the mother. The father imparted in his basic teaching at school a continuing intimacy with the Bible by means of both Scripture and the hymnal. The book of devotion used at home was J. Arndt's *Vier Bücher vom wahren Christentum* (Four Books of True Christianity; see above, 14). In the city school of Mohrungen, the young Herder received additional education. Soon his goal was to engage in theological studies. In his last Mohrungen years, he lived with the deacon (pastor) and poet Sebastian Friedrich Trescho (1733–1804), working as his *famulus*. The deacon, however, paid him little attention. Yet Herder could still make use of Trescho's considerably well-stocked library. The young man's insatiable hunger to read impressed Trescho. Even so, he suggested to the economically stretched parents that they should have him learn an honest trade. A Russian regimental doctor stationed in Mohrungen recognized Herder's special talents and took him to Königsberg when the Russian troops that had been located in East Prussia during the Seven Year War departed. The doctor sought to have Herder qualified as surgeon and promised him that he would receive the necessary education. The doctor attempted to arrange for him to study medicine in St. Petersburg. This plan fell through, because Herder blacked out during the first dissection. On the basis of a brilliant qualifying examination, however, he soon could take up study in the theological faculty in Königsberg. Free living accommodation in the *Collegium Fridericianum*, the residential home of a pietistic school, along with private lessons and before long employment, allowed him to achieve pedagogical success as an assistant teacher in the school. These resources financed his studies. Following the typical course of study, he pursued the basic philosophical studies at the time when Immanuel Kant (1724–1804) was still active as a private lecturer. Kant offered lectures during his "precritical" period in natural science and astronomy in addition to mathematics and philosophy. Kant familiarized his audience with scholars who included, among others, Alexander Gottlieb Baumgarten (1714–1762), the founder of aesthetics as a scientific discipline, David Hume (1711–1776), and Jean-Jacques Rousseau (1712–1778). Kant taught at the time that knowledge comes from experience, and for "practical philosophy" feeling and desire are the starting point. He argued that "natural religion" (which is independent of revelation), based on an indirect knowledge of God, defines moral acts. Even so, Kant's influence was limited to Herder's basic studies and should not be overemphasized. Just as important for him was probably his theological teacher, Theodor Christoph Lilienthal (1717–1782). In his hermeneutics lectures he took up S. J. Baumgarten's hermeneutics. Baumgarten granted a place to human experience in the truths of salvation and the Bible. Significant also was Herder's friendship with Johann Georg Hamann (1730–1788), the "magician of the north" (as he was named on account of his often dark prose). From Hamann he appropriated many ideas, for example, the thesis of poetry as the original language of humanity, and the familiarity with Shakespeare's *Hamlet* in the original text. However, his reactions to Hamann's Lutheranism were mixed, especially his stress on the fall of humanity and the "condescension" of God, that is, his lowering of himself to humans in Christ. In addition, Herder gained a far-reaching cultural orientation as a result of the stimulation of Hamann and the comprehensive lectures available in Königsberg concerning older and contemporary literature from all of Europe.

Hamann was also the one who arranged for Herder his first regular appointment as a "collaborator" (an assistant school master) in the cathedral school in Riga. At the end of 1764, he took up his position in the former Hanse city, now the main city of Livland, which had been under Russian rule since 1710. Riga still possessed a limited internal self-government and could preserve its German culture. In Riga he soon developed his method of teaching that engaged his students in an open-minded fashion. While unusual for the time, this approach won him their affection. They made available to him the homes of their parents, often well-to-do merchants. Georg Berens, who was a member of an influential family, became Herder's friend. Berens later often supported him financially. The bookseller Johann Friedrich Hartknoch became the lifelong publisher of his books. In 1767, when he received a call from the German Lutheran community in St. Petersburg to serve the newly founded Peter School, the council of Riga established for him, as an inducement for him to stay, the extraordinary position of preacher at both suburban churches. Herder then passed a theological exam and soon became the most popular preacher in Riga. In spite of all this, he still found time for a comprehensive reading of classical and modern literature. With the appearance of the anonymously written *Fragmenten über die neuere deutsche Literatur* (Fragments concerning the New German Literature), published by Hartknoch in 1766/1767, Herder entered the stage of a "man of letters."

In May 1769, Herder surprisingly asked the council to release him from his official responsibilities in order that he might take a lengthy educational journey. Although he guaranteed the city council that he would return, he never came back to Riga. He composed a *Journal meiner Reise im Jahre 1769* (Journal of My Travel in the Year 1769), in which he describes not the impressions of his travels but rather his readings along the way, his previous life, his ideas, and his plans. He accompanied by ship his friend Gustav Berens on a business trip to Nantes. He used the stay until October to engage in intensive readings of the French Enlightenment literature (Voltaire, Montesquieu, d'Alembert, and Rousseau, among others). He also composed a piece of his *Archäologie des Morgenlandes* (Archaeology of the Orient), which remained only in fragments (see below). Afterwards he traveled to Paris, where he became personally acquainted with Jean d'Alembert (1717–1783) and Denis Diderot (1713–1784), main representatives of the French Enlightenment (among other things, Diderot was editor of the famous *Enclyclopédie*). Owing to a lack of funds, Herder accepted a contract to accompany as teacher and minister the son of the prince-bishop of Lübeck, the hereditary prince of Schleswig-Holstein-Gottorp. This journey led him to Hamburg, among other places, where he became acquainted with Lessing, visited the pedagogue Johannes Bernhard Basedow (1724–1790), and became friends with the pious poet Matthias Claudius (1740–1815). With the prince, he traveled to different German courts, among others, the one in Darmstadt, where he came to know Caroline Flachsland (1750–1809) who would later become his wife. On account of his call to Bückeburg as the consistorial counselor and chief preacher, from Strassburg he sent his resignation to his former employer, but he remained there a longer time in order to undergo a painful but unsuccessful treatment for a chronic fistula of the eyes. While in his sickroom, he was visited daily by Johann Wolfgang Goethe (1749–1832), at that time a law student in Strassburg, for conversation. At the end of April 1771, he was in Bückeburg and presented an inaugural sermon in the baroque city church. Until 1776, he lived in the small state ruled by Count Wilhelm von Schaumburg-Lippe (1748–1777), who was especially interested in military matters. Thus, during this job Herder had scarcely any official obligations and little stimulation.

This period in Bückeburg is shaped by Herder's religious reflection, as a result of his contact with the pietistic Countess Maria (1744–1776), the resumption of an exchange of letters with Hamann, and a new correspondence that he commenced with the eccentric Zurich theologian, writer, and psychologist Johann Kaspar Lavater (1741–1801). In addition, Herder occupied himself with folk poetry, which included, among others, the alleged odes of the old Celtic legendary hero Ossian (which later were exposed as fraudulent), with Homer, and with the poetry of Friedrich Gottlieb Klopstock (1724–1803). During this period, his anonymously published *Auch eine Philosophie der Geschichte zur Bildung der Menschheit* (Also a Philosophy of History regarding the Education of Mankind [1774]) opposed the usually optimistic interpretation of history in the Enlightenment, as represented, for example, by Isaak Iselin's (1728–1782) *Geschichte der Menschheit* (History of Mankind [1768]). For Iselin, universal history, directed by God, moves forward steadily ("education") through the conquest of "superstition" to an enlightened morality. In contrast to this, Voltaire could recognize no clear progress in history. Herder, however, stressed progress in discontinuity: he did not consider the present to be the apparent high point and thus the standard for past periods, nor did he see an unplanned, eternal change between vices and virtues as did the skeptics. Rather, history is like a stream that is concealed in temporary twists from the wellspring to the sea, or to the changes of the ages of a person (*SW* 5:512–13). Important is the recognition of the intrinsic value of each period, if the thought of progress is not abandoned for the common course of history. The individual obtains the greatest emphasis, and therefore the early period becomes the "childhood" of humanity. This is compared to the patriarchal period, which is the golden age (481), although it certainly is not possible for a person to return to it. On the other side, although unobservable by us (559–60), is the history of the realization of the plan of God (567). It becomes recognizable through revelation, *Unterweisung des Vaters selbst an diese Kindhei*t (The Instruction of the Father Himself to This Childhood) (566). Likewise in

1774, the first volume of the *Ältesten Urkunde des Menschengeschlechts* (The Oldest Document of Men) appeared anonymously, in which this foundational thought is illustrated by the exegesis of the biblical primeval history of Gen 1. The second volume appeared in 1776. In addition, writings about the New Testament, including *Erläuterungen zum Neuen Testament aus einer neueröffneten morgenländischen Quelle* (Explanations of the New Testament from a Newly Discovered Source from the East [1775]), by which Herder sought to demonstrate his orthodoxy; the *Briefe zweener Brüder Jesu* (Letters of Two Brothers of Jesus [1775]); and a manuscript of *Johannes Offenbarung* (John's Revelation [1779], published in a revised form) were written during his time in Bückeburg. However, Herder sought to leave Bückeburg. Financial concerns, in spite of his promotion to superintendent, the atmosphere of the small city, and a conflict with his sovereign had spoiled his desire to remain. The attempts of the classical philologist Christian Gottlob Heyne (1729–1812) to enable him to be called as a professor to Göttingen failed in 1775 on account of objections from the theological faculty. Thanks to the intercession of Goethe, who was in Weimar, Herder received a call to become the Saxon-Weimar court preacher and general superintendent.

In Weimar Herder was received at first skeptically by his colleagues in office, because a freethinker had preceded him. However, his inaugural sermon for office removed all reservations: Herder was an exceptional preacher. Nevertheless, also in Weimar he failed to achieve a longed-for happiness. The mass of official duties overwhelmed him. He had the chief responsibility for all clergy and teachers of the state, had to conduct the inspection of the Weimar gymnasium, examined the theologians and teachers, sat on all committees of the upper consistorium as a member, and served as its vice president beginning in 1789, when he received a new call to Göttingen, which he rejected. Beginning in 1800, he had to be present at all meetings as the consistorium's president. He was significantly involved in churchly reforms (liturgy, hymnal, and others). In spite of many raises in remuneration, he still had to battle continual concerns about money, owing to the size of his family. His relationship with Goethe and his duke (Karl August, who reigned 1775–1828) remained ambiguous. Many things also impaired his sensibility, for he possessed a melancholic temperament. From his theological works of this period, especially important is *Briefe, das Studium der Theologie betreffend* (Letters Which Concern the Study of Theology [1780–1781]). Herder's main work on the philosophy of history, *Ideen zur Philosophie der Geschichte der Menschheit* (Ideas concerning the Philosophy of the History of Humanity), appeared in four parts during the years 1784–1791. He received sharp criticism from Kant. The thinking of both philosophers was very different, and Herder's style lacked the clarity required by Kant.

A disruption in his routine was occasioned by a trip to Italy (1788–89) at the invitation and in the accompaniment of the Catholic capitular F. H. von Dalberg (1752–1812). They traveled to Rome, where Herder joined the travel society of the widowed duchess Anna Amalia (1739–1807), then to Naples, and finally back to Weimar. The outbreak of the French Revolution in 1789 Herder (like many German intellectuals) initially regarded as positive. However, when the Jacobites instituted their reign of terror and King Louis XVI and Queen Marie Antoinette were executed in 1793, the early enthusiasm declined. Later, Herder became connected to the German national movement. His latest undertakings included the editing of a newspaper, *Adrastea* (1801), in which he wished to show to the new century the humanistic ideals of "truth and justice" from the progress of the past centuries. However, literary themes also played a considerable role in his contributions.

Herder's last years witnessed embittered disputations with his duke on account of the sovereign's refusal to recognize the nobility that the Bavarian prince elector had bestowed on him and because of different personal matters. But most of all, he faced the difficulties of an increasing infirmity. The crisis in health reached its climax in the early part of 1803, interrupted once by his experience of a joyful stay in Dresden. The return to Weimar with his burden of work caused the flaring up again of all of the old ailments. Several strokes led to a rapid decline in his physical powers. Herder died on 18 December 1803.

The numerous volumes of Herder's *Sämtliche Werke* demonstrate his productivity as an author who, while a full-time theologian, was no less a writer. His published works cover a variety of areas ranging from literary science to history to philosophy to theology. He was engaged in the entire sphere of the intellectual learning of the time. To all of these works, his handwritten bequest has to be added, although it has not yet been thoroughly explored.

For a long period, Herder stood in the shadows of Goethe and Schiller as a writer of classic works and Kant as a philosopher of the Enlightenment, and it is only recently that the uniqueness and weight of his thinking have been recognized. The foundations of his thought, which have been significant for the history of biblical interpretation, were apparent already in Königsberg. As a writer, Herder was assigned to the period of *Sturm und Drang*, and its style also impacted his theological work.

In the last years of his time in Riga, he worked on a manuscript that dealt with the biblical primeval history, *Über die ersten Urkunden des Menschlichen Geschlechts: Einige Anmerkungen* (Concerning the First Documents of the Human Race: Some Remarks, *Werke*, Bollacher et al. 5:9–178). It was long lost and remained unpublished until 1993. In Herder's opinion, Moses used ancient documents for his description of the primeval history, which already were available in written form. They in turn were based on still older traditions of a poetic character. "They are from the period of the traditions; and then everything was poetic" (*Werke* 5:26). The customary teaching of inspiration Herder rejects as fanciful. "God thinks without words or symbols"; therefore, "everything in the Bible is thoroughly human, including thoughts, words, series, and concepts. Every written thought of a human soul was thought before" (*Werke* 5:29). Herder sees this as not impairing the divine origin of the primeval history, for the author "was a holy person who built upon sacred tradition…, which came originally from an instruction of God to humans" (*Werke* 5:35). Yet, if the origin of the tradition is from God, we are nevertheless dependent on the author. In the fragments of an *Archäologie des Morgenlandes* (Archaeology of the Orient [1769]; *SW* 6:1–129), Herder turns again to the biblical narrative of creation (Gen 1:1–2:4). He proceeds from language, more precisely that of the church fathers (Origen, Jerome, and Augustine), to argue the well-known thesis that Hebrew (extended by Herder to the language of the "Eastern people") would be the primeval language of humanity. One must be able to empathize with the witnesses of this primeval language in order to be able to understand such an "original text" in its "innocence." "Thus one must step back into the time when the very ancient inhabitant of the lands of the East actually still sensed his universe as being both within this great blue hemisphere and also between heaven and earth" (*SW* 6:4). To understand a work from a distant past, "one must place himself into the spirit of its author, its public, its nation, and at least the spirit of its various parts" (*SW* 6:34). Instead of speaking of the divine origin and inspiration of Scripture and the truth contained in it, he mentions here a document composed by humans. Because it is poetry, emphasizing this fact is the important key to understand it. The historical distance, however, still remains known. Hamann's sentence from his *Aesthetica in nuce* (perhaps *Abriss der Ästhetik* [Abstract of Aesthetics], 1761), "poetry is the mother language of humanity," had deeply influenced Herder.

To be sure, the biblical text says especially something about man as creature and therefore as made in the image of God, an image that is based on freedom, capability of working, the ability to engage in language and education, and even the substance of its corporeal nature. The way to theology also leads through anthropology. Certainly, the human is also an animal (*SW* 6:25–28; cf. 54–55). If God in the creation of the human being gave to the human spirit a gift "to look into the nature of things and into the plan of creation" (*SW* 6:88), this occurs not through reason but rather through feeling. Feeling observes in the artistry of the creation the creator as artist. On the basis of pietism, this was absolutely a possibility, given the psychology of the Enlightenment!

Of the preparatory works, there followed in 1774 the first volume of the edited writing of the *Älteste Urkunde des Menschengeschlechts* (The Oldest Document of Humanity). It is at first glance not easily comprehensible. Its effusive style, aphoristic language, and numerous evocative signs impeded even the understanding of Herder's contemporaries. A closer examination, however, shows that Herder follows a precise plan and exegetically is definitely at the pinnacle of his time. After he has strongly criticized the present "schools" (natural-scientific criticism of the worldview of the primeval history, philosophical cosmology, and mystical-theosophical, metaphysical image of the divine [part 1, ch. 1; *Werke* 5:185–99]), he immediately engages in the interpretation of Gen 1. First he invites the reader to make certain the significance of the most important ideas "from the East" (200). The presupposition is that the early inhabitant of the east as a "simple natural human" combines sensory perception and feeling, for example, in viewing heaven and earth, which comprise for him the totality of all things. "The entire universe exists in *his* soul" (201). He apprehends the earth as the symbol of perpetual pillars and feels that the world before the creation was the dark abyss on which God's Spirit descends. The phrase "heaven and earth" is also a fundamental example of "parallelism," which here is grasped as a comprehensive, poetic element of style. Then the Word of God: "Let there be light!"—"and there was light," declares "God's epiphany in nature!" (205).

Surely Herder displays his thoughts as a complete picture comprehending sense, feeling, and understanding. In this manner, Herder moves through the text. In verses 26–27, when God is involved in the creating of humanity, Herder observes that verse 25, "and God saw that it was good," does not immediately follow the blessing, but rather the creation of humanity awaits the deliberation of God. "What then is the *sensory purpose of all this—unity*?" (230). This pause prepares for the creation of man in the image of God, through which the unity is first won. "What would the entire nature be in comparison to this *human soul—deliberating like*

God himself!" In the essential nature of the human person Herder includes the body: "the *erect, beautiful, sublime figure*," which, however, is but "the external veil and *picture of the soul!*" The sexes, man and wife, with their respective gifts. But human nature above all has to do with human action: "What gift of the creator, what *imitation* of the deity!" (232–33). This ideal of human nature is admittedly captured by the inhabitant of the East. He possesses the gift "to recognize these accomplishments as divinity and *to feel as if this were working in himself* … to be God on earth."To be sure, the reality here looks often otherwise: "Urban humans bent down to the dust, and to whom certainly the image of God is nothing more than the question in the catechism" (233). However, even if humans are animals according to their "perishable material," the ideal nevertheless is real in the statement: "Always, however, information and development are enough to live for *what we are*" (235–36).

The individual images possess a common, ever-present structure that, if one omits "everything that is unessential," for example, "daily tasks, blessing, name, and visualizing" (239), this portrait is still real. What is described in the first chapter of the Bible is "the primeval, most magnificent revelation of God … in nature," which can still be felt in the change from darkness to dawn that occurs each morning (239–41). From this experience, which Herder enthusiastically describes, the "portrait of the morning" (244), results the feeling of the presence of God. Nature is always creation! Herder treats the question of revelation in a separate chapter (ch. 4, 246–57) headed by the superscription, "Instruction beneath the Dawn." The idea of instruction, that is, the teaching by God, was well known in the Enlightenment. Herder, however, rejects the dominant opinion that God must reveal himself only through nature. Instead of this, it is the "rising dawn," the *image* of the "living natural man," in which "God's morning lesson takes place" (248). For "humanity in its childhood," this is the "method of God's teaching" (250, 248). "Thus God teaches! *Through images, facts, and events!* In the entirety of *nature* … everywhere that power strives and action appears—there is the all living God" (253). Herder reforms the principle of natural religion: it does not exist apart from revelation.

Herder completes these central thoughts through statements about the division of days, which leads to the Sabbath, a topic to which he devotes an entire chapter (ch. 7, 282–92). He now explicitly explains what he understands about "hieroglyphs" (267–82). During a time in which the Egyptian hieroglyphs had still not been deciphered, these were secret signs. Thus, he notes that the human being in the image of God is the "hieroglyph of creation" (292–94).

In the two additional main sections of the work, Herder traces the origin of the biblical history of creation. For different reasons, he determines that this portion of the history does not stem from Moses, but rather is older. Moses had appropriated in Egypt this "oldest document of humanity," which was originally common to all of the religions of the east. "It could be demonstrated that there were religions in Asia older than Moses, religions that dreamt of the creation of the world" (446). However, he decidedly rejects the thesis that they originated in Egypt (313–14). He seeks to adduce the evidence through an elaborate history of religions and comparative mythology of the East. Since neither cuneiform nor hieroglyphs could be deciphered, Herder could apply evidence used only in classical antiquity and the church fathers. Thus, there was no existing portrait to which he could turn. However, through this evidence, he anticipated the knowledge about the ancient Near Eastern high culture that was to be attained a hundred years later. Herder is of the view, however, that the document of creation in its Mosaic form has been preserved in its purest state, after Moses had appropriated in a ceremonial form the Sabbath for his people.

In a second volume, which appeared in 1776, Herder offers an interpretation of Gen 2:4–25 and the remaining primeval history. Herder understands Gen 2:4b–25 as an introduction to the "Garden Chapter" that follows in (496). The name of God as Jehovah-Elohim (in distinction to Elohim in Gen 1:1–2:4a and again in ch. 3) shows a different origin: it stems from the compiler (ibid.). Important for further criticism is Herder's new definition of the primeval history as "Sacred Sagas of the Prehistoric World" (superscription, 491). In contrast to his earlier evaluation of this literary section as "Allegory in a Fable" (*SW* 6:126), Herder sees this as history (*Werke* 5:566). The department of the first human pair he compares to the "nurslings of creation under the special care of the father" (ibid.). Children also speak with animals (568). The combination here of a traditional theological explanation of the fall of humanity with a natural interpretation is peculiar. Thus, the consequence of the eating of the fruit of knowledge of good and evil leading to the shame Adam and Eve experience in their nakedness (Gen 3:7) is explained as the transition to puberty among humans. In a further, more briefly composed section that treats the "progress of humanity" (*Werke* 5:622–60), chapters 4–6 of Genesis are entitled "a saga of households." Then the work of Herder breaks off, as others of his do, leaving the section incomplete.

A second comprehensive work on the Old Testament also remained an unfinished piece (1782–1783): *Vom Geist der Ebräischen Poesie* (Concerning the Spirit of Hebrew Poetry, *Werke* 5:661–1308), in which he returns to the themes of his earlier work. There he expands (in the first part in the mode of a fictional dialogue) the discussion to other sections of Genesis, Job, and different psalms. Poetry is now the main theme, which was mostly treated later in Old Testament criticism. Herder breaks new ground with his references to Hebrew poetry. While Robert Lowth (and other critics) still measured Hebrew poetic art by means of the standards of classical antiquity, Herder was the first to point to the unique form of Hebrew poetry and the high degree of poetic quality associated with it.

This is shown in a special piece, the translation and explanation of Canticles (*Lieder der Liebe* [Songs of Love], *Werke* 3:431–521). In contrast to the usual allegorical interpretation of this small book by Jews and Christians, Herder saw a collection of love songs of Solomon, arranged according to the growth of the love of this king. This explanation, taken over also by J. G. Eichhorn (who also gave up the authorship of Solomon), had become a prevalent one. Herder's *application* to the relationship between Christ and the church, as well as the individual, believing soul remained legitimate (*Werke* 3:518). This understanding of the book had legitimated it theologically (*Werke* 3:518) and consequently eased it into its place in the canon.

By approaching the Bible through the theology of creation, Herder wished to engage the rational criticism of the Bible as it was at the time especially voiced by Hume, the deists, and "the fragmentist" (Reimarus; see above). Herder was familiar also with the entire deist and rationalistic literature. His approach was an interesting attempt during the age of *Sturm und Drang* to shape a new form of apologetics, even if use of feeling that derived from pietism was not unknown in the Enlightenment. It was certainly not effective, which is evident in Herder's diction. One must also see, to be sure, that Herder does not speak of the incarnation (the word becomes flesh), which was so central to Hamann. The enthusiastic equation of Adam in the creation narrative as the image of God with the present human being shows no familiarity with the fracturing of human existence through sin. This is a point that corresponds to Herder's general interest in an application of the Bible to the contemporary hearer and reader. The access to revelation through the aesthetics of creation is strange to the Lutheran heritage, even though Herder does appeal to Luther. Recently, influences on Herder have been identified that emanated from the Enlightenment and rationalism. Others have wished, nevertheless, to recognize him as a genuine Lutheran theologian in a different situation. Thus, the theological judgment expressed about Herder is twofold. Nevertheless, his historical view of the Old Testament is correctly viewed as preparing the way for the appearance of the historical criticism of the Bible.

Nor is Herder forgotten when it comes to the study of the Gospels. It must be stressed that he knew and used the critical scholarship known at the time in New Testament exegesis, and he followed the historical approach to the Bible, which he shared with critical exegetes. Through his study he obtained new insights. In his work *Vom Erlöser der Menschen: Nach unsern drei ersten Evangelien* (Concerning the Savior of Men: According to our First Three Gospels], *Werke* 9.1:609–724), he expresses his opinion on the question of the relationship between the three Synoptic Gospels and stepping away from the popular thesis of a literary dependence. Further, he denies Lessing's hypothesis of a proto-Gospel that preceded all three Gospels and refers to the fact that the apostles originally spoke their proclamations (*Werke* 9.1:669–72, 682–83; cf. *SW* 19:281–383). The center of the Gospel was the affirmation that Jesus is the Christ who was previously announced by the prophets. When the need appeared, the three Evangelists wrote down independently of one another and each according to his methods the same oral traditions. We must "consider each one separately and regard each of them as if his only wish was to return to the time of early Christianity.... Matthew and John stand separately as *apostles* and *eyewitnesses*. *Mark* and *Luke* are *Evangelists*. With these words everything is explained" (*Werke* 9.1:684). As regards the relationship between the Gospels, it is necessary to say that "the Gospel of Mark is not abbreviated, but is its own Gospel. When the others have more or something different, however, this has been added to them, not, however, deleted in Mark" (*SW* 19:391). With this, Herder has produced an important contribution to the question, debated up to the present, about which is the oldest Gospel.

Herder clearly recognized the distinction between the Synoptic Gospels and the Gospel of John. In his writing *Von Gottes Sohn, der Welt Heiland: Nach Johannes Evangelium* (From God's Son, Redeemer of the World: According to John's Gospel [1797], *SW* 19:253–379), he stresses this Gospel's peculiarity. John must also have known the oral gospel (Herder regarded him as a disciple according to John 20:21). However, he formed his Gospel differently. "His Gospel is an entirely whole and personal work" (273). While the Synoptic Gospels are Palestinian and narrate many miracles corresponding to the folk character present there, John has retained only a few of these. Since the Christians had already separated themselves from the Jews, John consequently portrayed Jesus as the savior of the world and "showed in what sense he was the *Son of God*, the *Light of the world*, the *Shepherd of the nations*, and a source *of eternal blessing*, and thus made thereby … the ancient historical Gospel practical" (264; cf. 272). With the last word one encounters a central concern of Herder: he never allowed himself to be satisfied with a purely theoretical occupation with the Bible, but rather always sought to use it for his contemporaries and his community, whom he sought to "educate."

5.8. Improving the New Testament Text and Setting Forth the Synoptic Question: Johann Jakob Griesbach

Johann Jakob Griesbach was born in 1745 in Butzbach (Hessen), the only son of a pastor and a mother who was a learned pietist. She was the daughter of the pietistic theologian Johann Jakob Rambach. He grew up in Frankfurt am Main and studied theology in Tübingen, Leipzig (for a year), and Halle. In Halle he lived in the house of his teacher, Johann Salomo Semler, who enkindled his enthusiasm for textual criticism. Afterwards, he acquired a master's degree from the philosophical faculty and then, in 1768, undertook a study trip. This led him first to visit the different universities of Germany, followed by Holland, England, and France. A major purpose was to copy available New Testament manuscripts in the different libraries, for example, the library of the British Museum (today the British Library), the Bodleian Library in Oxford, the university library in Cambridge, and the royal library in Paris. These would furnish later material for text-critical works.

After his return in autumn 1770 and a period of preparation in his parent's home in Frankfurt, he was issued the *venia legendi* (allowance to give lectures) at the University of Halle in autumn 1771, on the basis of the work he did on the Gospel manuscripts used by Origen (see *History*, vol. 1). He was appointed associate professor in 1773. In 1775, he was called to the University of Jena as an *ordentlicher* (full) professor. He taught there until his death in 1812. Besides exegetical lectures on the New Testament (except the book of Revelation), through which he worked in four to five semesters, he gave lectures on church history and dogmatics, as well as New Testament introduction and hermeneutics. He spent a great deal of time assisting with the financial administration of the university and as the deputy of the district of Jena in the Weimar Diet (since 1782). His time often allowed him to produce only short treatises for the customary, festival programs (at Easter and Pentecost). Griesbach established friendships with Goethe and Schiller and had social contacts with other intellectual giants of his period.

The actual significance of Griesbach, however, lies in his critical editions of the New Testament, which, in addition to textual criticism, have strongly influenced Gospel research. His works originated mostly in Halle. To these belongs an edition of the text of the first three Gospels, printed in parallel columns for the use of students as a synopsis (1774). The Gospel of John and Acts followed in 1775. A comprehensive textual-critical edition of the New Testament appeared in two volumes in 1775 and 1777. In Halle also he produced the synopsis of the Gospels of Matthew, Mark, and Luke, likewise text-critically edited (1776). As the first New Testament textual critic in Germany, Griesbach declared that the traditional, standard text (Textus Receptus) contains errors in many places, a conclusion reached on the basis of better manuscripts. Many later editions depended on his text-critical work.

In regard to the questions still debated today—which may be the oldest of the Synoptic Gospels and what is the relationship of the three Gospels—Griesbach drew a decisive position. He was not the first person who engaged in the lively discussion of these issues during his time. For a long time, Augustine's opinion (*De consensus evangelistarum* [Concerning the Agreement of the Evangelists] 1.2.4) was viewed as the standard one: accordingly, Matthew is the oldest Gospel; Mark wrote a summary of the Gospel of Matthew but did not take into consideration Luke. It has been constantly attempted, since Tatian's *Diatessaron* was composed, to harmonize the four Gospels, since there could be only a single truth. Griesbach was the first one not to accept this principle. When he placed next to one another in his synopsis the three Gospels in their respective succession of pericopes, the agreements and differences in their arrangement especially caught his attention. In the sequence of pericopes, Mark sometimes followed Matthew, sometimes Luke, and at other times both. This appeared to him to be best explained by the view that Matthew had influenced Luke and both together had influenced Mark. Thus, Mark would have been the latest of the three. Griesbach expressed this argument in two Pentecost programs in 1789–90 (elaborated further in 1794). This interpretation has entered into the history of scholarship as the "Griesbach Hypothesis." After it was nearly totally superseded by the "two source theory" in the nineteenth century, some scholars have taken it up once again. There were additional explanations already during Griesbach's lifetime. These included the acceptance of shorter and longer individual accounts, which were edited by the Evangelists ("the fragment hypothesis"), the hypothesis represented by Richard Simon and later by Lessing that there was a primitive Gospel residing behind Matthew, and finally Herder's thesis (see above), which was designated as the "traditions hypothesis." That there was finally no single solution that continued without objections demonstrates the difficulty of the relationship of the Gospels to one another.

5.9. Explaining Miracles as Natural Events: Heinrich Eberhard Gottlob Paulus

Like other well-known theologians, Heinrich Paulus grew up in a pastor's home, that of a pious Swabian minister, and he experienced the typical education of a Swabian theologian. He was born in Leonberg in 1761. His father inclined toward a mystical piety practiced in small assemblies, especially following the early death of his wife in 1767, and was therefore dismissed from church service. The dismissal was also due to his writing in 1771 directed against the disbelief of nobles and government. His son Heinrich attended the lesser seminaries in Blaubeuren and Bebenhausen before studying in the Tübingen students' home (*Stift*), beginning in 1779. However, Tübingen professors influenced him less than the writings of Semler and Kant, which shaped his perspective. It was through the latter that he obtained a reasonable faith, which he proudly named "a thinking faith" or "rational faithfulness," differentiated from an "intuitive faith" (supernaturalism), which reckoned with a supernatural revelation of the secrets of belief.

Especially fascinating to Paulus was the theoretical knowledge of Kant's maxims, which had developed into three major critical works (*Critik der reinen Vernunft* [Critique of Pure Reason], 1781; *Critik der praktischen Vernunft* [Critique of Practical Reason], 1788; and *Critik der Urteilskraft* [Critique of Judgment], 1790). Kant stressed, in opposition to traditional metaphysics, which held that it was possible to reach a conclusion by moving from the sensory to the extrasensory world, that theoretical knowledge always moves within the sphere of appearance and is related to experience, which is ordered by categories of thought. The ideas of "soul," "world," and "God" as the Absolute are, however, taken for granted by means of pure reason itself, even though they possess no objective reality. The earlier, customary proof is rejected altogether as not sustainable. However, reason occurs, in its practical usage, in the question of what should be morally certain a priori (unconditionally) with respect to the fundamental precepts of God, freedom, and immortality. The moral precepts likewise are specified a priori through the "categorical imperative," to which should correspond the moral actions in which a person is engaged. *Religion innerhalb der Grenzen der blossen Vernunft* (Religion within the Limits of Reason Alone [1793]) became the basis on which Kant grounded the necessity of the transition to religion: the moral obligations were taken as divine commandments, because they were able to be understood as the will of a morally perfect, exalted creature.

Heinrich Paulus uses the epistemology of Kant in a pure form in his exegesis of the New Testament. However, he follows also his Tübingen teacher Gottlob Christian Storr (1746–1805), the head of the so-called older Tübingen school. Combined with the acknowledgement of Kant's maxims in principle, which served as the basis of morality, Storr wished to keep open the sphere of transcendental (*supernatural*) perceptions. These included the ideas of God and immortality. According to Storr, these may best be obtained from the New Testament and other historical documents of Christianity. Against pure rationalists ("naturalists"), who criticized the fundamental teachings of Christianity and with it the Bible, Paulus also sought to make certain, even when he did not share the supernaturalism of Storr, the unconditional believability of biblical witnesses, especially of the New Testament. Paulus emphasized the Synoptic Gospels of Matthew, Mark, and Luke, about which he had already written a three-volume commentary during the time he was professor of dogmatics and biblical exegesis in Jena (1793–1803; he first taught Oriental languages there beginning in 1789). He also adhered to this in later publications (especially the *Exegetischem Handbuch über die drei ersten Evangelien* [Exegetical Handbook on the First Three Gospels], 1830–1833 [*Hdb*], "cheap edition" [*WA*] 1842). He wrote a commentary on the Gospel of John only up to chapter 11 (1804). Much later he commented on some of the Epistles of Paul (1831–1833) and wrote a life of Jesus (1828) aimed at a broader circle of readers.

Paulus changed professorships by leaving Jena and moving to Würzburg. On account of the (temporary) dissolution of the theological faculty there during the time that the grand duke Ferdinand of Toskana was installed as ruler, he had to assume a position in the Bavarian school service (1807–1810). He was called to Heidelberg in 1811, where he remained until his death in 1851. For a long period of time, he was regarded as the leading New Testament scholar in Germany. In numerous political writings, he defended liberalism, which had a center in southwestern Germany. When he died at the age of ninety, he had seemed to his young contemporaries already for a long time an anachronistic figure.

Nevertheless, a long funeral procession of colleagues and students followed his coffin.

In regard to the relationship of the Gospels to each other, he followed in essence Griesbach: Matthew is the oldest Gospel, while Mark is only a "modified abbreviation" (*Commentary* 1.2:263) of Matthew and Luke. Independent of each other, these Gospels are based on a common, oral, ancient Gospel that possessed a different origin and compiled its own account (e.g., the Sermon on the Mount in Matt 5–7). Especially important for him was the fact that the reflections and narratives go back to eyewitnesses. Thus, these accounts possess a credible historical core. Further, the Gospel of John may be used as a historical witness, although it also contains reflections of the author in addition to the traditions that are transmitted by him (e.g., the Prologue in 1:1–18). The Gospel's historical traditions, however, go back to the witness of John, the disciple whom Jesus loved, and can fill in the interstices in the historical life of Jesus found in the other Gospels (see *Das Leben Jesu* 1.1:149–57). Fundamentally the Gospels are still so close to the events that one can trust them as reports about historical circumstances. To be certain, they are colored by the tradents and the Evangelists: Matthew was oriented to Jewish Christianity, Luke to pagan Christianity; and Mark wished to compare both tendencies to each other. In addition, the especially important point is that the modifications that underlie the narratives may go back to the understanding of the eyewitnesses of the events and the tradents.

The objective of the critical interpreter, therefore, is to filter out these misunderstandings and to set free the underlying historical facts concealed almost everywhere. Secondary and nonhistorical passages are found in only a few places. Aside from the reflections of the author of the Gospel of John, which have been mentioned, secondary passages are the ending of the Gospel of Mark in 16:9–20 (recognized as secondary today) and the concluding chapter (ch. 21) the Gospel of John. Others include especially the narrative of the watchers at the grave in Matt 27:62–66 and 28:2–4, 11–15, because these texts conflict with the understanding of what actually happened at the cross (see below, 209), as well as the text on Peter in Matt 16:18–19. This latter passage served to establish the Roman primacy regarding the papacy. Paulus is considered to be sharply anti-Catholic, as are most Protestant scholars of the Enlightenment!

A main objective of Paulus's interpretation is to reconstruct "purely historically" (to use his own words) the life of Jesus from the Gospels (see *WA* 1:xii). Since these Gospels, according to his interpretation, are mainly reports of eyewitnesses, this is possible without encountering many difficulties. If one explains everything that appears to be "mythical" or miraculous as due to the imperfect capacities of the knowledge of eyewitnesses and commentators, then the things they considered to be extraordinary can be interpreted in this fashion. For Paulus, who always refers to Kant, what is historically and actually a "fact" occurs "within observable nature" (*WA* 1:viii), that is, "as observed by the senses ... and transmitted." This holds good also for that which in the biblical narratives appears as a miracle. Paulus places great value on the view that "what is miraculous is also a fact" (*WA* 1:viii, xiv–xv). In this connection, one is to distinguish only between what actually happened and the reports of the tradents. What they could not explain and therefore interpreted as miracles can be explained by the modern interpreter. Paulus saw his "life's purpose" to reside in "seeking harmony between the original revelation of Christianity, as a fact that occurred, and the ever continuing religious deliberation" (*Hdb*, Preamble, vi). With this in mind, Paulus returned to an apologetic objective, as it was found already in Toland, when the latter wished to discover in Christianity nothing that was mysterious (see above). Only Kant now offered established standards for this type of investigation.

As he strings together and places the parallel passages side by side, Paulus obtains the basis for a "historical narrative of the Gospels," that is, a life of Jesus. To present a common understanding of this view, he composed a work that appeared later under the title *Das Leben Jesu*. To be sure, it is clear to him in view of the character of the Gospels that "an actually brief and comprehensive overview of the life of Jesus is not possible. The original tradents wished to take into consideration only the great events, which mainly deal with his person (*Leben Jesu* 1.1:65). However, Paulus believed that the life of Jesus may be established on the basis of the harmony of the Gospels that he produced. The Gospel of John, for example, is structured around three Passover festivals occurring during the three-year ministry of Jesus. Paulus argues that this structure is based on the arrangement of these three festivals by the individual witnesses of the Gospels. Thus, he is of the opinion that he can obtain a sufficiently precise portrait of Jesus.

This effort, informed by Kant's critical epistemology ("historical facts" may be obtained from sensory, comprehensive, normal, human experiences), undergoes its actual litmus test in the examination of the miracle stories. Entirely opposed to Paulus's own wishes, this attracted the greatest attention among his readers and critics. He remarked once: "I would prefer almost to denounce this activity, because it ... has all too often diverted the attempt to show ancient Christianity in its originally true form away from the practical, main work of all these efforts" (*Hdb*, Preamble, xxi). It is a possibility that actions that are described as miraculous by the Evangelists on account of their primitive faith in miracles, are to be designated as entirely and naturally explicable. Thus, Paulus deployed a simple explanation in his interpretation of the narrative of the healing of the two men possessed by demons in Mark 5:1–17. Jesus drove these demons into a herd of swine that proceeded to fall into the nearby lake. One of the demon-possessed men had caught sight of the herd of swine and, driven by his Jewish animosity toward swine and the opinion that his illness was caused by demons, cast himself into the herd. This herd, having been stampeded by anxiety, cast themselves down from the slope into the lake (*Leben Jesu* 1.1:230ff.). Typical of the interpretation of this and other healing stories is a psychological factor: the healings are for him "psychical works of trust in the Messiah, combined with a simple, though appropriate, type of treatment" (*Hdb*, Preamble, xxi). Thus, Jesus asks questions in the healing both of the two blind men and of the one who was mute because of possession by a demon (Matt 9:27–34). He asks the blind men: "Are you convinced that I can help you and wish that you by means of this conviction may be considered faithful?" Paulus remarks concerning this that, by touching their eyes, Jesus had recognized the possibility of healing and had provided precise instructions for treatment. Concerning the mute, the text says: "After the two blind men, a man who could not speak was brought to him. As soon as he had cast out the demon or as soon as his hallucination was remedied, he ventured to speak again" (*Leben Jesu* 1.1:249). The illness therefore is imagined.

Another possibility is that no miracle has occurred. Thus, in the feeding of the five thousand (Matt 14:13–22 par.), the crowd in the same area, for instance, was not satisfied through the miraculous multiplication of the few loaves and fishes, which were made available to the disciples, but rather through the clever action of Jesus. He saw to it that the poor and rich were embedded with each other so that the rich, who had brought their abundant portions with them, dispensed food to the poor (*Leben Jesu* 1.1:349ff.; cf. *WA* 2:205ff.).

The manner of explaining away the resurrection of the dead reported in the Gospels proceeded according to the same pattern throughout: the death had not actually occurred. Thus, for example, the daughter of Jairus (Matt 9:18–26 par.) in reality had only been unconscious (*Leben Jesu* 1.1:244ff.). The youth at Nain (Luke 7:11–17) lay on the bier and only appeared to be dead as he was carried to the grave. Jesus noticed his initial movements and that he was returning to consciousness. Jesus subsequently commanded him to arise (*WA* 1:716ff.; *Leben Jesu* 1.1:281–83). Lazarus, who had been too quickly entombed, came forth alive when Jesus caused the crypt to be opened (*Leben Jesu* 1.2:55–61).

Most significant for this practice is explaining the event of the crucifixion and the appearances of the risen Lord. Concerning these, Paulus remarks: Not that it would be possible to debate about the resurrection of Jesus, but rather one had to ask whether God may have "brought about its occurrence through the presently existing powers and means in the world order" (thus in natural ways) (*Leben Jesu*, 1.2:278). From the reports of the crucifixion and appearances of Jesus in the four synoptic Gospels under consideration, Paulus supposes that he is able to conclude that Jesus arose with his natural body. He appeared in this manner to the women, disciples, and other witnesses during the several weeks after his crucifixion (see esp. *Leben Jesu* 1.2:277ff.). In reality he was not dead, but rather only extremely weak, and he appeared to have died. Thus, he was placed in the tomb. Through a fortunate circumstance, he was not embalmed, owing to the Sabbath rest, for his brain and intestines otherwise would have been removed. Thus, Jesus secretly was removed from the grave, while Mary Magdalene believed that his body was stolen (John 20:13). It appears important to Paulus that only the hands of Jesus, and not also his feet, were nailed to the cross, since how could he have walked about with pierced feet for weeks (see *WA* 3:669)? The ascension of Jesus is not to be understood literally, but rather the statement of the two men dressed in white garments (Acts 1:11) meant only that, after his demise due to general weakness, Jesus was finally received "into the location and state of blessedness" (*Leben Jesu* 1.2:331).

By setting forth a rational explanation of the miracles, including the resurrection and ascension, Paulus reduces Jesus' life and work to that of a normal human being. However, he was to a certain degree extraordinary, though his activities and existence took place under natural circumstances. Paulus wishes to define the commissioning and message of Jesus in a new way over against the church's traditional "faith in inspiration." Thus, he shapes the "Preliminary Introduction" to *Leben Jesu* (1.1:1–64.) as the "Preparation for the Idea of Christ," which means a history of the idea of the Messiah. He pursues this concept throughout the Old Testament. Already in Abraham he finds a precursor to the representation of the "rational will," which he defines as "the combination of intentions and thoughts through the striving after perfection"

(*Leben Jesu* 1.1:15). After this, he traces the development of the idea of the Messiah from Moses to the Hasmoneans, eventually coming to speak about Jesus. Jesus is connected to the expectation of a "messianic spirit," which is finally shaped in Dan 7 as the "Son of Man" who has entered into a human body. Possessing the characteristics of intentionality and reason, he brought to realization "the messianic ideal that was worthy of divinity" (ibid., 55). The kingdom of God is defined in a purely moral way: "Jesus' Kingdom of God should be obedience to the desires of God who, through his deeds, effectuated salvation." In addition to this, Jesus commanded the "self-transformation of the customary human attitude" respecting faithful conviction. Paulus renders the word "faith" (*pistis*) to mean "that which God would desire," that is, "the idea of righteousness and goodness." The spirit (*pneuma*) is the "pure capacity of the will of reason,… in which the divine good, because it is good, is elevated to love" (57–59). Furthermore, Jesus has taken up the future hope in the return of the spirit of the Messiah for judgment and the final establishment of his kingdom. This hope, however, is bound up with the appeal for the faithful fulfillment of obligations, for this *instruction* is decisive for Jesus alone (60–64).

Further, Paulus does not allow himself to be diverted by the famous Pauline statements concerning justification: "that a person becomes righteous without the aid of the works of the law. Rather this occurs only through faith" (Rom 3:28). Paulus reinterprets this rationally: "the highest law comes into being only through the righteousness originating through faithful conviction in the mind" (*Des Apostels Paulus Lehrbriefe an die Galater—und Römer—Christen* [1831], 182). Paulus represents without restriction the optimistic depiction of humanity during the Enlightenment, according to which humans are able in and of themselves to accomplish good. Especially objectionable to him was the thought that Jesus gave himself to remove our guilt. Paulus maintains that nothing in the entire New Testament speaks of this.

If Paulus's historical competence and his effort to explain miracles was often praised during the Enlightenment, this is because Christianity of this new era began with the presuppositions of thought of the enlightened consciousness. Paulus did not take as his starting point the biblical faith of the Reformation, even when he expressly called on Luther (*Hdb*, Preamble, xliv). His biography testifies that his last attested words on his deathbed were, "I stand justified before God through the desire of the righteous one," and "There is another world."

5.10. Explaining Biblical Myth as a "Childlike" Manner of
Speech: Johann Gottfried Eichhorn and Johann Philipp Gabler

Johann Gottfried Eichhorn was born in 1752 in Dörenzimmern in the
vicinity of Heilbronn (in the principality of Hohenlohe-Öhringen), the
son of a pastor. After attending the city school in Weikersheim (where his
father had become the superintendent) and the gymnasium in Heilbronn
in 1767–1770, he studied Semitic and classical philosophy as well as theology, beginning in 1770 in Göttingen. Formative for him in addition to
the Orientalist scholar and theologian Johann David Michaelis (1717–
1791) and the scholar of universal history August Ludwig (von) Schlözer
(1735–1809), was especially the philologist of ancient languages Christian
Gottlob Heyne (1729–1812). In 1774, Eichhorn became the rector of the
gymnasium in Ohrdruf (in the duchy of Saxony-Gotha, today Thuringen). He graduated from Jena in 1775. In the same year, he became there,
at the age of twenty-two, the youngest professor of Oriental languages.
In 1788, he went to Göttingen, and for the rest of his life was professor of
philosophy. He died in 1827.

Eichhorn was an all-around scholar. He wrote several works about
world history and the history of literature, which, in addition to the Old
and New Testaments and different Oriental languages, were a part of his
rich program of instruction. In addition he produced some historically
specialized works. His scholarly work and lectures in Göttingen emphasized biblical topics. Among these, he published numerous reviews in
the two journals that he edited in succession, *Repertorium für Biblische
und Morgenländische Literatur* (Repertory of Biblical and Oriental Literature [1777–1786]) and somewhat more narrowly defined *Allgemeine
Bibliothek der biblischen Literatur* (General Library of Biblical Literature
[1787–1803]). Beginning in 1812, as the successor of Heyne, he edited the
journal *Göttingische Gelehrte Anzeigen,* which continues to this day. As a
Bible scholar he won enduring recognition for his work in the history of
the discipline.

This can be said especially of two spheres of scholarly work: his
research into myth and his pioneering of the form of the scholarly introduction to the Bible. Decisive for Eichhorn's judgment about the Old
Testament was his participation in the seminar on ancient mythology
held at Göttingen and directed by Heyne. In this seminar, Heyne treated
ancient poetic texts, above all the poetic works of Homer and Hesiod,
and he investigated the relationship between poetry and myth in classical antiquity. Previously the mythical material in these texts had been

regarded simply as poetic invention, often with an allegorical intention. Heyne, however, explained it in a revolutionary new way as a typical form of expression for the childhood of humanity. "All history and philosophy of early humanity has emanated from myths." He formulated this principle in his edition of (Pseudo-)Apollodorus (1783; 2nd ed., 1803, 14). The poets adapted the mythical materials and embellished them for poetic purposes. These poets were not the initial formulators of what they then transformed. Further, according to Heyne, allegory is principally a late development. Myths may not be explained allegorically. They were a *necessary* means of expression for the ancient period, which was characterized by the absence of knowledge, by the scarcity of the capacity for verbalization, and by the inability to disconnect oneself directly from the impressions of the senses. Heyne divided myths into two groups: (1) historical myths, which depicted historical events such as the founding of cities or the actions of a hero of the primeval period; and (2) philosophical myths, which contain speculative ethical or natural explanations in the form of cosmologies possessing similar contents.

Already by the age of twenty-three, Eichhorn produced his *Primeval History,* an interpretation of Gen 1:1–2:4a, and 2:4b–3:24. He published this anonymously in four parts in his *Repertorium für biblische and morgenländische Literatur.* His student Johann Philipp Gabler provided it with comprehensive introductions and notations in three volumes, newly appearing in 1790–93.

Gabler was born in Frankfurt am Main in 1753. His father was the *actuarius* (the legal director of administration) in the consistorium. The well-to-do father enabled his son to be instructed in reading, writing, religion, Latin, and Greek by a private tutor. At the age of ten Johann was sent to the gymnasium of his father's city. The dry method of cramming, which at that time was customary in the school, was mitigated, since his father gave him private exercises in philosophy, disputation, and coherent lectures. In addition, he was allowed to preach publicly as early as the age of sixteen, something that later was disallowed. Thus, he came to the university already proficient in several areas. From 1772 to 1778, he studied in Jena, primarily philosophy and then theology under Eichhorn and Griesbach. After he was promoted with a master's degree in 1778, he returned to Frankfurt for his churchly examinations and for additional instruction. From 1780 to 1783, he was a tutor in Göttingen. Here he had the opportunity to come to know Heyne, whose pioneering methods he appropriated. On the basis of his highly regarded work on 2 Cor 9–13 (1782), he was called to be a professor of philosophy and prorector of the

Archigymnasium in Dortmund. In 1785, he followed a call to the University of Altdorf, and in 1804 he moved to Jena, where he died in 1826.

The *Primeval History* in the ample comments of the new edition (1790–1793) is a work written by both Eichhorn and Gabler. In spite of many requests addressed to him to publish a new edition of his earlier work, Eichhorn had foresworn undertaking this activity, since he no longer agreed with his former interpretation especially of Gen 2–3. He had, however, approved the new edition written by Gabler. Both men are regarded in the history of interpretation as the founders of the "mythical school." To be sure, this was certainly more true of Gabler than of Eichhorn. As we are yet to see, in the first edition of the *Primeval History* there was a lack, to a large extent, of the necessary theoretical tools. Gabler, however, possessed a stronger theoretical mind, and formulated the necessary materials in his elaborate introductions and notations to the new edition.

Eichhorn was conservative inasmuch as he (at least in his early writing) still ascribed to Moses the authorship of Gen 1. His approach, however, was different from what had previously been the case. Earlier the discussion had been directed passionately to the theory of *accommodation*. It was asked especially whether Jesus actually shared the ideas of his Jewish contemporaries regarding angels, demons, the Messiah, judgment, and resurrection or had simply accommodated himself to these ideas in his own language. Could the Son of God actually have thought in a manner so time-bound to his own historical period? Analogous was the amount of truth attributed to the biblical primeval history by the critical rationalists ("naturalists") on account of the narratives' logical conflicts and especially their inconsistencies with the newest geological and cosmological knowledge about the origin of the earth and the universe. How could God create light and separate it from the darkness (Gen 1:3–4) before he had created the great heavenly bodies (the sun and the moon), which should distinguish between day and night (vv. 14–18)? How could creation be completed in six days when the newly discovered geology demonstrates a much greater age of the earth? The affirmation that Moses had accommodated himself in his description to the level of knowledge available to the Israelites at that time helped here just as little as the explanation that this all may be only free composition. One could not defend the authority of the Bible by this means from the approach of modern criticism.

The application to the Bible of Heyne's understandings of myth offered a way out. Heyne's theory about the myths of classical antiquity serving as the form of expression of traditional, mythical-bound human beings, overpowered intuitively by the emotion of the senses and unable to think abstractly, were typical in this respect for the childhood of humanity. This also could be said about the biblical myths. Among these, Eichhorn counted especially the sagas of the primeval history. With regard to Gen 1, he explains that Moses described the characteristics of creation in a manner corresponding to the ideas of his own time.

Eichhorn's writing *Urgeschichte: Ein Versuch* (Primeval History: An Examination), unaltered and republished by Gabler, is shaped in a simple manner in both its structure and purpose. As a text composed by a youth, it evidences a sanguine directness. Gabler was able to transmit Eichhorn's point of view of Gen 1 with only a few sentences. The main purpose of the chapter is stated succinctly: "Everything originates with God" (Introduction, 1:72). "Lacking a guide and leader and without map and travel book, I walked in my wandering to the holy temple of the revelation of God, and left to it to my good fortune" (1:141). Eichhorn accordingly advised his readers:

> Whoever wishes to investigate the Mosaic document of the creation of all things should not be aware of the expert opinion about it of others. … If he is, as is customary, not in this fortunate position, then he must forget everything that he has heard spoken, been taught, and dreamed as a pupil, a youth, and an adult … from knowledgeable and not unknowledgeable people. (1:140–41)

Immediately at the beginning he mentions the decisive points of view:

> How it is possible to maintain until the present time Moses' initial chapter to be nothing more than a simple narrative of origins and the construction of our earth, which consequentially places in order all parts of the observable world and outlines the origin of their succession, is to me something that always has been incomprehensible. Each mark appears to betray a brush of a painter's stroke, and not the stylus of a writer of history.… God is the originator of everything that is [see also 1:151–52]: this is the most important subject that the composer wished to execute. He therefore places himself in front of the innumerous series of created things and considers the main parts of each one in view of what the human eye can observe according to their origin and not in other ways as if he were a spectator of their coming into being. Therefore he speaks of all of these completely by means of what may be seen. (1:142ff.)

The parallels to Herder's *Ältesten Urkunde des Menschengeschlechts* (The Oldest Documents of Humankind; see above, 193–94), which was written at almost the same time, are obvious, even if Herder did not derive his views from Heyne but rather regarded all of this as poetry. The order of the works of creation "rests on this situation of the composer." This divides into three main parts, according to Eichhorn: "(1) First water and land, (2) then bodies in the water and on the land, and (3) finally, inhabitants of the water and the land" (1:143ff.). For the particulars of the division of the works into days, Eichhorn then addresses a more difficult reason. The creation of the light would be anticipated, because it would be necessary to observe creation. Two works must be added together to make one day, the creation of light called day and its separation from darkness called night. The author "gives the appearance of his being an observer of the great creation and sees in this situation all the major parts of the observable world originating in six days" (1:152). Gabler remarks concerning this (1:149 n. 1): the development of this plan "appears to me to be so natural that I always perceive it to be the sequence of the ideas of the ancient poet."

For the underlying hermeneutics, Eichhorn makes the comment that he wishes to attempt to deeply reduce the "developed spirit" of his reader "so much that it would be comparable to the child-like spirit of the first eon" (1:256). Later (*Einleitung in das Alte Testament* [Introduction to the Old Testament], 4th ed., 3:174–75) he formulates this more completely:

> Forget the century in which you live and the knowledge it offers you. If you are unable to do so, do not dream that you may enjoy the book in the spirit of its origin. The youthful age of the world, which it describes, requires a spirit that is deeply rooted in its depth; the first rays of the dawning light of reason do not bear the bright light of its complete days … without inward familiarity with the form of thought and conception of the uncultivated world … one becomes easily a betrayer of the book, if one wishes to be both its preserver and its interpreter.

This knowledge is acquired through acquaintance "with the earliest Greece and the uncultivated nations of more recent times…." The most recently obtained familiarity with people of nature who are still living today is just as much a source of opinion concerning the Old Testament as is the classical culture.

The second part of the *Urgeschichte* of Eichhorn (2.1:1–310) treats in particular Gen 2:4–3:24. The knowledge that we have to do with another "monument" that thus is to be separated from Gen 1 is presupposed by Eichhorn in reference to (Jean) Astruc (1684–1766) and J. F. W. Jerusalem (1709–1789) (2.1:10). He appropriates also from their interpretation the view that Moses could have used "ancient monuments" that Noah had saved over from the period before the flood (Gabler [n. 4] remarks that this is not possible, because writing was not invented so early). Eichhorn stresses immediately at the beginning the distance of the century of the interpreter from that of "gray antiquity": "here is finally a bright midday, when there is the first dawning of the awakening of human reason" (2.1:3–4). Entirely in the spirit of Lessing's book on education (see above), Eichhorn, who looks down from the height of enlightened reason, reckons with a steady higher development of the human spirit progressing from darkness to light. From here he develops a historical perspective, however, different from the previous efforts at analysis. "Completely as strangers in the customs, the language, and the way of thinking of the newer uneducated nations, most interpreters ventured to speak of the interpretation of the monuments by Moses, which originated from a time when humans were still looking towards their culture." In contrast to chapter 1, Eichhorn sees the style of Gen 2:4ff. declining. While there is shaped and then applied an artistic plan of the whole, "the narrative assumes" from 2:4ab "an artless way of proceeding" (14–15). The verses do not occupy the place that a more experienced narrator would have given them. The author must more frequently reach back to an anterior time that he had previously ignored. By means of the names of God, 2:4–3:24 distances itself clearly from chapter 4, because here the customary name "Jehovah (= common at this time, but resulting from an incorrect pronunciation) together with Elohim" is used, instead of simply "Jehovah" by itself in chapter 4. Chapters 2 and 3 hang closely together: "the same spirit of uncultivated antiquity and the same sensual concepts permeate both sections with equally strong rays" (18). One can recognize the age of the document, which had already existed for a long time prior to Moses, by its language: "it originated in a remote antiquity." Thus, it belongs "in the childhood of the world, where there was lacking to humans an overarching vista," so that "one therefore had to name parts in order to provide terms for the whole" (24). The author wished to say: "There was a time when there was nothing like it is now." He must express this through some common variations. For this he selected the green garment, which the earth takes on annually in the spring and in the fall again discards. He so shaped his wider description as necessities presented themselves to him. In order that it could turn green, the earth must initially be saturated by the rain and then tilled by the industry of humanity. For this he added: "for it had not yet rained and there was no human to till the soil" (Gen 2:5). "The next thought was: 'therefore all began to become as it is now'" (27). The variation has to begin in the air. Thus, the author spoke primarily of dew and related it to the earth. Therefore he said: "saturated the earth" (Gen 2:6). "Now our earth becomes green through the sweat of humans, who work it. Consequently the historian added: 'Jehovah formed therefore the man from the dust of the earth and blew into his nostrils the breath of life' (Gen 2:7)" (28–29). Eichhorn returns thus to the time of the "childlike" author and seeks psychologically to comprehend how this could have come to formulation. In so doing, he continually presupposes that a modern, enlightened writer would form the narrative with many exact, applicable, and consistent details. For example, Eichhorn remarks concerning the sentence "God allowed the animals to come to Adam in order to see what he would name them" (cf. v. 19) that "a writer from a cultured time would have used a more comprehensive form of expression": God placed Adam into the world of the animals. This gave him the opportunity to give them their names. "Should God actually have brought the animals in sequence to Adam? Was this necessary? Is it dignified enough? Did they not already run wild around Adam, since the time when God had him enter the world in Eden?" It is his lack of experience in the art of narrative that caused the writer to be guilty of failing to bring every idea together into the correct order. "From him speaks the simple, nonartistic nature" (31–32).

The rationalism of the Enlightenment makes a smooth transition at this point into the attempt at a historical consideration that takes the text in earnest in the context of the time of its origin. As a basic principle, Eichhorn formulates the following: "The closer a monument of antiquity stands to the youth of the world the more must the ideas of divinity ruling it differ from our own. These have greatly expanded over time and repeated revelation" (56). Eichhorn and Gabler make the effort psychologically to go behind the thoughts of the writer by trying to put themselves into his circumstances in life. To be sure they still reflect the Enlightenment's consciousness of superiority: "Finally, very imperfect, raw ideas about God reside at the basis of these documents ... so that He brings everything directly into the scope of reality, which must occur according to the arrangement God once has effected according to the course of nature" (56). "However, it is impossible for the narrator to think differently about the activities of the deity than he himself is capable of performing. Therefore, the deity continues each time to deliberate with himself. He goes personally to the place where he should act" (65). The author lets the deity act directly in every place "where he, according to our enlightened form of thinking, only indirectly acts" (79). According to Eichhorn, we have to do, if we understand it from the time of origin, with a "thoroughly true history," only rendered in this particular way (77). "Therefore, there can be neither mythology nor allegory" (79). In the following, he still presents several arguments against the acceptance of a myth. Obviously, in no way had he appropriated Heyne's understanding of myth! Gabler (nn. 36 and 37) remarks hereto: this could not be a "really true narrative." "The writer accepted already here a myth, namely, a historical one, even if he had not named it as such." The young Eichhorn makes a different assessment: "Away with all of these artificial exegetical maneuvers! One has to present only the concepts and language of the uneducated, sentient humanity: perhaps the fog disappears that until now covers the eyes of the interpreters" (96–97).

Eichhorn explains in similar fashion the narrative in Gen 3. The conversation of Eve with the serpent and the two humans with God are personified and dramatized thoughts: "Now doubts arise in the soul of Eve: 'Has God really said?' (cf. Gen 3:1). The series of thoughts, which now awaken within Eve, have been expressed in the old, vulgar human way of engaging in a conversation between the serpent and Eve" (154–57). Hebrew lacked a word for "thinking" but rather used the word for "speaking"! Thus, this is true of the personal intervention of God: "Everything which cannot be explained by an unenlightened human according to its initial origin or what happens when something is entirely unexpected he derives from a direct concurrence of God" (167–70). "And all things thereby—how natural! How commensurate with the childhood of the human age!" (181). Besides this, there becomes apparent to the enlightened person: "Admittedly this process of Eve's thought contains lowly, child-like ideas of God, if we measure this according to our superior knowledge, which millennia and repeated revelations have taught us" (183–84).

The transference of Heyne's mythical conception to the interpretation of Genesis must be ascribed mainly to the theorist Gabler. He especially expresses this in his comprehensive introduction to Eichhorn's *Urgeschichte*. There one finds a detailed debate with all other remaining, published interpretations of the biblical primeval history. The new edition can serve clearly as a handbook for the position of scholarship at that time. With Gabler it becomes clear that the efforts of his teacher, Eichhorn, as well as his own endeavors had at the outset an apologetic purpose. Against the orthodox, among whom he could list also the "naturalists," he stresses that he, as a Lutheran, has an obligation only to the books of confession of the Evangelical Lutheran Church, "and in these faith in the Mosaic six-day workweek is not compulsory" (Preamble, 1:xviii). Here Gabler also formulates his axiom that has become famous, although mostly has been misunderstood, about the separation of biblical and dogmatic theology (see below). This becomes for him a decisive principle: "Dogmatics must depend upon exegesis and not vice versa" (xv). He formulates expressly a confession of Christ according to Rom 1:16 (xx). Against the deists, who make sport of creation because of the six-day workweek, he underlines that there is no reason behind this: "It contains an admirable poetic painting of the entire world. Thereupon, one would have reason to make sport of the first account of our religion, only if we would wish to pass off this portrait for historical truth" (xxi).

In the following introduction (1:1–136), Gabler displays all of the previous, major interpretations, including the one by Eichhorn. He discreetly explains that he has another view, although the reasons brought forth against Eichhorn are not necessarily substantive ones (74). He responds to the most important objection that the Sabbath had not yet been introduced at the time of Moses by arguing that Gen 2:3 relates only to God's day of rest and not to any type of human Sabbath (82). Against Eichhorn, Gabler holds that the description of the Sabbath is much older than Moses (95). He points to the striking correlation with the older Egyptian and Phoenician sagas (97), a seminal perspective that points to future understanding. Egyptians and Phoenicians had possessed a tradition concerning the seventh day that was also common to Israel. Moses had taken over the division of the seven-day week from Egypt. With Spencer and Johann David Michaelis, he derives most of the religious and political organization of the Israelites from Egypt.

The second part of the primeval history appeared as a separate volume in 1792 (2.1:481–648). In his comprehensive introduction to this volume, Gabler describes in detail the theory of myth in its employment in the biblical, primeval history. In his earlier volume, he had required a uniform explanation of the mythical character of both chapters of Gen 2–3:

> There must have been the identical point of view and the same type of explanation in both chapters. However, one cannot understand the second chapter in this way, if one explains the third chapter as allegorical and imaginary. One chapter cannot be explained as history and the other as myth and vice versa.... The same point of view and form of explanation must be present throughout the document contained in both chapters. (2.1:2)

Later, in a fundamental discussion of myth, he explains:

> Myths are mainly sagas of the ancient world in the form of thought
> and language that was sensible at that time. In these myths, one may
> therefore not expect an event to be precisely described, as it actually had
> occurred, but rather only as it must have been thought to have occurred
> in and inferred from the sensory form that existed at that time. The
> event would have to have been reported and described in the pictorial,
> visible, and dramatic language, in which an event could be narrated at
> that time. Therefore, all narratives from the ancient world as well as on
> the initial origins of each people must necessarily be myths. The older
> the book the more myths it must contain. (2.1:482)

Fables, which originated from later expansions, are to be distinguished
from myths, although many also have called them myths. However, they
are a "later product of human fiction." Gabler appropriates also the division
between historical, poetic, and philosophical myths: "A historical myth is
one in which an actual event of the ancient world is delivered as a fact. Its
judgments and conclusions are presented in archaic language and a primitive form of thinking that is sensory, pictorial, visible, and appropriate for
its own period, but, in spite of this, expresses judgments and conclusions
as facts" (484). A true historical description, "as one today rightly requires
it of a careful historian," may not be expected of ancient myth. "Even so,
we can expect a historical base" corresponding to the poverty of ideas and
values of that time, as well as to the "great lack of knowledge of the natural
origin of things." It still is expressed in the "sensual form of thought" of
the primitive world. One must attempt to ascertain true history from the
description, outfitting, and "inner reality of the narrated event." "A myth is
poetic, if it is has been decorated with didactic additions and expansions,
or if the poetic genius has embellished and combined into an aggregate
several ancient myths that were dispersed in different locales." That is
also the case, if a myth was created by means of "artistic fiction." "A philosophical myth originated either simply out of pure speculation, or from
conjecturing about the origins of things in the world, or from thinking
about a variety of moral subjects. This was accomplished, when a philosophical thesis was clothed in a narrative." There may also be an actual
history residing at the basis of this type of myth, although the sage may
have expressed it to conform to his own ideas. This first class of myth may
be subdivided: "either one has thought something to have been the case ...
as one conceived it, or the history was only the hull for the philosophical
ideas contained in the mythical description" (482–90).

Thus, this allows the biblical, primeval history to be classified. If one
is correct in assessing this as myth, then, according to Gabler, its class

must be more precisely differentiated. Gabler considers it to be a historical myth. Paradise, the trees, the divine prohibition not to eat of the tree of knowledge, the snake, the detrimental activity of enjoyment of the fruit, the need for clothing, and the expulsion from the garden are seen as facts. Similarly to Eichhorn, Gabler finds a natural explanation for everything reported here.

He then sees that it is "necessary to take yet another step" (538). One has here a poetic or, still more probably, a philosophical myth, due to the speculation over the origin of evil (539–40). For this position he provides reasons in the subsequent elaborate explanation. In spite of this, Gabler judged later (with Herder and then also Eichhorn) that a historical factuality lies at the base. However, the speculation "of a wise man of nature" prevails over this first history of humans and the world, which expresses belief in this form of the origin of nature, humanity, and evil (587). Likewise (cf. the preface at 2.2:xxxi), he considers Gen 2–3 to be the philosophical theorem of an ancient sage. For distinguishing between historical and philosophical myth, he now explains, it is decisive which of these predominates in these chapters. Thus, a fact absolutely could lie at the basis of the philosophical myth, even if this is not the governing motif.

In the common work of both critics, the slightly older teacher and the student who always expressed his admiration for the teacher, the peculiar features of each come clearly to expression. Eichhorn is an exegete and a historian, while Gabler has stronger systematic inclinations.

As an author, Eichhorn has become known for more than composing his *Urgeschichte* (primeval history). He is recognized also for having written his introductions to both the Old and New Testaments. He is held to be the founder of this category of biblical scholarship. The *Einleitung in the Alte Testament* (Old Testament Introduction [three volumes, 1780–1783]) underwent four editions (and two unauthorized printings), and the fourth edition in 1823–1824 was expanded to five volumes. In a section taken from the foreword to the second edition, which is reprinted again in the fourth edition (1:iii–vi), Eichhorn elucidates once again his enlightened apologetic and historical intentions: the previous theological use of the Old Testament had sought out only religious ideas and rendered the eyes blind to its remaining content. This had been the case especially in regard to the question of the miracles of the Israelites, which some had acknowledged as true, while others had found them to be impossible, thus resulting in the mocking of these writings. With a more appropriate approach, however, it would quickly have become clear that only a misunderstanding of the language and form of thought, which the Bible held in common with all documents of a hazy antiquity, had incorporated the miraculous. It would have been different, "if they would have been made acquainted with the fact that they [the biblical Scriptures] have so completely described the history of the culture and enlightenment of an ancient people that there remain ... no other opportunities to provide for the important considerations of thousands of humans and of human history" (1:v–vi). Eichhorn chooses consequently the philosophical and historical approach to understanding the Bible by using Heyne's method for interpreting classical poetic works. A contemporary reader had written at this place on the margin of his copy: "theological use?" However, Eichhorn knowingly used a nontheological, cultural-historical approach and thereby introduced historical criticism according to the nineteenth-century standard), Eichhorn directed himself, in his own terms, to the habits of his contemporaries (vi). Therefore, he begins primarily (ch. 1) with a section mainly on Hebrew literature and on the origin, authenticity, and canonicity of the writings of the Old Testament. He unfolds there anew his thoughts on the childlike condition of the Hebrew people, whose education Moses sought to enhance, although without much success, through the gift of his law. Therefore, the crude condition of the people continued, without the development of a higher degree of knowledge, science, and philosophy. Thus, there was "no comprehensive view of the whole" (1:7). "Like all nations at the lower grade of education, the Hebrews engaged simply in singing and the writing of poetry." "Even the enlightenment of their priestly order stood only a few stages higher than the nation and never progressed ... to culture and science" (1:6–7). Such a tutor was indispensable for the childhood of this crude people and was therefore installed by Moses according to an Egyptian pattern. Later, to be sure, this became extremely harmful: "it obstructed the progress of knowledge ... and hindered it by being passed on to the entire nation" (1:9). The typical anticlerical position of the Enlightenment comes into view at this point! Greek culture, by contrast, existed in the period when humanity had already more matured into adulthood. Eichhorn even believes in a relapse of the Israelites after Moses. They could not grasp his heightened sense of monotheism and, on the contrary, became apostates during their journey in the wilderness and began to worship animals, and then in Canaan served many of the Canaanite gods. The artistic work that they had carried out in the desert, they forgot later on, requiring Solomon to hire foreign craftsmen to perform metalwork. All of this, however, must not lead to our contempt for the Scriptures, which we much more could put aside only with reverence and thanks. While they are not witnesses of the most rational religion of antiquity, they are valuable as a collection of authentic natural poetry and primitive temple songs. They are also worthwhile. The Hebrews had the most ancient of historians, since they originated in a hazy antiquity and were considerably older than the Greeks. Thus, they belong to those who produce the "invaluable documents for the history of human development." "Therefore, instead of mocking and despising them, we wish rather to thank fate for this still existing flowering of the oriental spirit" (1:16–17).

Eichhorn's theological valuation had therefore given way to an almost entirely cultural-historical, aesthetic treatment of the Old Testament, although he still retained elements of a supernatural viewpoint. The survival of the Hebrew literature in substantial sections "appears certainly a miracle of the age: how can this be explained in a natural manner?" (1:19).

More technical demonstrations follow these fundamental remarks. Thus, original Hebrew writings may have been collected in a library in the Jerusalem temple. The present collection certainly did not originate directly from there. The preservation of these works may have been due to an accident of good fortune (and the intervention of Cyrus; see Ezra 1). From private collections (among these were the prophetic writings), presumably an assortment of writings was placed in the new temple library (having begun with Ezra and later Nehemiah and then expanded by other patriots). During the postexilic period, the writings were carefully transmitted further, even though scribal errors crept into the texts.

In regard to the order of the collected books, Eichhorn next examines them in three parts. For his ideology, §9 is interesting (1:52–58): "Why can the composers of the Old Testament be designated as prophets?" It had come gradually into use to call the Old Testament authors prophets. Josephus built the reliability of the Hebrew histories upon this view by referring to them with this term. Eichhorn argues:

> The further we go back into the periods of the previous world, the less knowledge we discover humans have concerning the nature of things.... It took a thousand years before humans came to the insight that all changes hang together like links in a chain and until they could grasp the ideas of eternal, unalterable laws, according to which nature operates. They derive the idea that everything comes from the intervention of an unseen … mighty being. (1:53)

Following this, he concludes this chapter with a section on the language of the Old Testament. Eichhorn considers Job (already debated at this time) to be an ancient poetic writing, which may have been well established at the latest during the time of David. It was probably older, however, since its language can easily be derived from the ancient form of the Semitic language. The authenticity of the writings of the Old Testament (§14) Eichhorn wholeheartedly accepts. To be sure, the text has experienced many changes, and the writings have passed through the hands of redactors. This is true for the Books of Moses, which were arranged from Mosaic articles by a later hand. Samuel and the books of Chronicles underwent at least two editions. The book of Judges originally had only sixteen chapters. Five additional chapters were added later, because there was still room on the parchment. "Our Isaiah is a florilegium of different nameless prophetic poets, many of whom seem to have appeared first during the exilic period and who probably have written under the name of Isaiah in order that nothing be omitted" (1:93–94). While the name Deutero-Isaiah does not appear in his writing, Eichhorn still recognized that a case could be made for the late date of origin for the second part of the book of Isaiah. The only debate is whether Eichhorn is the first to have come to this position (or perhaps it was Johann Benjamin Koppe (1750–1791) in the notes of his German translation of R. Lowth's book about Isaiah (1779–1781).

The second chapter treats the history of the Old Testament text. The view that this chapter has been thoroughly and critically edited has generally prevailed. The third chapter deals with the tools to assist in the critical edition of the text. This chapter is very detailed, and it continues into and through the entire second volume. The third volume brings us to the second part of the work: the introduction to each of the individual books of the Old Testament. This evidences a later, classic structure for introductions. It has to do with age, time of origin, and circumstances of the period as well as the content of the individual books. For the Books of Moses, Eichhorn holds fast in the fourth edition to the Mosaic origin of these writings, although in the meantime doubts had intensified considerably against this view. The primary formulation of his argument is that it may not have been impossible for a written document to originate close to the time of 1500 B.C.E. owing to the antiquity of the Phoenician script. The question that is to be addressed to critical scholars is whether it is appropriate "to doubt purely on the basis of a priori reasons the authenticity of a monument of antiquity" (3:14). Eichhorn clearly remarks that he adheres to his position of Mosaic authorship even after forty years (3:15 n. h). He does not wish to change his position (de Wette remarked maliciously that he did so in order to save face), although he mentions all the new objections directed against him of which he was aware thereby demonstrating that he continued to follow the discussion. For the rest, he speaks of two "documents" in the Books of Moses while keeping his distance from Karl David Ilgen (1763–1834). Ilgen reckoned with two sources that used the name "Elohim" in the Joseph story (Gen 37; 39–48; 50). This problem is still debated today! Furthermore, Eichhorn believes in the antiquity and authenticity of these books, which, when read and interpreted as documents from the childhood of humanity, contain throughout credible historical messages. Eichhorn especially maintains that any doubt about the historicity of Moses is fallacious. "The view that there never was a Moses in the world who was the founder and lawgiver of the Hebrew State can result only from the intrusion of the most assiduous degree of skepticism" (3:178–79). Furthermore, Eichhorn holds that the book of Deuteronomy, in spite of all that had emerged in the meantime, expresses Mosaic ideas. In the rest of the volume, he reviews the remaining historical books up to and including Esther.

The fourth volume addresses the prophetic books. In regard to the prophets, Eichhorn stresses in the preamble (4:iii–xlvi) his preference for them in contrast to the Greek seers, although he censures the Hebrews for thinking that they derived all their skills from the intervention of a higher being. "They still hold that every evil in the world requires the punishment of the angry God, who must be appeased through confessions" (4:lxii). He also disapproves of their particularism of the prophetic books. The origin of the prophets may have derived from the predictions of wise men who were regarded in the early period as confidants of the deity. The prophets appeared like poets. Eichhorn stresses their ecstatic characteristics: "The deity fell mightily upon the inspired person, and what he did not know before this moment, he now speaks immediately out what he was taught by him" (4:7). Since there were already prophets before Moses, he administered their duties. He appointed them to be "heralds of things of truth, goodness, and beauty" (4:12). They should be responsible for the maintenance of his laws. As a consequence of their assignation, they must become the interpreters and commentators of Moses. That should offer them also personal protection. If they appealed to Moses, their person was sanctified and inviolable, and their life secured. But they became in the course of history concretely nationalistic in their perspective. The position of their nation, not the fortune of the world, mainly lay in their heart. However, they were also teachers "who gradually sought to provide the sensual religion of Moses a spiritual direction" (4:19). Since the Hebrews were a vulgar people, Moses could do nothing apart from gradually restraining their crude sensuality by means of his requirement of external customs, festivals, and sacrifices. His successors, the prophets, taught the people how to get rid of this burden and gradually to make superfluous all sacrifices, rites of purification, and chastisement with an ameliorated morality. The ideals of an enlightened religiosity were projected by Eichhorn onto the Old Testament prophets. Still, the prophets were for him only individually great souls, voices quickly dying away in a dead grove of trees. "At first the great teacher of humanity taught this with the voice of God, which will resound until the end of the times" (4:24).

Nevertheless, Eichhorn also has historical interests. In a later section (4:62–75) he treats the authenticity of prophecy and presents the means to determine the antiquity of prophetic statements. The genuineness of prophetic oracles is shown in their belonging to their respective periods. That Jeremiah, Haggai, and Zechariah were active in the same period is demonstrated by their common use of forms and also by their mistakes in language. Temporal distinctions are demonstrated also by the differences in language. To be sure, criticism may also separate the later sections in the ancient prophetic texts, and the contents may determine the respective periods of origin of the prophetic writings. The reasons for threats and promises are taken from the particular, temporal circumstances. However, these threats and promises are always rather general.

We pass over the subsequent individual descriptions of most of the prophetic books. Of special interest are the statements on the sections in the book of Isaiah that Eichhorn denied were authored by Isaiah the prophet. These included chapters 15; 16; and 24–27 in the first part of the book. In addition, chapters 40–52 of Isaiah were not composed prior to the Babylonian exile (4:82–90). Isaiah 36–39 consists of chapters taken from the historical narrative of the book of Kings (4:109). The result indicates: "All circumstances, it seems to me, lead to the view that our Isaiah may be an oracular anthology made after the Babylonian exile, the first basis of which was a collection of Isaianic prophecies" (4:114). When Eichhorn's *Einleitung in das Alte Testament* appeared in a fourth edition, the avant-garde had long since left him behind.

A similar portrayal is found also in Eichhorn's *Einleitung in das Neue Testament* (Introduction to the New Testament), which consists of five volumes that appeared between 1804 and 1827 (several published in a second edition). It is clearly arranged through its explicit structure and is especially of interest, because it shows Eichhorn's more advanced historical method.

According to Eichhorn, the first three canonical Gospels commonly originate from a single "primitive Gospel," although they did so independently of each other (cf. Lessing). In the sections in which all three concur, he accepts the view that they also had used a common source. For the sections containing texts that only two Gospels held in common or only one possessed, he also assumed that the Evangelists used written sources. While the ancient Gospel could have originated three to four years after the death of Jesus, the time of origin of the Gospel of Matthew, the first part of which is chronologically different from the rest, is uncertain. On account of the trinitarian baptismal formula in Matt 28:19, which departed from the original formula that had only the name of Jesus, the final form could not have originated from Matthew during the first generation of Christians. In respect to John (vol. 2), Eichhorn is quite conservative. He ascribes, according to tradition, all the writings bearing the name of John to the apostle John (the Younger), the son of Zebedee.

The first half of the third volume, in which Eichhorn was occupied with the letters of Paul, is methodologically of special interest. Eichhorn arranges the investigation of the individual letters consistently and concisely. He usually describes first the origin of the community to which each letter, according to its superscription, was directed. Then he seeks to combine the time period of the composition of the respective letters, based on the description of the book of Acts, with a specific moment of the missionary journeys of Paul. For the authenticity of each letter, he notes what the ancient church said (for example, that it left no doubt about the authenticity of a particular letter). And if it arises additionally that the letter "contains nothing that would contradict the location of the prophet at this time of composition and other temporal circumstances" (3:63–64, for 1 Thessalonians), its authenticity is secured. Even here Eichhorn's judgment is rather conservative. Almost all the letters belong to Paul, save the three so-called Pastorals: 1 and 2 Timothy and Titus. As regards these, however, he shows very astutely that not only is it matters of style, vocabulary, and train of thought that demonstrates that a letter is not Pauline or that speaks virtually against the Pauline form of writing, but also if the alleged circumstances that are accepted as the time and place of origin do not fit the travels of Paul.

Since few ideological specifications occur in the introduction to the New Testament, it looks generally more modern than does the introduction to the Old Testament. To be sure, the scholarship on this part of the biblical books in the nineteenth century quickly advanced and also often changed its points of view, so that Eichhorn even here appears to be surpassed toward the end of his life.

As regards Gabler, we have still to glance at his much regarded yet often misunderstood inaugural address as professor of theology in Altdorf in 1787, which bears the title "Over the Correct Distinction between Biblical and Dogmatic Theology and the Correct Determination of the Boundaries of Both" (in Latin). This was the first time that a differentiation was made between biblical theology and dogmatic theology. Gabler considered each to be a separate discipline and sought to determine their relation to each other. The kernel of this thesis consists in the argument that one must select from the Bible the general, continually valid ideas and separate them from those that are bound to their own time. One does this by means of historical investigation. When dealing here with the Bible, Gabler had in mind especially the New Testament, since he devalued the Old Testament for its particularity.

From these continually valid ideas, one must compile a biblical theology, which then can depict the divine basis for the determination of a Christian religion. It appears that Gabler appropriated the conception of the general ideas from the Leipzig philosopher, S. F. N. Morus (1736–1792). As Stoic terminology these ideas were, nevertheless, known long before the Enlightenment. Orthodox dogmatics may not, as previously happened, be mixed with biblical theology. Instead of this, biblical theology has to provide the common ideas from which dogmatics may be able to help in its own formulations. This occurs in two steps: first, to ascertain exegetically the teachings of the individual biblical authors, separated between the Old and New Testament, and then to ascertain through this means the "true biblical theology." What is discovered by this means must once again be examined in order to discover the actual fundamental ideas. These then constitute the "pure biblical theology," which unlocks the biblical teachings for dogmatics. This thesis factually contributed to the origin of a discipline of biblical theology, which, to be sure, would be developed for the first time in the twentieth century, as a result of the separation between Old and New Testament theology that eventuated in the nineteenth century. The discipline of biblical theology for the detailed treatment of the general ideas of the Bible was considered by Gabler but only in a very limited manner. The method of excerpting general ideas from the Bible, which then could be composed into a dogmatic system, owes much to the static thinking of the Enlightenment. As one of his students reported, Gabler in the year of his death still expressed in looking back at his views: "I have consistently assisted in restoring reason to its rightful place and have for a period of forty years aimed to develop a rational Christianity." To be sure, he denied being a rationalist in the sense of a skeptic ("naturalist"). He described his faith in Jesus in the following way: "I see in the statements of Jesus something that was divine, and have witnessed in him a divine teacher." It is also clear that Gabler's moral understanding of Christianity resulted from the heritage of humanistic Enlightenment.

As a theoretician of the mythical school, Georg Lorenz Bauer (1755–1806; 1789 professor for Oriental studies in Altdorf, later also of biblical criticism in the philosophical faculty, and then in 1805 in Heidelberg) still may be mentioned. He summarized the fundamental, mythical theory in his *Entwurf einer Hermeneutik des Alten und Neuen Testamentes* (Outline of a Hermeneutic of the Old and New Testament [1799]) and in his *Hebräischen Mythologie des Alten und Neuen Testamentes* (Hebrew Mythology of the Old and New Testaments [1802]).

6

BIBLICAL STUDIES AS A SCIENCE IN THE
NINETEENTH CENTURY

6.1. COMBINING REASON, AESTHETICS, FAITH, AND HISTORICAL
CRITICISM: WILHELM MARTIN LEBERECHT DE WETTE

Wilhelm Martin Leberecht de Wette was born in 1780 in the village of
Ulla, located between Weimar and Erfurt. His father was a pastor in Ulla.
The family name reveals a Dutch origin. When Wilhelm was a boy of
four, his family moved to Grosskromsdorf, near Weimar. As a student
in the gymnasium in Weimar, beginning in 1796, he came to know
Herder, who, as a general superintendent (see above, 194), administered
de Wette's examinations. De Wette also heard Herder's sermons, which
greatly affected him. As a teacher of Greek to the son of a French emi-
grant family, de Wette accompanied Herder in the winter of 1798–1799
on a journey to Geneva. Beginning at Easter in 1799, he became a law
student, having matriculated in the University of Jena located near his
home. He attended lectures also in other disciplines, which was customary at the time. During that time the important philosophers Johann
Gottlieb Fichte, Friedrich Wilhelm Joseph Schelling, and Georg Wilhelm
Friedrich Hegel were active there. However, Kant, especially his ethics of
obligation, made the greatest impression on de Wette. Kant brought the
teaching of the Enlightenment to its clearest expression. With Lessing, he
distinguished between contingent truths of history and necessary truths
of reason. A religion based on these referred in essence to morality. Major
dogmas of the church, including the Trinity and the resurrection of Jesus,
lost their meaning. Furthermore, the Bible, according to Kant, has to be
explained in its moral sense through the avenue of reason. This means,
consequently, that its readers must recognize how to behave according
to revelation. Still, other influences also affected the impressionable student, who was eager to learn. In the educational novel *Theodor oder des*

Zweiflers Weihe (Theodore or the Consecration of the Skeptic [1822]), de Wette appears to speak of his own internal development, although in an estranged fashion. He also heard lectures of Griesbach on the Gospels and of Paulus, who explained New Testament miracles by rational means. Although all of this captivated his understanding, the question that still moved him concerned the living God. However, he found here no answer. Therefore, the *Vorlesungen über die Methode des akademischen Studiums* (Lectures about the Methods of Academic Study [1802]) of Schelling (1775–1854) strongly influenced him. Schelling's audience was inspired by his thoughts about the necessity to see each subject in nature, history, and art as the manifestation of the absolute. From this, Schelling argued especially that freedom was the fundamental presupposition of each ethical action, while religion considered the origin of all things. In addition, myth was understood as a necessary form of religion; that is, it is an attempt, even if imperfect, to grasp the absolute. Finally, in 1802–1803, de Wette read Schelling's *Philosophie der Kunst* (Philosophy of Art). To be sure, Schelling's philosophy was not satisfactory in every respect to de Wette, who asked whether a human could be free, if the individual is only a part of the Absolute that is expressed in history. In a brief tractate (1801), *Eine Idee über das Studium der Theologie* (An Idea about the Study of Theology), de Wette turned toward the theological discipline. The study of theology should proceed from the consideration of art, which unlocks the feeling for the beautiful and the divine. Subsequently, the image of divine harmony in nature should be recognized. Finally, the look at history opens the eyes to God's works in all historical events. The reading of the Bible from this vantage point elevates one's mind through the inspired poetry of the psalmists, the characters of the prophets, Job's patience, and the piety of simple people present in the Old Testament. In the New Testament, it is especially the person of Jesus and the love and zeal of his disciples that inspire. These typical thoughts of Romanticism now led de Wette beyond the rationalism of the Enlightenment. These ideas together guided him on the way to a historical-critical interpretation of the Bible.

De Wette foreswore a churchly examination, thus leading to his break with his father. Instead of this, he prepared a dissertation, which earned him a doctorate in philosophy in March 1805. The brief dissertation bore a laborious Latin title translated as "Kritische Dissertation, durch die gezeigt wird, das 5. Mosebuch (Deuteronomium) von den übrigen Büchern des Pentateuchs verschieden und das Werk eines anderen jüngeren Verfassers ist" (Critical Dissertation Demonstrating That the Book of Deuteronomy

Is Different from the Other Books of the Pentateuch and Is the Work of Another, Later Author). This title indicates that his major intention was to demonstrate the special position of this biblical book. De Wette proceeds from the position, which he had earlier set forth, that Moses is not the author of the Pentateuch, that Genesis consists of two sources, and that Exodus through Numbers have several authors. Thus, in part 1, de Wette suggests that Moses left behind in Num 26:52–56 instructions concerning assignments in the division of the land and had appointed Joshua to be his successor in Num 27:12–23. Part 2 demonstrates that the beginning verses of Deuteronomy briefly summarize the content of the book of Numbers. Part 3 examines the characteristic style of Deuteronomy, pointing to more than thirty special phrases that prove that, several times, short verses of the earlier books are here treated at length. The comparison between Lev 26 and Deut 28 results in the fact that the peculiarity of Deuteronomy is not associated with speech, because Lev 26 also is a speech. Part 4 treats the religious character of Deuteronomy, which, according to de Wette, corresponds to later Judaism, for it is more mystical, superstitious, and subtle, and contains miracles, which are theologically explained. Part 5, which deals with the order of the cult, maintains that the demand for a central sanctuary is, together with the following regulations (as, e.g., for the Festival of Passover), an innovation of Deuteronomy.

An elaborate footnote (*Opuscula theologica*, 164 n. 5) compares the singular requirement to sacrifice in only one sanctuary with Lev 17:3–5, according to which all sacrifices are to be brought to the "tent of meeting," and with Exod 20:24–25, which presupposes numerous altars. Moreover, Samuel, Saul, David, and Solomon sacrificed in different places. According to de Wette, Num 17 is older than Deuteronomy. Here can be found also the thought that Deuteronomy could be the law book found in the Jerusalem temple during the time of King Josiah in 625 B.C.E. (2 Kgs 22).

To be sure this hypothesis later aroused a great deal of attention, although this was not the first time it had been mentioned. More important, however, is de Wette's comprehensive view of the historical development of Israel's religion, in which he for the first time fundamentally broke with the traditional picture that had been gleaned from the Pentateuch in its present arrangement. In the eyes of de Wette, Moses is no longer the creator of an encompassing order of religion and cult that was, from this time forward, valid for all Israel. Rather, the image transmitted by the Old Testament is the result of a protracted development that reached into the late period.

De Wette soon dealt with this more elaborately in his *Beiträge zur Einleitung in das Alte Testament* (Contributions to the Introduction to the Old Testament [1806–1807]). This work, according to the disclosure of Griesbach in his preamble (*Beiträge* 1:iii–vii), was the result of a fully new edition, which de Wette was constrained to make owing to the appearance of the third volume of the *Commentar über den Pentateuch* (Commentary on the Pentateuch) by the older and already well known Johann Severin Vater (1771–1826). De Wette had to be aware, shortly before delivering the manuscript to the publisher, that most of the arguments of his first draft jibed with those of Vater. Both composers held in common the interpretation that the Pentateuch was a collection of fragments that were brought together several hundred years after Moses by a collector. On the other hand, de Wette's writing, according to the witness of Griesbach (*Beiträge* 1:i–vi), contained many points that were unique. With the agreement of Vater, Griesbach advised de Wette that he should expand these parts of his investigation and publish them in an altered version.

De Wette initially reworked his dissertation in the summer of 1805, which appeared in 1807 as volume 2 of the *Beiträge*. Volume 1 had appeared in 1806 and begins with an enlarged critical examination of the books of Chronicles relative to their value as a source for the history of Israel's religion and worship. For these must draw "the most significant attention of the researcher of Israelite religion." With this argument, de Wette sets a benchmark for the subsequent century of Old Testament research. "Religion is the flower and fruit of the entire history of Israel" (*Beiträge* 1:4). Precisely in respect to religion and cult, however, the descriptions of the books of Samuel and Kings and those of Chronicles present entirely different views. According to Chronicles, worship since David was entirely both Mosaic and Levitical, while, by contrast, the books of Samuel and Kings point to "little, if any, of this Levitical, ceremonial essence of worship" and even contain "overall several traces of a non-priestly freedom from the cult" (5). The emphasis placed on the significance of religion reflects Schleiermacher's accentuation of pious self-confidence; however, de Wette would not come to know him personally until his time in Berlin. The negative evaluation of everything cultic, on the other hand, is the heritage of humanism and the Enlightenment. De Wette's position regarding Chronicles is forward-looking: through a comparison with the books of Samuel and Kings, it can easily be made clear that the books of Chronicles offer an ideologically colored picture of the history of Israelite worship. De Wette especially emphasizes: (1) their addiction to miracles; (2) their Levitical interests, that is, their preference

for the tribe of Levi, which they allow to play the leading role, where it did
not have one before; and (3) "the point, which is most interesting to us in
this investigation" (102), that is, what de Wette entitles "the retrieval of
the honor of the Jewish cultus" (ibid.). The Chroniclers' view relegates the
temple in Jerusalem to the position of serving as the central sanctuary for
all of Israel already in the time of David, to whom at least are attributed
the preparations for the building of the temple. These books are silent
about the existence of local sanctuaries in the earlier period.

Subsequently, de Wette brings together the results of his search for
the history of the Books of Moses and the giving of the law. An overview of the alleged early witnesses for the existence of the entire written
Pentateuch results in the first historically certain trace in the narrative
found in 2 Kgs 22. This recounts the discovery of the "Book of the Law"
in the temple of Jerusalem under King Josiah. Against Eichhorn, de
Wette defends his own interpretation that the book of Deuteronomy at
that time was largely unknown or just newly written. More precisely, he
incorporates the results of his dissertation without having actually cited
it. Thus, it is probably the book of Deuteronomy that is the text found
in the temple. This is further accentuated in the conjecture that the high
priest could have fraudulently produced this book. But de Wette qualifies
his statement: "I am still far from elevating this assumption to a position
of certainty, since to do so would cause me to violate the laws of history
(= historical certainty)" (179). Before this period, a "Law Book of Moses"
was unknown, while it is frequently mentioned in the later books of Ezra
and Nehemiah. De Wette finds especially important that the prophets
were totally silent about the Book of the Law. Jeremiah 7:22–23 is cited in
particular, since this prophet was not familiar with the regulations of the
book of Leviticus (184–85). An overview of the definite, preexilic reports
about the regulations of the Israelite cult (226–58) leads to the result that
overall there was no national sanctuary prior to the period of David and
Solomon and that even after the erection of the Jerusalem temple local
sanctuaries continued to exist. People continued to sacrifice on hills and
under trees in performing cultic actions that were not yet considered illegitimate. This entire "situation of license, dissoluteness, and debauchery"
continued until the discovery of the Book of the Law under Josiah.

In respect to the Pentateuch (the five Books of Moses), de Wette concludes from these observations that the tabernacle (the "tent of meeting")
as described in Exodus and Leviticus could not have originated in the
period of Moses. Furthermore, it was not possible for the comprehensive
laws of sacrifice and ceremonies to have been given by Moses. One can

still recognize traces of their gradual development in the Pentateuch. De Wette repeats his earlier observation concerning the book of Deuteronomy, that it originated later, independent of the four books that preceded it. He held the view that Deuteronomy was later than Leviticus. The regulations concerning the unity of worship first have been fulfilled under Josiah (to the "place, which Yahweh … had selected in order to cause his name to dwell there"; cf. Deut 12:5 and other places where, according to de Wette, the temple of Jerusalem was meant). In addition, the Passover was celebrated as a national festival for the first time during that period.

The second volume of *Beiträge* (1807), in which de Wette examined portions of the first four Books of Moses, is less significant on account of its literary assumptions than on account of its hermeneutical theses. In general, de Wette, similar to Vater, reckons with fragments, while in the Joseph story (Gen 37–50), he follows Ilgen's view about two continuous sources.

Fundamentally, de Wette distinguishes between historical sources and myths, under the motto, "truth is the first great law of history, and the love of truth is the first obligation of the historical critic" (*Beiträge* 2:1). Thus, he formulates the fundamental bases of historical criticism. The source of the knowledge of history is the report. The fundamental insight is that we never have before us the events themselves, but rather only the narratives about them. The purpose of the historian primarily is to interpret what has been narrated in order to understand the perspectives of the contributors to what has happened. A second step is the critical examination of whether the report is believable. In addition, the historian must have a further perspective on which individual, fragmented reports to gather into a whole. De Wette emphasizes that the historian may not exceed, individually and entirely, what is reported, for he is dependent on the report. He can fill possible gaps only by making assumptions. Here de Wette exhorts modesty, since "we cannot enter into the inner workshops of history … for each fact is a product of unending causes, which operate in secret" (9).

If what was narrated is accurately understood, one should then ask whether it is believable. This critical investigation, however, can proceed only in a negative manner, that is, to determine "whether the contributor wanted to deliver history and could have done so, whether his reports carried the imprint of truth, or whether errors and partiality entered into his description" (3). Criticism "is able only to abolish, but not to replace what is rejected; and it simply points out falsehoods, but it cannot recover the truth" (ibid.). The information of an eyewitness would be the best to have, but usually the historical critic must be satisfied with secondhand reports, which would require that the one making the report was not too distant from the events and heard them from reliable witnesses. In addition, impartiality is required of the reporter. His purpose must have been to narrate history.

De Wette rejects tradition as a source of history. It presupposes that ancient nations were interested in maintaining loyalty to the history of their fathers. Such a tradition, because it is patriotic, is uncritical and partial, for it fills in gaps in events with imagination. "An inner criterion for judging them does not exist" (17). This becomes apparent when these narratives contain miraculous elements, when God himself or through an angel speaks to humans, or when the narratives report processes that either contradict common experiences and natural laws or contain contradictions in themselves. Many statements reflect the argumentation of Reimarus, for example, when de Wette (173) speaks ironically of the failure of Pharaoh's political policy of extermination (Exod 1:22), if subsequently six hundred thousand men of military age could participate in the exodus.

Having moved critically through the Pentateuch based on these dicta, de Wette arrives, similar to Vater, at the conclusion that it "is rather useless as a source of history, or, rather does not exist as such" (398). Since the narratives about the patriarchs, Moses, the exodus, the giving of the law, and the wandering through the wilderness are mythical, we cannot know anything about these persons and events. He takes, however, a decisive step forward when he states that the Pentateuch nevertheless does not lose its importance: "On the contrary, it obtains a much higher value. Regarded as poetry and myths, it now appears as the most significant and elaborate object for the most important and most fruitful considerations," for it is a "product of the national religious poetry of Israel, in which are reflected its spirit, its patriotism, its philosophy, and its religion, and becomes therefore among the first sources of its history of culture and religion."

It is instructive to evaluate this change in the light of the somewhat older and contemporary interpretations of myth and poetry, which have already engaged us. De Wette certainly did not stand isolated in his position. When we think back on Herder, we see de Wette joining him in expressing an apologetic concern. Further, it is imperative for him to point back to the rejection of the Bible (the Old Testament) by the extreme rationalists ("naturalists"). He does that when he interprets the description of the Books of Moses as poetry. However, while Herder was directly concerned to obtain a *theology* of creation from the consideration of Gen 1–3, de Wette speaks in this connection rather of the "history of culture and religion" and the patriotic spirit of the Israelite nation found in these chapters. The distance of the historian, who de Wette at this point especially is, from his material thereby becomes clear. In comparison with (Heyne and) Gabler, de Wette speaks in a less differentiated manner about myth, which he compares to poetry. Gabler had appropriated, as we saw, Heyne's distinctions between historical, poetic, and philosophical myth and accepted in historical myth absolutely a historical kernel, concealed behind the clothing of a "childhood" means of expression of myth. To extract this kernel is the task of the historian. To recognize thereby a historical background in the Pentateuch is therefore possible. However, the demand for the impartiality of the historical commentator and the rejection of tradition as a historical source are excluded in de Wette's view of the Pentateuch.

Through his promotion de Wette had received the position of a private lecturer. He began his lectures in the winter semester 1805–1806. It was difficult for him to earn his living in Jena. Besides the small income from lectures and publications, a temporary stipend, collaboration on a journal, and translation work helped him along. He had married, but his wife, whom he loved died, in his arms after the stillbirth of their first child. This was a heavy blow, which, for a long time, he could not overcome.

In 1807, de Wette was named an associate professor in Heidelberg. He lectured there mainly on Old Testament themes, but also on biblical introduction and theology and New Testament literature. In Heidelberg he met as his colleague the philosopher Jakob Friedrich Fries (1773–1843), who showed de Wette a way out of his doubts about belief. These had oppressed him for a long time, as de Wette reports in his novel *Theodor*. With Fries he held frequent exchanges of thought during long walks on the bank of the Neckar, as he later tells. The topic above all was the role of reason and the problem that already had stirred Lessing: the contrast between common truths of reason and contingent truths of history (see above, 170). Fries distinguished between understanding and reason. Understanding is the ability to arrange the observations of the senses into an ordered whole. Reason, on the contrary, is related to ethical and aesthetic experience. It is connected with true revelation. Revelation in this sense, directed toward the ideal values of goodness, truth, and beauty, is the possession of all humans. The error with the earlier opposition between reason and revelation is that one related revelation to historical events and their mediation. This idealistic view had a liberating effect on de Wette. Historical revelation could now be evaluated by its relation to the eternal values by a reason that is related to ethical and aesthetic experience. Fries made use of his aesthetic-religious approach insofar as he emphasized "presentiment" (in contrast to knowledge) as an entrance to the realm of the supernatural (see *Wissen, Glaube und Ahndung*, [Knowledge, Belief, and Presentiment], 1805). De Wette's earlier, merely moral understanding of religion, as it was determined by Kant, now appeared to him as cold and lifeless. He was now overwhelmed by an aesthetic-idealistic approach, mediated to him by Fries.

In the year 1807, de Wette published his sharpest, youthful judgment about the relationship between Judaism and Christianity: *Beytrag zur Charakteristik des Hebraismus* (Contribution to the Characteristics of Hebraism). In following his own view, he treats the basic problem of the contrast between the ideal—that the innocent *must not* suffer and that he is inwardly free—and the adverse view of outward circumstances under which the innocent *must* suffer. This may have been written under the influence of Fries. Many psalms ("psalms of misfortune") treat this problem in laments, Job in the subjection to the will of God, and the preacher Solomon in the perception of the final vanity of life, while remaining attached to God. Likewise, the history of Israel consists of a chain of divine punishments, impotence, defeats, suppression, and a slow dying. The Old Testament bears witness to a religion of misfortune and of longing for a better order. This better order is maintained in Christianity as a religion of (even if interior) consolation. This was not de Wette's final judgment about "Hebraism." Some years later another picture becomes apparent.

In 1809, de Wette was named a full professor in Heidelberg. In the same year, he married for the second time, a widow who had an eleven-year-old son. This marriage did not turn out well.

The most important publication of de Wette's time in Heidelberg was his *Commentar über die Psalmen* (Commentary on the Psalms [1811]). In this volume, he expanded much of what he had written in a brief form in his *Beiträge*. There de Wette had taken up the question of the authenticity of the psalms. He had indicated that Eichhorn had already shown that, while not a few of the psalms had authors ascribed to them, the contents demonstrated that the psalms could not have originated with these authors (*Beiträge* 1:154). Especially the Davidic composition of many psalms appeared questionable. This necessarily resulted in doubts about the authorship of each psalm. The verification that a psalm originated from the indicated author becomes almost impossible owing to the contents. For de Wette, it is only the scholar of aesthetics who can determine and decide on the inner worth of each psalm, that is, what is original and what is but an imitation. To determine the author was of little interest to him: "if only the inner spirit breathes the youth of earlier centuries, then the earlier age is decided for it [i.e., the psalm]" (159).

In his Psalms commentary, which after its first publication in 1811 continued to have several, additional editions, both during and after his lifetime, de Wette characterizes the psalms as lyrical poetry. Thus, he regards the Psalter as a "lyrical anthology" (1856, 1–2) and offers a system of classification that anticipates much of Hermann Gunkel's later assignment of forms (see below, 355). This classification distinguishes: (1) "hymns, in which Jehovah is praised"; (2) "folkloristic psalms, containing reflections of the ancient history of the Israelites and the relationship of the people to Jehovah" (in this group he reckons Pss 78, 105, 106, and 114); (3) Zion and temple psalms; (4) royal psalms; (5) psalms of lamentation, which were divided mainly into individual and communal psalms, and in addition a series of smaller groups. De Wette does not want to treat the psalms only according to the conventions of historical criticism (although dominating his individual explanations are historical attributions, grammatical and lexical characteristics, and topical remarks). For the "religious researcher," de Wette sees the special significance of the Psalter in its role as an "excellent source of what is sentimental (that which is related to mental disposition) in the religion." For "religion is only present in true life and existence and is displayed in the feeling of the individual. If transmitted in dogmas and myths, it is already in effect petrified and ossified" (*Commentar*, 4). In connection with this de Wette cites even Luther's well-known expression, which is found in the preface: "Here you look into the heart of all the saints." However, with de Wette the approach is an essentially different one. With regard to the origin of the Hebrew artistry of poetry, de Wette rejects the assumption, widespread at that time, that is was related to Samuel's school of the prophets (see 1 Sam 10:5; 19:19–20). Although poetry may have been practiced in an ancient period (among others he mentions the Song of Deborah in Judg 5), he dates "very many" of the psalms late, that is, in the period of the exile and afterwards (*Commentar*, 10).

Much later in an addendum to his Psalms commentary, "Über die erbauliche Erklärung der Psalmen" (Concerning the Edifying Explanation of the Psalms [1836]), de Wette elucidated his principles of interpretation. He says there, especially in reference to the psalms, "that the edifying explanation must necessarily be grounded grammatically and historically, and contain the results derived from this." How this should happen is signified in the remark "that one must envisage exactly the situations in which the psalms were written, mark and revive the human in it, and from there rise to similar human situations and conditions ("Erklärung," 36). Formulated in modern concepts, an existential interpretation is demanded. The problem that authors and the concrete situations of the psalms' origins cannot be ascertained is regarded as by no means detrimental for de Wette: "I am now very inclined to believe that many psalms, especially the laments and poems of petition, have more general than special circumstances of Israelite life as background and subject." This is the basis of later form-critical research! Therefore, the quest to discover a concrete occasion, for example, in the life of David, is not only useless and unprofitable, but also mostly inadmissible." If it then results that "many writers lament, even if it is only in general, over the wickedness and godlessness of the one and the suffering and oppression of the other" (37), de Wette holds it appropriate that the practical, educational interpreter could remain with the transmitted attribution of a psalm, even when recognizing as a critical exegete that it is unsatisfactory.

De Wette then distinguishes between two main kinds ("compartments") of psalms. (1) There are those "which contain general ideas of God, including his nature, characteristics, activities, and will, and of humans and their relationship to God and to other humans. The latter are in part generally human and in part in common to the Old and New Covenant" (40). Here the edifying usage is simple, in which something is emphasized as also valid for us, for example, in Ps 23 trust in God's leadership. (2) There are also psalms that contain "the special, theocratic, folkloristic, and timely ideas of the Israelites concerning God and his relationships to the people of Israel and vice versa, of worshipful, human life, and so forth" (45). These produce an indirect, analogous kind of relationship. Thus, for example, the theocracy corresponds "in the facts of its establishment to the saving work of Christ, in its continued existence to the political-religious community, the Christian Church. This community consequently has exemplary significance. This community, which describes this saving work at a lower level of life, was established by the saving, revealing, and redeeming activity of God." (48).

Even if these are the convictions of the older de Wette, they continued to be the same, since his religious breakthrough: historical-critical interpretation and religious-philosophical interpretation are for him not opposites but rather are built, one upon the other.

In the summer of 1810, de Wette was called to a theological professorship in the newly founded University of Berlin where Friedrich Schleiermacher (1768–1834), among others, was his colleague. This call to the main city of Prussia was an honor that he could not hesitate to accept. In the first years there, he had numerous listeners and great success in teaching. Beginning in 1815, he came under the influence of pietism and more recent orthodoxy, the influence of which had steadily grown in Prussia. In addition, de Wette made himself (together with Schleiermacher) politically suspect, on account of his sympathies for the student movement, which, reaching its high point in the festival of Wartburg in 1817, strove to obtain more democracy and German unity.

That de Wette represented also during his time in Berlin a radical theology is clear from the book that appeared in 1813 with the Latin title *De morte Jesu Christi expiatoria commentatio* (Remarks concerning the Atoning Death of Jesus Christ). Here de Wette explains that neither the Old Testament nor Judaism nor Jesus himself had known something of the idea that the Messiah would die an atoning death for human guilt. That was solely formulated as a teaching by the disciples of Jesus and the early church. The pietistic orthodoxy naturally protested this interpretation.

In the same year, de Wette published for the first time his *Biblische Dogmatik des Alten und Neuen Testaments* (Biblical Dogmatics of the Old and New Testament) for use in lectures. Here de Wette found a new, central point of view from which he designs a biblical theology of the Old Testament. Expressly "proceeding historically," he ascertains as the point for connecting all teachings of the Old Testament the "moral idea of one God and one sacred will, which is freed from myth." To this idea belongs a subjective component, that is, the "love of truth and moral seriousness" (*Biblische Dogmatik*, 1831, §83, 63). From this follow, as the basis for the religion of the Hebrews, two features: "(1) an ideal universalism, the teaching of a highest, sacred God, and its associated ideas. Upon this is built (2) a symbolic particularism, the teaching of the theocracy" (§84, 64). After the succinct demonstrations of these themes (§§85–141), which were certainly elaborated in the readings, follow sections on the "Teachings of Judaism" and finally the history and teachings of Christianity (divided into the "Teachings of Jesus" and the "Teachings of the Apostles"). Characteristic is the overall negative evaluation of "Judaism," that is, the postexilic religion:

> Judaism is the unsuccessful recovery of Hebraism and the mixing of the
> positive, component parts of the same religion with strange mythological

and metaphysical teachings, in which was exercised a reflective understanding that lacked the living enthusiasm of feeling.... While Hebraism
was a matter of life and enthusiasm, Judaism is a matter of ideas and letters. (§142, 114)

Exactly this evaluation was to have in the following period a direct and
far-reaching effect. The departure from dogmatic ideas as one had in
orthodoxy still cannot be overlooked in this book. Only the contents have
been altered. It now concerns an "understandable perception and com-
pendium of religious ideas and opinions" (§38, 23).

In the Berlin period, de Wette came upon a new realization, which
decisively modified his faith. It is indicated in a dialogue of *Theodor*
(1:243–44) in which, motivated by one of his dialogue partners, the role
of Christ was newly defined. Previously, Christ was, in the mode of the
Enlightenment, understood as the ethical example and teacher of morality; now he became a "subject of feeling" or an "aesthetical symbol." De
Wette believed "that in looking at the limited temporal appearance of his
life, something is viewed that is still unlimited and eternal. There is something therein that remains, that is neither perceived with understanding
nor reached with action, but rather can be grasped only with feeling." To
the objection of a dialogue partner, that "Theodor" would assert thereby
the divinity of Christ, he responds that he actually does not want that, for
with this, "the purely aesthetic view becomes subjected again to reason."
He states: "It is my opinion that Christ presents himself to us as the image
of the highest spiritual sublimity and beauty, and thereby as the highest
religious symbol." The identity of the individuals hidden behind the fictional dialogue partners is a matter of some debate, but, in any case, de
Wette's aesthetic faith had been deepened.

The *Lehrbuch der historisch-kritischen Einleitung in die kanonischen
und apokryphischen Bücher des Alten Testaments* (Textbook of the Historical-Critical Introduction to the Canonical and Apocryphal Books of the
Old Testament [1817]; this had seven editions up to 1852). This originally
was designed to be an accompanying volume for corresponding lectures
on the Old Testament and on account of its succinctness needed also a
commentary. It had the main objective of summarizing the previous
critical results on the Old Testament, that is, what the predecessors of de
Wette, especially Eichhorn, had ventured (while at the same time correct-
ing parts of this past criticism). After the first and second main sections,
which traditionally were occupied with matters of the Old Testament
canon, biblical languages, and textual criticism, the third part became the

"special introduction," which dealt with individual Old Testament books. The results of *Beiträge* are already presupposed for the Pentateuch. In the course of time, de Wette had examined the secondary literature, so that, in the latest and sixth edition published during his lifetime (1844), he had given up the old theory of fragments and instead, following the more current position of his time, spoke of two major sources, the so-called *Urschrift* (primary source) with the divine name Elohim and the later, so-called Jehovist (in addition to Deuteronomy). On the whole, the work reflects, with its numerous references to the secondary literature, the contemporary position of criticism at the time, which de Wette carefully documents. Here he follows critical practice and points to the "inauthenticity" of many pieces, including those in the prophetic books. Thus, the origin of the inauthentic texts in the Pentateuch is considered to be later than the respective prophets.

For theological reasons, there had been already for some time expressions of suspicion and protests on the part of influential pietists against members of the Berlin theological faculty, including, among others, de Wette, something that made his position uncertain. The crisis broke out following the execution of Karl Ludwig Sand, a German student imbued with a high degree of patriotism who, in March 1819, had murdered the theatrical writer August von Kotzebue. De Wette wrote a letter of consolation to the executed youth's mother, but it was intercepted by the authorities. This occurred in a time of reactionary campaigns against the democratic student movement following the meeting in Wartburg. Thereupon, de Wette was discharged in October 1819 from Berlin. He moved to reside primarily in Weimar, while his wife and children went to Heidelberg. Without employment, he was supported financially by friends; he engaged in several trips during his time in Weimar, traveling, among other places, to Switzerland and Austria. In addition, he preached occasionally in the city church and wrote on different works. In 1821, he applied for a pastor's position that had become open in the Church of St. Katharine in Braunschweig. At this time he was already in Basel, when his call to a professorship in the university was pushed through, although against stiff opposition. Even though after his trial sermon he was unanimously selected to be pastor by the community of Braunschweig as the preferred choice on a list of candidates, the sovereign of the land (George IV of Hanover and England) rejected his appointment for political reasons. Thus, de Wette, in spite of the strong opposition that he expected from the university, along with a miserable salary, had no choice except to accept the position of a university professor in Basel. In 1822, he commenced his work at Basel. There, he was able to exist outside the reach of Prussian political power. That he had to work henceforth in a Reformed church he found to be less grave. There were several possibilities of being called to Strassburg or to Marburg, but they did not come to fruition, and he remained in Basel for the rest of his life, staying active and occupying himself with literary projects.

In regard to his family, de Wette was forced to endure numerous catastrophes. His second wife, Henriette, died in 1825, leaving him with his daughter, Anna. In 1833, he married for the third time, a well-to-do widow of a deceased pastor, Sophie von Mai. While in Basel, he did not escape many additional attacks by his conservative opponents.

De Wette composed a complete New Testament commentary in the years 1836–1848, the *Kurzgefasste exegetische Handbuch zum Neuen Testament* (The Compact Exegetical Handbook to the New Testament), altogether eleven volumes, most of which underwent at least a second edition. In respect to the mastery of the material, this is an enormous achievement. Nevertheless, de Wette was not breaking new ground in this area. He offered no new revolutionary insights, but rather worked carefully on the current position of critical scholarship. For every verse he considered, he registered carefully the interpretations of older and more recent interpreters and ranked them according to his own assessment.

De Wette was indefatigably active until the end of his life. His last illness was announced in a conference that he was directing, being the rector of the university for the fourth time. He died from an infection following a short period in his sickbed in June 1849.

6.2. Characterizing the Gospels as Myths: David Friedrich Strauss

David Friedrich Strauss was born in 1808 in Ludwigsburg, not far from Stuttgart, the son of a merchant. His lackadaisical father experienced little success in his business, but he knew Latin well and loved the poets Virgil, Ovid, and Horace, whom he read in their original texts. Theologically he inclined himself to orthodoxy, and in his old age to pietism, while his wife engaged in a life of rational, ethical Christianity.

For a father with few resources who strove to obtain for his gifted son a means to study, the typical way in Württemberg at the time was to follow the course of study to become a theologian. After attending the local Latin school, which the young Strauss completed as first in his class, he entered into the lower seminary in Blaubeuren, which at the time of the Reformation had been established as a boarding school within the walls of the earlier cloister of the Cistercians, which had been equipped especially to produce theologians for the state church. The way of life at this school was a cloistered one in which the daily course of activities was strongly regimented. In the fall of 1821, Strauss began the standard four-year education, which focused on the study of the ancient languages, including Hebrew. However, Ferdinand Christian Baur (see below, 276–85), whom Strauss encountered for the first time as an inspiring teacher, also taught courses in ancient religious history and interpreted the classical religions with psychological and mythological methods. Also popular as a teacher was F. H. Kern (1790–1842). Strauss was to meet both as his professors when he later studied in Tübingen.

In the year 1825, after having compiled an outstanding final exam in Blaubeuren, Strauss changed to Tübingen University, having been accepted in the famous Stift (the Tübingen Stift was a renowned hall of residence and teaching of the Protestant Church). The basic course of studies brought him little satisfaction. The professors, especially in philosophy, were insignificant, and most were poor pedagogues. Thus came together in a private circle of readers the Blaubeuren classmates who were now members of the Tübingen Stift: Strauss, Christian Märklin (1807–1849), and Friedrich Theodor Vischer (1807–1887), along with others. Kant was regarded as difficult and antiquated. Instead, especially inspiring was Romanticism. Thus one read, in addition to Schelling, the fascinating mystic Jakob Böhme (1575–1624) and the poets Tieck and Novalis. Ludwig Uhland was professor of German literature in Tübingen, while Eduard Mörike (1804–1875) was a fellow student in the Stift. Belonging to this time, in addition, were experiences such as the visits to Justinus Kerner (1786–1862), the poet who hailed from Ludwigsburg, in the vicinity of Weinsberg, where Strauss met a spiritualist (the "woman seer of Prevorst," Friederike Hauffe). Beginning in 1828, Strauss associated with a group inspired by Matthias Schneckenburger (1804–1848), at that time a Tübingen *Repetent* (graduate assistant) and later a professor in Bern. This group read Hegel's theory of religion set forth in his *Phänomenologie des Geistes* (Phenomenology of the Spirit [1807]). Strauss became familiar with Hegel's important distinction between religion and philosophy. Religion originated from *feeling* and then was completed in the form of a *concept*. The content of this is fully represented in images, symbols, and myths. In philosophy, the spirit represented principally the eternal, sensual, transcendent idea.

Meanwhile, in 1826 Baur was called as a professor to Tübingen to teach church history and the history of doctrine, and Kern, having a more conservative bent, dogmatics and apologetics. Strauss, who had taken up his main theological studies in 1827, found in Baur one of his preferred teachers, whereas the main representative of rational supernaturalism, Christian Friedrich Steudel (1779–1837), offered barren and boring lectures. Baur's advocacy for Schleiermacher occasioned the supernaturalists among the faculty, especially Steudel, to express their opposition to the deployment of feeling in the area of faith. This dispute caused Strauss to read Schleiermacher's works in private with the instruction of Baur. These included *Reden über die Religion* (On Religion: Speeches to Its Cultured Despisers [1799]), *Der christliche Glaube* (The Christian Faith [1821–1822]), and *Grundlinien einer Kritik der bisherigen Sittenlehre* (Fundamentals of a Criticism of the Previous Moral Teachings [1803]). Thus, he was well trained philosophically and theologically when he concluded his studies with his first theological exams in the fall of 1830 as the best student in his class. Thereafter, he spent a period of time as vicar in Klein-Ingersheim, a small rural community not far from Ludwigsburg. After nine months, he was called to become a *Repetent* in the seminary at Maulbronn, where he had to teach Latin, history, and Hebrew. At the same time he prepared for his philosophical promotion, at that time more of a formality, for which a short essay on the "Wiederbringung aller Dinge" (The Restoration of All Things) was sufficient. Before the acceptance of this work for promotion, however, he embarked on the educational journey to which he was entitled for receiving the first rank in promotion. He went to Berlin, where he hoped personally to hear Hegel. Having arrived there, he still had in mind Hegel's last lectures. But on November 15, when he paid an inaugural visit to Schleiermacher, he learned that Hegel had died suddenly the day before from cholera. Thus, he studied instead postscripts of his lectures and heard, in addition to Schleiermacher, P. K. Marheineke (1780–1846), the Hegelian. Strauss became acquainted also with Vatke (see below, 262–76), with whom he often met. In Berlin he conceived the plan for his famous *Leben Jesu* (*Life of Jesus*). In a letter to Märklein (Sandberger 1972, 195–97), Strauss describes his intentions: the planned disquisition should comprise three parts: an initial, traditional one in which he would describe the conventional life of Jesus, as it is depicted in the Gospels and should be the subjective model for the life of pious Christians; a second critical section, which would examine the historical value of the Gospels, which, by the way, do not stem from eyewitnesses, and which would emphasize the mythical component in the Gospels; and a third, dogmatic (more correctly a philosophy of religion) section, which would recover what had been destroyed, since Strauss saw "in the life of Jesus the consciousness of the church objectifying the human spirit as divine" (196). Since Schleiermacher at the moment did not offer his lecture on the *Leben Jesu*, Strauss read its notes along with the works of critical biblical scholars like de Wette, Griesbach, Gabler, and Eichhorn. In addition to these, he read individual essays in journals on the mythical methods, especially an anonymous contribution in the *Kritischen Journal der neuesten theologischen Literatur* (Critical Journal of the Newest Theological Literature), number 5 (1816), which required the implementation of the mythical, critical method in the New Testament, especially for the narratives of the Gospels. This appeared to have convinced Strauss finally of the necessity of such an investigation.

After a short trip, during which he visited some prominent theologians, Strauss returned in May 1832 to the Tübingen Stift. There he was contracted to serve as a *Repetent* with the offering of philosophical lectures. During three semesters he had stunning success as a teacher. He read first logic and metaphysics and described in an excursus Hegel's distinction between form and content and also its significance for theology and church. Thus, the description of the devil as a person would correspond to the conception of uneducated people, which science elevates into the idea of wickedness. The ascension of Jesus was for him a myth, having emerged from the conceptions present at the time. In the winter of 1832–1833 he read about more recent philosophy, and in the summer of 1833 about the history of morality. On account of differences with the professors of the philosophical faculty, who begrudged him his success and insulted him with unfair mockery, he chose to end this activity and remain active only in theology. At the same time, he wrote his *Leben Jesu,* the first volume of which he had ready for publication by the end of 1834. When the volume appeared in June 1835, a storm of indignation broke loose.

For Strauss, this also meant, besides the literary attacks that raged against him, primarily that he was transferred to the lyceum in Ludwigsburg as a teacher for classical languages. Strauss was forced to accept this decision. He succeeded only in that he was allowed to spend some weeks of further residency in Tübingen during which he could bring to conclusion his second volume, which would appear in October 1835. On account of the annoying job in the school and also a quarrel with his father, he quit his job in December 1836 and moved to Stuttgart. There he lived a while on the income derived from his book, which in 1837 appeared in a second edition. In the same year, he published three disputative writings against his opponents. He ventured the hope that he would still find a professorial post, and this induced him in the third edition of his *Leben Jesu* (1838–1839) to make some concessions to the dominant interpretation, among others, on the possible origin of the Gospel of John from an eyewitness.

Given that, he was finally offered the possibility of a professorship. In the Canton of Zurich, a liberal government in place since the July revolution of 1830 and driven by an anti-churchly sentiment called to office a radical theologian like Strauss in order to initiate social reforms in the church. The church, led by orthodox theologians, feared this, since it threatened the church's independence; they sought every possible means at their disposal to oppose his call. After two efforts had already failed, Strauss was finally issued the call in 1836 to be a full professor of church history and dogmatics. He accepted this invitation. Thereupon, however, there broke loose a storm of protests in Zurich. Pamphlets and articles quickly followed one after the other. A central committee of the opponents of Strauss was formed. Finally, a petition was submitted to the Canton's government, which demanded the annulment of the call of Strauss and the offer of the call instead to an orthodox professor. The petition was laid out publicly for signature in all the churches of Zurich and received an overwhelming majority of yes votes. Thereupon, the great counsel (the parliament) concluded in a special session that Strauss should be provided a pension prior to his entrance into his office. It became clear to him that he would have no further opportunity ever to succeed to a German chair.

Strauss now was reduced to becoming a private author. In the fourth edition of his *Leben Jesu*, which appeared in 1840, he withdrew the concessions he had made earlier in the third edition. He published a two volume work, *Die christliche Glaubenslehre in ihrer geschichtlichen Entwicklung und im Kampfe mit der modernen Wissenschaft* (The Christian Teaching of Faith in Its Historical Development and in the Battle with Modern Science [1840–1841]). In this work, he brings to an end what he had proposed in the conclusion of the *Leben Jesus*, that is, the outline of a speculatively grounded dogmatic theology. Although with good reason one could see this as the main theological work of Strauss and recognize that the *Leben Jesu* was only preparatory to this larger work, this two-volume writing had a disproportionately smaller success in contrast to the attack on Christianity by Ludwig Feuerbach (1804–1872) that appeared at the same time (*Das Wesen des Christentums* [The Essence of Christianity]). In his volume, Feuerbach maintained that in religion, including Christianity, humans projected only their own nature on the gods.

Strauss also worked part-time as a theater reviewer for the *Deutschen Courier* (German Courier), but this led to an unhappy episode in his private life. At one of the theater parties, to which he, on account of his position, was invited, he became acquainted with the well-known opera singer Agnese Schebest, whom, in spite of the warnings of almost all of his friends, he married in 1842. The marriage was not to last. Their differences in character, lifestyle, and interests were too great. In spite of the birth of two children, Strauss was divorced in 1847.

In 1848, Germany experienced a revolution. Strauss hoped that the revolution would lead to German unity under the leadership of Prussia, and he engaged in the liberal movement and wrote during the months of the revolution a series of political articles for the *Schwäbischen Merkur*. As a result of this activity, he was nominated as a candidate for the Frankfurt National Assembly, but he lost the election. By contrast, he was soon thereafter elected to the Württemberg parliament. Unsatisfied with the greater Germany (friendly to Austria), democratic, and republican tendencies of the liberal party of the government, he soon joined the conservative opposition and voted against all progressive proposals. Strauss took the next opportunity to abdicate his seat. His political attitude had no chance in democratic Württemberg, although this view would later prevail in Bismarck's Germany.

After years of restless itinerancy, Strauss settled down in Heidelberg in 1854 and spent six happy years there. He wrote a series of biographies, among others one about Ulrich von Hutten (1488–1523), the humanistic knight and poet and well known contemporary of Luther (1857). He also wrote a biography of Reimarus (1862) and another of Voltaire (1869). In 1860 he moved to Berlin owing to the continuing deterioration of his eyesight, and he underwent an ambulant eye operation. He lived in Berlin for a while with his old friend Vatke. Thereafter, he moved to Heilbronn, where at the time his children lived, and then in 1865, he moved to Darmstadt, where his daughter, who had recently married, was now residing. In the following years, during the time of disputes between Prussia and Austria, the victory over France, and the new founding of the empire under Prussian hegemony, he gained some popularity as a fervent, pro-Prussian German nationalist.

In *Das Leben Jesu für das deutsche Volk bearbeitet* (The Life of Jesus Edited for the German People [1864]), Strauss develops his interpretation of the Gospels as sources of the life of Jesus on the basis of the recently developed criticism of the Gospels. Subsequently he provides his sketch of the life of Jesus that was reconstructed from a mythological, critical view especially on the basis of the Gospels. As becomes clear in his concluding consideration, this had no theological significance for him. In reference to Lessing's thesis that accidental historical truths could never provide the proof for the necessary truths of reason (see above), Strauss argues for a "religion of humanity" in which the ancient, "primary picture of man as he should be resides in human reason" (37). This ought to replace the historical Christ. This ideal human portrait was to render the standard for human behavior.

Strauss's last comprehensive work, although it lacked unity, was *Der alte und der neue Glaube* (The Old and New Faith [1872]). This writing summarized his worldview at the end of his life. The first part, which deals with the old faith, answers the question "Are we still Christians?" with a resounding no. Jesus as a primitive fanatic cannot be worshiped by a progressive citizen! The second part describes the modern religion of humanity without a personal deity and without any hope in a personal immortality. In the third section, Strauss aligns with the worldview of Charles Darwin (1809–1882).

Strauss spent the last years of his life in Ludwigsburg. He died there on 8 February 1874 from a painful intestinal disease.

The significance of David Friedrich Strauss for New Testament criticism rests on his epoch-making work of 1835. The enormous furor that *Das Leben Jesu* produced at its appearance, is, at first glance, difficult to understand from our contemporary standpoint, since methodologically and content-wise he offered nothing stunningly new in his investigation of the Gospels. The mythological critical method had been developed before Strauss, and both Old and New Testament materials had been probed using this approach. New, however, was the radical nature of his approach, which he expanded to include the entire contents of the Gospels, nor did he shy away from the negative consequences his approach held for the Christian faith in his treatment of central literary pieces of the texts. The religious, philosophical standpoint of the author in the preamble (1:iii–x) and the conclusion (2:686–744) and the actual investigation of texts have to be separated from each other. This standpoint of Strauss did not have a bearing on the critical method operating in the main section of his exegesis. Here Strauss certainly took an important step in that he (along with de Wette) disapproved of the distinction between a historical and a philosophical myth (Introduction, §10, 1:41–46). For him the origin of myth is in no case dependent on a historical event that resides behind the mythical narrative (1:46). In distinction to the allegorical interpretation, with which Strauss compared his explanation, the sense of a mythical narrative did not result from a supernatural intrusion. Rather, myth in his view originated virtually unintentionally from the spirit of a people or a community (1:52). Its origin is no longer capable of being determined. It is developed in the course of oral tradition (1:74). That represents already a considerable step on the way to a purely secular understanding of the contents of the Gospels. Certainly, the purpose of a mythical explanation is "abandoning the effort to determine the historical reality of what is narrated to retain its absolute truth" (ibid.). The religious assertion of the Gospels' myths is formulated according to the Hegelian distinction as perception, and the philosophical concept is understood as a supertemporal idea. Strauss is able to summarize that "New Testament myths are to be understood as nothing different than the historically formed garments of early, pre-Christian ideas, which were patterned after undesigned poetic sagas" (1:75). "Saga" designates the composing of oral tradition. The early Christian interpretation of Jesus as the Messiah constituted the intrinsic motif for the origin of myths, which were components of a common myth taken as a whole. The Old Testament primarily provided the material for the mythical clothing of the life of Jesus. Everything that was spoken there about the ancient prophets had to be surpassed by the greatest prophet, and what was there prophesied as messianic had to be fulfilled in him (1:72–73).

In contrast to the title of the work, Strauss has no historical interest in the life of Jesus. His subject, rather, is the *description* of the life of Jesus in the four Gospels, which he treats in the exegetical, main part in three subsections. Here he follows, on the whole, a chronological order. The hotly discussed relationship between the Gospels holds no interest for him. As if it were a matter of course, he proceeds on the basis of the Griesbach hypothesis according to which Matthew is the oldest of the Synoptic Gospels. That allows him to begin with the infancy and childhood stories about Jesus. Here the contrast of the miraculous style of narrative with a historical report comes most clearly into view. Eichhorn already (*Einleitung in das Neue Testament* 1:630–31) had rejected the childhood stories as nonhistorical. This judgment holds true also for Strauss. At the same time a stratagem appears that runs through the entire interpretation of the Gospels. Concerning the individual pericopes, he places the uncritical interpretation of the orthodox and the supernaturalists besides the strictly naturalistic or psychological meaning of the rationalists, which explains away the miraculous (H. E.G. Paulus is often cited as the principal witness). He recognizes correctly that these two opposing ways of explanation still possess a common apologetic purpose, which is still to rescue the biblical statements as historical. An example is the first chapter concerning the announcement and birth of John the Baptist (1:79–104), where either the uncritical acceptance of every reported occurrence, such as the announcement of the birth by the angel and Zechariah's being struck dumb, may be literally believed to be historically true, or the explaining away of all miraculous features by means of natural explanations, as done by Paulus. Strauss's solution is to abandon such efforts and instead to accept the view that the saga has freely arisen in a manner analogous to the corresponding birth stories of Jesus. Patterns related to the example of the announcement of a son to an aged couple who had been childless for a long time are found in the Old Testament: the announcement of a son to Abraham (Gen 15), or to the parents of Samson (Judg 13), or to Hannah, the mother of Samuel (1 Sam 1–2) (I, 101–3). Since form critical viewpoints were still foreign to Strauss, he understands these examples as ones of direct dependence.

In the second section (1:307–730), Strauss handles the "History of the Public Life of Jesus," in which he traditionally begins with the encounter of Jesus with John the Baptist. Miracles that Jesus is said to have performed are primarily factored out, while what appeared to Jesus to have been miraculous is included. To this discussion belong especially the supernatural occurrences in the baptism of Jesus and the narrative of his temptation (ch. 2; 1:369–428). That Jesus subjected himself at all to the baptism of John, in view of the statement in Matt 3:6 that those who were baptized by John would have made a confession of sins, raises the question whether Jesus also would have made a confession of sins. Strauss answers the question with the view that Jesus included himself at least in the domain of general human sinfulness in the sense of Job 4:18 and 15:15 (1:374). In so doing, Strauss certainly overlooked the connection with Matt 3:13–17, where the Evangelist directly excluded this possibility. Therein a weakness of Strauss's description appears that becomes apparent elsewhere as well: isolating the pericopes from each other. In the baptism of Jesus, the supernatural features—the descent of the Holy Spirit in the form of a dove and the voice from heaven (Mark 1:10–11 par.)—are, on the basis of an "educated reflection" (1:376), to be understood neither simply literally as heavenly phenomena nor as stories having natural explanations (for example, the voice from heaven could have been thunder), especially because the reports of the Gospels are self-contradictory. Strauss considers, by contrast, the Old Testament examples of the heavenly voice, especially Isa 42:1, which revealed baptism to be a symbol of the Spirit corresponding to what is found in Judaism. He comes to the conclusion that these accompanying circumstances of the baptism of Jesus are purely mythical decoration and therefore are unhistorical (1:389).

A further example of a reputed miraculous occurrence with Jesus is the story of the temptation (Mark 1:12–13; Matt 4:1–11; Luke 4:1–13). The different sequences of the temptation in Matthew and Luke (which of these was the original continues to be debated even today), the alteration of locales for the temptation, how Jesus with the devil could cover such a wide distance, and especially the appearance of the devil in person are features that appear strange in this narrative. Also questionable is the identity of a mountain high enough that one could see all the kingdoms of the world. Finally the appearance of the angels at the conclusion, whose existence Strauss doubts anyway, is a question. Strauss describes the attempts at supernatural and natural (probably somewhat visual) explanation and comes to the mythical explanation: the conception of Satan could be brought forth from the Old Testament, and his appearance in bodily form and speech in dialogical form correspond to "the sentient manner of thought found in later Judaism" (1:421). Having him tempt the Messiah at his entrance into his final years was obvious in the tradition on temptation, likewise in the Old Testament (for example, Abraham in Gen 22:1; or the entire nation in Exod 16:4, among others). Moreover, the wilderness in the Old Testament was not only the place of temptation; there were other motifs similar to the tradition of the temptation of Jesus (hunger, provocation, the tempting of God, and the danger of idolatry), which stem from the wilderness tradition (§53, 1:429–45). The search for points of historical connection is therefore an endeavor that is out of place. Rather, this tradition treats myth; that is, it is a freely depicted composition.

Strauss also addresses the difference between the Gospel of John and the Synoptic Gospels, first by looking at the place of Jesus' activity (§53, 1:429–45). Whereas in the Synoptics Jesus is mainly active in Galilee and journeys for the first time to Jerusalem during his last Passover, John appears to know about several such pilgrimages to Jerusalem to attend the Passover. This demonstrates to Strauss that these different traditions represent two different purposes: namely, that Galilee or Jerusalem is presupposed as the actual place of Jesus' actions, while the other sphere provides the basis for the transitions to this place. Strauss's predecessors usually valued the Gospel of John more highly than the Synoptics and made numerous efforts at harmonization of the differences. Strauss notes primarily only that one must allow the opposition to remain constant. Similarly, in his subsequent reflections, he addresses the question of the probable duration of the works of Jesus, which is different in the Synoptics and John. John presents Jesus as having participated in three Passovers, while the Synoptics mention only one. Strauss seeks to discover in the difference between John and the Synoptics the number of Passover festivals in Jerusalem that Jesus attended. He puts forth also a number of certainties to which belong, among others, the self-understanding of Jesus that he was the Messiah (§§57–65; 1:463–519). Certainly it appears that Jesus was confident that he was the Messiah, since at the beginning he had simply announced the same message as the Baptist, that is, the kingdom of God has come near (Mark 1:14). It is important to Strauss that it was the purely spiritual, nonpolitical character of messiahship with which Jesus identified (§62). Strauss does not wish, however, to attribute preexistence to Jesus, as did John, or even to place the theme in the mouth of Jesus (§60). Strauss holds, rather, that the statements concerning the preexistence of the Messiah were shaped by contemporary Jewish interpretations of a preexistent wisdom. Another aspect in John is Jesus' relationship to the Samaritans. Strauss denies that the narrative of Jesus' encounter with the Samaritan woman at the well (John 4:4–30) has a historical kernel (§65).

Entirely different are the words of Jesus in the Synoptic Gospels. Here the view of Strauss is that "the granular speeches of Jesus were cut loose not infrequently from their natural connection due to the flood of oral tradition"; however, they "could not disintegrate." In this context one may see on occasion the extent to which Strauss was linked to the rational tradition of interpretation. We saw that Jesus was honored directly by the scholars of the Enlightenment as the teacher of a higher morality. Thus, Strauss also considers the words of Jesus to be original. Certainly both the Sermon on the Mount in Matthew and the Sermon on the Plain in Luke (Strauss spoke of the two redactions of the "address on the mountain"), similar to other longer speech complexes in the Synoptics, were pieced together from shorter sections by the Evangelists. This view was already known in critical exegesis before Strauss. Strauss likewise regarded the parables (§74) as authentic. In the event that simpler and more complete forms of the same parables occur, he sees the simple ones as original and the more expanded ones as resulting from the editing of the Evangelists.

Strauss judges the speeches in the Gospel of John differently. He takes them to be freely composed discourses by the Evangelist, except for where the Gospel has parallels with the Synoptics (1:675). This assessment is completely essential for his stunning new interpretation concerning the value of the Gospel of John as a whole. Whereas the entirety of previous scholarship on the Fourth Gospel traced it back to an eyewitness and therefore considered it to be the most authentic, Strauss reversed this relationship: the statements of Jesus, apart from those that were encountered in the Synoptic Gospels, are Johannine compositions containing merely the basic thoughts of Jesus' speeches that are "further expanded in an Alexandrian or mainly Hellenistic spirit." For this reason, one also looks to a relatively late time of origin for this Gospel.

In the second volume, Strauss initially considers the miracles of Jesus (ch. 9; 2:1–251). He begins with the casting out of demons (§§88–89). He explains this phenomenon in a psychological manner that parallels de Wette. Through purely psychic action, this type of psychically contingent illness was healed. And Jesus, with his authority, provided the best conditions (2:47). The more serious the symptoms of the illness, the more difficult it is to accept such a purely psychological healing (2: 48). Here Strauss follows the natural model of explanation of the rationalists. For the healing of lepers, however, he rejects Paulus's explanation of the healing in Mark 1:40–45 and parallels. Strauss postulates that this healing may already have been under way and that Jesus may only have declared that the convalescent was morally pure. Strauss takes this opportunity to criticize the rationalistic explanation as a fundamental ambiguity, since "not to differentiate between what is for us and what for the writer's own construal is usual and orderly" (2:55). The process is relegated, then, to the sphere of fable and to corresponding miracles in the Old Testament (Exod 4:6–7; Num 12:10ff.; and 2 Kgs 5). By contrast, Strauss thinks about the healing of the ten lepers, who, with the exception of the single Samaritan did not return to thank both God and Jesus (Luke 17:11–19). The point of the Samaritan as an example indicates that it is a transformed parable of Jesus.

Similarly, in the accounts of the healings of the blind (§91) and of the lame (§92), Strauss rebuts the often similar explanations of the "harmonists" (orthodox) and the rationalists and repeats his explanation that these events should be viewed as myth, that is, as one of the freely imagined narratives. He cannot recognize a historical background. With regard to the healings of the blind, the one in Jericho (Mark 10:46–52) is the original; the others are dependent on it and have increased the miraculous component.

The miraculous is even more extraordinary in the three narratives pertaining to the awakenings from the dead that are reported in the Gospels (§96). An additional increase in the miraculous elements can be observed from the narrative concerning the resurrecting of the recently dead daughter of Jairus (Mark 5:21–43 par.), to that of the youth of Nain, who had just been brought to the grave (Luke 7:11–16), to that of Lazarus, who already had lain in the grave for four days (John 11). Strauss again rebuts especially the rationalistic explanations (represented above all by Paulus). Looking back at the "stepladder of the miraculous," from the healing of one who is spiritually sick, to the bodily ill person, and finally to the raising of one already dead, he stresses: this is likewise "a stepladder of the unthinkable" (2:153). There were especially severe doubts raised by many factors in the Fourth Gospel. Above all is the question of why, if the raising of Lazarus was so decisive that it caused issuance of a death sentence by the Sanhedrin (John 11:47–53), it is completely unknown in the other Gospels (2:165). After the dismissal of the apologetic arguments brought forth by the orthodox and the rationalists, Strauss again returns to the "positive demonstration that without a historical basis the saga easily narrates that Jesus had raised persons from the grave." (171). The awaited resurrection of the dead, expected at the coming of the Messiah, was one basis for this type of account. Another was the Old Testament set of examples: the raisings by Elijah (1 Kgs 17:17ff.) and Elisha (2 Kgs 4:18ff.). Thus, Strauss reaches the conclusion that these New Testament instances of raisings of the dead resulted from the handling of analogous and free formations of Old Testament paradigms of myths, which had no historical background.

Strauss devotes three paragraphs (§§101–3) to the transfiguration narrative of Jesus (Mark 9:2–10 par.): the understanding of it as a miraculous, external occurrence; the natural interpretation; and his own explanation of the "event" as a myth.

> Thus, as always, we find ourselves here once again, where, after working through the circle of the natural explanations, we are led back to the supernatural. However, definitely repelled by it we are forced, because the text prohibits a natural explanation, and it is impossible to hold fast to the supernatural view fitting to the text for rational reasons, we must redirect our efforts to examine the statements of the text. (2:263)

He notes as a model the light radiating from the face of Moses when he descends from the mountain of God (Exod 34:29–35). In addition, Strauss detects a Jewish writing in which something similar is expected from the coming Messiah. Thus, the appearance of Moses and of Elijah as the precursor of the Messiah then follows as a matter of course. The purpose of the myth would be twofold: "first, the repeating of the transfiguration of Moses in Jesus in a more heightened manner, and second, the bringing together of Jesus as the Messiah with his two precursors" (2:273).

Of special interest for the adherents of the older Tübingen school understandably were Strauss's opinions about the resurrection and ascension of Jesus (§§133–38). With respect to the different reports of the

Gospels concerning the appearances of the resurrected Jesus, Strauss had to reject the blatantly rationalistic explanations that Jesus may in reality not have really been dead when he was taken down from the cross but rather was only extremely weak and later was able to revive (§136; cf. esp. 2:648–51). A problem is the question whether, after the resurrection, Jesus possessed a natural or supernaturally transfigured body (II, 643). A narrative such as John 20:19ff., according to which Jesus passed through closed doors and suddenly stood in the midst of his disciples, initiated a special discussion as to how it may have been possible for a material body to do this. Strauss arrives at the conclusion that the Evangelists could imagine the life of Jesus after the resurrection only as a supernatural one, his body only as a transfigured one (II, 643). For them, the touching of Jesus (John 20:24–28) also was entirely possible. To be sure, it was different according to Strauss, for in accordance with "our educated standpoint, which possesses a more precise knowledge of nature, the material body could not simply disappear" (2:644). A simple resuscitation of a dead body is not possible, since it would represent "a direct intrusion of God into the regular course of the natural life, and this would contradict the reformed views of the relationship of God to the world" (2:647). If one unsheathes the reality of the unanimously witnessed death of Jesus, there remain, proceeding from 1 Cor 15:5–6, only the psychological explanations of the appearances of the resurrected Christ as visions, as was the case with Paul. Thus, one must admittedly categorize many reports, such as the touching of his body, as unhistorical.

Similarly explained is the last important event from the life of Jesus according to the New Testament, the ascension (Mark 16:19; Luke 24:50–51; Rev 1:1–12; §§138–39), where the orthodox interpretation of a bodily ascension is similarly excluded, as is the weak rationalistic subterfuge. Both are unnecessary, if one sees that the ascension is only weakly attested (neither in Matthew nor in John; Paul himself was not aware of it in 1 Cor 15, since he would have to encounter Jesus still after this ascension!). A widespread interpretation (among others, Matt 26:64; 28:18, 20) may have imagined an unseen ascension of Jesus to the Father and nevertheless a continuing presence with his followers (taking into consideration only Ps 110:1). The fantasy of others envisaged, however, an observable ascension of Jesus to the clouds, from where, according to Dan 7, he would return as the Messiah.

Notwithstanding Strauss's criticism expressed along this line, one can determine his relative proximity to the rationalists. In the preamble to the second volume, he in fact expresses his thanks for the review of

the first volume by his "worthy old fellow countryman," H. E. G. Paulus
(4–5). Related to this are his conceptions about what corresponds to "our
standpoint comprised by a more precise knowledge of nature." He dis-
avows only the procedure of the rationalists, which was to rescue through
rational efforts of explanation the historicity of what was reported in the
Gospels. In this way, they are quite similar to the orthodox, who hold
fast to the reality of the miraculous. This corresponds to the impressions at that time, for Strauss, however, did not possess the knowledge of
modern times. Although he still could not know Darwin's work on the
origin of species (1859; German, 1863), natural science was, nonetheless,
an irreproachable authority already by 1835. Texts that contradicted it he
rejected as unhistorical. The thoroughly radicalized method of the mythical school, which was confined to *one* aspect, provided him the tool for
the classification of texts as myth. Strauss admits that the orthodox often
render the tendency of the texts differently. They do not see as questionable, however, the content that appears strange to readers of today. Strauss
assesses this content as myths.

Since he was faulted by the criticism that started at once for, among
other things, not having made clear what he understood to be myth, he
added in the introduction to the second edition of 1837 some sections
(§§13–15) in which he examines the possibility of myths in the New Testament. He elucidates the external and internal reasons and sets forth
criteria by which one could recognize what was mythical in individual
cases. Thus, it becomes clear that an account is not historical when it "is
incompatible with known and generally asserted laws of phenomena. To
these laws belong above all correct philosophical ideas as well as their
accord with all attested experience. The absolute causality never once
interferes with the chain of contingent causes of individual acts" (1837,
1:103). In cases where God himself directly or humans through supernatural action should have precipitated a phenomenon or event, then what
is narrated is not historical. In the background stands the "model of the
primeval artisan," according to which God set in motion the connection
of the cause and action only at the beginning of the world, and afterward
turned it adrift ("manifests himself … only in the production of the entire
complex of endless causations and their interaction").

To be sure, this does not mean that all the material of the Gospels
would be unhistorical. "The simple historical outline of the life of Jesus,
that he was reared in Nazareth, was baptized by John, had gathered
around him disciples, had moved around in the Jewish countryside teaching, was opposed everywhere by the Pharisees, had invited people to enter

the kingdom of the Messiah, at the end had succumbed to the hatred and envy of the Pharisaic party, and had died on the cross" (1837, 1:72) is by all means sustained. Added to these points is the view that Jesus' teaching was in essence correctly transmitted and that Jesus understood himself to be the Messiah. Admittedly, the historical character of the resurrection is discarded. There remain visions that can be explained psychologically.

On the whole, Strauss sees the Gospels' description of the life of Jesus to be determined by messianic motifs. They describe Jesus as the Messiah who has come. Strauss continues to seek examples for the individual characteristics of this description in the Old Testament. This was particularly the case with the narratives of miracles. Even if he overstated this understanding excessively, his observations still witness to his acumen. Even so, he could not yet draw fundamental results from these points.

An important conclusion is implicit in the theory of the unintentional and anonymous origin of the myths in the Gospels. With the orthodox teaching of their inspiration, their direct origin with God is cancelled. Instead of this, Strauss argues that the mythic Gospels are the expression of the worldview and attitude toward life of a people living in the distant past and an ancient community living among them in an Oriental culture (either a Jewish or an Alexandrian Hellenistic one). The association between reader and New Testament texts consists primarily in the fact that they are both witnesses of humans. The fundamental equality of all humans belongs to the basic interpretations of the Enlightenment. Another idea typical of the Enlightenment that we have already encountered in Lessing is that of progress. Thus there ensues an inescapable distance between the ancient texts and their modern readers. Already in the initial sentences of the introduction (1:1), Strauss points out:

> When a religion is supported by a written monument ... the confessor of a religion accompanies it through multiple and ever higher ascending stages of development and culture. There abounds sooner or later a difference between the spirit and form of every ancient document and the new culture for those texts, which at the same time are considered the holy books.

If one considers this, one will not be entirely astounded by the "concluding treatment," with which Strauss ends his work (§§140–47; 2:686–744). From the results of his investigation, he looks ahead to its effect on pious readers: "Everything that the Christian believed about his Jesus is destroyed. All of the exhortations which he created from this faith are revoked and all comforts are thereby stolen away....With abhorrence piety turns away from such enormous sacrilege" (2:686). Meanwhile, for Strauss ensued now the purpose "to recover dogmatically that which was critically destroyed" (ibid.). Now comes into play the idealistic philosophy in the sense of Schelling and Hegel. The purpose of mythical explanation is this: "while sacrificing the reality of what is narrated, it is important to retain its absolute truth" (1:52). Paradoxically, Strauss emphasizes now, against Schleiermacher's renouncement of these themes, that the resurrection (and ascension) of Christ were cornerstones of the Christian faith (2:718). However, as these cannot be historical facts, they must be interpreted idealistically. This succeeds only through a collective relationship:

> If the idea of the unity of divine and human nature is ascribed to reality, does this mean really that they once were present in an individual as never before nor after? That is certainly not the manner in which an idea is realized, to pour out into one example its complete fullness, but into a variety of examples ... this unity loves to expand its profusion.... Should it not rather be that the idea of the unity of the divine and human nature would be real in an unending, higher, and actual sense, if I grasp the whole of humanity as its materialization? Would this be the case, if I were to separate an individual human as such? ... Humanity is the incorporation of both natures, the God who has become human, who through finitude relinquished unending existence, and yet whose finite spirit recollects its eternity. This is the one dying, resurrected, and ascending to heaven. This originates in so far as he negates his natural state ... (and so forth). (2:734–35)

For the community, this "speculative Christology" (designated later as *Gattungschristologie*, "Christology of species," which represents a Christology that is both kenotic and moral) means that he must repeat "in spiritual ways the moments of his life, which he physically traversed" (2:732).

At first glance, this jaunt into speculation on the mythic meaning of the Gospels appears to be without any connection. However, one must recall that already with Schelling, who had developed the idea of myth of the Romantic age, and Hegel, who had contended that mythical speech is the expression of a deep-seated truth and transmits a religious knowledge that is identical to a philosophically obtained idea, had preceded Strauss. This does not yet, however, emerge with Strauss in the critical exegesis itself. There he treats myth much more as originating unplanned from the spirit of the primal community. Here Strauss was impacted by the rational treatment of myth ranging from Heyne to Gabler. This two-sided character of myth in Strauss is to be explained only from its prehistory, which also makes understandable the common structure of his work.

It has been correctly stated (Harris, 283–84) that the procedure of Strauss rests on a presupposition: there is no personal, extramundane God. Thus, there cannot be any otherworldly events that intervene in worldly occasions. If one does not share this presupposition, then all questions remain open. Also for Strauss himself, this highly speculative construction of thought possessed no enduring solution. He later abandoned the attempt. Nothing like this is found in the *Leben Jesu für das deutsche Volk bearbeitet.*

New Testament criticism already remarked quite early that Strauss's description is purely negative. He did not wish to give a description of the life of Jesus, as the title had wrongly allowed one to assume, but rather he intended only to destroy the historical credibility of most of the narratives in the Gospels. He left his readers in suspense about what myths can signify in a positive manner. Above all he waives the investigation of the literary structure of the Gospels, which had already been discussed since Griesbach, and treats them together on a single plane. To be sure, any fundamental insight into the sources of the Gospels had not been obtained at that time, yet even during the lifetime of Strauss decisive progress had been achieved in this field. Strauss himself offered some important contributions to this in that he was almost the first to have broken with the traditionally high value placed on the Gospel of John. He recognized that this Gospel was not to be used as a historical source for the life of Jesus. On the whole, modern scholars, in contrast to most of his contemporaries, may consider Strauss's *Leben Jesu* as one of the most important milestones on the way to the modern understanding of the Gospels.

6.3. Setting Forth a Biblical Theology in the Wake of Hegel and de Wette: Wilhelm Vatke

Wilhelm Vatke was born in 1806 in Behnsdorf (Province of Saxony) near Helmstedt, the son of a rationalist and Kantian-disposed pastor. He attended the village school and obtained his initial instruction in Latin and Greek from his father. After his father's death in 1814, his mother moved to Helmstedt with the two youngest children. There the young Vatke attended first the town's school and, from 1816 to 1821, studied in the gymnasium. After the death of several of her siblings, his mother also passed away in 1818. Beginning in autumn 1821 until 1824 Vatke was a student of the Halle orphanage. In the autumn of 1824, he began his study of theology in Halle, where he learned Hebrew and Oriental languages from Wilhelm Gesenius (1786–1842), who had become famous for his Hebrew lexicon. After the completion of four semesters, Gesenius recommended that Vatke transfer his studies to Göttingen, where he was to spend three terms. Afterwards he went to Berlin in April 1828. While there, Vatke regularly heard the lectures of Hegel before his death in November 1831. Although finding Hegel difficult to understand, Vatke acquainted himself with his historical idealism and religious philosophy. For this reason, he decided early on against accepting the views of Schleiermacher (with whom he continued to maintain a good personal relationship), along with the rationalists, the pietists, and the orthodoxy, who were influential in the faculty and later at the Prussian court. Soon he turned to the Old Testament. In this regard, he studied especially the works of de Wette, which he regularly mentioned later on. With his dissertation on Clement of Alexandria, which was accepted in 1830, he was promoted to a licentiate, and, as a *Privatdozent* (private lecturer), taught different subjects and until 1833 had a large audience who flocked to his lectures. In his younger years, he must have been a stimulating teacher. More and more he lectured about the Old Testament, the understanding of which he associated already in this period with Hegelian philosophy.

Already before the first volume of his work *Die biblische Theologie wissenschaftlich dargestellt* (Biblical Theology Critically Described) had appeared in 1835 (this should have made Vatke a professor), Schliermacher's death in 1834 altered Vatke's situation to his disadvantage. His prospects totally vanished after the appearance of his book. Orthodoxy, which in the faculty was represented formidably by Ernst Wilhelm Hengstenberg (see below, 286–98) and was influential at court due to the Romantic piety of the crown prince (later King Frederick William IV), continued to work to oppose the appointment of Vatke to a professorial chair. Together with his friend David Friedrich Strauss (see above), he was considered to be a dangerous opponent of the Christian faith. In 1837 he was appointed an associate professor (without a chair), a decision that had been nurtured along by the liberal thinking Minister of Culture, Education, and Religious Affairs Karl Freiherr von Altenstein (1770–1840), during the occasion of an absence of the crown prince. However, he continued in this post many long years without remuneration. He was free of financial woes only because he had in the same year married Minna Döring, the only daughter of a well-to-do merchant. With his nomination to a professorship, as it seems, a suggestion of Altenstein was made that he should not publish the planned further parts of the *Biblische Theologie*. Since Vatke followed his counsel, we have only the overall plan of the work and not its entire contents. In 1841 Vatke published a comprehensive work, *Die menschliche Freiheit in ihrem Verhältnis zur Sünde und zur göttlichen Gnade* (Human Freedom in Its Relationship to Sin and Divine Grace). In later years Vatke allowed nothing more to appear in print. After his death, manuscripts of lectures and other papers were edited to form a *Historisch-kritische Einleitung in das Alte Testament* (Historical-Critical Introduction to the Old Testament [1886]) and a *Religionsphilosophie* (Philosophy of Religion [1888]), although they received little attention. After 1850 he continued his lecturing for a long period to a slowly declining number of auditors and occupied himself with critical studies. He completely ceased these activities in 1876. Julius Wellhausen visited him at that time and was disappointed to find that he was interested only in music. In 1880 Vatke even received the honorary title of doctor of theology from the theological faculty in Jena. He died in the early part of 1882.

Vatke's *Biblische Theologie* has remained well known to this day, above all on account of its exegetical insights into the Old Testament. He had a purpose, however, that went beyond this. He wished to combine his work on the Old Testament with the historical and religio-philosophical insights that he believed he owed to Hegel's philosophy. He therefore prefaced the middle section with a complete introduction, in which he addressed the content and character of biblical theology, the religion and forms of its appearance in general, especially that of biblical religion, and the critical form of biblical theology. Later scholars, for example, Julius Wellhausen (see below, 311–25), in general took notice of only the first chapter, in which Vatke designed a critical history of the religion of the Old Testament. Vatke, however, wished to combine a historical-critical approach with a systematic understanding of religion. The Enlightenment's concept of a simple "historical truth," which proceeded from a partition between the subject and object, proves illusory, because, as Vatke recognizes correctly, nothing more could emerge than the determination of "how far the biblical teachings correspond to the leading ideas" (*Biblische Theologie*, 7).

> The objective character of our criticism cannot be reached, if one abstracts understandings from one's own critical perspective, waives entirely his own judgment and allows only the historical facts to speak. From this cannot follow a true understanding of history, because this always presupposes the connection of the given contents with a person's own thoughts.... By the same token just as little of this objective char-

acter is retained, when one abstracts the treatment of science from all fixed philosophical and dogmatic systems.... Rather, a standpoint must be selected, which regards all forms of spiritual life as elements of a great organism and tries to grasp every special standpoint as an integrating aspect of the whole. (13–14)

As the basis for the structure of this work, Vatke is served by Hegel's lectures on the philosophy of religion (see Hegel, *Werke*, vol. 15). From these lectures, Vatke adopts terminology, but not every individual detail. In Hegel's distinction between the concept and the idea of religion from its subjective and historical forms of appearance (cf. 17), which according to him, *develop* dialectically as a "living movement" of the concept of religion and "the progressive realization of its essential elements" (591), Vatke searches for an approach to a comprehensive view of Old Testament religion. To support such a holistic understanding of history and particularly the history of religion, Vatke discovers in philosophy that "in the consideration of history the different forms of the appearance of the spirit merge into the idea of the spirit itself" (16). From idealistic speculation Vatke derives the following definitions:

We distinguish between the *concept* and the *idea* of religion. "Concept" generally is thought of as the ideational totality of the possible aspects of development; "idea" by contrast is the reality of the concept in its unity with the object, with the human spirit, and with world history; or, to say the same thing, the concept of religion is its divine purpose, while the idea of religion is the achievement of this purpose in history. (18)

Thereby the following holds: "the historical course of religion may not contradict its concept or the concept contradict its historical course, and the harmony of both must actually be demonstrated" (vi). The acceptance of Hegel's idealistic philosophy (where Vatke refers to Hegel's *Encyclopädie der philosophischen Wissenschaften im Grundriss* [Encyclopedia of Philosophical Sciences in Outline], 1817 = *Werke*, vol. 6) comes to clearest expression in the definition of the processual character of history:

The eternal being, in the aspect of universality or of pure thought, distinguishes, namely, from himself the world of appearance, the outer nature and the finite spirit, as the aspect of particularity, and places himself as identical with the finite spirit as concrete spirituality, in the aspect of the particular. This entire spiritual process depicts both the self-consciousness of God in the spirit of humans and, conversely, the self-consciousness of the human spirit in God. (19)

The expansion of the absolute spirit revelation (of God) and knowing consciousness of humans coincide into one process. This in turn evolves in world and human history understood as an inner development. Thus, a subject–object relationship is avoided, and at the same time the distinction between God and the world is abrogated. The speculation (for Hegel originating from mysticism) ends (even if not clearly stated) in pantheism. In the process, corresponding to Hegel's philosophy of religion, three stages of development run through the evolvement of religion: beginning, flourishing, and decline. In the history of Old Testament religion one can observe only two historically precise periods: flourishing and decline (163); however the history of Old Testament religion and the history of New Testament religion stand opposite to each other as two main stages. In the original general plan, from which only a partial piece could be completed, a corresponding treatment of the Old Testament Apocrypha and the New Testament were to follow. This was intended to have two parts: "Therefore we have to treat in the first part the general concept and in the second part its reality in its particular historical form of appearance" (172). The perspective from which the entire history of religion is to be considered is its end point, which for Vatke is Christianity as the "absolute religion." The entire development moves toward this end (104). The stages of the development of consciousness correspond to the different stages of religion:

> This consciousness, first of all, is namely natural consciousness in the direct unity of the spiritual and the natural...; this consciousness is distinguished, secondly, from the natural, placing itself as a subject...; likewise the divine is situated therefore in the form of free subjectivity.... The consciousness is developed, thirdly, into self-consciousness, spirit, and unending subjectivity ... likewise the divine is therefore discovered as consciousness and spirit, which in its other form of finite subjectivity itself appears. (100)

From the philosophical presuppositions results also the intermediary function of biblical theology between the historical-critical disciplines of theology and the dogmatic-thetic disciplines (§§3, 4, 16). On the one hand, it gathers the results of the canon criticism and exegesis of the Bible and thereby is independent of dogmatics. On the other hand, it has in common with dogmatics and ethics a conceptual development.

Vatke's religio-philosophical presuppositions, therefore, provided standards for his view of Israelite religion. Methodologically he wants the "understanding of the inner essence of a religion" and its "historical appearance" "brought together into an organic unity." The scientific consideration could "require just as little … the deduction of the entire historical appearance of a religion from its general principles. On the other hand, it could recognize the purely empirical material as a scientific element, which it could assimilate in its directly given form" (121–22). He proceeds then, first of all (ch. 1, §§20–28, 177–599), to transmit a critical history of Old Testament religion and after that (ch. 2, §§29–43, 177–599) to treat the "general concept of Old Testament religion." In so doing he presupposes "that the understanding and, along with this, the description of biblical religion are mediated through the total development of the Christian spirit in the church and in science. Therefore, the inner form in which biblical religion is reproduced is not to be separated from the present standpoint of the spirit, which assumes the place of the subject" (155). Behind this formulation is concealed a hermeneutical recognition that looks very modern and already overcomes historicism: namely, there is no "objective" historical set of facts that are given, but rather all historical awareness depends on the perspective of the beholder.

With the concrete description of the critical history of Old Testament religion, however, Vatke seeks not to lose contact with the results of the newer criticism. He saw that the purpose of biblical theology, characteristic of the nineteenth century, was to describe Israelite religion in its historical development and not its individual ideas, which, as a second step, would be conceivable as a comparative task (164).

For him the "ascertainment of the factual" belongs, to be sure, not in the exercise of biblical theology; he wants to leave this task of discovering what is factual instead to historical criticism (as a science of assistance) (167). Apart from this, he follows de Wette for the most part, whom he regards as the leading authority of biblical criticism. Above all he agrees with de Wette's views of the early history of Israel. The fragmentary nature of the tradition and the practice of the narrators to place later events into the early period make it difficult to obtain assured findings about the "Mosaic period" (184–251). "The sagas of the religion of the patriarchs we preclude from the beginning. We do not dare to derive from the narratives of Genesis positive historical elements" (184). Thus, the events from the narratives of Genesis may not be characterized as positive historical expressions. Accordingly, Old Testament religion begins first with the exodus of the Israelites from Egypt. The Pentateuch's fiction that Moses may have created already the essentially religious institutions of Israel stands in opposition to the nomadic way of life of early Israel. While there is lacking a suitable historical background, "this does not cause one to be unaware of the presence of mythical and paraenetic features in the narratives, as well as the laws and admonitions of later origin." In addition, the largest component of the people had degenerated into the worship of false gods (in particular star worship). Behind the relevant narratives (Exod 32; Lev 10:1–5; Num 25; 21:4–9), Vatke assumes the presence of an ancient tradition (186). Especially important to Vatke is the witness of the prophet Amos concerning the wilderness period (Amos 7:25–26; confirmed by Ezek 20:7–8; 23:3, 8) as an authentic message (190). It is fundamentally true "that the prophet must be given more faith, since the prophets due to their impartial standpoint and historical coherence also had loyally retained the collective consciousness of the people" (194). Therefore, "their intimations, as few as they are, certainly … possess more historical value than the priestly legends of the Pentateuch" (187). By the way, the interpretation that most of the early Israelites were adherents of nature religion and idol worshipers was, in the structure of the Hegelian historical dialectic, an almost necessary presupposition of the transition to a higher stage: "The later religious view of the Hebrew people had therefore just … as well be grounded in nature religion … its empirical starting point the revelation of the divine ideality and holiness as its higher principle" (249). However, the historical-critical method also leads to these results: it was mainly false to follow the words of the Pentateuch literally. Following the way of negative criticism, one arrives at "only a few, but certain points" (203). If one looks at the Pentateuch as a whole, "soon the abstract, unhistorical character of the Mosaic state becomes visible" (205). The theocratic system (in which "God actually has his hands in the giving of the law, judgment and execution, and all the organs endued with the power of the state are only dependent mediators") is not truly a constitution of the state in the real sense, but rather "a religious outlook, consequence, and abstraction of already developed moral circumstances" (209). Since a great deal of agriculture and settled life was presupposed by the laws found in the Pentateuch, they cannot in this respect stem from Moses, for the history of the exodus and the sojourn in the wilderness presuppose that the Israelites were nomads in this period.

> One may not refer, therefore, to the notion of divine revelations in the evaluation of these laws, or to the assumption that they somehow reveal the same Mosaic period. They do not accomplish this requirement, since, if they had been revealed in the Mosaic period, they would not have fulfilled the next needs, which the divine wisdom would have to have to leap over several necessary instances of development. (214)

The laws about the cult and the priesthood in particular have no historical background. "They cannot be explained from the situation of the people at that time" (216). They developed much more in the later kingdom of Judah and were enforced in the period following the exile.

If Moses cannot have been the creator of the laws in the Pentateuch in their present form, it is possible to determine his role in a new way. If one goes back to the original meaning of "Torah" as divine instruction provided by means of revelation, Moses, like the prophets, can be designated as the recipient of divine revelations. "The Torah is nothing externally objective, but rather includes the general, religious, and moral consciousness, which has been revealed through Moses and all the following institutions of Jehovah." In place of the external form of the giving of the law in the form of commandments and prohibitions (which first originate from the period of the collection), there is to be ascribed to Moses and the prophets "the higher form of objectivity, that is, the revelation of the divine will, which replies to the human will as the norm." Thus, it follows that "Moses was a prophet and mediator of the covenant, which Jehovah concluded with the people." In spite of the chronological distance—a chain of prophets was demonstrable for the first time with Samuel—the common features between Moses and the prophets consisted "in the immediate activity that was free of a fixed institution and in the tendency mainly to introduce the divine law more in the human disposition and moral life than shaping it into the rigid letter. All those sent by God were in this respect spiritual *heroes*: Their justice was that of divine revelation, a higher objectivity" (226–28). This description is a projection: the Romantic, classical ideal of personality emerges in it, as it was constitutive for biblical exegesis into the twentieth century. On the other hand, Hegelian philosophy circumvents placing too much emphasis on individuality: " If then no individual, although designed to be a higher form of revelation, can step out of the common historical context, we may therefore not place too great a gulf between Moses and his contemporaries" (243). If the tradition would be correct, he would "have come when the time was not yet fulfilled, thus making him a far greater wonder than even Christ" (183). For Vatke, the position of Moses, the historical activity of whom he retains, is drawn only in this way and therefore fits within the course of the Old Testament history of religion, as it corresponds to the Hegelian scheme of development. If he is the recipient of revelation and therefore the intermediary of a new knowledge, he can, however, have had only limited significance, which inheres during his period of activity within the structure of the religious, collective development of his people.

We cannot go into the various details of Vatke's description of the subsequent periods, which posed considerable difficulties for his developmental approach. It is striking that Vatke, although he mastered the historical-critical method completely, was bound throughout by his scheme of development, so that there ought to have been a higher development observable in the period of the judges and the period of the Israelite and Jewish kings. However, this was not the case for Vatke. At the same time, he overlooks completely the scheme of apostasy, punishment, and repentance that determines the frame of the book of Judges. In addition, the time of the kings up to Jeroboam II (eighth century B.C.E.) appears more a period of transition "to the culminating point of the development represented by the period of the exile" (426). In general, Old Testament religion in this period is allowed only a limited religious knowledge.

> The identity of the divine and human will, set within the boundary of loyalty to the covenant, is still the abstract of law and obedience, not that of spiritual freedom. In order to achieve this latter point, the subject must be released from the moral substance or standpoint of the law, must know himself as free in its finitude, and then must sacrifice his own will to that of God's in order to rediscover it in a higher manner in God. This deeper dialectic could not find the concept of love ... from the viewpoint of the Old Testament. (425)

The "Assyrian period" for Vatke is therefore especially important, because in it the opposition between the ideal universalism and particularity was straightened out. Both of these come to awareness for the first time in viewing the divine rule of the world, and they could be "cultivated only in the dialectic of world history" (440). This occurred beginning with the eighth century: at that time "the historical and indirectly the religious horizon of the Hebrews underwent an altered form in that from now on they were drawn into the process of development of the great Asiatic kingdoms" (460). The "world position of the Hebrew State" (464) broadened this horizon. Here are found the speeches and writings of the prophets, especially of Amos, Joel, Hosea, Isaiah, and Micah (in each case only the authentic parts), which are evoked by grand events of history, but did not emanate from the usual process of the moral life" (467). "This depended on the religious spirit of the Hebrews accommodating itself to the altered sphere of actual life, on the raising of the objective dialectic of history on the basis of religious, ethical considerations, and on becoming thereby reconciled with its world.... The ones who put this into effect were the prophets" (466). While the majority of the people adhered to particularity and regarded Jehovah as only a national deity, the prophets recognized his universal guidance of history: "The world historical events eventuated directly as moments in divine resolutions; it was Jehovah, who terrified the nations, overthrew thrones of kings, strangled humans, and smashed idols. His activity coincided with the conduct of his historical executors" (471). "The works of the ancient prophets which are preserved for us describe the theocratic disposition most simply and deeply." They came to a "higher, self-conscious view..., which encompassed totality" (480). However, "since consciousness was in the process of living production and not yet at variance with its reality," the "elements..., which affect the purely inner and subjective side, may fail at the end of this period and in part at a time somewhat later." Since the end of the Jewish state and the destruction of Jerusalem by the Chaldeans (Babylonians) was not due to the exhaustion of the principle but rather came about more externally and accidentally, "the creative power of the religious spirit ... was not debilitated, but rather with time became even heightened" (499–500). The exile does not signify for Vatke a decisive break; now the spirit of the people developed, for the different catastrophes were in no way capable of fracturing "the culminating point of the principle" (520). Rather, pain had a decisively positive effect:

> The practical result of this dialectic for the present standpoint could admittedly consist only in still resignation and faithful hope; however, there occurred with this reflection the first step to a deeper grounding of subjective freedom, the moment of antithesis fell now in the movement of religious consciousness..., and for a further development it was required now only that the worldly appearance ... was destroyed more and more and thereby the spirit was directed to the pure inwardness and the transcendental sphere. (518)

Toward the end of the exile, the nameless prophet Second Isaiah generates a "lofty and deep perspective"—"in an objective consideration the highest standpoint, which the Hebrew principle has brought forth" (525). This high point, corresponding to the religio-philosophical view of Vatke, falls under the subject. "The view of the suffering and transfiguration of the servant of Jehovah depicts ... the most remarkable apprehension of salvation in the Old Testament and is therefore a prediction (but not the predication of Christ)" (531 n. 2). To be sure, Vatke, on the one hand, immediately constructs a restriction, which impeded one's seeing here an absolute high point of development. Yet this view has, on the other hand, "once more an abstract character, since an actual individual could not be considered as the innocent sufferer. Rather it was the servant in his ideal significance" (531–32).

It is characteristic for Vatke that in the Persian period which followed, he can find in no way a decline, although here the prophetic spirit passed "soon into the form of contemplative wisdom and reflection" (552), and "the gift of prophecy ... was extinguished" (562). Rather, "the ideal principle received its final perfection" in this period (552). The progress consisted in the fact that a community purified by worship could be established and develop its spiritual life in different directions. Two directions are highlighted: "the strongly legal on the one side and the freely reflecting on the other" (566). Further, the legal can be recognized as necessary and beneficial, although "the spirit had lost its creative activity" (567), even as the cult in its entirety was certainly not so rigid as the formulations of the law allowed one to assume.

Besides this, there were wisdom teachers and wisdom literature succeeding the prophets, since the presuppositions for their activity had ceased. "The commonality of both of these consisted in their striving to work subjectively through the religious content and to raise it to the actual consciousness of the community" (561). The wisdom literature is especially important, for it "lifted up the ancient conception of the spirit of Jehovah to the basis of pure thought." The philosophical background here once more is that the thought, the feeling, and the conception rise (i.e., transcend dialectically) to the higher form. Furthermore, the universal aspect was significant at the same time, for it broadened the standpoint "beyond the bounds of the moral spirit of the nation and understood the true and the good among all nations as the activity of the one wisdom." Admittedly, Vatke also stressed at this point once more the difference from "the prophetic spirit, which should be poured out over all, and even more from the spirit of the community according to the New Testament" (571).

Since the dialectical development at this point requires a phase of decline, Vatke, somewhat lacking in reasons for doing so, locates this in the "Macedonian and Maccabean period" (third and second centuries B.C.E.). "In religious matters, this entire period represents the transition from Old Testament religion to the later form of Judaism. The original productivity of the spirit was ruined, with the exception of some individual phenomena of lyrical ecstasy and reflective wisdom" (578). "Since now the voices of the last prophets had faded away and the initial exaltation of wisdom eventually was dampened, so criticism and reflection represented the midpoint of spiritual activity" (581). The origin of the synagogues, the conclusion of the canon, and the negative side of the dialectic in the book of Ecclesiastes and the positive one in Daniel could no longer be reconciled through the Old Testament principle.

For Vatke, the critical description of the course of the religious history of Israel is, however, not the main concern, but rather it serves as the "empirical basis" (591) of the verification of his religio-philosophical, fundamental theses, which he sets forth in the second chapter of his book (591–659). In this chapter he formulates the determination of the "concept" of Old Testament religion entirely in the terminology and system of Hegelian thought. This follows from the "totality of the appearing moments" and therefore from the "main forms of appearance as the inner movement of the concept" (591). Thus, it cannot be defined as a static entity, but rather only as the description of its consecutive phases.

Typically Hegelian is the determination of the general concept, which originates with a definition of God: "God is determined as pure subjectivity, which as the unending power defines every particularity as negative, and which as absolute wisdom and holiness combines the differences of the particular into a more simple and concrete identity." In addition, there is a dialectic: on the one hand, "the subjectivity … is essentially One; that is, it is in itself general and unending, and eliminates from itself every particularity." On the other hand, this unity is "not an abstract, empty identity, but rather a living process that comprises in itself differences" (594–96). Therefore, it contains in itself "as a concrete identity the difference of the general and particular. The composition of the particular in its totality is the act of the creation of the world" (600). "The general purpose of the world is the self-consciousness of general subjectivity." However, this is realized only in the human, intellectual nature "as the elevation to unending subjectivity" and "human intelligence as the image of the divine recognizes Jehovah" (611). Above we have pointed to the origin of the Hegelian system from mysticism. Here appears in particularly clear fashion intellectualized mysticism. The connection to the religious history of Israel is produced by seeking the "special or determined purpose" in the individuality of a certain people, concretely expressed "in the thought of the divine covenant and the covenant people" (613). These rest on the belief that Jehovah elected Israel to be his chosen nation and has guided its history providentially. However, the fundamental consciousness of Hebrew particularity consisted in the notion "that there is only one form of true religion, that is, the Hebrew religion, and that therefore all other forms … of religion are in themselves nothing." Christian particularity is different; though it recognizes the absolute religion only in the Christian Church, it presupposes the divine nature of humanity. Therefore, "the subordinated stages of the religion are to be seen only as estrangement from the originally comprised concepts and as points of opening for the divine education of humanity" (615). This interpretation is straightfor-wardly in line with Lessing and Hegel, for a religious history of humanity is involved.

Vatke describes the following three stages of the development of the concept of Old Testament religion through the corresponding "movement of self-consciousness" (641). The first stage, which is the simple gener-ality or the direct self-consciousness, reaches from Moses approximately to the eighth century b.c.e. This period is only slightly attested, because only the writings of the earliest prophets can be regarded as original documents from it. Here "the spiritual individuality" has "the character of immediate self-consciousness, to which its interior differences have not yet become objects in an impartial presentation." Since the older prophets knew themselves as directly determined by the same principle "as directly enlightened messengers of Jehovah," the concept of religion was "set as revelation but in its original form as direct self-consciousness, that is, absolute arousal" (645–46). Vatke judges "that the entire, objective formation of Hebrew religion in this first stage did not yet conform to the concept of the religious idea itself, neither in regard to the cult nor to the moral life, neither … in regard to the religious idea itself " (651). The second stage is that of "segregation or of self-consciousness, which evolves itself as objectivity" (643). This is the period extending from the eighth century to the end of the Babylonian exile. In addition to the writings of the older prophets, who can be counted also as witnesses of the transition to this stage, to it belonged especially also the "main content of the Pen-tateuch" (644). "In the second stage the simple commonality of concept diverges in its special moments, and the direct self-consciousness opens itself to the objective form of general consciousness" (652). In the first phase of this stage (eighth to seventh centuries) "the spirit was grasped in an ingenious unity with reality and in the direct production of the partic-ular content." In the second phase, the purpose confronted consciousness already in an independent form. This viewed now "its course in a clearly arranged manner and received with it a higher self-consciousness of its association with world history and its destination. The third stage, that of "the individuality or the concrete self-consciousness that reverted to itself

(643), in which now the subject reconciled itself with the objective (657) and developed especially a moral point of view (658), begins with Jeremiah and reaches its high point for the first time in the postexilic period, during which, in addition to the book of Proverbs, are counted especially Qoheleth and Job. When Vatke saw directly in these books, with their subjective reflection, the culmination of Hebrew religion, he stood in opposition to the negative evaluation of the late period in de Wette and especially Wellhausen at a later time. Moreover, Vatke did not in any way view the Old Testament priesthood negatively:

> It was certainly beneficial that the priesthood did not hold earlier a significant influence, since the higher principle was completely formed at this later time. Had it been earlier, the priesthood would have had to be grounded in the service of nature and superstition so that through this manner the free development of truth would have been inhibited.

Besides, the battle of the prophets against the priests had to do only with individual violations. "In contrast, it is impossible to prove that the prophets must have had to breach the barrier of mechanical formalities erected by the priests in order to establish the higher truth" (714).

In the third chapter (660–710), Vatke examines the "relationship of Old Testament religion to the stages of religion preceding it." For Vatke, nature religion is the presupposition of revelation: the acceptance of a primal revelation or primal wisdom cast aside as "unhistorical and lacking in any conception" (660). A battle begins between nature religion and Old Testament religion, which appears to have a self-conscious understanding of itself as revelation. Thus, there is a distinction between the origin of the name of God, which Vatke already recognizes was pronounced probably Yahweh (670), and the origin of Old Testament religion. Vatke assumes that the origin of the name came from the adoption in an earlier time of an original god of light from (Persian) upper Asia. In contrast, Hebrew monotheism (the term in Vatke's time was still used in an undifferentiated manner) was not borrowed from elsewhere but rather was revealed. Credit belongs to the Hebrews, "who knew and worshiped the highest God to the exclusion of all lower gods and all mythologies" (700). Therefore, Old Testament religion is identical neither with the concept of nature religion nor with the absolute religion, but rather is an "independent totality" (cf. 151).

Vatke was not the only interpreter of the Bible whom the speculative philosophy of Hegel brought under its spell. Its dialectic and the thought of development determined his view of the Old (and the New) Testament. For the modern reader, the Hegelian terminology impedes the understanding of Vatke's lectures on biblical theology. In spite of that, his thought has value for those who study him, for he was an entirely original observer to whom we owe many thoughtful insights into the Old Testament.

6.4. An Idealistic Perspective Investigating the New Testament by Historical Criticism and Understanding It as a Historical Method: Ferdinand Christian Baur

Ferdinand Christian Baur was the paradigm of a Schwabish theologian; his activity occurred in the close circle of his Württemberg homeland. He was born in 1792, the son of a minister in Schmiden near Stuttgart. He grew up there and in Blaubeuren. He passed through the process of education typical for a Schwabish theologian. He first attended the lower seminaries (cloister schools) in Blaubeuren and Maulbronn (1805–9) and concluded with the Evangelical Stift in Tübingen. As the best student of his age group, he completed his theological exams there in 1814. After a brief period as a vicar, he was soon called in 1816 to be a *Repetent* of the Stift. In 1817, he was called to be the professor of ancient languages in the lower seminary in Blaubeuren, where he continued until 1826. In 1821 he married a daughter of the doctor of the court from Stuttgart. His wife bore him two sons and three daughters. In contrast to the so-called older Tübingen school, which dominated the Tübingen theological faculty at the time and defended the authority of Holy Scripture against rationalism and the emerging school of historical criticism ("supernaturalism"), he began to open himself very early to modern views. He soon fell under the influence of Schelling, the idealistic philosopher of history who had developed his interpretation in his *System des Transzendentalen Idealismus* (System of Transcendental Idealism), which appeared in 1800. According to this volume, "history as a whole … is a progressive, gradual unveiling of the Absolute" (*AW* 2:603). The idea of development was nothing new, but probably his idealistic shaping was. For Baur, who therefore probably incorrectly appealed theologically to Schleiermacher, this meant the transition to a religio-philosophically grounded history of religion, which he described for the first time in his work *Symbolik and Mythologie oder die Naturreligion des Alterthums* (Symbolism and Mythology or the Nature Religion of Antiquity [1824–1825]). Here he understood Christianity to be the "absolute religion," giving it alone a place in a line of development.

The book made the young Baur well known at once, so he was called to Tübingen at the rank of full professor for historical theology, against the appeal of the faculty. Here he continued to work until his death in the year 1860. According to the standards of the time, by the time of his death, he was already a "venerable, aged man with white locks" (funeral elegy of Dean Georgi). His lectures included church history, history of doctrine, and symbolism of the New Testament. In addition, he was the morning preacher at the Stift's church. In the sphere of the history of religion, in addition to some shorter works, he also stepped forward with the volume *Die christliche Gnosis oder die christliche Religions-Philosophie in ihrer geschichtlichen Entwicklung* (Christian Gnosis or Christian Religious Philosophy in Its Historical Development [1835]). At that time, he already had come under the influence of the philosophy of history developed by Hegel, from whom he appropriated "the idea of process, through which God as the absolute Spirit mediates with himself and is revealed to himself" (*Gnosis*, 700). On the other side, Bauer became strongly influenced by the source-critical method of the historian Barthold Georg Niebuhr (1776–1831) and especially his work *Römische Geschichte* (Roman History [3 vols., 1811–1832]). Thus, Baur became a confident representative of historicism with its ideal of alleged objectivity. Thus, he says in the preamble to his work *Das Christenthum und die christliche Kirche der drei ersten Jahrhunderte* (Christianity and the Christian Church of the First Three Centuries [1853, *AW* 3:iv–v]: "My standpoint in one word is historical. This alone is the basis on which to set forth a given fact in so far as it is overall possible to be understood in its pure objectivity." From this statement, it certainly becomes clear that Baur had always been cognizant of the barriers to every type of historical awareness. The idealistic, overall view of history and precise textual criticism could never be read entirely on the same level, and Baur oriented himself in his later investigations ever more intensely to the text.

Baur is remembered primarily for his New Testament works. In 1831, his seminal essay, "Die Christuspartei in der korinthischen Gemeinde, der Gegensatz des petrinischen und paulinischen Christentums in der ältesten Kirche, der Apostel Petrus in Rom" (The Party of Christ in the Corinthian Community, the Antagonism between Petrine and Pauline Christianity in the Ancient Church, the Apostle Peter in Rome" [*AW* 1:1–146]), appeared. The starting point of this essay is 1 Cor 1:12, where Paul indicates that the community of Corinth is divided into four parties: the followers of Paul, of Apollos, of Cephas (Peter), and a group that called itself the party of Christ. The notion that Christ is the leader of a party is unthinkable, and also Eichhorn's opinion that it had to do with a group that denied apostolic authority is rejected by Baur. He conducts a penetrating investigation of the two Corinthian letters, and especially on the basis of 2 Cor 10–13, comes the conclusion that the party of Christ is an extreme wing of the party of Peter. This party sees itself directly associated with the earthly Jesus through this apostle by means of a legalistic interpretation of his teachings. According to this party, Paul, being called only by a vision (see Acts 9; 22; 26; Gal 1:1; and 1 Cor 9:1; 15:8), could not directly convey Christ to his followers. On the other hand, because he associates the people who were members of the party of Apollos with the party of Paul, Baur arrives at the thesis that in reality in Corinth there were two parties, one Jewish-Christian and one Gentile-Pauline. Baur saw now as his additional aim the ascertaining of their different intentions (*Tendenzkritik* [Criticism of Intentionality]) and on the basis of this could recognize dualism expanding the access to other New Testament writings and other early church sources.

According to Baur, we have to do with two

> completely opposite systems, which emerged from the antithesis between Judaism and Pauline Christianity. According to the first system (Judaism), revelation is only the general announcement of that which already existed earlier. The communication of what was divinely disclosed occurs only by way of external instruction. By contrast, according to the latter system (Pauline Christianity), revelation is a "new creation" [*kainē ktisis*], which, in the depth of one's own consciousness, must enable one to grasp the higher principle of life through the divine spirit. Christ is here only the teacher, there in the highest sense the savior. Here all religious worth is attributed to legal action, there to faith in the death of the savior. (1:74–76)

Baur could not yet correctly determine the significance of Christian enthusiasm opposed to Paul, since the phenomenon of Hellenism at that time had yet to be critically researched. However, his determined effort to detect the historical significance of the sources and his courage to discover far-reaching inferences of his observations is to be judged as essential progress.

Baur tested his approach in additional texts, among them the Letter to the Romans. In the title of the essay "Über Zweck und Veranlassung des Römerbriefs…: Eine historisch-kritische Untersuchung" (Concerning the Purpose and Cause of the Letter to the Romans…: A historical-critical Investigation [1836, *AW* 1:147–266]) appears for the first time the well-known modern expression for the method. Also here, what matters for Baur is thinking about "the purpose and the tendency of the letter, as well as the historical connections that have provoked the letter" (1:158). Since Baur contributes this methodologically important presupposition, he must determine also the concrete, external inducement for the letter in the affairs of the community (1:160). He sees the background of the letter as the conflict between Jewish and Gentile Christians in Rome: the Jewish Christians may have been concerned about the widespread admission of Gentile Christians due to the universalism and successful missionary activity of Paul, while the number of Jewish Christians remained almost stagnant. These Jewish Christians were afraid of the privileging of the Gentile Christians. The actual, difficult point is to be found not in the first eight chapters but rather in chapters 9–11, to which the opening chapters are only prefixed. In chapters 9–11, the apostle answers the question, "How may it be explained that the salvation appearing in Christ so great a part of the Jewish people did not share, seeing they have been the elect nation of God and the subject of all of the divine promises, while the Gentile Christians by contrast could receive the position left vacated by the former people of God?" (1:158). Paul would answer in the following way: (1) physical lineage means absolutely nothing; (2) it is due to the fault of the Jews, if they do not participate in salvation, which has to do with faith; (3) in spite of this God did not finally reject the Jews, for it may be only a temporary blindness. God has not dispensed with his call of them. Baur changes Paul into an analogous thinker:

> Nothing characterizes, however, his own manner of interpretation and description so much as the effort to place the concrete matter instead of considering it separately and lingering on empirically provided affairs.... He did not seek to set forth these affairs directly under the highest and most general point of view only to return again ... to the point, from which the consideration emerges, in order to apply what is general to what is empirically given. (1:176)

The Christian "principle" is newly formulated by Paul in a complicated concrete historical fashion. Here Baur proceeds from his previously adopted postulate of an opposition between Jewish and Gentile Christians. In the meantime, it has become clear that such a conflict did not exist in either the Corinthian or the Roman community, where at the time Jewish Christians scarcely dominated, even though at the beginning they had formed the kernel of the community.

Likewise in 1836 there appeared a treatise entitled *Die sogenannten Pastoralbriefe des Apostels Paulus aufs neue kritisch untersucht* (The So-Called Pastoral Letters of Paul Critically Investigated Anew). In this writing, Baur indicates that these letters (1 and 2 Timothy, Titus, and Philemon) cannot have been authored by Paul, because their intention, the rejection of Gnosticism, can refer only to a later period.

Baur completed and summarized these Pauline investigations in a work entitled *Paulus, der Apostel Jesu Christi* (Paul, the Apostle of Jesus Christ [1845]), which he, as the title suggests, intended to be a "contribution to a critical history of early Christianity." In spite of his love for detail, what mattered to him were the great historical correlations, as they presented themselves to him. The starting point in this study is the Acts of the Apostles, which Baur used as the source for the life and work of the apostle Paul, in spite of the critical work of Matthias Schneckenburger (1804–1848) that had appeared a short time before. Schneckenburger had pointed to the serious differences between the Paul of the book of Acts and the Paul of the letters (*Über den Zweck der Apostelgeschichte* [Concerning the Purpose of the Acts of the Apostles], 1841). Baur still granted to Acts the status of serving as a valuable source, certainly in the sense "that I can recognize in it no purely objective interest, but rather I am able to determine that it presents an altered description by means of a subjective interest" (*Paulus*, 8). Baur sees in Acts an apologetically intended work in its parallel presentation of the two apostles, Peter and Paul, which reflect the respective, major roles of each in the two groupings of chapters (chs. 1–12 and 13–28). It may be the purpose of the book to connect both apostles (and their disciples) as far as possible, whereby Paul is described as a Judaizing theologian, while the Jewish Christian apostle (Peter) observes in the first part the Pauline conventions concerning the equality of Jews and Gentiles. To further this intention, there is no mention of the scene between Paul and Cephas (Peter) in Gal 2:11–14. It is characteristic for Baur to inquire beyond the statement directly about the circumstances that would have led a disciple of Paul (presumably the author) to such a description. Baur comes to the thesis that this book must have been written at a time when "Paulinism had been so very much pushed back with a harshness and brusqueness … that only a softening, yielding position could preserve it against the powerful Jewish party opposing it, thus allowing its placement … in a … position of countervailing approval" (*Paulus*, 16). The presuppositions of such a thesis (especially the existence of a strong Jewish Christian party at the time of the origin of Acts) have long been recognized as untenable. Nevertheless, the question concerning the *Sitz im Leben* of the book is quite contemporary.

For Baur's interests in the history of doctrine, it is characteristic that the work in his last (third) section after the book of Acts and the Letters of Paul treats the *Lehrbegriff* (teaching) of Paul. The ideological approach of Baur certainly appears most clearly in this section. Thus, he states in a chapter with the heading "Das Christenthum als neues Princip der weltgeschichtlichen Entwicklung" (Christianity as the New Principle of the Development of World History):

> The relationship of Christianity to paganism and Judaism can only be determined as that of the absolute religion to the preceding forms which are subjected to it. It is the progress from slavery to freedom and from nonage to maturity, which is the case of the youth maturing into adulthood and from flesh to spirit.... In Christianity, man for the first time knows himself to be raised into the element of the spirit and the spiritual life. His relationship to God now becomes for the first time the relationship of spirit to Spirit. (*Paulus*, 232)

Here, Baur is entirely in agreement with Hegel, for whom the personal God of traditional Christian teaching is replaced by the idea of an absolute deity immanent in the world, who is understood admittedly not as static but rather is carried as the spirit by an inner movement, in which it itself is situated on the way to knowledge. Baur believes he finds these statements in the theology of Paul, where he sees the spirit as "the principle of Christian consciousness" (ch. 1) combined with the teaching of justification (chs. 2–3). However, he provides accordingly once more only what he himself feels in an alignment with idealism. Christ is "the principle of the community established by him" (ch. 4). While justification is related only to the individual, in Christ the reference to the community becomes clear. Behind this stands once more the sprit as the power that establishes the actual community (*Paulus*, 186–87).

Significant is also Baur's treatment "Über die Composition und den Charakter des johanneischen Evangeliums" (Concerning the Composition and Character of the Gospel of John), a journal article that appeared in sections in 1844 (reprinted in the *Kritischen Untersuchungen* [Critical Investigations]; see below). For the first time Baur addresses here the Gospels, after the *Life of Jesus* by his student, Strauss, had appeared. His procedure is methodologically interesting. He compares the inner character of the Fourth Gospel with the three preceding Gospels (the Synoptics,

Matthew, Mark, and Luke) and describes what, in his view, its historical value and theological significance are. Baur demonstrates that there are many reasons, which result in part from the comparison with the Synoptic Gospels and in part from inner contradictions, why the Gospel of John is unusable as a historical source. This derives from its purpose and intention, which Baur understands as "more speculative than historical," while "the composer of the Gospel (cannot be John the Son of Zebedee or the 'Beloved Disciple,' but someone who writes considerably later) lived more in the world of ideas than history" and "pronounced what were among his highest ideas, which moved the spirit filled with the absolute content of Christian consciousness" ("Composition," 474). The idea of the Logos is dominant for the Gospel of John. This idea is expressed in the Prologue (John 1) and especially in the speeches of Jesus. "In the speeches of the Johannine Jesus, we hear at the same time the composer himself. He both received information and expresses his own views, thus both something objective and something subjective flows into these speeches in alternating and indistinguishable ways" (ibid.).

While Baur denies any independent historical value to the Gospel of John (it appropriated only to a limited extent historical material from the Synoptic Gospels and from other traditions) and instead elaborates its theological self-reliance, he provides it with a specific role in the New Testament. John contains the content that receives Christian consciousness in the spirit. This secures for it a singular place among the Gospels.

In 1847, Baur followed with the summarizing work *Kritische Untersuchungen über die kanonischen Evangelien, ihr Verhältnis zueinander, ihren Charakter und Ursprung* (Critical Investigations of the Canonical Gospels, Their Relationship to Each Other, Their Character and Origin). In it he reprints his treatment of the Gospel of John, along with corrections made in response to critical reactions. Baur himself calls it the "main component of the present writing" (Preamble, iii). In addition, the main section dealing with the Gospel of Luke had been published previously (in the *Theologischen Jahrbüchern* [1846]). Here he had to rebuff above all the thesis held by the church fathers that the Gospel of the sectarian leader Marcion (see *History*, vol. 1) may have been a truncated version of the Gospel of Luke. He turns against the conservative position that the author is Luke the doctor who was the companion of Paul (Col 4:14, Phlm 24, 2 Tim 4:11; the debate about authorship continues today). It is decisive for Baur that the Gospel of Luke be seen as a writing evidencing a particular tendency. Its Pauline character, especially its universalism, which stands in contrast to the particularity of Matthew (Jesus is the savior of humanity, no longer only the Jewish Messiah), is obvious to him. Thus, this writing, too, conforms to the overarching opposition between Jewish Christianity and Gentile Christianity, which shapes for Baur the common portrait of ancient Christianity.

Baur does not consider the Gospel of Mark to be an independent Gospel, but rather only an abridgment of Matthew and Luke. It has dispensed with the prehistory (which Matthew and Luke offer in different ways), the Sermon on the Mount, and all other pieces from Luke, which distinguish it from Matthew. As concerns the proclivity of Mark, Baur regards "the character of the Gospel as indifferent and neutral in so far as it is also intermediary and conciliatory" (567). In his pattern of thought, Hegel's three steps appear: thesis, antithesis, and synthesis, but Baur never appropriates these in a strong form. Mark represents the third step.

Baur considers the Gospel of Matthew to be the oldest of the Gospels, in contrast to the dominant view of the time that Mark was older. He values most of Matthew as a historical source, above all its division into the two periods of Jesus' activity: a Galilean ministry and then the Judean ministry, which he regards as correct. Furthermore, Matthew is certainly not free of tendencies: its Jewish tendency, observable also in the rich occurrence of Old Testament citations is obvious. Central for the determination of the proclivity of this Gospel is Jesus' saying in Matt 5:17 that he came not to abolish the law, but rather to fulfill it (613). Baur draws from these observations a comprehensive conclusion about the history of primitive Christianity as a whole: it is self-evident to him that it, like "any ascertained historical event" (ibid.) must have a national origin. But in this there lies at the same time the source of a new idea, namely, the complete fulfillment of the law, which then establishes the relationship of God as Father to humans, typical of the Sermon on the Mount. Thus, an idea is born that, while directly grounded in Judaism, transcends it as "the principle that leads to a specifically different form of religious consciousness" (614). In the Beatitudes in the Sermon on the Mount, Baur discovers the essential kernel of ancient Christianity: "In this contrast between poverty and wealth, earth and heaven, and present and future, the Christian consciousness finds its purest ideal expression, as the ideal unity of all the oppositions that are forced upon temporal consciousness" (*Das Christenthum*, 1860, 26–27).

Baur inserts the primitive Christianity to which the writings of the New Testament testify into the framework of general church history (*Das Christenthum* [AW 3]). In the universalism of the Roman dominium of the world, he finds, remarkably enough, the actual first step toward

Christianity. He mentions further the pre-Christian religions, Greek philosophy, and only then Judaism (first section). It has been often noted that the person of Jesus is singled out from every other correlation, and his teaching is equated with the "absolute content of the Christian principle" (*Christenthum*, 32). "If one considers the process of the development of Christianity, thus it is only the person of its founder to which a complete historical significance adheres," and the teaching of Jesus contains "nothing that does not have a purely moral tendency" (34–35). These statements were explored in the lectures (see below) held in the same year, in which one finds this statement about Jesus, among others: "In the depth of his moral consciousness, he recognized himself as the son of God, insofar as the idea of morally good in its purity is constituted in his consciousness" (*Vorlesungen*, 118; cf. also 45, 64). Some have wished to attribute to a sudden influence of Kant Baur's turnabout, occurring around 1853, from his former, speculative view of the person of Jesus, to his view of Jesus as a teacher of morality, but there is no evidence for this. Rather, it appears that the old humanistic, Enlightenment view of Jesus as the teacher of morality again penetrated Baur's description, which had lost ground for a brief period to idealistic speculation. He follows finally, however, his own principle: the opposition between Pauline Christianity and Judaism finds its balance in the postapostolic writings of the New Testament, and the development then goes beyond the Gospel of John, which finally carries out the break with Judaism, and continues to the Catholic Church (second and third section).

Although here this development is accomplished beyond the canon, the *Vorlesungen über neutestamentliche Theologie* (Lectures on New Testament Theology, first held in 1853 and published posthumously) are confined to the writings of the New Testament. In moving beyond Gabler, Baur designates biblical theology here as a "purely historical criticism," which "from the beginning was directed to the historical, which is its essential element, as purely as possible in its description" (*Vorlesungen*, 1). Against the orthodox interpretation that the New Testament contains only revelation, Baur refers to the history of dogmatic theology, which describes mainly only what has been taught, not what is true in itself. Thus, New Testament theology asks only "what the writings of the New Testament contain as teaching" (33).

In the structure of the "Lectures," one notes that Baur, following the introduction, divides the description into two main sections: the first is a complete description of the teaching of Jesus (45–121), and the second consists of the teachings of the apostles, which encompasses the rest of the

New Testament. It is characteristic that the teaching of Jesus in the sense of a "moral, fundamental view" (*Vorlesungen*, 60ff.), at first is taken almost exclusively from Matthew, especially the Sermon on the Mount. Baur sees the midpoint of this teaching in the Beatitudes (Matt 5:3–12//Luke 6:20–26), with their emphasis on poverty (*Christenthum*, 26–27). The teaching of Jesus concerning his person, especially his messianic status, becomes more problematic. Baur confesses that this may be "the most difficult point of New Testament theology" (*Vorlesungen*, 75), an assessment that continues to be true today. It is clear that the Gospel of John can contribute nothing to this, since Jesus' statements about himself contain only the theology of the author. However, even in the Synoptics themselves it is necessary to distinguish between the original conception of Jesus and what his disciples taught about him following his death. Baur comes to the opinion that Jesus may have considered himself, above all, to be the Son of God, and he associates this view with his fundamental interpretation of the teaching of Jesus:

> In the depth of his moral consciousness, he recognized himself to be the Son of God, insofar as in his conscience the idea of the moral good was delineated in its purity, especially as he developed it in the Sermon on the Mount. As the Son of God he was the most perfect realization of this idea through his moral effort. (*Vorlesungen*, 188)

For the liberal theology of the nineteenth century following Baur, "the moral element, as it is given expression in the simple sentences of the Sermon on the Mount as the purest and best known content of the teachings of Jesus," is "the actual, substantial kernel of Christianity … providing the basis on which everything else can be built" (*Vorlesungen*, 64–65).

In the meantime it has become clear that this is a one-sided, untenable interpretation of the message of Jesus, especially because the eschatological horizon of his preaching had not yet come into view. An authentic alternative to Baur's theology did not emerge during his lifetime, and his theology was largely discredited, along with the entire Tübingen school founded by him. While almost all of his students were obstructed in their efforts to seek a theological career in a university, he himself remained personally unchallenged by this rejection. If one wishes to remember Baur's continuing inheritance, one must think of the historical-critical method founded by him. Separated from his speculative ideas, this inheritance prevailed in the subsequent period.

6.5. LIBERATING THE OLD TESTAMENT FROM RATIONALISM: ERNST WILHELM HENGSTENBERG

Ernst Wilhelm Hengstenberg was born in 1802 in Fröndenberg, the son of the Reformed minister of the village. The family later moved to Wetter (Ruhr). After a few years in the village school, Wilhelm, who was of delicate health, was privately instructed by his father, who was interested in many things. This private tutoring continued until 1819. Shortly after his confirmation by his father and his reception of an externally administered school certificate examination, he was able to enter the newly opened University of Bonn. Following the wishes of his parents, he studied theology, but also attended lectures on classical and Oriental philology as well as philosophy. By means of his work in the field of Arabic, he was promoted in 1823 to the degree of Doctor of Philosophy. In his public disputation, he defended several theses (Bachmann 1:328–29), including two concerning the Old Testament that stood out: the second thesis: "The theological explanation of the Old Testament is without value" and the seventh thesis: "In the collection of prophecies, which bear the name Isaiah, chapters 40–66 have one and the same author." The second thesis he soon revoked. It had been forced on him by his Doktorvater, the Orientalist G. W. Freytag (1788–1861) (Bachmann 1:97). The seventh and ninth theses ("The view of de Wette on the Pentateuch is false") suggest already the direction that his later interpretation of the Old Testament was to take. Soon afterwards, following the wish of the philosopher C. A. Brandis (1790–1867), he completed a translation of Aristotle's *Metaphysics*, which was subsequently published.

His visit to a worship service of the Herrnhuter community of brothers in Neuwied, where for the first time he experienced the living witness of a Christian community, strongly affected Hengstenberg. However, he remained throughout his life somewhat reserved in his view of pietism. Schleiermacher's *Glaubenslehre* he soon read after its appearance, but he did not feel convinced by its arguments.

After financing for study in Berlin fell through, an offer reached Hengstenberg to help out in Basel as an Orientalist. Soon he was also assigned to be the instructor in Arabic serving in Basel's Missions Seminary. In his private, especially historical theological studies, he turned increasingly from rationalism to Reformed theology as it was incorporated in the Augsburg Confession. Apart from that, he confessed Melanchthon and Calvin to be his most important theological master instructors. He often emphasized later that he came to his new theological views entirely independently—he had not experienced an awakening in a pietistic sense. Rather, this development, according to his own testimony, resulted from his being too much a sober man of reason.

Hengstenberg's goal from the beginning was Berlin. In autumn 1824, he was able to complete there his *Habilitation* in Oriental languages. In Berlin in the 1820s, as in other places, the movement of awakening that fought against rationalism, even in socially prominent circles, had greatly expanded. In addition to the well-known Baron H. E. von Kottwitz (1757–1843), the brothers von Gerlach (especially Ernst Ludwig [1795–1877] and Otto [1801–1849]) and numerous nobles also belonged to the movement. This reached even into the highest circles, including especially Crown Prince Friedrich Wilhelm, who later ruled as King Frederick William IV (1795–1861, reigned 1840–1857), and Princess Wilhelm Augusta (1811–1890), wife of the later king and kaiser Wilhelm I, both of whom sympathized with the movement. The most important rectories in Berlin were occupied by clergy who were among the "awakened." The estate owners, above all in Pommerania, supported the dispersal of these individuals among the peasantry. Their loyalty to the state, shaped by the epoch of restoration, followed the motto "Throne and Altar." This was certainly also the movement's weakness: it failed to a large extent to address the social questions occasioned by the beginning of the industrial revolution.

Schleiermacher and the Hegelian P. K. Marheinecke (1780–1846) served as full professors on the theological faculty of Berlin, since its establishment in 1810. Their conflicts from the beginning created internal tensions in the faculty. Hengstenberg soon found a lifelong friend and patron in the church historian August Neander (1789–1850), who was intimately associated with the awakening movement. In the early part of the year of 1825, Hengstenberg took his theological examination for his licentiate, was *habilitiert* (qualified to be an instructor), and began teaching in the winter semester as a *Privatdozent* (private instructor) in the field of Old Testament. The theses for his promotion to licentiate (Bachmann 1:333–34) illustrate his future fundamental positions concerning the Old Testament: Thesis 2: "The sense of the Old Testament is only one." Thesis 3: "The meaning, which the sense of the Old Testament transforms by means of allegory, owes its origin in part to unbelief and in part to the inability to defend religion." Thesis 4: "The idea of the Messiah in the Old Testament is no human discovery, but rather is truly from God; this idea is one and the same in all the prophets in every period, although its variety of details more or less derive from human weakness." Thesis 5:

"Those who deny that Isa 53 treats the Messiah do violence to the text." Theses 6–8 defend the antiquity and integrity of the book of Job. The basic theological interpretation of Hengstenberg appears immediately in the first thesis: "In order to understand the Old Testament, philology does not suffice: it requires a disposition, to which the glory of Christ is opened." Compare also theses 11 and 12: "Philosophers who wish to know more than Christ are idolaters," and "human reason is blind to divine matters."

Hengstenberg, however, lived in a difficult financial position, which led him to attempt by repeated efforts to gain support from ministerial appointments. Finally, beginning in 1826, after receiving a call from Rostock, he was named an associate professor, admittedly without a fixed salary. For the first time, at the end of 1826, he was granted a small yearly salary. The minister Altenstein attempted several times to remove him from Berlin for representing a theological-political direction that he regarded as threatening. He sought first to relocate Hengstenberg to Königsberg, and later to Bonn. With the assistance of his influential friends, however, Hengstenberg succeeded in avoiding both of these. In in 1828, when Count von Schönburg wished to call him to Glauchau to become superintendent, Hengstenberg placed before the minister an alternative: allow him to go or assign him the still open Old Testament chair of de Wette. Even though the crown prince became involved in the decision, in November 1828 Hengstenberg obtained the position of full professor of Old and New Testament exegesis. He had won the battle with Altenstein. By means of petition, the theological faculty in Tübingen soon awarded him the degree Doctor of Theology. The next forty years until his death, Hengstenberg occupied this chair in Berlin, for many years almost the absolute sovereign in the faculty and the most influential representative of New Orthodoxy in Germany.

Already in 1827, Hengstenberg was appointed the editor of the newly founded newspaper of the awakening movement, the *Evangelische Kirchen-Zeitung*. He was to edit it until his death. He developed it into a newspaper that was decisively antagonistic toward all opposing opinions, a position that gathered large numbers of followers of the awakening around it. Through the *EKZ* Hengstenberg became especially well known. Particularly noted by both followers and opponents were his forewords, composed at the beginning of each year, in which he typically proceeded from a biblical text to address the present situation. The Ministry had to endure the publication, although it viewed its appearance with extreme misgivings.

In the *EKZ*, Hengstenberg represented decisively his renewed Old Lutheran orthodoxy and his conservative political standpoint against the "rationalism" and the liberal theology of his time. He wished consciously to take up Luther and the Reformation. His weakness was that, at the same time, he appropriated the old Protestant understanding of Scripture that had become untenable while rejecting unilaterally the historical-critical view that had come to prominence in that period.

Hengstenberg was influential in faculty politics. His opinions and recommendations often proved decisive in the calling of professors to the Prussian universities, especially during the time when Karl Otto von Raumer (1805–1859) was Religion Minister.

Hengstenberg had to endure a great deal of suffering in his family. His wife, Therese, whose maiden name was von Quast, the daughter of a squire, died in 1861. Three of his five children died during their childhood, and the two remaining sons passed away during the height of their manhood from tuberculosis. Hengstenberg himself maintained his fragile health only by regular vacations and trips to baths. In 1867, before he was quite sixty-seven, he was afflicted with a protracted lung infection. His brother, Karl, attended him on his deathbed. Of his closest relatives, only his two-year-old granddaughter Therese and his very old mother-in-law, Frau von Quast, survived him.

Shortly before he was named to the post of full professor, Hengstenberg presented to the minister his first volume (1.2) of the work *Christologie des Alten Testaments und Commentar über die Messianischen Weissagungen der Propheten* (Christology of the Old Testament and Commentary concerning the Messianic Predictions of the Prophets). The third and final volume appeared in 1835.

In the introduction, Hengstenberg clearly and immediately set forth the dogmatic bases for his point of view: humanity, separated from God and already lost owing to original sin, could be reunited with God only through the sending of a divine savior, who removed through his suffering and death original sin and its consequences. Thus, the offspring of the first humans are justified by God, who granted to them the Holy Spirit as a new principle of life, and established against the kingdom of Satan a kingdom of God in the world. Finally the kingdom of darkness is entirely removed. "Why the sending of this divine savior, which was decided from all eternity, … did not immediately occur after the sinful deed and why four thousand years between the act of the fall and the fact of salvation had to pass" led him to conclude that "to fathom this does not belong to the innermost depth of human wisdom" (1.1:3). As a possible reason, one can still declare that humanity had first to be prepared for the coming of the savior in due manner. "All in all, the pagans were left to themselves" (4). Through the inner disruption of late antiquity, there awakened in humans the desire for a savior. With the Jews, God prepared for the appearance of a savior among their people. This began when God raised first Abraham and then his progeny to himself, and then entered into a special relationship with the nation as its king. He helped them by numerous wonders in their national history. Important also was the gift of the law, for: "Through the revelation of the law came the recognition of sin, and where sin is recognized, there is also the wish to be freed from it as well as the feeling for the need of salvation" (7). Now there is even among the pagans the message of an expected reconstitution (for which Hengstenberg cites historical, religious, and ancient sources). With the Hebrews, by contrast, there are statements about the coming of the redeemer. "These alone have the seal of divine authority and only are for us pure, free of any human additions." These are called the messianic predictions (according to Ps 2 and Dan 9:24–27). These were necessary in order that the temporally limited particularity of the theocrats might be overcome. They recognized "that the special relationship of God to the people of Israel may be only temporary," and one day a savior would appear in whose kingdom all nations would participate (16–17). The messianic proclamation should console one, move one to piety, and cause one to accept the Gospel of the forgiveness of sins, existing also in the old covenant. "The main purpose of messianic prediction, however, was to prepare for Christ, since he could be known as such from the comparison of prediction with fulfillment" (18). Therefore, Hengstenberg is especially concerned with the relationship of the Old Testament to the New!

In the second part of the first volume (which appeared first), Hengstenberg is occupied initially with the prophet Isaiah. In the section concerning the authenticity of chapters 40–66, Hengstenberg reports on the arguments against their authenticity and in so doing uses the historical-critical commentary of Wilhelm Gesenius (1786–1842). Interesting are a few of Hengstenberg's counterarguments for the authenticity of these chapters, in which he betrays no understanding of historical criticism. Most important for this process is the fundamental interpretation of prophecy: according to this all the prophets had "a double calling, in part to impinge on the present, and in part to issue proclamations concerning the future" (1.2:6). In the first place, Isaiah points to the law as the foundation of the old covenant, with the purpose of giving honor alone to God. The proclamation of the future up to the Babylonian imprisonment and the complete destruction of Judah must make the preaching's exhortations more striking, while the announcement of the freeing from the Assyrians and the return from the Babylonian exile could maintain the consolation of the pious. The messianic proclamations, however, with the promise of the man and God (Christ) who cancels sin and unites all peoples to engage in the adoration of God through the spirit, constitutes the kernel of the predictions (7–8). The prophet obtains here, in the ecstasy removed from every human obtuseness, a comprehensive insight: "The view of the freeing from Babylonian exile connects with the view of the freeing from sin and error through the Messiah." Therefore, the prophet's view is directed at times so unwaveringly toward this matter, that the near future is lost entirely from his sight. "Rising above time and space, he surveys from the heights, on which the Holy Spirit has placed him, the entire development of the messianic kingdom from small beginnings to glorious end" (171). For present observers the objection is obvious that this type of exaggerated interpretation causes prophecy to lose its grounding completely, so that its association with the respective historical situation no longer comes into view. This was not a necessary consequence of a confessional, theological attitude, for there were other confessional exegetes, for example, Franz Delitzsch (1813–1890), who offered thoroughly historical-critical results.

Hengstenberg devotes a special section to the problem of the suffering and atoning Messiah in the Old Testament (1.1:252–92), whereby he engages in disputation with de Wette's corresponding writing (see above). In this process, he deals in particular with Isa 53. Against those who maintained that the Israelites expected a Messiah who would be only a powerful earthly king, Hengstenberg remarked:

> The only ones who can confess this view are those who disregard the authority of our Lord whose holy mouth cannot lie and cannot err and who regard the authority of his apostles to be nothing, even though they were taught by Him about the meaning of the predictions of the old covenant and are led in all truth through the same spirit who speaks through the prophets. (1.1:254)

Hengstenberg always returns to a dogmatic position that historical evidence for the period from the contemporary sources (de Wette had adduced it from the early rabbinic literature) does not permit de Wette to prove his point.

Hengstenberg proceeds principally with two steps: first, he attests to the authenticity of the prophetic books; and, second, he examines christological statements in this corpus. He undertakes the first parallel to the appearance of the *Christologie* in a special series, which he obviously names in a deliberate opposition to the *Beiträge* of de Wette (see above, 234): *Beiträge zur Einleitung ins Alte Testament* (Contribution to the Introduction to the Old Testament). In the first volume (1831) he treats *Die Authentie des Daniel und die Integrität des Sacharjabuchs* (The Authenticity of Daniel and the Integrity of Zechariah). To demonstrate the authenticity of the book of Daniel was especially difficult due to the indications of its origin in the second century B.C.E. Here Hengstenberg's (weak) arguments against the objections of his opponents are less important than the positive reasons he presents for authenticity. Among these are the inclusion of the book of Daniel in the canon, which, according to Hengstenberg, occurred under Ezra and Nehemiah and provided the thoroughgoing recognition of its canonicity (237–57). Still more important here is the witness of Christ and the apostles (258–77). The circular reasoning is especially obvious when Hengstenberg presupposes the reliability of the Gospels and the other New Testament writings.

In the same series a two-volume work followed in 1836 and 1839: *Die Authentie des Pentateuch* (The Authenticity of the Pentateuch). Besides his *Christologie*, this work is usually seen as one of Hengstenberg's main writings. The earlier critical observations against the Mosaic authorship of the Pentateuch by Vater, Eichhorn, and de Wette led to a systematic tradition of pentateuchal criticism. Hengstenberg rejects these "rationalistic" theories and seeks to revive the orthodox interpretation by providing a chain of arguments against this criticism and in favor of the authenticity of Mosaic authorship. The work lacks a consistent disposition. His first presentation of evidence (*Authentie* 1:48–126) seeks to demonstrate the ostensible traces of the use of the Pentateuch by the prophets Hosea and Amos, as well as by the books of Kings. It is true that in Hos 12:4–5; 10:13; and Amos 2:7 a muted familiarity with traditions in the Pentateuch can easily be shown. Apart from these, however, numerous other examples of passages mentioned by Hengstenberg scarcely illuminate comparisons with pentateuchal verses. This makes clear the weaknesses of his reasoning: in no case is it proven that the prophets knew the Pentateuch in its final, written form. In the concluding discussion of the books of Kings (1:126–80), Hengstenberg maintains that, in the confrontation with the priests of Baal on Carmel, Elijah as well as these priests paid attention to the instructions of Lev 1:6–8 for the sacrifice of a steer. This is a pointed observation. Yet one could even at that time oppose it and still not deny that there may have been also in an earlier time fixed rules of sacrifice. Similar is the argument concerning 1 Kgs 21:3 in which Naboth may have had in mind the commandment of Lev 25:23 when he refused the offer of King Ahab to purchase his inherited vineyard. When it comes to the consideration of content, however, there is no evidence that there was at this early time a specific commandment written down that can be found in the present Pentateuch.

Central to pentateuchal criticism at that time were the different divine names of Yahweh and Elohim. Since Henning Bernhard Witter (1683–1715) and Jean Astruc, the occurrence of both divine names in Genesis provided the impetus for the differentiation of two sources. Eichhorn had treated it in a comprehensive way for the first time (see above). At least in respect to the E source (Elohist), a consensus on the separation of the source had been reached among critical scholars. Further, in addition to the differences in divine names, other distinctive features provided evidence for sources, including style, vocabulary, and theological content. De Wette had registered a summary of features in his *Einleitung* (see above, 235–37). Nevertheless, Hengstenberg undertook to defend, against this phalanx of critics, the authenticity and unity of the Pentateuch. He tried to show that the different use of the two names of God goes back not to different sources but rather to the distinctive significance of both of them. The prevailing interpretation that the name "Elohim" is the general term for God in the ancient Near East, while YHWH was especially the national God of Israel (Hengstenberg already was aware that the popular pronunciation of "Jehovah" at the time was not correct, but he retained it as the traditional one [1:226, n.; see also 230]). Hengstenberg rejects this with the reasoning that a national name for God could not have been used at the time of Moses, when there did not yet exist a nation Israel, and even earlier (he thinks of the primeval history in Gen 2–3). Rather, there are differences in content between the two names of God: Elohim may be a general divine name for God, which speaks of his omnipotence over all things as seen in his rule over nature, while YHWH designates a special name for "a certain figure, a distinctive personality" (1:293). In a comprehensive line of argument, Hengstenberg comes to the conclusion that the significance of the name is "being" (1:245). The transition from Elohim to YHWH occurs through revelation in history: Elohim becomes YHWH through historical actions; the "true religion necessarily must have a historical character" (I, 294). In Exod 34:6–7, where YHWH himself had made his fundamental nature known to Moses, "the moral features appear especially as the kernel of Jehovah's nature; Jehovah, not Elohim, is both the compassionate God and the judge" (1:295). Unmistakably, Hengstenberg is shaped by the worldview of the classical period and Idealism in his statements. His investigation implies that the occurrence of both of these divine names does not amount to different pentateuchal sources, but rather points to the distinctive meaning of a particular section on which the respective use of a name is contingent. He seeks to demonstrate this subsequently (1:306–414) in his working through the books and individual chapters of the Pentateuch—Genesis in particular—while the rest are treated more briefly. It is certainly clear in this movement through the Pentateuch that the main difference between the two names of God is not supported with concrete examples: on the one hand, as a definition, it is too nondescript, and, on the other hand, the arguments are not illuminated with specific passages. In the end (1:414), Hengstenberg maintains that the evidence he has set forth as the reason for the change of the divine names would have demonstrated both the authenticity as well as the unity of the Pentateuch. Subsequently,

> the constant implementation of the use of Elohim … from Gen 1 to Exod 6, which is connected similarly with its constant abstention from that point to the end, occurs only by the acceptance of one author who writes … according to a well considered plan. The hypothesis of ancient documents and the hypothesis of fragments are proven to be untenable, and thus we have reached a standpoint where it is easier to demonstrate Mosaic composition.

Hengstenberg attempts this in the second volume of his description. This volume treats especially anachronisms in the Pentateuch (statements that appear to argue against origin in the time of Moses) and the contradictions in content that critics had ascertained (2:179–338). Hengstenberg is extensively knowledgeable about these observations made since Ibn Ezra (see *History,* vol. 2). According to a classification of Vater (see above, 234), the following are anachronisms: (1) when the cities are referred to by names that occur in other books for the first time long after Moses; (2) when names, especially of places, are explained by additions that would have been redundant for the time of Moses; (3) when the usage appears that something survives "unto the present day"; (4) and when circumstances are presupposed that have eventuated after the time of Moses. Some more recent critics added more additional anachronisms of style or content. Hengstenberg, aware of these, introduced here additional, particular, orthodox views. While other defenders of the authenticity of the Pentateuch had necessarily allowed later modifications of some passages, he holds fast to his position: "We must even here be stronger than the opponents. Each acceptance of a major interpolation appears to us as extremely questionable, and even anachronisms, which rest only on an individual or at most a few words, we do not consider to be unimportant," for if the Pentateuch stems from Moses, no one should risk allowing it to be even lightly affected as a holy book (2:183). When one, however, allows interpolations, then one is forced to open oneself to various cases. Thus, Hengstenberg addresses at this point each individual example. When the city of Hebron is mentioned by this name in Gen 13:18; 23:2; and Num 13:23, according to Josh 14:15 and 15:13, this name was first preserved after Moses. Earlier, the city was called Kiriath-Jearim during the time of Abraham, as noted by Hengstenberg. He argues that its occurrence in Num 13:22 shows that Hebron was the original name, which was displaced for a while by Kiriath-Jearim. Then, later, the original name was recovered (2:187–92). As for the place-name Dan, mentioned in Gen 14:14 (Deut 34:1), it was not introduced until later when the Danites first conquered the city according to Josh 19:47 and Judg 18:29. Earlier it was called Laish and was given the name Dan after the conquest. Hengstenberg explains this by suggesting that there were two places named Dan in northern Canaan (2:192–94). While these are obviously implausible pretexts, Hengstenberg (against Vater) correctly points to the great antiquity of Bethel as a cultic place (2:202, etc.). The "Book of the Wars of the Lord" cited in Num 21:14 was a major stimulus for the critics of the Mosaic origin of the Pentateuch, for how should Moses, composing the Pentateuch in the wilderness, have read such a book and made excerpts from it? Hengstenberg explains that the book contained in verses 17–18 is a *psalm* (as also is the case in vv. 27–30), meaning that was a collection of psalms.

In addition, Hengstenberg takes very seriously the contradictions in the Pentateuch that speak against its unity and authenticity (2:346–47). (1) There are chronological contradictions. He solves these either through harmonization or by assuming a symbolic-pictorial significance. He avoids many problems by not even mentioning them. (2) There are different names and places in apparently parallel passages (e.g., Exod 17:1–2 par. Num 20:1ff. [2:378–84]—Hengstenberg assumes different events). (3) There are different names for the same places or persons in different passages, among others, the double name for the Mountain of God, Horeb and Sinai (2:396–99). Hengstenberg explains that Horeb may be the name of a range of mountains, while Sinai is the individual mountain in this range. (4) There are factual differences. To these, Hengstenberg reckons above all the descriptions concerning cultic themes, such as festivals (e.g., the time of the festival of the Passover [2:361ff.]) and cult personnel. Everywhere we observe a similar process: in seeking to enervate the objections raised by the critics against the authenticity (Mosaic origin) of the Pentateuch, he acutely recognizes their logical weaknesses, but not his own. He argues against the view that there are inconsistencies in the Pentateuch. Yet he succumbs to spurious argumentation occasioned by his fundamentalist guidelines.

Only in regard to the ancient Near Eastern criticism as it was practiced at that time was he on top of things. In the early nineteenth century, knowledge was limited essentially to Egypt. One is in debt to Napoleon I for the beginning of scientific research on ancient Egypt, for his expedition to Egypt in 1798–1799 was accompanied by a group of experts. Their observations, published in the years 1809–1826, offered a decisive stimulus for Egyptology, together with the decipherment of the hieroglyphs of the Rosetta Stone by T. Young and J. F. Champollion (1790–1832) in the year 1821. John Gardner Wilkinson had awakened a broad public interest in the new knowledge through his excavations of Egyptian graves and the publication of a fundamental work, *The Manners and Customs of the Ancient Egyptians* (3 vols., 1837), which also pointed to the significance of Egyptian archaeology for ancient Israel. Hengstenberg deserves credit for being the first to have scholarly evaluated, in his *Die Bücher Moses und Ägypten* (The Books of Moses and Egypt [1841]), the revolutionary results that Egyptian archaeology had to offer to Old Testament research. It is no wonder that Hengstenberg also turned them to his purposes: on the basis of the available written, architectural, and artistic evidence we now know well the life of the ancient Egyptians. If the Pentateuch presupposes the same circumstances of life, then this was, for Hengstenberg, additional evidence that the Pentateuch could not have originated later (in the period of the kings or the Babylonian exile). Hengstenberg seeks to demonstrate this by tracing historical and cultural reflections of Egypt in the Pentateuch (for instance, in the Joseph story and beyond this in many individual remarks) and by pointing to influences of Egyptian religion and morality on Israel's law in adopting or prohibiting them. As we saw (see above, 118), John Spencer (1630–1693) and John Marsham already in the seventeenth century set forth the thesis that Moses had appropriated the Torah from the Egyptians, thus providing ammunition for deistic criticism. Hengstenberg, who engaged in intense polemics against Spencer (*Authentie des Pentateuch* 1:iv–viii), sees the relationship differently, for it serves, by contrast, an apologetic purpose. Fundamentally, he has no misgivings in acknowledging a dependence in many individual cases, since for him the spiritual uniqueness of Israelite religion is maintained. As already noted, Hengstenberg thereby shows a remarkable knowledge of the pertinent data. To be sure, he confronts us additionally with valuable insights, as well as rather extensive, far-fetched arguments. On the whole his achievements are today obsolete.

In his *Christologie,* Hengstenberg engages extensively (2:401–581) with the problem of the seventy weeks of years in Dan 9:24–27. He appropriates for this the traditional messianic explanation, going back to the church fathers, that it has to do with Christ. With great complexity of erudition in respect to the ancient sources for the Persian Empire and on the basis of fundamental knowledge of exegetical literature, he finds in the statement a precise prediction of the coming of Christ, his death, and the destruction of the second temple by the Romans (70 C.E.). After earlier efforts to obtain from the data of the numbers a reckoning of the end of the world, this is an original solution. In the meantime, however, the book of Daniel had received an almost uncontested chronological interpretation that placed it in the time of the Maccabees and Antiochus IV Epiphanes (ruled 176–164 B.C.E.). Hengstenberg's procedure is similar in all these investigations: since he views the text from his own dogmatic position as existing essentially on the same plane and interprets all statements in their reference to Christ, he remains blind to any kind of separate dimensions of salvation *history.*

This applies even to his last lecture, which under the title *Geschichte des Reiches Gottes unter dem Alten Bunde* (History of the Kingdom of God under the Old Covenant), was published posthumously in 1869–71. A dogmatic sentence immediately at the beginning (1:2) characterizes the approach: "The middle point of the Resolutions of God for the salvation of humanity was from the beginning Christ." The history of the institutions of God's salvation falls into two halves: the time of preparation and the time of fulfillment. The most important distinction between the "economy" of the old and the new covenant consists in the following: the first is based on the promised Christ and the second on the Christ who appears. The old scheme of promise and fulfillment appears here through what naturally, above all, is made concrete in the prophets, but also through the typological view, which observes the correspondences between the results of the old and the new covenants. With Hengstenberg's principle of proceeding from individual sections of Scripture, he identifies the central aim of their edification and elaborates their interpretation, while the historical connection or even an inner historical development is lost.

Hengstenberg also published a series of commentaries on the New Testament writings, among others, the Gospel of John (1861–1864) and the Revelation of John (1861). He attributes all Johannine writings to the apostle John, the son of Zebedee. As one would expect, there occurs throughout these writings a harmonization: Hengstenberg does not see contradictions within the Synoptic Gospels but stresses that John transmitted the speeches of Jesus, not literally but analogously and correctly. The weight of Hengstenberg's work chiefly lay in the area of the Old Testament.

Hengstenberg's history of activity was unique. In Germany one remembers him at best as a figure of the history of theology during the nineteenth century. Although he was vested with a chair in Old Testament, his exegetical works are largely forgotten. It is different in the Anglo-Saxon world, particularly in the United States. Because the formerly conservative, Reformed press of T&T Clark in Edinburgh published English translations of almost all of Hengstenberg's great works—a record for German theological literature—the Lutheran Hengstenberg is especially well known among the conservative, Reformed churches, particularly in the United States. Charles Hodge (1797–1878), one of the most influential scholars at Princeton in the last half of the nineteenth century, was influenced by the decidedly conservative, theological climate at the university and elsewhere in the United States. He studied Hengstenberg, among others. This tradition continues to live. Even as late as 1956, Hengstenberg's *Christology* was newly edited in Grand Rapids.

6.6. DIRECTING HISTORICAL-BIBLICAL CRITICISM
TO POSITIVE RESULTS: HEINRICH EWALD

The son of a clothier, Heinrich Ewald was born in Göttingen in 1803 and, with the exception of a ten-year sojourn in Tübingen, he continued to reside in his hometown for the remainder of his life. It was likely his mother who sent him to the gymnasium. At the university, beginning in 1820 he studied classical philology, theology, and especially Semitic languages. His most important teachers were Eichhorn and Thomas Christian Tychsen (1758–1834). He was, however, already at the time a rather independent thinker. He soon earned the degree of Doctor of Philosophy with the acceptance of his dissertation, "Die Komposition der Genesis" (The Composition of Genesis), which was still conservative in outlook. After a short time as a teacher in a gymnasium in Wolfenbüttel, in 1824 he became a theological *Repetent* in Göttingen. In 1827, he became an associate professor and then, in 1831, was named a full professor. As an Old Testament scholar he served on the philosophical faculty, which at Göttingen was traditional! In 1833, he became a regular member of the Royal Society of the Sciences at Göttingen, and in 1836 the University of Copenhagen conferred on him an honorary doctor's degree in theology.

During these years, Ewald primarily delved further into Semitic languages and, beyond these, also Sanskrit. After works on Arabic poetry and grammar, he became well known for his *Kritische Grammatik der hebräischen Sprache* (Critical Grammar of the Hebrew Language [1827, etc.; new ed., *Ausführliches Lehrbuch der hebräischen Sprache des alten Bundes* [Detailed Textbook of the Hebrew Language of the Old Covenant], 1844, etc.; in addition a shorter *Anfänger-Grammatik* [A Beginner's Grammar]). This appeared in competition with the corresponding work of Wilhelm Gesenius (1786–1842). Ewald's basic principle that grammar depends on a precise exegesis of biblical Hebrew literature prepared him invariably for actual work in the Old Testament. In 1830, he married the daughter of the mathematician C. G. Gauss. Following her death in 1840, he wedded a second time.

In 1837, the state charter of the Kingdom of Hanover, enacted in 1833, was rescinded by the new ruler, Ernst August (1771–1851). The civil servants were released from their oath to the constitution. Seven Göttinger professors (the "Göttingen Seven"), among them Ewald, who could not reconcile themselves to this decision by reason of conscience, protested this action and were dismissed. However, the Württemberg king called him in the early spring of 1838 to a chair in Tübingen on the philosophy faculty. Ewald gave vent to his shock over these results in several political pamphlets. In 1841, he transferred to the theological faculty. While in Tübingen, he wrote his most important exegetical works. He continued there until 1848, when he, made miserable by the theological climate at Tübingen, was granted his request to return to Göttingen. However, the transfer to the theological faculty there was denied him in 1855. His immoderate polemic, which he theologically had now unleashed against the Tübingen school, was feared. Since his return to Göttingen, he launched his works in the New Testament so that he could keep up with the Tübingen theologians.

In 1867, when Ewald, after the merging of the Kingdom of Hanover into the Prussian state, was ordered to take his oath to the new ruler, he refused to do so and was dismissed, only with full salary. After a new political proclamation was issued in the autumn of 1868, the previous allowance for him to hold lectures was revoked. The outrage over the unjust Prussian annexation of Hanover drove him into the arms of the then newly founded Welfen party. Again he published a series of political pamphlets, addressed to the Prussians, Bismarck, and the German people. In 1869, he was elected to the Northern German (since 1871 German) Reichstag (parliament) as a member of the Welfen party, where he, to be sure, frequently appeared to be an unfortunate figure. For a lengthy period he was a German patriot. Beginning in 1848, following Jakob Grimm (1785–1863), he wrote all German and foreign words consistently with lower-case letters. In 1863, he belonged to the founding members of the liberal Protestant Association, even though he himself was by no means a liberal theologian. In an often extreme polemic, he also turned against the "unfree" (conservatives under the leadership of Hengstenberg who do not consider humans to be free of sin), opposed the "sin free" (those who view humans to be free from evil), and the "atheistic school," which he understood to consist of F. C. Baur and his students. He was active also in scholarship: he wrote a four-volume biblical theology: *Lehre der Bibel von Gott oder Theologie des Alten und Neuen Bundes* (Teaching of the Bible about God or the Theology of the Old and New Covenants [1871–1876]). He died in Göttingen in 1875.

During his lifetime, Heinrich Ewald was considered to be the most significant Old Testament scholar in Germany, whose particular authority allowed him to be forgiven his frequent instances of personal recalcitrance. In the context of the history of exegesis, he must be seen rather as a transitional figure, for essentially new knowledge was first won during the generation of his students. During his lifetime, however, he completed a comprehensive exegetical program. He began with the *Poetischen Büchern des Alten Bundes* (Poetic Books of the Old Covenant [on Psalms, Job, Proverbs, and Ecclesiastes; 1835–1839; 2nd ed., *Die Dichter des Alten Bundes* [The Poets of the Old Covenant], 1866). He completed this series in 1839 with an introductory volume in which he provided an introduction to Hebrew Poetry (later, *Dichtkunst* [Art of the Poets]).

This last volume contains a series of insights into Hebrew poetry that originated in an intensive engagement with the Psalms of the Old Testament and betrayed an intrinsic familiarity with the Bible. One is to keep in mind the presuppositions under which Ewald worked: exegesis of the Psalms was still in its infancy (Gunkel was the first to adopt the criticism of forms; see below, 355), while the science of poetry and meter even today has considerable problems with regard to their employment in the Hebrew Bible. Some foundations were laid by Lowth, while Herder had awakened, at least emotionally, an interest in Hebrew poetry. Ewald, however, as was the case in other matters, was very independent in his observations. Thus, he asserted that the versification in the songs in each case follows a meaning and therefore, in contrast to classical verse, is often irregular. This is the consequence of his view that poetry originates in thought (*Dichter* 1:1, 5–17). That he experimented, on the other hand, with accentuations and unstressed syllables as they occurred in classical verse is not surprising, since much in this area even today is uncertain. Against Hegel, who holds that the epic is the oldest poetic form, followed by lyric and drama, Ewald stresses "that the lyrical poetry or the song overall is the shortest form of poetry, which originates with any people" (17). Important are his observations on melody and the music used to accompany the songs (209–33). More uncertain, even until today, is the existence of strophes, which Ewald, beginning in 1828, believed was apparent. On the other hand, the conservative trait that permeates Ewald's entire Old Testament research already becomes clear here; he advocates with some degree of emphasis that the origin of a group of psalms was to be attributed to the personal composition of David (*Dichter* 1.2:3–7). Analogously, King Hezekiah was the author of Isa 38:10–20, while Exod 15 and Judg 5 are, in Ewald's view, very old psalms.

One of the main works of Ewald is his *Propheten des Alten Bundes* (Prophets of the Old Covenant), which his student, Julius Wellhausen, saw as his "exegetical, crowning achievement": "he was congenial to the prophets and he pressed deeper into their nature, more so than any of his predecessors" (*ThB* 27, 130–31). Ewald in the beginning provides a general description of the Old Testament prophets. Concerning the prophet who is commissioned by God as a speaker (thus Ewald explains the Hebrew word *nābî'*), he speaks on behalf of God and receives the divine word from God. Ewald notices "that this way necessarily leads beyond the limits where human and divine spirits encounter each other and … ignite the spark that expresses correctly the apposite idea about existing questions of human life" (9). This leads to the contemporary view that everyone "also today" should strive to reach the same aim with comparable certainty. No doubt, this flowing of the Spirit is an inner process, which a description cannot reach and a prophet cannot himself effectuate (21). Surely, "the prophet must speak what his God desires and how he wants it expressed" (9), whereupon the force and directness are alone the decisive difference for the prophetic. Today, such a powerful, eruptive prophecy is certainly no longer necessary: "Now, thanks to the prophets, the divine truths [i.e., the religious and moral ones …] are generally known and have become prevalent, and it is nearly only a matter of their correct relationship and exercise" (11). Pure doctrine was developed from the prophetic books, which now transmit for everyone the given truths (12). In spite of his criticism of the "Henstenbergians," Ewald is at heart a rather conservative Lutheran Christian!

Ewald also places prophecy in the context of history: he sees a development of three stages in which prophecy rises to an increasingly pure form (40–47). However, then comes a period of decline, which also encompasses the false prophets, even though there was, once again in the postexilic period, a flowering of genuine prophecy. For the recording of the prophetic books, Ewald is of the opinion that there already had been in earlier times a type of prophetic writing (49). To be sure, only the book of Ezekiel was preserved "as it proceeded from the prophet's own hand" (70–71; this was not questioned before the beginning of the twentieth century), and the book of Jeremiah approaches this. All others were already altered comparatively early. Further, he reckons with the possibility that there once may have existed a more comprehensive prophetic corpus of writings of which only broken sections are preserved. Ewald sees his task as placing these prophetic fragments in the period in which they originated. Therefore, he stresses the historical-critical aspect. By the same token, however, the meaning "as well as the skillful composition and artistry" of each fragment are important for him to recognize (84). The strength of his investigation lay in these features, not in his methodological criticism. In what were originally two, and later three volumes, he brings forth a thorough commentary on the entirety of the corpus of prophetic books.

This writing was in turn preliminary to Ewald's monumental seven-volume work *Geschichte des Volkes Israel* (History of the People of Israel), wherein he entered virgin territory. He continued this history through the sixty or seventy years that were covered by the New Testament and into the second century C.E., the Bar Kokhba Revolt (132–135 B.C.E.). Almost twenty years transpired between the appearance of the first and the last volume of what originally was to be a three-volume work. This history evidences an amazing knowledge of the Bible possessed by one person, even if the results—and not only by reason of the progress of critical knowledge—are generally out of date. Ewald's conservative bent is shown in the fact that he fiercely rejected the views of de Wette and Vatke concerning the criticism of the historical sources. Although he wished to describe the historical results appropriately, he also had a theological purpose behind his history. According to the section entitled "The End of This Entire History" (7:394–402), the history of Israel has a twofold outcome: Ewald is convinced that the nation of Israel came to an irrevocable end with the beginning of Roman rule. Everything that had developed in Israel of higher and eternal importance passed to Christianity, which emerged within it. Thus,

> no people of antiquity in the midst of its downfall has been discovered like this people to undergo such a transformation and to continue to live in the divine sense in the midst of its own transformed community as immortal. The history of no other people finished therefore so absolutely and so clearly according to divine imperative as did the history of this people.

That this end is final Ewald argues against those who think differently: "and only the highest degree of foolishness is found in the opinions still continuing today that this people who declined so would again be resurrected and continue their history" (395–96). That they continued in any way to be a people following Hadrian's victory over Bar Kokhba "no expert will maintain" (399). "Into Christianity was transmitted now all that was true, noble, and glorious of this ancient people, only in a greater manner. They were transformed in an aggrandized fashion" (394).

In a self-directed journal, the *Jahrbüchern der Biblischen Wissenschaft* (Annuals of Biblical Scholarship [1848–1865]), which Ewald produced for the most part himself, Ewald damned with scathing judgments most of the new literature appearing in Old Testament studies that dealt with biblical criticism. In essence he regarded the Bible as the single source of truth and was of the opinion that it is best to master its materials. His student Wellhausen found fault with his teacher, since he had failed to accept the methodological criticism developed by de Wette and Vatke. To be sure, in this criticism there was a little bias, owing to his association with both scholars.

6.7. Detecting the Sources of the Gospels through Historical-Critical Analysis: Heinrich Julius Holtzmann

Born in Karlsruhe in 1832, Heinrich Julius Holtzmann was the oldest of eight children of the Baden theologian Karl Julius Holtzmann, who was married to the daughter (Adelheid Sprenger) of a minister. At that time, Karl Julius was a teacher in a Lyceum in Karlsruhe. In 1847, the family moved to Heidelberg, where the father became the minister of the *Heiliggeistkirche* (Church of Holy Spirit) and a *Dozent* (private lecturer) of a preaching seminary. In 1856, the theological faculty bestowed on him an honorary doctorate. After his *Abitur* (high school diploma), Heinrich matriculated in 1850 in Heidelberg University to study theology. During a year of study in Berlin (1851–1852), he attended the lectures of all of the professors of theology there. In retrospect, he confessed that only Vatke actually was important for him. Holtzmann heard his lectures on *Historisch-kritische Einleitung in the Bücher des Neuen Testaments* (Historical-Critical Introduction to the Books of the New Testament), which the young student continued to find stimulating. At Heidelberg during that time, there was no actual expert in the study of the New Testament. When he finished his exams in the autumn of 1854, Holtzmann was a pastoral vicar in Badenweiler for three years. In 1858, he received his licentiate and obtained thereby permission to serve as an instructor on the theological faculty of Heidelberg. In 1859 he became a lecturer in the preaching seminary and began to offer lectures in New Testament as well as practical and historical theology. His volume *Kanon und Tradition* (Canon and Tradition [1859]) demonstrated his competence in practical and historical theology. However, he achieved a breakthrough in New Testament with the work *Die synoptischen Evangelien: Ihr Ursprung und geschichtlicher Charakter* (The Synoptic Gospels: Their Origin and Historical Character [1863]). He became an associate professor in 1861. In 1862, he received the distinction of an honorary doctorate from the Evangelical theological faculty in Vienna, which extended a call to him in 1865. Following his rejection of this invitation, he was named a full professor at Heidelberg.

A huge assignment fell to him with the editing of the unfinished *Bibelwerks für die Gemeinde* (Bible Work for the Community), which was left behind by C. K. J. von Bunsen (1791–1860). Consisting of nine volumes of a revised Luther text with notes, these were to comprise a division containing the history of the biblical books up to the life of Jesus. Holtzmann himself contributed important sections to this project. In addition to his students, he felt himself always mostly connected with the community. Furthermore, he was a contributor to the *Protestantenbibel Neuen Testaments* (The Protestant Bible of the New Testament [1872]), the *Bibellexikon* (Biblical Lexicon) of Daniel Schenkel (1813–1885), the *Lexikon für Theologie und Kirchenwesen* (Lexicon for Theology and Ecclesiastical Matters [1882; 3rd ed., 1895]), and the *Kurzen Bibelwörterbuch* (Short Biblical Dictionary), edited by the Old Testament scholar Hermann Guthe (1849–1936). Numerous journal articles and popular contributions served the same purpose.

Holtzmann worked as a liberal representative in the Baden parliament (1867–1871), where he addressed especially cultural problems and school questions. Controversy began to occur after the defeat of Austria by the Prussians in the war of 1866, in which Baden had fought on the side of Austria. Was Baden to ally itself with the German empire or with Austria? Holtzmann leaned in the direction of being congenial to Prussia. In the foundation of the "Protestant Association," Ewald, Schenkel, and he were among the founding members.

The Imperial Chancellery in Berlin was responsible for the newly founded University of Strassburg, located at that time in the imperial territory of Elsace-Loraine. When the theological faculty of this university proposed Holtzmann as a full professor, controversy broke out. The largely conservative Lutheran pastors of Elsace opposed his appointment and demanded a professor be appointed who represented their theological orientation. Kaiser Wilhelm I, who was responsible personally for the naming of full professors, delayed for a long time in giving his approval. He yielded to the request only when Holtzmann, at the demand of the Curator of the University, signed a declaration that he would not continue to be active in church politics. In Strassburg, where Holtzmann continued until his retirement in 1904, Holtzmann taught, as was customary at the time, not only his main field of New Testament but also dogmatics and early church history. He likewise published considerably in different areas: especially in the New Testament, but also systematics (along with Richard Rothe [1799–1867], the most significant Heidelberg dogmatician), church history, the history of religion, the philosophy of religion, and practical theology. In 1897, an honorary doctorate was bestowed upon him by the philosophical faculty, and in 1901 he prevailed in having accepted the *Habilitation* of his student, Albert Schweitzer (1875–1965), in spite of resistance and opposing views. In 1907, Holtzmann moved to his place of retirement in Baden-Baden. There he died in the year 1910.

Although Holtzmann also published comprehensive works on the epistles (Ephesians and Colossians in 1872; the Pastoral letters in 1880), he also dealt with Acts in the Hand-Commentar zum Neuen Testament (1890; 3rd ed., 1901) and with the Johannine literature (1891; 3rd ed., 1908), he has continued to be remembered especially for his knowledge of the questions concerning the Gospels. The relationship between the so-called Synoptic Gospels (Matthew, Mark, and Luke) is one of the most complicated problems in New Testament criticism, and the determination of which is the oldest Gospel has not been decided up to today. This indicates the difficulty that lies behind this issue. Through his careful interpretation, Holtzmann brought the long-standing discussion to a provisional conclusion. The negative result of the investigations of David Friedrich Strauss, bearing the misleading title *Das Leben Jesu* (The Life of Jesus), and the methodology related to it had revealed the ample defects of previous research: it lacked a sufficient knowledge of the sources. In his description, Strauss had proceeded from the so-called traditions hypothesis. His view that the Gospel narratives are, for the most part, mythology presupposes a lengthy phase of oral tradition. This was an anonymous process in the early community by which the mythically formed narratives about Jesus were developed. The question of the historical value of the tradition was raised now in a forceful manner, as a result of this view.

This methodological change goes hand in hand with a modification in the development of the history of ideas that perhaps was introduced around the same time. This was brought about especially by historians. B. G. Niebuhr (who wrote his Roman history during the years 1811–32) had based the history for the first time on a meticulous evaluation of the sources. The most prominent theoretician of so-called historicism, who regarded the purpose of his criticism to be to achieve the highest possible objectivity, was Leopold von Ranke (1795–1866). He formulated in the foreword of his first work, *Geschichten der romanischen und germanischen Völker von 1495 bis 1535* (History of the Roman and German Peoples from 1495 to 1535 [1824]), the famous statement that his effort did not have in view the task assigned previously to history, that is, to instruct contemporaries about history. Rather, "it will simply show how it actually was" (*Sämtliche Werke*, 1874, 33–34:7). This belief in objectivity attainable in historical criticism today we know is an illusion that reigned supreme throughout the entire nineteenth century. Thus, it influenced biblical criticism during this period to a great degree.

Following are some of the conclusions that the further criticism of the sources of the Gospels had to dispute. According to the greater knowledge provided by the criticism of the character of the Gospel of John, its value as a historical source appears to be ruled out. As for the other three Gospels, their materials parallel each other by half. This is demonstrated immediately when the respective sections of the three forms of the Synoptic Gospels are placed side by side. This group of parallel texts corresponds considerably to the content of the Gospel of Mark and contains for the most part narrative materials. In addition to this, there is material that largely consists of texts that have the character of sayings, which are found in the Gospels of Matthew and Luke. Conspicuous, to be sure, is their different arrangement: while this material appears to be strewn throughout the Gospel of Luke, in Matthew it is ordered by large complexes such as the Sermon on the Mount (chs. 5–7). Finally, there is special material, such as a series of parables in Luke and the two different birth and childhood stories of Jesus in Matthew and Luke.

Soon after the appearance of the work by Strauss, two critics almost at the same time came forward with their comments: Christian Gottlob Wilke (1788–1854) and Christian Hermann Weisse (1801–1866). After the philologist of ancient languages Karl Lachmann, Wilke was the first who argued against the Griesbach Hypothesis (see above) in his book *Der Urevangelist* (The Original Evangelist [1838]). This was a comprehensive investigation of the Gospels of Mark and Matthew, or at least the material common to them. Wilke concluded that Matthew is not the oldest Gospel, but rather it is Mark. Mark had already been written prior to the two other Gospels and provided significant portions of the other two, which are dependent on him. Weisse, who was interested in a variety of things, was in his main office a philosopher and represented an idealistic orientation. He contributed an important contribution to Gospel criticism in that he set forth for the first time a well-founded two-source theory. One source stemmed from a student of Peter, who had listened to the apostle's authentic narratives about Jesus and compiled his Gospel (*Die evangelische Geschichte kritisch und philosophisch bearbeitet*, 1838, 1:59–62). The Evangelists Matthew and Luke had used another source in addition to Mark. They used Mark as the predecessor for their narratives, which provided a fixed series of materials that gave evidence of their dependence; in addition they used a source that consisted mainly of sayings (*logia*) (see 2:1–180).

In addition to these two important representatives of the main theory, which Holtzmann came across when he followed his own description, he listed an entire series of other scholars who participated in the discussion. Holtzmann himself turned out his own work, *Die Synoptischen Evangelien* (The Synoptic Gospels), dating from 1863, which for a lengthy period provided a final consolidation of the previous results. The foreword is interesting (7–14), in which Holtzmann relegates his work on the Synoptic Gospels to the sphere of the critical introduction to the New Testament and defines it, with F. C. Baur, as a purely historical enterprise (even though at least in practice this presupposes a dogmatic standard through limiting the enterprise to the canon). The task is to open "the road to historical research with the means of criticism" (8). Certainly, it has to be defined as that of a theological lecture. Even more conspicuously, however, Holtzmann mentions in the introduction (§1), always still in the forefront in opposition to Strauss, that the final purpose of his investigation is to answer the question

> whether it may be at the time still possible to trace the *historical* form of someone to whom (namely Jesus) Christianity not only ascribes its name and existence, but also whose person has been made the middle point of Christianity and the center ... of its world view, in a manner that meets all correct requirements of the advanced historical-critical sciences.... In so doing, does this continued historical-critical research of this person satisfy all correct requirements of a scrupulous, historical criticism? (1)

Finally, this research has to do with the historical reconstruction of a life of Jesus. Holtzmann decides to renounce the Gospel of John for this type of historical description. Instead, he intends "thus to work with the Synoptic Gospels and to address the question whether or not they are capable of being used as sources for advancing a synoptic portrait of Christ." This requires that "a completely certain ... answer must follow" (8–9).

Holtzmann concretely supports the view of the existence of two Synoptic sources: one source, which he calls A and in 1863 still equates with a somewhat larger source that precedes the Gospel of Mark (he later gave up this thesis), and a sayings (*logia*) source, which he designates with the Greek siglum *L*. In order to reconstruct this source, one has to proceed from the Gospel of Luke (128–57), since Matthew assembled his large compositions of speeches, for example, the Sermon on the Mount (chs. 5–7), for the first time at a later period. At least this is supported by the points of view of the content. On the other hand, Luke presents the sayings source in a form in which the individual sayings are strewn throughout the Gospel. In the arrangement of the two sources, a clear residual of materials certainly remains that is unique to one or the other Gospels. To these unique materials belong especially the extensive childhood narratives in Matthew and Luke, which are fundamentally different from each other.

Certainly in opposition to his predecessors Weise and Wilke, Holtzmann allows an incremental interval between the two Synoptic Gospels and the time of Jesus, during which there were only oral traditions. In spite of that, he sought already in 1863 to offer a "Portrait of the Life of Jesus according to Source A" (§29, 468–96). Therein it may be possible "to give some kind of fixed portrait of the historical character of the person Jesus." He sees this as "decisive progress" against the Tübingen school

(469). Toward the end of his life, he once again composed a work about the historical Jesus, entitled *Das messianische Bewusstsein Jesu* (The Messianic Consciousness of Jesus) as a "contribution to criticism concerning the life of Jesus" (1907).

The principles of his interpretation of Jesus can be most clearly traced in the *Lehrbuch der neutestamentlichen Theologie* (Textbook of New Testament Theology [2nd ed., 1911]), published posthumously in the final version. The proclamation of Jesus assumes a central place in the first volume of this work, which Holtzmann places under the superscription "Jesus and Primeval Christianity" (ch. 1.2) in the frame of his chapters "The Religious and Moral Thought World of Contemporary Judaism" (ch. I, 1; with the inclusion of Alexandrian theology) and "The Theological Problems of Primitive Christianity" (ch. 1.3). It is characteristic of Holtzmann that Paul is not mentioned, but in the second volume he is assigned his own chapter. Pauline theology ("Pauline Thought," ch. 2.1) beside "Deutero-Pauline Thought" (ch. 2.2) and "Johannine Theology" (ch. 2.3) receives a place among the theological systems of thought. An aloofness is betrayed here, that is seen also in the foreword, which states that "the effort to make the New Testament thought world completely and suddenly a decisive component of our present thinking about God and the world is a totally impossible undertaking" (1:13). For Holtzmann, the proclamation of Jesus has the fewest difficulties. Among the presuppositions for the occurrence of this proclamation, it appears to him most important that he possessed "his own genius." Holtzmann arrives at this through his preoccupation with Jesus in the attempt "to conceive the occurrence and the accomplishments of a restless internal activity, while his personality [!] was developing and maturing." Further, for the description of the proclamation of Jesus, the typical principle of liberal Protestantism is constitutive: Working out the "moral content of the idea of God" (1:222), Jesus proclaims "that God's being is love" (1:220), and even in regard to sinners, of a God who "in and of Himself is compassionate" (1:221). In the life's work of Jesus this God is revealed. Although this has already been prepared beforehand in the Old Testament (Holtzmann points to Ps 103 and Isa 57:15) as an "ancient prophetic thought" (ibid.), for him, Jesus comes to rest "on the highest echelon of moral development, the Old Testament and related New Testament connections, which can only be found in gradually working out ... the moral content of the idea of God. Having arrived at the crest of development, the portrait of God is identified, however, only through his ethical associations with the human world" (1:222–23)—and no longer, as in the pre-Christian period, through the role of the god of nature. The "movement of religion from the metaphysical to the moral sphere" allows comparisons to be made with Socrates, Plato (who extolled the idea of the moral good to become the norm of the idea of God"), the Pythagoreans, and the Stoics. "Jesus by contrast draws directly from what is his very own self" (1:225). Religion and morality appear in a close, interchangeable relationship; this is conveyed especially in the two love commandments (1:227). In addition, the kingdom of God (1:248–95) is, according to Holtzmann, to be understood as an internal occurrence. The question whether the kingdom may be understood as present or future, he lets hang in the balance (1:292). On the whole, disregarding messianism, one is allowed to understand "that, what Jesus brought to the world were a deepening of Jewish consciousness of God and an ethical internalization that moved beyond conventional morality" (1:295).

In view of these ideas, it is consistent that Holtzmann in connection with the suffering and death of Jesus rejects the idea of vicariousness as incompatible with the self-understanding of Jesus. Holtzmann wants to concede nothing more than that Jesus may have recognized his unavoidable fate of death as inevitable—"it must be, therefore go forward!"—when the Son of Man desires to require from humans an identical self-sacrificial service of love (1:363). That the death of Christ was thereby reduced to the idea of a paradigm was criticized already by contemporaries (1:363 n. 2).

In the wake of Holtzmann, scholarship today accepts two sources: Mark, the oldest of the Gospels, and the sayings source (usually called "Q"). These are viewed by most scholars today as the original sources from which the two other Gospels, Matthew and Luke, were created. To be sure, this result is treated not as a fact but rather as a hypothesis. A high degree of probability is given to this hypothesis, although not clearly to every individual detail. In addition to the two sources, one must reckon with special materials both for Matthew and for Luke. In some few cases, the relationship between these two Gospels and the Gospel of Mark remains open for explanations.

However, there has been a minority of scholars who have held fast to the Griesbach Hypothesis. The most well known of these in the nineteenth century was H. U. Meijboom (1842–1933) with his Groningen dissertation of 1866, "Geschiedenis en critiek der Marcushypothese" (translated into English by J. W. Kiwiet, *History and Critique of the Marcan Hypothesis* [1933]). Representative in the twentieth century is William R. Farmer (*The Synoptic Problem* [1964] and other publications). However, their interpretation up to now has not prevailed.

6.8. Redetermining the Course of the History of Israel: Julius Wellhausen

Julius Wellhausen was born in 1844 in Hameln, the son of the pastor August Wellhausen (1808–1861). Julius remembered experiencing a pleasant youth with many contacts, even when his depressing family situation overshadowed his life. His father, a literate man who was an orthodox Lutheran and friend of the liturgical movement, was frequently ill and died at a young age. All of Julius's siblings died during childhood. After attending elementary school and a progymnasium (secondary school) in Hameln, Wellhausen came to Hanover to study in a lyceum. Beginning in 1862, he studied theology in Göttingen, although primarily without much satisfaction, and he was close to giving up this discipline. At Easter 1863, when he first accidentally came across Ewald's *Geschichte des Volkes Israel* (The History of the People of Israel; see above), he came under the influence of this Göttingen teacher, who was sniggered at in the faculty as a somewhat peculiar original. From this point on, Wellhausen increased his study of Hebrew, the basic elements of which he earlier had hardly mastered, and other Semitic languages. Without overlooking Ewald's weaknesses, he was fascinated by the seriousness of the latter's exegetical endeavors, linguistic knowledge, methodological meticulousness, openness, and sense for comprehensive historical perspectives. Wellhausen's critical insights certainly would later considerably exceed those of his teacher. In 1865 he passed his church examinations. After his activity as a house teacher in Hanover in 1865–1867, he returned to Göttingen, where he attended Ewald's class because of the demands of his feared Semitic language exercises. This class especially laid the foundations for Wellhausen's later knowledge of Arabic. Owing to political reasons, there eventuated finally a parting of company between the two. After 1866, Ewald became a fervent advocate of the Welfen party (see above), while Wellhausen, always the realist, leaned toward the cause of Prussia. Wellhausen declined when Ewald one day demanded that he declare that the Prussian king and Bismarck were rogues. With tears in his eyes, Ewald showed him the door.

In 1868, Wellhausen became the *Repetent* at the Stift, was promoted to a licentiate in 1871, and thereafter became a *Privatdozent* (private lecturer). In 1871, he published a carefully written, comparative investigation *Text der Bücher Samuelis* (Text of the Books of Samuel). As early as 1872, he was called to Greifswald as a full professor, obviously a compromise candidate between a liberal and a person of a "positive" direction in the theological faculty at the time. At his departure, the Göttingen faculty awarded him a doctorate in theology. In Greifswald he married the sensible daughter of a professor of chemistry. After a miscarriage and an operation, she was chronically ill, and thereafter, the marriage remained childless. In Greifswald, Wellhausen established a lifelong friendship with the famous U. von Wilamowitz-Moellendorf who was a philologist of ancient languages (1848–1931). Wellhausen's work *Die Pharisäer und die Sadducäer* (The Pharisees and the Sadducees [1874]) presents the thesis that the Pharisees were the churchly party, while the Sadducees were the secular party. Wellhausen's first literary-critical work, *Composition des Hexateuch* (Composition of the Hexateuch) appeared in 1876–1877, written initially in the form of journal articles. He published the planned continuation of the historical books (Judges–Kings) as a part of the fourth edition of F. Bleek's *Einleitung in das Alte Testament* (Introduction in the Old Testament), to which he was commissioned by his publisher. In later editions, Wellhausen brought together both parts. In 1878 he published his most famous composition, the *Geschichte Israels* (History of Israel; since 1883, *Prolegomena zur Geschichte Israels,* Prolegomena to the History of Israel). The commercial success of this book echoed throughout the public sphere. Initially, the skeptical publisher evidently had paid Wellhausen no honorarium. However, with the second edition in 1883, the book definitely fetched a rather handsome payment.

A planned second volume did not come to fruition at the time. At the beginning of 1879, Wellhausen entrusted the current referent in the ministry of culture and religion with his conflict of conscience. In 1880, Wellhausen offered without success his request that the minister approve his transfer to the philosophical faculty. Wellhausen resigned from the theological faculty in Greifswald in 1882. In his resignation request, Wellhausen writes that he has decided to leave his present office and to earn his *Habilitation* in Semitic languages in either Göttingen or Halle:

> I have become a theologian, because I am interested in the critical treatment of the Bible. It eventually came to me that a professor of theology has at the same time the practical task of preparing students for service in the Evangelical Lutheran Church and that I am not personally fit for this objective. Much more ... I render my hearers unfit for this office. (Cited from Alfred Jepsen, *Der Herr ist Gott: Aufsätze zur Wissenschaft vom Alten Testament* [Berlin: Evangelische Verlagsanstalt, 1978], 266).

Since Wellhausen remained a pious Christian his entire life, according to the opinion of all who knew him, the most illuminating explanation for this step was his extreme individualism, which could not allow him to correlate his views and actions with the institutional church. Disregarding the fact that he held as hopeless the current position of the orthodox as well as the liberal Protestant Church, he was also skeptical of the church as an institution. Therefore, he believed he could not serve it as an instructor. We shall see how this individualism also determined his view of the history of Israel's religion.

The Ministry did not drop him completely, but rather transferred him to Halle as an associate professor of Semitic philology. He spent three years in this post and was called to Marburg in 1885 as a full professor for Semitic languages, on the condition that he not engage in offering lectures on the Old Testament, out of respect for the theological faculty's Old Testament scholar W. W. Graf Baudissin (1847–1926). The latter, however, placed no value on such a "muzzling" of his colleague. Thus, Wellhausen soon offered Old Testament courses.

Semitic philology was now his official area of instruction. Since his interest in the current development of the knowledge of Assyrian/Babylonian continued to be limited and Aramaic appeared too close to the Old Testament, he became occupied in particular with the Arabic he had learned from Ewald. He was especially interested in pre-Islamic, Arabic studies, since there were possible parallels with early Israel. Wellhausen became as well known as an Arabist as he was as an Old Testament scholar. By means of a trip to Leiden, Paris, and London in the summer of 1880, he prepared himself for this new objective. He composed an introduction to an edition of a writing attributed to al-Waqidi (*Kitab al Maghazi* [The Book of the Wars]) on the wars of Muhammad in Medina (1882). Of his numerous works in this area, the third volume of the *Skizzen und Vorabeiten: Reste arabischen Heidentumes* (Outlines and Preliminary Works: Remnants of Arabic Paganism [1887; 3rd ed., 1961]) has become the best known. His major work, however, is considered to be his *Das arabische Reich und sein Sturz* (The Arabic Empire and Its Collapse [1902]), which treats the history of the Umayyads.

On account of the crisis that culminated in his departure from Greifswald, the planned second volume of the *Geschichte Israels* was deferred to an undetermined time. Wellhausen returned to this project once more, when he was called to Göttingen to hold the Old Testament chair as the successor of Paul de Lagarde (1827–1891). In the same year, he was accepted by the *Akademie der Wissenschaften* (Academy of the Sciences). Together with a volume of the *Skizzen und Vorarbeiten*, he brought out a translation of the *Kleinen Propheten* (Minor Prophets), which was accompanied by notes (1892; 4th ed., 1963). In 1894 his *Israelitische und jüdische Geschichte* (Israelite and Jewish History) appeared. Preliminary materials are in an article in the *Encyclopedia Britannica* on Israelite History (1881), the main part of which was printed in a private form in 1880 as well as published in German under the title *Abriss der Geschichte Israels und Judas* (An Abridgment of the History of Israel and Judah [1884]).

Wellhausen spent the remainder of his life in Göttingen. He had to fight against health problems throughout his lifetime. In addition to a chronic stomach illness, he experienced increasing deafness after about the age of sixty. Because he could no longer hear the contributions of his colleagues, he resigned from the *Akademie* in 1903. Early on, an agonizing arteriosclerosis afflicted him that during the last years of his life almost prevented him from working. In 1913, he let himself receive an emeritus status on account of issues of health. Nevertheless, he was described as a continually happy person, jovial, and in good humor, one who did not disown his idyllic agrarian origins.

Also in the area of the New Testament, to which Wellhausen turned following the conclusion of his Arabic work, he produced substantial writings. In 1903 and 1904, new translations appeared, including a succinctly composed commentary on the Synoptic Gospels. The results of his observations, gained directly from the text, almost without taking into consideration the comprehensive secondary literature already written up to that time, were integrated in an *Einleitung in die drei ersten Evangelien* (Introduction to the First Three Gospels [1905; 2nd ed., 1911]). *Das Evangelium Johannis* (The Gospel of John) followed in 1908. These were reprinted jointly in 1987 (*Evangelienkommentare* [Gospel Commentaries]). This demonstrates a continuing interest of specialists in his work. In addition, the Revelation of John (1907) and the book of Acts (1914) were taken into account. The New Testament works were less regarded, since they were written by one outside the discipline, although he brought important insights. In respect to the Synoptic Gospels, Wellhausen was a follower of the Markan hypothesis. More significant was his judgment concerning the life-of-Jesus criticism that had become a beloved child of liberal theology of the nineteenth century. He clearly recognized "that we do not have the material for a historical life of Jesus" (introduction to his *Evangelienkommentare*, 154). Even more important, he saw that the principle of the liberal life-of-Jesus criticism was mistaken: "If the crucified, resurrected, and returning one is Jesus the Christian Messiah, then he is not the teacher of religion. The apostolic Gospel, which preaches faith in Christ, is the authentic one, and not the Gospel of Jesus, which prescribes to the church its morality" (153). "Jesus Christ is the object of the message, and not its bearer" (147). Christianity is established on the resurrection of Jesus, which became certain to the disciples in their ecstatic visions (149). As concerns the Gospel of John, Wellhausen came to the conclusion in his volume *Erweiterungen und Änderungen* (Expansions and Revisions), that it is not a unit. On this basis he built his commentary. He divides the Fourth Gospel into a basic writing (A) and progressive modifications (B), the later of which he reckoned were an essential component of the speeches. He denied that the Fourth Gospel might have arisen under Greek (possibly Gnostic) influences: "It is indeed grown out of from Judaism, and yet still grew on its own soil, as genuine Christianity (*Das Evangelium Johannis*, 123). When Wellhausen died in 1918, his death came as a release. He had completed his life's work.

In retrospect, the major significance of Wellhausen lies in his role as an Old Testament scholar in the new determination of the factual and the chronological sequence of the sources of the Pentateuch and the new, revolutionary view of the course of Israelite-Jewish history won from source criticism. To be sure, he was not without predecessors. Already de Wette had produced preliminary work, especially through the assessment of Deuteronomy (see above, 233, 236). The Strassburg Old Testament scholar Eduard Reuss (1804–1891) in 1834 in a lecture about the so-called foundational writing (*Grundschrift*) of the Pentateuch, which he later named the Priestly writing (P) because of its priestly character, had already designated this strand (P) as the latest pentateuchal source. His student Karl Heinrich Graf (1815–1869), a gymnasium professor in Meissen, had completely substantiated this thesis in his work, *Die geschichtlichen Bücher des Alten Testaments* (The Historical Books of the Old Testament [1866]). Also Abraham Kuenen (1828–1891) in Leiden, where Wellhausen visited him in 1880, had published for the first time in 1868 the same thesis. Decisive for Wellhausen was the reading of Graf's work, to which the dogmatic theologian Albrecht Ritschl (1822–1889), had drawn attention in a visit to Göttingen in 1867. Wellhausen himself reports about how he experienced enlightenment in the following: In the beginning of his studies he had read the prophetic and historical books of the Old Testament, "having been attracted by the narratives about Saul and David as well as Elijah and Ahab, deeply stirred by the speeches of an Amos and Isaiah."

> However, I had a bad conscience, as if I had began with the rooftop instead of the foundation; for I did not know the law about which I heard spoken. Was it the foundation and presupposition of the remain-

ing literature? Finally, I summoned the courage and worked my way through Exodus, Leviticus, and Numbers, and even through Knobel's commentary [August Knobel, 1807–1863]. However, I waited in vain for the light, which should pour forth on the historical and prophetic books. Rather the law vitiated for me the joy of those writings; it did not bring them closer to me, but rather thrust its way only in a disturbing manner.… Then I incidentally came to learn…, that Karl Heinrich Graf pointed out that the law came after the prophets. While I knew almost nothing of the basis of his hypothesis, I was won over to it: I allowed myself to confess that Hebrew antiquity could be understood without the Book of the Torah. (*Prologemena*, 1905, 3–4)

When Wellhausen began with his investigations on the composition of the Hexateuch (the five Books of Moses and Joshua), H. Hupfeld (*Die Quellen der Genesis* [The Sources of Genesis], 1853) already had come to distinguish between three sources: the foundational writing (*Grundschrift*), which one usually held to be the oldest (on account of the divine name of Elohim, it was called the older Elohist), the later Elohist, and the Yahwist (named after Yahweh). Wellhausen suggested for the so-called foundational writing (*Grundschrift*) the abbreviation Q (*quattuor*—the writing of four covenants)—however, later the abbreviation P prevailed. The two sources of the Yahwist (J) and the Elohist (E) combined together by a redactor were placed together under the siglum JE (the "Jehovistic" work of history). Later added to these is Deuteronomy (Deut.), the fifth Book of Moses. In working through the Hexateuch, during which Wellhausen above all pays attention to the great outlines and does not seek a division of sources into the smallest details, results in the following: "From J and E, JE has flowed together to form JE. Deuteronomy was then connected. An independent work in addition is Q. Expanded into the Priestly Code, Q was then incorporated into JE + D, and from this originated the Hexateuch" (*Composition*, 1963, 207). The process of the binding together of JE with D Wellhausen conceives to have been accomplished by "the Deuteronomist, that is, the composer who has inserted the Deuteronomistic source into the Hexateuchal book of history, … and at the same time has edited the latter with the Deuteronomistic understanding." This portrait may already be abridged, since all sources may have had before their aggregation most likely several editions (J^1, J^2, J^3, etc.). In addition, Wellhausen had not been able to trace clearly the strands in the book of Numbers and Joshua (*Composition*, 207–8). For the historical books, Wellhausen reckoned with several writings larger than earlier sources, which were composed before their final redaction into books. All of the historical books were placed within an encompassing Deuteronomistic edition.

The investigation of the sources, to be sure, is not an end in itself, but rather seeks to make certain the basis for the reconstruction of the history of Israel that for Wellhausen is a history of religion.

The next step for Wellhausen consisted in securing the historical place of the Priestly code, that is, the Mosaic law, by means of wide-ranging investigations. This occurs in the *Prolegomenena zur Geschichte Israels*. The most important investigation is directed at the history of the cult (§1, 15–162). Here Wellhausen demonstrates that in the historical and prophetic books of the Old Testament there cannot be found any trace of a single, uniquely legitimate sanctuary as the Priestly code (P) presupposes (17–52). Much more the JE sources sanction the multiplicity of cultic places, while P presupposes the existence of the tabernacle (tent of meeting), which it traces back to the earliest period of Israel in the wilderness. Nothing of the sort, however, can be found in the historical tradition.

The same is true for sacrifices. For an exact determination of the development of sacrifices the sources are not sufficient (53). Still, the contrast between the older sources and Q is clear. The precise description of ritual as the subject of the Mosaic giving of the law, that is, the *when*, *where*, by *whom* and especially the *how*, is found in P. In JE it is to *whom* the sacrifice is made that is emphasized, Yahweh or the other gods. Knowledge of the ritual is presupposed. In addition, sacrifice is much older than the Mosaic law: already Cain and Abel, as well as Noah have sacrificed in the later, usual manner. Furthermore the character of sacrifice has been significantly changed through the centralization of the cult:

> In the ancient period, the worship of God was produced out of life and closely adhered to it. The sacrifice of Yahweh was a meal offered by human beings, significant for the lack of opposition between spiritual seriousness and worldly cheerfulness.… There are earthly relations, which receive consecration through sacrifice. To these correspond the natural occasions of festivity, presented by the variety of life. From year to year, fruit picking, corn harvest, and sheep shearing continued to return and yoke together the members of the household by eating and drinking before Yahweh. (74)

It was different after the centralization of the cult in Jerusalem: "If sacrifice was colored earlier through the type of its occasion, so it now had to have one and the same purpose: to be the medium of the cult. The breath of life was no longer cultivated through means of the cult; rather it had its own meaning.... The soul had leaked out, the shell remained.... The cult was spontaneous in antiquity, now it becomes a statute" (76).

Similarly, the character of the festivals is also changed. The three annual festivals of Mazzoth, Passover, and Tabernacles are originally bound with the harvest and the bringing of firstfruits. They also possess this character in the historical and prophetic books. In P they have lost this connection; they are denaturalized and historicized.

Likewise there can be determined for the priesthood a development from the preexilic period to the postexilic situation, which is observed in P. In P we find the distinction between the secular tribes and the spiritual tribe of Levi, and within that tribe between the sons of Aaron and the simple Levites. This is prepared by the precepts in Ezek 44:6–16, according to which only the sons of Zadok are to be the priests in the rebuilt sanctuary, while the Levites shall perform the religious tasks of common workers. That these were previously a matter for which foreign slaves of the temple were to attend shows "that the systematic exclusion of the holy from profane touching did not exist at all times" (117). In contrast to this, a professional priesthood is almost entirely lacking in the period of the judges. Sacrifices could be brought by private people, and there were priests only in a large sanctuary, a case by which alone Shiloh is known. Moreover, laity could be named priests. Levites very seldom exist. One finds only in Judg 17–18 a Levite acting as a priest. During the time of the kings, priests appear more frequently. However, they regarded the sanctuaries as their private possession. The centralization of the cult brought about a change. Since Deuteronomy could not enforce its demand that Levites should come from the closed local sanctuaries to Jerusalem in order to officiate at the temple (Deut 18:1, 6–7), there originated then a distinction between priests and Levites, which was codified by P (139–40). It is first in P that the high priest becomes the head of the hierarchy, a development derived from Aaron. That this high priest is now, at the same time, the head of the nation is the consequence of postexilic, foreign domination: "Before the perspective of the Priestly Code Israel is in fact not a nation, but rather a community. Worldly matters likewise are distant for them...; their life proceeds in service to the Holy" (144).

In the middle part of his book (section II, "History of the Tradition," 163–360), Wellhausen repeats essentially the results of his *Composition*, completed by the books of Chronicles. In the determination of their unhistorical character and the tendency to contrast with the books of Samuel and Kings, he could agree with the results of de Wette.

The motto from Hesiod is prefixed to this part: "The half is more than the whole." This indicates that, for Wellhausen, the preexilic tradition has more value than the canonical, final form, which the Deuteronomists, the Chronicler, and the Priestly writing had formed. He sees them parallel in their course of action: "The history of the pre-historical and the epic tradition therefore has entirely the same phases through which to progress as does the historical tradition" (360). A characteristic judgment on the Chronicler is offered: "What the Chronicler has made of David! The founder of the empire is become the founder of the temple and of worship, the king and hero at the head of his comrades at arms becomes cantor and liturgist as well as the leader of a cluster of priests and Levites" (176–77). For the historical books the following holds true: "What appears as the usual concept for the specific character of Israelite history and has charted the same particularly in the names of the *holy* history rests primarily on the additional repainting of the original picture" (291). In Judges, the placing together of the description of the war of Deborah in chapter 5 and chapter 4 and the two versions of the campaign of Gideon against the Midianites in Judg 8:1–3 and 8:4ff. demonstrate the character of these repaintings (236–39). In Judg 5 the conquest is prepared with human hands and with the negotiations between the tribes, while in Judg 4 the battle alone is an affair of Yahweh's doing. In Judg 8:4ff. Gideon undertakes his campaign as an act of blood vengeance, while in 8:1–3 the stimulus is a theophany. The canonical portrait of Israelite history has been transformed from an early secular history, viewed in a natural sequence of cause and effect, into a religious history. In the (Deuteronomistic) portrait, "grace and sin operate as though they were the most mechanical forces at work in the gears of results.… This pedantic supernaturalism, the *holy history* according to the formula, is not found in the original narratives" (230–31). By contrast, religion was a national affair in the period of the judges; Yahweh was especially sought out to be the one who provides aid in war.

In the concluding part ("Israel and Judaism," §3, 361–424), Wellhausen responds to objections against what is expressly named the Graf hypothesis. The motto stems from Rom 5:20: "The law appeared in the meantime." One of the chapters is treated in a manner that is very typical of Wellhausen ("The Oral and Written Torah," ch. 10, 391–409). With an explicit reference to Goethe, Wellhausen stresses in this section the significance of the spoken word over against the written text: "While ancient Israel does not lack the God-given foundations for the order of human life, they were not fixed only in written form. On a large scale, usage and tradition were seen as the institution of the deity" (393). In this regard, Wellhausen points to the issuing of the Torah of the priests, which primarily has had a legal character (see also "Israelite-Jewish Religion," 10). "The priests appear here as the foundation pillars of the spiritual order of things, not provided by their offering of sacrifices, but rather in their teaching of matters" (395). Further, the prophets, who are described by Wellhausen as great individuals, carried out their tasks without a previously given law: "The prophets have known no father, as is generally known (1 Sam 10:12); their significance rests on individuals" (397). In the description of prophecy, the statements of Wellhausen gain emphatic momentum:

> The element of life of the prophets is the storm of world history, which sweeps away the orders of humanity.... If the earth collapses in tremors, then they triumph, for Yahweh alone remains exalted. They do not preach about given texts, but rather they speak from the Spirit, which judges all and is judged by no one. Where do they ever lean on another authority for moral evidence, other than the basis of their own certitude? This belongs to the idea of the prophetic, and that is the authentic revelation that Yahweh, beyond every regular agency, addresses the individual.... All statements, which rise above the personal in the highest sense, in truth are the objective, i.e., the divine. It stands the test as such through the affirmation of the general conscience.... their credo is not in any book. It is a barbarism, in dealing with such a phenomenon, to debase its physiognomy with the law. (398)

Said in a more sober way: "It is an empty illusion that the prophets would have explained and interpreted the law" (ibid.). Wellhausen's concern is to show that the voice of the prophets has assumed the same rank that is usually ascribed to the law. It was never specified in any circumstance that the prophets were interpreters of the law.

Deuteronomy, according to the narrative in 2 Kgs 22–23, was the first expressly so-called Book of the Torah discovered in 621 B.C.E. during the reign of Josiah (thus according to de Wette). Indeed, while the book took up older, priestly materials, it is the first time that a book receives public standing. It attained this standing by the exile. Its emergence signified a decisive turn: "With the appearance of the law, the time-honored freedom ceased, not simply in the sphere of the cult..., but also in the region of the religious spirit. The law now existed as the highest, objective authority: this led to the death of prophecy" (402). After the temple was destroyed, the regulations of cultic practice were written down. Ezekiel began this process; the priests follow him, having composed Lev 17–26 (the so-called Holiness Code, a name that originates later). Beginning with this code, the work of priests continued for many years, leading finally to the Priestly code. The Priestly code was introduced under the governorship of Nehemiah by Ezra, the priest (Neh 8–10). This was arguably not an isolated writing, to be sure, but rather was already placed within the common structure of the Pentateuch (407).

In the concluding chapter, "The Theocracy as an Idea and as an Institution" (ch. 11, 409–24), Wellhausen returns yet again to the organization of the community, as it may have been created according to the principal meaning provided by Moses. However, "in truth, Moses is author of the 'Mosaic constitution' approximately in the same sense as Peter is the founder of the Roman hierarchy." In the periods of the judges and the kings, one may not observe anything that approaches such a constitution. In the history of ancient Israel nothing abounds

> more than the uncommon freshness and naturalness of their impulses. The persons who are active in the narratives appear of necessity according to their nature, whether men of God or murderers and adulterers. They are figures who come alive in the open, living air. Judaism, which had brought into reality the Mosaic constitution and consequently has enhanced it, did not allow individuality any room to play: in ancient Israel the divine law was not in the institution, but rather was present only in … the individuals. (410)

Subsequently, Wellhausen brings forth a short overview of the history of the Israelite-Jewish state, which originated from natural beginnings, and shows how, after its final collapse, it was refashioned as a cultic community gathered around the temple and the priesthood. "The mosaic theocracy … is itself not a state, but rather a non-political, artistic product created under unfavorable conditions through means of an eternally noteworthy energy…. It is in its nature closely related to the early Catholic church, whose mother Judaism in fact was" (421). And the cult had decisively altered the theocracy's character from that of the preexilic period: "The cult now is alienated from the heart…. It is rooted no longer in naiveté; it is a dead work … and after its life had been put to death, has been made into a devotee of supernatural monotheism" (423–24).

It is no wonder that, following the appearance of this book by Wellhausen, a fierce polemic broke out that proceeded not only from "positive" theologians and colleagues in the discipline but, as one would expect, also reached a broad church public. Certainly people were unable to understand the complex background of source criticism and requirements of content in Wellhausen's constructions when they reproached him for his sweeping ideas of development ("Darwinism"). Wellhausen responded with a vehement counter polemic in the preface of his second edition of the *Prolegomena* (1883), although he omitted it in later editions.

The *Israelitische und jüdische Geschichte* (Israelite and Jewish History) appeared for the first time in 1894. It was planned to be the second volume of a two-volume work, the *Geschichte Israels*, but now it was a self-contained work. Wellhausen based this work on the foundations established in his earlier *Prolegomena*. Wellhausen had already paraphrased, in his private printed edition of 1880 (see above, 314) the faith on which rested Israel's feeling of community as the later so-called covenant formula: "Yahweh, the God of Israel, and Israel, the People of God" (*Grundrisse*, 16; cf. also *Israelitisch-jüdische Religion*, 9/74). On the whole, Wellhausen distinguished three periods in this history, as he had done in his *Prolegomena*: (1) "Ancient Israel": Wellhausen characterizes it comprehensively in chapter 6, "God, World, and Life in Ancient Israel." (2) "The Prophetic Reformation" (ch. 9, 122–32): Wellhausen begins this chapter with Isaiah and ends it with the reform that had consequences in the sphere of the cult (131). (3) "The Restoration" (ch. 12, 153–65): It reaches from the end of the exile to Ezra-Nehemiah (ch. 13, 166–76). "The law" belongs to this period. It is here that we discover the assessment: "The cultus was the pagan element in the religion of Yahweh…, a constant danger for both morality and monotheism" (174). Although it was opposed by the prophets, it could not simply be abolished. The cultus became legally regulated in Deuteronomy and finally in the Priestly codex. Wellhausen's entire outline follows the main work of his teacher, Ewald, the *Geschichte des Volkes Israel* (History of the People of Israel), insofar as he continues to the chapter entitled, "The Gospel." Originally, Wellhausen's final chapter stood as the next to last chapter preceding "The Downfall of the Jewish Community." Wellhausen often reworked the chapter on the Gospel and placed it in later editions entirely at the end. Wellhausen offered the explanation (358, n. 1): "I have allowed this chapter to continue to stay, although I am not in full agreement with it." This he writes obviously on the basis of his work on the Gospels. However, one can allow him to apply what he still considers to be the main features of early Christianity. It is an unostentatious description of the appearance of Jesus, which knowledge of the text betrays. The concluding sentences often have been cited:

The stages of religion, like the stages of history overall, continue to exist beside one another. However, Jesus has not founded the church, but rather he has announced judgment against the Jewish theocracy. The Gospel is only the salt of the earth; where it wants to be more, there is less. It preaches the noblest type of individualism, the freedom of the children of God. (371)

There should be no lack of clarity about Wellhausen's own Christianity. What he believed, he has spoken in clear words.

With this in mind, there is also an unequivocal answer to the much-discussed question of which presuppositions of thought have led Wellhausen to his total view of the history of Israel. His description rests on the results of the literary investigations of the sources, which he himself partially extracted from the texts, and the results of criticism he himself had already in large measure predetermined. To be sure, source criticism was in itself never the primary purpose of his work, but rather only the necessary preparation for the entire picture that he obtained from its results. In this respect, in an age of historicism, he had understood himself completely as a historian. Much discussed especially was the question about the possible dependence of Wellhausen on Vatke and through Vatke on Hegel. For Wellhausen, the picture of a three-stage development of Israelite-Jewish (religious) history results: the early period from the judges to the time of the Israelite kings, the period of transition from the prophet Isaiah in Judah to the book of Deuteronomy, and the late period of Judaism shaped by the law up to the destruction of the Second Temple. Was the three-stage scheme of the philosophy of history developed by Hegel (thesis, antithesis, and synthesis) have been the inspiration for it? Already in the introduction to the *Geschichte Israels* Wellhausen has valued Vatke's book as "the most significant contribution to the history of ancient Israel that has been produced." Wellhausen's critics have taken up this statement, without considering the fact that what mattered for him regarding Vatke were his results in approaching the question of sources in the Old Testament, not his Hegelianism. Wellhausen had expressly confirmed this awareness of Hegel's possible influence in his letter of consolation to Vatke's son Theodor after the death of his father (see Benecke 1883, 627): "Hegelian or not: that is to me all the same, however your blessed father had a remarkably true feel for the individuality of matters." Wellhausen was not a philosopher, but rather a historian and theologian. As an exegete, he directed his polemics against dogmatics. In addition, chronological reasons also speak against a direct dependence on Vatke, for Wellhausen had become familiar with Graf's Hypothesis already by 1867 and was convinced by it long before he had familiarized himself with Vatke's book in 1874 as the precursor of Graf. Thus it was only later that Vatke's work became his own "main authority."

A classification in intellectual history is more possible than a philosophical one. A series of characteristics converge in Wellhausen's writings that are typical of the spiritual climate of the epoch in which Wellhausen worked. This is also the case in terms of the contents he expressed about the periods he described. We have already mentioned his extreme individualism. It presupposes his aversions to institutions such as the church and postexilic Judaism ordered by the Torah. In spite of this, his judgment is ambivalent, for he characterizes postexilic Judaism as individualistic, thus as directly opposite to earlier periods.

> In spite of this, religion began placing its center of gravity on the individual instead of the whole. In antiquity and all in all still even in the period of the great prophets, religion was the common possession of the nation, something both self-evident and natural. Now one born a Jew had to make himself Jewish by means of deliberate works. The community rests upon like-minded individuals who bear and sustain it. The ideal is righteousness.... Its kernel is ... individual morality. (*Grundrisse*, 102–3)

Wellhausen had in common with Herder the attribution of the emotive inclination to the original, poetic, and natural features found in the early period of Israel. However, he emphasized in opposition to Herder the character of ancient Israel as a "war-like confederacy"; the military encampment was at the same time the oldest sanctuary, thus "the cradle of the nation" ("Israelite-Jewish History," 23–24). Here one may detect the influence of Thomas Carlyle (see below) with his glorification of the heroic individuals. The subject of natural things as being original in contrast to sacred things, which are devalued as "supranaturalistic," signifies Wellhausen's appropriation of Romanticism's body of thought. At the same time, this reflects the new Protestant, anti-cultic impulse inherited from the Enlightenment, which Wellhausen (perhaps also in reaction to his father's view of the liturgy) had developed. This is the drawback of religious individualism. It leads to Wellhausen's description of the priestly writing's cultic order as something that was artificial. "A material, external opposition of holy and profane originated." Holiness "in itself is a rather empty, mainly antithetical concept" (420). Formulations like those cited above, including, among others, the view that the cultus may be the "pagan element" in Israelite religion, signify, in spite of every acutely reasoned, exegetical observation, a skewed and tendentious portrayal of the sources.

Another question is the critical assessment of Wellhausen's outline of history. Only a few years after his death, it was clear that he had excluded significant new insights that had come to light already during his time of activity. Virtually unconsidered were the series of spectacular archaeological finds of the second half of the nineteenth and the beginning of the twentieth centuries, discoveries that had contributed significantly to the emerging field of ancient Oriental studies. Although Nineveh, the major city of the Assyrian empire, had been excavated already in 1842–1850 (by P. E. Botta [1802–1870] and A. H. Layard [1817–1894]), which had led to the discovery of an increasing number of texts, and although he himself had acquired some knowledge of Akkadian, he took little notice of these spectacular advances in the development of the ancient Orient and their altering of the entire historical picture. Israel now appears as a latecomer in ancient Oriental history, and the significance of its surrounding environment was increasingly taken into consideration. Wellhausen remained untouched by this development and even by the discoveries of El-Amarna (1887), which included an exchange of letters from the fourteenth century B.C.E. between two Egyptian pharaohs, on the one hand, and their vassals in Palestine/Syria and other rulers in the Near East, on the other. He continued in his standpoint of the 1870s, in which literary criticism of the Old Testament remained in the center and Arabic language and culture became the embodiment of Orientalism. Moreover, he had not taken into consideration in an adequate way the accomplishments of the form-critical method. They would be established by the generation that followed with Gunkel at its head. That still was to remain a goal for the future. In the end, Wellhausen was a literary critic. He tacitly presupposed that the time of origin of the textual sources was identical with the age of their contents. The cultic law came to have primary significance when it, according to Wellhausen, was written down. Thus, the later discussion about oral or written tradition remained outside his horizon. He did not expressly deny the oral tradition, conceding, for example, that priests already played a significant role in the preexilic period.

Nonetheless, Wellhausen left behind a continuing heritage especially in the sphere of Old Testament research.

6.9. SEARCHING FOR THE ORIGINAL PROPHECY: BERNHARD DUHM

In the history of research, Bernhard Duhm can be regarded as the closest comrade-in-arms of Wellhausen, although he did not belong to his "school." Not only was Duhm Wellhausen's contemporary, but also his course of life led him into close proximity to Wellhausen during the same decisive period. In addition, they were close in their exegetical starting point and total theological approach. Duhm was born in Bingum in Ostfriesland, the son of a merchant and beer brewer. He felt connected to his home throughout his life, and he speaks of a happy childhood. It was not unusual that, after three years of instruction in Latin, Greek, and French under the tutelage of neighboring pastors, he immediately was accepted into the second class of the Aurich gymnasium. During this time in the gymnasium he was especially interested in Greek, history, and German literature. He also learned the elementary fundamentals of Hebrew. Beginning in 1867, he studied theology in Göttingen and also attended lectures in other fields, such as history, literature, psychology, and the history of philosophy. In theology, he attended mostly the lectures of Albrecht Ritschl, although he soon turned to the study of the Old Testament. Ewald's *Propheten des Alten Bundes* (Prophets of the Old Covenant; see above) was the first book he purchased, and Duhm heard Ewald's last lectures before he was prohibited from teaching owing to an injunction against him issued in 1868 that forbade him to teach theology. A friend—obviously it was Wellhausen—took him along to participate in Ewald's Arabic and Syriac exercises, although he soon had to miss them because of illness. He also attended Wellhausen's first lecture course as *Repetent* in the winter semester of 1869–70.

From the beginning of his career, Duhm expressed his greatest interest in the Old Testament prophets. In an unpublished treatment, which he used to apply for a post as *Repetent*, he treated the problem of the "Inspiration of the Prophets" on the basis of the question whether Deutero-Isaiah was a prophet or a poet. He answered: this man had indeed been gifted in the art of poetry, but was still a prophet. Duhm's Latin dissertation, which led to his licentiate in theology and then served as his *Habilitation*, which culminated in his appointment as a *Privatdozent* for Old and New Testament, broached his basic understanding of the Old Testament and guided him in his further work: "The Judgments of Paul concerning the Religion of the Jews." Here he upbraids Paul for not taking into consideration the prophets, psalmists, and wisdom teachers, all of whom were pious human beings. Yet Paul did not examine anything between Moses and Christ except the law (27, 36). The starting point for Duhm is the distinction between law and gospel in Lutheran dogmatics, which claims Paul as its crowning witness. Paul, on the one hand, identifies Judaism with the law, the violation of which leads to death, so that it had to be repealed through the gospel of Jesus Christ. On the other hand, he lays claim to Abraham as the father of the faith. He passes this to his children and finally to the Christians as the legitimate heirs. In so doing, however, Paul overlooks the true religion of the Israelites, who are the true successors of their father, Abraham, and have lived under one law. This is not the law of death, as Paul understands it but rather a gift of God for life, based on the election and the promise to the fathers (31ff.). Paul has in mind, however, particularly the Pharisees, and the law that convicts is equated with the Priestly law, which requires adherence to the external, ritual commandments. The true law, which is shaped by morality and leads to righteousness, can be found, for example, in the admonitions of Deuteronomy. Thus, for Duhm, one must distinguish between Judaism/Pharisaism as slavery under the ritual law and genuine Israelite religion in the form of Abraham's purely moral faith. We discover here as in Wellhausen the typical devaluation of the cultic realm during this period in the nineteenth century in favor of morality as well as the high value of religious personality: the prophets, psalmists, and wisdom teachers were pious humans!

When Duhm received both his promotion and *Habilitation* with this writing, he had already been at work on his first major composition, which appeared in 1875 with the illuminative title, *Die Theologie der Propheten als Grundlage für die innere Entwicklungsgeschichte der israelitischen Religion* (The Theology of the Prophets as the Fundamental Basis for the Internal History of Development of Israelite Religion). In the same year he received a stipend for two years. In the meantime, he was still a *Privatdozent*. When, in 1877, he applied for and received the appointment of associate professor, this followed some debate among the faculty. The decision in favor of Duhm was due to Ritschl's support and the high regard in which his authority was held. Duhm had to persevere for a lengthy period in this position. Then, in 1885, he received at least an honorary promotion from the faculty of Basel. Finally, he was named a full professor in 1889 in Basel. At the same time he received a contract to teach Hebrew at the gymnasium located there.

Duhm had to move to Basel alone with his three young sons, for he was already a widower. His wife, Helene, the daughter of a teacher in Bingum, whom he had married in 1877, had died in 1884. One of his sons, Hans Duhm (1878–1946) became an Old Testament scholar.

In Basel, Duhm felt increasingly at home and was a popular teacher among the students. These were years of rich literary productivity; Duhm was above all a composer of commentaries. In 1892, his volume *Das Buch Jesaja* (The Book of Isaiah), appeared in the series Handkommentar zum Alten Testament. He wrote additional commentaries in the Kurzen Hand-Commentar on the books of Job, Psalms, and Jeremiah (1897, 1899, and 1901). Since there was not enough space allotted in this latter series for the reproduction of full translations of texts, Duhm developed his own series, *Die poetischen und prophetischen Bücher des alten Testaments: Übersetzt in den Versmassen der Urschrift* (The Poetic and Prophetic Books of the Old Testament: Translated in the Meters of the Original Text). In addition to the translations of three commentaries (1897–1903) Duhm published the *Übersetzung des Buches der zwölf Propheten* (Translations of the Twelve Prophets [1904]). In commenting on this latter translation, Duhm offered numerous insights, which he published in 1911 in the journal *Zeitschrift für die alttestamentliche Wissenschaft* (appearing also as a separate printing). In addition, he wrote a separate commentary on the book of Habakkuk. Final among his works on prophecy was his general description of *Israels Propheten* (Israel's Prophets [1916; 2nd ed., 1922]).

Since there was no age limit imposed on active teaching at that time, Duhm remained in office until his death. He was still active in his eighties when he was to give a comprehensive offering of lectures during the winter semester of 1928–29. On 1 September 1928, however, he was run over by a car and killed.

In his early work *Die Theologie der Propheten* (The Theology of the Prophets), Duhm continued along the lines that were apparent in his dissertation, where he directed his attention for the first time toward prophecy, which from then on would become his life's theme. In regard to this topic, he begins with the difficulties of the traditional view that the period of the prophets followed that of the priests. When one reviews the content of the middle pentateuchal law, which Paul characterized appropriately as directed to the consequences of external rules, then one must necessarily ask how this compares to the faith of Abraham and to the prophets?

> If one, however, regards that the apostle's judgment of the law and the prophets leads to their having only limited worth, then it becomes necessary for one to explain how the inner religiosity and free morality of the prophetic period could grow from the law and the pressure of the

law that came from the external institutions and commandments of Mosaism. (14)

The fundamental motif of Duhm's approach emerges in contrasting the external with the internal, thus ritualism and morality and force and freedom. This leads him to abandon the traditional view of the history of Israelite religion: it is impossible to regard the period of the law as the first stage of development, followed by that of the prophets. In the second line of this consideration, the results of Graf's pentateuchal criticism come to his assistance. The dating of the literary sources is not the primary factor, but rather the consideration that a religion's interiority cannot have developed from forms that are determined by external rules and laws. Therefore, it is compelling to allow the religion of Israel to begin with the prophets (15). The second major motif of Duhm is his interest in the personality of the prophets, as well as that of the most important writers of history and poets (20–21).

In his overview of the history of the development of Israelite religion, which he places at the beginning of the book (36–71), he describes the oldest form of worship in Israel as one shaped by simplicity (51; cf. 60). In the midpoint of Israelite religion stands, in opposition to nature religion, the inclination "to comprehend God as a personality and to stand with him in moral association" (53). "An association, however, between two personalities is not directed chiefly to the unveilings of the nature of both, but rather to the confirmation of the disposition … and to the fulfillment of the obligations, which each places upon the partner" (74). The general influence of Kant is unmistakable here. On the other hand, Duhm separates himself from Kant when he remarks that it was well-nigh impossible to find a transition to personality by means of this abstract principle of morality, even as the interpretation of Lutheran orthodoxy of the Good is of little use. Instead of this, he holds "that morality is not exempt from the law of development" (107).

The idea of development plays an important role in the subsequent description of individual prophets, whom Duhm divides into prophets of the Assyrian, Chaldean, and Persian periods. The development of prophecy rests on "the idea of the moral personality, whose divinely created nature is an internal process that is conducted by God that produces a moral character" (103). "The bearers of religion are the prophets, whose conviction of a personal relationship with God should display to us their justice and their truth, for it is by them that religious and moral ideas are further developed" (170). Along this continuum Duhm inserts the individual prophets as he characterizes them through the types of their religion. Hosea (as also Zechariah) is a representative of the religion of sentiment, while Amos and Micah represent the ethical momentum, the rigor of moral judgment. Amos and Micah both turn against sacrifice and festival. For example, in Mic 6:1–6, the prophet opposes the people who are guilty of believing in a despotic God who requires sacrifice, for he is a moral being who wants only humility and moral conduct. "Amos and Micah raise religion from the sphere of nature to that of morality; from now on religion may develop more highly." However, even with Amos the idea of the moral personality is still missing, for morality still hovers "in the objective sphere of actions of justice and natural humanity." It is "still not grasped as the personal relationship between God and humans and as an action according to an inner, unifying purpose" (103). Yet the expectations of Isaiah show clearly that the prophecy of this period persists at a level where personal relationships are only possible between God and the people.

This imperfection is partially overcome by Jeremiah. He places the heaviest weight on a religion that is characterized by the "moral, spiritual community of the individual with God" (243). "His prophecy opens the period of subjective piety, in which the spiritual personality is made into the bearer of religion" (246–47). In addition, Jeremiah develops for the first time the idea of an all-encompassing plan of God for the entire world. He even ventures to speak of Nebuchadnezzar as the servant of God. Nevertheless, he continues to stand at the halfway juncture:

> If it had been possible for Jeremiah to discover the indispensable idea of an objective religious community for the pious individual, which stands over individual piety…, he would have prefigured Christianity and … for his theology has reminded us of the Christian ideas of the Kingdom of God and of the community. (251)

Here Duhm is distinguished from Wellhausen, whose consistent individualism he does not share. Rather, Duhm stands closer to Schleiermacher.

Ezekiel is dramatically different from Jeremiah. He too speaks of the majesty of God, but in a way that is different from Isaiah: "With Ezekiel the majesty of God is a object of terror, presses down humans deeply into the dust, and pushes God to the unreachable distance of transcendence" (260). Religion and morality lose their personal character; now decisive in the place of moral freedom and joy is the strong compliance with rules and customs. The program of the law in Ezek 40–48 combines theocracy with particularity, because it is limited to a single people. This "has already nothing more to do with prophetic religion; we find it present in the air of Judaism and the Talmud." "Ezekiel deserves the credit for transforming the idea of the prophets into law and dogmas and for having destroyed the spiritually free and moral religion" (263). The postexilic development, for Duhm, is mainly shaped by Ezekiel and not by Jeremiah: the religious personality takes a back seat, while the temple and sacrifice receive sacramental value. Ezra is the representative of extreme supernaturalism. Morality in religion is completely suppressed, while only the external laws of purity have remained.

Even Deutero-Isaiah cannot reverse this trend. As was the case for First Isaiah, so it is for him that the majesty of God stands in the middle of his message. He was the first to introduce the idea of election. However, his universalism loses any contact with reality. Since the idea of God absorbs his entire interest, Deutero-Isaiah virtually forgets to point to the moral obligations of the nation to God. Instead he directs his attention only to waiting for divine salvation and to solace. After Jeremiah, only the prophet could press forward, giving "back to the subject of religion … its full significance. In so long as it is merely God alone who acts and acts according to what he desires, then we discover ourselves on a precipitous slope, which leads to legal supernaturalism and materialism" (287).

Duhm's separation of the Songs of the Servant (Isa 42:1–7; 49:1–6; 50:4–9; and 52:13–53:12) from the rest of Deutero-Isaiah as a particular source was a groundbreaking view. He assumes that these songs could have originated as part of a description of the life of Jeremiah, which Deutero-Isaiah, however, substantially revised (287–301). With this he initiated a discussion about the special place and significance of these "Songs of the Servant of God," including the question of the identity of the Servant of God, a question that up to today has not lost its tension. Duhm's evaluation of these pieces is typical of his approach: similar to Hosea we have here a "purely religious standpoint," where righteousness, peace, salvation, and divine election are expected as divine gifts, acquired only through trust and patience. This is at the same time a step forward and a step backward: progress in the belief that God is to be regarded as the single source of righteousness, deficiency in understanding righteousness as a gift identical with salvation. The significance of the suffering of the Servant of God as vicarious for the sins of the people (Isa 53:5, 8, 10) is, for Duhm, "a sad externalization of religion" (297).

That these understandings were deeply rooted in Duhm and were not limited to his view of the prophets one may recognize by considering his popular lectures, which he published in brochures from time to time. Thus, the opposition between theology and true religion permeates his inaugural lecture given in 1899: "Über Ziel und Methode der theologischen Wissenschaft" (Concerning the Purpose and Method of Theological Criticism). The first example of a theological system is the Torah: Deuteronomy had erected for the first time a network of fixed rules, which stood in the way of the earlier free intercourse of the nation with God, although it had been collated with the best intention out of the demands of the prophets for a life in conformity with the will of God. There was a similar development in the Christian era: it was first Greek philosophy and later Roman legalism that generated the system of Scholasticism, which kept imprisoned to its speculation the power of life of the new religion. However, then something occurred, "for religion was not dead; rather it was regenerated in the heart of the German nation. The German prophet (meant here is Luther) had actually something new to bring, for he made the free personality into the subject of religion ... the Reformation had created the bases for a free humanity" (21). Corresponding to this credo, Duhm required of critical theology "above all the understanding of the original, religious personality, not simply the one who was creative, that is, the prophet, but also the receiving one, the 'believer'" (30). As an Old Testament scholar, Duhm is convinced "that the prophetic religion of ancient Israel will prove to be the standard religion, because it is the least influenced by priestly-theocratic inclinations" (27–28).

His popular work of his later years, *Israels Propheten* (Israel's Prophets) narrates the history of the prophets in the same way, only without the lengthy theoretical discussions. As a result of Wellhausen's criticism of his early work, Duhm gave greater weight to world history as the occasion of prophecy. The invasion of the Assyrian army may have prompted the prophets for the first time to struggle with the interior meaning of the events (*Israels Propheten*, 1922, 3). He explains that the role of prophecy in the inner history of Israel consisted of a three-stage development, which he attempted to discover in all prominent nations. In the prehistoric stage, the world is populated by demonic powers. In the historical or dynamistic period the nation is led by God himself, who works through prophets and prophetic heroes. When Israel wished to live "like the other nations" (1 Sam 8:5) and to conform to a life in a state with a king and his ministers, this came to a standstill. "Israel would have failed to fulfill its calling on behalf of humanity." But then, in the third and highest stage, another type of prophet appeared. These prophets did not pronounce salvation and victory but rather judgment and subjection. They took over the role that is granted to philosophers, statesmen, and poets in other nations; that is, they assumed "the leadership in the internal history of Israel" (7). Amos and Micah reject the cult; they "place on a purely moral basis the relationship between the nation and God" (140). They do not, however, replace religion with morality; humans who by means of visions and auditions stood in actual contact with God would not have done so. The concern of the classical prophets is "to free religion from sensuality … and to raise it on the heights of moral contact with free personalities" (142). Furthermore, Duhm regarded the postexilic period as a time of decline. He did not change his interpretation.

In the preface to his commentary on Isaiah, Duhm articulated principles that guided him in his commentaries on the prophetic books. These are still always worth reading. In order "to bring out what the authors actually say and wished to say," one should "attempt to penetrate as deeply as possible into the personality of the composer himself" (1922, 3). In this commentary, for the first time Duhm characterizes the prophets as ecstatics. The vision of the call of Isaiah in chapter 6 is an ecstatic experience; similarly to be recognized is Isa 8:11–15, which is among the most important passages, "for it permits us to have a look at the psychic side of Isaiah's inspiration" (82). Duhm's occupation with the psychology of the prophetic reception of revelation would remain an important theme of prophetic criticism into the 1930s. In addition, Duhm gives consideration especially to meter. "The poetic speech is the speech of the gods, who speak through the poets and the prophets" (*Israels Propheten*, 95). Duhm's appropriation of poetry remains entirely that of the Romantic Herder. Other ecstatic phenomena he regards with a considerable degree of mistrust. Both axioms, psychology and meter, combined with each other, lead to a more or less rigid selection of materials, which Duhm recognizes as original prophetic words. One of the most important marks of prophetic words is their poetic form, in contrast to prose sections, which he ascribes to later redactors. Of genuine interest for Duhm are only the original prophets. He attributes proportionately a great deal to each of the three prophets, Isaiah, Deutero-Isaiah, and Trito-Isaiah, but the result in the book of Jeremiah is more rigorous. Since Duhm recognizes as authentic to Jeremiah only stanzas of four lines with three + two accents, only a small portion of the material stands the test of authentication. Duhm represents in its earliest form the thesis of the three major sources in the book of Jeremiah (*Das Buch Jeremia*, x): (1) the authentic prophecy, (2) the Jeremiah biography composed by his scribe, Baruch (regarded as a valuable source), and (3) later additions from different periods. In Duhm's view, the latest of these goes down to the first century B.C.E.

When Duhm published his Psalms commentary in 1899, Gunkel had not yet undertaken his groundbreaking form-critical investigations of the Psalter. When Duhm's second edition came out in 1922, Gunkel's *Ausgewählte Psalmen* (Selected Psalms [1904]) had already appeared in four editions. However, form criticism did not leave any trace in Duhm's second edition. What was more interesting to him was the date of the origins of the psalms, and he inclined toward an extremely late dating for these texts. According to Duhm, the oldest psalm is Ps 137 from the time of the Babylonian exile.

> If there still exists in the Psalter equally old or even older psalms, thus they at least are not recognizable. No single psalm brings an impartial and unbiased reader to the position that it must be pre-exilic or even could be. By the same token I know of no psalm, which leads one to think of the Persian period. (*Die Psalmen*, 1922, 20–21)

Duhm dates the earliest psalms in the period after Alexander the Great (356–323 B.C.E.) and goes down to the second century. These evaluations have long been regarded as untenable, but Duhm continues to be remembered as a scholar of the prophets. His influence on this sphere was felt as late as the period following the Second World War, but lapsed for the first time with the newer interest in the tradition history of the prophetic books.

7
The History of Religion School

The decades between 1880 and the end of the Second World War brought for biblical criticism an unusually high number of new insights, especially concerning the New Testament. It was also unusual that a single institution of higher education, Göttingen University, formed the nucleus of this activity. In Göttingen, Albrecht Ritschl, because of the forcefulness of his personality, his intellectual acuity, and his rigorous systematic theology, exercised a phenomenal influence on his students. A circle of young theologians gathered around him during the last years of his life, all wishing for a university career, which for most began with a *Habilitation* in Göttingen. All were united in the belief that they must pursue new courses of understanding in moving beyond Ritschl. In addition to Ritschl, other personalities influenced the group. These included especially Bernhard Duhm, an associate professor in Göttingen during the years 1877–1888 (see above), who was an extraordinarily sociable man, and P. A. de Lagarde (1827–1891), who beginning in 1869 was a professor for Oriental studies in Göttingen. De Lagarde attracted only a few students to hear his specialized lectures; however, they were among the most gifted. In devoting a great proportion of his labor to the edition of texts, he planned a critical edition of the Greek Old Testament, which his student, Alfred Rahlfs (1865–1935), carried to completion. However, de Lagarde considered himself to be mainly a critical theologian. In open debate with Ritschl, he rejected justification and atonement as the fundamental teachings of Christianity. He considered these to be primarily teachings that arose during the Reformation. He opposed Pauline theology and instead emphasized the teaching of Christ. He also called for a national church, which, separated from the state, would overcome the schism caused by the confessions. For him theology is exclusively a "historical discipline." In his historicism he was in agreement with Duhm. Wellhausen also was honored as an example, although he distanced himself from the later so-called history of religion school.

The cohesion that developed among the members of Ritschl's group was sustained by their lives in the students associations. They would meet regularly in the convivial gatherings of the Academic Theological Association for weekly presentations at festive beer parties. Professors and individual lecturers would occasionally participate as guests. Beginning in 1892–1893, they met in the Evangelical fraternity "Germania" (where Bousset undoubtedly set the tone).

The spiritual father of the group was considered to be Albert Eichhorn (1856–1926), who was not particularly distinguished for his few publications or his career (as associate professor of church history in Halle and later in Kiel, where he took early retirement for reasons of health). Nevertheless, his personal influence was still considerable. In addition to him, other members of this small circle included Wilhelm Bousset, Hermann Gunkel, and Wilhelm Heitmüller (1869–1926). These were joined by additional members: Hugo Gressmann (1877–1927), Heinrich Hackmann (1864–1935), Rudolf Otto (1869–1937), Ernst Troeltsch (1865–1923), Johannes Weiss (see below), and Wilhelm Wrede (1856–1906). Beyond these there was an "open border" through which additional colleagues entered the program or stood close by it over the course of time.

The name history of religion school (*religionsgeschichtliche Schule*) was probably first used internally in 1903 by the members of the group. They were, however, only a loose circle of colleagues and friends who were bound together through common concerns and still more personal relationships. "History of religion" means primarily an investigation of the particular features of the Christian religion with historical methods. In the foreword to his *Reden und Aufsätze* (Speeches and Essays [1913]), Gunkel expressly guarded against the misunderstanding "that it engages mainly in the investigation to explain biblical religion by means of its associations with non-biblical religions.… We have from the very beginning understood under the expression 'history of religion' not the history of religions, but rather the *history of religion*" (5). The school shared this main interest with the rest of liberal theology and especially also with its predecessors Duhm and Wellhausen. Gunkel, Bousset, and others understood themselves to be thoroughly Christian theologians. However, their interest was directed now toward religion. Gunkel describes the intention of the young critics at that time: "We were infused by the thought that the final purpose of the work of the Bible may be to look the men of religion in their heart, to experience with them the innermost feelings, and to describe these sufficiently" (5–6). In a lecture delivered in 1919, Bousset stressed something like a theological testament: "We want all to have a Christian religion and Christian theology, not a general religion or global theology" (*Religionsgeschichtliche Studien*, 39). Naturally, criticism focused especially on the New Testament. Historicism shaped this approach as well, only it was handled in a still more radical fashion. This led to a second step, which was the comparison of religion with the religious environment of the New Testament. This is an important step, but the purpose was not to make these religions themselves the independent subject of the investigation. Thus, first one proceeded to study the so-called late Judaism, later also the Hellenistic environs. From this grew the demand to step beyond the limits of the biblical canon and to make out of New Testament theology a history of religion of primitive Christianity. Following the example of Bousset (see below), one can pursue this development. Included was an element that had already played a role in Herder and the mythical school, only now had methodological weight: folk piety and the cultus (as a practiced religion) moved into view as the bearers of religious tradition. Sociological and psychological points of view were introduced to the field of interpretation. Wellhausen's exclusive handling of sources along with their theoretical contents as the subject of historical research was therefore left behind. Wellhausen himself did not follow this development; he contined to regard it with skepticism.

7.1. Ascertaining the History of Israelite Religion and Sketching an Old Testament History of Literature: Hermann Gunkel

In 1862, Hermann Gunkel was born as the oldest son of the pastor Karl Gunkel, in Springe by Hanover. Hermann was raised with his younger brother, Karl, in Lüneburg, where his father relocated the year Hermann was born. Hermann always spoke of a happy youth. Life in a refined pastor's house shaped the adolescent. His grandfather also had been a pastor. Reading the books that were typical for youth of the educated middle class of the period, such as J. V. von Scheffel's *Ekkehard* and G. Freytag's *Bilder aus der deutschen Vergangenhe*it, awakened his historical interest as early as the seventh grade. Later he read the works of Ranke and Mommsen. In Lüneburg he attended the Johanneum Gymnasium and passed his *Abitur*. In the summer semester of 1881, he began theological studies at Göttingen. There he was numbered among the devoted students of Albrecht Ritschl; he learned Arabic and Syriac from de Lagarde; and he attended the offerings in other disciplines, especially German studies, history, and philosophy. Certainly, like other young theologians, he was displeased with a certain aspect in Ritschl's system. Ritschl portrayed Christianity like the picture of an ellipse, regarding one focal point to be the forgiveness of sins and the other to be the kingdom of God that as the "highest good" is in the possession of Christians and at the same time is an ethical-practical field of activity. But Ritschl's hearers criticized how forcefully he arranged New Testament sayings into this system. In 1882–1883, Gunkel went to Giessen for three semesters and heard lectures from different scholars, among them the famous church historian and historian of dogmatics Adolf Harnack (1851–1930) and the student of Wellhausen Bernhard Stade (1848–1906). Gunkel honored Harnack in the dedication of his commentary on Genesis (1901) as his most important theological teacher, save for his father. He did this in spite of the fact that Harnack kept his distance from the history of religion school. Gunkel, however, he came to learn historical criticism from him. After he returned to Göttingen, contact with the circle around Albert Eichhorn especially stimulated him. In the spring of 1885, Gunkel passed the first theological exams of the state church of Hanover. He spent the years 1884–1888 there, expanding his theological education and preparing his dissertation, which he submitted in Göttingen in 1888: *Die Wirkungen des heiligen Geistes nach der populären Anschauung der apostolischen Zeit und der Lehre des Apostels Paulus* (The Workings of the Holy Spirit according to the Popular View of the Apostolic Period and the Teaching of the Apostle Paul). He broke new ground in this dissertation by choosing not to follow the traditional teaching about the Holy Spirit, but instead to observe pneumatic phenomena, such as the psychological activities of the Spirit. The theological faculty viewed the results with obvious skepticism. Although he had passed his colloquium *magna cum laude,* they promoted him to licentiate only with *rite* (Latin for "duly," meaning to "pass"). When his father applied on his behalf to the minister of education that he should receive a *Dozent*'s stipend, this was granted for two years. This occurred, however, after an initial refusal because an unfavorable recommendation had been sent to the minister following a trial reading testing his competence to teach the field of "Biblical Theology and Exegesis" (Old and New Testament). Gunkel taught in Göttingen for only a semester, when, as it seems, he had to face a second set of difficulties with the faculty. The curator of the university relayed a ministerial directive to Halle suggesting that the theological faculty there should consider Gunkel for the position of associate professor. When this did not materialize,

Gunkel, nevertheless, received his *Habilitation* once again in Halle, probably owing to the suggestion of the rather assertive ministerial director in the Ministry of Culture and Religion, Friedrich Althoff (1839–1908) and became a private lecturer in 1889. Here he changed mainly to the Old Testament, for reasons that are not clear. He again received from the ministry a two-year stipend, which was later extended for two additional years. In Halle he again met Albert Eichhorn, who had received his *Habilitation* there in 1886. A circle of like-minded people gathered around the two. To Gunkel's friends belonged the Assyriologist Heinrich Zimmer (1862–1931), who came to Halle in 1890. He made accessible to Gunkel above all cuneiform texts in translation, which at the time largely broke new ground. In 1894, Gunkel received the title of associate professor. In the same year, he married Elisabeth Beelitz, the daughter of the preacher of the cathedral in Halle. In 1895, he was called to Berlin as an associate professor. An additional increase in rank was not possible in the kingdom of Prussia because of his theological position. In Berlin he engaged in substantial activity: his lectures, which taught exegetical methodology and transmitted the spirit of the Old Testament, found enthusiastic hearers. In addition, he offered numerous popular presentations, collaborated in the liberal *Christlichen Welt* (Christian World) and the series of *Religionsgeschichtliche Volksbücher* (History of Religion Popular Books; see below), and wrote more than three hundred articles for the first edition of the encyclopedia *Religion in Geschichte und Gegenwart* (Religion in History and Present), published by Mohr (Siebeck) in Tübingen. Gunkel was the editor for the Old Testament in this encyclopedia. His desire to make serviceable the results of critical biblical studies and to show that they may be of use to common people was especially responsible for this activity, not simply his need to earn additional income. During the semester vacations, he took part regularly in certain holiday courses in Jena as an instructor. In spite of this, not only did Gunkel feel rather pressured by his financial straits in Berlin, but he was also often ill. He felt liberated when, after the death of Stade in 1906, he received a call to Giessen to become a full professor. Although he had far fewer students there than he had had in Berlin, the liberal spirit of the small faculty did him good. In 1911, he received an honorary doctorate in philosophy, which the faculty of Breslau bestowed upon him. In the same year he was honored the same way by receiving an honorary doctorate in theology from Christiania (Oslo). The call of Bousset in 1916 (see below) brought a like-minded colleague to Giessen. Certainly, the difficult years of the First World War were to be endured.

The end of the war brought about a fundamental change in the policy of filling professorships by the Prussian Ministry of Culture and Religion. Carl Heinrich Becker (1876–1933) was named Undersecretary of State and later Minister by the new social democratic government. Against their will, he required the faculties of theology to appoint the previously neglected representatives of the history of religion school. This led to a call to Gunkel to serve on the faculty of Halle in 1920. Shortly before leaving Giessen, he had to deliver the funeral oration for his friend Bousset.

The last years in Halle brought Gunkel increasing health problems. In addition to heart, stomach, and intestinal ailments, he also suffered an advancing arteriosclerosis. After having undertaken, at the beginning of 1927, a study and recuperative journey to Italy, he then received an approved leave for the summer semester. He subsequently submitted a petition for his retirement on 1 October 1927, for reasons of health. The completion of his last work, the *Einleitung in die Psalmen* (Introduction to the Psalms), he entrusted entirely to his student Joachim Begrich (1900–1945), and it was finished by Christmas 1931. Another student of Gunkel was Hans Schmidt (1877–1953), his successor in Giessen in 1921 and then, beginning in 1928, in Halle. Schmidt, who was accompanied by a colleague, J. Ficker (1861–1944), tells of Gunkel on the eve of his death. "He spoke about whether he would ever be able to work again as he had previously. We both told him that if anyone had a right to rest, he did, and that his life's work lay in the form of both a closure and completeness for all eyes to behold" (*ThBl* 11 [1932]: col. 97).

In fact, his life's work was imposing. One could say that Gunkel blazed new paths in every field in which he worked, and in many cases methodologically broke new ground. Against a generation that had been represented by Wellhausen, he led scholarship to a completely altered outlook, especially in Old Testament research. One must, however, confess that his methodological approach has been almost completely forgotten in the present and overshadowed by a sort of return to Wellhausen in the form of the redaction history school. However, this development lies outside the scope of this study.

Gunkel's first significant work, *Schöpfung und Chaos in Urzeit und Endzeit* (Creation and Chaos in the Primeval Period and the End Time [1895]), in which he dealt with both chapter 1 of Genesis and Revelation 12, contained correspondingly an Old and a New Testament section (3–170, 171–398). They are bound together through commensurate superscriptions: "Gen 1, die Schöpfung in der Urzeit" and "ApJoh 12, die Schöpfung in der Endzeit." ("Gen 1, Creation in the Primeval Period" and "Revelation 12, Creation in the Endtime"). Gunkel assumes that Rev 12 has, as its background, the same chaos myth that lies behind Gen 1. In contrast to Wellhausen, who regarded Gen 1 as the free composition of the author of the Priestly source, representing a "single cosmogonic theory" (*Prolegomena*, 1957, 259), Gunkel pursues the tradition behind the chapter and finds its origin in the Babylonian creation myth, which had the customary opening at the beginning, *Enuma eliš* ("When the gods"), which provided the name of this epic. The first exemplar of this Babylonian epic, written on a clay tablet, was excavated in Nineveh in the palace of Assurbanipal in 1873. He was one of the last Assyrian kings (reigning from 669 to approximately 630 B.C.E.). Since then, numerous additional copies and fragments have been discovered. The archaeological discoveries in Mesopotamia strongly impacted most Old Testament scholars, especially after many texts had been found and at least provisionally deciphered. The similarity of the Babylonian creation myth to the biblical creation narrative in Gen 1 was striking. Since other ancient Oriental sources were not yet known, the acceptance of the Bible's dependence on this source was unavoidable. But how should this be explained? For the literary-critical school, their own narrow view stood in the way, since they were inclined to deal only with sources and their (mostly hypothetical) composers. Since the question of dating the sources stood in the center of their discussion, the assumption of a literary appropriation of the Babylonian precursors was debated on the basis of chronology (see Gunkel, *Schöpfung und Chaos*, 3–4). Gunkel introduced in his work a reliable alternative. Following the methodology of the history of religion school, he investigated first the biblical material: the priestly history of creation in Gen 1 and the apocalyptic vision of Rev 12, determined the foreign character of the statements encountered there, and inferred their Babylonian origin. The Assyriologist Zimmer examined and confirmed the result (10–11). Zimmer also added to the work a translation of the corresponding Babylonian texts ("Supplements," 401–28), which today is certainly out of date. In addition to Gen 1, Gunkel investigated other Old Testament passages in which a reflection of the battle with the chaos dragon and primeval sea is to be found (29–114). For the appropriation of this material, Gunkel reckons with a lengthy period of oral tradition, which, at the same time, reflects the great difference between the biblical and Babylonian descriptions of creation: "These narratives came to us in a more or less obscure form" (147–48). Gunkel estimates that this appropriation occurred during an early period. The Tel el-Amarna correspondence (see above, 325) had shown that the Egyptian pharaoh had communicated with his vassals in Palestine as early as 1400 B.C.E. by using cuneiform tablets written in the Babylonian language. Therefore, the Babylonian culture was known by the Canaanites at the time of Israel's entrance into the land, and the immigrants soon adopted Canaanite culture (151) and thereby came indirectly under Babylonian influence. The acceptance of a lengthy tradition also bridged the chronological distance between such an early Israelite familiarity with Babylonian materials and the relatively late composition of the Priestly creation history: "In the exploration of the myths and sagas, we have to reckon not only with writings and authors, but also far more with oral tradition. In addition, most carefully we have to distinguish overall between the time of the oldest document available to *us* for an idea and to the age of the idea itself" (235). "The sagas have already had before their literary formation a history in oral tradition, and this … prehistory is not to be obtained by literary criticism" (143). Gunkel reckons with two periods of significant Babylonian influence: a "pre-prophetic" one in the early period after the entrance into the land and a "post-prophetic" one, that is, exilic and postexilic (169). For him, it is important to stress that the transmitted mythical material became religiously significant for the first time in the late period, in which Israel's religion "had become so established that it was not possible to speak of a fundamental influence by Babylonian texts" (170). "Correspondingly, the enormous distance between the two accounts required a rather considerable period of time, before Gen 1 could finally have been influenced by the ancient Babylonian myth" (136). Gunkel agrees throughout with those "who are afraid even to name both reports together:" "The difference between the Babylonian myth and Gen 1 is so great in religious attitude and aesthetic coloring that they at first glance appear to have nothing in common" (29). Accordingly, although Gunkel emphasizes that the story of the primeval flood (Gen 6–8) corresponds to the Babylonian flood narrative, he nevertheless notes that in spite of

> a substantial similarity in details a significant difference between the two accounts exists.… Also here the idea of a direct acquisition of the Babylonian version by Gen 1 is far from likely. Rather, a period of time must have separated the two, since polytheism in the biblical story disappeared altogether , and the poetry of the Babylonian account eventually became in Gen 1 a prosaic narrative. (143–44)

It is also noteworthy that Gunkel attests to the idea of creation that was present in Israel was of great antiquity, although its actual significance for this people first occurred during the exilic period (156–63).

In the New Testament section, Gunkel proceeds in the same way. The criticism concerning the book of Revelation likewise had been determined by literary, critical aspects: there was the suggestion that it may be traced back to several Christian sources (D. Völter, 1882) or to a later, Christian editing of an originally Jewish document (E. Vischer, 1886). In order to substantiate his engagement with a single chapter of the book of Revelation, Gunkel follows the thesis of K. H. Weizsäcker (1892) that the book may have been assembled from many originally independent visions (194). The attention given to connections of content prompts him to add to chapter 12 also 19:11–20:3 to provide the conclusion of the vision of the dragon. At this point he reaches a new methodological insight. Instead of the historical, temporal, (allegorical) interpretation that his predecessors pursued, which had degenerated into pure guesswork and which he declares is "bankrupt" (233), he contends that one should pursue the history developing from both an underlying tradition and the literary critical division into different strata. In opposition to the traditional Christian explanation of Revelation 12 that regarded the chapter as referring to the birth of Christ and the ascension, Gunkel supposes (by reference to a talmudic passage) that a Jewish tradition serves as the background of the vision. In this way, Gunkel contends that one must go back behind the assumption of the Jewish tradition. The oral tradition leaves traces behind: "elisions, additions, and displacements, which later generations have carried out on the older materials" (256). In such "obfuscations" (ibid.), one recognizes the antiquity of a tradition. Gunkel discovers these types of characteristics in Rev 12: for example, the woman flees into the wilderness following the birth of the boy (v. 6).

> Why to the wilderness? The text says nothing concerning this. In spite of this omission it is still possible to explain this element: the wilderness is characteristic of that which is waterless. The woman, however, naturally flees there, where she feels secure from the persecutor. Therefore we conclude that the actual element in which the dragon is powerful is the water. (258)

This is confirmed additionally by two features: all at once the dragon pours after the woman a stream of water, which, however is swallowed by the earth (vv. 15–16), and finally he is sealed and bound in the primeval ocean (Abyss; 20:3). That the dragon directs his anger against the stars (12:4) shows that he is a monster of darkness. On the whole, the narrative is sketchy as it now stands. Why the dragon wishes to devour the newborn child is not clear. However, according to 12:5; 16:14; 19:12, 15, 16, he will one day become a ruler of the world and then will finally displace the dragon from its temporary sovereignty of the world. What the source is that enables the dragon to know about this and the impending birth, along with many other things, remains obscure.

In the search for the origin of the narrative, Gunkel gives himself up to the "aesthetic impression." For the concrete features, there "is a certain burning complexion characteristic of the symptom of a passionate, heated fantasy" (272). Analogies to this can be found in mythology. The narrative, which is obscured in many passages, may originally "have been more extensively colored, more mythological" (273). From the similarity to Daniel, Enoch, and earlier materials in the book of Zechariah, Gunkel indicates that what is found in the book of Revelation belongs to the previous apocalypses. Characteristics of these apocalyptic texts are cosmology and eschatology, angel speculations and visions (290), but also the belief in heaven and hell, and resurrection (291). These traditions do not stem from Judaism—which took the subjects primarily from paganism—nor do they derive from Greek traditions. There remain only Babylonian or Persian traditions. Although Gunkel will not automatically exclude Persian influence (293 n. 3), for Rev 12 he thinks that some traditions that are probably Babylonian can be identified. This is especially true for the number seven, which is the number of the spirits (Rev 1:4; 4:5; 5:6), the angels (8:2), and the astral gods (planets) with a Babylonian background (294–302). The twenty-four elders (Rev 4:4) go back to the twenty-four members of the divine council in Babylonian tradition (302–8). Gunkel reconstructs (cf. 257–270) the Babylonian myth underlying Rev 12 as follows (385–88): the child whom the dragon wishes to devour is the young god Marduk (the city god of Babylon); his mother is the dragon Tiamat, the goddess of heaven. While Tiamat wishes to devour the newborn child, the child confronts her and an eagle (an animal of Marduk?) instead redeems the boy by bringing him to heaven. Tiamat, who then pursues him, is slain by the heavenly army and cast into the Deep. Marduk attempts to wreak vengeance on his mother, but she saves herself by escaping into the wilderness. Even when today one views the background of the chapter differently, methodologically the approach of Gunkel brought entirely new perspectives to the text.

The way Gunkel assessed theologically the Babylonian influence on the Old Testament can be seen from his *Israel und Babylonien* (1903; *Israel and Babylon*, 1904, 25).

If then we should find real Babylonian elements in the history of Israel, … our faith should nevertheless rejoice.… We acknowledge cheerfully and honestly God's revelation wherever a human soul feels itself near its God, even though that be in the most arid and strange forms. Far be it from us to limit God's revelation to Israel!

The church fathers have thought of this in a grander way, for "in the great and noble heroes of Greek philosophy [they] have seen bearers of the seed of the divine Word, seed sown everywhere."

In *Zum religionsgeschichtlichen Verständnis des Neuen Testaments* (Concerning the History of Religion's Understanding of the New Testament [1903]), Gunkel again begins with the influence of ancient Oriental religions on Judaism, which he characterizes in certain ways as a "virtually syncretistic religion." Even so, while Judaism experienced foreign influences, it continued to preserve some of its specific characteristics, especially monotheism. His thesis is "that Christianity, born from syncretistic Judaism, also gives evidence of strongly syncretistic features" (34–35). One moves from the Old Testament, through Judaism, and to the New Testament (37). The material of the book of Revelation is originally of pagan origin, even though it had passed through Judaism (39). Again, this has to do with the number seven and the twenty-four elders, the *mythological* conception of the heavenly Jerusalem (Rev 21:10–27), and so on. In the Gospels, Gunkel finds, in addition to a stratum of narratives that "is generally good historical material" and at times contains also legendary material, a second stratum of mythical stories; these have to do actually with stories of gods or heroes, which one subsequently has assigned to Jesus" (64–65). To this mythical stratum, Gunkel assigns especially the childhood narratives, the story of the baptism, and the story of the temptation, as well as narratives of the appearances of the resurrected Christ, the ascension, and Christ's journey to hell (65–73). In the identification of these narratives as "mythical," one is often reminded of D. F. Strauss. For instance, Gunkel derives the celebration of Sunday from the festival of the sun god (73–76). He also seeks finally to explain the resurrection of Jesus in terms of the history of religion: in spite of some careful circumscriptions, he traces the idea, including the chronological designation "after three days" (where there are special parallels to the number three), back to the mythologies of ancient Oriental religions concerning the yearly dying and rising of the gods, which was transmitted through Judaism (76–83). But how can one assign such ideas to the crucifixion of Jesus, who died indisputably on the cross? Concerning this Gunkel remembers the Pauline teaching of baptism in Rom 6, according to which baptism is conceived of as death and resurrection. As a parallel to this, Gunkel names the Egyptian Isis mystery, which likewise wished to show the way from death to life in the mystical unification with the deity (83–84).

The concluding remarks show how a liberal theologian confronts the New Testament as a whole: in the Synoptic Gospels (85–96), "he arrives in a world in which he soon feels at home; here moves a spirit, which he understands quite well." The only thing foreign to him is "eschatology, especially the teaching of the resurrection of humans at the last days." Thoroughly different, by comparison, are the writings of Paul and John. "One may think only of ideas like rebirth, divine sonship in a metaphysical sense, atonement through the death of Christ, mystical association of Christ with the church, creation of the world by Christ" (86). Gunkel mentions especially once again faith in the resurrection and Christology as Oriental in origin. "The origin of Pauline and Johannine Christology is the problem of all problems of New Testament criticism" (89). The Pauline doctrine of salvation especially has pagan parallels. Everything that divine beings who descend to the earth normally do has been assigned to Jesus, "and that is, so we maintain, the secret overall of New Testament Christology" (93).

Gunkel comes to the conclusion: "Christianity is a syncretistic religion" (95; cf. 88). It is wrong to evaluate it only on the basis of the Gospels. Even so, he notes in a positive manner a surprising fact, given what has been said: Christianity originated in a time of world history when it stepped out of the Oriental realm into the Greek sphere. This is providential for it. Since it was ordained for many peoples, it has grown from the history of many peoples. He utters a citation from Otto Pfleiderer (1839–1908), the major theologian of liberal Protestantism (*Das Urchrisenthum*, 1902, 1:vii), who defines Christianity "as the necessary product of the development of the religious spirit of our genre, to whose education the entire history of the ancient world gravitates." That may be "the grandest and most solid apology for Christianity, which [on the historical standpoint—the addition of Gunkel!] one is permitted to think."

Already two years prior to the publication of the history of religion's understanding of the New Testament, his great commentary on Genesis appeared in print (1901). This volume, on which Gunkel had probably worked since 1897, turns one toward another world. Here, too, Gunkel breaks new ground methodologically. This is especially the case for literary critical methods. For the first time Gunkel turns to form criticism in this commentary. It is first in the second edition (1902) that he is able to refer to folkloristic literature, which is concerned with folktales, legends, and folk songs. The fairy tale, to which Gunkel dedicates a small writing (*Das Märchen im Alten Testament* [The Folktale in the Old Testament], 1917), already had been made popular in a Romantic spirit by the brothers Grimm (Jakob [1785–1863] and Wilhelm [1786–1859]) and their collection of "children and home folk tales" (1812–1814). Also important is their distinction between nature poetry and artistic poetry, whereby the legend is accorded a special place as a poetic form of narrative with a historical kernel. In addition, Gunkel had read the writings of Herder, whose concept of saga and poetry as the oldest human speech fascinated him. These essays, however, had submerged the criticism that around the middle of the century had been oriented mainly toward historical *sources*. And it was Gunkel who had initiated an entirely new beginning. Later on (1921) he once stated that his occupation with the Old Testament psalms for the first time directed him to research in literary history. In the third (and final) edition of his commentary (1910), he explored to a wider degree extratheological literature—folkore and legend. While Gunkel still often mentions "myths" in the first edition, he speaks more reticently in the third edition of only "faded myths" in the primeval history (primeval legends, xiv). From the definition "myths are stories of the gods that are in distinction to legends, whose active persons are humans," the conclusion arises: the actual character of Yahweh religion is not propitious to myths. This religion from its beginning is designed for monotheism; a story of the gods requires at least two deities (ibid.). Therefore, Gunkel speaks rather consistently of "legends."

Gunkel also considers legends that contain a historical kernel. A group of stories that he calls "historical" legends is found especially in the book of Judges, which tells about individual leaders. Besides these, there are "ethnographical" legends, such as those of Cain and of Ishmael, which concern the circumstances of peoples (xx). "Etiological" legends are those that seek to explain something (xx–xxv). To these belong "ethnological" legends, which explain the relationships of peoples by regularly tracing back the present circumstances to the activity of the primeval fathers, and "etymological" legends, which interpret the meaning of names (of peoples or geographical phenomena like mountains, wells, sanctuaries, and cities). Important are legendary cultic motifs, which explain the orders of worship. They are often especially connected to specified cultic places. In addition to all of these conspicuous motifs, there are also those that are inexplicable, which often are the main factors of a legend. Their frequency just in the legends of the fathers prompts Gunkel to assume in these cases the existence of older patterns, in which later additional topics of Israel have been inserted. This leads to the radical "judgment that the legendary materials treated in the legends of the fathers on the whole are neither of historical nor of etiological origin" (xxvi). In the first edition of his commentary, Gunkel was still inclined to adopt, if only with a degree of limitation, the influence of the Wellhausen school that the legends of the fathers deal with the first ancestors of the peoples, mostly Israel (*Genesis*, 1901). In the second edition, Gunkel had already departed from this and regarded the legends as inexplicable (*Genesis*, 1902, x). Later (1919) he declared that the tribal, historical interpretation originated from rationalism and has become antiquated. Already in the first edition, he had flatly moved away from the evaluation of legend by historical plausibility: "this poetry has another possibility than what applies in prosaic life" (*Genesis*, 1901, iv). It is wrong to confuse legends for lies. Rather, a legend is a special form of poetry, and "the poetic narrative is in a much better position than the prosaic one to become the bearer of religious ideas" (*Genesis*, 1901, ii).

Primarily what matters for Gunkel is, above all, the aesthetic evaluation of Old Testament materials:

> all the more significant than the literary-critical issues appear to me to be aesthetic and literary historical problems for which a rich field exists for our exploration.... Since the great Herder has proclaimed vividly the sovereignty of the Old Testament to the world, there never has been lacking among professional scholars in their entirety critics who gave testimony to the beauty of those creations. ("Ziele und Methoden der Erklärung des Alten Testaments" [Objectives and Methods of Explanation of the Old Testament], in *Reden und Aufsätze*, 22)

In addition to Reuss, Gunkel mentions here Wellhausen: "We walk in the paths of Herder and Wellhausen, when we subject the form of the various creation accounts of the Old Testament to special consideration" (ibid.). Gunkel gives the interpreter the following methodological task:

> primarily the exegete must experience strongly and deeply the aesthetic character of each single piece.... Then he should seek to couch what he has viewed in the most appropriate manner. Further, he should analyze the impression, which is thus received and secured, and then examine the question by which specific means the writer produced this result. (23)

The aesthetic consideration then becomes one of the history of literature, when the critic compiles his observations and resorts to a history. In this connection, it is most important to recognize the *genres* of Hebrew literature. It is necessary not to overlook the strangeness of ancient forms of expression in contrast to present ones. The aesthetic view, however, is not the final purpose: "for we are not aesthetes, but rather theologians" (24). To be sure, it remains unclear in regard to Gunkel how one should relate the beauty of form to religious content.

For the legends of Genesis, Gunkel asks "that each individual legend first be explained in and of itself. The more independent a narrative is the more certain it is that it contains the older form" (*Genesis*, 1910, xxxiii). This takes up a requirement expressed already by Wellhausen (*Prolegomena*, 1905, 334). It is the case in addition that "the shorter a legend is the more probable it is that it is contained in its older form" (*Genesis*, 1910, xxxiv). An example is the narrative of Hagar's flight (Gen 16). By contrast, the Joseph narrative (Gen 37; 39–48; 50) is comprehensive and rambling; Gunkel names it a "novella" (lv). In the meantime, Gunkel notes also a series of stylistic features that are peculiar to legends. Gunkel considers in the following way the tradition history of legends in Genesis in oral form (lvi–lxxx): some of the legends may not be genuinely Israelite, but rather may have entered into Israelite tradition from the outside. The primordial legends stem from Babylonia. Some of the Babylonian myths came into Canaan during the pre-Israelite period, and Israel would have come to know them when they came into contact with Canaanite culture (*Genesis*, 1910, 29). Gunkel discovers Egyptian influence only in the Joseph narrative. The legends of Abraham, Isaac, and Jacob are not at home in Canaan proper, but rather in the steppe. This connects with the fact that the oldest narratives describe the fathers not as farmers but rather as nomads, in particular sheep breeders. Nothing that is actually Canaanite is to be ascertained anywhere. The wider tradition has brought with it, then, all kinds of dislocations, as well as a certainly steady, if slow, adjustment to new relationships. Also to be noted is the development from the oldest, shortest legends (e.g., Gen 12:10–20) to the elaborate and latest of all, the Joseph narrative.

Most significant, however, is the history of religion. The figures of deities in the legends are quite varied: gods of places, family gods, the national god, and even the Lord of all peoples stand side by side. When we wish to comprehend what is actually Israelite, however, it is pivotal to discern what Israel made of this. It is essential to note that Israel "stamps upon the entire multiplicity of the ideas of God transmitted in the materials of the legends with its 'Yahweh' and by this means has eliminated the internal differences" (lxviii). On the other hand, the significant proximity of Gunkel to Herder and also the Enlightenment in his assessment of the early legends is clear:

> We believe that God is active in the world as the still, concealed background of all things;… We anticipate his workings in the marvelous bonding of things; however, he never appears to us as an active factor beside others, but rather steadily as the final cause of all things. However, it is entirely different in many narratives of Genesis. For example, God walks in paradise, creating humans with his own hands, and he closes the doors of the ark. (xi)

All this belongs to things "that speak against our better knowledge." They "are unbelievable to us." "We are in the position to understand something like that as the naiveté of ancient humans; however, we refuse to believe such narratives" (x–xi). Later, "a refinement of revelation" enters into the picture (lxix): While God still walks unsuspectingly among humans in the oldest legends, later it is a messenger of God who either appears or is present in a dream revelation.

The aesthetic approach to the narrative, as is the case with Herder, replaces the believing acceptance of the narratives as historical truth: "The major factor, however, is and continues to be the *poetic tone* of these narratives.… The legend is poetry by nature: it desires to rejoice, elevate, inspire, and touch." Gunkel highly values the legends aesthetically: they are "perhaps the most beautiful and deepest ones, which have been given on the earth" (xii).

In Genesis Gunkel distinguishes between two main groups of legends: the primeval legends and the legends of the fathers. To these are added hero legends, which are found in the following "historical" books (see *Die israelitische Literatur* [The Israelite Literature], 19).

Gunkel reckons further with groups of legends, which have already been arranged together in the oral stage (lii–liii). Such "wreaths of legends" are those of Abraham-Lot and Jacob-Esau-Laban. Also the sources of J and E are such collections in the written stage. It is worthy of note that Gunkel does not abandon the division of sources, but rather proceeds from it as a basic principle. "The division of these three 'literary sources' of Genesis is a common result of Old Testament criticism, which has worked on this for a century and a half" (lxxxi). In this summary, Gunkel refers to Wellhausen's *Prolegomena* as a "master work," a tribute that was not returned by Wellhausen.

Compared to the accusations that Gunkel had little interest in what is specifically Israelite in the final form of the legends, one can cite a host of contrary expressions that clearly indicate the especially high value he places on the religion of Israel. In opposition to the ancient creation myths, which at the same time tell of the origin of the gods, there is lacking in Gen 1 a theogony. "This observation therefore teaches one to recognize the majesty of the religion of Israel. The nations surrounding Israel believe in gods, who have originated in ancient times. Israel, however, has a God, who lives from eternity to eternity!" (*Genesis*, 1910, 124–25). "Accordingly, there is no greater opposition than between the multicolored, fantastic mythology of all these nations and the intellectually clear and sober supernaturalism of Gen 1." Such expressions thoroughly correspond to the piety of a liberal theologian of the period.

Gunkel later wrote another commentary of Genesis, *Die Urgeschichte und die Patriarchen* (The Primeval History and the Patriarchs [1911; 2nd ed., 1921]), in a series dedicated to the needs of pastors, teachers, and interested laity, *Die Schriften des Alten Testaments in Auswahl* (Selected Writings of the Old Testament). He also provided the plan for the series and selected the collaborators. More important are the three introductions that he contributed to the volume by Hans Schmidt, *Die grossen Propheten* (The Great Prophets [1915; 2nd ed., 1923]). His contributions bear the superscriptions "Geschichte Vorderasiens zur Zeit der grossen Propheten" (History of Asia Minor at the Time of the Great Prophets), "Die geheimen Erfahrungen der Propheten" (The Secret Experiences of the Prophets), and "Die Propheten als Schriftsteller und Dichter" (The Prophets as Writers and Poets). He also set forth his views of prophecy in the collection of essays *Die Propheten* (The Prophets [1917]). Gunkel's theological heart responded most directly to the sphere of prophecy, although, in spite of numerous essays, he did not publish any comprehensive, major work on prophecy. In his view of prophecy, he was a typical representative of his time. The Graf-Kuenen-Wellhausen school had rejected the earlier view that prophets were interpreters of the law. Instead, this approach had moved the personality of the prophets to the center of consideration, a position we saw above all with Duhm. A new point of view was the occurrence of ecstasy. In this connection, Gunkel points to Duhm's Isaiah commentary. Experiences of revelation that one observed with the prophets became the subject of psychological investigations.

What Gunkel had in mind above all are the so-called writing prophets: Amos, Hosea, Isaiah, Jeremiah, and Ezekiel. "To describe the life of the souls of these men must become our actual purpose in that which follows." "The fundamental experience of all prophecy, however, is 'ecstasy'" (in H. Schmidt, 1923², xviii). For this purpose, Gunkel calls on the stories of the ecstatic "schools of prophets" (1 Sam 10:5–16; 19:18–24 or the prophets of Baal on Carmel (1 Kgs 18:26–29). He seeks, time and again, to find ecstatic utterances in the prophetic words, so much so that in many instances he clearly exaggerates this principle. Gunkel likewise integrates the prophetic signs of activities under the ecstatic phenomena. Then comes a break in the description of the great prophets. Gunkel characterizes them in contrast to the schools in which the prophets appear, for example, 1 Kgs 22:5–6 These spiritual heroes, the great prophets, are not ecstatic but rather are "individuals of noble kind… Men of higher flight of thought and greater breadth of sight," "heroes" who speak about current political questions. Here the ideal personality enters once again. "And they have arrived by themselves at these issues" (xxix). Gunkel describes them as men of finer comprehension, who see coming out of a small cloud the approaching storm (1 Kgs 18:44). From the two types of prophets, those of salvation and others of disaster, the larger number are prophets of disaster. Following the appearance of the Assyrian danger in the eighth century, there were "writing prophets." "All of them have the fundamental conviction that they possess the thoughts of Yahweh." They receive "a superhuman cognition of the future." However, Gunkel regards the prophets more as independent intellectuals: "Thus we see therefore in the history of prophecy a change flowing from prophet to preacher and religious thinker" (xxx–xxxiii).

Gunkel ventures along new paths in the third introduction. Here he handles questions of the Old Testament history of literature. As the most important point of view in this sphere he mentions the question concerning the genre of a document. In the process he comes to an important insight, which in actuality contrasts diametrically with his previously expressed point of view. This is his understanding "that the genres in the literature of an ancient people play by far a greater role than they do today. Individual authors, in composing modern literature, for all the world seem to recede from this characteristic of antiquity in a way that at first is surprising to us." This is grounded in the customs of an ancient culture, in which the individual is involved to a greater extent by convention in the community and also speaks as a poet and writer in a style usual from time immemorial. This insight, as much as it establishes his generic criticism, Gunkel buries at once by stating, "To be certain, also ancient Israel has produced great writers of a personal, yes, very personal style that stands out." "That it produced such compositions

gives it its fame among the nations of the entire ancient Orient." Among
these were some of the prophets. "This peculiarity of the 'one' occurred
in Israel, but was not known in the rest of the Orient: the individual has
appeared" (xxxv).

In spite of this, he perceives important insights: that the prophets
originally were not writers, but rather speakers, and that in every instance
of their appearance one has to imagine their words always in a scene in
which they appear. "Whoever thinks about ink and paper in the reading
of their writings has lost the game from its very beginning. 'Hear' begins
their passages, not 'Read!'" The reader should attempt "to place them
into the middle of the life of the people of Israel, where they once have
spoken." From the customary beginning of the speech, "Thus Yahweh has
spoken to me," it may be concluded that "they usually are not accustomed
to speaking in ecstasy, but rather engage in discourse afterwards, when
they have become more tranquil" (xxxvi–xxxvii). One can recognize the
transition to the prophets as authors in Jeremiah's dictation to Baruch
(Jer 36) or in Isaiah's testimony of his oracle (Isa 8:16; 30:8). Amos may
have been a writer after his expulsion from the northern kingdom (Amos
7:12). Gunkel's concepts of the origin of a prophetic book are still strongly
shaped by literary critical patterns. He imagines that the prophet's words
were disseminated originally on short leaflets and then were assembled
somewhat haphazardly into "early collections" by students of the prophets. Therefore, they do not show any precise order. In many cases, oracles
of nameless prophets were appropriated by the shapers of the collections,
so that the final prophetic books "constitute a variegated world." It must
be the first objective of criticism to lift out originally independent passages. As a start, Gunkel reckons with statements of only two (Hebrew)
words, for example, Hos 1:8 ("not my people") and Isa 8:3 ("the prey
comes quickly, the booty hastens"). After this followed short sayings of
two or three long verses. It was only later that the prophets learned to
compose longer speeches.

As concerns the words of the prophets, Gunkel sees a line of development "from poetry to prose." Prophetic speech originally was poetry. The
transition to prose may probably be explained by the prophets' first being
ecstatics, then preachers, and finally religious thinkers (see above).

In a subsequent section (xlii–lxx), Gunkel assembles the variety of
prophetic genres. The major genres placed under the common designation of "oracle" (xlii) are visions (apparitions) and auditions (words).
Visions are disclosed in the form of reports. They are usually connected
with verbal revelations. Words by rule are divine words, which the

prophet delivers as a messenger. There can also take place a dialogue between the prophet and God. As regards content, the words are a problem for a classification by reason of the variety of complexities. Gunkel helps himself by the disclosure "that most of these genres are originally not prophetic. From the beginning on the prophets are not poets of songs, narrators of history, or preachers of the Torah." This means "that prophecy has appropriated in its development a very large number of alien forms" (xlvi). Gunkel sees this as a means for the prophets to come close to the heart of the people, when their own speech is no longer adequate.

> All the more, however, the question emerges as to the identification of the *actual prophetic form* by starting with what remains of it in the biblical texts. This must be the genre, which is clearly and specifically prophetic in terms of content and form. The main purpose of the prophets originally … was to engage in proclamation. Accordingly, we may expect the oldest prophetic style to appear in texts describing the future and are named by us as "promises" or "threats" depending on their content of either salvation or disaster. (ibid.)

These two major forms have continued to exist during the entire period of prophecy. From the abundance of forms that have been appropriated, two lines of development can be extracted: the prophets have become both poets and thinkers. For prophets of disaster, a special, significant form is the funeral dirge, while the hymn is important for the prophets of salvation. The latter is in particular frequently found in Deutero-Isaiah. When a prophet appropriates a communal lament, he positions himself as the representative of his people before Yahweh. To be an intercessor belongs to the traditional purposes of the prophet. Next to the threat, there is the "word of reproach," in which the reference to sins that have already been committed serves as the foundation of disaster. "This identification of sins has now become for the great prophets of disaster a major point of their entire activity"(lxii). The form of the "reproach" has developed from this. A further genre is the "speech of controversy," which results from the disputation of the prophets with their opponents.

Gunkel concludes his observations, only some of which we were able to single out, with the remark that the reader may "interpret" this delineation not as the "result of critical research," "but rather as an attempt to master the enormous amounts of material." For the rest, the history of literature may be a rich field; "may it be that the future will not lack for workers that will harvest its rich fruits" (lxx).

Gunkel himself has harvested rich fruits from this field, and this is the best-known aspect of his work. His first publications on the Psalter appeared in 1903, while his last work, comprising his most important writing, he had to leave unfinished for a student to bring to completion. Already by 1904 he had offered to the public his first major collection, *Ausgewählte Psalmen* (4th ed., 1917). In the year 1911 the publisher G. Ruprecht had given Gunkel a contract to prepare a revision of the psalms commentary for the series Göttinger Handkommentar. This enormous task, as he describes it in the foreword (*Die Psalmen*, 1968, 6), kept him busy for many years, before it could appear finally in 1926. And this was possible only by eliminating a still incomplete, comprehensive introduction. The responsibility for finishing this volume he had to give, during Christmas 1931, to his longtime assistant, Joachim Begrich (1900–1945). According to Gunkel's own wish, one should treat both the commentary and the *Einleitung in die Psalmen* as a *single* work. "The *Einleitung* offers a summary of the individual observations that were obtained in the commentary. These, however, rest on the overall understanding, which is carried forth in the 'Introduction'" (*Einleitung*, 1986, x). Thus, it is appropriate when we take into view each of these features.

In the nineteenth and the beginning of the twentieth century, there were many commentaries written on the psalms. However, although Flacius had already found it necessary to observe the literary forms of the biblical texts (see above, 13) and de Wette had already produced essays that classified psalms according to *Gattungen*, Gunkel was the first to record this objective methodologically and, in spite of many inconsistencies, to lay a fixed foundation for them. He was himself aware that there was certainly nothing "new to say that was previously unmentioned" (*Einleitung*, 9). Moreover, there is here certainly an ideological requirement in view when Gunkel declares in the foreword to his commentary (7): "I ... have held it to be my actual intention to describe the *content of the psalms*, and that is their religion." In so doing, Gunkel has especially the pious individual in view in consideration of the "piety of the psalms" (*Einleitung*, 27). This principle continued to have consequences for the determination of the forms in the *Einleitung*.

Gunkel does not limit his observations to the psalms collected in the Psalter, but also takes into consideration those encountered in other Old Testament books. Beyond these he also draws on ancient Near Eastern hymns as parallels and possible examples of influence. These were generally accessible in ample collections. A study such as that of Friedrich Stummer (1886–1955), *Sumerisch-akkadische Parallelen zum Aufbau alt-*

testamentlicher Psalmen (Sumerian-Akkadian Parallels to the Structure of Old Testament Psalms [1922]), though not perfect, already offered preparatory work.

It is especially important that Gunkel asks about the "life setting" (*Sitz im Leben*) of the psalms. Since their superscriptions are relatively late and appear to have been added to the individual psalms, they are not capable of saying anything about the worship of ancient Israel and its different occasions. What amounts to Gunkel's methodological principle is the following: "Primarily, one may ... collect only such poems which belong in their entirety to a fixed *occasion* in *worship* or at least derive from this." Additional requirements for Gunkel are a common "treasure trove of thoughts and voices" and a common style of "forms of speech" (*Einleitung*, 22–23). The major forms of the Psalter accordingly are the "hymn," the "community lament," the "individual lament," and the "thanksgiving of the individual." Additional forms, which Gunkel includes, are small in number of occurrences. These were included among the "smaller forms" (293), although the "thanksgiving psalm" could actually demand an equal place among the more frequently occurring forms. Its more infrequent occurrence Gunkel explains psychologically, which is largely unconvincing: "The human heart indeed turns often and happily toward God in offering lamentation and presenting a plea. However, following deliverance, one forgets to give thanks to the one who provides aid" (315).

For Gunkel, the division of these major forms is clear and, and he is able to specify in each case a typically common structure with clear stylistic marks of "forms of speech." He also distinguishes the units of meaning according to related motifs (cf. 26). Nevertheless, the classification of the psalms in individual cases definitely encounters difficulties. First, Gunkel gives consideration to the history of the forms. Not before one recognizes these can one understand that the investigation of the forms of the psalms is a history of literature (*Reden und Aufsätze*, 33). "In the oldest period, the individual poems were extraordinarily brief. This corresponds to the modest capability of the receptivity of each primitive generation." These poems continued to "increase" in size (27). In addition, Gunkel speaks of a "mixture of different forms," which goes back to a "removal of the forms from their original, concrete situations" (398). Today, one has to regard the ideal of an originally "pure" form rather as an abstraction that is far from being real. Actually, almost all of the present psalms are "mixed forms," in which elements of several ideal forms occur. While the oldest forms had their fixed place in worship, the later poets of the psalms "turned their backs" on the cult and "learned to sing songs..., which were no longer destined for use in public worship." This was due, in Gunkel's estimation, to the influence of the prophets. "And at the same time the enormous individualism of the prophets recurs here: the soul alone appears before its God" (30). Thus, in this way, noncultic "spiritual poetry" may have originated (ibid.; cf. also 398). And here Gunkel's heart pulsates! Especially in the laments of the individual Gunkel finds in this series of psalms at least some that are distanced from the cult, even if originally the form belonged to worship. His most significant student, the Norwegian Sigmund Mowinckel (1884–1965), rebutted this point. In his *Psalmenstudien* ([6 vols.; Kristiania: Dybwad, 1921–1924; repr., Amsterdam: Schippers, 1961], 1:137–38), he emphasized "that also the psalms of the lament which are transmitted in the current Psalter actually are cultic psalms." Indeed, this understanding is associated with the untenable thesis that the "enemies" in the psalms of lament may consistently be magicians. Mowinckel, however, correctly turns against a too narrow definition of the cult that understands it as having to do only with sacrifice. He also indicates that the laments considered to be remote from the context of temple worship still continued an association with this cult. This is noted in regard to the thanksgiving for salvation that is carried out. Most important, however, is the indication that in the psalms of lament we have to do with official cultic formulae. Thus, the "I" of the lament who speaks is "in general not a living individual of flesh and blood, but rather a type for the group of the pious." During the lifetime of Gunkel, this debate was not resolved, and it continues in some respects even today. There exists the "post-cultic" explanation of some psalms in addition to those that are cultic.

Additionally, Gunkel does not use uniform standards to gauge the forms of the Psalter. There is also a series of forms that he determines according to their content. To these belong the "songs of Yahweh's enthronement," the royal psalms, and the victory song. Furthermore, he devotes a special paragraph to wisdom elements in the psalms (§10, 381–97).

In spite of the many concepts that are linked to Gunkel's work, one may conclude that, through his breakthrough to new methods, including especially the history of religion approach to the Bible and form-critical research, he transmitted to biblical studies new understandings that continue to endure. This applies especially to research on the Psalter. In spite of this, also here new insights have subsequently been gained. Gunkel could still state: "An internal order among the individual psalms as a whole has not been transmitted to us" (3). Nevertheless, present criticism endeavors to discover a meaningful arrangement of adjacent psalms in the Psalter according to standard points of view that were decisive for the collection of these texts. This continuing research into the Psalter does not diminish in any way the significance of Gunkel's life's work.

7.2. Placing Primitive Christianity into the History of Religion: Wilhelm Bousset

Wilhelm Bousset was born in 1865, the son of a pastor in Lübeck. He was the oldest of four siblings. He had two brothers and a sister. In the orthodox parsonage, he experienced a happy childhood, as he himself reported (*Pastorenjungs* [A Pastor's Son [1919]). After passing his final examination in 1884 at the Katharineum Gymnasium in Lübeck, he engaged in theological studies at Erlangen for three semesters at the wishes of his parents. The faculty was known as a conservative Lutheran one at the time. At the same time, he studied under Ernst Troeltsch and learned to know him, which led to a continuing friendship. Bousset held himself at a distance from the Erlangen professors, including the well-known conservative New Testament scholar Theodor Zahn (1838–1933). The theology in Leipzig, where he studied during 1885–1886, left him likewise unaffected, in spite of the fact that he studied under Franz Delitzsch and the well-known, influential Lutheran dogmatic theologian C. E. Luthardt (1823–1902). Instead, he read Harnack (1851–1930) and Ritschl. In a serious conflict with his parents, he pressured them to allow him to study at Göttingen in the winter semester of 1886–1887. Without question it was Ritschl who finally convinced the young Bousset to study theology, especially the New Testament and Reformation history. Ritschl's systematic theology rather disappointed him.

Bousset remained in Göttingen for four years. After having taken his church exams in the summer of 1888 in Lübeck, he soon returned there in order to prepare for his examination for his licentiate. There he moved into the circle of young theologians from which later developed the history of religion school. Among those in the group who received his *Habilitation* was Bousset. The established professors at the time were concerned with this group, since they feared they would develop a "small theological faculty." Bousset presented first his *Die Evangelienzitate Justins des Märtyrers* (The Citations of the Gospels by Justin Martyr; for this early theologian, see *History*, vol. 1) and passed his licentiate exams. After his colloquium and public defense, he received his licentiate. But this accomplishment did not satisfy the faculty enough to award him a

Habilitation. Thus, Bousset spent two additional years in order to present a second treatise, this one having the title *Die Lehre des Apostels Paulus vom Gesetz* (The Apostle Paul's Teaching of the Law). This lecture led to his gaining permission to teach. However, he had a lengthy wait of five years before he received a regular position. Since his post as a private lecturer was not accompanied by remuneration, he continued to be willing to receive support that required sacrifices by his parents. He soon developed into a popular lecturer, since he shared the questions of the students and answered them empathetically. He also was fond of his personal contact with the students. Finally, after he had published several books, he was named in 1896 to the position of associate professor and received a modest salary. Now he could afford to marry Maria Vermehren of Lübeck, who was involved in the women's movement. It was a happy marriage, clouded only by the lack of children.

The early theological position of Bousset is presented in his book *Jesu Predigt in ihrem Gegensatz zum Judentums* (The Preaching of Jesus in His Opposition to Judaism). He wrote this book in 1892 as a response to the publication of the book by Johannes Weiss, *Die Predigt Jesu vom Reiche Gottes* (Jesus' Proclamation of the Kingdom of God; see below, 373). Although Bousset did not fundamentally deny the eschatological explanation of the message of Jesus by Weiss, he desired at least to modify it. Thus he set forth what he himself viewed as the major elements of Jesus' preaching. For this reason he belongs to the series of the scholars who engaged in research on the life of Jesus. It is especially worth noting the extent to which in this regard he proved to be a loyal disciple of Wellhausen. He explicitly remarks concerning Wellhausen's brief description, the "Geschichte Israels und Judas" (History of Israel and Judah), in the *Skizzen und Vorarbeiten I* (Delineations and Preparatory Works [1884]): "I owe especially from all the appropriate writings the most to the wonderful and grand description of Wellhausen in this outline" (10 n. 1). Bousset begins his portrayal of "late Judaism" with the period of the Maccabees and characterizes it as apocalyptic (10–11). This corresponds to Wellhausen. Bousset remarks: "In late Judaism there is no actual, living power, and no creative spirit. The basis of Judaism has ascended to a purely transcendent and resigned point of view that is characterized by a flight from the present world. This is coupled with a legal striving after holiness" (38). For Bousset, Judaism has developed in the apocalypse "a true aptitude for hate" (46 n. 2). Indeed, he attributes to Judaism in addition to the expansion of a worldview a change in the conception of God and the spiritualization of the prophetic future hope. However, this stands in tension with a narrow nationalism. The proclamation of Jesus is defined in principle, then, by its opposition to Judaism. This includes his speaking of God as the father, his demand for a new righteousness in the form of service to one's neighbors, his contest with legal casuistry, and a false worship following the spirit of the prophets (54). Jesus' "entire life" is characterized "by the feeling of an absolute opposition between his time and himself" (58). To be certain, Bousset was familiar also with the other side, according to which the lines of connection lead from Judaism to Jesus. Here one finds in Jesus an aversion to the world, which leads to his expectation of an imminent end of the world (65). A distance between Ritschl and Bousset lies in the following expressions in which the latter makes it clear that the work of culture (as work in the "kingdom of God") cannot be the final purpose of life. "No statement, can be taken as the starting point of dogmatics" (77). "Rather, finally the purpose of individual life consists in arriving at clearness about the last aims, in penetrating to its deepest reality" (74). It is here that Jesus' preaching is authoritative to a greater degree.

Bousset had to continue in his position as an associate professor for an unusual length of time. This was surely due in part to his political leanings, which made him suspicious in a Prussia under a conservative government. He came to this position in view of the social climate that was generated in Germany by industrialization. The situation of the uprooted masses of workers aroused in him sympathy and concern. They lived in the industrial quarters surviving on starvation wages in the context of social adversity, and the church, on account of its relationship with the partially authoritarian state government, was estranged from this social environment. Already as a student, Bousset was a disciple of the Prussian chaplain of the court, Adolf Stöcker (1835–1909), but this came to nothing as a result of the failure of the Christian Social Party. Later, Bousset attached himself to Friedrich Naumann (1860–1919) and became a member of a new party, the National Social Union, which, however, proved unsuccessful. Stöcker and Naumann both were alarmed by the strong increase in the number of Social Democrats. In the election for the empire's parliament in 1890, they received 1.5 million votes. Bismarck's "Socialists law" of 1878 had rather invigorated them. Stöcker and Naumann were especially alarmed by the prevailing anti-Christian ideology developing under the influence of Marxism. Beginning in 1874, one of the leaders, August Bebel (1840–1913), disseminated a new writing disposed to propaganda, entitled "Christentum and Sozialismus," according to which these two ideologies stand opposite each other like "fire and water." Stöcker and Naumann wished to counter this by the founding of a Christian, nationally minded, socially engaged movement, whose activity, however, would remain narrowly limited. In 1898 Bousset failed in an attempt to be a candidate for election to the parliament. Later the party merged with the left-leaning Liberal Federation. Naumann was elected as a representative to the parliament in 1907 and with a small group of like-minded representatives could introduce his agenda. In addition, one sought to work in common with the Social Democrats, who continued to increase in strength. Bousset participated also in the preparations of a further merger of all left-leaning liberals, leading to the chair of a commission. This merger led in 1910 to the formation of the Progressive People's Party. In the parliamentary election in 1912, this newly merged party had as its first chairman, Naumann.

This political activity made Bousset highly unpopular with the Prussian government, a fact that, in addition to his critical attitude toward church tradition, stood in the way of his academic career. Once even disciplinary measures against him were considered. A possible call to Heidelberg, where the faculty had recommended him for a chair in New Testament, fell through in 1897. He experienced a similar rejection twice in Leiden in 1903.

As a result of his collaborative work with his brother, Hermann (1871–1953), who was the business manager with the publishing house Gebauer-Schwetschke in Halle (Saale), later then with Mohr (Siebeck) in Tübingen, the series Religionsgeschichtlichen Volksbücher (Laymen's Books on the History of Religion) was published. To this series Bousset submitted popular contributions, entitled *Das Wesen der Religion* (The Nature of Religion [1903]) and *Jesus* (1904). An essential concern of his was the religious education of the laity.

Bousset was also engaged in liberal church politics. When the pastor H. Weingart was deposed from his office in 1899, because he denied both the bodily resurrection of Jesus and his divinity, Bousset collected writings of protest against this action. In spite of difficulties, he contributed to his party energetically as a member of the Hanover provincial synod (1905, 1912). In addition, he campaigned for the liberal General Evangelical-Protestant Missions Union. Despite his theological radicalism, he was actually a pious person.

In the meantime, after the publication of his major works, Bousset's scholarly reputation had grown outside of Germany. Above all one should mention his commentary *Die Offenbarung Johannis* (The Revelation of John [1896]), in which he pointed to numerous parallels from the history of ancient Oriental religions to the images of the Apocalypse. Also among his important works are *Die Religion des Judentums im neutestamentlichen Zeitalter* (The Religion of Judaism during the Period of the New Testament [1903]), the *Hauptprobleme der Gnosis* (The Main Problems of Gnosticism [1907]), and finally the description of the history of the faith in Christ in the ancient church, *Kyrios Christos* (1913). In Göttingen, his achievements were honored rather late (not before 1915). He was elected as a regular member to the Academy of Science. Finally, at the end of 1915, at fifty years of age, Bousset was called to a professorship that was open in the small theological faculty in Giessen, where Gunkel was dean at the time. He was to enjoy this position for only four years. While he was there, he was popular among the students as a compelling teacher.

Bousset's early death often has been associated with the results of the famine in the last years of the war and shortly thereafter, but this is medically uncertain. He died suddenly at his desk from a heart attack on March 8, 1920.

Die Religion des Judentums im neutestamentlichen Zeitalter (The Religion of Judaism in the New Testament Period) was a groundbreaking work. In the foreword of the first edition, Bousset explains "that the comprehensive description of late Judaism which I here have provided … can have only the significance of a first attempt" (*Religion des Judentums*, 1903, viii). Actually, it was not only something new at that time, but also became a standard work in the third edition redacted by H. Gressmann, which was reprinted in 1966. The interest in so-called late Judaism at the time of the turn of the century was rather intense (in reference to the wider history of Judaism one speaks today rather of "early Judaism"). Thus, Emil Schürer had written a well-known *Geschichte des jüdischen Volkes im Zeitalter Jesu Christi* (History of the Jewish People in the Period of Jesus Christ [1907]), in which the religious ideas of Judaism only constituted one aspect. Bousset was occupied with the periods of the Maccabean time (after 164 B.C.E.), continuing until the final defeat of the Jews by the Romans in 135 C.E. Something of the character of the work is indicated by the selection of the sources: Bousset mainly draws upon the intertestamental (Apocrypha) and Hellenistic Jewish literature, occasionally also on New Testament writings, while he scarcely refers to the later rabbinic writings from the Mishnah to the Talmud, as well as the Midrashim (commentaries on biblical books). Therefore, he was attacked from the Orthodox Jewish side (Felix Perles, rabbi in Königsberg, wrote a sharp critique), probably incorrectly, for Bousset explained also in the first edition of his work that he could use this material only with great reluctance, since there any systematic treatment of it was lacking. Therefore, it may be uncertain how far this material may have contained authentic views of early Judaism (44). Corresponding to the historical principle, he wished to support contemporary sources, which begin with the last few writings of the Old Testament, such as the book of Daniel, Psalms classified as Maccabean, the apocalyptic literature of Enoch, the book of Jubilees, the Testament of the Twelve Patriarchs, the Psalms of Solomon, 1 Maccabees, the Sibylline Oracles, the Life of Adam and Eve, the Ascension of Isaiah (Ascensio Isaiae), and, from the diaspora, the Letter of Aristeas, the Wisdom of Solomon, 2 Maccabees, and especially the works of Philo of Alexandria. There are also some apocalypses and the writings of Josephus (6–53).

From this itemization of texts one sees how Bousset saw Judaism in the periods handled by him. He demarcates this Judaism from later rabbinic Judaism, which begins to develop after the final defeat at the hands of the Romans in 135 c.e. The Judaism he describes is distinct from Israel in the Old Testament.

> There is found depicted a Jewish church and a worldwide expansion and comprehensiveness, in which the cult in the temple has declined in importance in comparison to the religion of the synagogue.... A sacred canon originated and an interpretation of Scripture developed based on fixed rules; the scribes became the theologians who have taken over leadership in the area of religion. (448)

Bousset entitles the second section of his work "The Development of Jewish Piety to the Church" (54–184), thus underlining the importance of this aspect. The word "piety" is to be accentuated, for Bousset often approaches this topic. In addition, he begins not with monotheism (a corresponding section he added first in the second edition), but rather with eschatology. Monotheism is the presupposition of "the great inheritance of the past" (291), although the apocalyptic background is much more central for the specifically late Jewish piety, faith, and hope. In apocalyptic the universal aspects are fundamental.

Besides this universalism, Bousset notes, however, also a continuing particularism in speaking of the national character of Judaism. He entitles the third section: "The national limit of the Jewish Religion" (185–276). In this sphere belong, among other things, the messianic hopes (199–229). At the same time, Bousset sees the particularism, however, as further diminished in apocalyptic (229–73). A new view of this and the future life originated in an all-encompassing worldview, associated with the idea of successive, cosmic periods and the expectation of the destruction of the world, cosmic renewal, and resurrection of the dead. "They stand disproportionately beside and above the old messianic thinking" (448).

In addition, Bousset claims to have observed a development toward individualism. He dedicates the fourth section to this, "Individual Faith and Theology" (277–404). "Overall ... religion begins to separate itself from national life, the life of the nations.... And here and there the principle of religious individualism awakens. The individual begins to demand his right and his place in life, and religion will procure for him the satisfaction of this claim" (451). Interest in the hereafter and in an individual final judgment arises. The deity becomes more spiritualized and further removed from everyday existence. On the other hand, cosmological speculations awaken in apocalyptic, and the old earthly messianic hopes continue to exist in different ways.

These strong alterations are considered in the concluding sixth section, "The Problem of Religions History" (448–93). There is the question whether these ideas may "still be grasped as a genuine development from the religion of the prophets and the psalms or whether one has to reckon with a manifold influx of foreign elements of religion" (449). This question is answered positively in terms of the latter. The so-called late Judaism is a syncretistic religion. On occasion this is because its character is an inferior imitation and uncreative: "The original spirit is missing" (ibid.). In addition, the period of Alexander the Great and the Diadochoi (the time of Hellenism) has been "a time of general amalgamation." "The boundaries of the nations disappear, when nations begin to speak a common language. This occurs in terms of external and spiritual features. The same ideas and thoughts pervade the nations, whose religions flow into one another. Should it have been that Judaism alone had not participated in these movements?" (450). Bousset did not trust the movement toward dissociation from Hellenism, which had been going on since the period of the Maccabees, would win out over time. For his entire description it is characteristic that he assessed Judaism from the sources of the period he examined, which were removed from later rabbinic orthodoxy. These sources were preserved only because they continued to be transmitted in the Christian sphere. Incidentally, he tends to regard late Judaism in its essence as a common phenomenon: "as great as the differences between ... Palestinian (Babylonian) Pharisaism and the (Alexandrian) Diaspora Judaism, unity prevails in the two forms" (2).

It is characteristic for Bousset that he seeks the pattern for Jewish apocalyptic in Iran (Persia) (475–93). He points to the dualism that is dominant in Iranian apocalypticism, to the savior known as Saoshyant (477), and to the speculations of Philo over the hypostases (independent personifications) of God, which correspond to Persian speculations about the divine Amesha Spentas. He compares the figure of the Son of Man and Philo's speculations (*De opificio mundi* §134ff.) on the first and second man (taking Gen 1 and Gen 2 side by side) with the conceptions of the primeval man of the environment and names, among others, the Iranian primeval man Gayomarthia. He designates the origin of this concept as "a great riddle of the history of religion" (348). For the conception of the "Son of Man," Bousset seeks to demonstrate that the supernatural appearance of the "Son of Man" in the Ethiopic book of Enoch and 4 Ezra 13 is completely new for the thought world of ancient Israel and does not likely go back to Dan 7:27, where this transcendent phenomenon collectively means Israel (248–55). In general, Bousset underscores that most of the parallels are between Jewish and Iranian apocalyptic, in spite of the fact that there are some differences. For Bousset, these themes do not consist in the esoteric speculations of eccentric literati, but rather are phenomena that belong to "the piety of the people and the masses" (492). Subsequently, history-of-religions research does not occupy itself with the history of ideas. A far-reaching goal of Bousset is announced in the brief remark that this new popular piety is "reflected in the New Testament, particularly the synoptic Gospels" (ibid.). Taking the long view of this matter, Bousset's work on late Judaism is considered to be a preparation for his concentration on the New Testament.

In the beginning, Bousset had allowed little possibility of Babylonian influence on Judaism (452–54). He later revised this judgment and viewed Babylonian astronomy as a positive influence but considered faith in demons and magic a negative influence on Persian-Hellenistic Judaism (1926, 475–78). Yet he continued to express the view that "one may accept *a priori* the existence of a much greater amount of essential influence of Iranian-Zarathustrian religion" on Judaism (1926, 478).

Bousset ends with the twofold statement that the concept of a future life did not succeed in clarifying "the fanatically national, particularistic, limited thoughts of the future found in Israelite religion. The religion of Judaism directly contains, therefore, a contradictory image." "One had to come who was greater than the apocalyptic thinker and the rabbinic theology. There had to happen in the Gospel a regeneration, before the seething chaos could arise once more and threaten the unity and vitality of a more authentic and true piety" (1903, 493). The judgment expressed concerning Judaism remains ambivalent. Finally, particularism prevailed: "Judaism remains a religion that is chained to a single people" (86). This decision occurred after 70 c.e., when in the Mishnah and the Talmud the tendency to exclusivity gained the upper hand, and Christianity became the heir of the worldwide Jewish mission and along with it universalism (ibid.). In the reproach of particularism, there is apparent one of the ideological specifications that Bousset shared with cultural Protestantism and that moved him to his one-sided judgment about Judaism. On the other hand, "Judaism has laid the groundwork of this in an honest manner ... by appropriating essential elements of foreign religion.... Finally, it is not the case that only one religion has contributed to the progress of Christianity, for it came into contact with the religions of the western cultures, in particular Hellenism" (493). One cannot accuse Bousset of anti-Semitism.

Just as important as Bousset's works in the history of religion is his research on the major problems of *gnōsis* (*Hauptprobleme der Gnosis* [1907]). In his introduction to this topic, he describes the status of Gnostic research at the time. The understanding of Gnosticism fluctuated between the conception represented especially by Harnack, in which *gnōsis* is seen to be a Greek philosophical movement that represents "an acute Hellenization of Christianity," and the opposite view, according to which Gnosticism has to be especially regarded as an Oriental religious worldview especially as observed in the cultic nature and myths. This history of religion view was, at that time, in its earliest stages. With his work, Bousset succeeded in leading it finally to its triumph in the study of religion.

In the individual chapters of his book, Bousset treats the Gnostic conceptions of the seven divine planets (ch. 1; Bousset considers this to have a Babylonian origin), the "mother," the "unknown father" (ch. 2; Bousset reflects on the Near Eastern mother deities and assumes a Persian origin for the "unknown" God), Gnostic—originally Persian—dualism (ch. 3), the motif of the primeval man (ch. 4; also here Bousset assumes an Oriental origin), the doctrine of the elements who turn into the hypostases (ch. 5), the form of the Gnostic redeemer (ch. 6, concerning which Bousset thinks of a myth of the Babylonian god Marduk; only later had this form been identified with the historical figure of Jesus Christ), and the cultic practice of Gnostic sects in the mystery religions (ch. 7). With this Bousset has supplied for the first time a common description of Gnosis as a special religion. It is, however, especially confusing and complex, because it shows itself as having split into countless sects. According to Bousset, the idea of the primeval man was originally alien to Gnosticism and was subsequently inserted into its major concepts (*Gnosis*, 331). Bousset formulates one of the most important results of his research in the concluding chapter (8), which summarizes the major teachings of the Gnostic system: "It is now rather remarkable that we can state rather clearly that a number of these sects for all intents and purposes represent a pagan religion. It has almost nothing, or nearly nothing, to do with Christianity, or it is veiled with an entirely thin Christian veneer" (323). By contrast, Bousset discovers in Gnosticism a dependence on the Old Testament in spite of its strongly anti-Jewish attitude.

Without question, Bousset's work in this period was a pioneering effort and has continued to be a standard source, offering for the first time a complete overview. In the interim, Gnostic research has certainly continued and has been invigorated through the discovery of new texts. Bousset's thesis of a pre-Christian origin of Gnosticism and the Oriental source of its motifs has become improbable, but there remains an impenetrable darkness concerning the beginnings of this movement.

Bousset's major work on the New Testament is his book *Kyrios Christos: Geschichte des Christusglaubens von den Anfängen des Christentums bis Irenäus* (Kyrios Christos: A History of the Belief in Christ from the Beginnings of Christianity to Irenaeus [1913]). This book may be put in its proper context when one takes into consideration the presuppositions of Bousset's worldview. These assumptions had been determined since his days as a student when he studied Thomas Carlyle. (Ernst Troeltsch [in Lüdemann and Schröder 1987, 23] reports that, at the time he and Bousset were students in Erlangen [1884–85], one usually read "the Romantics, Fichte, and Carlyle.") Thomas Carlyle (1795–1881) belonged to the writers *en vogue* in the nineteenth century. In 1897, Bousset published an extensive description of Carlyle in the journal *Christliche Wissenschaft*. Carlyle was attractive to him for two things: his emphasis on the great personality as the resourceful individual who is immediately connected to God and directs the course of history during creative moments, and his argument that in a revolutionary era stagnant forms are usually broken apart. Carlyle also argues that hero worship is the kernel of the entire social order. Carlyle, whose eyes were opened early by the social crisis in England during the Industrial Age in the first half of the nineteenth century, called on the leading personalities of his country to care for the needs of the working masses. Early on, this corresponded to Bousset's demonstrated social engagement (when he was still an adherent of Stöcker and used to read his "Reichsbote"). Revolutionary situations of crisis are reflected, for him, in apocalyptic images, which are not visions of a single person but rather the expression of a seething disposition of the masses, who envision the collapse of the older authorities and hope for a new order. This disposition prepares for the appearance of new leading figures.

In *Kyrios Christos,* Bousset shapes from these presuppositions his history of Christian faith. It is characteristic of the approach of the history of religion school that the boundaries of the canon were knowingly exceeded. In this volume, Bousset continues to examine the development of Christianity and its theology reaching to the church father Irenaeus (see *History,* vol. 1). As Bousset expressly declares in the foreword to the first edition, "one treats here the removal of the partition between New Testament theology and the dogmatic history of the primitive Church" (1921, iv). At the same time, the view to which Ritschl adhered, that the main propositions of the New Testament could be understood from those found in the Old Testament, is abandoned. Bousset instead sees the break much more in the fashion of the history of religion, that is, in the transition of Christianity into a pagan environment. "No event can be compared to this in its importance." Besides, Bousset was committed to researching, as had been done many times before, "the separation of the religious history of primeval Christianity from the common development of religious life that surrounds Christianity in the period of its early youth" (v). The demand for a history of primeval Christian literature already arose at the end of the nineteenth century in the work of scholars such as A. Eichhorn and G. Krüger. W. Wrede had required, in a lecture entitled "Über Aufgabe und Methode der sogenannten neutestamentlichen Theologie" (Concerning the Purpose and Method of So-called New Testament Theology [1897]), that this discipline treat living religion as the history of piety instead of presenting the teachings and dogmas of the New Testament.

Because Bousset saw the break in the transition of Christianity into a pagan environment, he regards the two initial chapters of his book, which treat the first three Gospels on the basis of the faith of the ancient church in Palestine and Jerusalem, as only the introduction or prelude to the volume's full description (ibid.). This applies only in respect to the structure of the work, for he makes it clear in the conflict with his critics (*Jesus der Herr* [Jesus the Lord], 1916, 94–95) that, in his view, "the figure of Jesus and the piety of the ancient community by all means are not achieved" in the Hellenistic communities. It should be mentioned that, in these chapters, Bousset holds, in opposition to his earlier view, the self-designation of Jesus as the "Son of Man" to be substantially a creation of the community (5, 35). An emphasis of his description can be found in chapter 3,

"The Pagan Christian Primitive Community" (75–104). While the titles of Christ (= Messiah) and the Son of Man were characteristic of the Palestinian and Jerusalem early community, they recede into the background later on. Their place is taken by the title *Kyrios* (Herr, "Lord"). Bousset seeks the history of religion origin of this title (91–99) in the Roman emperor cult, which had its prototypes in the Oriental-Hellenistic sphere, more precisely in Syria and Egypt. From there comes also the religious usage of the title as a designation of the deity. Added to that, Bousset wishes to establish that the title *Kyrios* may be given especially to the gods who stand in the center of a cult (98). Although Bousset does not use the expression "setting in life" (*Sitz im Leben*), he does argue that the cult of the first Hellenistic communities provides the context for Christian usage. On Sunday, the "Lord's Day," the community gathers together around the Lord on whose name they call. For this matter, Bousset reflects on the conclusion of the Philippian hymn in Phil 2:9–11. Besides the spiritually moving experiences of the gatherings for worship, which Bousset describes in a lively manner, they are important to him also as social phenomena. In the worship services, "those who believe in Christ gained the awareness of their unity and their unique sociological closeness." They experienced "the wonder of the community" (89). Bousset is certain that the Hellenistic community took the title *Kyrios* out of the environment and not out of the Old Testament (where it is to be found as a translation of *Adonai* in the Septuagint or Greek version). The way it came to this, according to his view, reflects Carlyle: it is a collective phenomenon. "These kinds of processes take place unconsciously, in the uncontrollable depth of the common psyche shared by a community; this launches out from itself and is, as it were, in the wind." "The young Christian religion, with the one Lord Jesus Christ, has faced the many lords of the Hellenistic cults with a formerly unheard of one-sidedness and with a bold defiance" (99). In *Jesus der Herr* (39), Bousset stresses once again "that even to me, when I position him in this milieu, the faith in the Lord of the early community appears as an enormously great religious deed." To be sure, for Bousset the tracing of the title back to the Lord of the Old Testament is *secondary*. Bousset lists the many Old Testament passages that appear with this title in the New Testament. In this way, he is able to bring the title into conformity with his theory (*Kyrios*, 101). In *Jesus der Herr*, Bousset concedes that what his critics have charged may be true: that his description may have been one-sided in favor of the Hellenistic-Roman milieu of the environment of the New Testament and that one perhaps may find in Paul "a good deal of the Old Testament and the

Gospel of Jesus" (76). The forms in which this asserts itself he regards as still problematic. The notion that the title *Kyrios* originates in the setting of worship has been regarded in contemporary scholarship as doubtful. This theory has too little support from New Testament texts.

Bousset follows another prototype of intellectual history in his assessment of Paul. He contrasts the "personal Christ-piety of the apostle Paul" with the community and worship-bound faith in *Kyrios*. Characteristic of this is "the intensive feeling of the personal affiliation and the spiritual connectedness with the exalted Lord" (104). For Bousset, Rom 6 is evidence that Paul takes up the sacramental event of baptism. This indicates that he was seized "by and liberates this cultic experience, which is only grasped in the contemporary climate as a mystery. He liberates this experience from the dullness of bondage, turns it into the personal sphere, and interprets it spiritually and morally, thus expanding it." The Pauline epistles provide Bousset with "the means to overhear this intimate process of the development of personal mysticism from the cultic mystic, which is so significant for the history of religion" (107). Bousset speaks in this manner of the "mysticism of Christ" and calls it a stage that moves beyond "cultic mysticism" in the stages of the history of religion. He thus regards Paul's "mysticism of Christ" as "cultic mysticism." Here once again is the frequently documented, negative evaluation of the cult that came to expression in the period of the Enlightenment. In the preceding section of his investigation, Bousset only seemingly overcame this negative view. Yet one can also point to the positive side of Bousset's assessment in his preoccupation with the philosophy of religion developed by J. F. Fries (see above, 238–39). Bousset condensed this in an essay he published in the *Theologische Rundschau* in 1909. Since Bousset had become familiar with the aesthetic, emotional approach of Fries to religion, a new perspective had been opened to him, which he combined with the aspects appropriated from Carlyle. The tendency is one of a conscious return to German Idealism. An authentic understanding of Pauline theology certainly could not grow from this. By contrast, Bousset declares that "the duplication of the object of faith," which may enter with the Pauline proclamation of faith in Christ, remains "a strong and burdensome riddle." (*Jesus der Herr*, 40). This view was in response to the criticism of his friend Paul Wernle (1872–1939), who accused him of speaking of Paul's mysticism of Christ in place of faith in Christ (*Jesus der Herr*, 40). When the assessment by the ancient church's apologists (esp. 1 Clement; see *History*, vol. 1) reflects this mystical characteristic, Bousset gives preference to them and also to the "Gospel of Jesus" over against the "Pauline-Gnostic faith in salvation." Thus, when religion appears foreign to humans due to the one-sided thinking about salvation, when it is subsumed by the power coming from above, and when the best and the highest possessed by a human stands in contrast to his natural being ... then the apologists certainly possess very little of this kind of religion. (*Kyrios*, 329)

Bousset treats the Johannine texts as a unity (ch. 5, 154–83). Faith in the Son of God as the light that illuminates the darkness is central. The statement in John 10:30 according to which Father and Son are one is important. Jesus is "the Son of God or God who wanders upon the earth" (159). Although the name of *Kyrios* is avoided, it is used by "vulgar Christianity, which is developed on Hellenistic, Oriental soil," when its members encounter the risen Lord in the service of the community (158). Still, there is also something human that remains. "The Word became flesh" (John 1:14). Bousset also speaks here of the mysticism of Christ. However, in contrast to Paul, its fire in this Gospel has almost been extinguished. On the other hand, it has become the "mysticism of God": "Deification takes place through the vision of God" (164) and is fulfilled in the image of the Son of God appearing on the earth (168). This is the *gnōsis* of the Gospel of John (171). In the background of the dualism of light and darkness stands the opposition between the Johannine community and the world, especially the Jews and the heretics. The distinction between the Pauline and Johannine mysticism of Christ consists in the fact that for Paul it was "the power of the spirit raging from heaven," while for John it was "the mild, radiating, warming, and fruit-bearing light" (181). The roots of this mysticism grow in the ground of Hellenistic piety, not in the preaching of Jesus and not in the Old Testament. Bousset finds prior images of this in the mystery cult, with the view of God as the highest point in the astronomical worldview. To be sure, this does not involve direct dependence, but rather points to the milieu from which Johannine piety is understood. Certainly there exists a connection to the Old Testament-Jewish tradition that continues in the assumption of the title of the "Son of Man" from Jewish apocalyptic (155–56).

In more recent discussion of the background of intellectual history regarding Johannine literature, there continue to be those who point to a Gnostic background, and others who stress the Jewish-Christian origin of this specific world of thought. Here Bousset was the inspirer, not the originator of the final answers.

Kyrios Christos is rightly considered the crest of the work of the history of religion school. The scope of the materials handled in this work deserves this honor. Although Bousset's theological point of view is strongly one-sided, as observed already by his contemporaries, his significance for New Testament scholarship remains and can scarcely be overestimated. While he opened to scholarship the wide horizon of the historical, religious environment of the New Testament, he also developed decisively new perspectives as well.

7.3. Interpreting Jesus' Proclamation of the Kingdom of God as the Announcement of the End Time: Johannes Weiss

Johannes Weiss was born in Kiel in 1863, the son of a professor of New Testament, Bernhard Weiss (1827–1918), and of Hermine Weiss, whose birth surname was von Woyna. He had two sisters and one brother. His father had just been called to a chair in Kiel prior to the birth of Johannes. While growing up in the house of his parents, he received their considerable support in the development of his talent and knowledge of music, which played a significant role in his life. His mother was gifted in both music and painting. Thus, he was raised in a cultured family. In 1877, he accompanied the family's move to Berlin, where his father had received a call. His inclinations to music, literature, and art struggled within him for a long time, but Karl Büchsel (1803–1889), the general superintendent who instructed him during his confirmation studies, awakened in him the desire to become a theologian. While in Berlin, he attended the Wilhelm gymnasium and received his *Abitur* there in 1882. In the summer semester of the same year, he began his studies in theology in Marburg. He came immediately into contact with the New Testament scholar Georg Heinrici (1844–1915) and the Old Testament scholar Wolf Wilhelm Graf Baudissin (1847–1926). In Heinrici's house, he also came to know Alexander Ritschl, a son of Albrecht Ritschl. This was the start of his ever-closer relationship with the Göttingen theologian and his family. At the same time, he made friends with a number of theological students, almost all of whom were disciples of Ritschl. On the advice of his father, he transferred to Berlin beginning in the winter semester in 1882–83 and from there went to Göttingen in the winter semester in 1884–1885. While in Göttingen he frequently visited the Ritschl home and was particularly close to him and his family. He often attended Ritschl's lectures and affiliated with the circle of young theologians who were established around Ritschl and came to be known, and we saw above, as the history of religion school. Having passed his first theological exams in February 1886, his student days came to an end. After a half year in Breslau, he fulfilled his military duties as a one-year volunteer in Potsdam and prepared himself for his examinations to become a licentiate. His work for becoming a licentiate, *Der Barnabasbrief kritisch untersucht* (The Letter of Barnabas Critically Investigated), was published in 1888. Afterwards he stood for the colloquium before the faculty and gave his public defense, for which he was awarded the *magna cum laude*. He then offered a trial lecture on "Exegese des Neuen Testaments" (Exegesis of the New Testament) and was awarded the *venia legendi* (instructor's permit). Between these events, he became engaged to Auguste Ritschl, whom he married in the summer of 1889, following the death of her father for whom he had cared during his final illness.

Weiss was the first of the "small Göttingen faculty" to complete his *Habilitation*. His personal association with Ritschl was combined with the latter's strong theological influence on him. Not only Weiss, but the entire younger, theological generation was gripped by Ritschl's understanding of the "kingdom of God" as a field of endeavor for ethical works. The relationship of this present, practical understanding of the idea helped to shape the later New Testament work of Weiss, which must now occupy us.

In the year 1890, Weiss was named an associate professor. The subsequent period led to the publication of his major work, *Die Predigt Jesu vom Reiche Gottes* (The Preaching of Jesus concerning the Kingdom of God [1892]). In 1895, he was called to a chair in Marburg, where he continued until 1908. It is worth noting that he, like Bousset (see above, 360), was active in F. Naumann's National Social Union. In 1896, he belonged to the founding members. Thus, he advocated a fundamental separation between the Gospel and politics. In an anonymous series of articles in the first year of Naumann's weekly paper, *Die Hilfe* (1895), he wrote under the fiction "Letters to a Worker" on the question, "Who was Jesus of Nazareth?" Here he stresses the fundamental strangeness of the situation and preaching of Jesus to the contemporary context and the program of Social Democrats. He was also active as a city councillor in Marburg from 1905 to 1908. He was the editor of the popular biblical series *Die Schriften des Neuen Testaments, neu übersetzt und für die Gegenwart erklärt* (The Scriptures of the New Testament, Newly Translated and Explained for the Present)—the outgrowth of the respected Old Testament series—and author of several of its commentaries. From his time in Marburg, there were reports of his inspiring teaching and his great interest in the personal condition of the students.

Weiss filled the New Testament chair in Heidelberg in 1908, when Bousset was passed over owing to the resistance of the conservative dogmatician Ludwig Lemme (1847–1927). This appointment brought Weiss to the city on the Neckar, where he spent the last years of his life. There Weiss expected also to have a better occasion for possible church involvement in the liberal Baden regional church. In regard to writing, he was at this time in the stages of the preparation of his last major work *Das Urchristentum* (Primitive Christianity). He was able to publish the first volume in 1914, but his serious illness from cancer made it impossible for him to finish the entire project. His friend, New Testament scholar Rudolf Knopf (1884–1920), edited the remainder of the work, which appeared posthumously in 1917. Weiss died in August 1914 at the young age of fifty-one.

Weiss is significant especially because of *Die Predigt Jesu vom Reiche Gottes*. On the one hand, Weiss's theological thinking emphasized the influence of the idea of the "kingdom of God," which was current in the field of ethics because of his teacher, Ritschl. Weiss's practical political engagement corresponded to this idea, and he verbalized it also theoretically. In the introduction to the first edition of his work, he (against the confessional theology of his day) advocates "not to take any more the justification doctrine of Paul, but the major thought of the preaching of Jesus as the starting point and center for the construction of systematic theology." One then could combine dogmatics and ethics. "The artificial isolation of religious experiences, 'the work of God on humanity,' from the religious, moral reactions of the individual, is a necessary consequence of the separation of both disciplines" (*Predigt*, 1892, 5; 1964, 217). The main thought of the proclamation of Jesus, the message of the kingdom of God, would be received in preaching, when it "seriously and enthusiastically calls together humans into the Kingdom of God. This is the community of those who are committed to God as King and Leader of their lives, and place their powers in his service" (6, 218).

Thus, it is even more remarkable how Weiss now sets to work in order to subject Jesus' message of the kingdom of God to historical examination. That the original meaning is different from its contemporary usage does not disturb him. In all spheres of spiritual life, ideas are used that in later generations are reshaped to have new meanings. Even so, one must continue to be conscious of this. This opens the way to a presupposition-free investigation when it comes to determining how Jesus may have originally understood the idea. It is necessary to penetrate to the "original historical sense, which Jesus associated with the words, 'kingdom of God'" (7, 229) without engaging in conflict with the present practice of the church. Thereby Weiss comes to far-reaching new understandings, which signified a turning point for New Testament criticism.

The first edition of the book, which comprised ony sixty-seven pages, had a sensational effect. In the second edition (1900), Weiss dispensed with the systematic introduction, undertook numerous modifications, and yet also attenuated and defused many of his sharply stated arguments. However, he continued to stand by his basic interpretation. Although in the meantime he realized "that the actual roots of the ideas of Ritschl reside among those of Kant and the theology of the Enlightenment" (Foreword to the Second Edition = 1964, xiii), he still considered their thoughts of the kingdom of God to be "that form of the teaching of faith, … which at most is adapted to bring near the Christian religion to our generation and … to awaken and cultivate a sound and powerful religious life as we require today" (xi).

A glance at the first edition shows in an impressive manner the innovation of his knowledge. After a brief overview of the sources, Weiss begins with the passage of Mark 1:15, where the message of Jesus is summarized: "The time is fulfilled and the kingdom of God has drawn near. Repent and believe the Gospel." The same message is applied by Jesus during his speech concerning the sending of the disciples in Matt 10:7; similarly, this idea occurs in the commission of the seventy-two in Luke 10:9. While formulated with different Greek verbs (Weiss assumes that the same Aramaic word existed in the primal text) the message in Matt 12:28 and Luke 11:20 has the same meaning. So far it appears clear: for Jesus, the kingdom of God is near. The strongest argument for this—that God's kingdom is imminent—is found in the first petition of the Lord's Prayer: "Thy kingdom come."

Now the question arises, "*In which sense* had Jesus already spoken of the presence" of the kingdom of God (1892, 13 = 1964, 221)? The passages that especially address this question are Matt 12:28 and Luke 17:21. These are explained by Weiss as having an apocalyptic perspective, according to which Jesus, as the bearer of the Spirit of God, leads the battle against the kingdom of Satan. Since the might of Satan in this battle is already broken, Jesus is able to speak in such passages of a kingdom of God that has already broken into history. "However, these are moments of lofty prophetic inspiration, where a consciousness of victory overwhelms him" (21, 223). In the background of this thinking stands the concept of a "twofold world," that of humans and that of angels; that is, the earthly events are only consequences or activity of the heavenly ones (1892, 26). These are, however, only isolated passages; most references to speak primarily of a future establishment of the kingdom. There is no evidence for the designation of Jesus in dogmatic theology as the "founder" of the kingdom of God. Instead, *the proclamation of the imminent coming of the kingdom of God* along with the battle against the kingdom of Satan is prominent in the activity of Jesus. Weiss stresses "that the same in principle does not differ, at least in the beginning, from the preaching of the Baptist" (24, 224). The call to repent and the announcement of the kingdom of God are two themes that coincide. This is important also in another respect: Jesus' entire activity is not messianic but rather is simply preparatory. Moreover, Jesus does not primarily lay claim to the title "Son of Man." "Since Jesus now is a rabbi and a prophet, he has nothing in common with the Son of Man, other than to issue the demand to become like him" (ibid.). Further, the words of Jesus at the Last Supper tell that he will no longer drink from the fruit of the vine until the kingdom of God is come (Luke 22:18). He will drink it anew with them in the kingdom (Mark 14:25). He possesses only an entitlement to the kingdom of God, nothing more (1964, 96). Jesus was no revolutionary. He warns against trying to bring about the kingdom of God by force (Matt 11:12). The one who is resurrected says to his disciples that the time and hour for its coming are reserved to the Father alone (Acts 1:7). Weiss brings forth detailed expressions about the final judgment, which, according to the message of Jesus, will be combined with the return of the Messiah and the establishment of the kingdom of God. (In the second edition these were significantly abbreviated.) The speeches in Luke 17:22–37 and Mark 13 provide the most detailed disclosure. The images that Jesus uses here must remain in their strangeness. In no case may they be "spiritually" reinterpreted (1964, 106). That God would renew the entire world in the messianic age was a view that was widespread in contemporary Judaism. Subsequently, the establishment of the kingdom on the earth is introduced by the judgment, a point that Jesus holds in common with John the Baptist.

Weiss explains contradictory statements of Jesus as the result of an "inconsistent form of popular thought" (1964, 113). Whereas Mark 9:42–48 especially presupposes that the hearers of Jesus, apparently still living at the time, will enter the kingdom of God ("for it is better that a bodily member be removed than for the entire body to be cast into hell"). This occurs in the story of the rich man and poor Lazarus (Luke 16:19–31). The impoverished Lazarus after his death immediately goes to Abraham's bosom, while the rich enters the place of torment. The thief on the cross, according to Luke 23:43, should "today" be with Jesus in paradise. In Weiss's view, the authentic words of Jesus occur here. Elsewhere (1892, 37 n. 1) he attributes the distinction admittedly to another source (ostensibly a Jewish Christian, Lukan source), according to which the righteous make the transition to the state of blessedness immediately after death. It remains unclear whether he imputes to Jesus the origin of the concept.

After Weiss has shown the peculiarity and different understandings of Jesus' proclamation of the kingdom of God in contrast to modern conceptions (Jesus' view is directed to the imminent coming of the kingdom—thus, an eschatological message) in the first edition, he finally returns once more to the difference from the contemporary worldview. This consists in "that we do not partake in the eschatological sentiment.... We do not pray any longer for the coming of grace and the passing away of the world, but rather we live in joyful confidence that also *this* world shall increasingly become the showplace of a 'humanity of God.'" Where this sentiment may not exist, "everything should be done in preaching and teaching in order to awaken it" (1892, 67 = 1964, 246). Weiss died in the beginning weeks of the First World War. He did not experience the terrible failure of the cultural Protestant expectations.

The acceptance of the work of Weiss varied. It was enthusiastically hailed by Albert Schweitzer as "the third great either-or in the Life of Jesus research." The first had been set forth by Strauss: either purely historical or purely supernatural. The second the Tübingen scholars and Holtzmann had struggled to reach: either a Synoptic or a Johannine Jesus. Now the third was "either an eschatological or noneschatological Jesus" (Schweitzer, *Geschichte der Leben-Jesu Forschung*, 232). Schweitzer himself pursued the same course, only more radically, in that he included the entirety of the acts of Jesus (*Geschichte*, 390–443). Other scholars pointed out that Weiss had improperly neglected the places that indicated that Jesus had regarded the kingdom of God as already arrived. But it was exactly on these passages that Weiss placed great importance. "This entwining of present and future, especially the statements about the present, cede the right caption to the dogmatic theologian. The idea of the Kingdom of God is the central concept of the Christian world view" (*Predigt*, 1892, 13 = 1964, 221). In spite of this attempt at compromise (it is still debated whether Jesus' proclamation points to a future kingdom or to one that already has broken into history), Weiss's treatment had an incisive impact on the description of the kingdom of God. Weiss had demonstrated, in contrast to the liberal interpretation of Jesus, how strange this proclamation had been. Contrary to his own intention, he had made clear that the school of Ritschl was wrong in its use of the concept of the kingdom in the Bible.

8

New Directions in the Twentieth Century

8.1. Letting God Be God in His Revelation in the Cross and Resurrection of Jesus the Christ: Karl Barth

Karl Barth was born on 10 May 1886, in Basel, the oldest son of Johann Friedrich (Fritz) Barth (1856–1912). The elder Barth was a teacher of theology at a school for preachers in Basel. The younger Barth's mother was Anna Barth, whose maiden name was Sartorius. Both grandfathers had been pastors in Basel. In 1891, Barth's father was called to the position of professor of church history at the University of Bern, although he lectured and published chiefly in the New Testament. Barth spent the greatest part of his childhood in Bern. While there, he attended the so-called *Lerberschule,* later Freies Gymnasium, which was a Christian private school in which his father taught religion. Here he passed through his entire schooling from the lowest class to the final examination for his certificate (*Maturität = Abitur*). He spent his first four semesters of theological study (1904–1906) at Bern, where he was inspired less by his professors than by his relationships in the student association, *Zofingia.* Among his fellow students at Basel, he came to know well Eduard Thurneysen (1888–1974), who was to be his closest, lifelong friend. Beginning in 1930, Thurneysen was professor of practical theology in Basel and later was an important representative of so-called dialectical theology. An interim examination (the *Propädeuticum,* preparatory exam) concluded this chapter of his studies. Afterwards, Barth went to study abroad (as a compromise with his father) for a semester in Berlin, where he studied with Harnack, Gunkel, and the dogmatic theologian Julius Kaftan (1848–1926). Harnack especially excited him. In regard to literature, he was occupied with Kant, Schleiermacher, and Wilhelm Herrmann. The summer semester (1907) he spent once more in Bern, as president of the *Zofingia*! Because of the pressure placed on him by his father, he finally went to Tübingen, where, however, he was not deterred from his liberal theological mind-set—as his father had hoped—by the significant Lutheran New Testament scholar Adolf Schlatter (1852–1938). It was first in Marburg, where he spent in 1908 his final semester, that he found *his* honored teacher, the dogmatic theologian Wilhelm Herrmann (1846–1922). In the autumn of 1908, Barth passed his second exam, was ordained by his father, and finally obtained a post in Marburg as the editorial assistant of Martin Rade (1857–1940). Rade edited the *Christliche Welt*, in which Gunkel, Bousset, and other liberal theologians published. Barth himself was now a convinced liberal!

In the years 1909–1911, Barth was active in his first church office as an assistant minister (*pasteur suffragant*) in the German-speaking congregation in Geneva. There he became engaged to one of his candidates for confirmation, Nelly Hoffmann. In 1911, he received the rectorate in Safenwil (Aargau). The ten-year period of activity in this community became fundamental for his theological development. The social relationships in this farmers' and workers' community came to affect him. The class opposition between some of the families of the factory owners and a majority of the extremely underpaid factory workers brought him to engage intensively in socialism and the movement of the labor unions. He began to hold lectures for the *Arbeitsverein* ("workers union"). Barth married in 1913, and his daughter Franziska was born in 1914. He later had four sons, two of whom (Christoph and Markus) became theology professors. He cultivated a close exchange of ideas with Thurneysen, when he received a rectorate in the neighboring community of Leutwil. With him, Barth learned to know interesting people, patrons like the well-to-do married couple Pestalozzi, and the socioreligious Zurich pastor Hermann Kutter (1863–1931), who was the representative of a "theocentric" (placing God at the center) theology. Through Kutter he also made contact with the socioreligious Leonhard Ragaz (1868–1945). The socioreligious movement at that time was widespread among Swiss pastors. Even so, Barth and Thurneysen maintained a certain inner reserve.

The outbreak of the war on 1 August 1914 signified for Barth a decisive, internal turning point. More terrible than setting in motion the event itself was

the dreadful Manifest of the 93 German intellectuals, who before the entire world identified with the politics of war espoused by Kaiser Wilhelm II and his chancellor Bethmann-Hollweg. And among those who signed their names, I must with horror also discover the names of nearly all of my teachers (with the honorable exception of Martin Rade!). An entire world of theological exegesis, ethics, dogmatics, and preaching, which I had held as credible, began to shake in its foundations. ("Nachwort," in Bolli, *Schleiermacher-Auswahl*, 293)

This "ethical failure," which Barth saw occurring in the Christian sanctioning of the war, led him to doubt not only his teachers but also their common theology. In the same way, he lamented the "failure of the German Social Democrats concerning the ideology of war." In spite of this, Barth joined the Swiss Social Democrats in 1915. Thereupon, he was addressed as "Comrade Pastor" by the workers of Safenwil. It became increasingly clear to him, however, because of the war and the continuing necessity to preach and teach that there must be something beyond (even Christian) morality and politics that he could say to his congregants in Safenwil. He received new stimulation from a visit by Christoph Blumhardt (1842–1919) in Bad Boll. His message to Barth was significant, for he spoke of Christian future hope and the expectation of the act of God as the radical renewal of the world. In the internal struggles as well as in the criticism of the bond of the Swiss church to the world, it became ever more important for Barth that in the Christian message God must be the center of importance. Especially in his reflection on the meaning of his preaching, he discovered that it was increasingly difficult, if not impossible, to speak adequately of God.

In the quest for a new theological foundation, this difficulty drove Barth and Thurneysen to attempt "a renewed learning of the theological ABC's that now would be more reflective than before, starting with an emphasis on the readings and interpretation of the writings of the Old and New Testaments" ("Nachwort," 294). In 1916, Barth began to turn to an intensive examination of the Epistle to the Romans, and he discovered there fundamentally new aspects. With the basic differentiation of the exclusive contrast between God and all things human and the kingdom of God as something new breaking in on all human efforts, Barth distanced himself not merely from liberal theology's departure from human religion, but rather also from pietism and religious socialism. In spite of disruptions, Barth produced from his notes a full-fledged commentary, which was published in December 1918. With lectures to the worker's union, however, he intervened again in politics and fell into a fierce conflict with the factory owners and the church administration.

To a large extent Barth became well known in Germany by means of the lecture that he presented in September 1919 to a socioreligious conference in Tambach (Thüringen) on the theme, "Der Christ in der Gesellschaft" (The Christian in Society [in Moltmann, *Anfänge* 1). In it he sharply demarcated Christ and the kingdom of God from all human conservative or revolutionary efforts, from piety and religion, and from religious socialism. However, Christ is still in society. "Christ is the unconditional new thing that is from above" (*Anfänge* 1:11). God's reign is directed to an attack against society, a protest against what exists, and judgment. Søren Kierkegaard (1813–1855), Leo Tolstoy (1828–1910), Friedrich Nietzsche (1844–1900), and Fyodor Dostoevsky (1821–1881) are for Barth the spokesmen for this protest, which he attributes to socialism, mysticism of the Middle Ages, the original Reformation, and Anabaptism (30). However, because God is the creator of the world, he is also its savior. Therefore, actual life can also become a parable, preeminently in the parables of Jesus, which are taken from everyday existence. Thus, one can "recognize in the worldly the analogy of the Godly and rejoice thereover" (24). God is Christ as judge and redeemer: here emerges already the later, mature theology of Barth. Barth, whose lecture made a strong impression on his hearers, who had been made uncertain and troubled by the postwar situation, obtained new friends here and soon thereafter elsewhere in Germany.

In 1920, Barth revised through additional studies his view of the Epistle to the Romans. The readings from Calvin, Kierkegaard, Nietzsche, Dostoevsky, and Franz Overbeck (1837–1905) as well as the influence of his brother, the neo-Kantian philosopher Heinrich Barth (1890–1965), who was a student of Plato and Kant, brought him back to rewrite his commentary on Romans. While Barth, in 1921, began to work on it, an invitation from Göttingen reached him, offering him a newly developed (honorary) professorship in Reformed church history. While his new interpretation was not yet finished, he accepted the offer, at the same time feeling that he was not fully prepared to undertake this office. In Göttingen, Barth was an outsider among the professors. Yet he familiarized himself with the heritage of the Reformation and developed his own theology, which, on account of its concentration on the Word of God was known as the "theology of the Word" or, because it dealt with the speech of humans with the sovereign God who confronted them, was named "dialectical theology." In 1923, Thurneysen, Friedrich Gogarten (1887–1967), and he founded the journal *Zwischen den Zeiten* (Between the Times), in which for the next ten years the theologians who were close to "dialectical theology" published their contributions. Based on an exegetical lecture on 1 Corinthians, Barth's commentary *Die Auferstehung der Toten* (The

Resurrection of the Dead) appeared at the same time. Barth held his first trimester lectures on dogmatic theology under the general rubric: "Dogmatic theology is the reflection on the Word of God as revelation, Holy Scripture, and *Christian proclamation.*" Barth emphasizes the last point. *Deus dixit* ("God has said") means "the revelation of God in and behind the Scriptures (*Karl Barth-Eduard Thurneysen Briefwechsel*, 2:251). The Scriptures are assigned a place between revelation and proclamation. The *Prolegomena zur christlichen Dogmatik* (Prolegomena to Christian Dogmatics [1927], again a fully new edition) received the subtitle *Die Lehre vom Worte Gottes* (The Doctrine of the Word of God).

In 1925, Barth followed a call to Münster to accept a chair of dogmatics and New Testament exegesis. There he immediately offered a major lecture course on the Gospel of John, followed by others on Philippians, Colossians, and a seminar on Galatians. In his last years in Münster, Barth (beginning in 1926 he was also a German citizen) became anxious over the internal political situation and the developments of the church in Germany. There were deep divisions within the circle of dialectical theologians.

In 1930, Barth was called to Bonn to accept a chair of systematic theology. With numerous students who came to Bonn to study under Barth, a period of prosperity for the Evangelical theology faculty in Bonn began. With an investigation concerning the *Proslogion* (Address) of Anselm of Canterbury (1033–1109) and his famous formula *fides quaerens intellectum* (faith seeking understanding), Barth provided (in 1931) the foundation for a new principle in his *Church Dogmatics.* This multivolume theology became his main work for the rest of his life. The new principle consisted in the fact that Barth oriented his theology strictly toward Christology. His was a theology of grace in Jesus Christ.

In 1933, Adolf Hitler assumed power in Germany. In the church battle that subsequently broke out, Barth wrote his combative *Theologische Existenz heute* (Theological Existence Today), in which he said that it would now be essential to "do theology and only theology." The teaching of the Deutsche Christen (DC, German Christians) he characterized as erroneous. When Ludwig Müller became the Reich bishop, the Deutsche Evangelische Kirche (DEK) received a constitution, and it seemed as if the Deutsche Christen would prevail. The infamous "Aryan paragraph" in the Prussian law for clergy and church officials decreed that non-Aryans and those who were married to non-Aryans would not be permitted to be employed in the service of the church. In connection with quarrels with Gogarten, because he had drawn close to the DC, Barth had ceased publishing their journal *Zwischen den Zeiten.* In its place he founded, together with his friend Thurneysen, the series Theologische Existenz heute. It was surprising that the DC was quickly ruined. A Pastors' Emergency League, later the *Bekennende Kirche* (BK, Confessing Church) was founded. The Free Reformed Synod met in Barmen at the beginning of 1934 and adopted a resolution written by Barth: "Declaration over the Correct Understanding of the Reformation's Confession in the German Evangelical Church of the Present." By the end of May, the first Confession Synod of the DEK took place and agreed to the "Theological Declaration" drawn up by Barth. The first thesis is stated in the following sentence: "Jesus Christ, as he is attested to us in Holy Scripture, is the one Word of God whom we have to hear, and whom we have to trust and obey in life and in death." In the writing entitled "No!" against the (probably misunderstood) early fellow combatant Emil Brunner (1889–1966), Barth turned sharply against any kind of natural theology and the "point of contact" viewed to be necessary by Brunner for the gospel in humans.

At the end of 1934, when Barth was required to sign the oath of allegiance to the Führer, he added the statement "in so far as I can answer it as an Evangelical Christian." This led to his suspension and, in the middle of 1935, he was finally retired. Directly after this he was named a full professor at Basel. His further academic activity he pursued while he was there, except for two semesters as a guest professor in Bonn in 1946 and 1947. During this period, he continued especially to offer lectures in dogmatic theology, which were then written down in numerous volumes of *Church Dogmatics*. At the end, however, the series was disrupted. From Switzerland, he participated by offering numerous statements that lamented the battle of the German church (later collected into a volume entitled *Eine Schweizer Stimme* [A Swiss Voice]), led the Swiss relief organization for distressed German scholars in Basel, and took care of emigrants. He was still active at the age of fifty-four in the Swiss Relief Organization. After the end of the war he declined to proceed against communism with the same sharpness. He cooperated with the national committee Freies Deutschland (Free Germany), which demanded, among other things, the taking of a position against the Vietnam War and requested the recognition of the borders in the East. Theologically important especially in the postwar period was his debate with his former fellow combatant Rudolf Bultmann (*Rudolf Bultmann: Ein Versuch ihn zu verstehen* [Rudolf Bulmann: An Effort to Understand Him], 1952). There were several important questions that Barth put to Bultmann. Through his participation in the Conference of the World Church in Amsterdam in 1948 and in conferences of preparation for the assembly in Evanston in 1951–1953,

Barth was introduced to ecumenical problems. It was not until 1962 that he was given the status emeritus. Advanced in age, he undertook a trip to Rome. In the last years of his life, he was afflicted with illnesses and underwent a number of operations. Barth died peacefully in the night of 8–9 December 1968.

The character of biblical interpretation of the young Barth one learns best from the second edition of his commentary, *The Epistle to the Romans*. The first edition had already indicated that Barth had broken with liberal theology. In the foreword to the second edition, when he spoke of what the two editions held in common, he reshaped what he had said in the brief foreword to the first edition (1922, 3–4). Although he does not regard historical-critical exegesis as superfluous, he does view it as only the preparation for the actual objective, the *factual* understanding of the Bible. He recognizes that historical criticism's accomplishments are worthy of attention. Yet he reproaches it, for having ceased at the point of "what stands there" (i.e., in the Bible). Understanding, however, comes from what it may have *meant* (1922, xi). In 1918 Barth had stated the purpose of interpretation: "one is to see through the historical the spirit of the Bible, which is the eternal Spirit." He was at that time still dependent on several Swabish theologians, especially F. C. Oetinger (1702–1782), J. A. Bengel, and Johann Tobias Beck (1804–1878) and their understanding of the Spirit. In both editions he reproached his liberal teachers, since their interpretation was too quickly reached: "For me, historical-critics should be more critical (2nd ed., xii). The older theory of inspiration was basically correct, "because it pointed to the activity of understanding itself, without which all preparation lacks value" (1919, 3). Later (*Die Auferstehung der Toten*, 1924, 5) he stresses expressly once more: "The disintegration of a prevailing historically and a prevailing theologically interested exegesis is certainly an imperfect situation." His own "attempt at a theological exegesis" he understands "as a necessary corrective" (ibid.).

In the criticism of earlier theology, the first edition already takes some important steps. Already at this point Barth contrasts the kingdom of God and the ancient kingdom of humans, which he also sees represented through "Church and mission, individual, intellectual competence and morality, pacifism and social democracy" (42). This criticism considers individualism, as well as all "religious activity and ecclesiasticism" (117), "idealistic moralism" (125) and its culture of personality. Barth sees in the "reevaluation of all values" the posing of the question of God (57) and stresses that "salvation comes from the creation of a new world in Christ" (108). He also speaks against the "legal" question of the "stirred up romanticist and individualist": "What should I do?" From being "in Christ" a new ethic emerges: "We stand in the consummation of the divine action" (264). The distance from the second edition is clear, however, especially in the treatment of Rom 8 (ch. 8, "The Spirit"). In the first edition (295–355) Barth explains the chapter in the time line "The Past," "The Present," and "The Future." In these three dimensions of time, the process of growth courses the way of a new history of the Word, which leads from Adam to Christ, and at the same time is the history of God. "In the Messiah" we no longer stand under judgment. "In Christ, however, is the divine, which must appear in our being, nature, talent, and growth" (295). The new humanity appearing in Christ is real and universal; in interpreting Rom 8:10–11 Barth speaks of the Spirit as "a sprout placed in us." The Spirit is "the dynamic principle through which an enclave of righteousness is created in us (8:3–9)." Barth here uses natural images, from which he later distanced himself. Revelation and history are closely oriented to each other. The world as a whole passes by means of the spirit to a liberation of the world, not, in contrast, to its destruction. In this connection, Barth cites Goethe: "No creature can decay to nothing! The eternal stirs forth in all" ("Vermächtnis" [Legacy]), and "World soul, come to penetrate us!" ("Eins und Alles" [One and All]) (330–31). Striking here are the relics of an idealistic view of history, which Barth later abandons. However, he himself had viewed his first attempt as a "preparatory effort."

After he had behind him the readings of Kierkegaard, Nietzsche, Dostoevsky, Heinrich Barth, and Overbeck, he could not continue to speak in this way. In the foreword to the second edition, Barth remarks that in this new edition "So to speak no stone will be left unturned." "The position taken at that earlier time has been moved to points, which are situated more ahead and there arranged anew and strengthened" (1922, vii). In the new interpretation, he proceeds from the inner dialectic of the matter. On the basis of Kierkegaard's statement concerning the "unending qualitative distinction" between time and eternity and with the passage that "God is in heaven and you are on the earth" (Qoh 5:1), his theme would now be "the theme of the Bible and of philosophy together": "the connection of *this* God to *these* humans, the connection of *these* humans to *this* God" (xiv; cf. 294). The presupposition that has to stand the test in Romans seems to be "that in the formation of Paul's ideas the equally simple as well as boundless significance of this relationship at least may have stood as equally sharp before his eyes as they are to me" (ibid.). Thus, Paul speaks of nothing other than "the permanent crisis of time and eternity" (xv).

In the second edition there is no continuing process of thought; since Barth comments on the Pauline text, there are numerous repetitions. The style is impressionistic. Barth reckons with a central point: the revelation of the distant God occurs on the cross and in particular in the resurrection of Jesus Christ, which breaks into history "down from above" and "between the times." Barth can compare this also to Lao-Tse's hole in the wagon wheel (236). There is an intersecting line between the two planes: "The known is the one which was created by God; however fallen from its original unity with God and therefore remains a world of 'flesh' in need of salvation...." This known plane is intersected from another that is unknown, ... the world of the original creation and the final salvation" (5). The first world is "in Adam," the second is "in Christ" (142). The intersection can be temporally determined in a precise way. This is comprised of the time of revelation and discovery, that is, the lifetime of the "historical" Jesus (5). The "critical moment" (42–43), in which "the absolute crisis" that God is for the world, breaks out, is the one of resurrection or of faith. (51). "In the resurrection, the new world of the Holy Spirit touches the old world of the flesh. However, it touches it like the tangent does a circle. While it touches, it does not intersect. It touches its boundary as the new world" (6). The "line of death," which the religious world "designates as the mere world of appearance," not only separates but rather identifies it as a sign for the eternal that resides behind it (106). Characteristic of the second edition is Barth's penchant for geometric comparisons, which serve to provide precision. Resurrection is an action that occurs in space and time, "before the doors of Jerusalem in the year 30, in so far as it 'occurred' there it was discovered and made known" (60). However, in another sense it is also *not* historical, for the appointment of the Messiah as the son of God is both *before* and *after* Easter; thus it is beyond time. The revelation and view of the unimaginable glorification of God in Jesus Christ is the resurrection of Jesus from the dead. As such, it is at the same time the *boundary* of eidetic human history and *encompasses* this history (183). However, there is no continuity to it, for should such exist for the empty tomb of the Synoptics or the appearance of the resurrected one in 1 Cor 15, the 150,000 years of human history would have "a right to a say in divine things," to which it is not entitled (184). An actual dilemma originates between these statements and what has already been cited, according to which the one to thirty years, the entire life of the historical Jesus, are the time of revelation. Following Overbeck, Barth speaks here of the "primal history" (5–6, and other places). Barth had later (*Kirchliche Dogmatik* 1.2:55–56) distanced himself from the punctuality appearing here: John 1:14 ("the Word became flesh...") is not sufficiently borne in mind. At the end stands the judgment of God as the "end of history.... History is finished. It will not be continued" (51). For Overbeck history, including that of Christianity, was the history of decline. On the other hand, history has a character that portends: "we allow the law, the Bible, and religion in its reality to address history, 'to witness' (3:21) about its own meaning" (92). Thus, profanely seen, senseless history obtains "meaning as a parable, as a witness (3:21), as a reflection of the entirely other world, of the entirely other humanity, and of the entirely different history, as a parable, a witness, and a reflection of God" (82; cf. 41, 53–54, 65, 71, 94, 105–8, 138, 147, 156, 202, and other places). In the interpretation of Rom 8:20–21, Barth cites Calvin: "There is no element and no particle of the world, which does not hope for resurrection, having grasped a recognition of its present misery." "Emptiness" of the cosmos (as Barth translates it; better is "futility") is not the last word: the suffering, to which are subjected all things created by God in this world of separation, is still placed on hope, "hope in the unimaginable *unity* of creator and creature that is restored through the cross and resurrection of Christ" (292–93).

Therein resides the paradox in that which is put in force by God: God is "entirely other." Barth says this in separating himself from liberal theology: "Therefore, not actions, experiences, and the unimaginable character of a God," who, like the resurrection, "signifies the *pure* negation and therefore the *beyond* of the 'here and now,' the negation of the negation, the beyond for the 'here and now' and the 'here and now' for the beyond signifies the death of our death and the non-being of our non-being." Barth discovers God in the same word in all three places: "on the periphery of Plato, on the edge of the art of Grünewald and Dostoevsky, on the margin of the religion of Luther" (118). From Plato stems dualism. In regard to Grünewald, Barth thinks of the finger with which John the Baptist points to the one crucified on Grünewald's altar, an image that Barth had hanging in his study. However, that is important: directly as the crucified one he makes alive, he is the savior. "And even the non-knowledge of what God knows, is the knowledge *of* God, the consolation, the light, and the power" (294).

This is made possible in Jesus, an emphasis made by Barth. In Jesus "erupts the unity of God."

> Placed in Jesus are the coordinates of eternal truth, binding here what customarily diverges: humanity and humanity, parting in ways that cus-

tomarily will flow in different directions: humanity and God. In the light of this crisis, God is known, honored, and loved … by having ripped asunder time and eternity, human righteousness and God's righteousness, the "here and now" and the beyond in Jesus in unambiguous ways. Yet they are also combined in him and also in God, united also in unambiguous ways. (88)

In alluding to Overbeck, Barth names Jesus as the Christ of "primeval history" (5, and other places). While the entire interest is concentrated on Jesus, the negation, indispensable for Barth in the battle against liberal theology, is still only preparation for this position.

One will have to understand the exposition of the Epistle to the Romans, especially in the second edition, as a writing of conflict of the young Barth by which he had to create room for the discussion. This makes understandable the frequent, excessive abruptness of many of the formulations in this volume. He did not repeat them later. The writing closest to this is Barth's 1923 reading of 1 Cor 15 in the framework of the Letter of 1 Corinthians (*Die Auferstehung der Toten* [The Resurrection of the Dead]). In this presentation Barth seeks to demonstrate that the letter possesses a common structure, which courses its way to its high point in chapter 15. "Resurrection of the dead" means not least of all "the origin and truth of all that is, known and possessed, and the reality of every *res* [matter], all things, and the eternity of time" (62). It limits the enthusiasm of the Corinthians. In addition, Barth contests energetically the apparitions of the resurrected one in the tradition of the community transmitted by Paul in 15:3–7. This tradition possesses the character of a historical witness, for this word "appeared" could be understood "only as revelation or, if not, it is not understandable at all.… The resurrection is only the witness of God's revelation as the actual, authentic Easter message" (79). It would be interesting to compare Bultmann's understanding of the resurrection as a nonhistorical event (see below, 403) to Barth's view. Bultmann's view follows the course of Barth's interpretation in several similar statements. For example, it could be irrelevant whether the tomb was empty (78; see above), or whether the virgin birth occurred ("The Wonder of Christmas," *KD* 1.2:187–219). Barth distinguishes there between "miracles," "extraordinary events within this our world," and "wonders," which are absolutely "signs of God, who is the Lord of the world, that limit absolutely our world as the created world" (216). The latter is Barth's meaning, and he knowingly places this sign in parallel to that of the empty tomb. These two "wonders" are the demarcations of the beginning and end of

Jesus' life (199). Barth distinguishes the position of the (liberal) theologians, who deny the reality of the virgin birth, from those who leave open whether one is to recognize this sign as a wonder effectuated by God. Should one conclude thereby that according to their meaning the virgin birth did not actually occur (O'Neill, *Authority*, 277)? And should one say that "Barth's system is a pure humanism which believes that the salvation of humanity lies in the acceptance of the irrational?" (O'Neill, 282). Not so, if one attributes to revelation and faith its own findings alongside those of the observable, history, and reason. To rescue revelation and faith is Barth's major intention, and one should evaluate him on this basis.

Barth speaks about religion in his discussion of Rom 7 (1922, 211–53) under the theme, "Freedom." The superscriptions for this chapter are "The Limits of Religion," "The Meaning of Religion," and "The Reality of Religion." Religion is equated with the law. Barth comes to the conclusion that the religious human is the human in *this* world, and "the reality of religion is the human horror before himself " (252), a conscious antithesis to the conviction of the nineteenth century about religion and Christianity as the highest religion.

There remains the matter of the significance of the Bible for Barth's major work, *Church Dogmatics*. A comparison with the orthodox form of dogmatics, with which we have become familiar in Johann Gerhard, demonstrates a parallel in design insofar as Barth introduces his work with the teaching of the Word of God "as the criterion of dogmatics." Certainly, Barth is to be differentiated from the orthodox model (and draws nearer to harbingers like Luther), in that he treats a threefold form of the Word of God (*KD* 1.1, §4): the proclaimed, the written, and the revealed Word of God. Preaching is primarily granted the preference among the three, because "the event of real proclamation is the determining function of the life of the Church beyond all others" (*KD* 1.1:89). But then, after all, the Holy Scripture, the written Word of God, admittedly also a temporal entity, yet "superior to it in dimension" (103) is placed alongside it. It reflects what God's already occurring revelation is, for the written word is canon, *regula fidei* ("rule of faith"), and norm of faith. As such, it is binding, for it is identical to the word of the prophets and the apostles. That it is the written prophetic and apostolic word constitutes its preeminence and obligation as compared to the modern human word. In contrast to the Catholic interpretation, Barth understands apostolic succession as the church in relationship to the Bible: "It [apostolic succession] is directed toward the canon, therefore according to the prophetic and apostolic word as the necessary rule of every word prevailing in the church" (106). The Bible, however, also has a center as regards content: "The prophetic and apostolic word is the word, witness, pronouncement, and preaching of *Jesus Christ*" (110). The sentence "Jesus Christ is the only Word of God" (cf. also the Barmen Confession, thesis 1) is based on the Scriptures (*KD* 4.3:102). Certainly, the Bible is "not itself or by itself God's occurring revelation," but rather it *testifies* to the occurring revelation, as the proclamation promises the future revelation. "This promise ... rests, however, on its manifestation in the Bible" (*KD* 1.1:114). For itself, the Bible does not claim any authority. "One therefore pays the Bible a pernicious and even unwelcome honor, when one identifies it directly ... with revelation" (115). For this reason, Barth distances himself from the older theory of inspiration as we found it in J. Gerhard. In spite of this, Scripture has a fundamental significance in *Church Dogmatics*. As the first concrete demand of dogmatic theology, Barth formulates "that its investigations, sentences, and confirmations must have a *biblical mindset*." In the prolegomena to dogmatics, which is contained in volumes 1.1–2 of *KD*, Barth grants to the doctrine of the Trinity (the three in one, Father, Son, and Holy Spirit) an important place (§§8–12), which he situates, however, at the beginning of the pattern of revelation. In the concluding chapter, which is especially devoted to revelation (§§13–15), the christological emphasis is clear: likewise the first thesis (§13; *KD* 1.2:1) contains the sentence "The incarnation of the eternal Word, Jesus Christ, is God's revelation," and indeed "according to the Holy Scripture." The pouring out of the Holy Spirit, which enlightens us through the knowledge of the word and points to the reality of revelation (§16, Thesis; *KD* 1.2:222) is subjective. Subsequently Barth deals in detail with the Holy Scripture (§19; *KD* 1.2:505–98). Its classification is determined by the two coordinates, the first of which already emerges in the superscription of §19: "God's word for the Church" (505). Barth was aware of the final word *Dogmatik* (dogmatics), in distinction from the first word, *Kirchliche* (church) in *Church Dogmatics*, according to which he determined the church to be the legitimate space for God's revelation and demarcated himself from the individualism of liberal theology. The church is certainly not to be identified with any of the contemporary, existing, corporate churches. The other coordinate is the Holy Scripture. It is God's (written) word, "as it has become and will become the witness of God's revelation to the Church through the Holy Spirit" (ibid.). However, it is not "God's Word on the earth in the same way as Jesus Christ" (570). The eternal presence of him is concealed as the Word of God, above all in the witness of the prophets and the apostles. Since this witness is earthly and chronologically human, it requires the activity of the Holy Spirit, the promise, and faith to become effectual (ibid.). This means, however, on account of the criterion of the freedom of God, that it necessitates "the free attribution of the free grace of God," for which one must pray (ibid.). For his understanding of the inspiration of the Bible, Barth calls especially upon the Reformers, Luther and Calvin (577). On the other hand, the hardening of orthodoxy, which declared the inspiration of the Bible to belong to its *nature* and to be therefore available, he regards as already being part of the process of secularization (580). The sentence, the Bible is God's word, is therefore not to be reinterpreted from a sentence about God's being and activity in the Bible to a sentence about the Bible as such (585). The Word of God, therefore, is not an inherent characteristic of every book, chapter, and verse of the Bible. It happens only concretely, when this or that biblical context is speaking to us as authentic witness. However, "[w]e remember, in and with the church, that the word of God already has been heard in this *whole* book, in all its parts. We expect therefore to hear again the word of God in this book." That this may actually be the case, however, is the "free decision of God" (*KD* 1.2:589).

Barth sees the New Testament together with the Old Testament as a single entity. He follows in this way the Reformed tradition that goes back to Calvin (see *History*, vol. 3). Barth places the time of the Old Testament under the superscription "The Period of Expectation" (*KD* 1.2:77–111). The Old Testament period is the period of the expectation of revelation. The one who is expected is Jesus Christ. Only in this respect can we maintain that revelation takes place in the Old Testament (79). Among the New Testament books that make this into a theme (Matthew, James, Hebrews, Luke, and also John!), Barth discovers in Paul the broadest attestation "that Christ as the one who was expected was also revealed in the period of the Old Testament," a sentence that he designates as "axiomatic" (*KD* 1.2:81). That this was self-evident since the time of the primitive church, Barth ascertains from an overview from Ignatius to Lutheran orthodoxy, whereupon Luther receives the word in an exceedingly elaborate manner. Conversely, he criticizes Old Testament research, that, in spite of all the abundance of its treatment of problems, still did not meet the requirements of theology. The character of Old Testament *piety* or the demonstration of a historical connection of the Testaments is still not identical with the unity of revelation. "It has therefore nothing to do with a historical relationship between two religions, but rather … here and there with the unity of *revelation*." The failure of research leads necessarily to dogmatic theology going its own way in an unconcerned manner (*KD* 1.2:86–87).

In combination with certain dogmatic themes, one comes to a "post-critical" interpretation of Old Testament texts. Thus, in regard to the doctrine of election ("God's Gracious Election," *KD* 2.2:, ch. 7, 1–563) there is the exegesis of Gen 4; Lev 14:4–7; 16:5–6; Saul and David; and 1 Kgs 13. Regarding the doctrine of atonement (*KD* 4.1), §60 contains "Human's Pride and Fall" (395–573), embedded in shorter sections concerning Gen 3, four Old Testament texts of meditation (Exod 32:1–6 [470–79]; 1 Sam 8–31, the history of Saul [485–94]; 1 Kgs 21 [503–8], and Jeremiah [520–31]). The "breaking of the covenant" through the making of an image of a bull in Exod 32 is a more severe incident placed by Barth in connection with Exod 19:3–4 ("the divine event of revelation" [470]) and Exod 32:7–8 (Moses as intercessor, the renewal of the covenant). The worship of the image of the bull as an act of apostasy occurring directly after the resplendent revelation stands as an example of "those occurrences in the history of Israel that have taken place as the opposite of the fidelity, grace, and compassion of its God. It is the painful contradiction of its entire existence" (474). This formulation characterizes at the same time Barth's common judgment expressed concerning Old Testament Israel, as it is also articulated elsewhere in *Church Dogmatics*. Peculiar is Aaron's characterization in this place: he stands for the institutional priesthood (which is placed in the critical light of prophecy since the time of Amos). In so doing the priesthood "lacks an independent relationship to God" as well as "an independent commission to the people" (475). Indeed, the clergy are virtually the exponents of the sin of the people, although they alone are at fault. Here appears the well-known anticlericalism, shaped by the Reformed tradition, which we have already frequently encountered in his view of the history of Saul, especially in the characterization of it as an "episode" that depicts a final result, which is as "bleak as possible." Here he follows Martin Noth's *Geschichte Israels* (1950). He sees Saul's history as the "classical Old Testament depiction" (485) of human megalomania. Barth does not consider the fact that this description is tendentious (Deuteronomistic), nor does he consider the literary breaks. This is naïve, not in the sense of being precritical, for Barth had critical teachers, but rather in the sense of a conscious postcritical naiveté. The preceding treatment of the history of Saul and David is never mentioned under the theme "the elected and the rejected" in *KD* 2.2:404–34, in which the dogmatic (New Testament and early church) interpretation of Israel's kingship provides a background and depicts a pattern (*typos*) of the kingship of Christ, in *KD*

4.1. This is an indication of the aphoristic character of the exegeses in the systematic work.

8.2. Interpreting the Message of the New Testament Existentially: Rudolf Bultmann

Rudolf Bultmann was born in 1884 in Wiefelstede (Oldenburg), the oldest son of a Lutheran pastor and later church councillor, Arthur Bultmann. After attending elementary school in Rastede (1892–1895) and the classical gymnasium in Oldenburg (1895–1903), he studied theology in Tübingen (1903–1904), Berlin (1904–1905), and Marburg (1906–1907). He passed his first theological exams in the Oldenburg high consistory and was active during the same year as a teacher in the Oldenburg gymnasium and for some time as a house teacher. From 1907 to 1916, he served as *Repetent* for New Testament at an institution for stipend recipients in Marburg, having been called there through the efforts of Johannes Weiss, who would supervise his licentiate work. There were some additional obligations in preaching. In the years 1907–1910, Bultmann wrote his licentiate work, for which Heitmüller officially served as referee. This work appeared under the title "The Style of Pauline Preaching and the Cynic-Stoic Diatribe." With the work "The Exegesis of Theodore of Mopsuestia" (see *History*, vol. 2; first printed in 1984), he received his *Habilitation* in 1912 for the field of New Testament. He lectured from then on as a private lecturer until he was called to the position of associate professor in Breslau in 1916. He could not participate in military service during World War I because of hip trouble. In Breslau he wrote, following on preparatory works on which he labored for a long time, *The History of the Synoptic Tradition* (see below) and married Helene Feldmann (1892–1973). In 1920, he became the successor to Bousset in Giessen and was called to teach there as a full professor. In 1921, he left for Marburg, where he took the chair of Heitmüller. There he worked until he became emeritus in 1951. Bultmann died in Marburg in 1976.

The first significant work of Bultmann, *Die Geschichte der synoptischen Tradition* (The History of the Synoptic Tradition), appeared in 1921. Around this time, three works concerning form criticism of the Gospels, appearing later than similar works having to do with the Old Testament, were published independently of each other. In *Der Rahmen der Geschichte Jesu* (The Frame of the History of Jesus [1919]), Karl Ludwig Schmidt (1891–1956) taught that the entire geographical and chronological connection was a secondary framing of the individual pericopae. In the same year Martin Dibelius (1883–1947) published *Die Formgeschichte des Evangeliums* (The Form Criticism of the Gospel). Opposite to the procedure of Dibelius, who introduces a picture of the primitive Christian community and from this context describes the origin of the gospel tradition in its individual forms, Bultmann proceeds initially from individual parts. He analytically arranges at the outset their forms in their genres. In doing so, he borrows from Gunkel's assignment of parts of the tradition to their respective life situations (see *Synoptische Tradition*, 4). He classifies the materials of the Gospels into "I. The tradition of the words of Jesus [8–222] and II. The tradition of the narrative materials" (223–335). He divides the words of Jesus first into (a) apothegms (sayings) (8–73), which are words that are placed in the brief frames of a scene (e.g., a contest speech, or when a question is addressed to Jesus). Often, especially in "biographical" sayings, they are ideal scenes. These sayings cannot be used biographically in reconstructing a "life of Jesus." Free-floating words of Jesus were added to already existing scenes; most of them end with an apothegm. "The interest in apothegms resides entirely in the saying of Jesus" (66). (b) Words of the Lord. To these belong *logia* (words in which Jesus appears as a wisdom teacher), prophetic and apocalyptic words, legal words, and community rules. On the history of tradition, Bultmann follows the critical line of scholarship (originally he wished to dedicate the book to D. F. Strauss!): in a great number of cases the words are not originally those of Jesus, but rather are the creation of the community. This is true even for "I-sayings" (161–79). Bultmann seeks to demonstrate that these sayings later were assigned to Jesus chiefly by the Jewish or Hellenistic community. The sayings of the Lord were formulated predominantly not on Hellenistic soil, but rather were originally Aramaic, which was the language of Jesus and his Palestinian disciples. Similarly with the parables (179–222), among which Bultmann distinguishes with A. Jülicher example narratives and allegories, Bultmann assumes numerous creations of the community or alterations. He notes, however: "When there is a contrast to Jewish morality and piety and a specifically eschatological mood, characteristic for the pronouncement of Jesus, and where, on the other side, a lack of any specifically Christian feature can be found, one most easily may have a genuine parable of Jesus" (222). With this understanding comes a criterion of authenticity that is still used to this day. This criterion, however, has its weaknesses, for if Jesus was a Jew—something that was later an important point for Bultmann (see below)—one could expect to have something specifically Jewish emanate from some of his sayings. More recently, there actually are critics who, by contrast, wish to overturn the understanding of Jesus in terms of his Jewish nature (see below).

In part 2 (223–348) Bultmann treats the tradition of narrative materials, and in part 3 (348–92) there is an examination of the redactional material. Yet this is not a consistent redaction history, which would be a later development in the interpretation of the Gospels. Yet Bultmann formulates important insights, which are significant for a new evaluation of the character and intentions of the Gospels: they are the writings of early Christian proclamation of the *kērygma*, that is, the message of Jesus as the Christ. "The Christ who is proclaimed is not the historical Jesus, but rather the Christ of faith and of the cult." Therefore, the death and resurrection of Christ stand in the center as the acts of salvation. The emphasis is on the history of the passion and Easter. In baptism and the Lord's Supper, the realities of salvation become actualized for the believer. "The Kerygma of Christ is therefore a cult legend, and the Gospels are expanded cult legends" (396). Bultmann demonstrates that the requirements of preaching, disputation with the non-Christian world, the order of the community, and the interpretation of Scripture (the Old Testament) are the decisive agencies that have formed the tradition.

The results of the form criticism of the Gospels dealt a decisive blow to the liberal life-of-Jesus theology. The idea of the formation of the Gospels from many small individual traditions and their combination with proclamation made it impossible for the Gospels to be used as a historical source to reconstruct the figure of an earthly Jesus who could serve as a moral paradigm. This recognition led Bultmann to a new theological orientation, which appeared in his "Ethische und mystische Religion im Urchristentum" (Ethical and Mystical Orientation in Early Christianity [1920; Moltmann, *Anfänge* 2:29–47]). Assigning himself to "liberal theology" (41), Bultmann regards as fundamental the distinction drawn by his teachers, who belonged to the history of religion school. They differentiated between the ancient Palestinian community and the Hellenistic community. It is an important thesis (though not entirely new) "that Jesus belongs to the conclusion and fulfillment of the history of Judaism [likewise the Palestinian, primitive Christianity; 'a Jewish sect,' 36, 42], while something new begins with Paul and the Hellenistic community" (35). In Hellenistic Christianity, which could be designated as a "mystical, cultic religion," the "cult deity" is "identified with the historical person Jesus of Nazareth. The Palestinian community honors him as a prophet and teacher and expects him as Son of Man" (36–37). The person of Paul fulfills a connecting function. His piety unifies ethical and mystical religion. The community of Christ, which is experienced in the Spirit, is the center of Pauline piety. The history of religion school had already spoken of "mysticism." However, the fruits of the Spirit add the factor of moral change (39).

From his biblical observations, Bultmann then draws theological consequences. He concedes the deficiency of historical criticism in its religious and churchly results. But he responds that "it never was nor can be the purpose of historical critical theology to establish piety, but rather the objective ... is to lead to self-understanding" (41). With respect to the present inclination to mysticism, historical criticism is able to contribute to the clarification of the consciousness of the period in which a biblical text is composed. The next objection, that liberal theology had wished to set forth the "historical Jesus," thus making a historical person the norm of piety, is legitimate, also in its content: "The most extreme mistake of 'liberal theology,' in my opinion, was the confusion of a religiously colored moralism with ethical religion" (44). In Bultmann's view, the authentically religious plays only a very small role with the historical Jesus. Bultmann defines religion as does Rudolf Otto (1869–1937, whose main work was *Das Heilige* [The Holy], 1917). Religion is the encounter with the "entirely other," the "God who confronts humans in their experiences of obedience to the good" (45).

The movement to a new form of theology, which Bultmann had obtained from his exegesis independent from K. Barth and the other "dialectical" theologians (although he mentions Gogarten approvingly), is clear here, even if this is still not sharply articulated.

He does take a more explicit position in the contribution "Die liberale Theologie und die jüngste theologische Bewegung" (The Liberal Theology and the Latest Theological Movement; in *GV* 1:1–25). In the meantime, Karl Barth had brought out the second edition of his commentary on Romans, and the dialectical movement had gathered around the journal *Zwischen den Zeiten* (1923–33). Bultmann was a regular contributor to this journal. He now formulated his theology in a much clearer fashion: "The subject of theology is God, and the reproach against liberal theology is that it has treated, not God, but humans. God signifies the radical negation and abrogation of human; the theology which has God as its subject is able therefore to have for its content only the *logos tou staurou* [the word of the cross] (cf. 1 Cor 1:18)" (*GV* 1:2). Liberal theology is to be reproached, since it has sought to evade this scandal. The effort of liberal theology to attach the revelation of God in history especially to the historical Jesus, who becomes, like other figures, the bearer of revelation, is censured by Bultmann as "historical pantheism," which is closely related to nature and intermundane pantheism (5). However, in doing this, one does not proceed from the connection of relationship. In regard to the different portraits of Jesus, it is common that they are able only to reflect interpersonal experiences, whereas "God's otherness, his otherworldliness, means the abrogation of everything human, of his entire history" (13; cf. 18). Furthermore, activity in the enterprise is not simply worship. This is "only for the one who surrenders under divine judgment and then in obedience to God takes up work in the world." God "connotes the total abolishment of the human being . . . the judgment for the human being" (17–18). Liberal theology has not taken this seriously. The wish to assert oneself is its basic sin. *At the same time*, judgment is also grace; both occur in one element. When a human being stands before God, he is a sinner and yet knows at the same time that divine grace is for the sinner. At this moment, Bultmann knows himself to be close to Barth, Gogarten, and their circle.

The fundamental decisions of Bultmann are mirrored in his additional works. In regard to his booklet *Jesus* (1926, and later editions), it is characteristic that he treats not the life of Jesus but rather Jesus' proclamation. The discussion is not about the figure of Jesus, for "I am certainly of the opinion that we are not able to know much at all about Jesus as a person, since the Christian sources are not interested in this" (*Jesus*, 11). Bultmann engages in presenting in an introductory fashion some of his deliberations about the historical understanding: in distinction from the examination of nature, where one is able to state what exists, the one who considers history has to "say to himself that he is himself a part of history and therefore turns to a connection (a connection of effect), in which he himself is linked with his own being." Therefore he says "with each word about history ... at the same time something about himself" (7). This points to Bultmann's continuing interest in the hermeneutics of history, which is sustained up to his late essay "Das Problem der Hermeneutik" (The Problem of Hermeneutics [1950], *GV* 2:211–35).

As an interpreter of the New Testament, Bultmann came into prominence especially with his commentary on John (1941), which was for a lengthy period of time the standard for the understanding of this Gospel. He provided here concrete answers to the main problems of this Gospel. (1) The obviously disturbed condition of the text requires adjustments. For example, chapter 5 must change places with chapter 6, since the former takes place in Jerusalem, while in 6:1 Jesus is positioned on the other side of the Sea of Galilee. It can be debated if Bultmann has rearranged too many texts. (2) The question concerning the sources of this Gospel is also perplexing. There are few contacts to the Synoptic Gospels. The result is that John must have had his own sources. Apart from a hymn reworked by the evangelist to serve as the Prologue (John 1) and the history of the passion (John 18–20), there are the "Signs (*Semeia*) Source," which is a collection of miracle stories, beginning in 1:35 and ending with 20:30–31, and points to its own number of miracles (2:11; 4:54), as well as a collection of "speeches of revelation." A churchly redaction has added to the finished Gospel the reference to the sacraments (19:34b–35) of baptism (3:5) and the Eucharist (6:27–59), since they had not been mentioned previously.

From where, however, does the theological peculiarity of the Gospel of John originate? John is rather distant from the primitive community and its problems, as well as from the actions of Jesus. The "Jews," with whom the Gospel fights, are the representatives of the unbelieving world. Nor is there any direct connection to Paul. By contrast, characteristic of John is the dualism between "light" and "darkness." The "Gnostic redeemer myth" offers a parallel to the Gospel. According to this myth, a divine figure from the world of light is sent down to the earth, which is ruled by the demonic powers of darkness, to free and bring back home the sparks of light, which have been captured in human bodies. In human form, the redeemer reveals by his speeches and teaches humans, in whom sparks of light dwell, to recognize their true identity and how to find their way back to the world of light. In the Gospel of John a similar example is recognizable: according to John 1 the Logos (the "Word"), dwelling with God in the beginning, comes to the earth. Sent by the Father to the world below, the Logos fulfills his commission in obedience. He reveals himself in his speeches and makes a division between the blind, who continually misunderstand him, and his own, who recognize him and receive from him the truth. After fulfilling his work, he ascends back again, the cross being his exaltation and glorification, and he will draw to himself his own. Indeed, there are also differences from the Gnostic myth that should be noted. In John this myth lacks both the cosmic aspect of the understanding of the world and the idea of the sparks of light dwelling in human beings, of which one only has to be reminded. Instead of these, Jesus is the Word who requires the decision of faith. The Gnosis recognized the non-worldliness of God and the lost condition of humanity. Therefore, John could tie the two together. John introduces Jesus (in the "I am" words) as the true light, the true bread, and the true vineyard. Revelation here is radically grasped as the call of Jesus to himself, and no longer as the message of teachings concerning the world and humanity. Humans are not taken out of the world, but rather are placed in the position of having to make a decision whether or not to believe in Jesus and to be obedient to his commands. In this way existence from which the worldly is removed takes place.

Bultmann was occupied also with Paul from the time of his dissertation in 1910 to the commentary on 2 Corinthians, which he published in 1976 shortly before his death. In his early works, he made use of "experience" and "mysticism" with the approach of the history of religion school. In his essay "Das Problem der Ethik bei Paulus" (*Exegetica*, 36–54), however, he understands the contrast between statements narrowly standing beside one another, the first according to which one who is justified no longer lives in the flesh, but rather is alive in the spirit (as Gal 5:25). The admonition, which stands in the immediate context, to fight against sin (Gal 5:13–24) is indicative and imperative, no longer as an antithesis but rather as an expression of antinomy: justification is an act of God on human beings. Justification does not result in the alteration of one's moral character; rather, it is a judgment of God and, like obedience, can only be something that is believed. In his portrait of Paul, Bultmann has implemented the turning point and discovered the pathway to Reformation theology. Later he accentuates his meaning, for example, in his essay "Die Bedeutung der 'dialektischen Theologie' für die neutestamentliche Wissenschaft" (The Significance of Dialectical Theology for New Testament Criticism [1928], *GV* 1:114–33), in which he stresses that a text is to be understood in each case "from its understanding of human existence" (129). "Body" (*sōma*) designates then "the historical being, which … has both possibilities to be determined by God or by sin" (130–31). The unity of the human is not to be seen as substance, but rather as historical, meaning "that to a human being God's demand is issued."

Between this and the earlier statements one may note Bultmann's intensive collaboration with Martin Heidegger (1889–1976) during the latter's activity as a professor of philosophy in Marburg (1923–1927). In the year Heidegger was called to Freiburg im Breisgau, his major work, *Sein und Zeit* (Being and Time), appeared. Heidegger's analysis of human existence as "being in the world" offered Bultmann the opportunity to create a theological anthropology, in which God determines the meaning of existence (i.e., "existential"). Through this the character of Bultmann's hermeneutic was determined from this time forward.

In "Die Bedeutung des geschichtlichen Jesus für die Theologies des Paulus" (The Significance of the Historical Jesus for the Theology of Paul

[1929], *GV* 1:188–213), Bultmann resolutely repudiates the idea that Jesus' proclamation was relevant for Paul. Jesus does encounter human beings including Paul, but it is in the proclamation about Jesus Christ. The one who is preached is the Lord. The theologian Paul says something different: the primal sin of humanity is the desire to assert oneself against God. The Jews have misused the law in this regard (196). Only God is able through grace to deliver humanity. The human being remains the one who is the recipient of this act of grace. To be sure, this theology corresponds in its basic motif to the polemic of Jesus. Moreover, Jesus distinguishes between justice and the will of God, showing that one can present no achievement before God. However, Jesus has not developed a theoretical ethic.

While it was in no way the main point in Bultmann's theology, his thesis of "demythologization" caused the greatest sensation in the churches and the public and generated a long-lasting debate. This term shaped by Bultmann obfuscated the understanding of what he meant. While it was not before 1941 that he first formulated this thesis, it has in its theological roots a longer prehistory. Bultmann paved the way for it in the essay "Religion und Kultur" in 1920 (*Anfänge* 2:11–29), in which culture, which in the spheres of science, art, and morality is ruled by reason, is, for Bultmann, separate from religion. This was due to the influence of Marburg Neo-Kantianism (their representative, Paul Natorp [1854–1924] was the teacher of Heidegger!) and of his theological teacher Wilhelm Herrmann (1846–1922). Religion is the matter of the individual. It is, in modifying the definition of Schleiermacher, "the consciousness of the most absolute dependency" (*Anfänge* 2:17–18). As such, it is experience in which occurs an encounter with a power to which the "I" can totally subject and addict itself (25), something like the experiences of trust and love (23). Religion is neutral toward culture, science, art, and also morality. From Neo-Kantianism stems also the statement of "objectification" in which these spheres are placed before the eyes as the subject of rational analysis, something that, according to Bultmann, does not apply to religion.

In the essay on "demythologization" ("Neues Testament und Mythologie" [New Testament and Mythology], 1941), this separation continues to be maintained. At the same time, the understanding of myth present in liberalism since the Enlightenment has its effects. Bultmann contrasts the modern understanding of reality with the three-story worldview of myth envisaged in the Bible, the corresponding Jewish apocalyptic, and the Gnostic redeemer myth. Bultmann initially describes the acts of salvation preferably with examples from the letters of Paul: "One cannot use electric light and a radio and in cases of illness demand modern medicinal and clinical means of treatment and at the same time believe in the world of spirits and miracles of the New Testament" (new printing, 1985, 16). If this cannot be expected from a modern human, the question must be posed for the Christian proclamation "whether the proclamation of the New Testament has a truth that is independent of the mythic world view" (14). Yet New Testament criticism can be theologically relevant only if it "results by necessity from the situation of modern human beings" (18). To make it relevant "it would then be the assignment of theology to demythologize the Christian proclamation." To the doctrines not understood by modern humans, Bultmann attributes also the idea of death as punishment for sin and the affirmation of the vicarious atonement achieved through the death of Christ.

Given this situation, both the theologian and the *teacher* have to face the task of demythologization. In answer to the criticism of Bultmann's formulation (something delayed by the events of the war, but intensely exerted during the postwar period), one must stress his concern for an adequate language of the preacher vis-à-vis the community "and those whom he wants to attract for the community" (21). The solution consists in interpreting myth "not cosmologically, but rather anthropologically or better, existentially" (22). That means that the mythology of the New Testament is "not to be examined for its objectified sense, but rather for the understanding of existence articulated in its ideas" (23).

In his additional statements, Bultmann builds on this foundation: "A. The Christian self-understanding" (32–38), and "B. The act of salvation." Human existence is characterized (1) outside faith and (2) in faith. A person is outside faith, because he lives from what is disposable and is worn down by cares (1 Cor 7:32ff.), and since the available is perishable and deteriorates into extinction. Authentic life, by contrast, is that which is lived apart from what is disposable, "according to the spirit," in faith. This signifies trust in God's grace that forgives sins, a sense of ease from every worldly thing that is disposable, and distance from the world. Above all life in faith is not a state. Rather, the imperative is added to the indicative, and the decision to believe is to stand the test in every concrete situation. In these statements, Bultmann summarizes some features of Pauline theology. For the description of the event of salvation (B), the fundamental recognition is understanding that human beings cannot liberate themselves, but rather are made free only by an act of God (45). Contrary to philosophy, Bultmann stresses that the natural human being is given to trust in what is mortal, or, in the language of the New Testament, he is a sinner, because he lives in hubris. The sense of the Christ event (50), therefore, is the belief that the human is liberated from himself. Freedom from sin is the freedom of obedience and devotion to the other (Rom 13:8–10; Gal 5:14). Thus, decisive for the New Testament is the act of God, which principally makes possible faith and love (52).

Subsequently (52–63), Bultmann explores the question of whether the Christ event may be a mythological occurrence. These expressions especially have led to the sustained debate over the program of demythologization in the church and in theology. For Bultmann there is "no question that the New Testament conceives of the Christ event as a mythological occurrence," even though Jesus Christ is a historical figure. Thus "historical and mythic are here peculiarly interlaced." Next to the historical event of the cross, "stands the resurrection, which is in and of itself no historical event." These affirmations along with other, partially contradictory statements could be abandoned when one asks "whether the mythological language simply means the significance of the historical figure, Jesus, and his history, that is to say, brings to expression the prominence of this history as a form and event of salvation" (53). This is shown primarily in the event of the cross, which as an act of salvation is certainly not a mythical event, when for faith its presence is experienced as a liberating judgment of humanity in the sacraments and in the concrete execution of the life of the believer. This is, however, also not as a historical event, but rather because the crucified at the same time is proclaimed as the one resurrected.

It holds good for the resurrection that the proper language can only be the "expression of the significance of the cross." This is because it cannot be regarded as a historical event. Bultmann had already come to this conclusion by means of the form-critical investigation he pursued in his *Geschichte der synoptischen Tradition*. Nor can this event be a "verified miracle," although it is described in this way often in the New Testament, for example, in the legends of the empty tomb and the accounts of Easter as well as in 1 Cor 15:3–8 (according to Bultmann an unfortunate argumentation) (58). As a mythic event it is unbelievable, and as an objective result "it cannot be regarded as an objective event, even though there were so many witnesses." It is "itself the subject of faith," and it is this, "because it is an eschatological event" (59). Because the participation of Christians in this event is proven (as Bultmann indicates in 2 Tim 1:10; 2 Cor 5:14–15; 1 Cor 15:21–22; Rom 6:4–5, 11, among others) "in the concrete performance of life," thus the resurrection is similarly believed as the significance of the cross. Bultmann formulates in a pointed way: "Resurrection faith is nothing else but faith in the cross. They both are an event of salvation" (60–61). This statement often has been criticized, because the resurrection as an event is to be taken on its own weight. There is one question: "How do we come to the point that one is to believe in the cross as an event of salvation?" According to Bultmann there is only *one* answer: "because it is preached to be a salvific event and because it is proclaimed with the resurrection. Christ, the one crucified and the resurrected one, confronts us only in the word of proclamation and nowhere else. The faith in this word is precisely the Easter faith." We "cannot place the question of legitimation" vis-à-vis the Word of God (61). Bultmann here distinguishes between the fact, which the historian can determine, and the word of proclamation, in which the resurrected one alone is encountered. In this sentence, "The resurrection of Christ is not a historical event" (ibid.). As such, only the Easter faith of the disciples is comprehensible. In the preaching of the word, the apostle also proclaims that the church belongs to the eschatological event.

These statements are only understandable from Bultmann's fundamental concern, and that is to comprehend faith as an existential activity in which as a believer I grasp not a fact that is the object of my knowledge ("objectivizing"), but rather that I allow God to act upon me. In the subsequent, intense outbreak of contention that was especially ignited by Bultmann's evaluation of the Easter faith, which, misunderstood, is seen as a denial of the resurrection, this concern was often not taken sufficiently into consideration. Rather, Bultmann's ambition was recognized to enable the Gospel to be understandable in terms of the modern picture of the world by removing its outer garment of an outdated, ancient portrait of the world. Another question is whether he had described sufficiently the modern picture of the world or whether he had presupposed a modern view that already had become obsolete. (1) The scientific view of the world has decisively changed, in macrocosm through Einstein's theory of relativity and in microcosm through research into atoms. (2) An alteration in the evaluation of myth has recently entered into research, which, under different facets and specific conditions, concedes it to be an independent understanding of reality along with that of science. Even if this is not recognized everywhere in biblical criticism, it nevertheless still strongly impacts Bultmann's influence.

As heir of the history of religion school, Bultmann demonstrates that he also has composed his own history of primitive Christian religion: *Das Urchristentum im Rahmen der antiken Religionen* (Primitive Christianity in the Framework of Ancient Religions [1949]). There primitive Christianity appears as a "syncretistic phenomenon" (§5.1, superscription), which is shaped by the Old Testament, Judaism, Greek religion and philosophy, and Hellenism.

Bultmann crowned his work on the New Testament with his *Theologie des Neuen Testaments* (Theology of the New Testament [1953]), in which he compiled his findings. His specific principle is shown in the work's design: he does not integrate the preaching of Jesus into his New Testament theology but rather places it at the beginning, in the first part, under "Presuppositions and Motifs of New Testament Theology" (1–34). The first sentence reads: "The preaching of Jesus belongs to the presuppositions of the theology of the New Testament and does not constitute a part of it" (§1; 1). Here are found the themes of "The Kerygma of the Primitive Community" (34–66) and "The Kerygma of the Hellenistic Community before and at the Time of Paul" (67–186). The second part (187–445) treats the theological concepts of Paul (187–353) as well as the theology of both the Gospel of John and the Epistles of John (354–445). The third part is somewhat lacking in unity: under the common superscription "The Development of the Ancient Church" are intermittently treated systematically ordered themes like "Christology and Soteriology" (§58; 507–51; passages are taken from the post-Pauline and early church writings) and ethics ("The Problem of the Christian Conduct of Life," 552–84). In the "Epilegomena," (postscript, 585–600), Bultmann explains the twofold purpose of a New Testament theology: to display the *kērygma* (the [believed] message) and the theological statements in their distinctive features, although both are never fully separated from one another (588).

As the large number of editions of this work demonstrates, it has been an important handbook for a long period of time. The interest in Bultmann and his program of demythologization has decreased only in recent times, as newer developments have taken his place.

8.3. Outlook

It is difficult to outline the new developments in a brief section. In general, one is able to say that the area of what may be designated biblical interpretation in a critical sense has diversified considerably during the wider course of the twentieth century and continues to do so in the early part of the twenty-first century. Further, much of the critical study of the Bible has not been considered here. In addition, the practical contact with the Bible is an extensive field, which must remain unexamined in this study. This diversity resides primarily in the fact that the parties involved in the discussion have considerably increased. As a consequence of two world wars, the monopolization of biblical exegesis by German-speaking scholars as it had once existed has ended, and the developments of biblical criticism in other lands, especially among Anglo-Saxon, Scandinavian, and Dutch scholars, have caught up. Since the encyclical of Pope Pius XII, *Divino afflante Spiritu* (Inspired by the Divine Spirit [1943]), Roman Catholic criticism of the ancient texts of the Bible has been free to develop. Especially the Dogmatic Constitution on Divine Revelation (*Dei verbum* [The Word of God]), issued during the Second Vatican Council (1965), freed scholars from their chains of official instruction. Many spheres of Roman Catholic critical biblical interpretation since that time have succeeded in producing many leading positions. In addition, Jewish exegetes increasingly produce studies worthy of note. Through the general multiplication of high schools and institutions, together with the places equipped for teaching and criticism of the Bible, the number of participants in biblical criticism and the publications developed from them have hugely increased. This is shown by the occasionally vast number of participants in international congresses on biblical studies. While an increasing specialization has developed a considerably extensive range of approaches, at the same time the possibilities of cross-disciplinary dialogue have been further limited. No one can adequately become familiar with the flood of new publications in every year in the sphere of biblical criticism.

The development of the past half century was characterized primarily by the emergence of new methods. Tradition history followed form criticism. Its pioneer was Martin Noth (1902–1968), a student of Albrecht Alt (1883–1956). His theses established especially the "Deuteronomistic History" (Deuteronomy–2 Kings; *Überlieferungsgeschichtlich Studien* [Studies in the History of Traditions]). Another student of Alt, Gerhard von Rad, summarized the results of his life's work in his *Theologie des Alten Testaments* (Old Testament Theology). Worthy of note is his separation between the "historical traditions of Israel" (preceded by a "Survey of the History of Yahweh Faith" [vol. 1]) and the "prophetic traditions of Israel" (vol. 2; Psalms and Wisdom are separate and placed under "Israel before Yahweh" [The Answer of Israel] at the conclusion). In the intensely discussed program, the "recounting" of Israel's historical traditions reveals a conservative tendency.

At the same time, Alt and Noth were the main representatives of the territorial history of Palestine, which combined an interpretation of the biblical texts (especially in Joshua) with topography and archaeology. The critical view toward the possible historical evaluation of the results brought them into opposition with William Foxwell Albright (1891–1971), who sought to employ archaeological discoveries to confirm biblical accounts and who founded an influential school. Recently the interest in biblical archaeology has been employed in the illustration of political history, which is related strongly to the social development and anthropology of the Near East and especially the Canaanite culture of the Late Bronze and Iron ages. In addition, the expression "biblical archaeology" has been brought into discussion.

In Old Testament exegesis, redaction criticism has followed form and tradition history criticism. In redaction criticism the focal points of literary criticism, which already had been thought to have reached their conclusion, are surprisingly revived, even if with different interests. Earlier literary criticism had been interested in penetrating the texts to discover the earliest sources, especially in the Pentateuch, and to separate them from the later, "secondary" materials. Now the emphasis falls on their combination and transformation by redactors who were especially interested in the final form of the text resulting from their efforts. The work with sources (the older ones of literary criticism, makes Wellhausen's work again contemporary!) and the interpretation of the process of redaction as a literary activity that takes place at the "scribal desk" are both methods that have certain things in common.

A consequence of this is also the opinion that the final form of the biblical texts is decisive for interpretation, so that the earlier forms are no longer interesting. Thus, different exegetical methods are developed: the first is narrative criticism, which analyzes the text as narrative and is not concerned with the delineation of sources. The methodological basis is a literary theory according to which a text has meaning as a text without regard for the place of origin or for the author's point of view. An example is Robert Alter, *The Art of Biblical Narrative* (1981). Mark Allan Powell, Cecile G. Gray, and Melissa C. Curtis (*The Bible and Modern Literary Criticism* [1992]) provide a bibliography. The second is structural exegesis. It has developed as a special form of narrative exegesis under the influence of the linguists F. de Saussure and A. J. Greimas and pursues the linguistic structure of sentences in texts of biblical prose. This discussion was often conducted in the journal *Semeia*. The same is true for the countermovement of deconstruction, proceeding from the anti-metaphysical philosophy of Jacques Derrida and likewise applied to biblical texts. Anthropological, social-scientific, and political features play a role. The third method refers to the theological maxim that biblical interpretation occurs within the structure of the biblical canon. This has led to "canonical exegesis," which was most ably represented by Brevard S. Childs (1923–2007). His works led from exegesis (*Exodus*, 1974), to Old and New Testament theologies, to a general biblical theology (*Biblical Theology of the Old and New Testaments*, 1992). As a student of Karl Barth, Childs proceeded from Barth's "theology of the Word of God."

The period following World War I also brought about a reawakening of Old and New Testament theology (we have already mentioned the works of Bultmann and von Rad), which in the course of the nineteenth century had begun entirely as a history of religion. Walter Eichrodt (1890–1978) offered a systematically constructed *Theology of the Old Testament* (1933–1939) as did Ludwig Köhler (1880–1956). Since then, increasing numbers of new studies have appeared, especially in the United States. Some of the most recent examples are Otto Kaiser, *Der Gott des Alten Testaments* (The God of the Old Testament [2 vols., 1993–1998]), Rolf Rendtorff, *Theologie des Alten Testaments* (2 vols., 1999–2001), and Walter Brueggemann, *Theology of the Old Testament* (1997).

Some forms of biblical interpretation take a consciously one-sided approach for ideological purposes. To these belong the "political theology," which, in Germany, was represented by Dorothee Sölle in contesting Bultmann (*Politische Theologie: Auseinandersetzung mit Rudolf Bultmann* [Political Theology: A Dispute with Rudolf Bultmann], 1977; 2nd ed., 1982). She appropriates especially the "liberation theology" of South America, along with Marxist and feminist exegesis. Another theory that proceeds from an ideological orientation is the so-called reader-response criticism, which proceeds from the idea that the questions addressed to the text must be those of interest to the reader, since the views of the author cannot be demonstrated and the intentions of the readers may be variable (Stanley E. Fish, *Is There a Text in This Class? The Authority of Interpretative Communities* [1980]). This principle admittedly calls into question the authority of the Bible as a witness of a message *and* the community that therefore carries it as an address to the readers.

One debate that has emerged is whether the approach to the study of the Old Testament should focus on Old Testament theology or on the history of Israelite religion. It was instigated by the work of Rainer Albertz, (*Religionsgeschichte Israels in alttestamentlicher Zeit* [A History of Israelite Religion in the Old Testament], 2 vols, 1992). He argued that examining the history of Israelite religion is more sensible and even more theological than an Old Testament theology (1:37–38; see esp. the *Jahrbuch für biblische Theologie* 10 [1995]). An "either-or" approach to this debate, however, may not be applicable. Both forms of description make their own particular sense. There is no question that there can be also a secular interest (historical, archaeological, and linguistic) in the Old Testament in addition to the theological one. Outside the continent of Europe, there are numerous religious faculties and institutes, as well as biblical departments, that function outside of theological faculties. Since the Bible imposes on its readers the demand to give witness to faith, an integrated understanding, to be sure, is indispensable. Thus, institutionally separated understandings are hardly trend-setting (against Eckart Otto, *Der Stand der alttestamentlichen Wissenschaft* [The Position of Old Testament Criticism], 1991, 27–28).

Modern Jewish criticism inclines toward the historical approach through the history of religion and archaeological interpretation of the Bible. Not overtly theological, however, is the direction stemming from German Judaism, which is represented by the following Jewish scholars: David Hoffmann (1843–1921), Yehezkel Kaufmann (1889–1963), Menahem Haran (b. 1926), and Jacob Milgrom (b. 1923). They agree in emphasizing that the Priestly document in the Pentateuch was of great antiquity and possesses the highest authority for the Jewish life of faith.

A similar development to what has occurred in the Old Testament can be observed in biblical exegesis of the New Testament. Old approaches reappear. This is the case primarily for the Life of Jesus research. Bultmann's student Ernst Käsemann (1906–1998) placed the topic once more on the table in his contribution "Das Problem des historischen Jesus" (The Problem of the Historical Jesus, 1953). "No one can evade arbitrarily and with impunity this problem, which has been handed down in tradition from the fathers. And that the representatives of liberal theology today widely no more are acknowledged as such does not change the fact that they are nevertheless this for us" (*Exegetische Versuche und Besinnungen*, 187–214, esp. 195). In contrast to the systematic designs of the teachers, one is now "frequently impelled ... to reach back to the preceding field of historical efforts and reflections" (7). Above all this may be justified "inasmuch as the Gospels ascribe their Kerygma ... however, even to the earthly Jesus" (ibid.). Since then research has continued to develop in numerous ways. Thus, the debate has not ended as to whether the proclamation of the kingdom of God by Jesus, as Johannes Weiss (see above) and Albert Schweitzer thought, was "eschatological," that is, directed to a *future* reign of God, or was even apocalyptic, or was "present," that is, has in view the presence of the kingdom already on the earth. More recent theories understand the parables of Jesus as metaphors shaped by wisdom for the kingdom of God that already has broken into history. The standard for the authentic words of Jesus has changed from the "criterion of difference" (a statement is authentic if it varies from contemporary Judaism and early Christianity; see Bultmann, above, 395–96) to sociohistorical interests. This latter approach integrates Jesus within the context of what was then contemporary Judaism and comprehends his appearance by comparison to related phenomena of the period. This has led already to a Jewish interpretation of Jesus (among others, David Flusser, *Jesus* [1968] and Geza Vermes, *Jesus the Jew* [1973]). There is also discussion of whether Jesus claimed for himself christological titles of majesty, thus indicating that he possessed a messianic consciousness of himself. Especially debated in this regard is the concept of the "Son of Man" (see Volker Hampel, *Menschensohn und historischer Jesus* [The Son of Man and the Historical Jesus], 1990). Associated with this is whether Jesus knew about his suffering beforehand and understood himself to be one who vicariously suffered for the sins of others. All of these questions have not been definitively answered.

In addition, after Bultmann, not a few "theologies" of the New Testament have appeared. While Hans Conzelmann (1967) continued to develop Bultmann's approach, Werner Georg Kümmel (1969), Joachim Jeremias (1971), and Eduard Lohse (1974) included the message of Jesus in New Testament theology. By contrast Andreas Lindemann (1975) limited this to the interpretation of the message of Easter. This debate is still not resolved.

In his *Biblische Theologie des Neuen Testaments* (Biblical Theology of the New Testament [3 vols., 1990–1995]), Hans Hübner consciously operated from the principle of "a theology, the subject of which is the entire Bibl..., that seeks to encompass both Old and New Testaments" (1:14). He proceeds by examining the interpretation of the Old Testament in the New. He sees the relationship between the Testaments in both continuity and discontinuity and uses this as his manner of treating New Testament texts. Most of the newer investigations of a common biblical theology proceed in the opposite fashion, that is, from the Old Testament to the New. Therefore, there are models of salvation history, typology, "promise and fulfillment," traditions history, and the bridging of the two Testaments by means of common theological concepts. One is also able to say here that the development is still not completed, and the different efforts have illumined only some of the aspects of interpretation. How and whether a biblical theology is possible is still discussed in a controversial fashion.

However, the task remains to make newly accessible to the church the *entire* Bible in its indissoluble connection.

To describe these developments individually would at least require an additional volume in this series. However, for such an enterprise the chronological and intellectual distance is not great enough, since we currently are engaged in discussions that are yet unfinished. Later generations must write this new description.

Selected Resources and Readings

1. Lutheran Hermeneutics in Germany

1.1. Matthias Flacius Illyricus

Works
Clavis scripturae seu de sermone sacrarum literarum. 2 vols. Frankfurt: Pauli, 1719.
De ratione cognoscendi sacras literas. Edited by Lutz Geldsetzer. Düsseldorf: Janssen, 1968.

Literature
Barton, Peter. "Matthias Flacius Illyricus." Pages 277–93 in vol. 2 of *Reformationszeit.* Edited by Martin Greschat. Gestalten der Kirchengeschichte 6. Stuttgart: Kohlhammer, 1981.
Baur, Jörg. "Flacius—Radilkale Theologie." *ZThK* 72 (1975): 365–80.
Keller, Rudolf. *Der Schlüssel zur Schrift. Die Lehre von der heiligen Schrift bei Matthias Flacius Illyricus.* Hannover: Lutherisches Verlagshaus, 1984.
Moldaenke, Gunter. *Schriftverständnis und Schriftdeutung im Zeitalter der Reformation I: Matthias Flacius Illyricus.* Stuttgart: Kohlhammer, 1936.
Preger, Wihelm. *Matthias Flacius Illyricus und seine Zeit.* 2 vols. Erlangen, 1859–1861. Repr., Hildesheim: Olm, 1964.
Schwartz, Karl Adolf von. *Die theologische Hermeneutik des Matthias Flacius Illyricus.* Munich: Mößl, 1933.

1.2. Johann Gerhard

Works
Loci theologici cum pro adstruenda veritate tum pro destruenda quorumvis contradicentium falsitate per theses nervose solide et copiose explicate.

Edited by Johann Friedrich Cotta. 20 vols. Tübingen: Cotta, 1762–1781.

———. 9 vols. Jena: Steinmann, 1610–1623. Repr., edited by Eduard Preuss. Berlin: Schlawitz, 1863–1870.

LITERATURE

Baur, Jörg. "Die Leuchte Thüringens. Johann Gerhard (1582–1637). Zeitgerechte Rechtgläubigkeit im Schatten des Dreißigjährigen Krieges." Pages 335–56 in *Luther und seine klassischen Erben: Theologische Aufsätze und Forschungen*. Tübingen: Mohr Siebeck, 1993.

Hägglund, Bengt. *Die heilige Schrift und ihre Deutung in der Theologie Johann Gerhards*. Lund: Gleerup, 1951.

Kirste, Reinhard. *Das Zeugnis des Geistes und das Zeugnis der Schrift: Das testimonium Spiritus sancti internum als hermeneutisch-polemischer Zentralbegriff bei Joh. Gerhard in Auseinandersetzung mit Robert Bellarmins Schriftverständnis*. Göttingen: Vandenhoeck & Ruprecht, 1976.

2. THE BIBLE IN ENGLAND FROM THE SIXTEENTH TO THE EIGHTEENTH CENTURIES

GENERAL

Reventlow, Henning Graf. *The Authority of the Bible and the Rise of the Modern World*. Philadelphia: Fortress, 1985.

2.1. THOMAS CARTWRIGHT

GENERAL

Emerson, Everett H. *English Puritanism from John Hooper to John Milton*. Durham, N.C.: Duke University Press, 1968.

Frere, Walter Howard, and Charles Edward Douglas, eds. *Puritan Manifestoes: A Study of the Origin of the Puritan Revolt with a Reprint of the Admonition to the Parliament and Kindred Documents, 1572*. London: SPCK, 1907; 2nd ed., 1954. Repr., New York: Franklin, 1972.

Lake, Peter. *Moderate Puritans and the Elizabethan Church*. Cambridge: Cambridge University Press, 1982.

WORKS

Anonymous (Cartwright, Thomas?). *A Christian Letter of Certaine Eng-*

lish Protestants ... unto That Reverend and Learned Man, Mr R. Hoo, Requring Resolution in Certinae Matters of Doctrine. Middelburg: Schilders, 1599. Repr., Amsterdam: Theatrum Orbis Terrarum; New York: Da Capo, 1969.

A Brief Apologie of Thomas Cartwright against All Such Slaunderous Accusations as It Pleaseth Mr Sutcliffe in Seuerall Pamphlettes Most Iniuriously to Loade Him With. Middelburg: Schilders, 1596. Repr., Amsterdam: Theatrum Orbis Terrarum; New York: Da Capo, 1970.

A Directory of Church-Government Drawn Up and Used by the Elizabethan Presbyterians. London: Wright, 1644. Reprinted in, Albert Peel and Leland H. Carlson, eds. Cartwrightiana. Elizabethan Nonconformist Texts 1. London: Allen & Unwin, 1951.

LITERATURE

Pearson, A. F. Scott. Thomas Cartwright and Elizabethan Puritanism. Cambridge: Cambridge University Press, 1925. Repr., Gloucester, Mass.: Smith, 1966.

2.2. THOMAS HOBBES

WORKS

De cive; or, The Citizen. Edited by Howard Warrender. Oxford: Clarendon, 1984.

The English Works of Thomas Hobbes Now First Collected and Edited by Sir William Molesworth. Edited by Bernard Orchard and Thomas R. W. Longstaff. 11 vols. London: Bohn, 1839–1845. Repr., Aalén: Scientia, 1962.

Leviathan. Edited by with an introduction by John Charles Addison Gaskin. Oxford and New York, 1996.

Leviathan. Translated by Jutta Jutta Schlösser. Edited by Hermann Klenner. Philosophische Bibliothek 491. Hamburg: Meiner, 1996.

Leviathan; oder, Stoff, Form und Gewalt eines bürgerlichen kirchlichen Staates. Edited by Wolfgang Kersting, Berlin: Akademie, 1996.

Leviathan; or, The Matter, Forme and Power of a Commonwealth Ecclesiastical and Civil. Edited by Michael Oakeshott, Oxford: Blackwell, 1946. Repr., Collier Classics in the History of Thought. New York: Collier Macmillan, 1962.

Thomae Hobbes Malmesburiensis opera philosophica quae latine scripsit omnia, in unum corpus nunc primum collecta studio et labore Gulielmi

Molesworth. 5 vols. London: Bohn, 1839–1845. Repr., Aalén: Scientia, 1962.

Vom Menschen; Vom Bürger. Edited by Günter Gawlick. Philosophische Bibliothek 158. 2nd ed. Hamburg: Meiner, 1966.

LITERATURE

Bowle, John. *Hobbes and His Critics: A Study in Seventeenth Century Constitutionalism.* New York: Oxford University Press, 1952.

Braun, Dietrich. *Erwägungen zu Ort, Bedeutung und Funktion der Lehre von der Königsherrschaft Christi in Thomas Hobbes' "Leviathan".* Vol. 1 of *Der sterbliche Gott oder Leviathan gegen Behemoth.* Zürich: EVZ-Verlag, 1963.

Farr, James. "Atomes of Scripture: Hobbes and the Politics of Biblical Interpretation." Pages 172–96 in *Thomas Hobbes and Political Theory.* Edited by Mary G. Dietz. Lawrence: University Press of Kansas, 1990.

Förster, Winfried. *Thomas Hobbes und der Puritanismus: Grundlagen und Grundfragen seiner Staatslehre.* Berlin: Duncker & Humblot, 1969.

Gauthier, David P. *The Logic of Leviathan.* Oxford: Clarendon, 1969.

Glover, Willis Borders. "God and Thomas Hobbes." *Church History* 29 (1960): 275–97. Repr. as pages 141–68 in *Hobbes-Studies.* Edited by Keith C. Brown. Oxford: Oxford University Press, 1965.

Hood, Francis Campbell. *The Divine Politics of Thomas Hobbes: An Interpretation of Leviathan.* Oxford: Clarendon, 1964.

Johnston, David. *The Rhetoric of Leviathan: Thomas Hobbes and the Politics of Cultural Transformation.* Princeton: Princeton University Press, 1986.

Kersting, Wolfgang. *Thomas Hobbes zur Einführung.* Hamburg: Junius, 1992.

Koselleck, Reinhart, and Roman Schnur, eds. *Hobbes-Forschungen.* Berlin: Duncker & Humblot, 1969.

Macpherson, Crawford Brough. *The Political Theory of Possessive Individualism: Hobbes to Locke.* Oxford: Clarendon, 1962.

McNeilly, Frederic S. *The Anatomy of Leviathan.* London: Macmillan, 1968.

Mintz, Samuel I. *The Hunting of Leviathan: Seventeenth Century Reactions to the Materialism and Moral Philosophy of Thomas Hobbes.* Cambridge: Cambridge University Press, 1962.

Röd, Wolfgang. "Thomas Hobbes (1588–1679)." Pages 280–300 in vol. 1 of *Klassiker der Philosophie.* Edited by Otfried Hoffe. Munich: Beck, 1981.

Rogow, Arnold A. *Thomas Hobbes: Radical in the Service of Reaction.* New York: Norton, 1986.

Schnur, Roman. *Individualismus und Absolutismus: Zur politischen Theorie von Thomas Hobbes (1600–1640).* Berlin: Duncker & Humblot, 1963.

Strauss, Leo. *The Political Philosophy of Hobbes: Its Basis and Its Genesis.* Chicago: University of Chicago Press, 1963.

Tönnies, Ferdinand. *Thomas Hobbes: Leben und Lehre.* Stuttgart: Frommann, 1925.

Warrender, Howard. *The Political Philosophy of Hobbes: His Theory of Obligation.* Oxford: Clarendon, 1957.

Willms, Bernard. *Die Antwort des Leviathan: Thomas Hobbes' politische Theorie.* Politica 28. Neuwied: Luchterhand, 1970.

———. *Thomas Hobbes: Das Reich des Leviathan.* Zürich: Piper, 1987.

2.3. JOHN LOCKE

WORKS

The Correspondence of John Locke. Edited by Esmond S. de Beer. 8 vols. Oxford: Clarendon, 1976–1989.

Epistola de tolerantia: A Letter on Tolerance. Edited by Raymond Klibanski. Oxford: Clarendon, 1968.

An Essay concerning Human Understanding. Edited by Peter H. Nidditch. Oxford: Clarendon, 1975.

An Essay concerning Human Understanding. Edited by Kenneth P. Winkler. Indianapolis: Hackett, 1996.

Essays on the Law of Nature. Edited by Wolfgang von Leyden. Oxford: Clarendon, 1954.

Filmer, Robert. *Patriarcha and Other Writings.* Edited by John P. Sommerville. Cambridge: Cambridge University Press, 1991.

A Paraphrase and Notes on the Epistles of St. Paul to the Galatians, 1 and 2 Corinthians, Romans, Ephesians. Edited by Arthur Wainwright. Oxford: Clarendon, 1987.

Two Tracts on Government. Edited by Peter Laslett. Cambridge: Cambridge University Press, 1967.

The Works of John Locke. New, corrected ed. 10 vols. Aalén: Scientia, 1963.

Zwei Abhandlungen über Regierung: Nebst "Patriarcha" von Sir Robert Filmer. Translated by Hilmer Williams. Halle : Niemeyer, 1906.

LITERATURE

Aaron, Richard I. *John Locke*. 2nd ed. Oxford: Clarendon, 1955.

Ashcradt, Richard, ed. *John Locke: Critical Assessments*. 4 vols. London: Routledge, 1991.

Bourne, Henry R. Fox. *The Life of John Locke*. 2 vols. London: King, 1876. Repr., Aalén: Scientia, 1969.

Brandt, Reinhard. "John Locke (1632–1704)." Pages 360–77 in vol. 1 of *Klassiker der Philosophie*. Edited by Otfried Höffe. Munich: Beck, 1981.

Cranston, Maurice. *John Locke: A Biography*. London: Longmans, 1957.

Euchner, Walter. *Naturrecht und Politik bei John Locke*. Frankfurt am Main: Europäosche, 1969.

Harris, Ian. *The Mind of John Locke: A Study of Political Theory in Its Intellectual Setting*. Cambridge: Cambridge University Press, 1994.

King, Peter, and Lord King. *The Life and Letters of John Locke*. London: Bell & Sons, 1884. Repr., New York: Garland, 1984.

Macpherson, Crawford Brough. *The Political Theory of Possessive Individualism: Hobbes to Locke*. Oxford: Clarendon, 1962.

Marshall, John. *John Locke: Resistance, Religion and Responsibility*. Cambridge: Cambridge University Press, 1994.

Spellman, William M. *John Locke*. New York: St. Martin's, 1997.

Yolton, John William. *John Locke: A Descriptive Bibliography*. Bristol: Thoemmes, 1998.

———. *John Locke and the Way of Ideas*. Oxford: Oxford University Press, 1968.

———, ed. *John Locke: Problems and Perspectives—A Collection of New Essays*. Cambridge: Cambridge University Press, 1969.

2.4. JOHN TOLAND

GENERAL

Hunter, Michael, and David Wootton, eds. *Atheism from the Reformation to the Enlightenment*. Oxford: Clarendon, 1992.

Lechler, Gotthard Victor. *Geschichte des englischen Deismus*. Stuttgart: Cotta, 1841. Repr., with a foreword and bibliographical references by Gunter Gawlick. Hildesheim: Olms, 1965.

Weinsheimer, Joel C. *Eighteenth Century Hermeneutics: Philosophy of Interpretation in England from Locke to Burke*. New Haven: Yale University Press, 1993.

WORKS

Christianity Not Mysterious. Repr. with an introduction by Günter Gawlick. Stuttgart-Bad Cannstatt: Frommann, 1964. [Orig. 1696]
Letters to Serena. Repr. Stuttgart: Frommann, 1964. [Orig. 1704]

LITERATURE

Daniel, Stephen H. *John Toland: His Methods, Manners, and Mind.* Kings-
ton, Ont.: McGill-Queen's University Press, 1984.
Sullivan, Robert E. *John Toland and the Deist Controversy.* Harvard Historical Studies 101. Cambridge: Harvard University Press, 1982.

3. THE BATTLE FOR THE TEXT OF THE BIBLE

3.1. ELIAS LEVITA, LOUIS CAPPEL, AND THE BUXTORFS

WORKS

Anonymous (Louis Cappel). "סוד הניקוד נגלה": *Hoc est arcanum punc-
tationis revelatum, sive De punctorum vocalium et accentuum apud
Hebraeos vera et germana antiquitate, Diatribe.* Edited by Thoma
Erpenio. Leiden: Maire, 1624.
Buxtorf, Johannes (father). *Tiberias sive commentarius Masorethicus tri-
plex, historicus, didacticus, criticus … recognitus, et additamentis non
paucis hinc inde locupletatus à Johann Buxtorfio Fil.* Edited by Johann
Jakob Buxtorf (son). Basel: Buxtorf, 1665.
Buxtorf, Johannes (son). *Johannis Buxtorfi, Filii, Tractatus de punctorum
vocalium, et accentuum, in libris Veteris Testamenti hebraicis, orig-
ine, antiquitate et authoritate oppositus arcano punctationis revelato
Ludovici Capelli.* Basel: Sumptibus haeredum Ludovici König, 1648.
Levita, Elias. *Sefer Masoret ha-Masoret: Liber traditionis traditionum.*
Basel, 1539 = *The Massoreth Ha-Massoreth of Elias Levita.* Hebrew,
with an English translation and notes by Christian David Ginsburg.
London: Longmans, Green, Reader & Dyer, 1867.

LITERATURE

Burnett, Stephen G. *From Christian Hebraism to Jewish Studies: Johannes
Buxtorf (1564–1629) and Hebrew Learning in the Seventeeth Century*
SHCT 68. Leiden: Brill, 1996.
Laplanche, Francois. *L'écriture, le sacré et l'histoire: Érudits et politiques
protestants devant la Bible en France au XVIIe siècle.* Amsterdam:
APA-Holland University Press, 1986.

Schnedermann, Georg. *Die Controverse des Ludovicus Cappellus mit den Buxtorfen über das Alter der hebräischen Punctation.* Leipzig: Hinrichs, 1879.

Smend, Rudolf. "Der ältere Buxtorf." *ThZ* 53 (1997): 109–17.

Weil, Gérard E. *Elie Lévita: Humaniste et Massorète (1469–1549).* StPB 7. Leiden: Brill, 1964.

3.2. JOHN MILL, JOHANN ALBRECHT BENGEL, JAKOB WETTSTEIN

WORKS

Bengel, Johann Albrecht. *Gnomon Novi Testamenti.* Tübingen: Schramm, 1742; 2nd ed., 1759; 3rd ed., 1773. [Many new editions, often abbreviated without textual critical notes]

Wettstein, Johann Jacob. *Jo. Jacobi Wetstenii Epistola ad virum plurinum venerandum H. Venema.* Amsterdam: Adrianum Slaats, 1754.

———. *Libelli ad crisin: Atque interpretationem Novi Testamenti.* Edited by Johann Salomo Semler. Halle: Trampe, 1766.

———. *Novum Testamentum Graecum.* 2 vols. Amsterdam: Dommer, 1751–1752. Repr., Graz: Akademische Druck, 1962, 1969.

LITERATURE

Brecht, Martin. "Johann Albrecht Bengels Theologie der Schrift." *ZThK* 64 (1967): 99–120.

———. "Johannes Albrecht Bengel und der schwäbische Biblizismus." Pages 193–218 in *Pietismus und Bibel.* Edited by Kurt Aland. Witten: Luther, 1970.

Fox, Adam. *John Mill and Richard Bentley.* Oxford: Blackwell, 1954.

Horst, Pieter Willem van der. "Johann Jacob Wettstein nach 300 Jahren: Erbe und Auftrag." *ThZ* 49 (1993): 267–81.

Hulbert-Powell, Charles Lacy. *John James Wettstein 1693–1754: An Account of His Life, Work, and Some of His Contemporaries.* London: SPCK, 1938.

Merk, Otto. "Von Jean-Alphonse Turrenti zu Johann Jakob Wettstein." Pages 89–112 in *Historische Kritik und biblischer Kanon in der deutschen Aufklärung.* Edited by Henning Graf Reventlow, Walter Sparn, and John Woodbridge. Wolfenbüttler Forschungen 41. Wiesbaden: Harrassowitz, 1988.

Mussies, Gerard. "Wettstein (Wetstenius), Johann Jakob." Pages 394–399 in vol. 3 of *Biografisch lexicon voor de geschiedenis van het Neder-*

landse protestantisme. Edited by Doede Nauta et al. 6 vols. Kampen: Kok, 1988.

4. FRANCE AND THE NETHERLANDS IN THE SEVENTEENTH AND EIGHTEENTH CENTURIES

4.1. RICHARD SIMON

WORKS

Histoire critique des principaux commentateurs du Nouveau Testament, depuis le commencement du Christianisme juque à nôtre tems. Rotterdam: Leers, 1693. Repr., Frankfurt am Main: Minerva, 1969.

Histoire critique des versions du Nouveau Testament, ou on l'on fait connoître quel a été l'usage de la lectures des livres sacrés dans les principales églises du monde. Rotterdam: Leers, 1690. Repr., Frankfurt am Main: Minerva, 1967.

Histoire critique du Texte du Nouveau Testament. Rotterdam: Leers, 1689. Repr., Frankfurt am Main: Minerva, 1968.

Histoire critique du Vieux Testament. Rotterdam: Leers, 1678; 2nd ed., 1685. Repr., Frankfurt am Main: Minerva, 1967.

Nouvelles observations sur le texte et les versions du Nouveau Testament. Paris: Boudot, 1695. Repr., Frankfurt am Main: Minerva, 1973.

LITERATURE

Bernus, Auguste. *Richard Simon et son Histoire critique du Vieux Testament: La critique biblique au siècle de Louis XIV.* Lausanne: Bridel, 1869. Repr., Geneva: Slatkine, 1969.

Margival, Henri. *Essai sur Richard Simon et la critique biblique au 17e siècle.* Paris: Maillet, 1900. Repr., Geneva: Slatkine, 1970.

Mirri, Francesco Savemo. *Richard Simon e il metodo storico-critico di B. Spinoza.* Firence: Le Monnier, 1972.

Reventlow, Henning Graf. "Richard Simon." Pages 9–21 in vol. 2 of *Klassiker der Theologie.* Edited by Heinrich Fries and Georg Kretschmar. 2 vols. Munich: Beck, 1981–1983.

———. "Richard Simon und seine Bedeutung für die kritische Erforschung der Bibel. Pages 11–36 in *Historische Kritik in der Theologie.* Edited by Georg Schwaiger. Beiträge zu ihrer Geschichte. Göttingen: Vandenhoeck & Ruprecht, 1980.

Steinmann, Jean. *Richard Simon et les origines de l'exegese Biblique.* Paris: Desclee de Brouwer, 1960.

Stummer, Friedrich. *Die Bedeutung Richard Simons für die Pentateuchkritik.* ATA 3/4. Munster: Aschendorff, 1912.

4.2. BARUCH DE SPINOZA

WORKS

Briefwechsel. Translation and notes by Carl Gebhart. 3rd ed. Edited by Manfred Walther. Hamburg: Meiner, 1986.

Ethica ordine geometrica demonstrata/Die Ethik in geometrischer Methode begründet. Edited by Konrad Blumenstock. Pages 84–587 in vol. 2 of *Opera/Werke.* Darmstadt: Wissenschaftliche Buchgesellschaft, 1980.

Opera quotquot reperta sunt. Edited by Johannes van Vloten und Jan Pieter Nicholas Land. The Hague: Comitum, 1914.

Opera. Edited by Carl Gebhardt. 5 vols. Heidelberg: Winter, 1925–1987.

Politischer Traktat: Lateinisch-Deutsch. Translated and edited by Wolfgang Bartuschat. Philosophische Bibliothek 95b. Hamburg: Meiner, 1994.

Tractatus theologico-politicus. Translated by Samuel Shirley. Leiden: Brill, 1989.

Tractatus theologico-politicus/Theologisch-politischer Traktat. Vol. 1 of *Opera/Werke.* Edited by Günter Gawlick and Friedrich Niewöhner. Darmstadt: Wissenschaftliche Buchgesellschaft, 1989.

LITERATURE

Breton, Stanislas. *Politique, religion, écriture chez Spinoza.* Lyon: Profac, 1973.

Breton, Stanislas. *Spinoza: Théologie et politique.* Paris: Desclée, 1977.

Colerus, John. *Spinoza, His Life and Philosophy.* New York: American Scholar Publications, 1966.

Delf, Hanna, et al., eds. *Spinoza in der europäischen Geistesgeschichte.* Studien zur Geistesgeschichte 16. Berlin: Hentrich, 1994.

Freudenthal, Jacob. *Spinoza, sein Leben und seine Lehre,* Stuttgart: Frommann, 1904 = *Spinoza: Leben und Lehre.* Edited by Carl Gebhardt. Heidelberg: Winter, 1927.

Garrett, Don. *The Cambridge Companion to Spinoza.* Cambridge: Cambridge University Press, 1996.

Gründer, Karlfried, and Schmidt-Biggemann, Wilhelm, eds. *Spinoza in der Frühzeit seiner religiösen Wirkung.* WSA 12. Heidelberg: Schneider, 1984.

Harris, Errol E. *Salvation from Despair: A Reappraisal of Spinoza's Philosophy.* The Hague: Martinus Nijhoff, 1973.

Lucas, Jean-Maximilian. *La Vie et l'esprit de M. Bénoit de Spinoza.* Amsterdam: Charles le Vier, 1719.

Malet, André. *La Traité théologico-politique de Spinoza et la penseé biblique.* Paris: Belles Lettres, 1966.

Meinsma, Koenraad Oege. *Spinoza und sein Kreis: Historisch-kritische Studien über holländische Freigeister.* Berlin: Schnabel, 1909.

Moreau, Pierre-François. "Les principes de la lecture de l'Ecriture sainte dans le Tranctatus Theologico-Politicus." Pages 119–31 in *L'écriture sainte au temps de Spinoza et dans le système spinoziste.* Group de Recherches Spinozistes, Travaux et Documents 4. Paris: Presses de l'Université de Paris Sorbonne, 1992.

———. *Spinoza: Versuch über die Anstößigkeit seines Denkens.* Frankfurt am Main: Fischer-Taschenbuch, 1994.

Nassen, Ulrich, ed. *Klassiker der Hermeneutik.* Paderborn: Schöningh, 1982.

Piepmeier, Rainer. "Baruch de Spinoza: Vernunftanspruch und Hermeneutik." Pages 9–42 in *Klassiker der Hermeneutik.* Edited by Ulrich Nassen. Paderborn: Schöningh, 1982.

Smith, Steven B. *Spinoza, Liberalism, and the Question of Jewish Identity.* New Haven: Yale University Press, 1997.

Specht, Rainer. "Baruch Spinoza (1632–1704)." Pages 338–59 in vol. 1 of *Klassiker der Philosophie.* Edited by Otfried Höffe. Munich: Beck, 1981.

Strauss, Leo. *Spinoza's Critique of Religion.* New York: Schocken, 1965.

Walther, Manfred. *Das Leben Spinozas: Eine Bibliographie.* Hannover: Witte, 1996.

Zac, Sylvain. *Spinoza et l'interpretation de l'Ecriture.* Paris: Presses Universitaires de France, 1965.

4.3. Pierre-Daniel Huet (Huetius)

Works

Censura philosophiae Cartesianae. Kampen: Cotti, 1690. Repr., Hildesheim: Olms, 1971.

Demonstratio evangelica ad serenissimum Delphinum. Paris: Michallet, 1679; 2nd ed., 1680; 3rd ed., 1690; 4th ed., 1784.

Mémoires: 1718. Introduction and notes by Philippe-Joseph Salazar. Paris: Klincksieck, 1993.

Lettre-traité de Pierre-Daniel Huet sur l'origine des romans: Edition du Tricentenaire 1669–1969. Edited by Fabien Gégou. Paris: Nizet, 1971.

Traite philosophique de la faiblesse de l'esprit humain. Amsterdam: Du Sauzet, 1723.

LITERATURE

Dupront, Alphonse. *Pierre-Daniel Huet et l'exegese comparatiste au XVIIe siècle.* Paris: Leroux, 1930.

Espenberger, Johann Nepomuk. *Die apologetischen Bestrebungen des Bischofs Huet von Avranches.* Freiburg im Breisgau: Herder, 1905.

Gégou, Fabienne. "Un érudit du Grand Siècle. Pierre-Daniel Huet, traite du gay sober." Pages 359–68 in *Melanges d'histoire litteraire, de linguistique et de philologie romanes.* Edited by Charles Rostaint. Liège: Association Intercommunale de Mecanographie, 1974.

Guellouz, Suzanne, ed. *Pierre-Daniel Huet (1630–1721): Actes du colloque de Caen (12–13 novembre 1993).* Biblio 17. Paris: Papers on French Seventeenth Century Literature, 1974.

Tolmer, Leon. *Pierre-Daniel Huet (1630–1721): Humaniste-Physicien.* Bayeux: Colas, 1949.

5. THE BIBLE IN PIETISM AND THE GERMAN ENLIGHTENMENT

5.1. PHILIPP JACOB SPENER

WORK

Pia desideria. Edited by Kurt Aland. 3rd ed. Kleine Texte für Vorlesungen und Übungen 170. Berlin: de Gruyter, 1964.

LITERATURE

Aland, Kurt. "Bibel und Bibeltext bei August Hermann Francke und Johann Albrecht Bengel." Pages 89–147 in *Pietismus und Bibel.* Edited by Kurt Aland. Witten: Luther-Verlag, 1970.

Brecht, Martin. "Philipp Jacob Spener, sein Programm und seine Auswirkungen." Pages 281–389 in *Der Pietismus vom siebzehnten bis zum frühen achtzehnten Jahrhundert.* Edited by Martin Brecht. Geschichte des Pietismus 1. Göttingen: Vandenhoeck & Ruprecht, 1993.

Chi, Hyeong-Eun. *Philipp Jakob Spener und seine Pia desideria: Die Weiterführung der Reformvorschläge der Pia desideria in seinem späteren Schrifttum.* Frankfurt am Main: Lang, 1997.

Schmidt, Martin. "Philipp Jacob Spener und die Bibel." Pages 9–58 in *Pietismus und Bibel.* Edited by Kurt Aland. Witten: Luther-Verlag, 1970.

Wallmann, Johannes. "Philipp Jacob Spener." Pages 205–23 in *Orthodoxie*

und Pietismus. Edited by Martin Greschat. Gestalten der Kirchengeschichte 7. Stuttgart: Kohlhammer, 1982.

Wallmann, Johannes. *Philipp Jacob Spener und die Anfänge des Pietismus.*
2nd ed. BHTh 42. Tübingen: Mohr Siebeck, 1986.

5.2. AUGUST HERMANN FRANCKE

WORKS

*Manuductio ad lectionem scripturae sacrae historicam, grarmnaticam et
practicam una cum additamentis regulas hermeneuticas de affectibus,
et enarrationes ac introductiones succinctas in aliquot epistulas Pauli-
nas complectentibus.* Halae: Zeitler, 1693; 3rd ed., 1709.

*Praelectiones hermeneuticae, ad viam dectre indagandi et exponendi
sensum scripturae sanctae studiosis ostendam.* Halle: Orphanotro-
pheum, 1723.

Werke in Auswahl. Edited by Erhard Peschke. Witten: Luther-Verlag,
1969.

LITERATURE

Brecht, Martin. "August Hermann Francke und der Hallische Pietismus." Pages 439–39 in *Der Pietismus vom siebzehnten bis zum frühen
achtzehnten Jahrhundert.* Edited by Martin Brecht. Göttingen: Vandenhoeck & Ruprecht, 1993.

Deppermann, Klaus. "August Hermann Francke." Pages 241–60 in
Orthodoxie und Pietismus. Edited by Martin Greschat. Gestalten der
Kirchengeschichte 7. Stuttgart: Kohlhammer, 1982.

Peschke, Erhard. "August Hermann Francke und die Bibel: Studien zur
Entwicklung seiner Hermeneutik." Pages 59–87 in *Pietismus und
Bibel.* Edited by Kurt Aland. Witten: Luther, 1970.

———. *Bekehrung und Reform: Ansatz und Wurzeln der Theologie August
Hermann Franckes.* Arbeiten zur Geschichte des Pietismus 15. Bielefeld: Luther-Verlag, 1977.

———. *Studien zur Theologie August Hermann Franckes.* 2 vols. Berlin:
Evangelische, 1964–1966.

5.3. JOHANN CHRISTIAN EDELMANN

WORK

Sämtliche Schriften in Einzelausgaben. Edited by Walter Grossmann. 12
vols. Stuttgart-Bad Cannstatt: Frommann, 1969–1986.

LITERATURE

Grossmann, Walter. *Johann Christian Edelmann: From Orthodoxy to Enlightenment.* The Hague: Mouton, 1976.

Mönckeberg, Carl. *Hermann Samuel Reimarus und Johann Christian Edelmann.* Hamburg: Nolte, 1867.

Schaper, Annegret. *Ein langer Abschied vom Christentum: Johann Christian Edelmann (1698–1767) und die deutsche Frhaufklärung.* Marburg: Tectum, 1996.

GENERAL

Schweitzer, Albert. *The Quest of the Historical Jesus.* Translated by W. Montgomery et al. Minneapolis: Fortress, 2001.

5.4. HERMANN SAMUEL REIMARUS

WORKS

Die vornehmsten Wahrheiten der natürlichen Religion. 3rd ed. Hamburg: Bohn, 1766. Repr. Edited by Günter Gawlick. 2 vols. Göttingen: Vandenhoeck & Ruprecht, 1985.

Allgemeine Betrachtungen über die Triebe der Thiere. Edited by Jürgen von Kempski. 2 vols. Göttingen: Vandenhoeck & Ruprecht, 1982.

Apologie oder Schutzschrift für die vernünftigen Verehrer Gottes. Edited by Gerhard Alexander. 2 vols. Gesammelte Schriften 5. Frankfurt am Main: Insel, 1972.

Kleine gelehrte Schriften: Vorstufen zur Apologie oder Schutzschrift für die vernünftigen Verehrer Gottes. Edited by Wilhelm Schmidt-Biggemann. Veröffentlichungen der Joachim-Jungius-Gesellschaft der Wissenschaften Hamburg 79. Göttingen: Vandenhoeck & Ruprecht, 1994.

The Principal Truths of Natural Religion Defended and Illustrated, in Nine Dissertations. Translated by R. Wynne. London: Law, 1766.

Vernunftlehre. Edited by Frieder Lötsch. New printing of the 1st (1756) ed., with references to the 3rd (1766) ed. Munich: Hanser, 1979.

Vindicatio dictorum Veteris Testamenti in Novo allegatorum. Edited by Peter Stemmer. Gesammelte Schriften 20. Veröffentlichungen der Joachim-Jungius-Gesellschaft der Wissenschaften Hamburg 47. Göttingen: Vandenhoeck & Ruprecht, 1983. [Orig. 1731]

LITERATURE

Boehart, William. *Politik und Religion: Studien zum Fragmentenstreit (Reimarus, Goeze, Lessing).* Schwarzenbeck: Martienss, 1988.

Gawlick, Günter. "Hermann Samuel Reimarus." Pages 299–311 in *Die Aufklärung*. Edited by Martin Greschat. Gestalten der Kirchengeschichte 8. Stuttgart: Kohlhammer, 1983.

Lachner, Raimund. "Reimarus, Hermann Samuel." *BBKL* 7:1514–20.

Schetelig, Johann Andreas Gottfried, ed. *Auktionskatalog der Bibliothek von Hermann Samuel Reimarus*. Hamburg: Reimarus-Kommission der Joachim-Jungius-Gesellschaft der Wissenschaften, 1978. [Orig. 1769 and 1770]

Schmidt-Biggemann, Wilhelm. *Hermann Samuel Reimarus: Handschriftenverzeichnis und Bibliographie*. Göttingen: Vandenhoeck & Ruprecht, 1979.

Schultze, Harald. "Reimarus, Hermann Samuel (1694–1768)." *TRE* 28:470–73.

Stemmer, Peter. *Weissagung und Kritik: Eine Studie zur Hermeneutik bei Hermann Samuel Reimarus*. Veröffentlichungen der Joachim-Jungius-Gesellschaft 48. Göttingen: Vandenhoeck & Ruprecht, 1983.

Walter, Wolfgang, ed. *Hermann Samuel Reimarus 1694–1768: Beiträge zur Reimarus-Renaissance in der Gegenwart*. Göttingen: Vandenhoeck & Ruprecht, 1998.

General

O'Neill, John Cochrane. *The Bible's Authority: A Portrait Gallery of Thinkers from Lessing to Bultmann*. Edinburgh: T&T Clark, 1991.

5.5. Gotthold Ephraim Lessing

Works

Die Erziehung des Menschengeschlechts. Edited by Louis Ferdinand Helbig. Bern: Lang, 1980.

Sechs theologische Schriften Gotthold Ephraim Lessings. Introduced and interpreted by Wolfgang Gericke. Berlin: Evangelische Verlagsanstalt, 1985.

Werke. Edited by Herbert G. Gopfert. 8 vols. Munich: Hanser, 1979.

Literature

Aner, Karl. *Die Theologie der Lessingzeit*. Halle: Niemeyer, 1929. Repr., Hildesheim: Olms, 1964.

Batley, Edward M. *Catalyst of Enlightenment: Gotthold Ephraim Lessing: Productive Criticism of Eighteenth-Century Germany*. Bern: Lang, 1990.

Bollacher, Martin. *Lessing, Vernunft und Geschichte: Untersuchungen zum Problem religiöser Aufklärung in den Spätschriften.* Tübingen: Niemeyer, 1978.

Mann, Otto. *Lessing: Sein und Leistung.* 2nd ed. Berlin: de Gruyter, 1965.

Schilson, Arno. *Lessings Christentum.* Kleine Reihe 1463. Göttingen: Vandenhoeck & Ruprecht, 1980.

Schmidt, Erich. *Lessing: Geschichte seines Lebens und seiner Schriften.* 4th ed. 2 vols. Berlin: Weidemann, 1923.

Sichelschmidt, Gustav. *Lessing: Der Mann und sein Werk.* Düsseldorf: Droste, 1989.

Smend, Rudolf. "Lessing und die Bibelwissenschaft." Pges 298–319 in *Congress Volume: Göttingen, 1977.* VTSup 29. Leiden: Brill, 1978. Repr. as pages 74–92 in idem, *Epochen der Bibelkritik: Gesammelte Studien 3.* BevT 109. Munich: Kaiser, 1991.

———. *Lessings Nachlaßfragmente zum Alten Testament.* Göttingen: Vandenhoeck & Ruprecht, 1979. Repr. as pages 93–103 in idem, *Epochen der Bibelkritik: Gesammelte Studien 3.* BevT 109. Munich: Kaiser, 1991.

Thielicke, Helmut. *Vernunft und Offenbarung.* 3rd ed. Gütersloh: Bertelsmann, 1957 = *Offenbarung, Vernunft und Existenz: Studien zur Religionsphilosophie Lessings.* Gütersloh: Bertelsmann, 1967.

5.6. Johann Salomo Semler

Works

Abhandlung von freier Untersuchung des Canon. Edited by Heinz Scheible. Gütersloh: Mohn, 1967. [Orig. 4 vols., 1771–1775]

Apparatus ad liberalem Veteris Testamenti interpretationem. Halae: Hemmerde, 1773.

Beantwortung der Fragmente eines Ungenannten insbesondere vom Zweck Jesu und seiner Jünger. Halle: Erziehungsinstitut, 1779.

Evangelische Glaubenslehre. 3 vols. Edited by Siegmund Jacob Baumgarten. Halle: Gebauer, 1759–1760.

Geschichte der Religionspartheyen. Edited by Jacob Baumgarten Siegmund. Halle: Gebauer, 1766.

Letztes Glaubensbekenntnis über natürliche und christliche Religion. Königsberg: Nicolov, 1792.

Versuch zu einer freien theologischen Lehrart zur Bestätigung und Erlauterung seines lateinischen Buches. 2 vols. Halle: Hemmerde, 1777.

LITERATURE

Hess, Hans Eberhard. "Theologie und Religion bei Johann Salomo Semler: Ein Beitrag zur Theologiegeschichte des Jahrhunderts." Diss. Kirchl. Hochschule Berlin, 1974.

Horning Gottfried. *Die Anfänge der historisch-kritischen Theologie: Johann Salomo Semlers Schriftverständnis und seine Stellung zu Luther*. FSThR 8. Göttingen: Vandenhoeck & Ruprecht, 1961.

———. *Johann Salomo Semler: Studien zu Leben und Werk des Hallenser Aufklärungstheologen*. Tübingen: Niemeyer, 1996.

Lüder, Andrem. *Historie und Dogmatik: Ein Beitrag zur Genese und Entfaltung von Johann Salomo Semlers Verständnis des Alten Testaments*. BZAW 233. Berlin: de Gruyter, 1995.

5.7. JOHANN GOTTFRIED HERDER

WORKS

Sämtliche Werke. Edited by Bernhard Suphan et al. 33 vols. Berlin: Weidmann, 1877–1913. Repr., Hildesheim: Olms, 1967–1968.

Werke in Zehn Bänden. Edited by Martin Bollacher et al. 10 vols. Frankfurt am Main: Deutscher Klassiker, 1985–2000.

LITERATURE

Bultmann, Christoph. *Die biblische Urgeschichte in der Aufklärung: Johann Gottfried Herders Interpretation der Genesis als Anwort auf die Religionskritik David Humes*. Tübingen: Mohr Siebeck, 1999.

Haym, Rudolf. *Herder nach seinem Leben und seinen Werken*. 2 vols. Berlin: Weidmann, 1880–1885. Repr., Berlin: Aufbau-Verlag, 1958.

Heinz, Marion, ed. *Herder und die Philosophie des deutschen Idealismus*. Fichte Studien Supplementa 8. Amsterdam: Rodopi, 1991.

Herms, Eilert. "Herder, Johann Gottfried (1744–1803)." *TRE* 15:70–95.

Otto, Regine, ed. *Nationen und Kulturen. Zum 250. Geburtstag Johann Gottfried Herders*. Würzburg: Königshausen & Neumann, 1996.

Poschmann, Brigitte, ed. *Bückeburger Gesprache über Johann Gottfried Herder 1979*. Schaumburger Studien 41. Rinteln: Bösendahl, 1980.

———, ed. *Bückeburger Gespräche über Johann Gottfried Herder 1988*. Älteste Urkunde des Menschengeschlechts. Rinteln: Bösendahl, 1989.

Sauder, Gerhard. *Johann Gottfried Herder 1744–1803*. Hamburg: Meiner, 1987.

Willi, Thomas. *Herders Beitrag zum Verstehen des Alten Testaments*.

Beiträge zur Geschichte der biblischen Hermeneutik 8. Tübingen: Mohr Siebeck, 1971.

5.8. JOHANN JAKOB GRIESBACH

WORKS

"Commentatio qua Marci Evangelium totum e Matthei et Lucae commentariis decerptum esse monstrantur." Pages 103–35 in *Johann Jakob Griesbach: Synoptic and Text-Critical Studies 1776–1976*. Edited by Bernard Orchard and Thomas R. W. Longstaff. SNTSMS 34. Cambridge: Cambridge University Press, 1978.

Opuscula academica. Edited by Johann Philipp Gabler. 2 vols. Jena: Frommann, 1824–1825.

LITERATURE

Delling, Gerhard. "Johann Jakob Griesbach: Seine Zeit, sein Leben, sein Werk." *ThZ* 33 (1977): 81–99.

Dungan, David Lee. *A History of the Synoptic Problem: The Canon, the Text, the Composition, and the Interpretation of the Gospels*. Winona Lake, Ind.: Eisenbrauns, 1999.

Johnson, Sherman E. *The Griesbach Hypothesis and Redaction Criticism*. SBLMS 41 Atlanta: Scholars Press, 1991.

Lang, Maruike Helene de. "De opkomst van de historische en literaire kritiek in de synoptische beschouwing van de evangeliën van Calvijn (1555) tot Griesbach (1774)." Diss., Leiden, 1993.

Metzger, Bruce M. "Griesbach, Johann Jakob (1745–1812)." *TRE* 14:253–56.

5.9. HEINRICH EBERHARD GOTTLOB PAULUS

WORKS

Des Apostels Paulus Lehr-Briefe an die Galater- und Römer-Christen. Heidelberg: Winter, 1831.

Des Apostels Paulus Ermahnungs-Schreiben an die Hebräer-Christen. Heidelberg: Winter, 1831.

Exegetisches Handbuch über die drei ersten Evangelien. 3 vols. Heidelberg: Winter, 1830–1833. *Handbuch über die drei ersten Evangelien: Wohlfeile Ausgabe*. 3 vols. Heidelberg: Winter, 1842.

Die freie religiöse Aufklärung, ihre Geschichte und ihre Häupter. Darmstadt: Leske, 1843.

Das Leben Jesu als Grundlage einer reinen Geschichte des Urchristentums. 2 vols. Heidelberg: Winter, 1828.

Philologisch-kritischer und historischer Commentar über das Evangelium des Johannes. Lübeck: Bohn, 1804.

Philologisch-kritischer und historischer Commentar über die drei ersten Evangelien. 3 vols. Lübeck: Bohn, 1800–1802.

Skizzen aus meiner Bildungs- und Lebens-Geschichte zum Andenken an mein 50jähriges Jubiläum. Heidelberg: Groos, 1839.

LITERATURE

Burchard, Christoph. "H. E. G. Paulus in Heidelberg 1811–1851." Pages 222–97 in vol. 2 of *Semper apertus.* Edited by Wilhelm Doerr. 6 vols. Berlin: Springer, 1985.

Graf, Friedrich-Wilhelm. "Frühliberaler Liberalismus: Heinrich Eberhard Gottlieb Paulus (1761–1851)." Pages 128–55 in *Aufklärung. Idealismus.* Vol. 1 of *Profile des neuzeitlichen Protestantismus.* Edited by Friedrich-Wilhelm Graf. Vormärz, Gütersloh, 1990.

Reichlin-Meldegg, Karl Alexander von. *Heinrich Eberhard Gottlob Paulus und seine Zeit nach dessen literarischem Nachlasse, bisher ungedrucktem Briefwechsel und mündlichen Mittheilungen dargestellt.* 2 vols. Stuttgart: Verlags-Magazin, 1853.

Reventlow, Henning Graf. "Eberhard Gottlieb Paulus (1761–1851)." Pages 211–225 in *Gottes Recht als Lebensraum: Festschrift für Hans Jochen Boecker.* Edited by Hans Strauss and Eckard Schwab. Neukirchen-Vluyn: Neukirchener, 1993.

5.10A. JOHANN GOTTFRIED EICHHORN

WORKS

Einleitung in das Alte Testament, 3 vols. Leipzig: Weidmann, 1780–1783; 4th ed. 5 vols. Göttingen: Rosenbusch, 1823–1824.

Einleitung in das Neue Testament. 4 parts in 5 vols. Leipzig: Weidmann, 1804–1827.

Einleitung in die apokryphischen Schriften des Alten Testaments. Leipzig: Weidmann, 1795.

Die hebräischen Propheten. 3 vols. Göttingen: Vandenhoeck & Ruprecht, 1816–1819.

Urgeschichte. Edited with an introduction and notations by Johann Philipp Gabler. 2 parts in 3 vols. Altdorf: Monath & Kußler, 1790–1793.

LITERATURE
Hartlich, Christian, and Walter Sachs. *Der Ursprung des Mythosbegriffs in der modernen Bibelwissenschaft.* Schriften der Studiengemeinschaft der evangelischen Akademien 2. Tübingen: Mohr Siebeck, 1952.
Sehmsdorf, Eberhard. *Die Prophetenauslegung bei J. C. Eichhorn.* Göttingen: Vandenhoeck & Ruprecht, 1971.
Smend, Rudolf. "Johann Gottfried Eichhorn." Pages 71–81 in *Theologie in Göttingen.* Edited by Bernd Möller. Göttingen: Vandenhoeck & Ruprecht, 1987. Repr. as pages 25–37 in idem, *Deutsche Alttestamentler in drei Jahrhunderten.* Göttingen: Vandenhoeck & Ruprecht, 1989.

5.10B. JOHANN PHILIPP GABLER

WORK
Kleinere theologische Schriften. Edited by Theodor August Gabler. 2 vols. Ulm: Stettin, 1831. Repr., Munich: Hieronymus, 1980.

LITERATURE
Knierim, Rolf. "On Gabler." Pages 495–556 in *The Task of Old Testament Theology.* Edited by Rolf Knierim. Grand Rapids: Eerdmans, 1995.
Merk, Otto. *Biblische Theologie des Neuen Testaments in ihrer Anfangszeit: Ihre methodischen Probleme bei J. Ph. Gabler und G. L. Bauer und deren Nachwirkungen.* MThSt 9. Marburg: Elwert, 1970.
Sæbo, Magne. "Johann Philipp Gabler at the End of the Eighteenth Century: History and Theology." Pages 327–35 in *On the Way to Canon: Creative Tradition History in the Old Testament.* Edited by Magne Sæbo. JSOTSup 191. Sheffield: Sheffied Academic Press, 1998.
Smend, Rudolf. "Johann Philipp Gablers Begründung der biblischen Theologie." *EvT* 22 (1962): 345–57. Repr. as pages 104–16 in idem, *Epochen der Bibelkritik: Gesammelte Studien 3.* Munich: Kaiser, 1991.
Wittenberg, Gunther H. "Johann Philipp Gabler and the Consequences: In Search of a New Paradigm for Old Testament Theology." *OTE* 8 (1995): 103–28.

6. BIBLICAL STUDIES AS A SCIENCE IN THE NINETEENTH CENTURY

Rogerson, John William. *Old Testament Criticism in the Nineteenth Century: England and Germany.* London: SPCK, 1984.

6.1. WILHELM MARTIN LEBERECHT DE WETTE

WORKS

Beiträge zur Einleitung in das Alte Testament. 2 vols. Halle: Schimmelpfennig, 1806–1807. Repr., Hildesheim: Olms, 1971.

Biblische Dogmatik des Alten und Neuen Testaments. Berlin: Realschulbuchhandlung, 1813; 3rd ed., 1831.

Commentar über die Psalmen. Heidelberg: Mohr & Zimmer, 1811; 5th ed., 1856.

De morte Jesu Christi expiatoria commentatio. Berlin: Ex libraria Scholae realis, 1813.

Dogmatik der protestantischen Kirche nach den symbolischen Büchern und älteren Dogmatikern beider Konfessionen. 3rd ed. Berlin: Reimer, 1840.

Kurzgefasstes exegetisches Handbuch zum Neuen Testament. 2 vols. in 3. Leipzig: Weidmann, 1836–1848.

Die Psalmen. Heidelberg: Mohr, 1823.

Opuscula theologica. Berlin: Reimer, 1830.

Theodor oder des Zweiflers Weihe: Bildungsgeschichte eines evangelischen Geistlichen. 2 vols. Berlin: Reimer, 1822; 2nd ed., 1828.

Über die erbauliche Erklärung der Psalmen. Basel: Wieland, 1836.

Das Wesen des christlichen Glaubens. Basel: Schweighauser, 1846.

LITERATURE

Rogerson, John William. *W. M. L. de Wette, Founder of Modern Biblical Criticism: An Intellectual Biography.* JSOTSup 126. Sheffield: Sheffield Academic Press, 1992.

Rohls, Jan. "Liberale Romantik. Wilhelm Leberecht de Wette (1780–1849)." Pages 233–50 in *Aufklärung. Idealismus.* Vol. 1 of *Profile des neuzeitlichen Protestantismus.* Edited by Friedrich-Wilhelm Graf. Vormärz, Gütersloh, 1990.

Smend, Rudolf. "Wilhelm Martin Lebrecht de Wette." Pages 44–58 in vol. 1 of *Theologen des Protestantismus im 19. und 20. Jahrhundert.* Edited by Martin Greschat. Stuttgart: Kohlhammer, 1978. Repr. as pages 38–52 in idem, *Deutsche Alttestamentler in drei Jahrhunderten.* Göttingen: Vandenhoeck & Ruprecht, 1989.

———. *Wilhelm Martin Leberecht de Wettes Arbeit am Alten und Neuen Testament.* Basel: Helbing & Lichtenhahn, 1958.

6.2. DAVID FRIEDRICH STRAUSS

WORKS

Die christliche Glaubenslehre in ihrer geschichtlichen Entwicklung und im Kampfe mit der modernen Wissenschaft. 2 vols. Tübingen: Osiander, 1840–1841.

Hermann Samuel Reimarus und seine Schutzschrift für die vernünftigen Verehrer Gottes. Leipzig: Brockhaus, 1862.

Das Leben Jesu kritisch bearbeitet. 2 vols. Tübingen: Osiander, 1835; 2nd ed., 1837.

Life of Jesus. Translated by J. L. MacIlraith. London: Temple, 1890.

Streitschriften zur Vertheidigung meiner Schrift über das Leben Jesu und zur Charakteristik der gegenwärtigen Theologie. Tübingen: Osiander, 1841.

LITERATURE

Backhaus, Gunther. *Kerygma und Mythos bei David Friedrich Strauß und Rudolf Bultmann.* Hamburg-Bergstedt: Herbert Reich Evangelischer, 1956.

Barth, Karl. *David Friedrich Strauß als Theologe.* ThSt 6. Zürich: Verlag der Evangelischen, 1948.

Graf, Friedrich Wilhelm. *Kritik und Pseudo-Spekulation: David Friedrich Strauß als Dogmatiker im Kontext der positionellen Theologie seiner Zeit.* Munich: Kaiser, 1982.

Harris, Horton. *David Friedrich Strauss and His Theology.* Cambridge: Cambridge University Press, 1973.

Hartlich, Christian, and Walter Sachs. *Der Ursprung des Mythosbegriffs in der modernen Bibelwissenschaft.* Schriften der Studiengemeinschaft der evangelischen Akademien 2. Tübingen: Mohr Siebeck, 1952.

Lange, Dietz. *Historischer Jesus oder mythischer Christus: Untersuchungen zu dem Gegensatz zwischen Friedrich Schleiermacher und David Friedrich Strauß.* Gütersloh: Gütersloher Verlagshaus, 1975.

Sandberger, Jörg. F. *David Friedrich Strauß als theologischer Hegelianer.* SThGG 5. Göttingen: Vandenhoeck & Ruprecht, 1972.

Ziegler, Theobald. *David Friedrich Strauß.* Strassburg: Trübner, 1908.

6.3. WILHELM VATKE

WORKS

Die biblische Theologie. Vol. 1: *Die Religion des Alten Testaments.* Berlin: Bethge, 1835.

Die menschliche Freiheit in ihrem Verhältniss zur Sünde und zur göttlichen Gnade wissenschaftlich dargestellt. Berlin: Bethge, 1841.

Wilhelm Vatkes Religionsphilosophie oder allgemeine philosophische Theologie. Edited by Hermann G. S. Preiss. Bonn: Strauss, 1888.

LITERATURE

Benecke, Heinrich. *Wilhelm Vatke in seinem Leben und seinen Schriften.* Bonn: Strauss, 1883.

Brömse, Michael. "Studien zur 'Biblischen Theologie' Wilhelm Vatkes." Diss., Christian-Albrechts-Universität, Kiel, 1973.

Perlitt, Lothar. *Vatke und Wellhausen: Geschichtesphilosophische Voraussetzungen und historiographische Motive für die Darstellung der Religion und Geschichte Israels durch Wilhelm Vatke und Julius Wellhausen.* BZAW 94. Berlin: de Gruyter, 1962.

Smend, Rudolf. Universalismus und Partikularismus in der alttestamentlichen Theologie des 19 Jahrhunderts." *EvTh* 22 (1962): 169–79. Repr. as pages 117–127 in idem, *Epochen der Bibelkritik: Gesammelte Studien 3.* BevT 109. Munich: Kaiser, 1991.

6.4. FERDINAND CHRISTIAN BAUR

WORKS

Ausgewählte Werke in Einzelausgaben. Edited by Klaus Scholder. 5 vols. Stuttgart-Bad Cannstatt: Frommann, 1963–1985.

    Vol. 1: *Historisch-kritische Untersuchungen zum Neuen Testament.* Introduction by Ernst Käsemann. Stuttgart-Bad Cannstatt: Frommann, 1963.

    Vol. 3: *Das Christenthum und die christliche Kirche der drei ersten Jahrhunderte.* Introduction by Ulrich Wickert. Stuttgart-Bad Cannstatt: Frommann, 1966.

Die christliche Gnosis oder die christliche Religionsphilosophie in ihrer geschichtlichen Entwicklung. Tübingen: Osiander, 1835. Repr., Darmstadt: Wissenschaftliche Buchgesellschaft, 1967.

Die christliche Lehre von der Versöhnung in ihrer geschichtlichen Entwicklung von der ältesten Zeit bis auf die neueste. Tübingen: Osiander, 1838.

Kritische Untersuchungen über die kanonischen Evangelien. Tübingen: Fues, 1847. Repr., Hildesheim: Olms, 1999.

Paulus, der Apostel Jesu Christi: Sein Leben und Wirken, seine Briefe und seine Lehre. Stuttgart: Becher & Müller, 1845. English: *Paul the Apostle* of Jesus Christ: His Life and Works, His Epistles and Teachings. Peabody, Mass.: Hendrickson, 2003.

Symbolik und Mythologie; oder, Die Naturreligion des Alterthums. 3 vols. Stuttgart: Metzler, 1824–1825.

"Über die Composition und den Charackter des johanneischen Evangeliums." Theologische Jahrbücher 3 (1844): 1–91, 397–475, 615–700.

Vorlesungen über neutestamentliche Theologie. Edited by Ferdinand Friedrich Baur. Leipzig: Fues, 1864. Repr. with an introduction by Werner Georg Kümmel. Darmstadt: Wissenschaftliche Buchgesellschaft, 1973.

LITERATURE

Barnikol, Ernst. Ferdinand Christian Baur als rationalistisch-kritischer Theologe. Berlin: Evangelische Verlagsanstalt, 1970.

Georgii, Decan, et al. "Worte der Erinnerung an Ferdinand Christian von Baur." Tübingen: Fues, 1861.

Köpf, Ulrich, ed. Historisch-kritische Geschichtsbetrachtung: Ferdinand Christian Baur und seine Schüler. Sigmaringen: Thorbecke, 1994.

Steck, Karl Gerhard. "Ferdinand Christian Baur." Pages 218–32 in Die neueste Zeit. Edited by Martin Greschat. Gestalten der Kirchen Geschichte 9.1. Stuttgart: Kohlhammer, 1985.

Wetzsäcker, Karl. Ferdinand Christian Baur: Rede zur akademischen Feier seines 100. Geburtstages am 21. Juni 1892 in der Aula in Tübingen. Stuttgart: Frommann, 1892.

6.5. ERNST WILHELM HENGSTENBERG

WORKS

Die Authentie des Pentateuch. 2 vols. Berlin: Oehmigke, 1836–1839. English: Dissertations on the Genuineness of the Pentateuch. 2 vols. Translated by J. E. Ryland. Edinburgh: T&T Clark, 1847.

Dissertations on the Genuineness of Daniel and the Integrity of Zechariah. Translated by B. P. Pratten. Edinburgh: T&T Clark, 1847. [Orig. 1831]

Christologie des Alten Testaments und Commentar über die Messianischen Weissagungen der Propheten. 3 vols. in 4. Berlin: Oehmigke, 1829–1835. English: Christology of the Old Testament: And a Commentary on the Messianic Predictions. Translated by Theodore Meyer and James Martin. 4 vols. Edinburgh: T&T Clark, 1858–1868. Repr. with a foreword by Walter C. Kaiser Jr. Grand Rapids: Kregel, 1970.

A Commentary on Ecclesiastes. Evansville, Ind.: Sovereign Grace, 1960. [Orig. 1859]

Egypt and the Books of Moses; or, The books of Egypt. Translated by by R. D. C. Robbins. Edinburgh: T&T Clark, 1845. [Orig. 1831]

Geschichte des Reiches Gottes unter dem Alten Bunde. 2 vols. Berlin: Altenberg, 1869–1871. English: *History of the Kingdom of God under the Old Testament.* 2 vols. Edinburgh: T&T Clark, 1871–1872.

Das Hohelied Salomonis. Berlin: Oehmigke, 1853.

Die wichtigsten und schwierigsten Abschnitte des Pentateuchs erläutert. Berlin: Oehmigke, 1842.

LITERATURE

Bachmann, Johannes. *Ernst Wilhelm Hengstenberg: Sein Leben und Wirken nach gedruckten und ungedruckten Quellen.* 3 vols. Gütersloh: Bertelsmann, 1876–1892.

Davis, Daniel Clair. "The Hermeneutics of Ernst Wilhelm Hengstenberg: Edifying Value as Exegete." Diss. theol. Göttingen, 1960.

Kramer, Wolfgang. "Ernst Wilhelm Hengstenberg, die evangelische Kirchenzeitung und der theologische Rationalismus." Diss. phil. Erlangen, 1972.

Taylor, James Carol. "Ernst Wilhelm Hengstenberg as Old Testament Exegete." Ph.D. diss. Yale University, 1966.

6.6. HEINRICH EWALD

WORKS

The Antiquities of Israel. Translated by Henry Shaen Solly. London: Longmans, Green, 1876. [Orig. 1848]

A Grammar of the Hebrew Language of the Old Testament. Translated by John Nicholson. London : Whittaker, 1836. [Orig. 1827]

Geschichte des Volkes Israel bis Christus. 7 vols. Göttingen: Dieterich, 1843–1859. English: *The History of Israel.* Translated by Russell Martineau. 5 vols. London: Longmans, Green, 1869–1874. [Orig.]

Die poetischen Bücher des Alten Bundes. 4 vols. Göttingen: Vandenhoeck & Ruprecht, 1835–1839; 2nd ed., *Die Dichter des alten Bundes.* 4 vols. Göttingen: Vandenhoeck & Ruprecht, 1866.

Die Propheten des Alten Bundes. 2 vols. Stuttgart: Krabbe, 1840–1841; 2nd ed., 3 vols., 1867–1868.

Syntax of the Hebrew Language of the Old Testament. Translated by James Kennedy. Piscataway, N.J.: Gorgias, 2005.

LITERATURE

Ebach, Jürgen. "Ewald, Georg Heinrich August (1803–1875)." *TRE* 10:694–96.

Perlitt, Lothar. "Heinrich Ewald: Der Gelehrte in der Politik." Pages 157–212 in *Theologie in Göttingen: Eine Vorlesungsreihe*. Edited by Bernd Möller. Göttingen: Vandenhoeck & Ruprecht, 1987. Repr. as pages 263–312 in *Allein mit dem Wort: Theologische Studien*. Edited by Hermann Spieckermann. Göttingen: Vandenhoeck & Ruprecht, 1995.

Rogerson, John. "Ewald, Georg Heinrich August (1803–1875)." Pages 363–64 in vol. 1 of *Dictionary of Biblical Interpretation*. Edited by John H. Hayes. 2 vols. Nashville: Abingdon, 1999.

Wellhausen, Julius. "Heinrich Ewald." Pages 61–81 in *Festschrift zur Feier des hundertfünfzigjährigen Bestehens der Königlichen Gesellschaft der Wissenschaften zu Göttingen*. Berlin: Weidmann, 1901. Repr. as pages 120–38 in *Grundrisse zum Alten Testament*. Edited by Rudolf Smend. ThB 27. Munich: Kaiser, 1965.

6.7. HEINRICH JULIUS HOLTZMANN

WORKS

Die Entstehung des Neuen Testaments. Halle: Gebauer-Schwetschke, 1904.

Evangelium, Briefe und Offenbarung des Johannes. HCNT 4. Freiburg im Briesgau: Mohr, 1891 = *Evangelium des Johannes*; *Briefe und Offenbarung des Johannes*. 3rd ed. HCNT 4.1–2. Tübingen: Mohr, 1908.

Lehrbuch der historisch-kritischen Einleitung in das Neue Testament. Freiburg im Briesgau: Mohr, 1885; 2nd ed., 1892.

Lehrbuch der neutestamentlichen Theologie. 2 vols. Freiburg im Briesgau: Mohr, 1897; 2nd ed., Tübingen: Mohr, 1911.

"Die Markus-Kontroverse in ihrer heutigen Gestalt." *AR* 10:18–40, 161–200.

Das messianische Bewusstsein Jesu: Ein Beitrag zur Leben-Jesu-Forschung. Tübingen: Mohr, 1908.

Die Synoptiker, Die Apostelgeschichte. HCNT 1. Freiburg im Briesgau: Mohr, 1889 = *Die Synoptiker*; *Die Apostelgeschichte*. 3rd ed. HCNT 1.1–2. Tübingen: Mohr, 1901.

Die synoptischen Evangelien: Ihr Ursprung und geschichtlicher Charakter. Leipzig: Engelmann, 1863.

LITERATURE

Bauer, Walter. *Heinrich Julius Holtzmann: Ein Lebensbild*, Giessen: Töpelmann, 1932. Repr. as pages 285–341 in idem, *Aufsätze und kleine Schriften*. Edited by Georg Strecker. Tübingen: Mohr Siebeck, 1967.

6.8. Julius Wellhausen

Works

Abriß der Geschichte Israels und Judas. Skizzen und Vorarbeiten 1. Berlin: Reimer, 1884.

Analyse der Offenbarung Johannis. Berlin: Weidmann, 1907. Repr., Nendeln, Lichtenstein: Kraus, 1970.

Die Composition des Hexateuchs und der historischen Bücher des Alten Testaments. Skizzen und Vorarbeiten 2. Berlin: de Gruyter, 1885. 4th ed., 1963.

Einleitung in das Alte Testament von F. Bleek. Edited by Julius Wellhausen. 5th ed. Berlin: Reimer, 1886.

Einleitung in die drei ersten Evangelien. Berlin: Reimer, 1905.

Evangelienkommentare. Berlin: de Gruyter, 1987.

Das Evangelium Johannis. Berlin: Reimer, 1908.

Das Evangelium Marci: Übersetzt und erklärt. Berlin: Reimer, 1903.

Das Evangelium Matthaei: Übersetzt und erklärt. Berlin: Reimer, 1904.

Grundrisse zum Alten Testament. ThB 27. Edited by Rudolf Smend. Munich: Kaiser, 1965.

Israelitische und jüdische Geschichte. Berlin: Reimer, 1894; 9th ed., 1958.

Die kleinen Propheten übersetzt mit Noten. Skizzen und Vorarbeiten 5. Berlin: Reimer, 1892 = *Die kleinen Propheten: Übersetzt und erklärt*. 3rd ed. Berlin: Reimer, 1898; 4th ed., 1963.

Kritische Analyse der Apostelgeschichte. Berlin: Weidmann, 1914. Repr., Nendeln, Lichtenstein: Kraus, 1970.

The Pharisees and the Sadducees: An Examination of Internal Jewish History. Translated by Mark E. Biddle. Macon, Ga.: Mercer University Press, 2001.

Prolegomena zur Geschichte Israels. 6th ed. Berlin: Reimer, 1905. English: *Prolegomena to the History of Ancient Israel: With a Reprint of the Article Israel from the Encyclopaedia Britannica*. New York: Meridian, 1957.

Literature

Frenschkowski, Marco. "Wellhausen, Julius." *BBKL* 13:716–27.

Perlitt, Lothar. "Julius Wellhausen." Pages 33–37 in *Tendenzen der The-*

ologie im 20. Jahrhundert. Edited by Hans Jurgen Schultz. Stuttgart: Kreuz, 1966.

———. *Vatke und Wellhausen: Geschichtesphilosophische Voraussetzungen und historiographische Motive für die Darstellung der Religion und Geschichte Israels durch Wilhelm Vatke und Julius Wellhausen.* BZAW 94. Berlin: Töpelmann, 1962.

Smend, Rudolf. "Julius Wellhausen." Pages 166–80 in vol. 1 of *Theologen des Protestantismus im 19. und 20. Jahrhundert.* Edited by Martin Greschat. Stuttgart: Kohlhammer, 1978. Repr. as pages 45–58 in *neueste Zeit 2.* Edited by Martin Greschat. Gestalten der Kirchengeschichte 10.1. Stuttgart: Kohlhammer, 1985. Repr. as pages 99–113 in Smend, *Deutsche Alttestamentler in drei Jahrhunderten.* Göttingen: Vandenhoeck & Ruprecht, 1989.

6.9. Bernhard Duhm

Works

The Twelve Prophets: A Version in the Various Poetical Measures of the Original Writings. Translated by Archibald Duff. London: Black, 1912.

Das Buch Hiob. KHC 16. Freiburg im Breisgau: Mohr, 1897.

Das Buch Jeremia. KHC 11. Tübingen: Mohr, 1901.

Das Buch Jesaja. HKAT 3/1. Göttingen: Vandenhoeck & Ruprecht, 1892; 4th ed., 1922.

Israels Propheten. Tübingen: Mohr, 1916; 2nd ed., 1922.

Die Psalmen. KHC 14. Tübingen: Mohr, 1899; 2nd ed., 1922.

Die Theologie der Propheten als Grundlage für die innere Entwicklungsgeschichte der israelitischen Religion. Bonn: Marcus, 1875.

Über Ziel und Methode der theologischen Wissenschaft. Basel: Schwabe, 1889.

Literature

Reventlow, Henning Graf. "Die Prophetie im Urteil Bernhard Duhms." *ZThK* 85 (1988): 259–274.

Smend, Rudolf. "Bernhard Duhm." Pages 114–28 in idem, *Deutsche Alttestamentler in drei Jahrhunderten.* Göttingen: Vandenhoeck & Ruprecht, 1989.

7. The History of Religion School

General

Lüdemann, Gerd, ed. *Die "Religionsgeschichtliche Schule": Facetten eines theologischen Umbruchs.* Studien und Texte zur Religionsgeschichtlichen Schule. Frankfurt am Main: Lang, 1996.
Lüdemann, Gerd, and Martin Schroder. *Die religionsgeschichtliche Schule in Göttingen: Eine Dokumentation.* Göttingen: Vandenhoeck & Ruprecht, 1987.

7.1. Hermann Gunkel

Works
"Einleitungen." Pages ix–lxx in Hans Schmidt, *Die großen Propheten.* Die Schriften des Alten Testaments in Auswahl 2.2. Göttingen: Vandenhoeck & Ruprecht, 1915; 2nd ed., 1923.
Genesis. Translated by Mark E. Biddle. Macon, Ga.: Mercer University Press, 1997. [Orig. 1901]
Einleitung in die Psalmen: Die Gattungen der religiösen Lyrik Israels. Completed by Joachim Begrich. Göttingen: Vandenhoeck & Ruprecht, 1933; 6th ed., 1986. English: *Introduction to Psalms: The Genres of the Religious Lyric of Israel.* Translated by James D. Nogalski. Macon, Ga.: Mercer University Press, 1998.
Israel und Babylonien: Der Einfluß Babyloniens auf die israelitische Religion. Göttingen: Vandenhoeck & Ruprecht, 1903. English: *Israel and Babylon: The Influence of Babylon on the Religion of Israel.* Translated by E. S. B. Philadelphia: McVey, 1904.
Die israelitische Literatur. Darmstadt: Wissenschaftliche Buchgesellschaft, 1963.
Die Propheten: Die geheimen Erfahrungen der Propheten; die Politik der Propheten; die Religion der Propheten; Schriftstellerei und Formensprache der Propheten. Göttingen: Vandenhoeck & Ruprecht, 1917.
Die Psalmen. HKAT 2/2. Göttingen: Vandenhoeck & Ruprecht, 1926; 5th ed., 1968.
Reden und Aufsätze. Göttingen: Vandenhoeck & Ruprecht, 1913.
Schöpfung und Chaos in Urzeit und Endzeit : eine religionsgeschichtliche Untersuchung über Gen 1 und Ap Joh 12. Göttingen: Vandenhoeck und Ruprecht, 1895. English: *Creation and Chaos in the Prime-*

val Era and the Eschaton: A Religio-historical Study of Genesis 1 and Revelation 12. Translated by K. William Whitney Jr. Grand Rapids: Eerdmans, 2006.

Zum religionsgeschichtlichen Verständnis des Neuen Testaments. FRLANT 1. Göttingen: : Vandenhoeck & Ruprecht, 1903.

LITERATURE

Klatt, Werner. *Hermann Gunkel: Zu seiner Theologie der Religionsgeschichte und zur Entstehung der formgeschichtlichen Methode.* FRLANT 100. Göttingen: Vandenhoeck & Ruprecht, 1969.

Müller, Hans-Peter. "Hermann Gunkel." Pages 241–55 in vol. 2 of *Theologen des Protestantismus im 19. und 20. Jahrhundert.* Edited by Martin Greschat. Stuttgart: Kohlhammer, 1978.

Rabenau, Konrad von. "Hermann Gunkel." Pages 80–87 in *Tendenzen der Theologie im 20. Jahrhundert.* Edited by Hans Jurgen Schultz. Stuttgart: Kreuz, 1966.

Schmidt, Hans, ed. *Eucharisterion: Studien zur Religion und Literatur des Alten und Neuen Testaments.* FRLANT 36. Göttingen: Vandenhoeck & Ruprecht, 1922.

Smend, Rudolf. "Hermann Gunkel." Pages 345–55 in vol. 2 of *Giessener Gelehrte in der ersten Hälfte des 20. Jahrhunderts: Lebensbilder aus Hessen.* Edited by Hans Georg Gundel, Peter Moraw, and Volker Press. Veröffentlichungen der Historischen Kommission Hessen 35.2. Marburg: Elwert, 1982. Repr. as pages 160–72 in Smend, *Deutsche Alttestamentler in drei Jahrhunderten.* Göttingen: Vandenhoeck & Ruprecht, 1989.

7.2. WILHELM BOUSSET

WORKS

The Antichrist Legend: A Chapter in Christian and Jewish Folklore. Translated by A. H. Keane. Atlanta: Scholars Press, 1999. [Orig. 1895]

Der Apostel Paulus. Halle: Gebauer-Schwetschke, 1906.

Hauptprobleme der Gnosis. FRLANT 10. Göttingen: Vandenhoeck & Ruprecht, 1907. Repr., 1973.

Jesu Predigt in ihrem Gegensatz zum Judentum: Ein religionsgeschichtlicher Vergleich. Göttingen: Vandenhoeck & Ruprecht, 1892.

Jesus der Herr: Nachträge und Auseinandersetzungen. FRLANT 23. Göttingen: Vandenhoeck & Ruprecht, 1916.

Die jüdische Apokalyptik: Ihre religionsgeschichtliche Herkunft und ihre Bedeutung für das Neue Testament. Berlin: Reuther & Reichard, 1903.

Kyrios Christos: Geschichte des Christusglaubens von den Anfängen des Christentums bis Irenaeus. Göttingen: Vandenhoeck & Ruprecht, 1913; 2nd ed., 1921. English: *Kyrios Christos: A History of the Belief in Christ from the Beginnings of Christianity to Irenaeus.* Translated by John E. Steely. Nashville: Abingdon, 1970.

Die Offenbarung Johannis. KEK 16. Göttingen: Vandenhoeck & Ruprecht, 1896; 6th ed., 1906.

Die Religion des Judentums im neutestamentlichen Zeitalter. Berlin: Reuther & Reichard, 1903; 2nd ed., 1906 = *Die Religion des Judentums im späthellenistischen Zeitalter.* HNT 21. Revised and edited by Hugo Gressmann. 3rd ed. Tübingen: Mohr, 1926; 4th ed., 1966.

Religionsgeschichtliche Studien: Aufsätze zur Religionsgeschichte des hellenistischen Zeitalters. Edited by Anthonie Frans Verheule. NovTSup 50. Leiden: Brill, 1979.

Unser Gottesglaube. Religionsgeschichtliche Volksbücher 5/6. Tübingen: Mohr, 1908.

What Is Religion? Translated by Florence B Low. London: Unwin, 1907.

LITERATURE

Berger, Klaus. "Nationalsoziale Religionsgeschichte: Wilhelm Bousset (1865–1923)." Pages 279–94 in *Kaiserreich.* Vol. 2.2 of *Profile des neuzeitlichen Protestantismus.* Edited by Friedrich Wilhelm Graf. Gütersloh: Mohn, 1993.

Merk, Otto. "Wilhelm Bousset." Pages 105–20 in vol. 2 of *Giessener Gelehrte in der ersten Hälfte des 20. Jahrhunderts: Lebensbilder aus Hessen.* Edited by Hans Georg Gundel, Peter Moraw, and Volker Press. Veröffentlichungen der Historischen Kommission Hessen 35.2. Marburg: Elwert, 1982. Repr. as pages 159–74 in *Wissenschaftsgeschichte und Exegese.* Edited by Rolf Gebauer et al. BZNW 95. Berlin: de Gruyter, 1998.

Murrmann-Kahl, Michael. *Die entzauberte Heilsgeschichte: Der Historismus erobert die Theologie 1880–1920.* Gütersloh: Mohn, 1992.

Schmidt, Johann Michael. "Bousset, Wilhelm." *TRE* 7:97–10.

Verheule, Anthonie Frans. *Wilhelm Bousset: Leben und Werk—Ein theologiegeschichtlicher Versuch.* Amsterdam: Van Bottenburg, 1973.

7.3. Johannes Weiss

Works

Earliest Christianity: A History of the Period A.D. 30-150. Translated by Frederick C. Grant. New York: Harper, 1959. [Orig. 1917]

Die Predigt Jesu vom Reiche Gottes. Göttingen: Vandenhoeck & Ruprecht, 1892; 2nd ed., 1900; 3rd ed., 1964. English: Jesus' Proclamation of the Kingdom of God. Translated, edited, and with an introduction by Richard Hyde Hiers and David Larrimore Holland. Philadelphia: Fortress, 1971.

Die Schriften des Neuen Testaments neu übersetzt und für die Gegenwart erklärt. 2 vols. Göttingen: Vandenhoeck & Ruprecht, 1907-1908.

Literature

Lanert, Berthold. Die Wiederentdeckung der neutestamentlichen Eschatologie durch Johannes Weiß. Texte und Arbeiten zum neutestamentlichen Zeitalter 2. Tübingen: Francke, 1989.

Schäfer, Rolf. "Das Reich Gottes bei Albrecht Ritschl und Johannes Weiß." ZThK 61 (1964): 68-88.

Schweitzer, Albert. The Quest of the Historical Jesus. Translated by W. Montgomery et al. Minneapolis: Fortress, 2001.

8. New Directions in the Twentieth Century

8.1. Karl Barth

Works

"The Christian's Place in Society." Pages 272-327 in idem, The Word of God and the Word of Man. Translated by Douglas Horton. New York: Harper, 1957.

"Exegesis of 1 Kings 13." Pages 393-409 in vol. 2/2 of Church Dogmatics. Edited by G. W. Bromiley and T. F. Torrance. 14 vols. Edinburgh: T&T Clark, 1936-1977.

Karl Barth-Eduard Thurneysen Briefwechsel. 2 vols. Zürich: Theologischer Verlag, 1973-1974.

Die kirchliche Dogmatik. 5 vols. in 14. Zollikon: Verlag der Evangelischen Buchhandlung, 1932-1970. English: Church Dogmatics. Edited by G. W. Bromiley and T. F. Torrance. 5 vols. in 14. Edinburgh: T&T Clark, 1936-1977.

"Nachwort." Pages 290–312 in *Schleiermacher-Auswahl*. Edited by Heinz Bolli. 2nd ed. Gütersloh: Mohn, 1980.

The Resurrection of the Dead. Translated by H. J. Stenning. New York: Arno, 1977.

Der Römerbrief. Bern: Bäschlin, 1919; 2nd ed., 1922. English: *The Epistle to the Romans*. Translated by Edwyn C. Hoskyns. London: Oxford University Press, 1963.

Rudolf Bultmann: Ein Versuch ihn zu verstehen. ThSt 34. Zollikon-Zürich: Evangelische, 1952.

Literature

Bächli, Otto. *Das Alte Testament in der kirchlichen Dogmatik von Karl Barth*. Neukirchen-Vluyn: Neukirchener, 1987.

Busch, Eberhard. *Karl Barth: His Life from Letters and Autobiographical Texts*. Translated by John Bowden. Philadelphia: Fortress, 1976.

Merk, Otto. "Karl Barths Beitrag zur Erforschung des Neuen Testaments." Pages 149–76 in *Wissenschaft und Kirche: Festschrift für Eduard Lohse*. Edited by Kurt Aland and Siegfried Meurer. Texte und Arbeiten zur Bibel 4. Bielefeld: Luther-Verlag, 1989.

Moltmann, Jürgen. *Anfänge der dialektischen Theologie*. 2 vols. Munich: Kaiser, 1962–1963.

Trowitzsch, Michael, ed. *Karl Barths Schriftauslegung*. Tübingen: Mohr Siebeck, 1996.

Smend, Rudolf. "Nachkritische Schriftauslegung." Pages 215–37 in *Parrēsia: Karl Barth zum 80. Geburtstag am 10. Mai 1966*. Edited by Eberhard Busch. Zürich: EVZ-Verlag, 1966. Repr. as pages 212–32 in idem, *Die Mitte des Alten Testaments: Gesammelte Studien 1*. Munich: Kaiser, 1986.

8.2. Rudolf Bultmann

Works

"Ethical and Mystical Religion in Early Christianity." Pages 221–35 in vol. 1 of *The Beginnings of Dialectic Theology*. Edited by James M. Robinson. Translated by Louis De Grazia and Keith R. Crim. 2 vols. Richmond: John Knox, 1968.

Exegetica: Aufsätze zur Erforschung des Neuen Testaments. Tübingen: Mohr Siebeck, 1967.

Glauben und Verstehen: Gesammelte Aufsätze. 4 vols. Tübingen: Mohr Siebeck, 1933–1965. English: *Faith and Understanding*. Edited with an introduction by Robert W. Funk. Translated by Louise Pettibone Smith. New York: Harper & Row, 1969

Die Geschichte der synoptischen Tradition. Göttingen: Vandenhoeck & Ruprecht, 1921; 7th ed., 1967. English: *The History of the Synoptic Tradition.* Translated by John Marsh. New York: Harper & Row, 1963.

Geschichte und Eschatologie. Tübingen: Mohr Siebeck, 1958; 2nd ed., 1964.

The Gospel of John: A Commentary. Translated by G. R. Beasley-Murray. Philadelphia: Westminster, 1971.

Jesus. Tübingen: Mohr Siebeck, 1926. New edition. UTB 1272. Tübingen: Mohr Siebeck, 1983; 3rd ed., 1994.

New Testament and Mythology and Other Basic Writings. Edited and translated by Schubert M. Ogden. Philadelphia: Fortress, 1984.

Primitive Christianity in Its Contemporary Setting. Translated by R. H. Fuller. New York: Meridian, 1956.

The Second Letter to the Corinthians. Translated by Roy A. Harrisville. Minneapolis: Augsburg, 1985.

Theologie des Neuen Testaments. Tübingen: Mohr Siebeck, 1953; 9th ed., 1984. English: *Theology of the New Testament.* Translated by Kendrick Grobel. 2 vols. New York: Scribner, 1951–1955.

LITERATURE

Backhaus, Gunther, ed. *Kerygma und Mythos bei David Friedrich Strauß und Rudolf Bultmann.* Hamburg-Bergstedt: Herbert Reich Evangelischer, 1956.

Bartsch, Hans Werner, et al., eds. *Kerygma und Mythos.* Vols. 1–7.1. Hamburg: Reich, 1948–1978.

Conzelmann, Hans. "Rudolf Bultmann." Pages 243–47 in *Tendenzen der Theologie im 20. Jahrhundert.* Edited by Hans Jurgen Schultz. Stuttgart: Kreuz, 1966.

Evang, Martin. *Rudolf Bultmann in seiner Frühzeit.* BHTh 74. Tübingen: Mohr Siebeck, 1988.

Fries, Heinrich. "Rudolf Bultmann (1884–1976)." Pages 297–317 in vol. 2 of *Klassiker der Theologie.* Edited by Heinrich Fries and Georg Kretschmar. 2 vols. Munich: Beck, 1981–1983.

Jaspert, Bernd. *Sackgassen im Streit mit Rudolf Bultmann: Hermeneutische Probleme der Bultmannrezeption in Theologie und Kirche.* St. Ottilien: EOS Verlag, 1985. Repr. as pages 311–79 in idem, *Theologie und Geschichte: Gesammelte Aufsätze 3.* EHS 23/671. Frankfurt am Main: Lang, 1999.

Klein, Gunter. "Rudolf Bultmann." Pages 404–19 in vol. 2 of *Theologen des Protestantismus im 19. und 20. Jahrhundert*. Edited by Martin Greschat. Stuttgart: Kohlhammer, 1978. Repr. as pages 52–69 in *Die neueste Zeit*. Edited by Martin Greschat. Gestalten der Kirchen Geschichte 10.2. Stuttgart: Kohlhammer, 1986.

Marlé, René. *Bultmann und die Interpretation des Neuen Testaments*. Konfessionskundliche und kontroverstheologische Studien 4. Paderborn: Verlag Bonifacius-Druckerei, 1959; 2nd ed., 1967.

Nethöfel, Wolfgang. *Strukturen existentialer Interpretation: Bultmanns Johanneskommentar im Wechsel theologischer Paradigmen*. Göttingen: Vandenhoeck & Ruprecht, 1983.

Schmithals, Walter. "Bultmann, Rudolf (1884–1976)." *TRE* 7:387–96.

Stegemann, Wolfgang. *Der Denkweg Rudolf Bultmanns: Darstellung der Entwicklung und der Grundlagen seiner Theologie*. Stuttgart: Kohlhammer, 1978.

8.3. Outlook

Albertz, Rainer. *A History of Israelite Religion in the Old Testament Period*. Translated by John Bowden. 2 vols. Louisville: Westminster John Knox, 1994.

Alter, Robert. *The Art of Biblical Narrative*. New York: Basic, 1981.

Baldermann, Ingo. *Religionsgeschichte Israels oder alttestamentliche Theologie?* Jahrbuch für Biblische Theologie 10. Neukirchen-Vluyn: Neukirchener, 1995.

Brueggemann, Walter. *Theology of the Old Testament: Testimony, Dispute, Advocacy*. Minneapolis: Fortress, 1997.

Childs, Brevard S. *Biblical Theology of the Old and New Testaments: Theological Reflection on the Christian Bible*. Minneapolis: Fortress, 1992.

Flusser, David. *Jesus*. Translated by Ronald Walls. New York: Herder & Herder, 1969.

Fish, Stanley E. *Is There a Text in This Class? The Authority of Interpretative Communities*. Cambridge: Harvard University Press, 1980.

Hampel, Volker. *Menschensohn und historischer Jesus*. Neukirchen-Vluyn: Neukirchener, 1990.

Hermisson, Hans-Jürgen. *Alttestamentliche Theologie und Religionsgeschichte Israels*. Forum Theologische Literaturzeitung 3. Leipzig: Evangelische Verlagsanstalt, 2000.

Hubner, Hans. *Biblische Theologie des Neuen Testaments*. 3 vols. Göttingen: Vandenhoeck & Ruprecht, 1990–1995.

Käsemann, Ernst. "Das Problem des historischen Jesus." Pages 187–214 in vol. 1 of *Exegetische Versuche und Besinnungen*. Edited by Ernst Käsemann. Göttingen: Vandenhoeck & Ruprecht, 1964.

Kaiser, Otto. *Der Gott des Alten Testaments*. 3 vols. Göttingen: Vandenhoeck & Ruprecht, 1993–2003.

Kümmel, Werner Georg. *The Theology of the New Testament according to Its Major Witnesses: Jesus-Paul-John*. Translated by John E. Steely. Nashville: Abingdon, 1973.

Lindemann, Andreas. "Jesus in der Theologie des Neuen Testaments." Pages 27–57 in *Jesus Christus in Historie und Christologie: Neutestamentliche Festschrift für Hans Conzelmann zum 60. Geburtstag*. Edited by Georg Strecker. Tübingen: Mohr Siebeck, 1975.

Lohse, Eduard. *Grundriß der neutestamentlichen Theologie*. Theologische Wissenschaft 5. Stuttgart: Kohlhammer, 1974; 2nd ed., 1998.

Noth, Martin. *The Chronicler's History*. Translated by H. G. M. Williamson. JSOTSup 50. Sheffield: JSOT Press, 1987.

———. *The Deuteronomistic History*. JSOTSup 15. Sheffield: University of Sheffield, Dept. of Biblical Studies, 1981.

Otto, Eckart. "Der Stand der alttestamentlichen Wissenschaft." Pages 9–28 in *Bibel und Christentum im Orient*. Edited by Eckart Otto und Siegbert Uhlig. Orientalia Biblica et Christiana 4. Glückstadt: Augustin, 1991.

Powell, Mark Allan, Cecile G. Gray, and Mellisa C. Curtis. *The Bible and Modern Literary Criticism: A Critical Assassment and Annotated Bibliography*. New York: Greenwood, 1992.

Rad, Gerhard von. *Old Testament Theology*. Translated by D. M. G. Stalker. 2 vols. New York: Harper & Row, 1962–1965.

Rendtorff, Rolf. *The Canonical Hebrew Bible: A Theology of the Old Testament*. Translated by David E. Orton. Leiden: Deo, 2005.

Reventlow, Henning Graf. *Problems of Old Testament Theology in the Twentieth Century*. Philadelphia: Fortress, 1985.

Sölle, Dorothee. *Political Theology*. Translated by John Shelley. Philadelphia: Fortress, 1974.

Vermes, Geza. *Jesus the Jew: A Historian's Reading of the Gospels*. Philadelphia: Fortress, 1973.

Index of Names and Places

Index of Subjects

Index of Biblical References